Using SuperCalc®5

2nd Edition

James T. Perry, Ph.D.

Joseph G. Lateer

que®

CORPORATION

LEADING COMPUTER KNOWLEDGE

Using SuperCalc®5
2nd Edition

Library of Congress Catalog No.: 89-60242

ISBN 0-88022-404-5

92 91 90 89   6 5 4 3 2 1

Interpretation of the printing code: the rightmost double-digit number is the year of the book's printing; the rightmost single-digit number is the number of the book's printing. For example, a printing code of 89-1 shows that the first printing of the book occurred in 1989.

Using SuperCalc5, 2nd Edition, is based on Version 5 of SuperCalc and can be used with all previous versions.

DEDICATION

To my wife, Nancy Carroll Perry
—J.T.P.

To my wife, Nancy Lazzaretti Lateer
—J.G.L.

Publishing Manager

Lloyd J. Short

Product Director

David Maguiness

Production Editor

Steven L. Wiggins

Editors

Mary P. Arthur
Luanne R. Blackburn
Jeannine Freudenberger
Alice Martina Smith

Technical Editor

David Lively

Editorial Assistants

Fran Blauw
Stacie Lamborne

Indexed by

Brown Editorial Service

Book Design and Production

Dan Armstrong   Jennifer Matthews
Brad Chinn   Cindy L. Phipps
Cheryl English   Joe Ramon
David Kline   Dennis Sheehan
Lori A. Lyons   M. Louise Shinault

*Composed in Garamond and Excellent #47
by Que Corporation*

ABOUT THE AUTHORS

James T. Perry, Ph.D.

Jim Perry received his Ph.D. degree in Computer Science from The Pennsylvania State University and his B.S. degree in Mathematics from Purdue University. Over the past 20 years, he has been a professor of computer science and information systems at several universities and also has consulted extensively. He has published several articles and books including *A User Friendly Guide to CP/M with an Introduction to dBASE II*, *CP/M for the Kaypro with an Introduction to dBASE II*, *A User's Guide to dBASE II*, and *Understanding Oracle*. Dr. Perry is currently an associate professor in the School of Business at the University of San Diego located in San Diego, California.

Joseph G. Lateer

Joe Lateer, born in Champaign, Illinois, has developed a thorough background in business in his lifetime. Raised in a family business, he attended the University of Illinois and majored in finance and minored in accounting. After several years in accounting in the aerospace business, he returned to study at San Diego State University and achieved an M.B.A. in Information Systems. Thoroughly entranced with the uses of the personal computer in business, he has been designing and implementing systems, training personnel, and developing an expertise in the field in both the aerospace industry and medical products industry. He has authored *Understanding Oracle*. Currently, he is in charge of information systems for La Jolla Technology, Incorporated, located in San Diego, California.

CONTENTS AT A GLANCE

TABLE OF CONTENTS

4   Formatting a Worksheet 73

II Learning SuperCalc's Intermediate Features

6 Adding Another Dimension: Linked Spreadsheets 149

III Creating Reports and Graphs

9 Creating Reports with /Output.................. 279

IV Using Advanced Features

ACKNOWLEDGMENTS

Much time and effort has gone into the research for and writing of this book. Through the thousands of hours we have spent with SuperCalc5 and its recent predecessors, SuperCalc4 and SuperCalc3, we have been impressed with SuperCalc5's power and versatility.

We thank Ed Holub, who helped us a great deal by providing a well-structured analysis of SuperCalc's comprehensive set of financial functions.

There are several people at Que Corporation who have contributed to this effort and deserve special mention. Steve Wiggins painstakingly edited chapters and figures and double-checked chapters for technical accuracy. Our main Que contact, Dave Maguiness, has been helpful throughout the process. He checked our progress frequently (often several times each week—ugh!), and he pushed, poked, and prodded us when we needed it (and a few times when we didn't). His sense of humor provided the needed relief in an often-stressful writing environment. Lloyd Short, responsible for managing the entire effort, was available when we needed him. He provided us with valuable suggestions and help at crucial times, and he pushed various Que people "off the dime" on our behalf more than once.

Three special people at Computer Associates graciously and enthusiastically supported our writing efforts. Hillary Martinson answered our sometimes esoteric questions and recorded bugs we discovered. Daniel Real, "product champion," provided us with each new beta copy of SuperCalc5 within days of its birth. Richard Goodhue, SuperCalc product manager, always responded to our phone calls, provided answers to our many questions, and directed us to other Computer Associates technical resources. Our job would have been much more difficult without the cooperation and assistance of these key people.

We appreciate the patience required of our families and demonstrated by them during this entire project. The Perry children, Jessica, Stirling, and Kelly, have been exceptionally patient in allowing their father to be alone to think and write on weekends and early mornings. Both of our Nancys have been remarkably understanding while we spent countless hours planning, outlining, writing, rewriting, and editing the manuscript. Without their support and cooperation, we would not have attempted to write this book.

James T. Perry
Joseph G. Lateer
San Diego
1989

*T*RADEMARK
*A*CKNOWLEDGMENTS

Que Corporation has made every attempt to supply trademark information about company names, products, and services mentioned in this book. Trademarks indicated below were derived from various sources. Que Corporation cannot attest to the accuracy of this information.

1-2-3, DIF, Lotus, Symphony, and VisiCalc are registered trademarks of Lotus Development Corporation.

Ashton-Tate, dBASE, dBASE II, dBASE III, and Framework are registered trademarks and dBASE IV is a trademark of Ashton-Tate Corporation.

COMPAQ is a registered trademark of COMPAQ Computer Corporation.

CP/M is a registered trademark of Digital Research Inc.

DESQview is a trademark of Quarterdeck Office Systems.

Enable is a trademark of The Software Group.

EPSON is a registered trademark of Epson America, Inc.

Hercules Graphics Card is a trademark of Hercules Computer Technology.

IBM is a registered trademark and IBM ProPrinter XL is a trademark of International Business Machines Corporation.

InSet is a registered trademark of INSET Systems Inc.

LaserJet is a trademark of Hewlett-Packard Co.

Microsoft, MS-DOS, and Multiplan and are registered trademarks of Microsoft Corporation.

PostScript is a registered trademark of Adobe Systems Incorporated.

PrivacyPlus is a trademark of United Software Security, Inc.

Sideways is a registered trademark of Funk Software, Inc.

SuperCalc is a registered trademark and AnswerScreen, Computer Associates, and SuperData Interchange are trademarks of Computer Associates International, Inc.

WordStar and MicroPro are registered trademarks of MicroPro International Corporation.

CONVENTIONS USED IN THIS BOOK

A number of conventions are used in *Using SuperCalc5*, 2nd Edition, in order to help you learn the program. Information you are asked to type is printed in **BOLDFACE** or set off in a line by itself. SuperCalc accepts most information in either upper- or lowercase; where case is important, it is noted in the text. The first letter of each command, which you type to invoke the command, is printed in a boldface capital letter. /**G**lobal,**K**eep,**Y**es means that you press /**GKY**.

Words printed in all uppercase include file names, range names, functions, modes, macro keywords, and cell references.

Labels from the spreadsheet are printed as they appear on-screen and in *italic*. Graphics options and quotations from the screen are printed in a `special typeface`.

References to keys are as they appear on the keyboard of the IBM PC. Keys that are pressed simultaneously are hyphenated. For example, Ctrl-Break means that you press Ctrl and hold it while you tap Break. Keys that are pressed in sequence are joined by +. End + Home means that you press End and then press Home.

Introduction

SuperCalc®5 is the latest update to one of the oldest spreadsheet packages on the market. With each release, the product is enhanced greatly, and it remains a leader in the spreadsheet market. This release by Computer Associates™ International, Inc., is no exception.

With SuperCalc's good documentation, on-screen help facilities, easy installation, portability, excellent database, multiple and multipage spreadsheet capability, and three-dimensional graphics features, you soon will become comfortable using this electronic tool to solve a wide variety of problems in your applications.

Who Should Use This Book?

This book can serve both as a SuperCalc tutorial and as a reference to the program's comprehensive set of tools. People who plan to use a spreadsheet package for the first time, persons who have used previous SuperCalc releases but want to learn about Super-Calc5, and current SuperCalc5 users who want to see examples of applications can find useful information in this book. Whether you have no spreadsheet experience or you are an experienced SuperCalc user, we believe that this book will help you. We suggest numerous ways SuperCalc can save you time, help organize your work, and provide a more structured approach for making decisions.

What Is in This Book?

Many chapters of *Using SuperCalc5*, 2nd Edition, are organized around comprehensive central applications. The descriptions of these models follow the sequence of commands you use to create the spreadsheet. These major examples are accompanied by specific examples that demonstrate particular features. Showing what SuperCalc can do in practical applications enhances your understanding and demonstrates the usefulness of SuperCalc and its commands.

Part I

Chapter 1 defines spreadsheets and explains how they are used and why. The chapter outlines the evolution of spreadsheets, from the original "visible calculators" to a set of functionally related integrated programs, and points out the enhancements added to Super-Calc5. The text explains when you should consider using a spreadsheet package and why SuperCalc is a good choice. In addition, some important questions are posed for you to consider as you develop your own worksheets.

Chapter 2 presents the basic structure and terminology of SuperCalc. You learn to perform several fundamental spreadsheet activities with SuperCalc, including invoking SuperCalc, moving around the spreadsheet, writing on the spreadsheet, saving a copy of your spread-sheet on a disk file, printing the spreadsheet, and leaving SuperCalc. A sample spreadsheet involving an automobile loan gets you up and running quickly on SuperCalc.

Chapter 3 continues the spreadsheet example introduced in Chapter 2, and you learn to enter simple formulas as labels. After locking the formulas, you can use the /**C**opy command to create cloned cells. Cell naming and the print command are also discussed as the chapter takes you through an easily understood example, which you print later.

Chapter 4 demonstrates the variety of ways you can alter the display of data on the screen. This formatting is important to you in the early stages of creating worksheets. You see the rich variety of display techniques, such as formatting column widths, establishing default display formats, and centering labels. You learn the flexibility you gain by using Super-Calc's user-defined formatting parameters for both values and dates to mix and match until you get the display you want. Understanding the options for formatting cells is essential to creating clean, easily understood spreadsheets that convey your information quickly.

Chapter 5 discusses the important topics of relative and absolute cell addressing and the utilities provided to speed the process of building worksheets by copying, block manipulating, and editing. The chapter emphasizes visual methods of cell referencing using POINT mode. By combining many of the techniques described in this chapter, you can gain mastery of SuperCalc, decrease your development time, and develop more flexible worksheets.

Part II

Chapter 6 introduces the topic of multipage and multiple spreadsheets. Introduced in SuperCalc5, spreadsheet linking and referencing multiple spreadsheets are two of the most important changes in SuperCalc. You will learn how to use the //**S**preadsheet command, how to create multipage spreadsheets, how to hide spreadsheet pages, and how to write link formulas that connect open and disk-resident spreadsheets. Several comprehensive multipage and multiple spreadsheet consolidation examples are illustrated.

Chapters 7 and 8 both are devoted to SuperCalc's functions because of the large number of functions provided with the program. Chapter 7 presents five categories of functions: statistical functions, arithmetic functions, logical functions, calendar functions, and three of the index functions (LOOKUP, VLOOKUP, and HLOOKUP). These functions are described within the structure of a project management example. Some techniques for developing dynamic spreadsheets also are discussed, and the /**A**rrange command is introduced.

Chapter 8, the sequel to Chapter 7, discusses financial functions, including lifetime annuities, periodic annuities, onetime investments, investment by period, and depreciation. The index functions are also presented with practical examples. String, special purpose, and trigonometric functions are explained here as well. The complexity and power of the financial functions are shown in several simple layered examples that demonstrate specific results from the specific function. Also included in this chapter are common investment questions. Because these functions address all sides of most investment decisions, you learn which function best meets your needs.

Part III

Chapter 9 explains how to use the /Output command. The chapter begins with a description of the main features of /Output and covers the basics of handling output, including sending it to the printer. The remaining portion of the chapter focuses on the options provided with SuperCalc to make your output truly presentation-quality.

Chapter 10 introduces SuperCalc's excellent graphics capability. Several aspects of creating graphs are discussed, including the settings in the Global Graphics menu. Many SuperCalc graph types are demonstrated. Three-dimensional graphics are shown.

Part IV

Chapter 11 covers SuperCalc's macro capability. You first learn macro structure, commands, and syntax. You then work through a step-by-step tutorial on creating, debugging, saving, and executing macros. Throughout the chapter, you see how the helpful LEARN mode automatically generates macros from what you type on the keyboard.

Chapter 12 describes the database features of SuperCalc. Methods are explained for creating database records, adding and deleting records, and reorganizing a database. Posing queries and extracting results from database searches using the //Data command are illustrated with a real estate sales example. Techniques for both simple and complex queries are given. The many database statistical functions in SuperCalc also are covered. Finally, the numerous special purpose data analysis and manipulation commands are presented, including distribution and regression analysis commands, matrix manipulation commands, data parsing commands, and data table creation commands.

Chapter 13 describes SuperCalc's rich set of auditing commands. You will learn how to spot problems in design or layout, identify formulas that reference empty or text cells, trace cell relationships, highlight named ranges, and locate and replace cell data. The //Test command and its many spreadsheet auditing tools are thoroughly described.

Chapter 14 discusses two major topics: how to transfer information between SuperCalc and other popular software products, and how to install and use other software add-in products. Several import and export examples are given, including importing and exporting dBASE® files, importing text files from remote computing sources into a spreadsheet, and loading and saving 1-2-3® spreadsheets.

Appendixes

Appendix A explains PrivacyPlus™, supplied with SuperCalc5, which uses the National Bureau of Standards Data Encryption Standard (DES) to provide a secure means to encrypt and decrypt any DOS file. You can invoke PrivacyPlus from DOS or make it memory-resident so that you can invoke it with a key combination. You learn how to lock files (rendering them unreadable) with your own password and how to transform files back into plain text.

Many commands from previous releases of SuperCalc have been retained as "hidden commands." Appendix B lists several of the most frequently used hidden commands along with their equivalent commands in SuperCalc5.

How Do You Use This Book?

Throughout this book, a large number of figures and other illustrations show actual screen displays produced by executing SuperCalc commands. Seeing a command and its resulting output can reinforce good learning. Many figures, therefore, have been carefully placed throughout the chapters. All figures that represent SuperCalc displays are produced with the utility package InSet® and are exact replicas of the worksheet seen on-screen.

We have used several different applications as illustrations. These applications have been chosen for their business usefulness.

We hope that this book will increase your interest in SuperCalc and your understanding of the capabilities of spreadsheet packages. By using the familiar but varied examples, you may find new applications for SuperCalc and new ways to manage your existing applications. As you move further into the package, you will find even more uses for SuperCalc and techniques to shorten your learning curve. We also hope that these 14 chapters and two appendixes become the opening chapters of your long-lasting and satisfying experience with SuperCalc.

Part I

Learning the SuperCalc Spreadsheet

Includes

SuperCalc5: The Revolution

Getting Started: Some Preliminaries

One Time through a Spreadsheet

Formatting a Worksheet

Becoming More Proficient with SuperCalc

SuperCalc5: The Revolution

SuperCalc5 is the culmination of many years of evolution in the spreadsheet industry and several enhanced releases to the original SuperCalc. With the changes introduced in SuperCalc5, the word *revolutionary* appropriately describes the software package.

A revolution implies overcoming problems and shortcomings and creating new methods to accomplish tasks more effectively. In every way, SuperCalc5 can be called revolutionary. Several dramatic new commands and capabilities incorporated into SuperCalc5 go far beyond mere "enhancements" or minor software updates. For example, SuperCalc5 contains an extensive collection of integrated spreadsheet auditing and debugging commands, not merely add-in tools. SuperCalc5's graphing and slide generation commands represent an exponential improvement over its predecessor, SuperCalc4. Perhaps the most exciting new capabilities introduced in SuperCalc5 are multipage spreadsheets and multiple spreadsheet linking.

At the same time, Computer Associates has kept in mind the installed base of over one million SuperCalc users. Computer Associates went to great pains to maintain compatibility with previous SuperCalc programs. For example, SuperCalc users can run all the new SuperCalc5 features on existing hardware. SuperCalc5 does not require a 80286 or 80386-based computer in order to run. PCs with just 512K of memory and dual 360K drives can run SuperCalc. In addition, several of the commands from previous versions of SuperCalc, that have been improved and renamed, remain as *hidden* commands, lessening the learning curve. For example, the /View command has been replaced by the vastly more capable //Graphics command. However, users can still invoke /View, because it has been maintained and is available as a hidden command.

Computer Associates has incorporated and improved many of the best features of other successful spreadsheets on the market. For example, users who are familiar with 1-2-3 can work with SuperCalc in 1-2-3-compatibility mode. By issuing the /Global,1-2-3 command, the familiar 1-2-3 menu is displayed. You can execute all of the 1-2-3 Version 2.01 commands (such as /Worksheet, /File,Retrieve, etc.) directly from SuperCalc.

Before learning the details of the program, you should know the guidelines to follow when developing electronic worksheets. These guidelines can help you determine how to use spreadsheets in your everyday life.

Some Spreadsheet Basics

The SuperCalc5 spreadsheet is a package of computer programs written to provide a quickly accessible active working area divided into 255 columns and 9,999 rows. This description sounds like a two-dimensional matrix, right? Well, that is basically what a spreadsheet is, with numbered rows and columns. The SuperCalc spreadsheet has rows numbered 1 through 9,999 and columns lettered A through IU. However, there's a third dimension. SuperCalc5 supports up to 255 spreadsheets, each with up to 255 pages in memory—the third dimension.

Cells

The intersection of each column and row is referred to as a *cell*. Each cell is identified by its column and row coordinates. The upper left corner cell coordinates, A and 1, combine to make the cell *address* A1. The bottom right cell coordinates, IU and 9999, are written as IU9999. Cells on other pages are identified by a page number followed by a cell address or cell range. For example, you can reference cell B5 on page 2 from any page of a spreadsheet with the cell reference 2!B5. Cells in other spreadsheets (either in memory or on disk) are referenced by another level of qualification: a spreadsheet name. Cell B5 on page 1 of a spreadsheet named DIVISION is referenced from the current spreadsheet cell by the *link* reference DIVISION!1!B5.

Like organic cells, these spreadsheet cells can grow, but the growth is in the number of characters (letters or numbers) each cell displays. You can vary the size of the cells from 0 to 127 characters. On a display screen 80 characters wide and 25 lines long, therefore, you can view 20 rows and from 1 to 75 columns of the total spreadsheet working area at any one time (depending on your column-width selections). SuperCalc uses the remaining rows and columns for borders and for a *dialog panel* at the bottom. The dialog panel is used to display menus, enter data, and show worksheet statistics. If you have an EGA monitor, you can view up to 43 rows; VGA monitor users can view 50 rows on the console.

Access to the Spreadsheet

Computer Associates provides simple keyboard-movement controls to move around the active working area. Think of using these controls and keyboard movements as similar to changing your field of vision as you look at different areas of a large document lying on your desk.

The keyboard-movement keys drive a *cell pointer*. The cell holding the cell pointer is high-lighted in reverse video to make the cell pointer easy to see. Although information is dis-played in that cell, you enter data in an entry line on the same screen, just below the spreadsheet.

Cell Contents

Cell entries can contain numbers, text, or formulas. Of these three, formulas provide the most power to the spreadsheet. Following basic mathematical rules, formulas can contain numeric constants, cell references, range names, text strings, and functions. Formula functions were originally simple commands that combined the steps of a common but complex mathematical formula (such as the present net value calculation). SuperCalc5 now has so many of these functions that they are grouped into special categories for reference.

The Fundamentals of Speed

Several other utilities are as important to the success of spreadsheet software as is the visible matrix structure. With the spreadsheet's copying features, for example, you can copy data quickly from one cell to another cell, to a range of cells, or to other spread-sheets and spreadsheet pages. SuperCalc provides other utilities to help you work effi-ciently: ways to insert, delete, and move rows, columns, blocks of cells, and ranges of pages in a spreadsheet; ways to blank, protect, and unprotect cell ranges; and ways to load, save, and consolidate data from multiple spreadsheets stored on disk or in memory.

By generating cell entries using spreadsheet utilities, you can speed routine aspects of worksheet creation. Spreadsheets often consist of recurring data structures. The most common occasion for repeated structure, for example, is over a duration of time, such as a 30-day period or a 12-month period. Another recurring structure is a set of similar calcu-lations repeated for multiple sets of data. SuperCalc lets you take advantage of repeated structures in developing your spreadsheet. Once you have defined one structure (perhaps a column of figures for one month of financial activity or a sales summary for one of several products), creating the remaining similar structures is a matter of copying and editing cells instead of creating new structures.

You also can make many commands apply to a single cell, an entire row or column, a contiguous range of cells, an entire spreadsheet, a range of spreadsheet pages, or a group of spreadsheets. This power is most effective when you are formatting your worksheet. For example, to format all numeric values in your worksheet to appear with dollar signs and two decimal places, you can enter a single global command. Aligning all the cost catego-ries against the left edges of the cells requires only one command for the entire range.

Almost any spreadsheet package contains features that ease your workload. SuperCalc, however, has capacities that facilitate more accurate and sophisticated uses of your data.

A Brief SuperCalc History

The original SuperCalc program has had many enhancements over the years. In 1983, the original developer, Sorcim, was acquired by Computer Associates International, Inc., a mainframe software company. Sorcim was merged with Information Unlimited Software, another Computer Associates acquisition, and called Sorcim/IUS. In 1985, the name was changed to Computer Associates. Throughout this process, the company continued to upgrade the products to keep current with the industry and to take advantage of the increasing power and flexibility of the personal computer.

In the process of improvement, however, the program designers have avoided making SuperCalc more cumbersome or difficult to use. The software requires no elaborate installation procedures and uses many hardware features automatically. Installation is accomplished through the main SuperCalc menu rather than a separate installation program. A series of sample programs is included to demonstrate the more important and complicated features of the system.

SuperCalc's command-sensitive help screens simplify your use of the product. At each level of commands, information relating specifically to any program problem you might have is only a single keystroke away. After reviewing the on-line help, you are returned to where you were (at READY mode or in a command string) so that you can continue your work. This context-sensitive help is a valuable feature for first-time users.

SuperCalc5 is the seventh significant release of the original SuperCalc program. The first SuperCalc program was one of the earliest spreadsheets on the market. SuperCalc was similar in design to the original VisiCalc spreadsheet but, unlike VisiCalc, was available for the CP/M operating system. The basic structure has remained the same through all the revisions, with the command line and status line situated below the main spreadsheet.

SuperCalc5

Compatibility has been a hallmark of SuperCalc throughout its existence. SuperCalc5 continues that commitment by maintaining full compatibility with earlier SuperCalc releases. Additionally, SuperCalc5 bridges to the large computer environment through compatibility with its mainframe counterpart, CA-SuperCalc.

With an installed base of over a million SuperCalc users, Computer Associates has incorporated in SuperCalc5 exciting new features that respond to the market demand for a top-notch spreadsheet product. Major enhancements found in SuperCalc5 include multiple and multipage spreadsheets (linking), production-quality graphics, comprehensive debugging and auditing features, coexistence with 1-2-3, presentation-quality output, an add-in manager, and support for engineering and scientific applications. Yet all these new features require no extraordinary hardware support. SuperCalc5 has the same hardware requirements as SuperCalc3 and SuperCalc4: an IBM® PC (8088-based machine or compatible) with 512K memory and two 360K floppy disk drives. An overview of SuperCalc5's features is shown in table 1.1.

Table 1.1
Overview of SuperCalc5's Features

Computer Requirements	*Graphics Support*
Runs on a PC or XT	3-D bar, pie, area, and line
Does not need color/graphics interface	Curve fitting (best fit)
	Scatter/polar graphs
	Graph output to film recorders
Multiple/Linked Spreadsheets	GSS driver support
	Slide service available
3-D spreadsheets	
Linked spreadsheets in memory	*Output Support*
Links to disk with formulas	
Spreadsheet alias names	Complete laser/PostScript support
	Direct, menu-driven printer attributes
1-2-3 Coexistence	Fonts, shading, boxes, grids, and lines
	Automatic double underlining
Optional 1-2-3 menu	ASCII extended character set
Links to 1-2-3 spreadsheets	
Both 1-2-3 and host macros	*Performance Enhancements*
Import preserves macro syntax	
	Auto link to LAN devices
Debugging/Auditing Features	Compatible mainframe version available
	Selectable cell or range recalculation
Over 75 auditing and debugging functions	Interruptable recalculation
Spreadsheet map view	
Auto step-through macros	

Multiple and Multipage Spreadsheet Support

SuperCalc5 contains a new feature called *multisheets with hot links* (a *link* is a reference to a cell not on the current page). This new feature provides two types of linking: page (or three-dimensional) linking and spreadsheet linking. Page linking allows you to create a spreadsheet with several pages and link data in those pages to a summary or consolidated page. You can save all of the linked pages and the summary page under a single file name. A spreadsheet can contain up to 255 pages, subject to the amount of conventional and expanded memory you have. SuperCalc supports the LIM Expanded Memory Standard (EMS) 4.0 permitting up to 32 megabytes of memory.

SuperCalc5 also supports links to other, independent, SuperCalc or 1-2-3 spreadsheets. In addition, links can be made to spreadsheets stored on disk, allowing you to reference information in large spreadsheets without affecting memory or performance. Up to 255 SuperCalc and 1-2-3 spreadsheets may be referenced. If you are on a network, you can reference SuperCalc and 1-2-3 spreadsheets located anywhere within that network. Up to three spreadsheets and spreadsheet pages that are memory-resident can be viewed on-screen at once (see fig. 1.1).

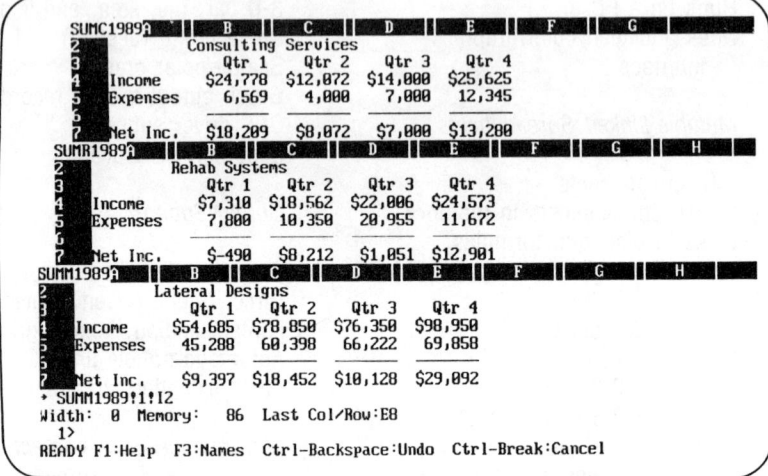

Fig. 1.1.

Three-dimensional and linked spreadsheets.

Production-Quality Graphics

Perhaps the most dazzling new enhancement in SuperCalc5 is its vastly improved graphics. SuperCalc5's graphics capabilities rival those of stand-alone graphics packages. Over 100 two- and three-dimensional chart and graph types are available, including pie, bar, stacked bar, area, and polar graphs. You also can produce high-quality transparencies and slides with bulleted phrases and words—word charts. Graphs and charts can be grouped, over-lapped, and clustered. Hundreds of graph and chart variations are available. Figure 1.2 shows a monochrome example of a three-dimensional area graph.

SuperCalc5 supports more graphics devices than previous versions, including VDI and CGI drivers for capturing images on film. You can have your graphics produced on slides and other output media by taking advantage of Computer Associates Graphics Service. State-of-the-art high-resolution monitors are supported, including large-screen monitors and VGA monitors.

Comprehensive Debugging and Auditing Features

SuperCalc5 includes an integrated, comprehensive debugging and auditing capability. Because spreadsheets are often large and complex and are used in making critical business

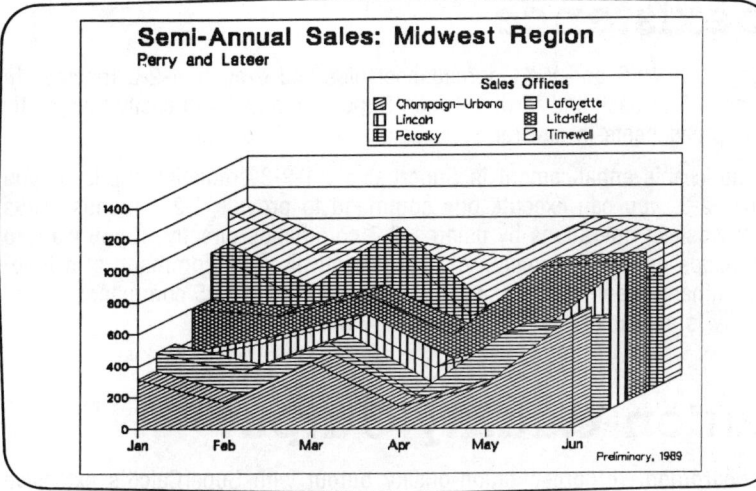

Fig. 1.2.

Presentation-quality graphics.

decisions, a simple method to audit spreadsheets is an essential tool. Invoked by typing //**T**est, you can use auditing to point out relationships between cells, highlight errors, and provide macro development and diagnostic aids. An overview of spreadsheet patterns and formulas is provided by the formula and map views of spreadsheets. Highlights are provided for cells whose contents change as a result of changing other cells. This is a valuable aid in visually spotting dependent and errant cell relationships.

Auditing features help you to develop correct macros. You can analyze line-by-line macro execution, set conditional and unconditional breakpoints, and produce a variety of audit reports. Figure 1.3 shows an example of a spreadsheet with highlighted cells and details shown in the audit detail box.

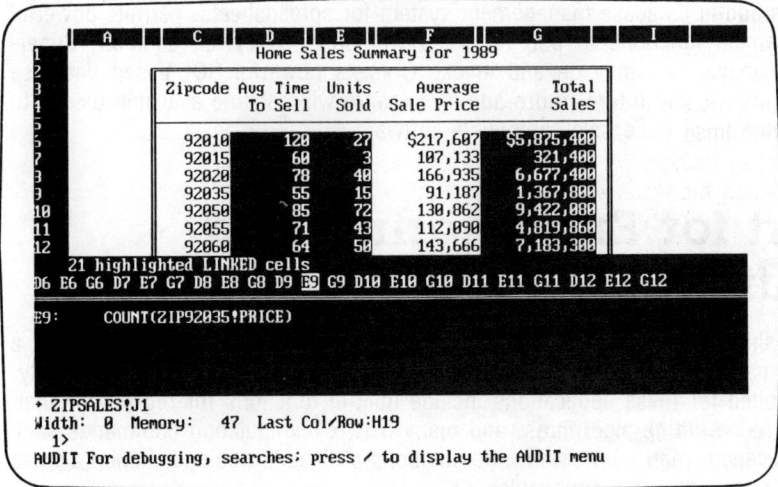

Fig. 1.3.

Comprehensive debugging and auditing tools.

1-2-3 Coexistence

SuperCalc can read 1-2-3 WKS and WK1 spreadsheet files and execute 1-2-3 macros. In addition, you can move files back and forth between SuperCalc and 1-2-3 easily by directly loading and saving spreadsheets in several SuperCalc and 1-2-3 formats.

Perhaps the most noticeable enhancement is SuperCalc5's 1-2-3 emulation mode. If you are migrating from 1-2-3, you can execute one command to provide 1-2-3 menus. Thus you can execute spreadsheet operations by using 1-2-3 commands directly. If you want to execute 1-2-3 commands only occasionally, you can selectively (one command at a time) turn on the 1-2-3 command menu and subsequently execute SuperCalc5 commands. All of the 1-2-3 functionality is available in this "compatibility mode."

Presentation-Quality Output

You can produce boardroom- or presentation-quality output with SuperCalc5's extensive support for both HP LaserJet™ and PostScript® laser printers. The impressive features include various fonts, lines, boxes, grids, and shading. SuperCalc5 also can take advantage of the special fonts provided with today's extensive array of output devices. You can print ready-to-use reports including, for example, 1040 tax forms identical to those provided by the Internal Revenue Service (ugh!). You can print profit-and-loss statements on a laser printer to produce camera-ready copy for annual reports. One menu option reports the total width of a spreadsheet (in characters) so that you can adjust the output font size before printing your spreadsheet.

Add-In Software Manager

An add-in manager allows third-party software to coexist with SuperCalc5. Silverado, Computer Associate's add-in database management system for spreadsheets, permits powerful database management functions to pop up when you press a key. In addition, SuperCalc5's add-in manager can manage and invoke Oracle's powerful SQL-based database management system. In the future, more add-in software will become available to add to the powerful collection of SuperCalc-compatible software.

Support for Engineering and Scientific Applications

Although spreadsheets have their roots in business applications, SuperCalc5 provides a large set of commands and functions that serve the engineering and scientific community. Functions well suited for these applications include built-in functions for regression analysis, choices for curve-fitting algorithms, and many matrix manipulation commands such as matrix multiplication, matrix inversion, and solutions of linear equations. SuperCalc can handle up to 90 equations with 90 variables.

Many graphing capabilities are aimed directly to the engineering and scientific user. For example, you can produce log-log and semi-log scaling when producing plots. With Super-Calc you can easily generate graphs produced with polar coordinates.

Other Advanced Features

Many important and sometimes subtle features are evident in SuperCalc5. You can specify recalculation ranges to limit and accelerate spreadsheet recalculation. Another feature, automatic memory squeezing, uses a unique memory saver algorithm to eliminate formula duplications. A special Undo key reverses unintentional commands and data entries and can be enabled or disabled as desired. Personal configuration files allow you to save and automatically restore many settings you have established as your personal preferences. Extensive import/export capabilities enable you to directly access many common file formats, including dBASE III files. You can directly query a dBASE file to select particular records that meet your criteria. Written in assembly language, SuperCalc5 performs functions quickly and efficiently.

Spreadsheet Security: PrivacyPlus

When you store your spreadsheets on a LAN file server or on a computer used by others, unauthorized individuals may have access to your files. Happily, SuperCalc solves that problem by including a special program called PrivacyPlus. This program encrypts files and renders them nearly impossible to decipher. Using the National Bureau of Standards-approved *Data Encryption Standard* (DES), PrivacyPlus can be invoked from DOS or can be memory-resident and invoked by pressing a key. You can encrypt any type of file: Super-Calc5 spreadsheets, software, dBASE database files, DOS utility programs, or WordStar® files. The encryption process uses a password you specify (from 3 to 32 characters) to encrypt a single file.

PrivacyPlus is a welcome addition to the growing number of products that are included with SuperCalc5. PrivacyPlus provides the needed security tool to protect confidential or private information from inadvertent or malicious disclosure to unauthorized users.

Applications for SuperCalc5

A host of applications can use SuperCalc5 spreadsheets. If you plan to use the program for business, SuperCalc5 can replace the more mundane tasks, leaving you with more time for analysis, decision making, or other more interesting and challenging duties.

If you are an accountant, for instance, you can incorporate that last-minute change in your statement and make your deadline without staying late. Budgeting, compiling actuals, and special reporting are all possible. Some of your greatest savings will occur when you must prepare periodic reports that incorporate many tables in the body of the text. You can develop such tables using SuperCalc5, store them in a disk file, and import them into a word processor to be printed.

In marketing and sales, SuperCalc5 can forecast sales, price the products, track quotes or sales by salesperson, analyze competitors, create questionnaires, or track business expenses. In manufacturing, you can quickly modify production schedules, analyze line and capacity problems, and record shipments. If your task is inventory control, you will find that calculating turns and forecasting reorder points were never before so simple.

If you are investment minded, you can use the program to manage property, call in data from various news sources, and perform investment analysis. If you are in education, whether teaching or learning, you can use SuperCalc5 to track grades; to generate statistical analysis of test scores; and to act as a tool in various business subjects such as accounting, finance, operations research, and economics.

If your interest lies in SuperCalc5 for home use, you can make a check register that posts to a budget and reconciles your bank balance. You can keep track of business expenses, forecast your income tax for the year, produce tax forms on your laser printer, and use the program to store databases for such things as mailing lists.

No matter what your type of application, SuperCalc5 can offer you several ways to save time and make otherwise ordinary projects more interesting. The program also will give you time to do other tasks that were never possible because of numerous recalculations and time constraints.

Worksheet Planning

As you become more involved with SuperCalc, you will find more varied uses. Some worksheets will take more thought and design preparation than others. If you are creating a "quick and dirty" report to be used only once, you need less preparation than if you are creating a fully integrated multiple-exhibit budget system. You can compose the former as you go, but the latter involves preparatory design steps.

Before you begin to develop your worksheets, you should answer the following list of questions. The questions are in future tense because you will be thinking of the answers before you begin creating a worksheet. The way you answer these questions will guide your worksheet development:

1. Will the worksheet be for you only or for others as well?

2. Will the worksheet be reused periodically as an input form (a *template*)?

3. Will the worksheet be subject to frequent structural changes?

4. Will the worksheet be part of a *consolidation*, comprising other spreadsheets referenced by link formulas?

5. Will the purpose of the worksheet be for analysis or for data storage?

6. How much will be riding on your worksheet (for example, winning or losing a proposal)?

Spreadsheet basics soon will be second nature to you, and you will be looking for more efficient means of developing quick, flexible, and comprehensive worksheets. In general, do what we constantly remind ourselves to do: "Keep it simple and clean." If you follow this rule, your worksheets will be more efficient to use, easier to understand later, and less cumbersome to calculate. You also can then make a faster transition to more advanced procedures.

Chapter Summary

SuperCalc5 is a powerful state-of-the-art integrated spreadsheet program. The spreadsheet, graphics, database management, and file-translating features are well-structured around the main spreadsheet display to give you tools for quick analysis and solutions to your business problems. The new features in SuperCalc5, including many new macros, a host of new and advanced functions, production-quality graphics, and multiple and multipage spreadsheet support, keep SuperCalc at the forefront of the industry.

Computer Associates' commitment to compatibility with previous releases of SuperCalc and other standard file formats makes file conversion painless. The program's automatic hardware-detection feature and not-copy-protected floppy disk masters make installation easy. And memory management and efficient coding make SuperCalc5 a sleek contender in the spreadsheet market.

Chapter 2 is a gentle introduction to SuperCalc5. You will learn some fundamental spreadsheet terminology, how to create a relatively simple spreadsheet, and how to enter text and numeric values to create a simple but useful spreadsheet. Other fundamental operations covered in Chapter 2 include saving a spreadsheet, loading a new spreadsheet, printing a spreadsheet, and leaving SuperCalc.

2

Getting Started: Some Preliminaries

This chapter describes how to invoke the SuperCalc program, print a spreadsheet, and leave the program. In addition, you will learn how to move the cell pointer, enter text data, and execute SuperCalc commands. After learning less than a dozen specific commands, you will be able to enter data, load new spreadsheets, and execute commands, such as the Help command, which displays on-line information. The chapter also provides several important definitions that will be used throughout the rest of the book.

When you finish this chapter, you will have used a "corner" of SuperCalc. You will be able to create, print, and save several useful spreadsheets. This chapter and its commands and activities serve as a springboard for the SuperCalc commands explained in chapters that follow.

If you have used SuperCalc4 or 1-2-3, you will find that SuperCalc5 is similar to those integrated spreadsheet packages. All the features available in SuperCalc4, for example, are retained in SuperCalc5. Many of the SuperCalc commands are similar to commands in 1-2-3 and so are easily recognized. Moreover, you can have SuperCalc display Lotus 1-2-3 commands by typing **/1** or by executing the **/G**lobal,**1**-2-3 command.

Note: The following sections contain important preliminary information about SuperCalc. Actually using SuperCalc to reproduce the screens and activities described in these sections will be very helpful to you. We suggest, therefore, that SuperCalc already be installed before you read further. Then, at convenient stopping places in your reading, perform the activities described and compare your results with ours.

Invoking SuperCalc

Having installed SuperCalc either on a floppy or a hard disk system, how do you execute the program? The file name of SuperCalc is SC5. (If you are using a hard disk, you must first log into the directory containing the SuperCalc files.) If you have a color monitor, type **SC5** to invoke the full-color options of SuperCalc. If you have a monochrome monitor system, such as a COMPAQ® or IBM monochrome system, type **SC5/BW** to invoke Super-Calc in black-and-white (BW) display. Although you can execute SuperCalc on a mono-chrome system by typing only **SC5**, some of the spreadsheet details are not always displayed satisfactorily because various colors do not display well on a monochrome moni-tor. The cell cursor, for example, is often difficult to locate on a monochrome monitor when SuperCalc is invoked by typing only **SC5**. All commands and most cell contents can be typed in either uppercase or lowercase. When a particular case is required, we make a special note of it.

When you press Enter, SuperCalc springs to action and first displays the Computer Associates International, Inc., logo and directions about how to proceed (see fig. 2.1).

Fig. 2.1.

The SuperCalc splash screen.

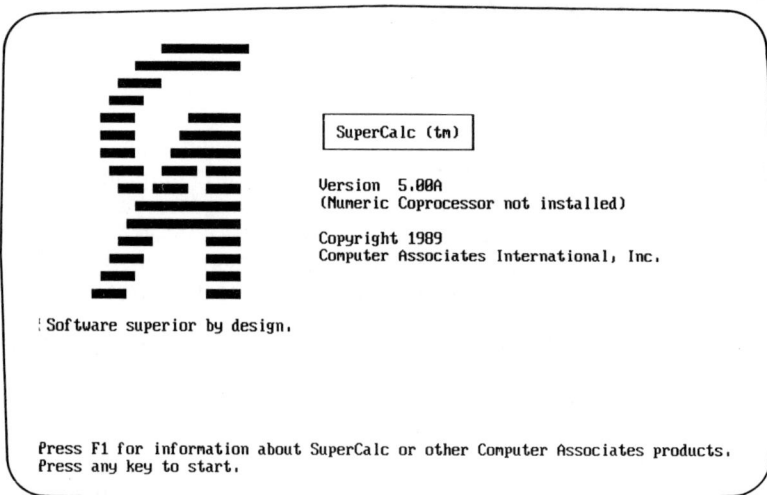

```
                          ┌────────────────────┐
                          │  SuperCalc (tm)    │
                          └────────────────────┘

                            Version  5.00A
                            (Numeric Coprocessor not installed)

                            Copyright 1989
                            Computer Associates International, Inc.

    Software superior by design.




    Press F1 for information about SuperCalc or other Computer Associates products.
    Press any key to start.
```

On a floppy disk system, you will be prompted to insert in drive A the second SuperCalc disk (*Product 2*). When you press Enter, you see on the screen a blank spreadsheet that can be filled with all sorts of information. Before placing any information on the spread-sheet, however, you need to know the structure of the blank spreadsheet and how to move around the spreadsheet.

Figure 2.2 shows the blank spreadsheet produced when SuperCalc is first invoked. Later, you will learn how to call up a previously created spreadsheet when you invoke SuperCalc. For now, however, start with a ''clean slate'' and examine the spreadsheet's structure.

To ensure a uniform, easily understood method of discussing different parts of the Super-Calc spreadsheet, we use certain words and terms throughout the remainder of the book. The following section defines several of these terms; the terms and definitions are consis-tent with those used by Computer Associates in the user's manual that accompanies the software. In addition, we examine the structure of the spreadsheet.

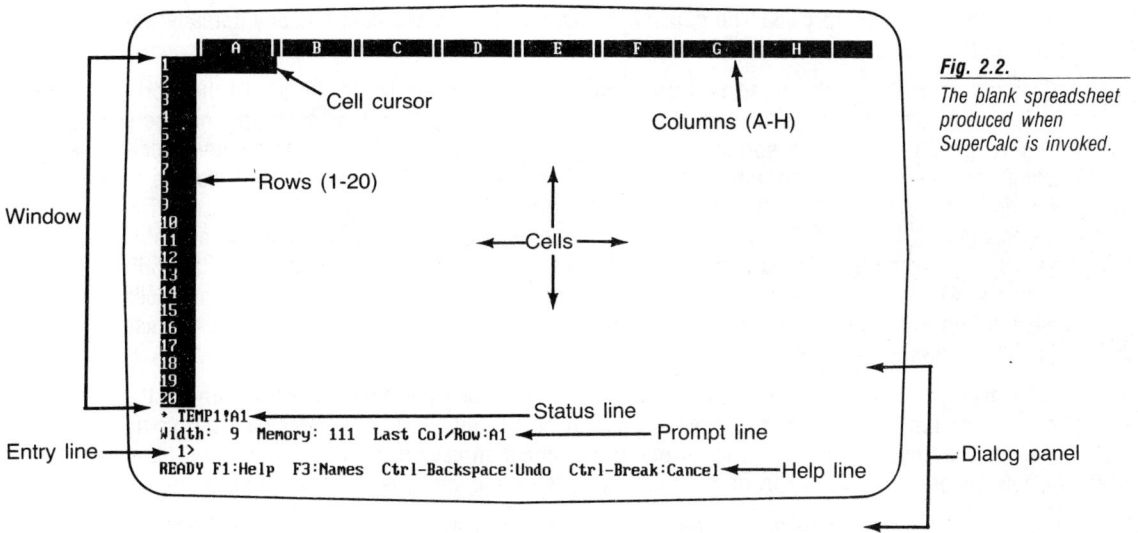

Understanding the Structure of the Spreadsheet

The SuperCalc spreadsheet displayed is composed of the following parts (see fig. 2.2):

1. Cells and the cell cursor
2. A dialog panel consisting of four lines:
   a. Status line
   b. Prompt line
   c. Entry line
   d. Help line

These parts are described in the paragraphs that follow.

Cells and the Cell Cursor

The part of the worksheet containing values, formulas, and characters that you enter or that SuperCalc computes is called the *window*. The spreadsheet window is composed of *cells*. The spreadsheet shown in figure 2.2 contains a total of 160 visible cells (20 rows by 8 columns). If you have an EGA or VGA monitor, you can see either 43 or 50 rows, respectively. You will learn how to "zoom" to these larger sizes in later chapters. Many more spreadsheet cells are available for use; however, not all of them can be displayed simultaneously. A SuperCalc spreadsheet can contain up to 9,999 rows and 255 columns for a total of 2,549,745 cells! The maximum number of rows and columns any spreadsheet can contain, however, is limited by the amount of memory in your computer.

Cells are uniquely numbered so that they can be referred to easily. At the top of the worksheet are column letters (A through H in fig. 2.2), and along the left side are row numbers (1 through 20). Because a spreadsheet can contain data in all 255 possible columns, columns are labeled beginning with A through Z. The next column is labeled AA. Columns to the right of AA are labeled AB through AZ, BA through BZ, CA through CZ, and so on. The last column is IU. On computers with smaller memories, the actual last column available varies. For example, the rightmost spreadsheet column is BK for machines with 256K memory. Machines with larger memories can access most or all of the 255 columns. Cells are referred to individually by a combination of column letters and row numbers. Examples of cell addresses are A20, B54, and CA34.

Whenever you want to place a value in a particular cell, use the *direction keys* to move the *cell cursor* until it is positioned over the cell to be altered. You then enter data by typing the information and pressing Enter or one of the direction keys to terminate the entry. Later in this chapter, you will learn more about using the direction keys to move the cell cursor.

Another way of reaching the desired cell immediately is by pressing the F5 function key, specifying the cell address, and pressing Enter. This command is called the GoTo command. Pressing F5, typing **M27**, and pressing Enter causes the cell cursor to jump directly to cell M27. You also can type the equal sign (=) and specify the cell address to jump to a cell.

The Current Cell and the Status Line

Immediately below the last row visible on the worksheet, the *status line* displays information about the location and contents of the current cell (see fig. 2.3). The seven different parts of the status line show the following information:

1. Cursor direction indicator
2. Spreadsheet name
3. Current cell address
4. Cell-entry format options
5. Protection indicator
6. Data type
7. Cell contents

The first character on the status line indicates the direction the cell cursor will move when you press Enter after entering data in a cell. This *cursor direction indicator* always shows the direction of the immediately preceding cursor movement, but you can alter the direction to help you enter data in a complete row or a complete column. You can also press the direction keys to alter the direction of movement. Pressing the down-arrow key after

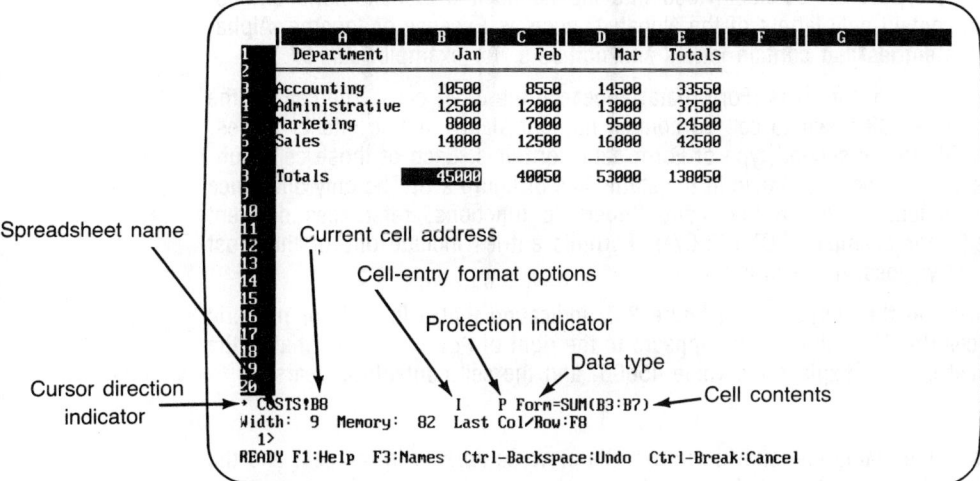

Fig. 2.3.
The status line.

typing in data enters the data into the current cell and moves the cursor to the cell below in the same column.

The second portion of the status line shows the *spreadsheet name* (COSTS in fig. 2.3). Spreadsheets being created for the first time are assigned a name beginning with TEMP (for example, TEMP1, TEMP2, etc.). That name indicates the name of the current spreadsheet being viewed. You can change this name at any time with the //**S**pread-sheets,**R**ename command.

The next item, the *current cell address*, indicates the current cell address of the cell cursor in column-row notation (B8 in fig. 2.3).

Immediately following the current cell address is the *cell-entry format options indicator*. This notation reveals any special formats of the current cell (any formats that differ from the default settings). Cell B8 has been formatted with the **I**nteger option (I in the status line).

The *protection indicator* is to the right of the cell entry format option. In figure 2.3, the P indicates that the current cell (B8) is protected (cannot be altered). The protection indicator is left blank for unprotected cells.

The last two components of the status line are the *data type* indicator and the *cell contents* indicator. Assuming four possible values, the data type indicator appears as one of the following:

Ctrl=	Control text (nonprinting text, preceded by I)
Form=	Formula entry (numbers or formulas)
Rtxt=	Repeating text
Text=	String text (labels, words, etc.)

Three of the four types (Form, Rtxt, and Text) appear in figure 2.3. Cells A1 through E1, for example, contain *Text* data (often called labels by spreadsheet users). Rtxt, which stands for *Repeating text*, is contained in cell A2 and is repeated in cells B2 through E2.

Rtxt and Text entry types can be subdivided into *alphabetic* and *alphanumeric* entries. Alphabetic entries contain only letters of the alphabet, such as *Expense* or *Income*. Alphanumeric entries are entries that contain letters and numbers, for example, *Jan 87*.

Two of the several kinds of formulas (Form data) appear in the other cells. The cells in the block ranging from cell B3 down to cell E6 contain numeric data—simple integer values. Cells B8 through E8 are the second type of Form data: formulas. Each of those cells contains a formula similar to the one shown in the status line of figure 2.3. The only difference is that the SUM function, one of the many SuperCalc functions, references different sequences of cells (for example, SUM(C3:C7)). Formula entries include one of the most frequently used entry types: numeric entries.

Form= is displayed on the status line in figure 2.3, indicating that a formula or numeric value resides in cell B8. The cell contents appears to the right of Form=. Notice that in the figure, spreadsheet cell B8 displays the value 45000, and the cell contents appears as

    SUM(B3:B7)

The cell contents in the status line shows the formula or value *entered* in the cell, and the spreadsheet cell displays the *computed result* of the formula evaluation.

The Prompt Line

Below the status line is the *prompt line*, which displays information about the entire spreadsheet (see fig. 2.4) or gives command prompt information (see fig. 2.5).

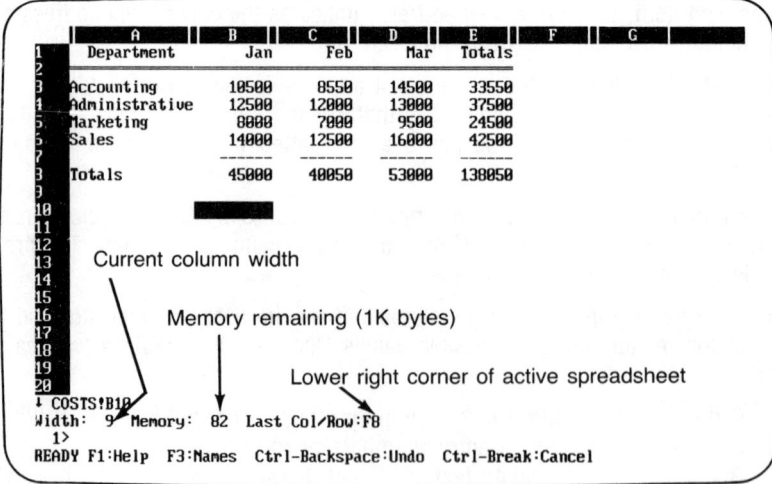

Fig. 2.4.

The prompt line displaying size and location information.

Width shows the width of the current cell (and thus the entire column). In the spreadsheet in figure 2.4, the value is 9. The column where the cell cursor is positioned is 9 characters wide, the default setting in SuperCalc. Memory is the amount, in thousands of bytes, of high-speed memory available. The value 82 in this spreadsheet indicates that approximately 82,000 bytes of memory remain available for spreadsheet cells. `Last Col/Row` holds the address of the lower right corner of the active spreadsheet. The cell address F8 means that no cells to the right of column F or below row 8 have been given values. If you think of a spreadsheet as a map with directions of north, south, east, and west, the `Last Col/Row` cell is the southeast corner of the spreadsheet. When a spreadsheet command is executed, the spreadsheet information is replaced by *command prompt* information (see fig. 2.5).

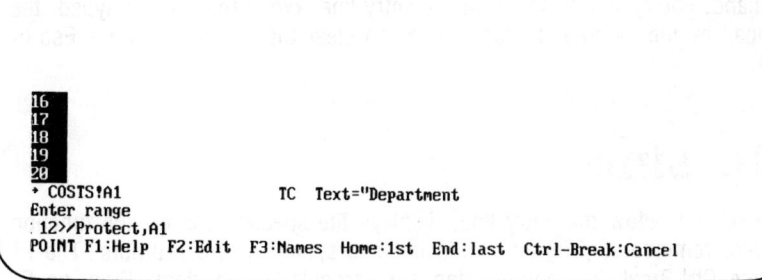

Fig. 2.5.

The prompt line displaying command options.

The Entry Line

Whenever you enter something other than a SuperCalc command or a cell-cursor-movement command, you are entering data into a cell. Located below the prompt line, the *entry line* shows the actual text, formulas, numbers, or control characters being entered in a spreadsheet cell. The *edit cursor* is activated and moves along the entry line. An example of data being entered on the entry line is the text label *First Quarter Sales* shown in figure 2.6. The number at the beginning of the entry line (20) is the position of the edit cursor on the entry line.

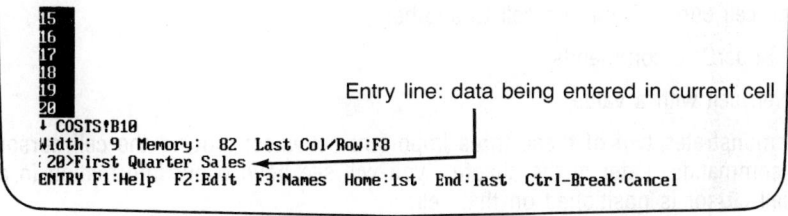

Entry line: data being entered in current cell

Fig. 2.6.

The entry line.

To enter data into a cell, you first type the data on the entry line. You then press Enter to move the data into the spreadsheet cell at the cell cursor.

As you type the data on the entry line, you can edit the data with the arrow keys if you have not yet pressed Enter to insert the data into a cell. If you have already pressed Enter, you can edit the data by invoking the EDIT mode. First, press the F2 function key to invoke EDIT mode; then use the direction keys to move the cursor to the character(s) to be altered. For example, the left-arrow key moves the edit cursor left in the entry line without deleting characters. The backspace key starts from the right end of the line and deletes characters. The Del (delete) key deletes characters to the right of the cell cursor. Press the Ins (insert) key to insert characters any place in the line. Notice that when Ins is pressed, the edit cursor changes from an underline to a square. Pressing the Home key moves the cursor to the leftmost position in the input line; pressing the End key moves the cursor to the rightmost position.

When you press Enter, the entry line is cleared, the value typed on the entry line is transferred to the appropriate spreadsheet cell, and the cursor position changes back to 1.

To execute a command, you type a slash (/) on the entry line. When the slash is typed, the status line is replaced by the command prompt line. To clear the entry line, press Esc or Ctrl-Break (cancel).

The Help Line

The *help line*, located just below the entry line, displays the special uses for the function keys, help messages, reminders, program mode indicators, and macro prompts. The F1 function key and the Ctrl-Break key combination are particularly important. Pressing F1 displays several screens of help information. The Ctrl-Break combination cancels the current activity—either canceling and clearing the entry line or canceling the current command. The status, prompt, entry, and help lines appear at the bottom of the screen as shown in figure 2.6. (The help line is the last line shown.)

Working in the Spreadsheet

To start using a blank spreadsheet, you must know how to perform three fundamental operations:

1. Move the cell cursor from one cell to another

2. Execute SuperCalc commands

3. Fill a given cell with a value

This section demonstrates two of these three important activities: moving the cell cursor and executing commands. Later in the chapter, you will see how to put information in a cell once the cell cursor is positioned on that cell.

Moving the Cell Cursor with the Direction Keys

You move the cell cursor around in the spreadsheet by pressing various *direction keys*. SuperCalc has two kinds of direction keys. One kind is indicated by *control-key sequences*, produced by pressing and holding the key marked ''control'' or ''Ctrl'' and simultaneously pressing a letter key. For example, to move the cell cursor to the right, hold down the Ctrl key and press the letter D. To move the cell cursor to the left, press the Ctrl key and the letter S. This sequence of key movements is abbreviated to the notation Ctrl-S. Ctrl-E and Ctrl-X move the cell cursor up and down, respectively.

The arrow keys also move the cell cursor. These arrow keys are located to the right of your keyboard in the numeric keypad. In this book, the words *up, down, left,* and *right* indicate the cell-cursor-movement direction. The instructions "Press the right direction key" and "press the left direction key" direct you to press a cell-cursor-movement key (either Ctrl-S and Ctrl-D or left arrow and right arrow, respectively). Pressing a right direction key moves the cell cursor to the right by one column. Pressing the down, left, or up direction key also moves the cell cursor in the appropriate direction.

Home and End are two additional direction keys on the numeric keypad. Home moves the cell cursor from its current position to the top left corner of the worksheet (cell A1). Pressing End and then Home moves the cursor to the lower right corner of the active portion of the spreadsheet.

Try using the direction keys. First, press Home so that the cell cursor is in cell A1. Now use the right and down direction keys to move from one cell to another. Notice that the only things that change on the displayed worksheet are the cursor direction indicator (the cursor moves, of course) and the current cell address, on the status line.

You can move the cell cursor quickly to the lowest right portion of the active worksheet by pressing two keys: End and then Home. This key sequence goes to the lowest and farthest right *occupied* cell (see table 2.1).

Table 2.1
Cell-Cursor-Movement Keys

Key	Resulting Cursor Movement
Arrow keys	Up, down, right, or left one cell (or use Ctrl-E (up), Ctrl-X (down), Ctrl-D (right), and Ctrl-S (left))
Home	To cell A1
End + Home	To the bottom right cell of active spreadsheet
End + arrow	To the last occupied cell in the direction of the arrow key pressed
Tab + arrow	To the first occupied cell in a series of occupied cells in the direction of the arrow key. When the last occupied cell is reached, Tab + arrow moves the cell cursor to the edge of the entire spreadsheet.
Backtab + arrow (Shift-Tab + arrow)	To the last occupied cell in a series of occupied cells in the direction of the arrow key. When the last occupied cell is reached, Backtab + arrow moves the cell cursor to the edge of the entire spreadsheet.
Return or Enter	To the next cell in the direction of the last cell cursor movement

Table 2.1—*Continued*

Key	Resulting Cursor Movement
PgUp	To the same relative position one screen (window) up or until row 1 is reached
PgDn	To the same relative position one screen (window) down or until the last row is reached
Ctrl-left arrow	To the same relative position one window to the left or until column A is reached
Ctrl-right arrow	To the same relative position one window to the right or until the last column is reached
Ctrl-Home	To the top left corner of the current window
Ctrl-End	To the bottom right corner of the current window
F5 or =	To the cell specified after F5 or =. Press Enter to complete the GoTo command.
F6	To the other window of a split screen. F6 is termed the *window switch command.*
Ctrl-F5	To a specified spreadsheet name
Ctrl-F6	Switch spreadsheet windows (between several memory-resident spreadsheets)
Ctrl-minus	Go to preceding page or spreadsheet
Ctrl-plus	Go to next page or spreadsheet
Ctrl-=	Enter the name of a spreadsheet to display
End-Ctrl-End	Go to the last page of the current spreadsheet
End-Ctrl-Home	Go to the first page of the current spreadsheet
Tab-Ctrl-End	Go to the first page of the last sheet on the Open Spreadsheet Directory
Tab-Ctrl-Home	Go to the first page of the first spreadsheet on the Open Spreadsheet Directory
Tab-Ctrl-plus	Go to the first page of the next spreadsheet on the Open Spreadsheet Directory
Tab-Ctrl-minus	Go to the first page of the preceding spreadsheet on the Open Spreadsheet Directory

Scrolling the Worksheet

To move the cell cursor to cell F5, start at the Home position (press Home) and press the right-arrow key four times and the down-arrow key five times. Voila! The cell cursor has moved, and the status line indicates that the active cell is F5.

You can see that moving the cell cursor to a cell some distance from the current position (to column AW from the Home position, for example) becomes difficult when you use the direction keys. SuperCalc answers this problem with the *scrolling keys*. Like the simple direction keys, a scrolling key moves the cell cursor in one of four directions. However, the cursor movement occurs in "big chunks." The whole worksheet scrolls right, left, up, or down. The right-scroll sequence is accomplished by holding down the Ctrl key and pressing the right-arrow key. To scroll the cell cursor to column AW from the Home position, hold down Ctrl and press the right-arrow key six times.

Executing SuperCalc Commands

Commands accomplish tasks such as sorting rows or columns, formatting cells, printing spreadsheets, and performing various other duties. You type commands on the same entry line used to enter data for the cells. However, SuperCalc distinguishes between cell data and commands by the first letter typed on the entry line. You invoke the command line by typing the slash (/) or the double slash (//). When SuperCalc recognizes the slash on the entry line, the program replaces the status and prompt lines with the *command prompt lines*, listing the available commands. An illustration of the command prompt lines is shown in figure 2.7.

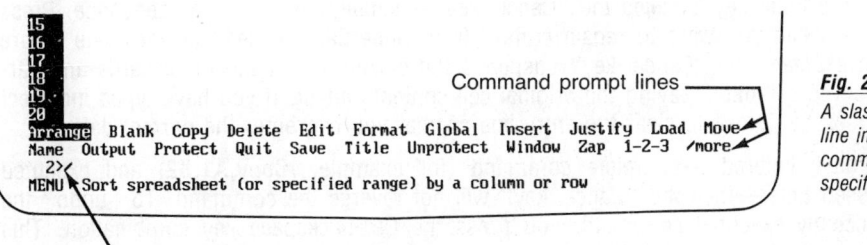

Command prompt lines ─────

Fig. 2.7.
A slash on the entry line indicating that a command is being specified.

Slash indicates a command is being entered

Following the slash on the entry line, you type the single letter specifying the required command. For example, the command entry /**S** invokes the /**S**ave command. If you press the slash key and then the F1 function key, you see an AnswerScreen™, a help display containing a brief explanation of the commands. A sample help screen is shown in figure 2.8. The Help command is discussed in greater detail later in the book.

What if you inadvertently press some other command letter and accidentally tell SuperCalc to execute the wrong command? Or what if you are typing a numeric value and discover that it is incorrect? Does SuperCalc have a convenient way to cancel an incorrect command or erase a bad data entry line? Yes!

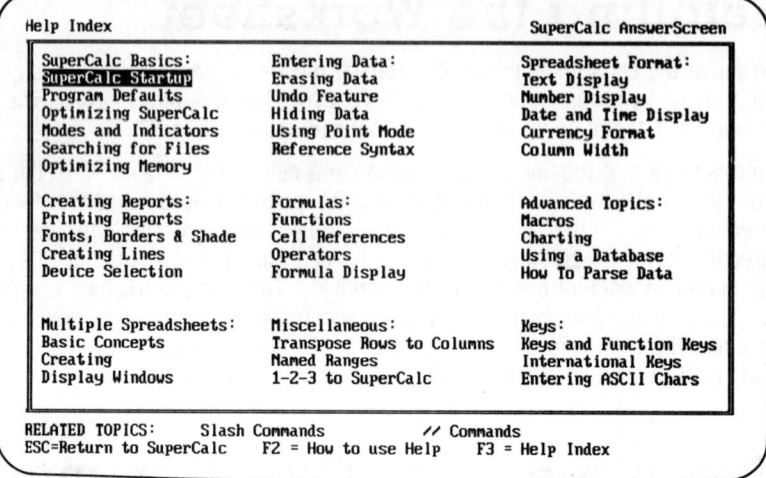

Fig. 2.8.

A help display (AnswerScreen).

Canceling a Command or Entry

Occasionally (or perhaps frequently at first), you may find that you have told SuperCalc to execute the wrong command or that the data you typed is incorrect. Such mistakes happen. SuperCalc offers you two ways to reverse what you have most recently done: pressing the "Cancel key" or pressing the Undo key.

The key that aborts the command request that appears on the entry line *before* you have pressed the Enter key is called the "Cancel key"—actually the Ctrl-Break sequence. Press Ctrl-Break when you want to regain control from SuperCalc or clear an entry line before you press Enter. The "Cancel key" suspends the current command or discards any partially entered cell data, leaving the original cell contents intact. If you have typed incorrect data, press Ctrl-Break to clear the entry line so that you can enter the correct data.

If you have entered a complete command (for example, /**C**opy,**A1**,**B2**) and executed it—pressed Enter—then the "Cancel key" will not reverse the command. To "undo" the most recently executed command, you press the Ctrl-backspace key combination. This Undo feature allows you to reverse any command. Pressing Ctrl-backspace restores the spreadsheet to its form before the most recent command; however, you can reverse only the most recently executed command. For the Undo feature to be active, you must execute the /**G**lobal,**O**ptimum,**P**resent,**U**ndo command sequence prior to the current SuperCalc session. The /**G**lobal commands are described throughout the book.

In addition, you can press the Esc key to cancel the current *option* of a given command, but not the entire command. For example, if you have typed

/**C**opy,**A1**,**B5**

you can press Esc to erase the rightmost entry on the Entry line (B5), back to the rightmost comma.

You now have enough information to begin creating a worksheet. The following section shows you how to use the SuperCalc commands and cursor-movement keys to begin building your first worksheet.

Building a New Spreadsheet

You can practice using SuperCalc by beginning to build an automobile loan worksheet that will determine a monthly payment for a loan at various interest rates for several different durations (in years). Before plunging ahead and creating this worksheet, look at its finished version to get an idea of where you're headed (see fig. 2.9).

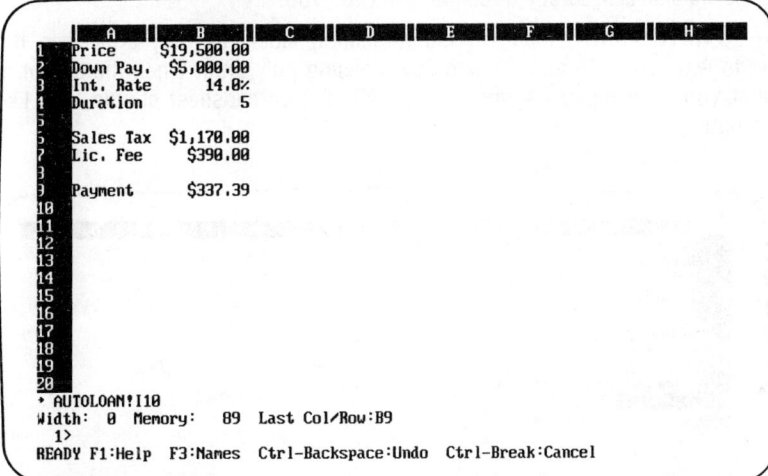

Fig. 2.9.

Completed AUTOLOAN worksheet.

In this chapter, you begin building a worksheet that looks exactly like the one shown in figure 2.9. You will put this worksheet in final shape in Chapter 3, so follow along with your copy of SuperCalc and perform all the steps here.

The automobile loan worksheet will, when finished, allow you to "plug in" different values for the down payment, interest rate, and loan duration to determine the value of the monthly payment (*Payment* in fig. 2.9) with various combinations of those three variables. The worksheet also calculates the amounts of the sales tax and license fee.

Entering Labels into the Worksheet

You begin by entering labels as text data. The seven labels to enter in the worksheet appear in the first column of the worksheet in figure 2.9. With the cell cursor positioned in cell A1, type **Price** exactly as you see it and press Enter. Notice that cell A1 now contains the label *Price*.

Note also that the cell cursor has moved one cell to the right, to cell B1. SuperCalc "assumes" that the cell cursor will move in the same direction that it has been moving. Because you have not yet moved the cursor, the initial default movement is to the right. You can, however, change the default direction. Because column A is to be filled with labels, you want the cell cursor to move down column A. To do that, move the cursor from B1 to A1 with the left-arrow key and then press the down arrow. This operation does two things:

1. Positions the cell cursor in the cell to be filled

2. Sets the default cell cursor direction to down

With the cell cursor in cell A2, type the text value **Down Pay.** and press the down arrow or Enter. The label *Down Pay.* is entered in the cell, and the cell cursor moves to cell A3 for data entry in that cell. You have discovered an important and efficient way to enter data into cells: letting the default cell cursor direction work for you.

Continue moving down column A, filling in the remaining labels as they appear in the figure. Remember to leave cells A5 and A8 blank by pressing only Enter when the cursor is in these cells. After you have typed **Payment** in cell A9, the spreadsheet should look like the one shown in figure 2.10.

Fig. 2.10.

AUTOLOAN worksheet with labels entered.

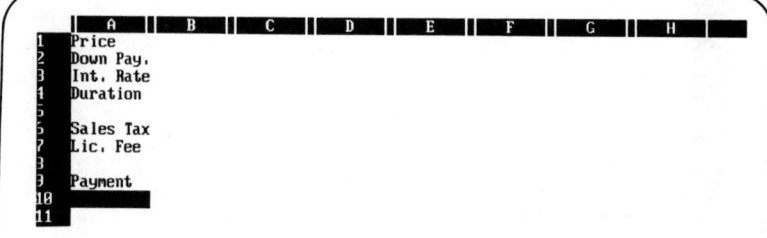

Entering Numeric Data into the Worksheet

Next, you enter numeric values as the *independent variables*. These values do not depend on other parts of the worksheet; instead, other values are determined by the independent variables. For example, the amount of the sales tax depends on the value entered for the price of the car.

Move the cursor to cell B1. This time, however, instead of using the arrow keys, type =**B1** on the entry line and press Enter. Earlier in the chapter, you learned that the equal sign (=) preceding a cell address is a quick way of moving to cells that are not adjacent to the current cell. This GoTo command does not alter the cursor direction indicator. However, because data is to be filled in from the top of column B down, the current direction is what you need.

To enter numeric data, simply type the value and press Enter. First, enter **19500** as the automobile's price. The cursor then moves to cell B2. Enter the value of **5000** for the amount of the down payment, and press Enter once more. (We will not include the direction to press Enter much more because this instruction is implied when you are entering numeric or text data.) Next, enter the value **.14** in cell B3. Finally, enter the value **5** in the cell adjacent to *Duration*. This time, however, after you have typed **5** and pressed Enter, press Enter once more to leave cell B5 blank.

Wait a minute! The partial worksheet doesn't look exactly like the worksheet in figure 2.9. Why not? You need to tell SuperCalc to format numeric values to display two places after the decimal point and floating dollar signs (formatting is explained further in Chapter 4.) At this point, without row or column indicators, the automobile loan worksheet should look like the worksheet in figure 2.11.

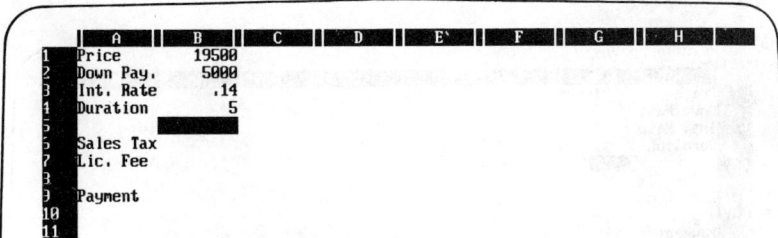

Fig. 2.11.

AUTOLOAN worksheet with labels and unformatted independent numeric variables.

A good deal of work has been accomplished so far, but a few more tasks are required to make your current version of the AUTOLOAN spreadsheet look like the spreadsheet in figure 2.9. The major information yet to be added includes values for *Sales Tax*, *Lic. Fee*, and *Payment*. Because these three values are computed from formulas, further discussion about them is delayed until the next chapter. Now, you need to know how to save the work you have done so that you can come back later to "fine tune" the worksheet.

Saving and Reloading the Changed Spreadsheet

You should form the good habit of saving the work you have entered in your spreadsheet. Always save a spreadsheet before you leave SuperCalc at the end of a session. In that way, you will always have a copy of the latest version of any spreadsheet. Save your work with the straightforward SuperCalc command /**S**ave.

Saving a Spreadsheet

To invoke the /**S**ave command, type /**S** (either uppercase or lowercase) on the entry line. Notice that as you type **S**, SuperCalc fills in the complete word *Save* and supplies a comma. Most commands are invoked by typing the slash (/) and one letter (others are invoked by typing two slashes and one letter). Or you can type /, use the arrow keys to highlight the proper command on the command prompt lines, and press Enter. After you enter the /**S**ave command, the last three lines of the dialog panel at the bottom of the spreadsheet appear as follows:

```
Enter Filename
 12›/Save,TEMP1
  FILE  F1:Help  F2:Edit  F3:File list  Ctrl-Break:Cancel
```

The command prompt and entry line indicate that a spreadsheet name can be typed. Because this is a new spreadsheet, type the name **AUTOLOAN** to specify the file name under which to save the spreadsheet, and then type a comma. (You must supply the comma because SuperCalc cannot predict how long the file name will be.) Notice that the default spreadsheet name TEMP1 is replaced with AUTOLOAN.

Because you should save the entire spreadsheet rather than just the values or parts of it, press Enter, which invokes the default **A**ll on the prompt line. (You also can type **A**.) Figure 2.12 shows the spreadsheet and dialog panel prior to your pressing Enter.

Fig. 2.12.

Invoking the /Save command.

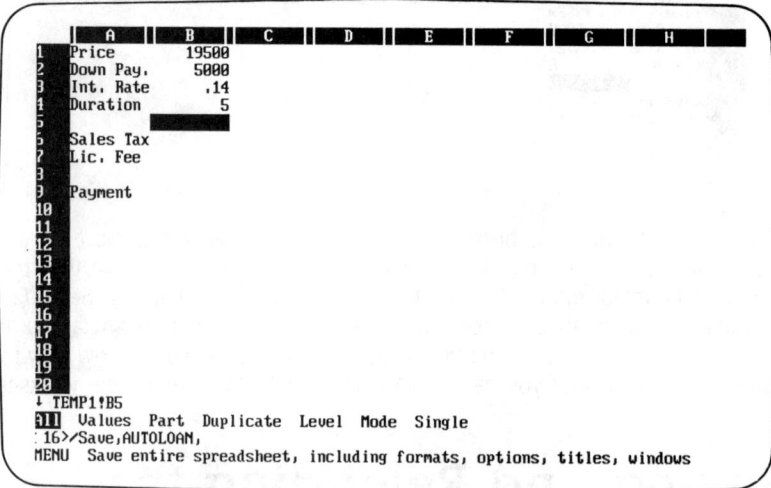

When you press Enter to choose **A**ll, SuperCalc saves all your work in a new file called AUTOLOAN.CAL. (SuperCalc supplies CAL as a default file extension.) The file is saved on the default disk: drive A for floppy disk computers or drive C if SuperCalc was first invoked from drive C. Now you have a copy of the spreadsheet that can be used later to add more data or print the results.

Loading Another Spreadsheet in SuperCalc

Suppose that you want to work on another spreadsheet and abandon the one currently displayed. You can clear the present worksheet from the console and work on a previously stored one. The /Zap command completely erases the current spreadsheet in preparation for loading a new spreadsheet. The /Zap command is executed by typing /Z. SuperCalc then asks whether the entire spreadsheet is to be erased, as shown in the following prompt, entry, and help lines, which appear at the bottom of the screen:

```
No  Yes  Save  Page
6›/Zap,
MENU  Do not clear the spreadsheet — return to ready mode
```

By pressing **Y** for **Y**es, you instruct SuperCalc to go ahead and erase the entire spreadsheet from memory. The disk file containing the spreadsheet is not affected—only the loaded (memory-resident) spreadsheet is erased. Note that because the suggested default is **N**o, the spreadsheet is not erased if you press only Enter. Before loading a new spreadsheet, however, you should erase the current spreadsheet. Otherwise, the two spreadsheets (the current one being displayed and the new one being loaded) can combine in unwanted ways.

The second and final step in loading a new worksheet is to execute the /**L**oad command. As with all SuperCalc commands, the slash indicates that a command is being entered. Following the slash, type **L**. The prompt, entry, and help lines displayed are

```
Enter Filename
15›/Load,AUTOLOAN
FILE  F1:Help  F2:Edit  F3:File list  Ctrl-Break:Cancel
```

The cursor is positioned to the right of the suggested spreadsheet name (AUTOLOAN). To load a spreadsheet called MORTGAGE.CAL, you erase the suggested file name by typing **MORTGAGE** and a comma. Before you press the comma key, the prompt, entry, and help lines are changed to

```
Enter Filename
15›/Load,MORTGAGE
EDIT  F1:Help  F3:File list  Ctrl-Break:Cancel
```

After you type **MORTGAGE** and the comma, the prompt line reads

```
Replace  All  Values  Consolidate  Part  Names  Graphs  Single
```

Generally, you want to load the entire spreadsheet. If this is the case, type **A** to indicate **A**ll as your choice. SuperCalc then loads the spreadsheet and clears the status and entry lines.

A second way to clear the current spreadsheet from memory (and the screen) and load a new spreadsheet from disk, all in one operation, is by issuing the /**L**oad command with the **R**eplace option. The **R**eplace option, the suggested default, performs the same function as the /**Z**ap command followed by the /**L**oad,*sheetname*,**A**ll command. The **R**eplace option clears memory and then loads the new spreadsheet.

Loading a Spreadsheet from the DOS System Prompt

If your disk holds spreadsheets from previous work sessions, you can load one of these spreadsheets when you first execute the SuperCalc program. When you type the name of the spreadsheet immediately following **SC5**, SuperCalc automatically loads the named spreadsheet. The following examples show this technique using both a computer with two disk drives and a computer with one disk drive and a hard disk.

If your computer has two disk drives and an A› appears on the screen, you should place the SuperCalc system disk in drive A and your data disk in drive B. You may, for instance, type the following:

SC5 B:AUTOLOAN

Press Enter. In one operation, SuperCalc executes and loads the file AUTOLOAN.CAL (stored on the disk in drive B).

If you have a hard disk, you probably have a C› on the screen (or whatever drive designation your hard disk has). First, you should change to the directory that contains your SuperCalc program files by typing, for example,

CD \CALC5

and pressing Enter. Next, you can type

SC5 C:\CALC5\DATA\SHEETS\AUTOLOAN

and press Enter. This command is based on the assumption that CALC5 is the subdirectory that contains the SuperCalc program files, and that C:\CALC5\DATA\SHEETS\ is the subdirectory that contains the file AUTOLOAN.CAL. Again, in one operation, SuperCalc executes and loads the file.

Whether you have two disk drives or one disk drive and a hard disk, the normal initial display screen shown in figure 2.1 is bypassed.

Printing the Spreadsheet: The /Output Command

The final results of a spreadsheet computation are usually printed or included in a report. You use the /Output command to send a file to the printer or to a disk file.

If you are working with SuperCalc as you read these instructions, load the AUTOLOAN worksheet. You execute the /Output command, like other commands, by typing / followed by the first letter of the command. Several choices appear on the prompt line: **P**rinter, **F**ile, **A**ttributes, **G**rid, **L**ines, and **N**ew-page. Because you want to print the file, press **P** (or Enter). Figure 2.13 shows the prompt line that appears.

Several choices are displayed. To produce printed output, select the first choice, **R**ange. (All the options will be described in later chapters.)

A *range* is one or more cells for which an operation is to take place. A range can be a single cell, several (or all) cells in the same row or column, or a rectangular block. A range consisting of a row or a partial row is identified by specifying the leftmost and rightmost cell addresses separated by a period or a colon (C12:H12). A range consisting of an entire or partial column is given by the cells at the top and bottom of the column separated by a colon or period (A2:A20). A rectangular block range of cells is identified by the cell addresses of either pair of cells at opposite corners of the block. Examples of four ranges that identify the same block are A10:D15, D15:A10, A15:D10, and D10:A15.

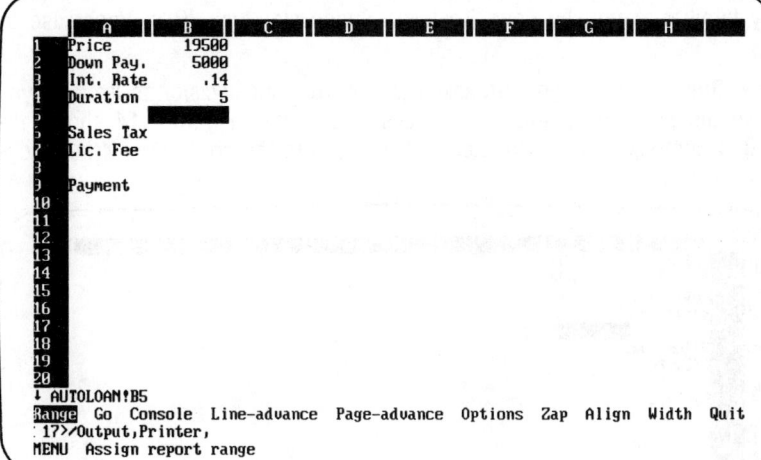

Fig. 2.13.

Selecting printer output.

Like all SuperCalc commands requiring range addresses, the output range is a pair of cell addresses separated by a colon (:). The range specifies the boundaries of the spreadsheet to be printed. After you press Enter or **R** to select the **R**ange option, enter the upper left and lower right spreadsheet corner addresses to define the spreadsheet area to be printed. Because the entire spreadsheet is to be printed, you use the cell range A1:B9. (An easy way to specify the entire spreadsheet is to press the Home key, type a colon, and then press the End and Home keys. This guarantees that the entire active spreadsheet range is specified.) The entry line now reads

        28>/Output,Printer,Range,A1:B9

To complete the specification of the range to be printed, type a comma (,). The main /**O**utput command prompt and menu lines then appear again (see fig. 2.13). The final step necessary for printing a spreadsheet is to press **G** to select the **G**o option. The following messages are displayed:

                        Insert paper and press any key
        Printing...

You press any key to start printing. If the printer is not turned on or is out of paper, SuperCalc detects the situation and displays a warning message. After printing is completed, the /**O**utput command line disappears, leaving a blank entry line.

Leaving SuperCalc: The /Quit Command

Once you have printed your spreadsheet, SuperCalc restores the command line to the familiar form of a list of the major commands. To leave SuperCalc and return to the operating system to carry out other tasks, use the /**Q**uit command. The way you invoke a command is probably familiar to you by now. To leave SuperCalc, type /**Q** in uppercase or lowercase.

Having invoked the /**Q**uit command, you are asked to confirm your decision to leave. If you decide not to leave the program at this time, press **N** or Enter. Figure 2.14 shows the screen after the /**Q**uit command has been executed, but before the confirming **Y** keystroke is entered.

Fig. 2.14.

*Leaving SuperCalc with the /**Q**uit command.*

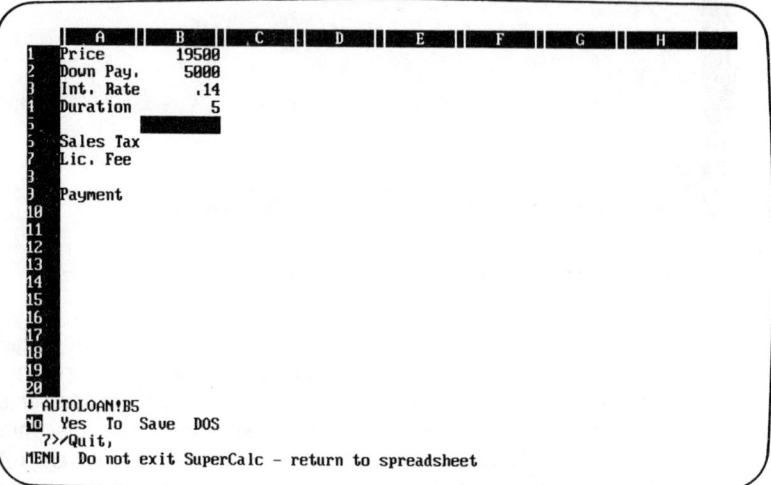

Chapter Summary

This chapter has lead you through several fundamental SuperCalc activities and commands. The chapter describes how to invoke SuperCalc, how to enter numeric and label information into spreadsheet cells, and how to save your spreadsheet. In addition, you have learned how to print a spreadsheet and load another spreadsheet. Having these fundamental spreadsheet skills, you are equipped to proceed to create more complicated and interesting spreadsheets.

In Chapter 3, you will abandon this spreadsheet and move on to a similar, more informative AUTOLOAN spreadsheet. When the AUTOLOAN spreadsheet is completed, it will contain the information you need to answer "what if" questions, such as, "What if the interest rate changes to 10 percent?" "What about a loan duration of 3 years?" "What if the down payment is decreased to $2,000?"— and so on.

3

One Time through a Spreadsheet

This chapter shows you how to develop a complete spreadsheet from the AUTOLOAN worksheet you began in Chapter 2. You will give the worksheet the capability to compute loan payments. You can then reorganize the worksheet into two sections so that independent variables are located in an area separate from computed results. The top section of the spreadsheet will contain purchase price, down payment, and annual interest rate —data supplied by the spreadsheet user. The lower section of the spreadsheet will contain values computed from the independent variables supplied in the first section.

The loan payment calculations you use in this chapter are common business calculations. Serving as a basis for many different kinds of loan payments, this spreadsheet can be modified to suit your particular needs. For example, you can use the model to compute monthly home-mortgage payments. First, you enter your house purchase price, down payment, and interest rate. Then, by altering the loan-duration values in the second half of the spreadsheet to 20, 25, and 30, you can have the spreadsheet calculate monthly payment amounts for 20-, 25-, and 30-year mortgages.

You also will learn to create formulas and use SuperCalc's capabilities to build flexible spreadsheets for many different situations. Good spreadsheets can be used easily by persons less familiar with such spreadsheets. The activities introduced in this chapter provide a professional-quality spreadsheet model that can be used repeatedly with new values to answer questions such as ''What if the interest rate drops to seven percent?'' or ''What would the payments be for a five-year automobile loan for $18,500?''.

Techniques such as protecting spreadsheet cells, formatting cells to display information more attractively, and building general spreadsheets are introduced and reinforced in this chapter. You learn more about various cells, such as text, repeating text, textual values, and formulas. You are also introduced to the arithmetic operators: addition ($+$), subtraction ($-$), multiplication (*), division (/), exponentiation ($\hat{}$ or **), percent (%), and unary minus ($-$). In addition, a section of this chapter describes cell referencing: absolute and relative addressing. You also see examples of the /**N**ame, /**C**opy, /**P**rotect, /**U**nprotect, and /**F**ormat commands. Once you have mastered the concepts in this chapter, you should be able to build your own useful spreadsheets with SuperCalc.

39

Understanding the Cell Types

The simple AUTOLOAN spreadsheet introduced in Chapter 2 contains labels and simple numeric values. Up to this point, all the labels and four of the numeric-valued cells have been filled in. The labels, such as *Down Pay.* and *Price*, are text, so they reside in *text* cells. The values in the second column, such as 19500 and 5000, are considered *formulas*, although the values are simple numeric values. Formula cells also can contain actual formulas: cell references, functions, numeric constants, and combinations of these formulas joined by arithmetic and logical operators.

Text-data entry is described in Chapter 2. *Textual data* and *repeating text* are both created using text (alphabetic) characters. The differences between text data, textual values, and repeating-text data are described in sections that follow.

Repeating-Text Cells

Repeating text is just what the name says: text that is repeated in any number of consecutive cells. Repeating text starts in the current cell and moves to the right across *empty* cells (cells without data) until the text reaches the last column or an occupied cell. You can use repeating text to create long lines that separate parts of a spreadsheet. Repeating text can consist of one or several characters. For example, the repeating text − − − − ! produces a string resembling the WordStar ruler line:

    − − − − ! − − − − ! − − − − ! − − − − !

This line repeats until the next occupied cell to the right is reached.

You enter repeating text with an apostrophe (') as the first character, followed by one or more characters. The status line indicates repeating text by displaying Rtxt = '. You can stop the repeating text by moving the cell cursor to any cell to the right, typing another apostrophe, and pressing Enter.

Formula Cells

Formulas are an important part of a spreadsheet because they perform the calculations. You enter formulas in some cells and values in others. If you change the values in the cells, the computer recalculates the formulas and displays the new (computed) values.

A *formula* is an expression consisting of cell references, functions, and operands that can be combined with arithmetic and logical operators. (Note that a formula can contain several functions, which are covered in Chapters 7 and 8.) A formula can be one of five types: a textual value, a date value, a special value called Not Available, an error value, or a numeric value (see table 3.1). When a cell contains a formula, the status line displays the following formula indicator: Form = .

Table 3.1
Five Types of Formula Entries

Formula Type	Sample Entries
Date	DATE(10,17,89)
	MONTH(TODAY)
	TODAY + 60
Textual	("OCTOBER")
	("Category 5")
	("Systems Engineer")
Not Available	NA
	NA + TODAY
Error	ERROR
	37/0
Numeric	SUM(A1:A5)/26*AB42**7
	PRICE − DOWN PAYMENT
	0.52*27/A1
	TODAY − DATE(12,7,1941)

Textual Values

Textual values are similar to text data. Textual cell values consist of characters that can be referenced in formulas or displayed by formulas. Popular uses of textual values include formulas that use lookup tables for months of the year or days of the week. You enter a textual value by enclosing it in quotation marks and enclosing the quoted expression in parentheses. For example, to enter the word *Thursday* as a textual value, type the following expression, and press Enter:

("Thursday")

Note that textual values are different from text data. If you enter "Thursday in a cell, the cell's value is displayed as Thursday, left-justified in the cell. On the other hand, suppose that you enter the following textual value (including the parentheses):

("Thursday")

This entry is displayed right-justified in the cell. Textual values are commonly used as labels in spreadsheets. Textual values often are placed in areas called tables, which are referenced by SuperCalc functions and formulas. (Text data and textual values can be used interchangeably. Earlier versions of SuperCalc did not permit certain functions to be performed with text data; thus textual data was used for table lookup values, for example. The distinction in SuperCalc5 is miniscule, but we have included discussion of textual values because it is a *hidden* data type that is supported for upward compatibility.) Chapter 7 illustrates several uses of textual values and tables.

You can include up to 240 characters within the quotation marks for textual values. The characters can include digits, special characters such as punctuation, and alphabetic characters.

Date Values

Date reference functions, as well as several date entry functions, display data in month/day/year format. (These functions are described in Chapter 7.) Although expressed in numeric form, a date value is not a numeric entry.

Not Available and Error Values

You can specify the special *Not Available* formula value by typing **NA** in a cell. SuperCalc always displays the value N/A for such cells. When developing a spreadsheet, you can enter **NA** in cells of incomplete models as reminders that these cells have yet to be defined. You can later fill in these cells.

An error message (ERROR) is displayed in any cell that returns a value that your computer cannot calculate. Usually, the error-type formula cell is a result of a mistake rather than an intentional entry. For example, if you enter the formula **25/B2** into cell A1 and cell B2 is blank, ERROR is displayed (in red on color monitors) in cell A1.

Numeric Values

Numeric values are the most frequently used of the five formula data types. These numeric values can be further subdivided into several classes, including simple numeric values (47.53); arithmetic formulas (76+C25); simple cell references (C5); and arithmetic formulas containing cell references, numeric values, function references, and cell names (PMT(PRINCIPAL,INTRATE/12,DURATION*12*5)). A formula is limited to 240 characters.

Refining and Expanding the Spreadsheet

The AUTOLOAN spreadsheet from Chapter 2 illustrates many of the remaining sections of this chapter. Figure 3.1 shows the spreadsheet once more. This simple spreadsheet serves as the starting point for more refinements.

The AUTOLOAN spreadsheet already has labels and simple numeric values filled in. The four values entered so far are the automobile price in B1, the proposed down payment in B2, the loan interest rate in B3, and the loan duration (in years) in B4. These values or variables are called *independent* variables because they do not depend on one another and are used to compute other values.

The worksheet uses the four independent variables in different combinations to determine the values of the *dependent* variables: sales tax, license fee, monthly payment, and amount to be financed. These four dependent variables need the four independent variables to obtain values. For example, the sales-tax value depends on the automobile purchase price (stored in cell B1). Likewise, the monthly payment cell gets its value from an arithmetic formula using the purchase price, down payment, interest rate, and loan duration.

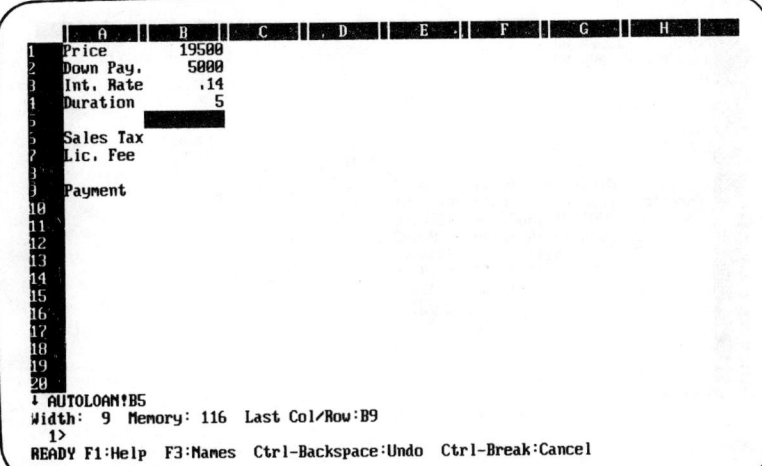

Fig. 3.1.
AUTOLOAN
spreadsheet.

You cannot enter values directly into the dependent cells. Instead, you insert formulas that *derive* (compute) values. The derived values are computed from values stored in other cells (both independent and previously computed dependent values).

Improving Appearance and Convenience

To make your AUTOLOAN spreadsheet more versatile and easier to use, you can give it a "face lift." The worksheet's final form displays independent (user-entered) values at the top of the spreadsheet. Similarly, the values that are computed from the user-entered values are displayed in the lower portion of the spreadsheet. Figure 3.2 shows the completed AUTOLOAN spreadsheet in its final form.

Because you are going to make several changes to the AUTOLOAN spreadsheet, start with a clean slate. You should become familiar with the /Zap command, which erases a currently displayed spreadsheet to leave you with an empty spreadsheet. If the spreadsheet has been loaded from a disk file, the disk file is not erased, however; only the memory-resident form of the file is erased. (The //Spreadsheets,Zap command clears *all* memory-resident spreadsheets and is used when you have several co-resident spreadsheets loaded. This command is described in Chapter 6.)

Normally, you probably would not completely erase a spreadsheet to modify it. The changes to AUTOLOAN are so extensive, however, that the most efficient way to make them is to start from scratch. Furthermore, not much information has been entered on the spreadsheet so far, so little effort is lost.

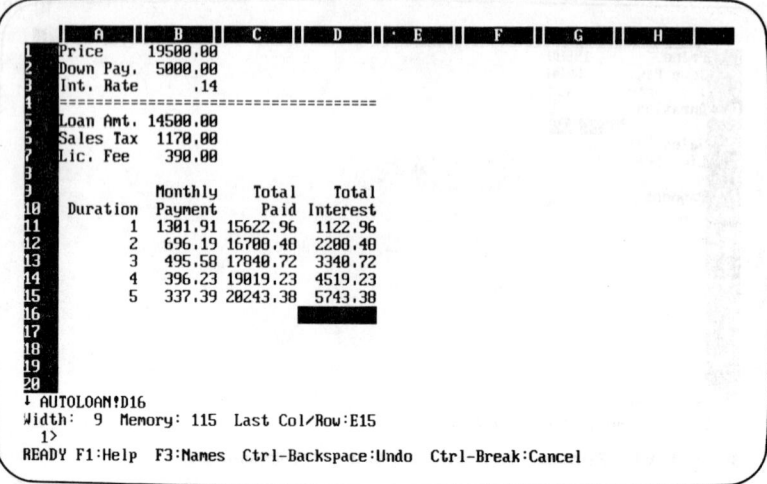

Fig. 3.2.

The revised AUTOLOAN spreadsheet.

To erase the spreadsheet, type **/Z** and then **Y**. The command just before typing **Y** is shown in figure 3.3. Notice that the highlighted option on the prompt line is **Y**es because the right-arrow key has been pressed once to position the highlight there.

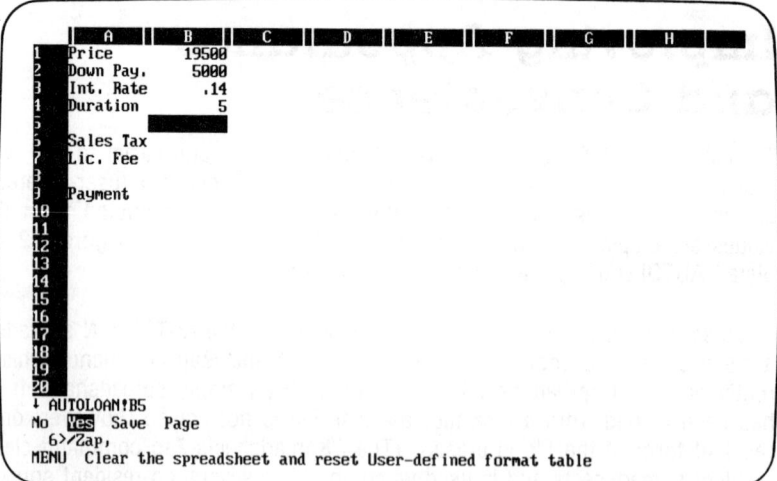

Fig. 3.3.

Erasing the AUTOLOAN spreadsheet with /Zap.

To re-create the label entries, move to cell A1 by pressing the Home key, and, using figure 3.2 as a guide, fill in the text entries as they appear in the figure. Type **Price** and press Enter. Move to cell A2 and type **Down Pay.** Continue to fill in the remaining text entries including the column labels **Duration**, **Monthly Payment**, **Total Paid**, and **Total Interest** in rows 9 and 10 (refer to fig. 3.2). Don't be concerned about justifying the column labels within the column; that is discussed later. Also, don't try to type the dashed line shown across the fourth row. That special entry is described in the following section. Fill in the three numeric values by typing **19500** (no commas) in cell B1, **5000** in cell B2, and **.14** in cell B3. These three cells are the independent values used by other formulas in the spreadsheet. The formulas are to be created and stored in the lower portion of the spreadsheet.

Entering Repeating Text

As explained previously, by entering repeating text, with only a few keystrokes you can create a line across a row in your spreadsheet. The repeating text in the fourth row of the AUTOLOAN spreadsheet separates the input portion of the spreadsheet from the computed, dependent portion. Move to cell A4 and type

     ' =

Press Enter. The first character in repeating text must be an apostrophe ('). (If you entered a quotation mark ("), the single equal sign would not repeat.) Move to cell E4, type an apostrophe, and press Enter. This apostrophe terminates the repeating text so that it does not appear beyond column D. Figure 3.4 shows the spreadsheet entries made so far.

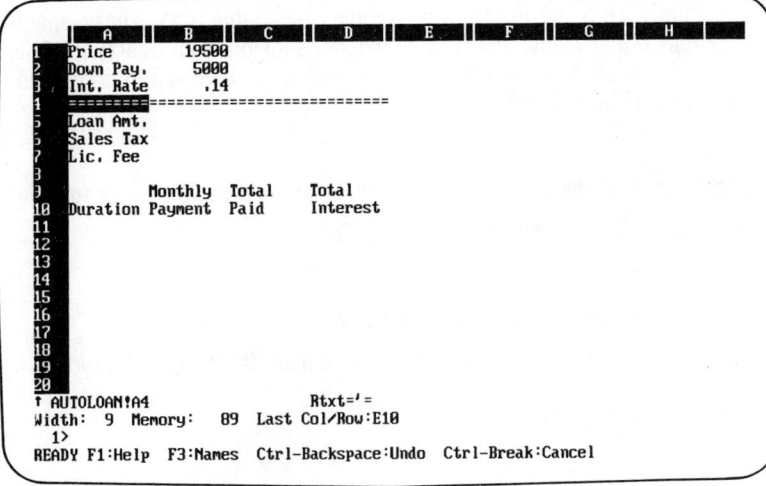

Fig. 3.4.

AUTOLOAN spreadsheet with labels, repeating text, and numeric values.

Entering a Simple Formula

The first formula to be entered is the value of the amount of the loan to be financed. This formula is placed to the right of the label *Loan Amt.* in cell B5. Move to cell B5 by executing the GoTo command: press the F5 function key, type the address **B5**, and press Enter.

What formula do you enter for the computed loan amount, and how do you enter the formula? The loan amount (*Loan Amt.*) is derived from the general formula sales price − down payment

SuperCalc, however, does not yet understand the words *sales price* and *down payment*. (Later, you can make this adjustment with the /**N**ame command.) You must construct a formula that refers to the cell containing the price and subtracts the value in the down payment cell from the value in the price cell.

To refer to a cell, such as the price cell, specify its location as a column-row coordinate. The price cell is referred to as B1 in the formula; the down payment cell is referred to as B2. The formula, therefore, for the loan amount (*Loan Amt.*) cell at B5 is

B1 − B2

Type the preceding formula into cell B5, and press Enter. The value of the expression is displayed in the cell, and the status line when the cursor is on cell B5 displays

Form = B1 − B2

This status-line display shows the contents of the cell and its form.

Using Arithmetic Operators

Six basic arithmetic operators are used in creating formulas (see table 3.2). These operators have levels of importance that follow algebraic precedence for order of operation. This precedence dictates the calculation order when several operators are involved in an expression. Suppose that a cell contains the formula

A1 − B2*C3**D4

Operator precedence dictates that the order of evaluation of the expression be as follows:

1. Determine the value of C3 raised to the power of D4.

2. Multiply this result by B2.

3. Subtract the result obtained from the value of cell A1.

Table 3.2 gives the order of precedence of each operator, ranked from highest to lowest.

Unary minus refers to an entry such as

−17*B1

and is equivalent to the expression −1*17*B1. The sign is called *unary minus* because the minus ''flips'' the sign of the single number or expression that follows it (−B2, for example).

Parentheses deserve special attention. Whenever parentheses occur in expressions, they alter the normal rules of precedence listed in table 3.2. The parentheses in the following expression, for example, change the order in which the expression is evaluated:

(A1 − B2)*C3**D4

Any expressions enclosed in parentheses are evaluated before any other expressions. The expression enclosed in parentheses (A1 − B2) is computed before the expression C3**D4.

Table 3.2
Arithmetic Operator Precedence from High (1) to Low (4)

Operator	Precedence	Meaning of Operator
−	1	Special unary minus. When written preceding a cell reference or a number, causes the sign to be changed (to positive or negative).
ˆ or **	2	Exponentiation, or "raise to a power"
%	3	Percent. Written between two values, and identical to division by 100.
*	3	Multiply two values
/	3	Divide one value by another
+	4	Add two values
−	4	Subtract one value from another

You can also nest parentheses, as in

$((A1 - B2)*C3)**D4$

In this case, you begin with the innermost set of parentheses and work outward.

The Percent Arithmetic Operator (%)

The next formula to enter on the AUTOLOAN spreadsheet is the sales tax in cell B6. Super-Calc must compute the value of the formula as six percent of the value in B1. Percent (typed as %) is an arithmetic operator, and the formula can be entered as

6%B1

This notation expresses the meaning of the formula (six percent of cell B1). You also can enter **B1*0.06**—the two statements produce the same result.

If you stored the formula 6%19500 in the sales tax cell, a change in purchase price could not alter the sales tax cell value. This formula would not allow "what if" questions because the sales tax cell would be locked into a fixed price. If, however, you enter in cell B6 the formula 6%B1, the program can always compute a value for sales tax. If the purchase price cell changes, the sales tax (a dependent variable) changes as well.

The license fee cell, B7, is similar to the sales tax cell. Enter the formula

2%B1

The result of entering these formulas is seen in figure 3.5.

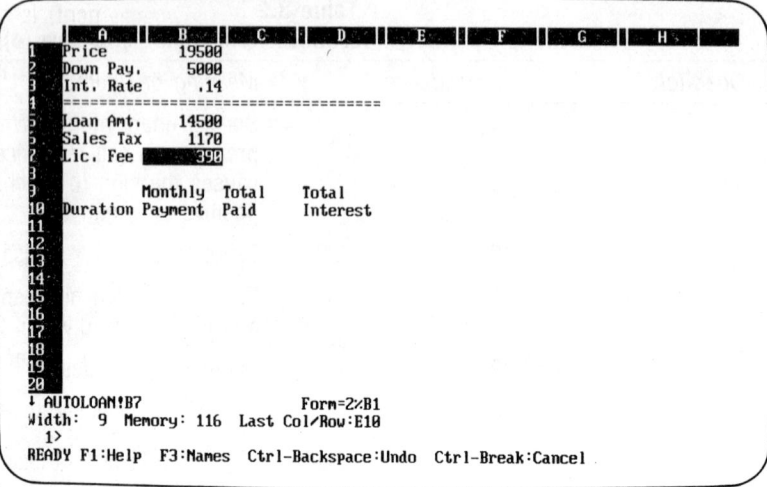

Fig. 3.5.

AUTOLOAN spreadsheet after three formulas are entered.

Other Arithmetic Operators

Although SuperCalc provides a function to compute periodic payments (see Chapter 7), you also can compute periodic payments by entering a formula with several arithmetic operators. This somewhat complex formula is not entered into the AUTOLOAN spreadsheet but is used here to illustrate how some of the arithmetic operators work.

The monthly payment or periodic payment formula can be written with the following algebraic formula:

$$\text{Monthly Payment} = \frac{LA*MIR}{1-(1+MIR)**(-12*DU)}$$

This general formula containing algebraic variables (LA, MIR, DU) can be translated and entered as a SuperCalc formula by substituting cell references for loan amount (LA), monthly interest rate (MIR), and duration (DU). The SuperCalc formula is

B5*(B3/12)/(1−(1+B3/12)**(−60))

Using Relational Operators

A *relational operator* compares two expressions to determine whether the relationship is true or false. The value 1 is displayed for true and 0 for false. A relational expression does not usually appear in a cell by itself, but as a part of an IF expression, such as

IF(B2>B1,ERROR,B1−B2)

In this IF expression, the relational expression B2>B1 determines whether cell B2 is greater than B1. The expression asks the question, "Is the value for down payment greater than sales price in the AUTOLOAN example?'' If B2 (down payment) is greater than B1 (purchase price), a data entry error has occurred, and the IF expression displays the message ERROR. Otherwise, the value of B1 − B2 is computed and displayed. The six relational operators and their meanings are listed in table 3.3.

Table 3.3
Relational Operators

Relation	Meaning
A1 < B1	Less than. The expression is true (1) if A1 is less than B1. Otherwise, the expression is false (0).
A1 = B1	Equal. The expression is true if A1 equals B1. Otherwise, the expression is false.
A1 <= B1	Less than or equal. If A1 is less than or equal to B1, the expression is true. Otherwise, the expression is false.
A1 > B1	Greater than. The expression is true if A1 is greater than B1. Otherwise, the expression is false.
A1 >= B1	Greater than or equal. If A1 is greater than or equal to B1, the expression is true. Otherwise, the expression is false.
A1 <> B1	Not equal. If A1 does not equal B1, the expression is true. Otherwise, the expression is false.

The relational operators = and <> can be used to compare all five data types. The other four relational operators compare only numeric or data-valued expressions. Expressions in a relational expression can be complex, including functions, arithmetic operators, and numeric values.

Unlike arithmetic operators, all relational operators are alike in precedence. In an expression, however, all arithmetic operators are evaluated before any relational operators because all arithmetic operators take precedence over all relational operators. Several examples of formulas containing relational and arithmetic operators appear in later chapters. Relational operators are evaluated from left to right in any expression containing more than one of them.

Naming Cells To Simplify References

The /Name command, first included in SuperCalc4, aids in writing easy-to-remember (*mnemonic*) formulas. /Name is an especially helpful SuperCalc command that lets you assign names to a cell or any block (rectangular group) of cells. Once you have assigned a name, you can use the name instead of a cell reference in formulas, without altering the worksheet. Creating cells with formulas containing cell names takes less work; and when you must reference a cell, remembering the cell's name is easier than remembering its location—for example, LOAN AMOUNT rather than B5.

You use cell names in the AUTOLOAN worksheet. The names appear in several formulas, such as the monthly payment formula (where names replace the relative references to the loan amount, interest rate, and duration cells). Once a model monthly payment formula is written with named references, you can copy this formula to the remaining four monthly payment cells that correspond to loan durations of two through five years.

After a named range is created, it replaces all the cell references (single cells and ranges) in the spreadsheet. For example, if the name SALES PRICE is assigned to cell B1 and DOWN PAYMENT is assigned to cell B2, the following formula replaces the original (B1 − B2) formula:

SALES PRICE − DOWN PAYMENT

Furthermore, SALES PRICE replaces any cell reference to B1 in any formula, and DOWN PAYMENT replaces B2. Similarly, if the name 3RDQUARTER is defined for cell range C1:C5, any formula containing SUM(C1:C5) is replaced with SUM(3RDQUARTER) automatically.

Invoking the /Name Command

The /Name command is executed to create or delete names by choosing /Name. A menu then appears giving several choices:

Create Delete Labels Table Zap

Create assigns a name to a cell or range of cells. **D**elete removes a previously assigned name and replaces it with its cell-range address. **Z**ap removes all cell and range names, replacing names with their corresponding cell-address references. The **L**abels option, a special purpose name-creation selection, uses existing text fields in the spreadsheet as internal names assigned to rows or columns. The **T**able option places the names and assigned cell ranges into the spreadsheet.

Assigning Names: /Name,Create

To create a named range, you select the **C**reate option by pressing **C** or (because **C**reate is the default) simply pressing Enter. Then type the name, give the cell range, and press Enter. Names can be up to 32 characters long and can contain letters, digits, and underscores, as well as a leading backslash. Lowercase letters can be entered, and they are automatically translated to uppercase. Thus, the names *amount* and *AMOUNT* are identical. Names may not contain only digits (digits must appear with letters). Although names can contain spaces, multiple spaces are compressed into one space, and leading and trailing spaces are eliminated. Names that differ only in the number or placement of spaces are considered identical.

Names such as I3, D25, and A15 are permitted, but they obviously conflict with cell addresses. When you create names that are the same as cell addresses, SuperCalc displays a warning message. Similarly, if names conflict with SuperCalc functions (for example, SUM, AVERAGE), a message warns you of a potential name conflict. Cells or functions are not accessible when their names have been assigned by the /Name command, so be careful to avoid assigning names that are column designators or SuperCalc function names. (Chapters 7 and 8 cover functions.) If you assign the name DATE to a cell, for instance, you cannot use the DATE function in other cells of the same spreadsheet. Assigning names containing blank characters (for example, SALES PRICE, ASSET VALUES, INTEREST RATE) is always safe because SuperCalc functions (and column addresses) do not contain blanks in their names.

In the AUTOLOAN spreadsheet, important cells are assigned names that will aid future creation of mnemonic formulas. The names and their associated cell ranges are listed in table 3.4.

Table 3.4
Names Assigned to Cells in AUTOLOAN Spreadsheet

Name Created	Cell Address
SALES PRICE	B1
DOWN PAYMENT	B2
INTEREST RATE	B3
LOAN AMOUNT	B5
DURATION	A11
PAYMENT	B11
PAID	C11

To assign the name SALES PRICE to cell B1, you execute the /Name command

/Name,Create,SALES PRICE,B1

You then press Enter. By now you are aware that only the first letter of each command and menu entry need be typed, so the preceding command is actually entered by typing

/NCSALES PRICE,B1

You complete the command by pressing Enter. Figure 3.6 illustrates the display just before Enter is pressed. The remaining names shown in table 3.4 are created in a similar fashion.

After names have been assigned, they replace corresponding cell addresses in formulas that were entered before the names were created. For example, when the spreadsheet cursor is positioned in cell B5, the following formula appears on the status line (in the dialog panel):

```
Form=SALES PRICE-DOWN PAYMENT
```

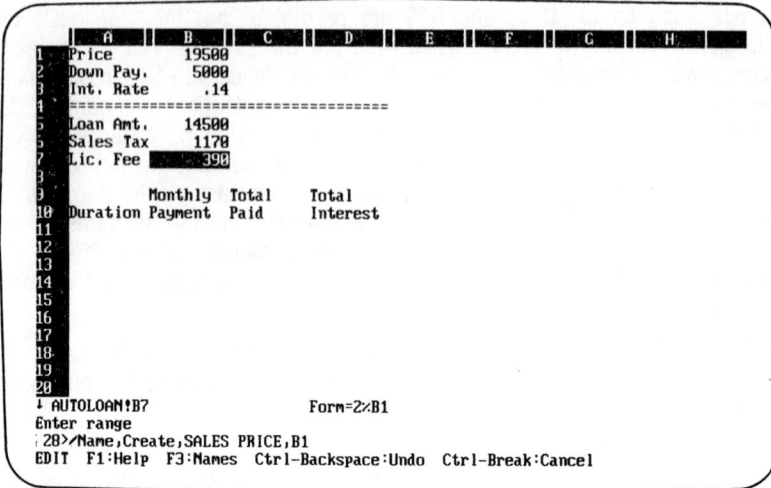

Fig. 3.6.

Assigning a cell name.

Reviewing Named Ranges

You can review range names and their assigned cells in one of two ways. One method is to view their definitions in the Named Range Directory. The second method is to store range names in your spreadsheet. Both techniques are explained in this section.

The Named Range Directory displays all the named ranges that have been defined for the spreadsheet. Accessed from READY, ENTRY, EDIT, or POINT modes, the Named Range Directory appears when you press the F3 function key. As you move the cursor to the desired name (see fig. 3.7), the range or cell address of the highlighted name is displayed in the status line.

To exit from the Named Range Directory, you press the Esc (escape) key. You press the F4 function key to enter on the entry line the *range* of the current selection. You press the Enter key to enter the *name* of the selection. When a row and a column of each cell in a named range have been defined as absolute, the name appears preceded by a dollar sign. In all other cases, the name is displayed without a leading dollar sign.

If you have created several range names, you may want to document the names within the spreadsheet. The /**N**ame,**T**able command performs this task. Creating a named range table is easy, but you want to be careful about its placement in your spreadsheet: be sure that the named range table will not overwrite any existing spreadsheet data.

To create a named range table, select the /**N**ame,**T**able command. When SuperCalc asks for the location for the table, indicate the spreadsheet cell range where you want the table to appear (a single cell address will do). Press Enter to complete the command. SuperCalc writes a table consisting of all your range names in one column and the referenced ranges in a column to the right. In figure 3.8, the command

/**N**ame,**T**able,**F2**

is used to place the range name table in cells F2 through G8.

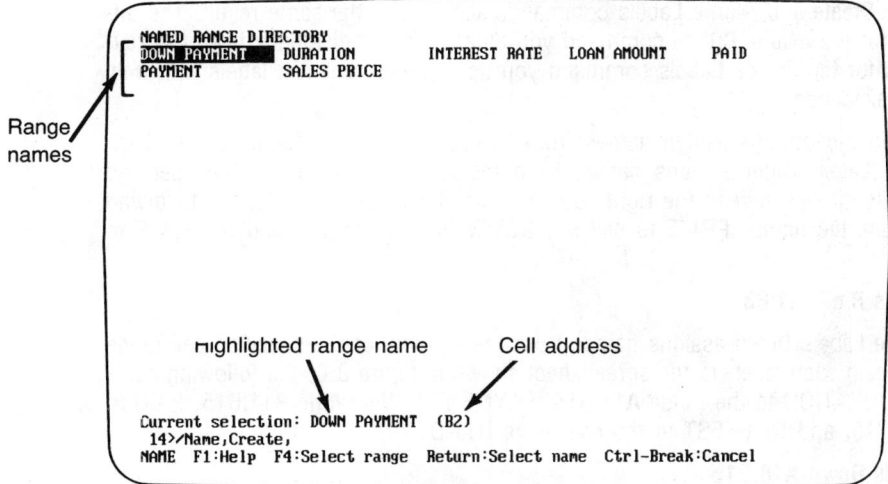

Range names

Fig. 3.7.
The Named Range Directory.

```
NAMED RANGE DIRECTORY
DOWN PAYMENT     DURATION        INTEREST RATE   LOAN AMOUNT     PAID
PAYMENT          SALES PRICE




                  highlighted range name        Cell address




Current selection: DOWN PAYMENT  (B2)
  14>/Name,Create,
NAME  F1:Help  F4:Select range  Return:Select name  Ctrl-Break:Cancel
```

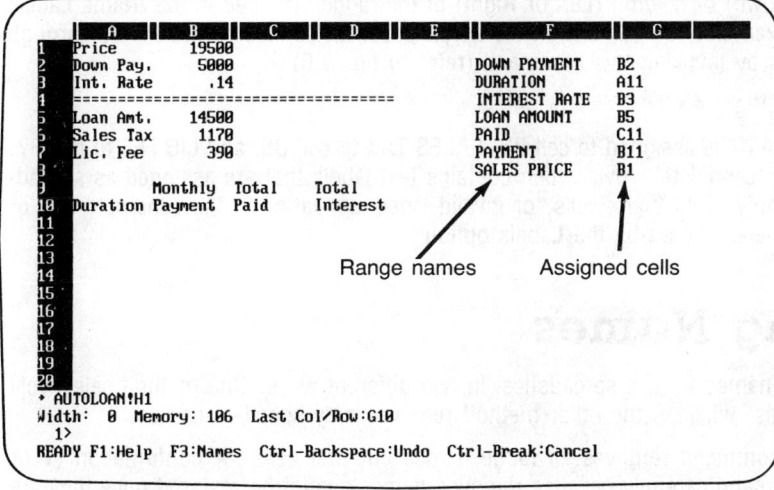

Fig. 3.8.
Displaying range names in a spreadsheet.

```
       A       B       C        D        E          F            G
1  Price     19500
2  Down Pay.  5000                             DOWN PAYMENT    B2
3  Int. Rate   .14                             DURATION        A11
4  ===================================         INTEREST RATE   B3
5  Loan Amt. 14500                             LOAN AMOUNT     B5
6  Sales Tax  1170                             PAID            C11
7  Lic. Fee    390                             PAYMENT         B11
8                                              SALES PRICE     B1
9           Monthly  Total    Total
10 Duration Payment  Paid     Interest
11
12
13
14
15
16
17
18
19
20
+ AUTOLOAN!H1
Width:  0  Memory: 106  Last Col/Row:G10
  1>
READY F1:Help  F3:Names  Ctrl-Backspace:Undo  Ctrl-Break:Cancel
```

Range names   Assigned cells

Creating Names Using Existing Labels

A series of names can be assigned to a neighboring range of cells by executing the /**N**ame,**L**abels command. This operation can save steps when names to be assigned appear in the spreadsheet as labels in a row or a column. For example, the four names DURATION, PAYMENT, PAID, and INTEREST (refer to fig. 3.6) can be assigned by one /**N**ame,**L**abels operation to cells A11, B11, C11, and D11, respectively.

Both the /Name,Create and /Name,Labels commands accomplish the same result. The difference is that for the /Name,Create command you enter names individually from the keyboard, whereas for the /Name,Labels command you use spreadsheet text labels with only one command execution.

Four basic command options assign names from spreadsheet labels: **R**ight, **D**own, **L**eft, and **U**p. /Name,Labels,Right assigns names from the *leftmost* column of the specified block to the cells in each row to the right. Using figure 3.6 as an example, the following command assigns the names PRICE to cell B1, DOWN PAY to cell B2, and INT RATE to cell B3:

   /Name,Labels,Right,**A1:B3**

Similarly, /Name,Labels,Down assigns names from the *top* row of the specified cell range to the cells beneath each label. In the spreadsheet shown in figure 3.6, the following command assigns DURATION to the range A11:A15, PAYMENT to the range B11:B15, PAID to the range C11:C15, and INTEREST to the cell range D11:D15:

   /Name,Labels,Down,**A10:D15**

The /Name,Labels,Left and /Name,Labels,Up commands operate in a similar way.

Keep in mind that spreadsheet labels to be assigned as cell names must be in the perimeter row (**U**p or **D**own) or column (**L**eft or **R**ight) of the range specified in the /Name,Labels command. For example, you can assign the spreadsheet labels located in cells B5 through B7 as cell names by invoking this command (refer to fig. 3.6):

   /Name,Labels,Right,**A5:B7**

The name LOAN AMT is assigned to cell B5, SALES TAX to cell B6, and LIC FEE to cell B7. Column A is the "candidate" row, which contains text labels that are assigned as spreadsheet names. Empty cells, blank cells, or invalid labels appearing in the candidate row or column of labels are ignored by the **L**abels option.

Deleting Names

You can remove names from a spreadsheet in two different ways. One method selectively removes all names, whereas the other method removes only specified names.

The /Name,Zap command removes all range names but first asks for confirmation (**Y** or **N**). Use this command carefully because removed names cannot be restored once they are "zapped."

To remove only specified range names, use the /Name,Delete command. You then specify the particular range name to be removed and press Enter. Not only is the range name deleted, but the corresponding cell range replaces all occurrences of the name. The **Z**ap operation acts in a similar way, replacing all named ranges with their corresponding cell-range addresses. Before you begin either deletion operation, you should first check assigned names in the Named Range Directory.

Entering More Formulas

Before proceeding, you must enter four additional formulas as models for the AUTOLOAN spreadsheet. The model formulas will be copied to other cells. These formulas correspond to the *Duration*, *Monthly Payment*, *Total Paid*, and *Total Interest* columns (refer to fig. 3.6). First, you move the spreadsheet pointer to cell A11 and enter **1**. You then move to cell C11 and enter the formula

DURATION*12*PAYMENT

Next, you move to cell D11 and enter the formula

PAID−$LOAN AMOUNT

Press Enter after each formula is typed. The monthly payment formula is the only remaining cell in row 11 to be defined.

Relative and Absolute Cell References

Notice the dollar sign prefix to the name LOAN AMOUNT in the preceding formula. The dollar sign indicates an *absolute* reference. All cell references up until now have been *relative* references—in the form of either named or regular cell references. Absolute and relative cell references are described in detail in Chapter 5, but they are introduced briefly here because cell references help streamline formula creation and copying operations.

Absolute references are cell references that are not adjusted when formulas containing these references are copied to other cells. Conversely, when relative references are copied to other cells, they are changed to refer to cells in the same relative position to the cell holding the reference. Relative cells are always adjusted unless you specifically tell Super-Calc not to adjust them. By incorporating absolute references in formulas that are to be copied to other cells, you can avoid the task of remembering to adjust certain cell references and not to adjust others. Because formulas referencing the LOAN AMOUNT cell (cell B5) never should be altered in any copy operation, any reference to LOAN AMOUNT should be absolute (for example, $LOAN AMOUNT or $B$5).

A cell may be referenced in four ways, ranging from relative to absolute. For example, the license fee formula shown in figure 3.5 (cell B7) references cell B1 with the formula 2%B1. The absolute reference form would be 2%$B$1 with a dollar sign preceding both the column and row components of the reference. Between the relative reference (B1) and the absolute reference ($B$1) forms are the two intermediate forms ($B1 and B$1), which are not wholly relative or wholly absolute. Both intermediate forms contain an absolute component and a relative component.

Examples of absolute, mixed, and relative cell references are

Cell Reference	Explanation
B1	Relative reference (relative)
$B1	Column absolute, row relative (mixed)
B$1	Column relative, row absolute (mixed)
$B$1	Both column and row absolute (absolute)

You can see the importance of absolute and relative forms of cell references when a cell is to be copied to another cell. (The /Copy command is described in detail later in this chapter). If the formula 2%B1 were copied from cell B7 (as in fig. 3.5) to cell B8, the cell reference would normally be adjusted to refer to cell B2 (2%B2). Cell B8 would display the computed value of 100 (two percent of the down payment). This answer would be a mistake. On the other hand, copying the formula 2%$B$1 from cell B7 to cell B8 would not alter the absolute address reference; the new formula would still display two percent of the sales price. More examples of absolute and relative cell references are provided throughout the remainder of this chapter.

The PMT Function

Instead of entering the complicated monthly payment formula provided previously, you can use the SuperCalc function (predefined formula) PMT.

The PMT function computes a periodic payment using three input *parameters*. The parameters are supplied to the PMT function in a list enclosed in parentheses. This list, called an *argument* list, is typed after the function name. The general form of the PMT function with parameters is

PMT(principal, periodic interest rate, number of periods)

In this example, the parameter *principal* is the amount borrowed, *periodic interest rate* is the interest rate for each period, and *number of periods* is the number of payments made over the loan's lifetime. The PMT function amortizes the loan amount over the period; that is, the amount of the periodic payment includes both principal repayment and interest payment. When the last payment has been made, the principal balance owed will be reduced to zero. Home-mortgage payments and auto-loan payments are examples of loan amortizations.

The PMT function computes annual, monthly, weekly, and daily payment amounts (any repayment frequency) depending on the parameters you supply. Table 3.5 shows examples of the PMT function for several different repayment frequencies (varying numbers of periods). The loan amount, annual interest rate, and loan duration are held constant for each example to illustrate how the periodic interest rate adjusts for different repayment frequencies (daily, weekly, and so on).

Table 3.5
Examples of PMT Function for Different Repayment Frequencies

Loan Amount:	$10,000	
Annual Interest Rate:	12%	
Duration:	5 Years	
Repayment Frequency:		
Daily	PMT(10000,0.12/365,5*365)	$7.29
Weekly	PMT(10000,0.12/52,5*52)	$51.19
Monthly	PMT(10000,0.12/12,5*12)	$222.44
Annually	PMT(10000,0.12,5)	$2,774.10

Place the monthly payment function into cell B11 on the AUTOLOAN worksheet (refer to fig. 3.2), by typing the formula

PMT($LOAN AMOUNT,$INTEREST RATE/12,DURATION*12)

In this example, the monthly interest rate (the second parameter) is the annual rate divided by 12, and the number of payments (monthly) for the life of the loan is given in months (12 months per year times 5 years). After you type the PMT function and press Enter, the value 1301.913 is displayed.

To complete the duration field, move the cursor to A11 and enter **1**. Move down to cell A12 and enter **2**. Continue this sequence until cells A11 through A15 contain the values 1 through 5, respectively.

Move to cell C11 and enter the formula

DURATION*12*PAYMENT

The preceding formula computes and displays the entire amount paid for the loan duration. Enter the total interest paid formula by typing the following formula into cell D11:

PAID − $LOAN AMOUNT

Figure 3.9 shows the spreadsheet after the three formulas in cells B11, C11, and D11 have been entered. The cell cursor is in cell B11 so that the underlying formula is displayed on the status line.

All that remains to complete the spreadsheet is to fill in cells B12 through D15. In this application, you can use the /Copy command to copy formulas and values from one or more cells to one or more other cells. The next section describes the /Copy command and shows it moving the model formulas in cells B11 through D11 down their respective columns to fill in rows 12 through 15.

Fig. 3.9.

Formulas entered for the first row of the table.

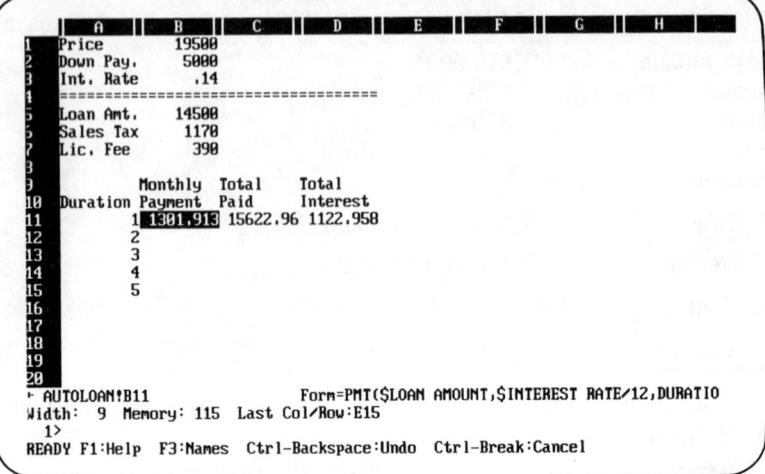

	A	B	C	D	E	F	G	H
1	Price	19500						
2	Down Pay.	5000						
3	Int. Rate	.14						
4	=================================							
5	Loan Amt.	14500						
6	Sales Tax	1170						
7	Lic. Fee	390						
8								
9		Monthly	Total	Total				
10	Duration	Payment	Paid	Interest				
11	1	1301.913	15622.96	1122.958				
12	2							
13	3							
14	4							
15	5							
16								
17								
18								
19								
20								

```
+ AUTOLOAN!B11            Form=PMT($LOAN AMOUNT,$INTEREST RATE/12,DURATIO
Width:  9  Memory: 115  Last Col/Row:E15
   1>
READY F1:Help  F3:Names  Ctrl-Backspace:Undo  Ctrl-Break:Cancel
```

Copying Formulas to Other Cells

Worksheets usually contain cells with formulas that differ only in the cells referenced to compute a value. You can see examples of these cells in the AUTOLOAN worksheet (see fig. 3.9). The formula that calculates the monthly payment can be duplicated four times to occupy a total of five rows (rows 11 through 15) of column B. The only difference among these five monthly payment formulas is that each formula references a different "duration" cell. The formula in cell B11 references a loan duration of one year, and the remaining formulas reference duration values that increase from two years to five years.

Knowing that the formulas in those five cells are identical in form (but not in the cells referenced), you can avoid creating five different formulas by writing one model formula and then duplicating it in other cells. The command to duplicate the formulas is the /Copy command. Like a photocopying machine, /Copy can reproduce as many copies of a cell's contents as you need. You simply specify the source (or original cell), select the target (or receiving cell) locations, and tell SuperCalc to reproduce the source cell.

The /Copy command is quite easy to use. The command can copy a single cell, a partial row or column, an entire row or column, or a block of cells. The /Copy command also can copy a graph description to another graph (this use is explained with the discussion of SuperCalc's graphing capabilities).

One Cell to Several Cells

To complete the AUTOLOAN spreadsheet, you could enter from the keyboard several more formulas in the *Monthly Payment*, *Total Paid*, and *Total Interest* columns in each of the 12 additional cells. However, because the three sets of formulas (one set for each column) are identical except for cell references, the formulas can be copied down through their respective columns with only minor (and automatic) cell reference adjustments.

The /**C**opy command can copy a single source cell to several cells if you specify the source cell to be copied, the range of cells to receive the copies, and, optionally, parameters that indicate whether or not to adjust the cell references from the source formula.

In the most elementary form of /**C**opy, place the spreadsheet cursor in cell B11 to copy this source formula down the next four cells in the *Monthly Payment* column. To begin executing the /**C**opy command, first type /**C**opy. The prompt and entry lines are shown in figure 3.10.

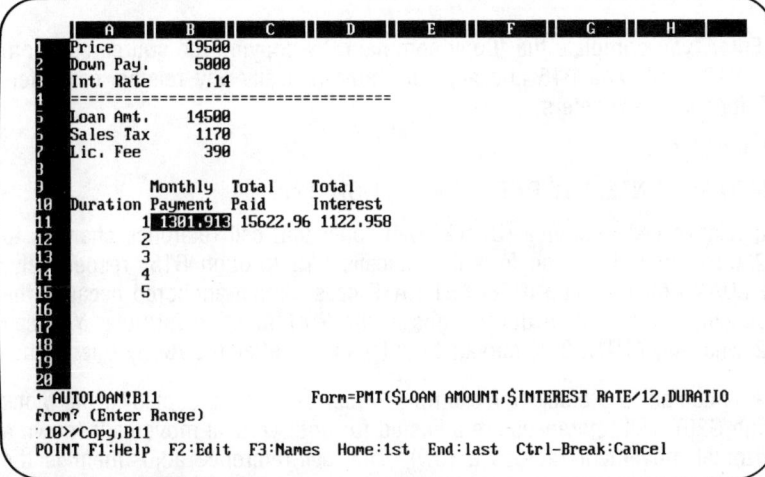

Fig. 3.10.

Preparing to copy a source cell to multiple cells.

Because the spreadsheet cursor is positioned on B11 (the cell to be copied), B11 appears as the source cell on the entry line. Next, press the comma key to terminate specification of the source-cell range (a single cell). SuperCalc next requests the destination cell range. Using the POINT method, move the spreadsheet cursor down to cell B12 and press the period to fix, or *anchor*, the beginning of the cell range. Use the down-arrow key to move to the *last* cell in the target (destination) range (B15). You could type the destination cell address range, but pointing highlights the cell range, visually verifying your accuracy. The entry line now contains

/**C**opy,B11,B12:B15

The entry line shows that B11 is the source cell and that cells B12 through B15 are the destination range. Figure 3.11 illustrates the spreadsheet with the destination range highlighted just before the Enter key is pressed.

Fig. 3.11.

*Specifying the
destination range for
the /Copy command.*

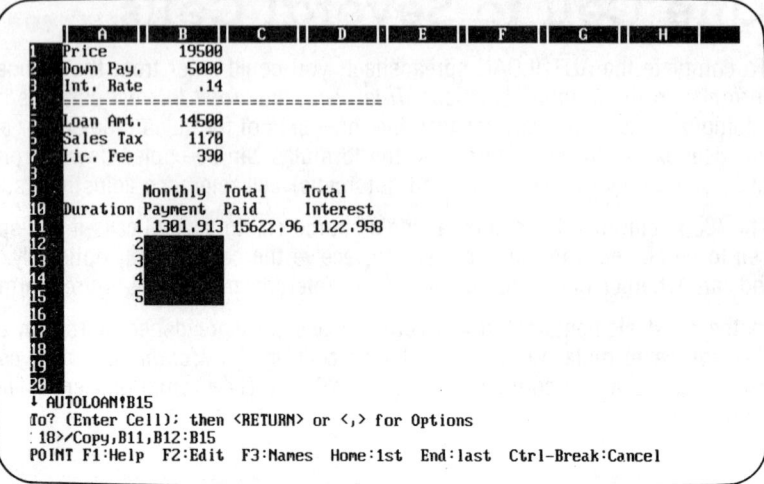

When you press Enter, you complete the /Copy command by copying the source cell from B11 to cells B12, B13, B14, and B15 and adjusting automatically any relative cell references in the PMT function parameters.

Because the PMT function

    PMT($LOAN AMOUNT,$INTEREST RATE/12,DURATION*12)

contains only one relative cell reference (DURATION), only that cell reference changes to refer to cells A12 through A15 for the formulas in cells B12 through B15, respectively. References to the LOAN AMOUNT and INTEREST RATE cells remain anchored because the references were specified with leading dollar signs in the PMT function formula. You can see in figure 3.12 what the AUTOLOAN spreadsheet looks like after the /Copy operation.

When a single cell is copied to a block (for example, when cell C22 is copied to the block of cells C22 through G26), cell references are adjusted for both vertical movement (down a column) and horizontal movement (across a row). This cell-reference adjustment is the default.

Figure 3.13 illustrates how cell references are automatically adjusted by the copy operation. In this example, cell C22 contains the formula C21 + B22. When you execute the copy operation

    /Copy,**C22,C22:G26**

the formula is adjusted for both vertical and horizontal formula movement. Look at cell E24, for example. The adjusted sum is

    E23 + D24

Because cell E24 is in row 24, the source cell row reference to cell C21 has been increased by 2 to 23. Likewise, the column reference of C in the source cell has been increased by two columns to the column reference E. The second source cell in the sum formula

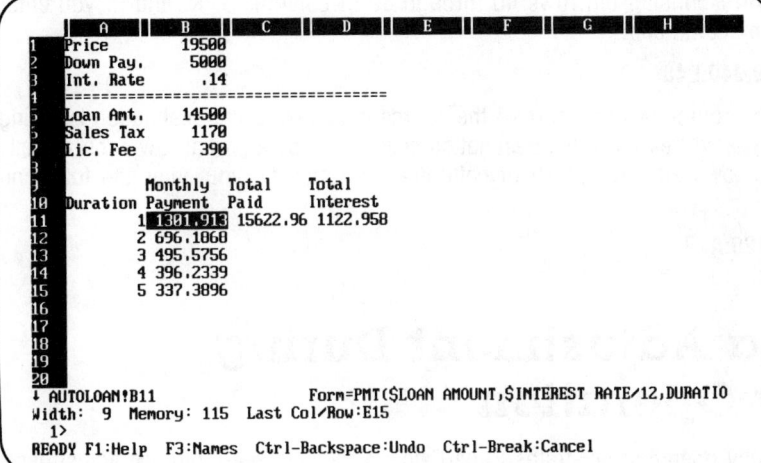

Fig. 3.12.

AUTOLOAN spreadsheet after the /Copy operation.

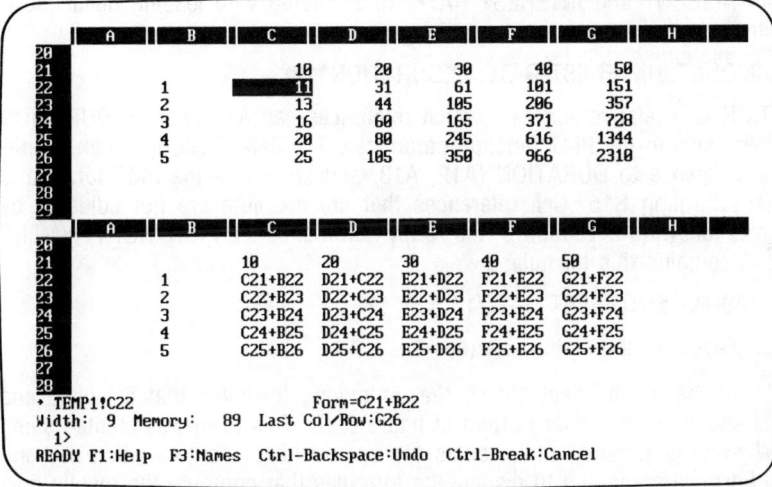

Fig. 3.13.

Formulas adjusted by vertical and horizontal movement (/Copy).

(source cell reference B22 in cell C22) has been increased by two columns and two rows: D24. Notice that the upper window shows the displayed values (for reference) and the lower window shows the adjusted formulas.

Partial Rows and Columns

When the source is a partial column, the source column is copied to the destination columns by designating the top (column) cells. For example, to copy a partial column

A20:A29 to the corresponding ten rows 40 through 49 of columns J, K, and L, you enter the following /Copy command:

/Copy,**A20:A29,J40:L40**

Similarly, when the source is a partial row, the source is copied to the destination by using only the *leftmost* cell addresses of the destination cells. To copy a partial row such as cells A1 through C1 to rows 20 through 70 of columns A through C, you enter the following /Copy command:

/Copy,**A1:C1,A20:A70**

Formula Adjustment During a Copy Operation

The preceding /Copy operation illustrates SuperCalc's automatic cell-reference adjustment. This function allows you to copy the same basic formula and adjust the relative cell references. Recall the MONTHLY PAYMENT formula in cell B11 (refer to fig. 3.12) where the named cells LOAN AMOUNT and INTEREST RATE were entered with leading dollar signs indicating absolute addresses:

PMT($LOAN AMOUNT,$INTEREST RATE/12,DURATION*12)

However, DURATION is a relative address, which references cell A11 initially. DURATION has no leading dollar sign in the PMT function parameter. The default /Copy action, therefore, adjusts each reference to DURATION (A12, A13, and so on) as the PMT formula is copied to cells B12 through B15. Cell references that are absolute are not adjusted by /Copy. For example, following execution of the /Copy command, the MONTHLY PAYMENT formula in cell B13 contains this formula:

PMT($LOAN AMOUNT,$INTEREST RATE/12,A13*12)

This formula is displayed on the status line (see fig. 3.14).

The lower portion of the spreadsheet shows the underlying formulas that calculate and display the results shown in the upper portion of figure 3.12. This form was created using the SuperCalc /Window command, which splits the spreadsheet into two windows, and using the /Global,Formula command to display the formulas that compute the results normally displayed. The /Window and /Global commands are described in Chapter 5.

Observe that although references B5 (LOAN AMOUNT) and B3 (INTEREST RATE) are unchanged, the cells references in the third argument (for example, A12*12 and A13*12) of the PMT function have been adjusted from their original source cell reference of A11 (named DURATION).

When cell references should remain anchored, either the No-adjust or Ask options should be specified for /Copy. No-adjust causes all cell references to be copied without adjustment to the destination cells. The Ask option lets you adjust or not adjust each cell reference in a source cell to be copied. Figure 3.15 shows the /Copy options. You invoke the /Copy options by typing a comma after the destination cell range on the entry line (for example,

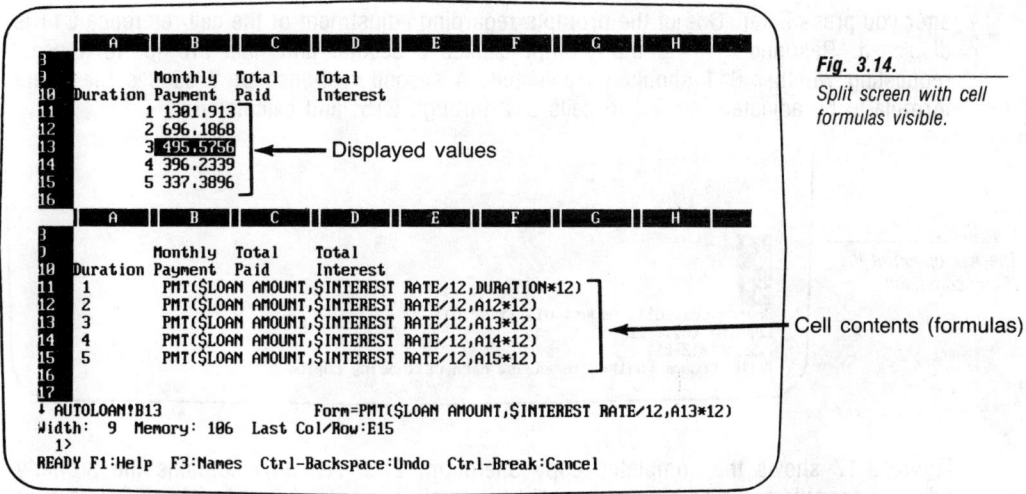

Fig. 3.14.
Split screen with cell formulas visible.

the third comma in /Copy,**C11,C12:15,**). If you press Enter after specifying the destination range, the cell(s) are copied immediately to the destination range—no /Copy options are allowed or displayed on the prompt line.

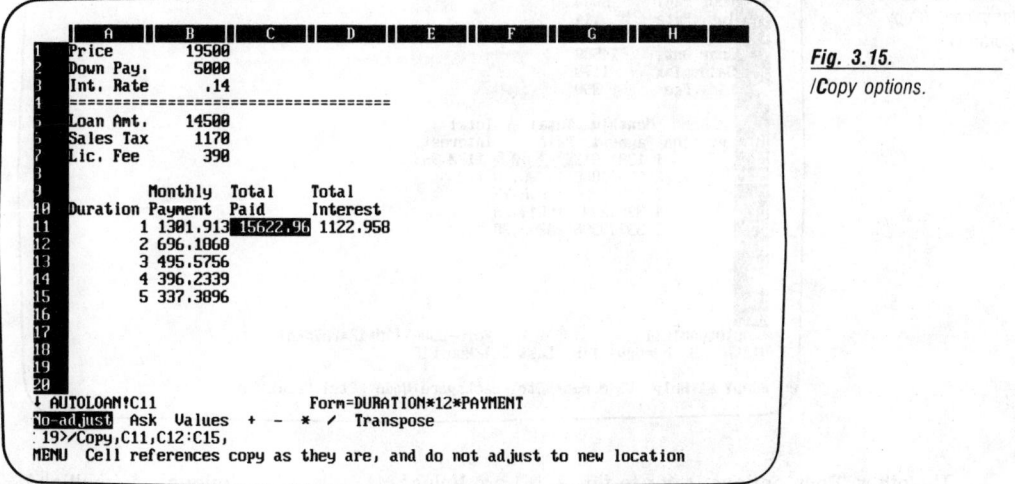

Fig. 3.15.
/Copy options.

Figure 3.15 also illustrates the display before copying the ''Total Paid'' source cell (C11) down to cells C12 through C15. The default option, **N**o-adjust, is highlighted. Because the source cell formula

DURATION*12*PAYMENT

contains relative cell references that must be adjusted for each new cell, the **A**sk option is chosen (although all cell references are to be adjusted). Figure 3.16 shows the dialog panel after you press Enter. One of the prompts regarding adjustment of the cell reference C11 is displayed. Responding **Y** to the prompt causes a second and final prompt to appear, requesting whether B11 should be adjusted. A second response of **Y** causes the entire formula to be adjusted, copied to cells C12 through C15, and calculated.

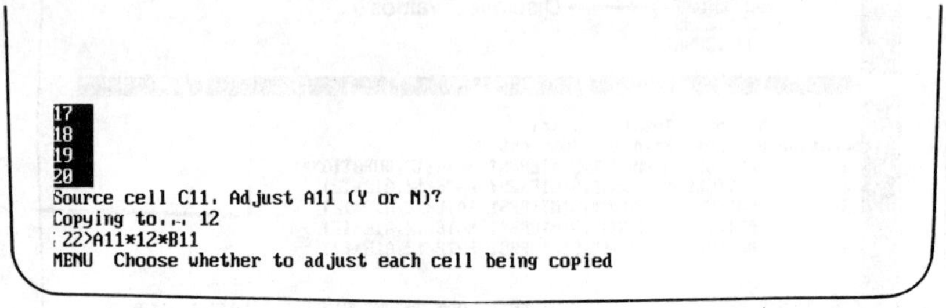

Fig. 3.16.

*The **A**sk option of the /**C**opy command.*

```
17
18
19
20
Source cell C11. Adjust A11 (Y or N)?
Copying to... 12
: 22>A11*12*B11
MENU  Choose whether to adjust each cell being copied
```

Figure 3.17 shows the completed copy operation. Each cell now contains the properly adjusted formula and displays the value of the total payment amount for the life of each of five loan durations.

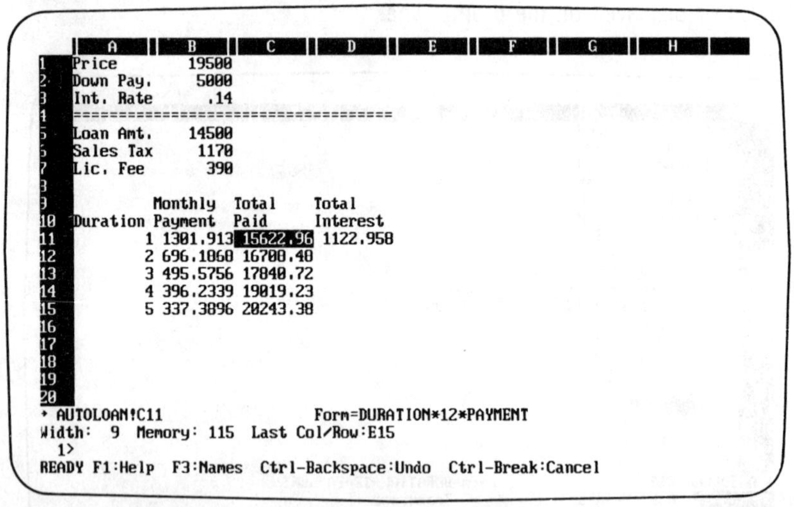

Fig. 3.17.

*Completed /**C**opy operation.*

```
    A        B       C       D      E      F      G      H
1  Price     19500
2  Down Pay.  5000
3  Int. Rate   .14
4  =========================================
5  Loan Amt.  14500
6  Sales Tax   1170
7  Lic. Fee     390
8
9          Monthly Total    Total
10 Duration Payment Paid     Interest
11      1 1301.913 15622.96 1122.958
12      2 696.1060 16700.40
13      3 495.5756 17840.72
14      4 396.2339 19019.23
15      5 337.3096 20243.38
16
17
18
19
20
* AUTOLOAN:C11              Form=DURATION*12*PAYMENT
Width:  9  Memory: 115  Last Col/Row:E15
   1>
READY F1:Help  F3:Names  Ctrl-Backspace:Undo  Ctrl-Break:Cancel
```

The other /**C**opy options (refer to fig. 3.15) are **V**alues, + (plus), − (minus), * (multiply), / (divide), and **T**ranspose. The options are displayed on the status line:

    No-adjust Ask Values + − * / Transpose

Values copies literal values—not the underlying formulas (the contents) used to compute values. Plus (+) adds each source cell value to the value in the corresponding destination cell, placing the sums into the destination cells. Minus subtracts the value in each source cell from the value in the corresponding destination cell. The difference (expressed as a value) is stored and displayed in the destination cell. The multiplication and division options are similar: the values in the destination cells are replaced with the products or the quotients, respectively, of the source and destination cells. The **T**ranspose option causes a row to be transposed to columns, and vice versa.

To complete the *Total Interest* column of the AUTOLOAN spreadsheet, move to cell D11 and enter

    /Copy,**D11,D12:D15**

Controlling Alteration of Cells

A protected cell or group of cells (a block) cannot be altered in any way; it cannot be edited, copied into, or reinitialized to new values. Once you have created and tested a spreadsheet, you can use the **/P**rotect command to shield all cells or selected cells whose contents should not be altered. By using protection, you prevent any attempt to alter protected cells.

On monochrome monitors, protected cells appear in lower intensity than unprotected cells. On color monitors, protected cells appear in yellow. When the spreadsheet cursor is positioned over a protected cell, the status line displays the character P to the left of the cell contents:

    AUTOLOAN!C13   P Form=A13*12*B13

Any attempt to alter a protected cell causes the following warning message to appear at the right end of the status line:

    Protected entry

You will find many occasions for using protection. For example, when your spreadsheets are to be used by other persons who may have different data, you should consider protecting cells. Spreadsheets used by anyone who did not create them will probably have both protected and unprotected parts. Typically, any cells that compute a result using references to other cells are *dependent* cells that should be protected. Cells whose values are entered from the keyboard are *independent* cells and should remain unprotected. To understand this concept better, protect critical cells in the AUTOLOAN worksheet—cells that other users should not inadvertently alter.

To remove protection from one or more cells, you use the **/U**nprotect command. Working in the opposite way from the **/P**rotect command, **/U**nprotect reverses cell protection back to the default condition: an unprotected cell available for change.

Protecting Cells: /Protect

To learn how to protect cells, begin by extending protection to all the cells in the AUTO-LOAN spreadsheet. In the next section, you can leave the input (independent) cell area unprotected so that the spreadsheet can be used as a model or template, allowing changes to be made to the values of SALES PRICE, DOWN PAYMENT, and INTEREST RATE.

To protect all the cells in the spreadsheet, enter the /Protect command and type the range, as follows:

/Protect,**ALL**

Note that rows or columns containing protected cells cannot be deleted (try /Delete,**C** or /Delete,**R**).

Removing Protection: /Unprotect

Because all cells are now protected in the AUTOLOAN worksheet, no changes of any kind can be made to cells in the block defined by the cells A1 through D15. Potential AUTO-LOAN template users, however, will want to experiment with various down payments, interest rates, and sales price values. Therefore, cells B1, B2, and B3 must be unprotected. To remove protection from the appropriate cells, type

/**U**nprotect,**B1:B3**

Figure 3.18 shows the spreadsheet before you press Enter to complete the /**U**nprotect command.

Fig. 3.18.

Unprotecting a block of cells.

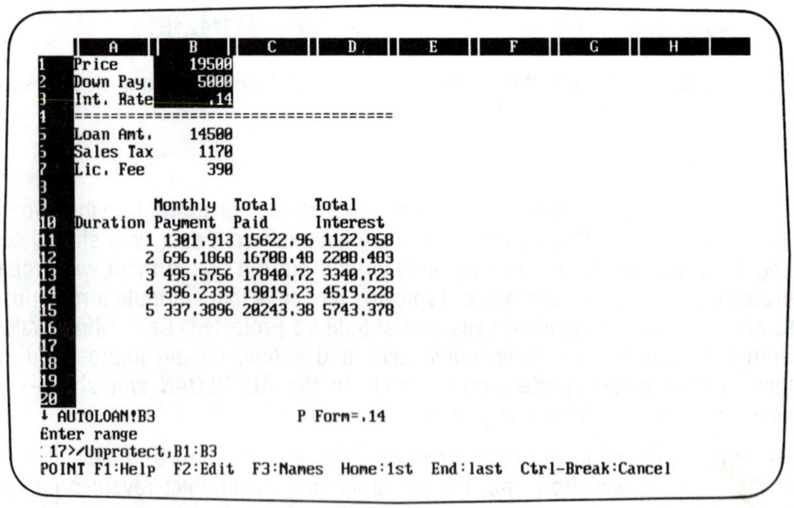

```
        A        B        C        D        E        F        G        H
1  Price      19500
2  Down Pay.   5000
3  Int. Rate    .14
4  ====================================
5  Loan Amt.  14500
6  Sales Tax   1170
7  Lic. Fee     390
8
9             Monthly  Total    Total
10 Duration  Payment  Paid     Interest
11         1 1301.913 15622.96 1122.958
12         2 696.1060 16700.48 2200.483
13         3 495.5756 17840.72 3340.723
14         4 396.2339 19019.23 4519.228
15         5 337.3896 20243.38 5743.378
16
17
18
19
20
↓ AUTOLOAN!B3              P Form=.14
Enter range
: 17>/Unprotect,B1:B3
POINT F1:Help  F2:Edit  F3:Names  Home:1st  End:last  Ctrl-Break:Cancel
```

If you discover mistakes in spreadsheet formulas that are protected, you do not have to execute the /Unprotect command before making changes to the formula. Instead, executing the following command temporarily disables the protection mechanism:

/**G**lobal,**P**rotect

You can make your corrections and then reinstate protection over the original cells throughout the spreadsheet by executing /**G**lobal,**P**rotect again to toggle protection back on. **G**lobal,**P**rotect is a toggle, which means that executing /**G**lobal,**P**rotect a second time reinstates protection—much like a light switch turns lights on and off.

Moving Directly to Unprotected Cells

Defining protected and unprotected areas of a spreadsheet results in the added (and welcome) capability of restricting cursor movement to only unprotected cells. Others using your spreadsheet can be directed to cells within the input areas of the spreadsheet and avoid protected cells, which should not be changed. The /**G**lobal,**T**ab command is the special toggle command that permits this restricted cursor movement.

Normally, pressing any of the arrow keys causes the cursor to advance to the appropriate cell. You can, however, restrict this arrow-key movement by issuing the command

/**G**lobal,**T**ab

This command alters the Tab value to *on* and restricts all cursor movement to unprotected, nonblank cells. A spreadsheet user can then enter a new value and press the arrow key to move to the next input cell. Because the Tab value is a toggle, you can switch it on or off (the default) by the /**G**lobal,**T**ab command.

If you execute /**G**lobal,**T**ab for the AUTOLOAN spreadsheet (see fig. 3.18), the cursor's movement is restricted to cells B1, B2, and B3, the input cells. This restriction eliminates the question often posed by people using models created by others, ''Which cells do I need to fill in to use this spreadsheet model?''.

Formatting Your Spreadsheet

The /**F**ormat command alters the form in which the data is displayed. Among the command's many options are the capabilities to display numbers in scientific notation and in dollars-and-cents format, to center text data, to align all data on either the left or right side of a column, and to hide data from view. (Additional format options are discussed in detail in Chapter 4.)

In this section, you can see two fundamental formatting options: displaying certain text-data values as right-justified, and displaying all numeric cells formatted with two places after the decimal point. Notice the word *displaying* in the preceding sentence. SuperCalc actually maintains numeric data to several decimal places of accuracy, but the program displays only two digits (rounded) following the decimal place. These options also improve the appearance of the AUTOLOAN spreadsheet. Remember, protected cells cannot be changed, so before formatting, disable global protection.

Formatting Numeric Cells

You can use the /Format command to alter the appearance of a block of numeric cells by typing

/Format,Entry,**B1:D15,$**

Notice that you must temporarily disable protection to format protected cells. Execute /**G**lobal,**-**,**P**rotection to disable protection before executing /**F**ormat. The **$** format option causes numeric cells to display two digits after the decimal place. This action also causes information to be placed in blank cells that are in the specified range, terminating repeating text from cells B4 through D4. To restore the appearance of the double line, use the command /**B**lank,**B4:D4**.

Right-Justifying Selected Text Cells

By default, all text entries are left-justified in their respective cells. To right-justify cells in particular rows, you specify the row range and then type **TR** (**T**ext**R**ight). The /**F**ormat command that right-justifies text cells in rows 9 and 10 of the AUTOLOAN worksheet is

/**F**ormat,**R**ow,**9:10**,**T**ext**R**ight

Figure 3.19 shows the AUTOLOAN spreadsheet after you have issued both of the preceding /Format commands. (See Chapter 4 for more information on formatting.)

Notice that all labels (text) in rows 9 and 10 are now right-justified in their fields. Compare these labels with the ones shown in figure 3.18.

Restricting Data Input: //Restrict

Introduced in Release 1.1 of SuperCalc4, the //**R**estrict command is especially useful when you want to confine data input operations performed by others to a specific area of your spreadsheet. By executing //**R**estrict (note the double slashes), you can build a logical "fence" in the spreadsheet around any rectangular area that is to be filled with input values.

//**R**estrict goes beyond the protection provided by the /**P**rotect command. /**P**rotect prevents spreadsheet users from altering protected cells, but this command does not prevent users

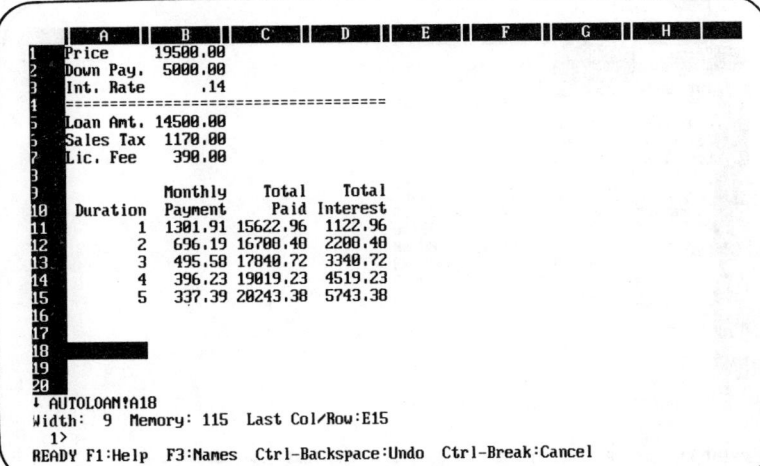

Fig. 3.19.

AUTOLOAN spreadsheet after formatting.

from moving (wandering) to protected cells or from attempting to alter noninput cells. //**R**estrict, on the other hand, helps those who use your spreadsheet models by confining all cell cursor movement and data entry operations to the restricted range—those cells that the user is to fill in.

To illustrate the usefulness of //**R**estrict, invoke the //**R**estrict command to confine input to the three unprotected cells B1, B2, and B3 in the AUTOLOAN spreadsheet shown in figure 3.19. Unlike the SuperCalc commands described previously, two slashes must be typed on the entry line to execute the //**R**estrict command. After you type the double slashes, the prompt line displays the commands

    Add-in Data Export File Graphics Import Macro Network Restrict
    Spreadsheets Test

Press **R** to select //**R**estrict. Next, specify the restricted cell range by typing the addresses of the two corner cells in the range or by using the POINT method (see fig. 3.20). Once you have specified the restricted range, complete the command by pressing Enter.

Immediately, SuperCalc scrolls the spreadsheet so that the upper left cell of the restricted range is displayed in the upper left of the screen (see fig. 3.21). Notice also that the program mode indicator on the help line has changed to INPUT. In INPUT mode, only data can be entered—not commands.

Cell-cursor movement is restricted to the three input cells. Pressing the left-, right-, up-, or down-arrow keys repeatedly (and in any combination) restricts cell-cursor movement to cells B1, B2, and B3. Pressing the down-arrow key repeatedly, for example, moves the cursor to cell B2, then to cell B3, and back to cell B1. The Home and End keys operate in a similar way. Press Home to go to the upper left cell of the restricted range (cell B1 in the example), and press End-Home to go to the lower right cell (cell B3). The PgUp, PgDn, Tab, Backtab, and F5 keys are inactive in the INPUT mode and do not move the cell cursor.

Fig. 3.20.

Specifying the restricted range.

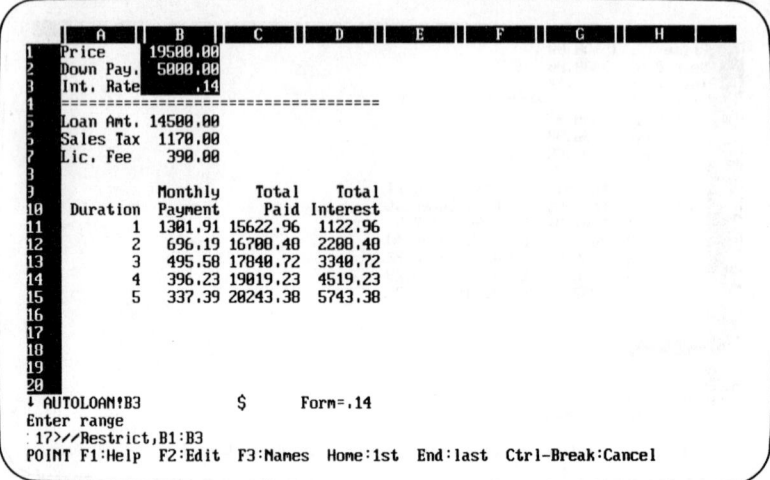

```
     A      B      C       D      E     F      G      H
1  Price    19500.00
2  Down Pay, 5000.00
3  Int. Rate    .14
4  =====================================
5  Loan Amt. 14500.00
6  Sales Tax 1170.00
7  Lic. Fee   390.00
8
9           Monthly    Total    Total
10 Duration Payment     Paid  Interest
11      1   1301.91 15622.96  1122.96
12      2    696.19 16700.40  2200.40
13      3    495.58 17840.72  3340.72
14      4    396.23 19019.23  4519.23
15      5    337.39 20243.38  5743.38
16
17
18
19
20
↓ AUTOLOAN!B3          $       Form=.14
Enter range
 17>//Restrict,B1:B3
POINT F1:Help  F2:Edit  F3:Names  Home:1st  End:last  Ctrl-Break:Cancel
```

Fig. 3.21.

*Spreadsheet after //**R**estrict is entered.*

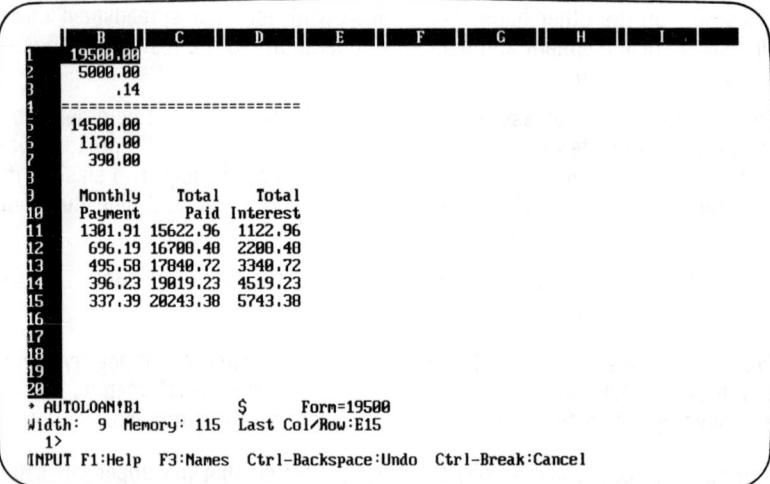

```
     B      C       D      E     F      G      H      I
1  19500.00
2   5000.00
3      .14
4  ============================
5  14500.00
6   1170.00
7    390.00
8
9  Monthly    Total    Total
10 Payment     Paid  Interest
11 1301.91 15622.96  1122.96
12  696.19 16700.40  2200.40
13  495.58 17840.72  3340.72
14  396.23 19019.23  4519.23
15  337.39 20243.38  5743.38
16
17
18
19
20
↑ AUTOLOAN!B1          $       Form=19500
Width:  9  Memory: 115  Last Col/Row:E15
   1>
INPUT F1:Help  F3:Names  Ctrl-Backspace:Undo  Ctrl-Break:Cancel
```

Try entering data into the cells, and use the arrow keys to move around the restricted area; get a feel for how //**R**estrict confines cursor movement and data entry to those cells. Also, try to enter a command (for example, /**P**rotect) in any of the input cells. Notice that if you type /, the slash is treated as text and can be entered into a cell directly.

To exit from INPUT mode, you press either Esc or Enter when the entry line is empty. The program is restored to READY mode. (The current mode is always shown in the lower left corner of the dialog panel.)

Chapter Summary

The initial steps for creating SuperCalc spreadsheets have included entering labels to identify data, entering formulas to permit various input data to be entered and results to be displayed, and establishing fundamental format operations to refine the displayed data. Separating the spreadsheet into protected and unprotected sections helps other spreadsheet users use your spreadsheet models easily. Cell naming helps you to construct sophisticated spreadsheets, reduces the need to remember cell references, and promotes more error-free spreadsheet development. You can use relative and absolute cell references in formulas that are to be copied when some cell references are to be adjusted and some are not.

Having learned several of the frequently used SuperCalc commands, you have the fundamental tools needed to build practical and useful spreadsheets. The next chapter presents more details about the /Format command, which is used to refine the display form of data and to provide a full range of display formats that enhance spreadsheet readability.

4

Formatting a Worksheet

The first spreadsheets could be used only in specific situations and could not be altered for other uses. When VisiCalc was first released, not even the column widths could be varied. New formatting capabilities, in particular, have provided the tools needed to make spreadsheets applicable in many different situations. The newest spreadsheets' capabilities to center text, to add comma delimiters to large numbers, and to display numbers with various decimal places have helped spreadsheets evolve from a tool that just generated numbers to a tool that creates presentation-quality displays of information.

At the first level of menu choices, SuperCalc offers a /Format selection to access both the global formatting commands and the column, row, and entry-range format commands. This system makes these commands more accessible than in previous spreadsheet programs. SuperCalc also offers user-defined formats, which provide users with a way to customize formats for numbers, date, and time.

You are ready to begin formatting a SuperCalc worksheet. This chapter describes how to define the worksheet defaults and how to make exceptions to the global default format settings. You should familiarize yourself first with SuperCalc's default format settings and then learn how to change them to fit your own needs. Through an example of a quarterly income statement, you learn how to manipulate column widths, display data labels, and display data in various forms, such as percentages and dollars. The chapter ends with the new /Justify command and a discussion of the /Global,Optimum command and other format-related /Global commands.

Understanding the Default Settings

SuperCalc is one of the most flexible spreadsheet programs on the market. In all areas of the program, various options affect display and print settings, memory usage, cursor-movement characteristics, and calculating and sorting orders.

To save your having to define each setting before you start developing your spreadsheet, SuperCalc includes the most general or common settings as the defaults. The start-up default settings include column width, alignment of numeric and alphanumeric entries, cell display formats, and a variety of general spreadsheet settings affecting cursor movement, text entry, and border and formula display. For example, when you call up SuperCalc and the blank spreadsheet display appears on the screen, you can see that each column is nine characters wide, the default setting for column width.

Most of the default settings affect the form of the worksheet display and can be accessed through the Format menu. To access the menu system from the main directory, type a slash mark (/). The menu selections are arranged in alphabetical order with **F**ormat on the top row. Select the **F**ormat option by moving the command cursor to **F**ormat and pressing Enter. As a quicker alternative, you can type **/F** for **/F**ormat. The Format menu is shown in figure 4.1.

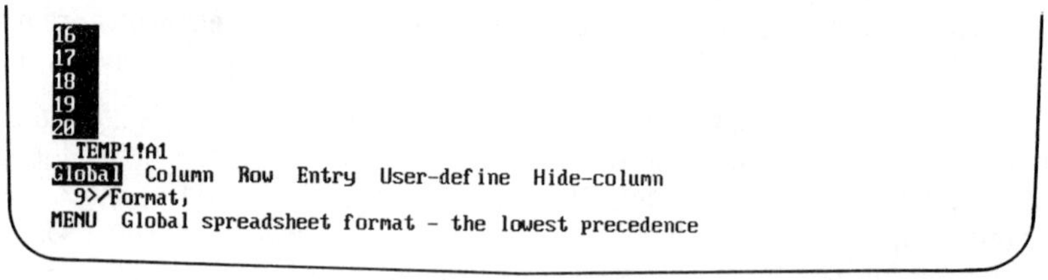

Fig. 4.1.

The Format menu.

```
16
17
18
19
20
  TEMP1!A1
Global  Column  Row  Entry  User-define  Hide-column
  9>/Format,
MENU  Global spreadsheet format - the lowest precedence
```

Through the Format menu, you can define the format settings for the spreadsheet as a whole; for one cell entry within the spreadsheet; or for a variety of column, row, or cell groupings. You can affect the format of a cell by defining a **G**lobal setting, a **C**olumn setting, a **R**ow setting, or a range or cell **E**ntry setting. Through **U**ser-define you can access the format customizer, and with SuperCalc5 you can hide one or more columns from view and access by selecting **H**ide-column and selecting the column(s) to hide.

A cell can have only one of the four types of formats at a time, so SuperCalc handles them in order of priority. This precedence of formatting (from high to low) is

1. **E**ntry
2. **R**ow
3. **C**olumn
4. **G**lobal

You cannot use a /**F**ormat,**G**lobal command for a cell that is already formatted with an **E**ntry, a **R**ow, or a **C**olumn command. If you format a row one way and a column another way, the cell at the intersection of that row and column is formatted according to the **R**ow format command. If you have already formatted a cell with the **E**ntry command, a **C**olumn or **R**ow format command does not affect that cell.

You can eliminate the precedence issue by avoiding the /**F**ormat,**R**ow command as much as possible and using the /**F**ormat,**C**olumn command only for adjusting the column widths. The **E**ntry function can be just as effective for most situations.

When you begin your spreadsheet, make sure that the default or global settings are appropriate for the worksheet you are developing.

Global Default Column Width

When you type **G** after /**F**ormat, the Format Global menu appears on the prompt lines (see fig. 4.2). Familiarize yourself with this display because you will use it often. These format options show up in several places within the Format menu structure.

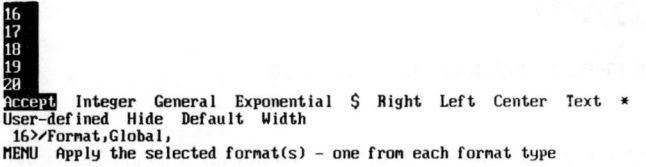

Fig. 4.2.

The Format Global menu.

The first setting you may want to change is the nine-character global default column width. Move the command selector to **W**idth by using the arrow keys or the space bar or by pressing W. Your display now matches figure 4.3. At this point, you can select a global column width ranging from 0 to 127 characters. The width you specify sets the maximum number of characters that can appear in any cell.

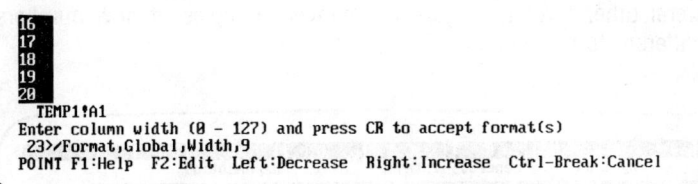

Fig. 4.3.

The Format Global Width menu.

With SuperCalc, you can choose a new cell size in two different ways. In the first method, you can type the cell width you want and press Enter. The display then changes to reflect your new choice and leaves you in READY mode. In the second, more visually oriented way, you can use POINT mode to choose the cell width you want (see the help line of the dialog panel at the bottom of fig. 4.3). Each time you press the left- or right-arrow key, all columns widen or narrow one space, respectively.

Selecting the cell width in POINT mode is more efficient than typing the cell width you want. This method is especially effective when data is already entered in the worksheet and you want the column width to fit the data. Although extreme changes in width are more quickly made by typing the new number, with POINT mode you can quickly fine-tune your display.

You can experiment by changing columns to several different widths. Notice that if you make a column less than three characters wide, the column letters disappear. Because the screen displays a total width of 76 characters, you may have to trade off between column width and the number of columns displayed. When the width of a column is made more than 76 characters (the maximum display width), the columns appear to stop growing.

When you begin working on a blank worksheet, you probably can make only a rough estimate of the best column width, which is fine. Often, you will need to change the column width later so that you can fit all the data on one printed page. You can change the global default settings at any time during construction of the worksheet, and the display will change to conform to the new format setting for all columns not specifically formatted with the /Format,Column command.

Default Format

Move to the Format Global menu by entering, in READY mode,

/Format,Global

Your display again matches figure 4.2 with all the options displayed. Use the space bar or press the appropriate arrow key to move the command pointer through the options. Notice the explanatory notes at the bottom of the screen as you move the pointer. Each help tip relates to the option on which your pointer is located.

The Accept option on the Format Global menu also could be named Quit or Exit; choosing this option moves you to the next higher menu level (the main Format menu, in this case). Of the next four options—Integer, General, Exponential, and $ (fixed to two decimal places)—the General format least alters the appearance of the stored number. Therefore, the General format option is the SuperCalc default setting. Besides the General format, SuperCalc provides several other formats. Figure 4.4 shows examples of how numbers appear displayed with different format options.

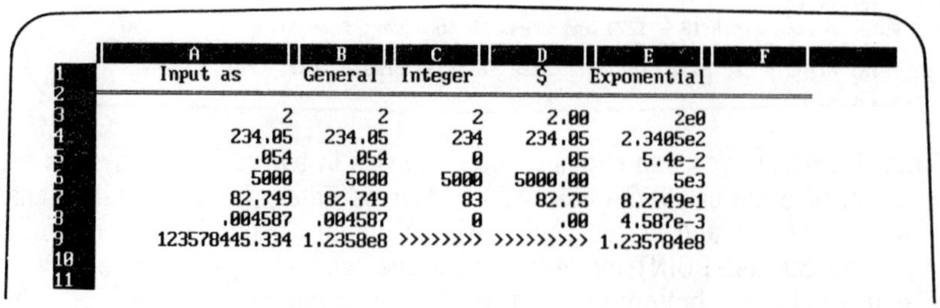

Fig. 4.4.

SuperCalc's numeric format options.

	A	B	C	D	E	F
	Input as	General	Integer	$	Exponential	
	2	2	2	2.00	2e0	
	234.05	234.05	234	234.05	2.3405e2	
	.054	.054	0	.05	5.4e-2	
	5000	5000	5000	5000.00	5e3	
	82.749	82.749	83	82.75	8.2749e1	
	.004587	.004587	0	.00	4.587e-3	
	123578445.334	1.2358e8	>>>>>>>>	>>>>>>>>>	1.235784e8	

General Format

In most cases, the **G**eneral format displays numbers exactly as they are entered. If the number typed into a cell exceeds the column width for that cell, however, SuperCalc rounds off any fractional portion of the number and applies the **E**xponential format to the number to make it fit. If the minimum possible form of the **E**xponential format does not work, a column-width spillover indicator (››) is substituted. For example, the following transformation will occur on the number 2345.045 as it is displayed in various column widths:

Column Width	9	8	7	6	5	4	3
Value	2345.045	2345.05	2345.0	2345.	2345	2e3	››

In figure 4.4, in row 9 the number 123578445.334 is entered in each cell. Because column B is only eight characters wide, the number in cell B9 appears as 1.2358e8.

Integer Format

As you can see in figure 4.4, the **I**nteger format (column C) rounds the entered number and displays it as a whole number. For example, 82.749 rounds to 83 in cell C7. Remember, however, that the stored number remains unchanged. For that reason, the rounded sum of a list of stored values is different from the sum of the rounded displayed values. In Chapter 7, you learn how the ROUND function, incorporated into a worksheet, can safeguard against this effect. Still, you probably should not format the entire worksheet in the **I**nteger format before the contents are well defined.

$ Format

The **$** format is a workhorse for financial data. Although this format is called the dollar format, a dollar sign does not appear in the cell. All numbers are displayed with two decimal places and without comma separators. Like the **I**nteger and **E**xponential formats, **$** rounds numbers for display—something to keep in mind when you want accuracy.

The **$** format lines up the decimal points throughout the column (see fig. 4.4). This uniformity is pleasing to the eye and eases working with long columns of data.

Exponential Format

The **E**xponential format, which is used more frequently in science and engineering than in finance and accounting, helps display very large and very small numbers. When any cell is formatted this way, the first nonzero number is displayed to the left of the decimal point, and as much of the remainder as possible is displayed between the decimal point and the exponent indicator (e). To the right of the *e* is the number of places that the decimal was adjusted, either positively (left) or negatively (right).

For the large number in row 9 of figure 4.4, compare the display in the **G**eneral format column (nine characters wide) with the display in the **E**xponential format column (11 characters wide). In the **G**eneral format column, the number is precise only to four decimal places. In the **E**xponential format column, the number is precise to six decimal places. Both numbers have been adjusted by eight powers of ten, but the columns have different widths.

If the number is an average size, the **E**xponential format does not save much in length because the exponent information takes up two or three spaces (depending on whether the adjustment was left or right). In row 5 of figure 4.4, the number .054 requires a wider column for exponential display ($5.4e-2$) than for any of the other formats.

Default Alignments

The alignment format options affect the location of the display within the cell. Both numbers and text can be aligned three different ways.

Numeric Alignment

From the Format Global menu (refer to fig. 4.2), the **R**ight, **L**eft, and **C**enter options affect the alignment of numeric data within the cells. The default value is **R**ight because this alignment was an accepted standard long before computers and spreadsheets were invented. You should be comfortable with right alignment and probably will not need to adjust the global default to left alignment. Some situations, however, may require setting the value to **L**eft or **C**enter. For example, in an outline or some other text-related task, the numbering scheme might look better with an alternative alignment. The spreadsheets in figure 4.5 are shown using the SuperCalc5 multiple spreadsheet display technique. They are the same spreadsheet as in figure 4.4, but set to **L**eft alignment on the top and **C**enter alignment on the bottom.

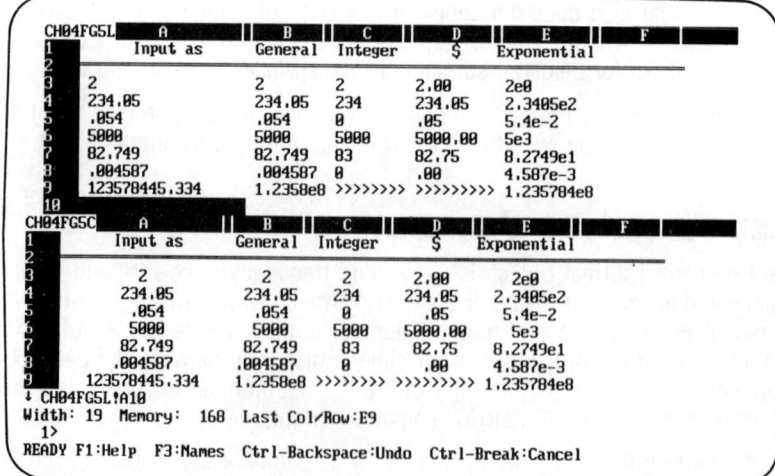

Fig. 4.5.

*Numeric formats displayed with **Left** (top) and **Center** (bottom) alignments.*

Because the decimal is no longer aligned in the $ column, you can see that neither of these alternative formats is effective for financial data.

Text Alignment

Text alignment has its own menu. To get to the text alignment options from the Format Global menu, move the menu pointer to **T**ext or press **T** (refer to fig. 4.2). A menu appears with the following options:

    Left Right Center

Left alignment is the default text alignment for two reasons. Because text usually begins against the left edge of a page, text should line up on the left edges of the cells. In addition, unlike numbers, which are displayed as overflow (›››››››) if they exceed the column width, characters can spill over into the cells to the right if those cells are empty. This feature is extremely valuable.

If the text alignment is switched to **R**ight alignment, the text does not spill over. The right end of the text string aligns against the right side of the cell, and the text string display is cut off at the left edge of the cell so that you cannot see the beginning of the string. When you do use **R**ight alignment of text, perhaps for labels, make sure that the column width is wide enough to display all the text.

Text that exceeds the width of a cell formatted to **C**enter alignment spills over to the cells to the right and appears to be left-aligned within the cell. A text string shorter than the column width is centered within the cell.

Figure 4.6 shows the three text alternatives, all entered in column A. For each alternative, you see a short text string, a text string that exceeds the column width, and a repeating text string. The Short Text Strings group is self-explanatory. In the Long Text Strings section, the third line demonstrates the odd appearance of right alignment. You can see how the string is truncated 24 characters from the end of the string. The third section, Repeating Text Strings, shows the effect of the different alignment options on the text function RTEXT, which you access by first entering a single quotation mark (') before entering your text string.

The double and single quotation marks are useful tools. In SuperCalc, everything that is not recognizable as a numeric value, a formula, or a function is considered a text string and is automatically stored with a double quotation mark (") preceding it. If you enter double quotation marks in the first character place in the entry, you force SuperCalc to consider what you enter as a text string. This instruction is necessary when you want to enter a text string that is identical to a numeric string or cell reference. For example, if you enter the date string **10-5-88** into a cell without preceding the string with a double quotation mark, SuperCalc identifies the entry as a formula and displays −83 (10 minus 5 minus 88) rather than the string you expected. Or, if you enter the string **A1** into a cell, the value stored in cell A1 appears because the string is automatically interpreted as a cell reference. For repeating text, enter a single quotation mark instead of a double quotation mark at the beginning of the text string, and the string that follows is repeated across the screen. Rows 2, 8, and 14 of figure 4.6 are examples of a common use of repeating text.

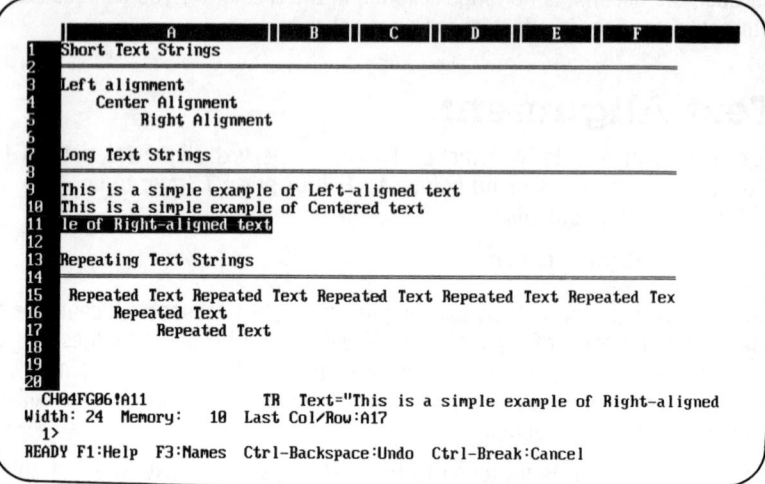

Fig. 4.6.

*Text alignment: Left,
Center, Right.*

If the cell is not formatted with **L**eft alignment, the repeat format—as in cells A16 and A17—appears as a normal text string, not as a repeating text string.

In a worksheet, you usually end up with a variety of text alignments. Handling more than one text alignment is explained in the section "Overriding the Defaults: Formatting Cells and Cell Groups."

Specialty Formats

The Format Global menu, shown in figure 4.2, contains two specialty formats. The linear format (*) is an option for displaying numeric data as a series of asterisks in line. Like numeric formats, these asterisks are displayed only for the width of the cell; they do not spill over to the cells to the right. You can use this format for creating simple graphs, but the linear format is not an appropriate choice for a global default setting.

The **H**ide format hides the contents of a cell. In specific cases, such as hiding a portion of a range before printing, this format can be quite useful; but it is less useful as a global default. Unlike the **H**ide-column option on the main Format menu, with the **H**ide format the column remains displayed and you can access the cell, but no data appears in the cell. If you use the **H**ide-column option, the entire column disappears and is not accessible. You may want to use the **H**ide format to conceal some information on the spreadsheet before printing or to hide an interim working cell that does not need to be seen on the final output. If you do not want to show an entire column on the final output, use the **H**ide-column option. You also can define the column width as 0 and the column will not show but is accessible. Either way, the column can be referenced but does not appear on the printed page or on the screen.

The Default Option

The **D**efault option on the Format Global menu is a reversing command. If you do not like the settings you have changed, choosing **D**efault is a quick way to return to the original values of **G**eneral format, UserDate1 format, **L**eft text alignment, **R**ight numeric alignment, and columns nine characters wide.

Defining Your Own Numeric Formats

The **U**ser-defined option on the Format Global menu is a useful tool. If none of the format choices on this menu (**I**nteger, **G**eneral, **E**xponential, or **$**) fits your needs, SuperCalc has designer formats.

With earlier versions of SuperCalc, you could vary seven display characteristics in eight different combinations; with the introduction of SuperCalc4 Version 1.1, you can vary eight display characteristics. More importantly, though, the definition and selection process for these eight combinations has undergone a face-lift.

Selection of a User-Defined Format

The eight **U**ser-defined settings do not have the same initial configuration, so you don't have to modify them immediately for use. To select a **U**ser-defined format, select **U**ser-defined on the Format Global menu, bringing up a menu with the following two options:

```
Number   Date
```

Selecting **N**umber from this menu brings up eight numbers representing the eight numeric formats you can customize:

```
1  2  3  4  5  6  7  8
26›/Format,Global,UserNumber
```

The new terminology, UserNumber, is necessary to differentiate the **U**ser-defined numeric formats from the date formats (titled UserDate), which are discussed in the following section. Whichever number you select from the dialog panel by using the menu selector or by typing directly is attached to the end of the string to mark this format (for example, UserNumber3).

The help line displays

```
Current:  $-11,111,111.11  No 0
```

If you move the menu selection cursor through the eight choices, you will see the help line change to display the number formatted using each setting. This helpful feature saves you from remembering the format of each of the eight settings. The No and O after the number refer to the Zero as Blank setting and Scaling Factor setting, which are discussed in more detail later in this chapter.

To change the looks of these eight settings, you must back out of the Format Global menu by pressing Esc three times. Doing so leaves you at the main Format menu again, as shown in figure 4.1.

The fifth option on the Format menu, User-define, takes you to where you can change these eight custom formats.

The Two Designer Menus

In previous versions of SuperCalc, the User-define option was called Define. That selection, although removed from the menu in favor of this more user-friendly command, is still accessible by typing D at the main Format menu. If you use an older version of SuperCalc and were just getting comfortable with the old method, it is still in place. The old directly updateable Format Define menu is shown in figure 4.7.

Fig. 4.7.

The traditional user-defined format screen.

```
                    User-defined formats
                    1  2  3  4  5  6  7  8

    Floating $      Y  Y  Y  Y  Y  N  N  N

    Embedded Commas Y  Y  Y  Y  N  Y  Y  N

    Minus in ( )    N  N  Y  Y  N  N  Y  N

    Zero as Blank   N  Y  N  Y  N  N  N  N

    %               N  N  N  N  N  N  N  Y

    Decimal Places  2  2  2  2  0  0  0  2

    Scaling Factor  0  0  0  0  0  0  0  0



     TEMP1!A1
    Yes or No ?
     16>/Format,Define,
    MENU  Precede numbers w/currency symbol
```

This menu is less effective than the new menu because you cannot alter the Before and After display and you cannot select Float under Minus. (These options are discussed later.) In contrast, the screen and the menu options that appear when you select the menu option User-define,Number are shown in figure 4.8.

This screen provides more direct feedback about what your setting will look like, and a menu system is included to help you step through the modification process. The last selection on the menu shown in the figure, Zap, is for resetting the formats to the current program defaults.

```
USER-DEFINE NUMBER FORMAT MENU

Format        Currently Defined Format                Zero as   Scaling
Set                                                   Blank     Factor
  1.   $-11,111,111.11                                  No         0
  2.   $-11,111,111.11                                  Yes        0
  3.   (    $11,111,111.11)                             No         0
  4.   (    $11,111,111.11)                             Yes        0
  5.   $-11111111                                       No         0
  6.   -11,111,111                                      No         0
  7.   (   11,111,111)                                  No         0
  8.   -1111111111.11%                                  No         0




  TEMP1↑A1
  Quit  1  2  3  4  5  6  7  8  Zap
   28>/Format,User-define,Number,
  MENU  Finished defining formats; return to /Format menu
```

Fig. 4.8.

The user-friendly User-Define Number Format menu.

Options Available for User Definition

To see how easily you can modify the eight formats displayed in figure 4.8, select **1** to modify that format set. The menu shown in the dialog panel of figure 4.9 appears.

```
  TEMP1↑A1
  Quit  Before  After  Thousands  Minus  Percent  Decimal  Zero  Scaling
   30>/Format,User-define,Number,1,
  MENU  Finished defining formats; return to /Format menu
```

Fig. 4.9.

The user-definable options.

Before and After

Before and **A**fter allow you to attach a currency string to either the left or right end of your numeric value. You have three options available when you select either of these options:

    Default   None   Enter

If you purchased SuperCalc in the United States, the original program defaults for **B**efore and **A**fter are the dollar sign ($) preceding and no character following the number. You can change the default setting by going to the Global Optimum Present menu, which is discussed later in this chapter. Selecting **N**one eliminates any character string from being displayed next to the number. The third option, **E**nter, allows you to enter a new character string of up to 15 characters, to be displayed either before or after the value.

Because of this **E**nter option, you can enter any denomination or currency value you want. If you are dealing in commodities, you can type

/Format,**U**ser-define,**N**umber,**1**,**A**fter,**Bushels**

and the word *Bushels* attaches to the value, such as

    100 Bushels

Lettered currency values, such as SF for Swiss Franc or the British Pound Sterling sign (£, entered by pressing Alt and typing the number **156**), are also now possible.

Thousands

Thousands alters the display to place a thousands delimiter every three places to the left of the decimal point, to make a number more readable. One million appears as 1,000,000 if **Y**es is selected under this option and as 1000000 if **N**o is selected.

Minus

Selecting **N**o for the **M**inus option displays a negative number with a minus sign attached to the left of the number, such as −15. Selecting **Y**es or **F**loat causes a negative number to appear enclosed in parentheses, as is common in accounting. The only difference between **Y**es and **F**loat is the location of the parentheses. For example, with **Y**es, −15 in a right-justified column 10 characters wide looks like (15). With **F**loat, the same circumstances cause −15 to look like (15).

Percent

Adding percentage (%) columns to a handwritten worksheet is so time-consuming that many times the task is avoided. But adding percentages in SuperCalc is simple enough to make this option a useful analytical tool.

In **P**ercent format, the cell content is multiplied by 100, and a percent sign (%) is appended to the right of the displayed number. For example, the number 1 is displayed as 100%. Because the calculation is performed before display, this format not only improves the appearance of your spreadsheet but also saves you time. You do not need to add a formula to each percentage cell in order to divide the contents by 100.

Decimal

With the **D**ecimal option, all values can be rounded to a fixed decimal display ranging from zero to seven places. If you enter **0**, you obtain the same result as if you were using the **I**nteger format from the main Format menu. Entering **2** is the same as using the **$** format from the main Format menu.

Because you must make a selection from 0 to 7 for this setting, all cells formatted with this UserNumber format will appear with the same number of decimal places. To display two numbers with all of the eight definable options except the decimal place the same requires using two of the UserNumber formats.

Zero

Zero as Blank (shortened to `Zero` in the menu) can be set to **N**o or **Y**es. With the **Zero** option, any cell content that evaluates to zero does not display—a blank cell appears instead. This feature is useful for unused sections in a worksheet. With zeros hidden, the worksheet looks less cluttered, and the relevant cells can be identified more easily.

Scaling

Like **D**ecimal, **S**caling can be set from 0 to 7. Zero, meaning no scaling takes place, is the default setting for this option. Setting it to a number besides 0 enables scaling. This setting causes decimal place rounding to continue to the left of the decimal point. For example, if you enter **2**, two integer places to the left of the decimal point are eliminated from the display and the remaining number is rounded to the nearest tenth.

The effects of this feature on the value 1,234,567 can be seen in figure 4.10. Each time the scaling factor is increased by 1, one less power of 10 is displayed. This option is useful in formatting the labels in graphs (covered in Chapter 10) and can be used to make a page less cluttered by eliminating zeros. How many times have you seen the messages `($000 omitted)`, `($000000 omitted)`, or `In Millions`? With this scaling factor, you can easily omit these zeros. With fewer zeros, more columns can fit on the page.

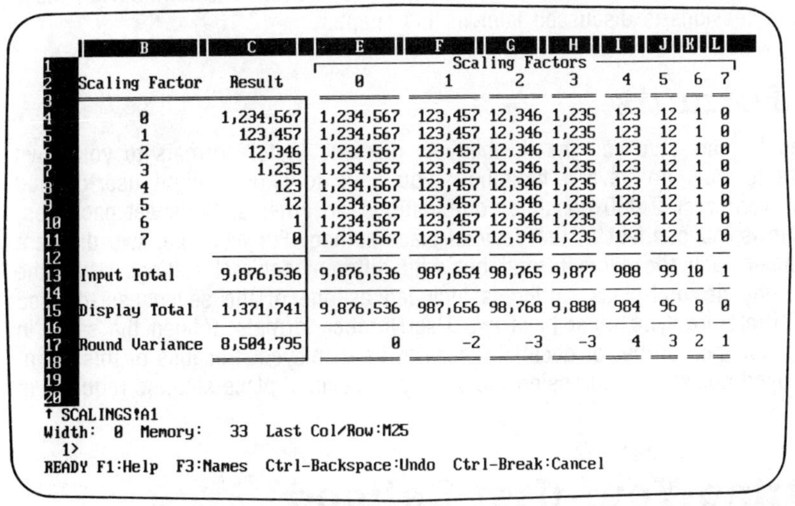

	B	C	E	F	G	H	I	J	K	L
1			Scaling Factors							
2	Scaling Factor	Result	0	1	2	3	4	5	6	7
3										
4	0	1,234,567	1,234,567	123,457	12,346	1,235	123	12	1	0
5	1	123,457	1,234,567	123,457	12,346	1,235	123	12	1	0
6	2	12,346	1,234,567	123,457	12,346	1,235	123	12	1	0
7	3	1,235	1,234,567	123,457	12,346	1,235	123	12	1	0
8	4	123	1,234,567	123,457	12,346	1,235	123	12	1	0
9	5	12	1,234,567	123,457	12,346	1,235	123	12	1	0
10	6	1	1,234,567	123,457	12,346	1,235	123	12	1	0
11	7	0	1,234,567	123,457	12,346	1,235	123	12	1	0
12										
13	Input Total	9,876,536	9,876,536	987,654	98,765	9,877	988	99	10	1
14										
15	Display Total	1,371,741	9,876,536	987,656	98,768	9,880	984	96	8	0
16										
17	Round Variance	8,504,795	0	-2	-3	-3	4	3	2	1
18										
19										
20										

↑ SCALINGS!A1
Width: 0 Memory: 33 Last Col/Row:M25
1>
READY F1:Help F3:Names Ctrl-Backspace:Undo Ctrl-Break:Cancel

Fig. 4.10.
User-defined scaling variations.

Rows 13 and 15 of figure 4.10 give the sums of the preceding seven rows in the column. The results illustrate the limitation of this format. Without rounding the underlying cell values to match the display, the numbers in a sum do not seem to add up. In this figure, the rounded sum of the cell contents varies from the sum of the rounded display by as much as four (line 17).

Uses of User-Defined Number Formats

Changes to a user-defined format are retroactive. Whenever you change these settings on the design screen, you affect all worksheet cells that have been formatted with the same user-defined format.

Even without saving your customized user-defined formats as program defaults with the /Global,Keep command (discussed later in this chapter), the modified formats are stored with your worksheet when saved to disk. So you can have a different set of special formats for each worksheet. One worksheet may require three decimal places, whereas another may use a different set of currency values.

To erase a worksheet but retain the special custom formats you created, you can use the command

/Zap,Contents

The Contents option is no longer displayed on the menus as it was in previous versions of SuperCalc. The option remains functional, though, when you execute it by typing C at the Zap menu. If you execute the normal /Zap,Yes command, all your user-defined settings return to SuperCalc's global defaults. With this special version of the command, your designer formats are preserved for further use during your current session. Saving these formats for future sessions is discussed later in this chapter.

Mixing Formats

The user-defined formats give you the flexibility to mix and match formats to your own liking, but these formats do have a limitation: you have to choose eight user-defined number formats from over 2,000 possible combinations. In other spreadsheet packages, the format setting is independent of the decimal-place setting. For example, two different cells can be defined with the same format but with different decimal settings. With the SuperCalc style, the decimal-place setting is included as one of the seven user-defined format options. Therefore, you must have two UserNumber formats defined the same in every way except for the number of decimal places to be displayed. Because of this, eight settings can be used quickly in addressing the variety of decimal place settings required in a worksheet.

Configuring Your User-Defined Number Format Options

Perhaps the idea of choosing eight formats from over 2,000 combinations is a bit over-whelming. Some combinations, however, can be easily ruled out. For example, although you can define a setting to display both a dollar sign and a percentage sign, in reality, the dollar and percentage formats are mutually exclusive: a value is never displayed with a dollar sign on the left and a percentage sign on the right.

Other combinations duplicate the predefined settings. For example, if you choose no dollar sign, no commas, no parentheses, zero display, no decimal places, and no scaling, you duplicate the predefined Integer format.

Some settings are rarely used. Percentages, for instance, usually range in value from 0 to 100, so you do not normally need comma delimiting or negative parentheses.

Some of these designer formats greatly affect column-width settings and may not be practical. Negative numbers in parentheses are visually pleasing but occupy two spaces in the cell. Even when the number is not negative, it is offset to the left one space to line up with any negative numbers displayed in the column. Furthermore, the Thousands display can add several spaces to the minimum necessary for the column width. Both of these options added to the Before and After formats require a sizable column width to accommodate them. This large width limits the number of columns that can appear on the screen at one time.

Judicious use of column and row labels within the worksheet can eliminate the need for the Before, After, and Percent formats when spreadsheet width is a consideration. If a column is labeled with a dollar sign, a dollar sign need not appear in each entry. Eliminating the dollar sign in the columns also makes your worksheet less cluttered.

A Sample Setting of the Eight UserNumber Formats

Figure 4.11 is an example of an all-purpose setting that may be a good combination for you to use until you decide how you want to set up the user-defined formats to best meet your needs. From these default settings, you can tailor an individual worksheet format.

```
USER-DEFINE NUMBER FORMAT MENU

Format          Currently Defined Format              Zero as    Scaling
Set                                                    Blank      Factor
  1.    -11,111,111.1                                    No          0
  2.    (   11,111,111)                                  No          0
  3.    -11,111,111.1                                    No          0
  4.    -11,111,111.11                                   No          0
  5.    (   11111111.1)                                  No          0
  6.    (   11111111.11)                                 No          0
  7.    (   $11,111,111)                                 No          0
  8.    -1111111111.11%                                  No          0
```

Fig. 4.11.

Sample user-defined settings.

Compare the settings in figure 4.11 with the default settings shown in figure 4.8. Notice that the Zero as Blank and Scaling Factor settings are not defined for any of the eight formats. Furthermore, one percentage format is usually adequate for a worksheet, leaving seven alternatives for regular numeric values.

UserNumber1 is a "plain vanilla" setting for displaying one decimal place. UserNumber2 and UserNumber7 are both set to zero decimal places (display values as an integer) because of the number of other options they have set. Embedded commas widen a number one space per thousand; displaying a minus in parentheses adds two spaces to the width; and in the case of UserNumber7, an added dollar sign adds one space to the width.

UserNumber3 and UserNumber4 are identical except for the difference in decimal places. Both formats include comma delimiters but do not enclose negative values in parentheses. On the other hand, UserNumber5 and UserNumber6 do not include commas but enclose negatives in parentheses. UserNumber5 is designed for one decimal place and UserNumber6 for two decimal places. This example demonstrates how quickly you can use up your eight formats handling different decimal place settings.

Finally, UserNumber8 is the percentage format, set to show only one decimal place, no embedded commas (rarely would you get a percentage in the thousands), and negatives appearing with a minus to keep the required column width to a minimum. This setting, like the others, does not use the Scaling Factor and does not display a zero value as blank.

Defining Your Own Date Formats

A completely new system for date formatting was added to SuperCalc4 Version 1.1. In addition, time formatting has been added to SuperCalc5, allowing you to choose alternative ways to display time functions. All the date and time formats fall within the User-define system. You can display a date in virtually any way you can imagine (except for maybe MCMLXXXIX).

With this system, you can design eight different ways to display calendar functions within a cell storing a calendar function. You also can alter the default time format for displaying time functions. To format a worksheet globally so that all dates appear as the format defined for UserDate3, you type

/Format,Global,UserDate3

Like the UserNumber format, an example of each format is displayed in the help line below the entry line to remind you of what you are getting. This reminder eliminates a great deal of experimenting and recalling on your part.

Unlike the date portion of the format, you do not have to activate the user-defined time format. You can display time only in one way throughout your spreadsheet. Once you alter the time format in the User-Define Date Format menu, the new format takes effect throughout your spreadsheet.

Customizing Your UserDate Formats

As with the UserNumber formats, to redefine the user-defined date and time formats you select **U**ser-define on the main Format menu. But instead of selecting **N**umber, you select **D**ate; the screen shown in figure 4.12 appears.

```
USER-DEFINE DATE FORMAT MENU

        Format                    Example (using March 8, 1980  7:09:10 AM)
    1.  _BM/BD/YYYY                      3/ 8/1980
    2.  DD-MMM-YY                       08-Mar-80
    3.  DD-MMM                          08-Mar
    4.  MMM-YY                          Mar-80
    5.  MM/DD/YY                        03/08/80
    6.  MM/DD                           03/08
    7.  YY-MM-DD                        80-03-08
    8.  DD.MM.YY                        08.03.80
    T.  BH:TT:SS_AM/PM                   7:09:10 AM

        Use M, BM, MM, MMM, MMMM or R  for month
        Use D, BD, DD,                 for day
        Use Y, YY, YYYY                for year
        Use WWW, WWWW                  for weekday
        Use BH, HH                     for hour
        Use BT, TT                     for minute
        Use BS, SS                     for second
        Use A/P, a/p, AM/PM, am/pm     for clock
  SCALINGS↑A1
 Quit  1  2  3  4  5  6  7  8  T  Zap
 26>/Format,User-define,Date,
 MENU  Finished defining formats; return to /Format menu
```

Fig. 4.12.

The User-Define Date Format menu.

Listed in ascending order are the eight UserDate formats with the syntax of the format (called the *token string*) in the left column and an example of the syntax based on March 8, 1980, in the right column. To modify one of the token strings, you select its number from the menu shown (**1–8** or **T**) and edit the string by using the F2 editing functions (see Chapter 5) or by retyping the string the way you want. SuperCalc interprets each letter in the token string.

Defining the Syntax of the Date Formats

The syntax of the token strings is traditional and is easily understood from the on-screen documentation. The key letters considered by SuperCalc (regardless of capitalization) are D, M, Y, B, and R for dates and H, M, and S for time.

Defining the Month

The key letter (token) in defining the month portion of a date is, naturally, M. Using M alone causes the actual number of the month to appear without considering spacing for single- or double-digit month numbers. Used as MM, the number of the month appears with a leading zero if it is single digit (01 for January), as demonstrated in UserDate5 and

UserDate6 in figure 4.12. Used as MMM, a three-letter abbreviation (Jan.) appears instead of the month number. Used as MMMM, the full month name appears.

Other letters also help to describe a month. The letter R causes the month to appear in Roman numerals (I for January). B, when used as BM, causes the leading zero to be blank for the single-digit months (1 for January), but the number will be spaced like a double-digit number.

The month can be combined into the displayed date in any order, and SuperCalc converts the first recognizable interpretation of the letter M or R into a date. Any occurrence after that will be shown as text. This practice is true of all the date components.

Defining the Day

The key letter in defining a day is D. It can appear in any part of a date token string. Using a single D trims the date to a single-digit number where appropriate; DD shows the leading zero; and BD spaces the date like a double-digit number but converts any leading zeros to blanks.

Defining the Year

The letter Y is key in defining the year value. When Y is used alone, all dates except 00–09 appear as double-digit, and 00–09 appear as 0–9 (single-digit only). Defined as YY, a leading zero appears where appropriate. Defined as YYYY, the full four-digit year appears except when the column width is too narrow; then the year is shortened automatically to two digits.

Adding Text to the Format

Other text, including spaces (which appear as a low-intensity underline on the entry line), may be added to the token string to format the date in a special way. For example, the token string

To"d"a"y"'s "D"ate = _D_MMMM_YY

is displayed as

Today's Date= 5 June 90

The quotation marks are used around the *d*, *y*, and *D* so that SuperCalc will not interpret them as date tokens.

Defining the Time

You can display time with only a few variations. The most basic option is 12- or 24-hour format. This option is controlled through the Global menus by typing

/Global,Optimum,Present,Time

Then select one of the two options: **12**hr or **24**hr.

On the User-Define Date Format menu, the default format looks like this:

    BH:TT:SS_AM/PM

The AM or PM will appear only if you have chosen the **12**hr option under the Global menus. You can substitute a B for the first T or S, as was done for the hours (BH instead of HH). Thus single-digit time elements include a blank space. You also can omit all or any part of the format, and you can choose from AM/PM, am/pm, A/P, or a/p to display the 12-hour format.

Overriding the Defaults: Formatting Cells and Cell Groups

So far, this chapter has focused on global Format settings, which affect the entire spreadsheet. All the **F**ormat options that relate to global defaults can also affect specified sections of the spreadsheet, such as a range of columns or rows or a single cell or group of cells. To give you a feeling for the kind of formatting you will encounter in a typical spreadsheet, a sample income statement is used to illustrate the discussion in this section.

Creating a Quarterly Income Statement

After you make any initial changes to the default settings, you can begin developing the worksheet. SuperCalc allows you to tailor the specific ranges as you go. Figure 4.13 is an example of a simple income statement that requires a variety of formats. To learn the formats involved, follow along and create an identical income statement on your own system.

As you develop this worksheet, you may notice several variations in column width, text alignment, and numeric display. Because no single format is dominant in the income statement, default /Format,**G**lobal worksheet settings of **G**eneral format, **T**ext Left, numbers **R**ight, and column width of 10 are adequate for beginning the spreadsheet. The user-defined formats displayed in figure 4.11 are used in this example.

Formatting Column Widths

Usually, the first thing you must change when creating a new worksheet is the individual column widths. For the income statement, you will modify both description columns (containing labels) and data columns.

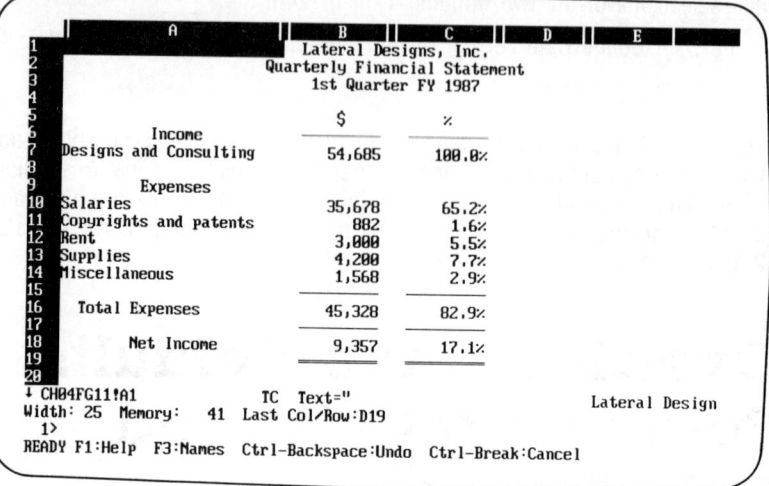

Fig. 4.13.

Income statement using a variety of formats.

Description Columns

Many times, the first column, A, contains the row descriptions or labels for the data input. Because descriptions can be lengthy text strings, column A needs to be widened. In Super-Calc, text strings can overrun the right end of their cells if the cells to the right are empty. You do not want strings to run over, however, because you want to put data in column B. Therefore, column A must be wide enough to accommodate all the row labels.

A good starting column width for column A in the income statement is 25 characters. From that width you can quickly fine-tune the width as you enter individual titles, add abbreviations where necessary, and at the end, consider the effect of all the column widths on the overall display.

To change the width of the first column to 25, press the Home key, which moves the cell pointer to A1. Type **/F** to get to the main Format menu. Instead of selecting **G**lobal at this point, as you did before, select the **C**olumn option. SuperCalc then prompts you to define a column range. The entry line shows

        17>/Format,Column,A

Because the cell pointer is in the first column, A is already entered as the column range. The default display is the letter of the column where the cell pointer is located. If you move the cell pointer to another column, the command string changes to reflect the new column. In this case, press Enter to accept that range. The Format Column menu appears.

Move the menu selector to **W**idth and press Enter, or simply type **W**. The current cell width is displayed automatically, and the system prompts you either to enter a new column width or to press the left- or right-arrow keys to decrease or increase the column width.

Because the 25-character column width is more than twice the size of the current width, you can enter the number 25 more quickly than you can use the arrow keys. When you press Enter, the width of column A changes to 25.

Data Columns

To see a helpful feature of SuperCalc, suppose that column B and column C need to be 11 characters wide instead of the default 9. Once more, choose

/Format,Column,A

At this point, you must enter a range of columns rather than a single column. Because the cell pointer is in A1, move the cell pointer right to point to column B. The following display line appears:

     `17›/Format,Column,B`

Now press the period or colon key; the display changes to look like this:

     `19›/Format,Column,B:B`

This range is now defined as a single-column range anchored on column B instead of the single column B. If you move the cell pointer to column C, the display changes to

     `19›/Format,Column,B:C`

As you can tell from this exercise, you can use POINT mode to point out column and row ranges just as you do a cell range. When you press Enter, the main Format Column menu appears. Select **W**idth to change these two columns to 12 characters wide. The display prompts for a column width, and the command string reads

     `27›/Format,Column,B:C,Width,9`

Because the current setting and the new setting differ by only three characters, press the right-arrow key three times to adjust the width. Notice that the two columns selected expand to 12 characters wide. If you press Enter, you will be back to READY mode.

Formatting the Alignment of Cell Contents

The spreadsheet is now formatted so that column A is 25 characters wide, columns B and C are 12 characters wide, and the remaining columns are 9 (the default). Now you are ready to enter the worksheet title headings.

A Hidden Tool: The Blank Character

One text-alignment tool, the blank character, is not in the Format menu selections. By using blank characters, you can store as a specific text character an area that appears blank on the screen. In any text alignment, you can make text strings begin at any location within the cell by entering a double quotation mark (") and a number of spaces in front of the text (use the space bar). This tool is handy when you want to center titles at the top of the worksheet (see fig. 4.13). Keep in mind that blank characters on the ends of character strings, however, are not kept; the text entry is assumed to end with the last nonblank character.

The titles that appear centered in columns B and C are actually entered in cells A1, A2, and A3, with various numbers of blanks preceding the titles. If you entered the same titles in B1, B2, and B3, you would have to center them farther to the left of the center of the income statement because column A is so wide. When printed, the income statement titles would appear offset to the right on the printed page.

To center the titles, enter them with 27, 23, and 28 leading blanks, respectively. You can adjust any of these figures three different ways: by retyping the entire cell contents, by using the /Edit command, or by pressing the F2 (Edit) function key to edit the entry. Editing is described in detail in Chapter 5.

Another alternative for centering these titles was first added in Version 1.1 of SuperCalc4. Enter each title in its own row and use the command

> /Justify,Single,**A1:F3**,Center

This command centers the titles within the range you specify. Be careful, because rejustifying the titles to the left edge does not work the same way as adding blanks; all three strings will be combined in one string. Other uses for /Justify are discussed later in this chapter.

You also can use blank characters to center row headings. *Total Expenses* in A16 is not formatted with the TextCenter format. The labels *Income* (A6), *Expenses* (A9), and *Net Income* (A18) are formatted as TextCenter, but the label *Total Expenses* is indented by using the default format and typing a double quotation mark, two spaces, and then the label itself.

Centered Text

You also may want to center other types of text. In figure 4.13, the column headings and the section headings are centered. To format these particular cells, move the cell pointer to C5. The quickest way to format the contents of B5, C5, A6, B6, and C6 is to format the row range 5:6. From the READY prompt, enter

> /Format,**R**ow,**5**

Above the entry line, the prompt reads

> Enter row range of 1 to 254 or R for Remaining rows (> 254)

This command has two variations, depending on the row being formatted. Within the first 254 rows of the spreadsheet, an individual row can be formatted. For rows 255 through the end, however, all the rows must be formatted as a group. This second option of /Format,**R**ow is useful if you are working with a large database with identical records in each row. Otherwise, this command is primarily effective within the first 254 rows. Use the /Format,**E**ntry command, designed for formatting a range of cells, for the remaining rows.

Because rows 5 and 6 are within the first 254 rows of the spreadsheet area, they can be formatted as a range by the /Format,**R**ow command. At this point, press a period or a colon to anchor the range at row 5 and move the cell pointer down one row. The entry line should look like this:

```
16›/Format,Row,5:6
```

By pressing Enter, you complete the range definition section of the command. The comma that appears after the range indicates that the definition is complete, and a new menu appears.

This new menu is similar to the menus for the /**F**ormat,**G**lobal and /**F**ormat,**C**olumn commands, but with one difference: this menu has no **W**idth option. Only one width can be defined per column, and widths cannot vary within a column. The width option cannot be used when you are formatting a range of rows.

From this menu of choices select **T**ext. The next menu has choices of

```
Left   Right   Center
```

Left is the default. For these rows, select **C**enter and press Enter twice to return to the main Format menu. Now, enter the title and column-heading text in the cells you have formatted.

The remainder of the cells in the row headings column are formatted in the default **L**eft alignment except for A9 and A18 (see fig. 4.13). In your worksheet, enter the rest of the headings without leaving the correct relative positions. For A9 and A18 (*Expenses* and *Net Income*), enter the text strings without spaces so that the strings line up on the left edges of their cells. You next will center these lines.

Now move the cell pointer to A9. From the READY prompt, choose

```
/Format,Entry,A9,
```

The Format Entry menu is displayed above the entry line. This menu is identical to the Format Row menu and can address the same range as the **R**ow option by selecting an entire row as the range. As you can see, this **E**ntry option can be used for all format settings except column width.

Select **T**ext and then **C**enter from the next menu, and press Enter. The command string looks like this:

```
28›/Format,Entry,A9,TextCenter
```

Press Enter and repeat the sequence for A18 (*Net Income*). The letter sequence is

```
/FEA18
```

Press Enter. Type **TC** and press Enter.

By choosing **A**ll in the range section of the **E**ntry command, you can affect the entire worksheet without affecting the format of blocks, rows, or columns that you might add later (as the **G**lobal option does).

Note that if a blank cell is formatted with the /**F**ormat,**E**ntry option, the cell is no longer considered blank. For more efficient memory and disk management, SuperCalc does not activate or store a cell until something is entered into it. When you format a cell by using

Entry, SuperCalc activates the cell in order to store the format information in the cell. So a double-quotation text entry, text = ", is stored in the blank cell to be tagged with the new format. Although the cell still looks blank, on the status line, the full cell contents appear as

```
TC      text = "
```

This display indicates that this particular cell is formatted as TextCenter. With the format stored in the cell, the format is carried forward along with the cell contents when that cell is copied to another cell.

Displaying Cell Contents with Format Codes

All operations presented so far in this chapter have dealt with formatting cells that contain text. Now you are ready to look at numeric formatting options.

Numeric Formats and Alignments

The defaults for numeric display are **R**ight alignment of numbers and **G**eneral format (display numbers exactly as typed). In the income statement, only whole-dollar, integer inputs have been used. Column C contains percentage calculations displayed to one decimal place.

Remember to be careful when considering how many decimal points you want displayed on a worksheet. Although a number is displayed with no decimal places, the numeric value can be stored in the cell in an original form of up to 16 decimal places. This discrepancy becomes a problem when you are adding this number to a list of numbers for a total value. SuperCalc adds the stored forms of the numbers, not the displayed value. The total figure is correct but appears incorrect because the displayed values in the arithmetic operation show rounded results for individual cells. Methods for solving this problem using the ROUND function are discussed in Chapter 7. Meanwhile, be aware of this possible discrepancy.

You can use the /Format,Entry command to format the numeric section of the worksheet. Move the cell pointer to B7, the first cell of the $ column. From the READY prompt, enter

    /Format,Entry,B7

To point to the range of cells you want to format, press the period to anchor the beginning of the range at B7 and then move the cell pointer to B18 where the *Net Income* total is displayed. Now that your range is set as B7:B18, press Enter to display the **E**ntry options above the entry line, as shown in figure 4.14.

Although the alignment is already **R**ight, press **R**. The entry line looks like this:

    28›/Format,Entry,B7:B18,Right,

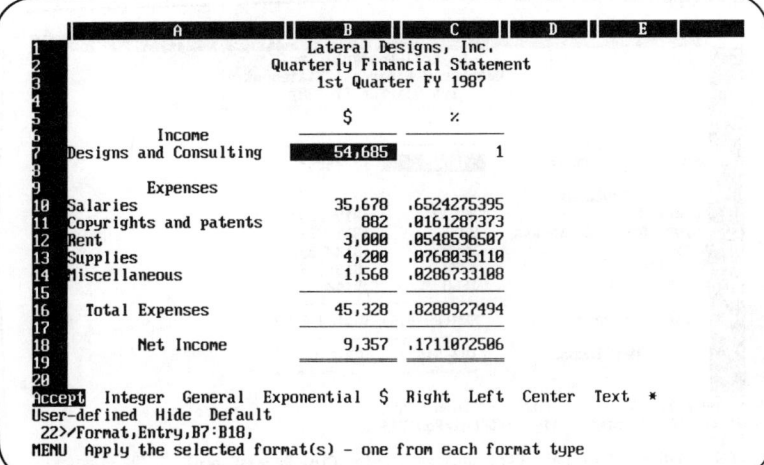

Fig. 4.14.

The Format Entry menu.

The alignment and format type you choose do not affect each other, so at one time you can enter a variety of format options for this cell range. If you enter contradicting selections (for example, **L**eft and then **R**ight) because you either made a mistake or changed your mind, the last selection takes precedence over the one entered earlier in the command string.

After selecting **R**ight, press **U** to select a **U**ser-defined format. These two choices appear: **N**umber and **D**ate. Select **N**umber to display a menu that has eight numbers. To make your income statement look like figure 4.13, press **2**. You have selected the UserNumber2 format from figure 4.11. The command entry line looks like this before you finally press Enter:

```
40›/Format,Entry,B7:B18,Right,UserNumber2,
```

Formulas

To test the format and alignment of range B7:B18, enter some numbers into the worksheet and try entering the formulas. The formulas used in this worksheet are shown in figure 4.15. The /**G**lobal,**F**ormulas option shows the formulas behind the displayed figures. With this option, the numbers appear left-justified, as do the formulas, because numbers are considered formulas too.

SuperCalc automatically identifies the SUM formula if the syntax is correct. To enter the SUM formula shown in B16 in figure 4.15, move the cell pointer to the total-expense cell (B16). From the entry line, type

```
SUM(
```

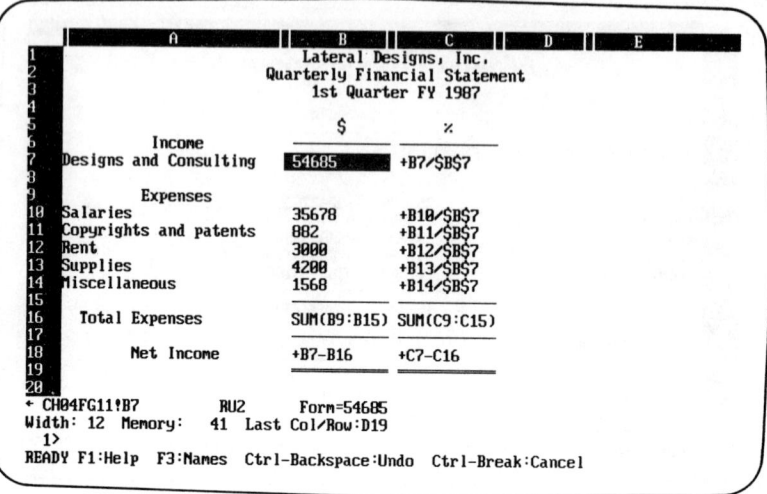

Fig. 4.15.

Formulas used in the income statement.

After typing the left parenthesis, move the cell pointer to the salaries row in column B. To anchor the beginning of the point range, press the period. The command line looks like this:

```
10>SUM(B9:B9
```

After you enter the colon, the cell pointer remains at the beginning cell of the range (B9) until you move it down to the cell containing the subtotal line (—————), the last cell you want to include in that SUM formula. With the range in the formula defined as B9:B15, type the closing parenthesis, **)**.

If the solution that appears in the cell is 45,328, you entered the formula correctly. If not, move through the steps again. If the formula appears as a text string in the cell, such as

```
text="SUM(B9;+B15)
```

you have made a syntax error (in the example, a semicolon rather than a colon). SuperCalc cannot recognize the contents of the cell as a formula.

Pointing

Range pointing should be used whenever possible. Pointing helps you create your formulas and ranges faster and, by providing a visual confirmation, ensures greater accuracy. SuperCalc recognizes a possible pointing situation and automatically puts you in POINT mode whenever you begin to point to a cell.

In some cases, however, you might still type the range coordinates, especially if you use named ranges in place of actual cell references. Mixing absolute references (for example, $B$7) and relative references (for example, B7) also may dictate circumstances when direct entry is required. The dollar sign indicates an absolute reference, which means that the reference will remain the same when the formula is copied to another cell. (Absolute references and your options for entering them are discussed in Chapter 5.)

Percentage Cells

Because you have an absolute reference ($B$7) in C7, you can use the /Copy command to copy that formula quickly to the rest of the cells in that column. If cell C7 were formatted with the /Format,Entry command, the cell format would be copied to the target cells as well.

As alternatives, you can use the /Format command to have the entire column displayed in percentage format, or you can format that range of cells after the formula has been copied to them. If you use the /Format,Column command, the format does not carry forward when the formula is copied to another column.

Figure 4.16 displays the income statement with column C still formatted in General format. If a cell is formatted with the /Format,Entry command, an abbreviation of the format is displayed as part of the cell contents in the dialog panel. You can see an example of this display in figure 4.16. The cell pointer is in A1, and the TC indication appears in the current cell status line at the bottom of the screen. If that cell were formatted with UserNumber2 format, U2 would appear in that cell.

```
           A               B         C        D      E
                     Lateral Designs, Inc.
 1                 Quarterly Financial Statement
 2                     1st Quarter FY 1987
 3
 4                        $         %
 5
 6          Income
 7   Designs and Consulting  54,685        1
 8
 9          Expenses
10   Salaries            35,678   .6524275395
11   Copyrights and patents  882   .0161287373
12   Rent                 3,000   .0548596507
13   Supplies             4,200   .0768035110
14   Miscellaneous        1,560   .0286733100
15
16      Total Expenses   45,328   .8288927494
17
18      Net Income        9,357   .1711072506
19
20
+ CH04FG11!A1            TC  Text="               Lateral Design
Width: 25  Memory:   41  Last Col/Row:D19
  1>
READY F1:Help  F3:Names  Ctrl-Backspace:Undo  Ctrl-Break:Cancel
```

Fig. 4.16.

Percent column displayed in General format.

To finish the numeric formats, select the method you want to use to format column C to UserNumber8 (%). You have three choices.

If you choose to set the Global default to display percentages, the command string is

/Format,Global,UserNumber8

If you want to format the entire column to the percentage format, the command is

/**F**ormat,**C**olumn,**C**,**U**serNumber**8**

Finally, if you want to use the **E**ntry option, the command is

/**F**ormat,**E**ntry,**C7:C18**,**U**serNumber**8**,

The values in column C are now displayed as percentages.

Toggling the /Global Worksheet Settings

The /**F**ormat commands are not the only commands that influence your worksheet format. Some of the /**G**lobal commands also affect formats. Still another group of /**G**lobal commands affects your movement around the worksheet.

Instead of the Format menu, select the Global menu:

/**G**lobal,

Figure 4.17 shows what your screen now looks like. Of the many /**G**lobal options, however, only a few affect the format of the worksheet.

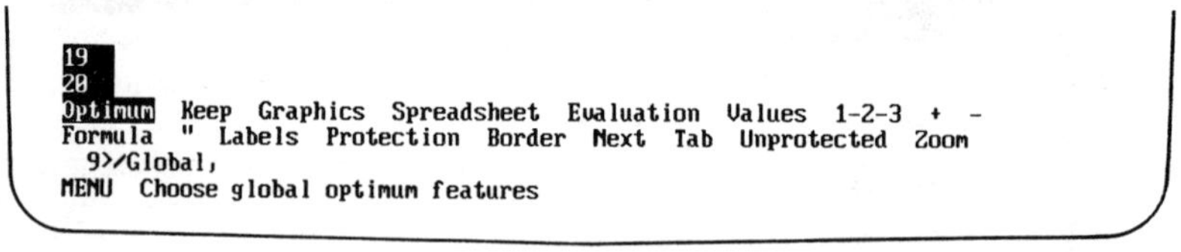

Fig. 4.17.

The Global menu.

```
19
20
Optimum  Keep Graphics Spreadsheet Evaluation Values 1-2-3 + -
Formula  " Labels Protection Border Next Tab Unprotected Zoom
    9>/Global,
MENU  Choose global optimum features
```

With the **F**ormula, ", **L**abels, **B**order, **N**ext, **Z**oom, and **K**eep selections, you tailor the appearance of and the movement in SuperCalc to your own liking. These selections work like toggles. Highlighting any of those menu selections (in white with a color display or in high-intensity with a monochrome monitor) indicates that the option is enabled. An option that remains yellow or displays normal intensity is disabled. The **O**ptimum option is a grouping of several format and configuration settings.

Optimum Spreadsheet Conditions

The /**G**lobal,**O**ptimum command, like the /**G**lobal command in general, covers several areas that affect your overall use of SuperCalc. To get to the Global Optimum menus, type

/**G**lobal,**O**ptimum

Two choices appear: **P**resent and **N**ext. All the **O**ptimum choices under **P**resent affect conditions during your current SuperCalc session. All choices under **N**ext will not take effect until you change the setting, save it to your configuration file, and reenter SuperCalc using the new configuration. The settings that most directly affect the spreadsheet format appear under the **P**resent option which when selected, displays the screen shown in figure 4.18.

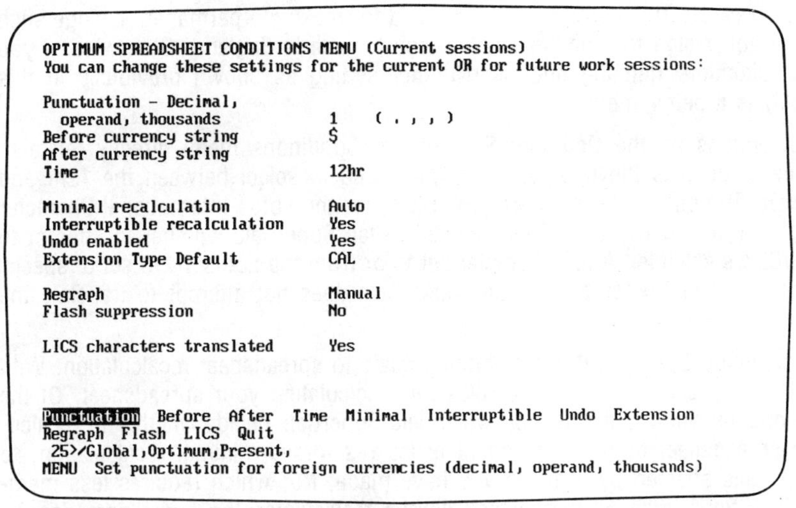

```
OPTIMUM SPREADSHEET CONDITIONS MENU (Current sessions)
You can change these settings for the current OR for future work sessions:

Punctuation - Decimal,
     operand, thousands          1     ( . , , )
Before currency string          $
After currency string
Time                            12hr

Minimal recalculation           Auto
Interruptible recalculation     Yes
Undo enabled                    Yes
Extension Type Default          CAL

Regraph                         Manual
Flash suppression               No

LICS characters translated      Yes


Punctuation Before After  Time  Minimal  Interruptible  Undo  Extension
Regraph Flash LICS Quit
   25>/Global,Optimum,Present,
MENU  Set punctuation for foreign currencies (decimal, operand, thousands)
```

Fig. 4.18.

The Optimum Spreadsheet Conditions menu (changes take effect in the current session).

The first choice on this menu, **P**unctuation, has to do with three different punctuation marks used throughout SuperCalc: the decimal delimiter, the function operand, and the thousands delimiter. You can redefine the decimal delimiter as a comma rather than a decimal point. You can redefine the *operand*, which is the punctuation mark you use to separate the components of a function [for example, IF(a>b,c,d) or IF(a>b;c;d)], to be a period, a semicolon, or the default comma. You can redefine the thousands delimiter to be a period or a blank space rather than the American standard comma. Using this command, you can choose among eight different combinations of these settings. Table 4.1 lists the eight options.

Table 4.1
The Eight Punctuation Choices

Number	Decimal	Operand	Thousands
1	.	,	,
2	,	.	.
3	.	;	,
4	,	;	.
5	.	,	space
6	,	.	space
7	.	;	space
8	,	;	space

The **P**unctuation selection, along with the next two options, **B**efore and **A**fter, make Super-Calc functional worldwide by providing alternative formats for displaying currency and values. The **B**efore and **A**fter options allow you to change the currency symbol from the

American dollar sign to any other character. You can have the currency display before a number by selecting **B**efore or after a number by selecting **A**fter. This prefix or suffix can be more than one character. Thus, if you are dealing in Japanese yen, you can define the suffix JY and any cell formatted with the UserNumber setting for displaying a suffix will automatically display JY. This command is best used for making a permanent change such as changing the dollar sign to a pound sterling sign for use in England. Otherwise, if you have a special situation, defining one UserNumber setting as shown previously in this chapter probably is a better method.

Two additional options on the Optimum Spreadsheet Conditions menu directly relate to formatting. One of them is the third option, **T**ime, used to select between the **1**2hr and **2**4hr time format. The other related selection is **L**ICS, for the Lotus International Character Set. This toggle, which by default is **Y**es, is used to tell SuperCalc whether to attempt to translate SuperCalc's extended ASCII character set to or from the Lotus 1-2-3 set of special characters. If you select **N**o for this option, SuperCalc does not attempt to translate the characters.

Three of the remaining **O**ptimum,**P**resent settings relate to spreadsheet recalculation. With the **M**inimal option, you can redefine the rules for recalculating your spreadsheet. Of the three possible options, **A**uto is the default, which lets SuperCalc decide whether to recalculate the entire spreadsheet or only dependent cells; **Y**es forces minimal recalculation, to recalculate only cells affected by changes you have made; **N**o, which requires less memory, uses the traditional recalculation, which always recalculates the entire spreadsheet. **I**nterruptible determines whether you can interrupt the recalculation process, and **R**egraph is useful in a dual monitor setup to determine whether the graph on the second monitor is redisplayed on each recalculation of the spreadsheet.

Undo is a new option in SuperCalc5. As in many word processors, if you have **U**ndo enabled, you can undo your last command. This feature is helpful but memory-costly. It can cut your available memory in half because SuperCalc5 has to keep in memory a "before" and "after" picture of your spreadsheet. If you select **E**xtension, you can change the format of the saved spreadsheet from SuperCalc format (file extension CAL) to Lotus 1A (extension WKS) or to Lotus 2.1 (extension WK1). **F**lash is a setting to change the colors on a color monitor from the traditional SuperCalc combination to another set that works more effectively with memory-resident programs.

The other menu of **O**ptimum settings, under the **N**ext option, further affects memory (**M**emory, **B**oundary, **E**xpanded) and video use (**V**ideo, **A**ttribute, **G**raphics, and **D**ual). The screen that appears when you select /**G**lobal,**O**ptimum,**N**ext is shown in figure 4.19.

Formula Display

An enabled **F**ormula selection (refer to fig. 4.17) tells SuperCalc to display the underlying formulas of all cells in the spreadsheet. This option was used in figure 4.15 to show the formulas behind the income statement.

```
OPTIMUM SPREADSHEET CONDITIONS MENU (Future sessions)
You can change these settings for FUTURE work sessions only:
1. Save spreadsheet. 2. Select new settings. 3. Enter /Global,Keep then /Quit.

                         Current setting:        Future setting:
Memory usage             Fast                    Fast
Boundary of spreadsheet  Auto                    Auto
Expanded memory          All                     All

Video                    IBM                     IBM
Attribute                Auto                    Auto
Graphics enabled         Yes                     Yes
Dual monitors            Yes                     Yes




→ TEMP1↑A1
Memory  Boundary  Expanded  Video  Attribute  Graphics  Dual  Quit
 22>/Global,Optimum,Next,
MENU  Controls whether excess memory is used for performance or data
```

Fig. 4.19.

The Optimum Spreadsheet Conditions menu (changes take effect in the next session).

Double Quotation Marks

If the ″ (double quotation mark) option is enabled, you must enter a double quotation mark on the entry line before entering any type of textual data. This option is disabled by default because SuperCalc automatically determines what type of entry you have entered and adds a double quotation mark before a text entry.

Labels Display

You use the **L**abels option if you prefer to see the *names* of ranges you are using in formulas instead of the *cell coordinates* of the range. You can display any enabled range names used in formulas in the spreadsheet. If the option is disabled, the actual cell or column range definitions appear on the screen. Assume that the range B7:B19 is named EXPENSES. With this option enabled, such a cell formula might read as

    SUM(EXPENSES)

When the option is disabled, that same formula appears as

    SUM(B7:B19)

Border

The **B**order toggle allows you to enable and disable the row and column borders on your worksheet. Typically, you use the borders enabled as you construct your worksheet, but after the worksheet is defined, you may want to eliminate borders to make the display look less cluttered.

Zoom

Zoom is a new **/G**lobal setting in SuperCalc5. With EGA- or VGA-compatible monitors, you can see either 43 lines (EGA) or 50 lines (VGA) of text rather than the traditional 25 lines. Figure 4.20 shows the income statement with **Z**oom enabled.

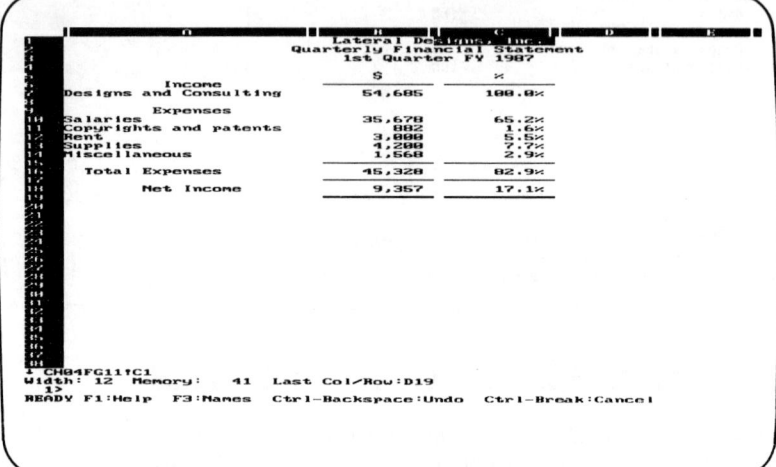

Although everything appears smaller in this mode, the number of rows visible is a benefit that offsets the smaller character size. If you want to see 38 rows of your spreadsheet at once or, with a split screen, two 19-row spreadsheets, the narrower rows are worth the smaller size.

Next

The **N**ext option affects only the cursor movement around the screen and does not change the format of the spreadsheet. With **N**ext enabled (the default setting), the cursor advances to the next cell each time you press Enter. For example, if you are entering a column of numbers, you can type a number and press Enter; the cell pointer advances to the cell below.

SuperCalc keeps track of the last cursor movement direction and assumes that you want to continue in that direction. If you move from A1 to B1, type something in B1 and press Enter, the cursor advances to C1. The current cursor-direction arrow appears at the far left end of the status line and indicates which way the cell pointer will advance the next time you press Enter.

If you disable the **N**ext option, the cell pointer remains in the same cell, requiring you to move the cell pointer with a direction key. Disabling **N**ext is recommended when you are using macros (see Chapter 11).

Keep

The **K**eep option saves the global settings you have defined as the default SuperCalc settings. Settings that can be kept within SuperCalc include

- /**F**ormat,**G**lobal settings
- /**G**lobal settings (except **T**ab and **P**rotect)
- Several /**O**utput,**O**ptions settings
- The currently logged disk drive in the File List menu
- The **U**ser-defined format settings

If you fail to select the **K**eep option after changing one of the listed settings, the setting will change only for the current session instead of remaining the program default for future settings.

All default settings are stored within a configuration file. The original settings are stored in a file named SCC.OVL. By typing

/**G**lobal,**K**eep,**Y**es

you create on the currently logged drive a file named SC5.CFG, which contains your altered settings. Alternatively, you can type

/**G**lobal,**K**eep,/*pathname*/*filename*

and store the configuration as SC5.CFG on another drive or subdirectory, or as a completely different file name on either the currently logged drive or another drive or directory. Doing so is especially useful if SuperCalc is installed on a network or if you share your computer with several users who all want their own settings. Also, for example, you can have stored under different names special combinations of settings to handle extremely large spreadsheets of different user-defined settings. To keep a combination of settings relating to a large spreadsheet, you could type

/**G**lobal,**K**eep,**T**o,**BIG**

To access these settings, instead of typing SC5 to access SuperCalc, you would type

SC5/BIG

SuperCalc would load the large matrix settings. Alternatively, now in SuperCalc5 you can retrieve a previously defined configuration by selecting

/**G**lobal,**K**eep,**F**rom,*filename*

You can retrieve all the settings, only the spreadsheet settings, or only the graphics settings.

Other /Global Options

Because the other /**G**lobal commands address a variety of functions, they are discussed with the system to which the commands are most directly related (for instance, graphics, printing, calculation orders, or multiple-iteration problems).

Word Processing with /Justify

As previously mentioned, a formatting tool first included with SuperCalc4 Version 1.1 is the command /Justify. This command provides you with the means to mold the text (not values) in a range of cells in order to fill the space within that range based on left, center, or right justification.

One of the things that make spreadsheets different from word processors is that instead of having one large bucket for storing text or values, you have hundreds of small buckets in which to place each individual text or value for individual manipulation. Word processing is used to mold a text into a whole, whereas spreadsheets are usually used to manipulate text (and values) individually. But what is a benefit for manipulating the data independently (using individual cell storage) sometimes creates problems for dealing on an aggregate level.

The /Justify command is a first step toward bridging the gap between word processing and spreadsheets, and this command can be used to perform simple word processing. During the execution of the /Justify command, SuperCalc shuffles the text to fit into the range of cells you have specified—even if fitting means moving the text to a different cell to accomplish the task. What results is an action that greatly resembles the reformatting command in a word processing program that reformats text inside new margins.

To demonstrate one use of this command, suppose that you wanted to create a quick memo to someone and did not have a word processor available or did not feel like leaving the comfort of your spreadsheet program. Figure 4.21 is an example of such a memo.

Fig. 4.21.

An example for use with /Justify.

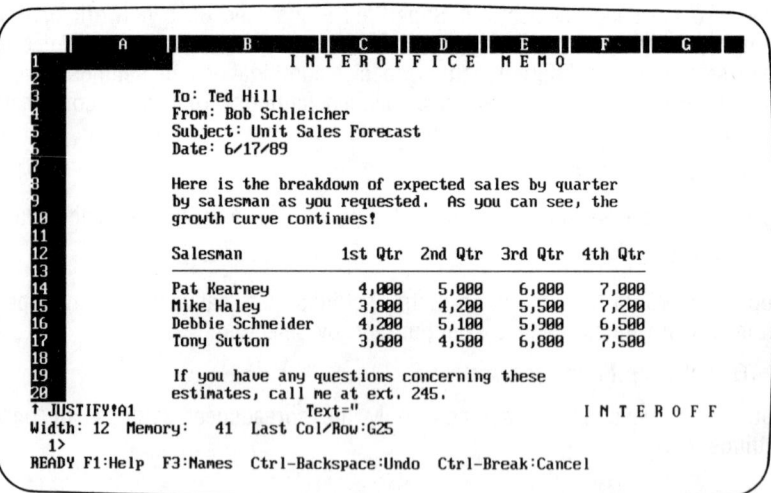

The memo involves both text and numbers, so using the spreadsheet is helpful for the data portion. Creating the rest of the document is greatly simplified by using the /Justify command. You can use it to center the interoffice memo title at the top of the screen; you can enter the first paragraph as if you are using a word processor without pressing Enter at the end of each line; and you can reformat the paragraph as you need to.

To demonstrate the **W**ord-wrap option of /**J**ustify, figure 4.22 shows the first paragraph of the memo being entered in the spreadsheet using /**J**ustify,**W**ord-wrap.

```
          B        C       D      E       F      G       H
 8 Here is the breakdown of expected sales by quarter by salesman
 9
10
11
12 Salesman          1st Qtr 2nd Qtr 3rd Qtr 4th Qtr
13
14 Pat Kearney        4,000   5,000   6,000   7,000
15 Mike Haley         3,800   4,200   5,500   7,200
16 Debbie Schneider   4,200   5,100   5,900   6,500
17 Tony Sutton        3,600   4,500   6,000   7,500
18
19 If you have any questions concerning these
20 estimates, call me at ext. 245.
21
22
23
24
25
26
27
↓ JUSTIFY↑B9
Width: 17  Memory:    41  Last Col/Row:G20
    4>as
ENTRY F1:Help F2:Edit F3:Names Home:1st End-Arrow:last Ctrl-Break:Cancel
```

Fig. 4.22.
The spreadsheet while entering text with Word-wrap.

To duplicate this memo entry, make sure that you have /**G**lobal,**N**ext enabled, which causes the cell pointer to advance automatically from cell to cell. Then go to cell B8 and select

   /**J**ustify,**W**ord-wrap,**R**ange

Press the period, point from your current cell (B8) to cell B10, press Enter, and then press **G**o. The screen changes to make B8 the upper left corner of the spreadsheet (see fig. 4.22), and the status message in the lower left switches from READY to WRAP, which means that you are ready to enter the text. When you begin entering text, the mode then switches from WRAP to ENTRY. After you enter a line of text (65 characters), the cell pointer automatically advances to cell B9. The next word you enter is shown at the beginning of the text string without your having to press Enter—just as if you were using a word processor. The text is entered with a "ragged right" look.

After completing the entry, press Home to view the entire memo. As you can see, the text runs too far to the right. You could have avoided this initially by selecting **W**idth and overriding the default of 65 with the 52-character width you wanted.

Instead, use /**J**ustify,**S**ingle as a method of rearranging previously entered text. Select the Justify menu again. The menu has the following three choices:

   Single Multiple Word-wrap

Select **S**ingle because you have only one paragraph of text to modify. The other option, **M**ultiple, acts similarly to **S**ingle, but when a blank or non-text row is encountered within the range, **M**ultiple honors that spacing and reinserts it within the new arrangement. In other words, you use **M**ultiple if dealing with more than one paragraph of text. After selecting **S**ingle, the following menu appears:

   Left Center Right

This menu (as does the Format Text menu) means that you can make the text left-justified against the left edges of the cells, right-justified against the right edges of the cells, or centered within the column. For the memo heading (INTEROFFICE MEMO) you would select **C**enter, but when justifying a paragraph, **L**eft makes more sense in order to format the text with a ragged right edge.

After selecting the alignment, you are prompted for a range to justify. Make sure that you define enough room for the program to accomplish its task or else the message

```
Not enough room for justify
```

appears. This message means that the defined range has too few spaces available to contain the long string entered into cell B8. Figure 4.23 shows the memo with the range defined by pointing. The range must be the resulting output range, not the input range. The text is currently stored in cells B8 and B9 and extends out 65 characters. The text should be reorganized to three lines of 52 characters each (B8:F10).

Fig. 4.23.

The /Justify range defined.

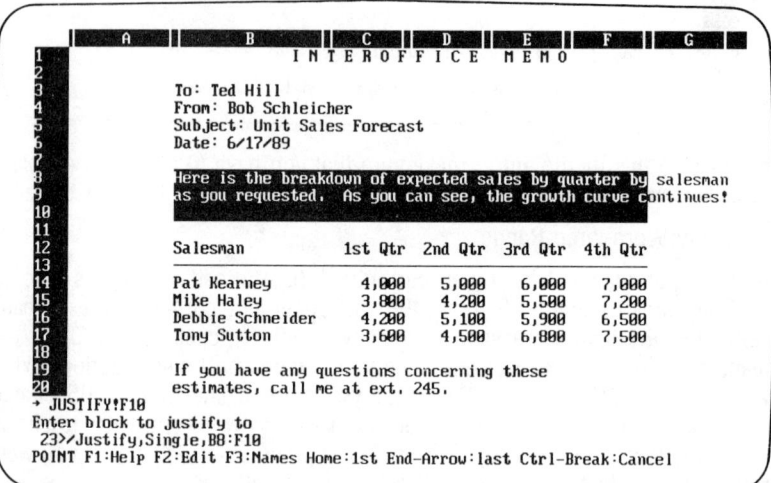

The result of the /Justify command on this range makes the memo look like the one shown in figure 4.21. Notice that all text is moved to fit within the defined range (B8:F10). Text is moved to a different cell when necessary and remains correctly spaced.

This command is not limited to simple memos. You will find yourself using /Justify when you have text comments, numbered directions, outline processing, or when you document the spreadsheet or a spreadsheet macro. /Justify,**W**ord-wrap (for original entry) and /Justify,**S**ingle,**L**eft (for rearranging your text as necessary) give SuperCalc two of the necessary tools to make it an effective (although simple) word processor.

Chapter Summary

Flexibility in formatting is the key to deriving useful information from a mass of numbers. SuperCalc provides the flexibility and easily accessible formatting tools to present data clearly and effectively. In this chapter, you have learned how to change column widths, cell-content alignment, and numeric formats. You have learned to use the **U**ser-define format screen to customize a numeric format when **G**eneral, **I**nteger, **$**, or **E**xponential will not do. Finally, you have learned how to use the Global menu selections that relate to formatting and to use the new command /**J**ustify.

Using these formatting commands along with the methods for speeding up your spreadsheet development covered in Chapter 5 will help you gain enough skill in SuperCalc to produce accurate, presentation-quality information.

5

Becoming More Proficient with SuperCalc

Creating spreadsheets with SuperCalc reduces time spent on mundane tasks, increases the accuracy and sophistication of analyses and forecasts, and makes your work look more professional. By learning how to enter data and formulas into the cells and how to format, print, and save information to disk, you achieve a useful level of knowledge about the program. SuperCalc also provides sophisticated tools and techniques that achieve long-term benefits and great time savings. You can gain additional value from SuperCalc by effectively using all its tools. Besides that, you may even find these tools fun to use.

This chapter presents new techniques for minimizing the number of keystrokes and increasing your worksheet accuracy, tools to speed up worksheet construction, and tools to reduce the need to revise and modify worksheets. You also see ways to use the /Title and /Window commands so that you can keep an eye on "the big picture" of your spreadsheet.

Saving Time with SuperCalc

In most parts of SuperCalc, you can achieve a result in several different ways. Cell referencing is a good example. You can refer to a cell by an absolute reference, a relative reference, or a name of your choice. You choose the method that enables you to expand your worksheet most efficiently. The following sections discuss optimizing your keystrokes, range pointing, and using the SuperCalc tools.

Using Fewer Keystrokes

Cell-pointer positioning and command and file selecting also can be done several ways. SuperCalc5 uses most of the cell-pointer movements introduced in early SuperCalc releases (Ctrl-E, -S, -D, and -X) and also incorporates all the efficient cursor-movement keys from IBM-compatible keyboards, such as PgUp, PgDn, Scroll, End, and Home. Using the cursor keys effectively can help decrease the number of your keystrokes. For example, to move from cell A1 to cell A21, you can use any of the following methods:

1. Press the down-arrow key 20 times.

2. Press Ctrl-X 20 times.

3. Press the PgDn key once.

4. Press F5 or =, and type **A21**, invoking the GoTo command, which takes you directly to that cell.

Using these keyboard controls reduces keystrokes. Furthermore, by using the cursor-control keys to help select commands, files, cells, and ranges, you can

- Increase the accuracy of your worksheet

- Decrease the instructions you must remember

- Speed the construction of your worksheet

SuperCalc5 introduces multipage spreadsheets and multiple displayed spreadsheets. Therefore, learning to use the special function keys, such as Ctrl-F3 through Ctrl-F7, Ctrl-plus and Ctrl-minus, Tab-Ctrl-plus and Tab-Ctrl-minus, and Tab-Ctrl-Home and Tab-Ctrl-End in layered spreadsheets is especially important. These movement keys are discussed in detail in Chapter 6.

Taking Advantage of On-screen Reinforcement

SuperCalc highlights commands and ranges with reverse video to show you what your fingers are doing. This reinforcement reduces the "thinking time" you must spend in many areas. Instead of recalling commands from memory, you merely select from the choices in front of you. Instead of typing your range choice, you can point to the range on-screen. In addition, instead of trying to remember the range names and files on your disk, you select them from a list on-screen.

Using SuperCalc Tools

SuperCalc provides excellent tools for creating and modifying your spreadsheets. The /Copy command can speed worksheet development more than any other command in SuperCalc. In addition, the /Insert, /Delete, /Move, and /Blank commands make up a whole set of tools to simplify spreadsheet preparation. As you develop more complex worksheets, you will be able to take advantage of title-locking and window-splitting tools for dividing information into workable segments.

Addressing for Speed and Flexibility

In SuperCalc, the default method for addressing cells is relative addressing. In addition, SuperCalc offers two optional cell-addressing techniques: absolute addressing and range naming. These two options provide a way to avoid the cumbersome /Copy and /Replicate commands of previous SuperCalc versions.

Relative Cell Addressing

Before discussing the two specialty cell-addressing techniques—absolute addressing and range naming—let's look at the default addressing technique: relative cell addressing. A relative address combines the column letter and row number coordinates. For example, A1 is the relative address for the top left cell of the spreadsheet. The term *relative* refers to the way this reference is used in formulas. Consider the following formula entered in cell B1:

   +A1

The formula appears to say, "Place the value in A1 into B1." However, a more accurate interpretation is "Place into the formula cell, the value entered in the cell one column to the left of the formula cell."

The two interpretations do not differ in relation to this isolated cell (B1). Suppose, however, that the formula +A1 is copied from cell B1 to C1. Now the difference in interpretations is clearer. The relative reference changes to +B1. When copied, the formula does not continue to refer to A1 but refers to the address of the cell one column to the left of the cell containing the formula.

Absolute Cell Addressing

As explained in Chapter 3, in an absolute cell address, both column and row coordinates are preceded by a dollar sign ($). For example, an absolute reference to cell A1 is

   +$A$1

Entered this way, cell address A1 does not change when the formula is copied to any other cell in the worksheet. Unlike the relative form of a formula, +A1, the formula +$A$1 always is interpreted as "Place the value entered in A1 into the formula cell."

An advantage of this cell-addressing feature is that a formula need not be completely relative or completely absolute. Both the column and row address in the absolute version of the formula $A$1 have dollar signs preceding them. However, you can mix these dollar signs within the formula to create $A1 or A$1. In the first case, the column address is absolute, but the row number is variable. In the second case, the row address is absolute, and the column address is relative. These mixed addresses are appropriate when you copy a formula to a block of cells.

Mixing Addressing

Figure 5.1 demonstrates the effects of several different types of cell referencing when a simple formula is copied to another cell. The left half of the screen shows the cell contents (either a value or a formula), and the right half shows the displayed results.

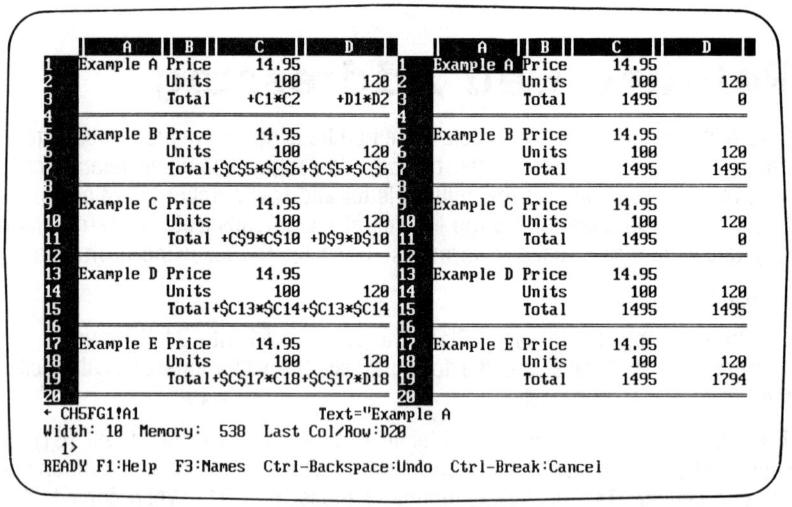

Fig. 5.1.

Examples of the effects of copying with absolute and relative addresses.

```
   ║   A   ║ B ║   C   ║   D   ║   ║   A   ║ B ║   C   ║   D   ║
1  Example A Price    14.95           1  Example A Price    14.95
2          Units     100       120    2          Units     100       120
3          Total   +C1*C2    +D1*D2   3          Total    1495         0
4                                     4
5  Example B Price    14.95           5  Example B Price    14.95
6          Units     100       120    6          Units     100       120
7          Total+$C$5*$C$6+$C$5*$C$6  7          Total    1495      1495
8                                     8
9  Example C Price    14.95           9  Example C Price    14.95
10         Units     100       120    10         Units     100       120
11         Total  +C$9*C$10 +D$9*D$10 11         Total    1495         0
12                                    12
13 Example D Price    14.95           13 Example D Price    14.95
14         Units     100       120    14         Units     100       120
15         Total+$C13*$C14+$C13*$C14  15         Total    1495      1495
16                                    16
17 Example E Price    14.95           17 Example E Price    14.95
18         Units     100       120    18         Units     100       120
19         Total+$C$17*C18+$C$17*D18  19         Total    1495      1794
20                                    20
← CH5FG1↑A1                Text="Example A
Width: 10  Memory:   538  Last Col/Row:D20
    1>
READY F1:Help  F3:Names  Ctrl-Backspace:Undo  Ctrl-Break:Cancel
```

In Example A, a relative address (+ C1*C2) is used in cell C3 to calculate the extended total, 1495. This formula is entered by these steps:

1. Move the cell pointer to C3.

2. Press +.

3. Press the up-arrow key to move the cell pointer up two rows to C1 (pressing the arrow key puts you in POINT mode).

4. Press *. The cell pointer moves to C3.

5. Move the cell pointer up one row to C2.

6. Press Enter.

In Example B, the formula is the same, but absolute addresses are used rather than relative addresses. To make +C5 an absolute address in the formula in C7, follow these steps:

1. Move the cell pointer to C7.

2. Press +.

3. Move the cell pointer to C5.

4. Press F4 (the absolute reference toggle) once.

    Step 4 changes the reference C5 to $C$5, which is the absolute version of the reference. Continue entering the formula:

5. Press *.

6. Move the cell pointer up one row to C6.

7. Press F4 once (to make the address absolute).

8. Press Enter.

The only steps added are 4 and 7, which convert the formula references to absolute references.

In Examples C and D, the steps are identical except that at steps 4 and 7, you must press F4 twice for Example C and three times for Example D. Each time you press F4 at cell C11, the address changes in the following ways:

Default	C9
F4 one time	$C$9
F4 two times	C$9
F4 three times	$C9
F4 four times	C9

The formulas in Examples C and D are mixtures of absolute and relative cell references. In C11, the row addresses are absolute ($9 and $10), and the column addresses are relative (C). As a result, when copied to another cell, the column references in this formula change, but the row addresses remain the same (cell D11). In C15, the opposite is true; the column addresses are absolute ($C), and the rows are relative (13 and 14). With this variation, the row addresses change if copied to another row; but the column references remain unchanged even if copied to another column (cell D15).

Example E mixes address types in a different way. The first address ($C$17) is completely absolute, and the second address (C18) is completely relative. When copied, the first reference in this formula ($C$17) remains unchanged, but the second reference (C18) changes to reflect the formula's new location.

As you can see from the right half of the screen in figure 5.1, the effects of the five examples of addressing are not apparent in the totals in column C because they all return the correct answer (1495). The differences become apparent only when each formula is copied to a column to the right, where the formula is to be used with another number of units (120). You want to multiply the price from column C by the new unit amounts in column D to get a total based on the second quantity.

Of the five examples, only Example E ends up with the relationship you want (C17*D18) and the correct amount (14.95*120 = 1794). The calculation is correct because the relative relationship (amount) is defined with a relative address and the constant relationship (price) is defined with an absolute address. In Example B, both cell references remain unchanged because they are absolute. The mixed addresses in Examples C and D both are wrong—the first because both column addresses are relative and the second because both column addresses are absolute.

To decide which combination of references to use in each situation, you must consider the following points:

1. Whether you will want to copy the formula to another cell or range of cells

2. Which cell addresses, if any, should remain the same and which addresses should change with location

3. How the relationships in the formulas will change in the target cells

In most circumstances, the mixture will be like Example E, where one or more references within a formula remain the same and one or more references vary according to their location. With multiple row and column copies, ensuring the correct relationship can be tedious. If done correctly, however, correct referencing will save you from repeatedly entering similar formulas in different cells.

Using Mixed Addressing

To demonstrate a practical use of mixed addressing, let's look at the formulas behind the income statement example begun in Chapter 4. Invoke /Global,Formula to display the formulas shown in figure 5.2. The percentage column (C) shows a common use of absolute referencing. The function of the percentage column is to evaluate what percentage of the total income each item is. The current row in column B, therefore, is the numerator of the formula, and the value in cell B7 is the denominator.

By anchoring the denominator with an absolute address in cell C7, you can copy the formula to the remainder of the cells, thus avoiding unnecessary typing. If, however, the denominator were not anchored and you copied the formula from C7 to C10, the formula in C10 would be

   + B10/B10

The solution of this formula is 1.

You can enter the formula another way that works just as well. Because you are copying down a single column, only the row needs to be absolute. The formula in cell C7 can be entered as

   + B7/B$7

This formula means "Divide the value in the cell one to the left in the current row by the value of the cell in row 7 of the column one to the left of the current cell." This formula is more relative than the following formula:

   + B7/$B$7

This formula means "Divide the value in the cell one to the left by the value in B7."

```
┌─────────────────────────────────────────────────────────────┐
│   │        A        ║    B    │    C    │    D    │   E   │   │
│ 1 │              Lateral Designs, Inc.                      │
│ 2 │            Quarterly Financial Statement                │
│ 3 │                 1st Quarter FY 1990                     │
│ 4 │                                                         │
│ 5 │                         $          %                    │
│ 6 │          Income                                         │
│ 7 │Designs and Consulting   54685     +B7/$B$7              │
│ 8 │                                                         │
│ 9 │          Expenses                                       │
│10 │Salaries                 35678     +B10/$B$7             │
│11 │Copyrights and Patents    882      +B11/$B$7             │
│12 │Rent                     3000      +B12/$B$7             │
│13 │Supplies                 4200      +B13/$B$7             │
│14 │Miscellaneous            1560      +B14/$B$7             │
│15 │                                                         │
│16 │   Total Expenses     SUM(B9:B15) SUM(C9:C15)            │
│17 │                                                         │
│18 │      Net Income       +B7-B16    +C7-C16                │
│19 │                                                         │
│20 │                                                         │
│ ↓ INCSTAT!A1           TC  Text="              Lateral Design│
│Width: 25  Memory:   98  Last Col/Row:C19                    │
│  1>                                                         │
│READY F1:Help  F3:Names  Ctrl-Backspace:Undo  Ctrl-Break:Cancel│
└─────────────────────────────────────────────────────────────┘
```

Fig. 5.2.
The income statement with formulas displayed.

Because one dollar sign is adequate for correct copying, the first formula, +B7/B$7, is probably the safer option. You should use the fewest possible absolute references so that you can be flexible in future expansion or alteration. In this example, you may want to create another section for the second quarter results in columns D and E. With the relative column reference in the denominator of the formulas in column C, this whole column of formulas can be copied to column E and still be valid. Cell E7 will contain

+D7/D$7

If the other version of the formula (+B7/$B$7) were copied, cell E7 would contain

+D7/$B$7

Each value for the second quarter would be divided by the revenue from the first quarter—a step that would definitely confuse management!

Usually, a cell that needs a completely absolute reference is easily identified. Common examples are a principal amount or an interest rate that is referenced throughout the spreadsheet or any variable assumption that you set apart for easy changing. In these cases, an absolute reference minimizes the possibility of the reference's being changed as you modify the spreadsheet.

The uses of mixed references are less obvious and take more thought. Mixed references usually are appropriate wherever a pattern or group of calculations is used repeatedly on several items. Examples of this situation are the income statement totals, which vary over time; sales analysis on several sales regions of a company, where the variation is geographic; and stock market analysis, which varies by business entity. Used with forethought, the absolute reference tool can effectively speed your spreadsheet development.

Named Ranges

Another cell addressing alternative is the named range. As you recall from Chapter 3, you can use the /Name,Create command with a name of your choice (up to 32 characters) to identify a cell or range of cells. Then you can substitute that name for the range address in any range-definition area of the worksheet.

You also can define a named range as absolute or relative. A name preceded by a dollar sign ($) is an absolute reference. Without a dollar sign, the name is a relative address.

If a worksheet formula references a cell address within a named range, that formula is changed to display the name. If the reference is an absolute reference, the formula changes to the name displaying the dollar sign. For example, if cell A1 is named START, any cell reference to $A$1 is changed to $START.

This naming option is similar to the range-naming capabilities of 1-2-3, but SuperCalc has its own style and capabilities. For example, the F3 key, which calls up the Named Range Directory, provides an easy way to find the name you want and insert that name into a formula or command.

Pointing for Visual Verification

In POINT mode you can use the pointer and cursor-movement keys to select an action or location from a set of actions or locations displayed on-screen. POINT mode provides visual verification. SuperCalc enhances the value of this method by highlighting selections with reverse video or different colors. This feature serves as a link between your eyes and fingers so that you do not need to look away from the screen so often.

Pointing helps the less experienced typist because on-screen selection and confirmation eliminates much worksheet-development typing. Instead of choosing the cells to include in a formula and then looking from the entry line to the keyboard to type the cell address, you can use the cell pointer keys. Because these pointer keys are easily reached and identified, your eyes stay fixed on the spreadsheet area to verify your selections.

SuperCalc incorporates this support tool into all parts of the package. One of the major areas is in the command selection process. After typing a slash (/) to enter the menus, the SuperCalc POINT mode lets you move the command cursor around the command menu to make a selection. After you become skilled with the package, you may want to return to the much faster way of entering the first letters of the commands; but having the choice is handy.

The command line is not the only area for pointing and selecting. You can use POINT mode to point to the file you want to load; to select a page within the spreadsheet or to select which spreadsheet (up to three) you want to display; to change the file directory or subdirectory when you are using a hard disk; to select a name you want to use in a formula; or to select various printer, color graphics, and display characteristics. You can point to cell ranges for copying, deleting, inserting, printing, naming, arranging, moving, blanking, and formatting. To increase the accuracy of POINT mode, when you point to a cell range, SuperCalc displays the entire range in reverse video (on a monochrome monitor) or bright blue (on a color monitor).

Using Key Controls

SuperCalc provides a variety of pointer and cursor-movement keys. These special control keys are designed to let you take advantage of your computer's keyboard to speed up your movement around the spreadsheet and to reduce the number of keystrokes required to operate SuperCalc. In some cases, a key's function is similar to or even duplicates another movement key. This duplication allows you to choose the key you are most comfortable with and to keep using some cursor-movement keys you learned in previous versions of SuperCalc. Key controls contribute to faster spreadsheet development, better on-screen assistance, and simplified computing.

Using F3 and F4 for File and Name Selecting

For visual verification in loading a file or selecting a range name, you must understand how to use function keys F3 and F4. Keep in mind that the functions of these keys change according to the mode you are in and where you are on the command line. For example, you can use F4 to cycle through the possible relative and absolute addressing formats. With the /Load command, however, you press F4 to change the default disk or directory to the disk or subdirectory where you are currently looking for a file.

The F3 key also can be used in different ways. At the file name prompt of the /Load command, the name of the currently loaded spreadsheet appears by default. If you want a new spreadsheet but are unsure of the name, press F3 to produce a screen similar to figure 5.3, to help locate the file you need. F3 also can be used for calling up the Named Range Directory if you are entering a formula, or for identifying a From or To range in a command string. If you are in the Graphics Name menu, F3 also displays a list of graphs available to retrieve, store, or delete.

In figure 5.3, the entry in the upper left corner reads ‹DIRECTORIES›. This word is followed by a list of files in the currently logged directory. When you press Enter once while the selector is highlighting this option, the display changes to ‹FILES›, and a list of subdirectories appears. If you press Enter again, the display returns to ‹DIRECTORIES›, and the file names are shown again. You then can use the arrow keys to select the file you want to load.

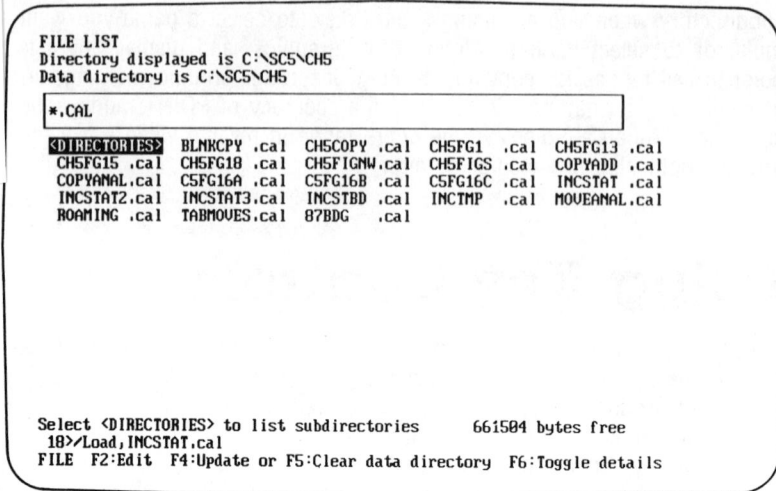

```
FILE LIST
Directory displayed is C:\SC5\CH5
Data directory is C:\SC5\CH5

*.CAL

<DIRECTORIES>  BLNKCPY .cal   CH5COPY .cal   CH5FG1   .cal   CH5FG13 .cal
CH5FG15 .cal   CH5FG18 .cal   CH5FIGNW.cal   CH5FIGS .cal   COPYADD .cal
COPYANAL.cal   C5FG16A .cal   C5FG16B .cal   C5FG16C .cal   INCSTAT .cal
INCSTAT2.cal   INCSTAT3.cal   INCSTBD  .cal  INCTMP   .cal  MOVEANAL.cal
ROAMING .cal   TABMOVES.cal   87BDG    .cal




Select <DIRECTORIES> to list subdirectories      661504 bytes free
18>/Load,INCSTAT.cal
FILE  F2:Edit  F4:Update or F5:Clear data directory  F6:Toggle details
```

If after looking at the various files on the disk, you want still more information about them, press the F6 key. This key changes the display to provide a more detailed list of all the files with CAL extensions and the contents of cell A1 in the spreadsheet. If you press F6 once more, the screen returns to its original form.

After you move the selector to the desired file name, press Enter. The spreadsheet screen reappears with the file name entered into the command string for you.

You can handle named ranges the same way. At any time, other than with the /Load command, you can press F3 to bring up the Named Range Directory (see Chapter 3). When you move the selector to the named range you want and press Enter, the main spreadsheet screen is displayed again. Notice that the name of the range has been inserted into the command string. You do not have to remember the exact spelling of the ranges because you can select the one you want from a comprehensive list.

In SuperCalc5, you can point to pages and spreadsheets by pressing Ctrl-F4, which brings up the Open Spreadsheet directory, just as you would select a file or range name to use. You can point to different sheets even within formulas by pressing Ctrl-plus or Ctrl-minus to move to the page, anchoring the page with an exclamation point, and pointing to the cell in the spreadsheet. These steps will result in a formula such as

$+2!A1+3!A1+4!A1$

which adds the values in cell A1 in spreadsheets 2 through 4. A more complete discussion of multipage spreadsheets is in Chapter 6.

Anchoring a Range with the Period or the Colon

The period (.) and the colon (:) are important to range pointing, especially when you are defining a multicell range. When you get to the range-definition section of a command-string entry, the current cell address of the cell pointer is displayed by default. When you move the cell pointer, the cell reference in the command line changes to match the location of the cell pointer.

The period or colon anchors the beginning of the range you are defining. That is, when you press the colon or period key, you are telling SuperCalc that you are defining a range address rather than a single cell address. To demonstrate this technique, suppose that figure 5.4 shows a blank spreadsheet where you want to execute a simple /Unprotect command on a range. After you move the cell pointer to B2 and invoke the /Unprotect command, the single cell address B2 is entered by default on the command line (see fig. 5.4).

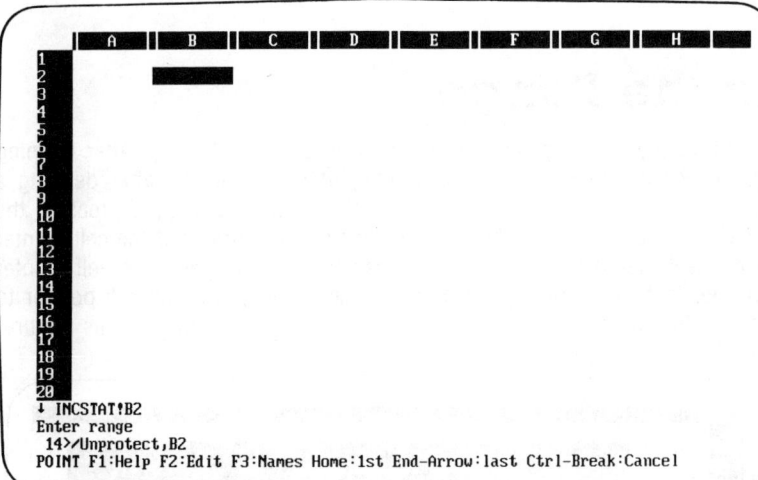

Fig. 5.4.

A cell-pointing example.

Suppose that you want to unprotect the range B2:H20. When you move the cell pointer, the cell address changes. To prevent this change, press either the colon key or the period key (on the main keyboard or on the numeric keypad). The following command string then appears:

    /Unprotect,B2:B2

SuperCalc has redefined that single cell address as a single-cell range address. The address to the left of the colon is anchored; when you move the cell pointer, the address to the right of the colon changes to reflect the cell pointer address. If you move the cell pointer to H20, the screen looks like figure 5.5. Notice that the defined range is highlighted on-screen with reverse video.

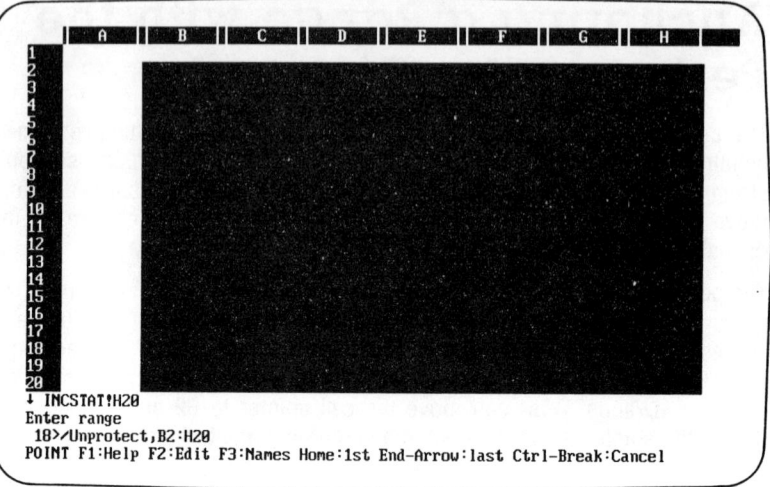

Fig. 5.5.

The defined range.

Viewing the Range

SuperCalc has added a range-viewing feature to use with range anchoring. After defining the full range, you may want to change the beginning of the range. Or after defining a range larger than the screen, you may want to view cells in the undisplayed areas of the range. Press the period once. The highlighted block remains the same, but the cell pointer moves clockwise to the lower left corner. If you press the period again, the cell pointer moves to the upper left corner. Pressing the period twice more moves the cell pointer to its original location in the lower right corner. Figure 5.6 shows a diagram of this feature.

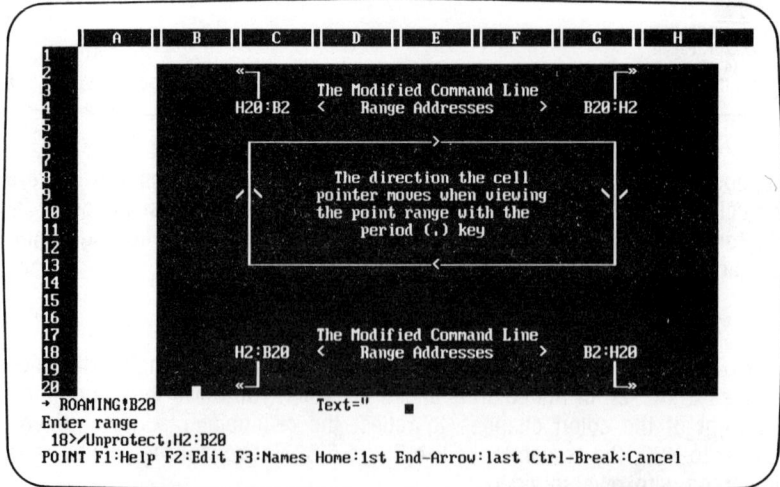

Fig. 5.6.

Viewing the range with the period key.

With the pointer at a corner, you can adjust the size of the range by stretching it left, right, up, or down for the desired effect. Notice that as you change the cell pointer location in the range, the range definition of the command is changed on the entry line as well. The command range changes to show the current cell pointer location as the ending address (after the colon). The other address on the entry line changes to show the address of the cell in the opposite corner of the range. In this way, you can anchor the first half of the range, leaving the second half free to adjust by the direction you move the cell pointer.

When you first define the range, B2 is the anchored address—the second address changes as you move the cell pointer to H20. By pressing the period key once, you change the anchored address to H2 (as shown in the entry line of fig. 5.6). You now can change the range to any size, but cell H2 will always be one corner of the range. Pressing the period again changes the address to H20:B2, and cell H20 becomes the fixed (anchored) cell, which will always define one corner of the range. Pressing the period a third time makes B20 the anchored cell, and the cell pointer moves to cell H2. Pressing the period one last time returns the cell pointer to the original location (H20) with B2 as the anchored cell.

Using the period for moving around a range is especially effective for checking the print range entered in the /Output command. Because printed ranges usually exceed your screen size, this technique is especially helpful to see quickly the range you have entered. You simply call up the range and press the period key four times to see the four corners of the range. If the range is not what you want, you can adjust the size from any of those four corners, as you go. You will find this timesaving option handy to avoid printing something that was defined incorrectly.

Using the End Key with the Direction Keys

The End key, located on the numeric keypad of any IBM-compatible keyboard, can be used with the direction keys—the left, right, up, and down arrows on the numeric keypad—to move the cell pointer to the extreme edges of the spreadsheet. When you press the End key, the program goes into END keyboard mode. END appears in the dialog panel and remains visible until you complete the movement or press the End key again.

Pressing any arrow key while the program is in END mode sends the cell pointer to the last cell of the worksheet in the direction you have chosen. If you press the up-arrow key, the cell pointer always moves to row 1 of the current column. Likewise, if you press the left-arrow key, the cell pointer moves to column A of the current row. In both cases, pressing the direction key completes the movement, and you are taken out of END mode.

For example, to define an entire spreadsheet as an output range, from cell A1 you anchor the range by pressing the period key once. Then you press the End key once to initiate END mode, and press the down-arrow key once to go to the last row of the active spreadsheet. Press the End key again to recall the END mode, and press the right-arrow key to move the cell pointer to the bottom right corner of the range (and spreadsheet). This technique works faster than pressing the down-arrow key through each row and the right-arrow key through each column. Using END mode helps the spreadsheet (and your fingers) keep up with your mind and saves time with SuperCalc.

Using Tab and Shift-Tab

The Tab and Shift-Tab (BTAB, or BackTab) keys are similar to the End key. They put the program into a keyboard mode so that you can use an arrow key to move quickly to another area. Their mode selections are displayed in the dialog panel as TAB and BTAB; as with END mode, the indicator remains in the panel until the movement is complete or the key is toggled off.

In TAB mode, the arrow keys direct the cell pointer to the beginning of the next set of nonblank cells; in BTAB mode, the cell pointer moves to the next end of a contiguous range of nonblank cells. If the cell pointer is in the last set of nonblank cells, pressing an arrow key in either TAB or BTAB mode moves the pointer to the end of the spreadsheet. For example, pressing TAB or BTAB and the right-arrow key moves the pointer to the right edge of the spreadsheet.

Look at the display in figure 5.7. Blank rows and columns separate the blocks of text. TAB and BTAB modes speed movement between the blocks. If you press the right arrow, the cell pointer moves to the first column of the next group with each successive keystroke. If you use BTAB mode (invoked by holding down the Shift key and pressing Tab) and the right arrow, the cell pointer moves first to the last of the current group of columns and successively to the last column of each group, and finally to the last column of the worksheet.

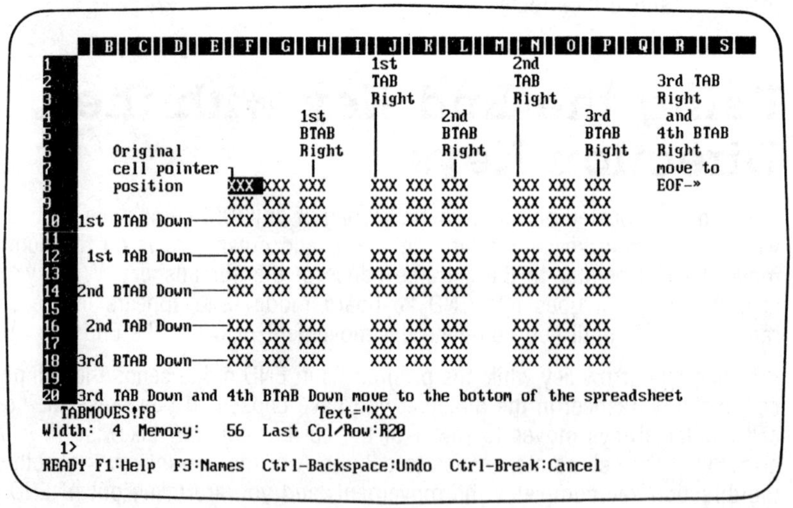

Fig. 5.7.

Demonstration of the TAB and BTAB movements.

Although a bit awkward because of location, the Tab key and the Shift-Tab combination can be helpful in moving swiftly to specific cells in a large worksheet.

Using the Home Key

By pressing the Home key, you move the cell pointer directly to cell A1 from any cell in the spreadsheet. This feature can be helpful, considering that SuperCalc can have 9,999 rows and 255 columns. When you press the End key and then the Home key, the cursor moves to the lower right corner of the active spreadsheet.

As an example, you can define a print range by pressing the Home key to get to A1, pressing the period key to anchor the range, and then pressing the End-Home key combination to move the cell pointer to the lower right corner of the active spreadsheet. This use of the Home key works even faster than the End-direction key method described previously. These alternative key combinations also demonstrate the flexibility you have in choosing the most convenient method to move around the spreadsheet.

Paging around the Worksheet

Another set of movement keys—PgUp, PgDn, Ctrl-left arrow, and Ctrl-right arrow—are used to step up, down, across, and back through the worksheet one page at a time. In this context, a *page* is an area of the worksheet that fits in the display window. Paging up or down repositions the cell pointer in the same relative location on the screen, but up or down 20 rows.

In the same way, if the worksheet columns are all sized to fit seven columns on the display, you can move seven columns to the left or right by pressing Ctrl-left arrow or Ctrl-right arrow.

Using the Forgotten Control Keys

Created in the pre-IBM compatibility days, SuperCalc originally used a set of alphabetic keys as control keys for cell-pointer movement. Computer Associates has maintained compatibility with the original cursor-movement keys. You can still use Ctrl-E, -X, -S, and -D to move the cell pointer one cell up, down, left, and right, respectively.

Don't ignore these control keys. For example, a classic problem with the 84-key IBM-compatible keyboard is having only one numeric keypad for both moving the cursor and entering numbers. You move between the two actions by pressing the NumLock key, which always seems to be toggled wrong. The control keys offer a simple solution that you may want to try. Table 5.1 presents a summary of all the movement keys.

Table 5.1
Summary of the Cell Pointer Movement Keys

Movement Key	Use
Right, left, up, and down arrows	Move the cell pointer up, down, right, or left one cell, respectively.
Home	Move the cell pointer to the top left cell (A1).

Table 5.1—*Continued*

Movement Key	Use
End-Home	Move the cell pointer to the bottom right cell.
End-arrow	Move the cell pointer to the last occupied cell in the direction of the arrow key.
Tab-arrow	Move the cell pointer to the first cell of the next group of contiguous cells in the arrow key's direction, or else to the edge of the worksheet.
BackTab-arrow	Move the cell pointer to the last cell in a contiguous group of cells, and then to the last cell in the next group or else to the edge of the worksheet.
PgUp and PgDn	Move the worksheet up or down one page in the same relative position in the display.
Ctrl-left arrow and Ctrl-right arrow	Page left or right one window, leaving the cell pointer in the same relative position in the display.
Ctrl-Home	Move the cell pointer to the upper left cell of the current window.
Ctrl-End	Move the cell pointer to the lower right cell of the current window.

Using the /Copy Command

The /Copy command is a good example of the evolution of SuperCalc. In previous Super-Calc releases, two commands, /Replicate and /Copy, did only a portion of what the new version of the /Copy command can do. And a new option, Transpose, has been added to SuperCalc5. Now you can copy one cell to another cell or to a block of cells. And with relative and absolute cell addressing, copying in SuperCalc can be one of the most useful tools for increasing your efficiency.

To learn the simplified /Copy command, consider the income statement introduced in Chapter 4. Suppose that you want to add an area for the company's second quarter results. Because the basic structure for the second quarter is the same as for the first quarter, you first copy the data ranges and column headings from columns B and C to columns D and E.

At the prompt, you can invoke the /Copy command by typing /C. SuperCalc then prompts you to enter a From (source) range. To point to the range, move the cell pointer to cell B5, which contains the column heading information. As the cell pointer moves, the command string changes to reflect the current cell location:

    /Copy,B5

To change B5 from a single cell to a single-cell range, press the period or colon key. This action anchors the beginning of the range to B5 and sets up B5 to the right of the colon. The command string now is

/**C**opy,B5:B5

Now you can point to the rest of the range. By moving the cell pointer to the lower right corner of the source, or From, range (C19), you highlight the range with reverse video (see fig. 5.8). At this point, you can move the pointer to any corner of the range by pressing the period key. Press Enter to define the first range.

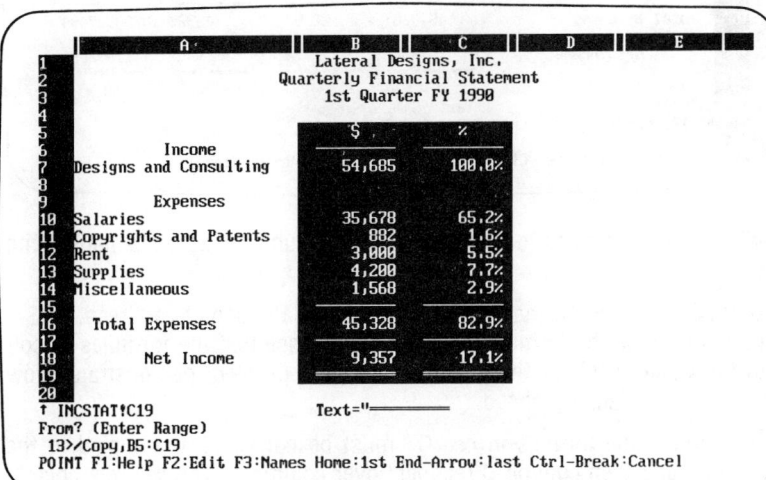

Fig. 5.8.

The From range defined.

The command prompt now asks for the To (target) range. The entry line reads

/Copy,B5:C19,B5

The default To range is the cell address of the cell pointer at the start of the command. In the next step, you move the cell pointer to the cell that defines the upper left corner of the target area, or To range. In this case, the cell is D5.

The program now has all data necessary to complete a simple copy. A range of 2 columns by 15 rows is defined as the From range. The command processor can copy the range to a range of the same size, starting with the upper left corner cell where the cell pointer is positioned. In other words, you have to define only the beginning of the target range; SuperCalc "assumes" the rest. When you move the cell pointer to D5 and press Enter, you duplicate the original block in the new range (see fig. 5.9).

The worksheet looks good, but a formula problem and a format problem remain. Because columns B and C were formatted with the **C**olumn format, these formats do not carry forward to the new range. To make D and E look the same as B and C, you must format column D with the user-defined format for displaying numbers with column delimiters, without decimal places (like an integer), and with negatives in parentheses; and you must

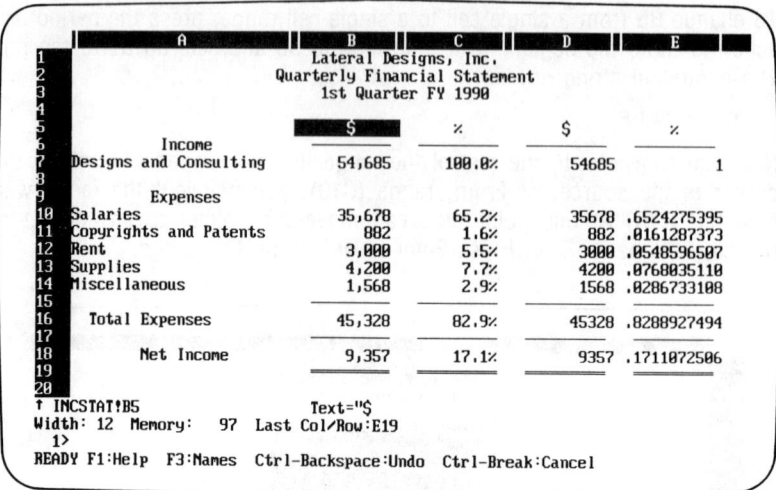

Fig. 5.9.

The income statement after the copying operation.

format column E with the user-defined format for displaying numbers as percentages with one decimal place.

The formula in column C is set up so that the denominator is an absolute address, $B$7. Using /**G**lobal,**F**ormula to toggle the formula display, you can see that the formulas in column E still refer to the value in B7 for the denominator. This problem demonstrates how you can avoid extra work by planning ahead.

To fix the incorrect formula, the formula in cell C7 must be corrected and copied to the remainder of the column, and then column C recopied over column E. The cell reference in the formula in cell C7 should be mixed (B$7) rather than absolute ($B$7) so that you can copy this column to column E or another percentage column if the situation arises. Although entering +B7/B$7 in E7 would suffice, instead enter

    ROUND(B7/B$7,3)

The ROUND arithmetic function makes the calculated value of the cell match the displayed value. In this case, the solution to the formula B7/B$7 will be rounded to three decimal places. This format will match the number being displayed in percentage format with one decimal place, because the percentage format automatically multiplies the stored value by 100, thereby moving the decimal point two places to the right. Using the ROUND function to make the underlying value match the displayed value improves the accuracy of the formula and eliminates rounding errors. The ROUND function is discussed in fuller detail in Chapter 7.

Once the new formula is entered into B7, the cell should be copied through the current column. You type

    /**C**opy,C7

The cell pointer should be positioned at the From cell (C7). You do not have to define a single cell as a range, so press Enter to bring up the prompt for the To range.

To define the beginning of the To range, move the cell pointer down two cells to C9. Because you are executing a one-to-many copy, you must define the entire target range. Press the colon or period to define the To range as C9:C9. Move the cell pointer to the *Miscellaneous* row (row 14) to change the To range to C9:C14. The To range is now completely defined. To copy the new formula to the rest of the range, press Enter.

The new formulas also should be copied to the column E percentage cells, to incorporate the ROUND function into the column E range and make the spreadsheet more uniform. Perform this copy by copying range C9:C14 to cell E9. Notice how much time this /Copy command can save in both expanding and revising the worksheet.

The Copying Options

Although absolute referencing has eliminated the need for several /Copy options for most copying, some options available with this command may help you in some circumstances or take the place of the absolute and relative referencing methods described. To use a /Copy option, enter a comma after defining the To cell.

All the options discussed in this section also can be used with the /Load command to load a file or file range from the disk into the worksheet. In these situations, thinking of /Load as a copy operation from an external range or spreadsheet may be helpful.

No-adjust

Absolute referencing was not available in earlier releases of SuperCalc. When you copied formulas in these earlier versions, the addresses in the formulas were adjusted automatically. To keep the formula from adjusting during the process of copying or replicating, the No-adjust option overrode the default of Adjust so that the formula addresses remained the same in the target cells. This option has been carried forward to SuperCalc, although absolute addressing is available to replace the No-adjust option.

To use No-adjust, enter a comma after defining the To cell. The following menu of choices appears:

```
No-adjust Ask Values + - * / Transpose
```

Select No-adjust and press Enter. The source cell's text and formulas are copied to the target cell, and the formulas remain identical to the source formulas.

Ask

The Ask option lets you choose the addresses you want adjusted for the target cell and the addresses you do not want adjusted. To demonstrate this option, suppose that cell E7 in the income statement worksheet in figure 5.9 is completely relative-address formula, as in prior releases of SuperCalc—instead of +D7/D$7, the formula reads +D7/D7. To copy +D7/D7 to the remainder of the cells in column E, use the Ask option because the formula is mixed (one relative address and one absolute address).

After defining the source (From) cell and the target (To) range, select the **A**sk option by typing a comma. SuperCalc then prompts

```
Source Cell E7. Adjust D7(Y or N)?
Copying to . . . E
22›+D7/D7
```

The first address in the source cell is highlighted on the command line. SuperCalc is asking whether to adjust this cell in the target formulas. Because the numerator is the address to be adjusted to the current row number, the answer to this prompt should be **Y**es. The display then changes slightly to

```
Source Cell E7. Adjust D7(Y or N)?
Copying to . . . E
25›+D7/D7
```

In this prompt, the second address in the formula is highlighted, and the **A**sk prompt now asks whether you want this second address to be adjusted relative to each target cell or to remain D7 in all the target cells. When using **A**sk, you have to consider which cell address is highlighted and how the question relates to what you are trying to accomplish. As the number of cell addresses increases, so does the number of questions and the possibility of error.

With SuperCalc's capability to copy from one cell to a range of cells in one step, the **A**sk option does not work with mixed references. This option can copy a single cell to multiple columns or rows only if the references are either completely absolute or completely relative. Otherwise, you must use the old two-step approach.

With relative and absolute addressing, these tedious adjustments can be avoided by a little planning. Usually, you can determine ahead of time which cell references will be useful as absolute addresses. For clarity, you can even give names to the absolute reference cells.

Values

The **V**alues option converts formulas to actual values during the copying process so that the solution to the formula, rather than the formula, appears in the target cell. You can use this option when copying a cell or range over itself or to another location in order to convert the formulas to values.

Because values require less memory than formulas, this option helps speed calculations and allows you to enter larger worksheets in the same amount of memory.

/Copy Arithmetic

The remaining four options, +, -, *, and /, stand for add, subtract, multiply, and divide, respectively. By selecting one of these options, you can perform consolidation arithmetic with two ranges of numeric values or consolidate one range with itself. Figure 5.10 shows the use of the four options on a range of cells that all start out containing the value 100 in B3.

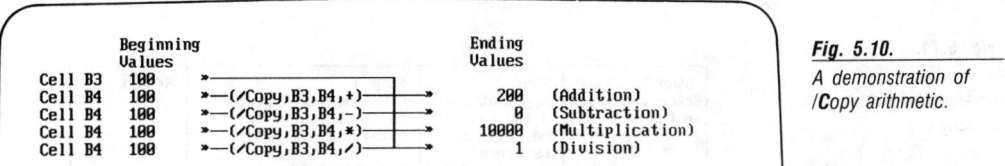

```
              Beginning                        Ending
              Values                           Values
    Cell B3   100      »
    Cell B4   100      »—(/Copy,B3,B4,+)———→      200   (Addition)
    Cell B4   100      »—(/Copy,B3,B4,-)———→        0   (Subtraction)
    Cell B4   100      »—(/Copy,B3,B4,*)———→    10000   (Multiplication)
    Cell B4   100      »—(/Copy,B3,B4,/)———→        1   (Division)
```

Fig. 5.10.

A demonstration of /Copy arithmetic.

In the first situation, a value of 100 is stored in B4 to which the 100 in B3 is added. The result (200) is stored in B4 in place of the 100. If the value in B4 is subtracted, the new value in B4 is 0 (100−100). In turn, the multiply option in row 3 produces 10,000 (100*100) in B4, and the last option (/) results in 1 (100/100) being stored in B4. Because these characters are options, they are always the last step in the /Copy command. The command starts to execute as soon as you press one of the four operator keys (+, -, *, or /).

Because of the way the /Copy command processes and because you can copy a range over itself, you can use these options to create numbering systems. Of these four arithmetic options, the add (+) option probably is used most for this process. For example, if you want to create a list numbered from 1 to 10, you enter a 1 in cell A1, and in A2 enter the formula

+A1+1

Copy this formula from cell A2 to the range A3:A10. You then have a list of values from 1 to 10 created by a series of formulas, each referencing the cell above and adding that value to the result.

Figure 5.11 illustrates the + option method that SuperCalc provides as an alternative to the formula method. The + option produces a value, rather than a formula, in each cell. Three steps are required for creating a numbered list with /Copy. You must issue the /Copy command twice: first, to create the base values in each cell (step 2) and, second, to add values to create the list (step 3).

Copying formulas over themselves with the Values option also gives you values in the cells. This process, however, takes twice as much effort as the + option.

The arithmetic options require numeric values in both the source cell and the target cell; therefore, you must begin a list by entering a 1 in the top cell of the list, as indicated in step 1 of figure 5.11 (in this case A1). Then copy that cell to the range A2:A10 (step 2 of the figure). Step 2 shows the To range during the /Copy. Now you have a column of 1s that you want to convert to a list from 1 to 10.

Step 3 shows how you must copy the range over itself but with an offset of one cell. First, move the cell pointer to A1; to invoke the /Copy command, type

/Copy,A1

At the From prompt, point to range A1:A9 and press Enter. The From range is the first nine cells of the column. At the To prompt, move the cell pointer down one cell to A2. This movement defines the top of the To range (which is all that you need to define). Next,

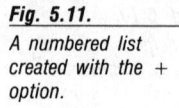

Fig. 5.11.
A numbered list created with the + option.

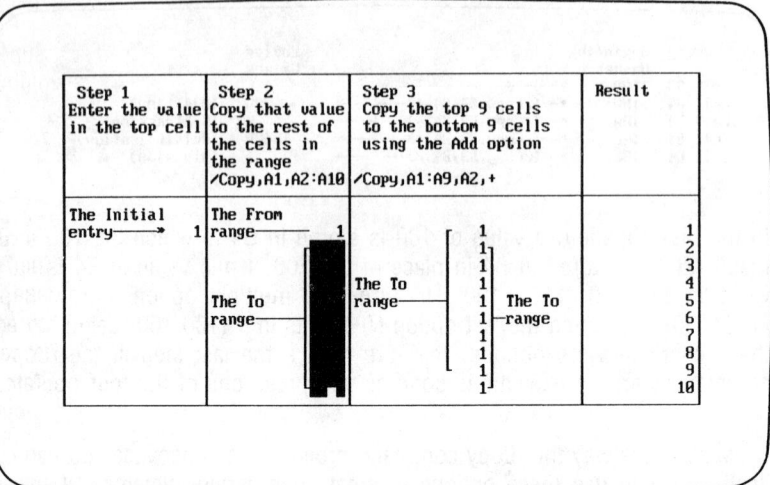

Step 1 Enter the value in the top cell	Step 2 Copy that value to the rest of the cells in the range /Copy,A1,A2:A10	Step 3 Copy the top 9 cells to the bottom 9 cells using the Add option /Copy,A1:A9,A2,+	Result
The Initial entry⟶ 1	The From range⟶ 1 The To range⟶	The To range⟶ 1 1 1 1 1 1 1 1 1 The To range	1 2 3 4 5 6 7 8 9 10

press the comma to call up the /Copy options. From the options, select + to indicate that you want the From range added to the To range; then press Enter.

After the command string is completed, the action begins. The column of 1s created in step 3 is converted to the finished product, seen in the *Result* column. This process is the equivalent of 19 single copies. The first cell of the From range (A1) is added to the first cell of the To range (A2); 1 and 1 are added, and the result—2—is stored in A2. Next, the second cell of the From range (A2, which now contains a 2) is added to the second cell of the To range (A3) and the result—3—is stored in cell A3. The process continues for the next 7 cells.

The /Copy command executes one cell at a time, and the result is immediately stored for use as input to the next step in the operation. This action produces a list of numbers from 1 to 10.

After several practices, you will get the feel for this process, which works with block ranges as well. This copy process is a quick way to create a numbered list, and less memory and calculation time are needed to store numbers in each cell than to store formulas.

Transpose

This option is a new addition to SuperCalc5 and a powerful one, too. Before Transpose, SuperCalc offered no quick way to copy a column of text or values into a row. So once you committed your design to a direction, you were in for a major overhaul or some fancy use of the index function to convert it to the other direction. Now an entire row, column, or block can be transposed with a single command. For example, if you enter the months of a year down column A (A1:A12) and decide instead that you want them across the top of your worksheet (A1:L1), all you have to do is enter

/**C**opy,A1:A12,A1,**T**ranspose

The months will be copied across row 1 from column A. Because SuperCalc has many more rows than columns, you cannot copy too large a block from a column to a row. This option also works for an entire block of values.

Things To Consider When You Copy

SuperCalc's data storage methods add some considerations to using the /**C**opy command. To increase performance and reduce calculation time and memory usage, SuperCalc does not store any information about blank or unused cells. When you copy a range that contains blank cells, the blank cells are ignored, leaving unchanged the cells in the same relative position in the To range. However, not all ranges that appear blank are blank. If the "blank" cells in the From range have been formatted with the **E**ntry option, they are no longer blank. If you move the cell pointer to a cell formatted with the **E**ntry option, in the status line you will see

Text=

To store the formatting information for the cell, SuperCalc creates a blank text string in the cell. Because of this feature, and because this entry formatting is carried forward with the /**C**opy command, these cells write over the cells in the To range.

For example, if the unformatted data in column A of figure 5.12 is copied over the data in column B, the result looks like the display in column C. However, if the data in column E is formatted with the command

/**F**ormat,**E**ntry,E1:E20,**G**eneral

and is copied over the data in column F, the result looks like the display in column G.

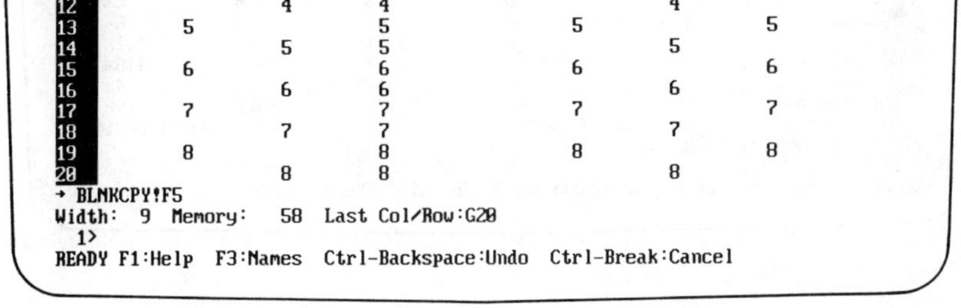

Fig. 5.12.

The effect of copying a blank text string.

If memory is not a problem and you are accustomed to 1-2-3's method, you can format the worksheet with

/Format,Entry,All,General

The /Copy command then works like 1-2-3's.

In another formatting case, if the source range is formatted with the Column or Row formatting option, the format is not carried over to the target range. This happened in the income statement example (refer to fig. 5.9). When the ranges from columns B and C were copied to D and E, the new data was unformatted.

Occasionally, you will be surprised by the result of a copy. When you use the + option to generate a list of numbers, the range is copied over itself. If you copy a range to a cell within the range without the + option, the first cell or row of the From range is copied to every cell. Therefore, be careful when copying a range to a cell within the range.

Revising and Restructuring Your Spreadsheet

SuperCalc provides a variety of commands for revising and restructuring your worksheet size and content. To see how these commands are used, you will modify the income statement from figure 5.9. Instead of the revenue combined on one line, you will itemize revenue with a subtotal for total income, and break out the miscellaneous category into four additional categories. The result of this adjustment looks like figure 5.13.

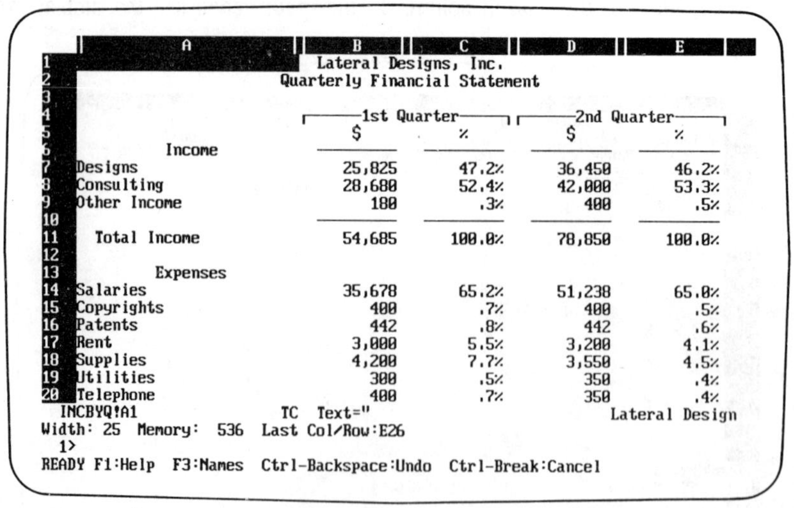

Fig. 5.13.

A more complex income statement.

	A	B	C	D	E
1		Lateral Designs, Inc.			
2		Quarterly Financial Statement			
3					
4		┌─1st Quarter─┐		┌─2nd Quarter─┐	
5		$	%	$	%
6	Income				
7	Designs	25,825	47.2%	36,450	46.2%
8	Consulting	28,680	52.4%	42,000	53.3%
9	Other Income	180	.3%	400	.5%
10					
11	Total Income	54,685	100.0%	78,850	100.0%
12					
13	Expenses				
14	Salaries	35,678	65.2%	51,238	65.0%
15	Copyrights	400	.7%	400	.5%
16	Patents	442	.8%	442	.6%
17	Rent	3,000	5.5%	3,200	4.1%
18	Supplies	4,200	7.7%	3,550	4.5%
19	Utilities	300	.5%	350	.4%
20	Telephone	400	.7%	350	.4%

```
    INCBYQ!A1         TC   Text="                      Lateral Design
Width: 25  Memory:  536  Last Col/Row:E26
   1>
READY F1:Help  F3:Names  Ctrl-Backspace:Undo  Ctrl-Break:Cancel
```

The /Blank Command

The first command for revising your spreadsheet is /**B**lank.

/**B**lank is a straightforward command that can be compared to using an eraser on a handwritten worksheet. You can clear a single cell, a range of cells, an entire column, or all unprotected cells in the worksheet with the /**B**lank command. This command erases both the cell content and the **E**ntry formatting within the cell. In most cases, you should use this command to blank the target range before executing the /**C**opy command.

To convert the original income statement format (refer to fig. 5.2) to the quarterly statement in figure 5.13, the worksheet titles should be changed. To eliminate the third title line, *1st Quarter FY 1990*, move the cell pointer to A3 and choose

/**B**lank,A3

The dialog panel now looks like figure 5.14.

```
↓ INCBYQ!A3            H       Text="                              1st Quarter F
Enter range: then <RETURN> or <,> for Options
 10>/Blank,A3
POINT F1:Help F2:Edit F3:Names Home:1st End-Arrow:last Ctrl-Break:Cancel
```

Fig. 5.14.
*The dialog panel for the /**B**lank command.*

When you press the Enter key, you eliminate the cell contents. As an alternative, from anywhere in the spreadsheet you can enter

/**B**lank,**3**

The entire third row will be blanked out.

The /Insert Command

You use the /**I**nsert command to modify a worksheet already containing information. With this command, you can insert blank rows, blank columns, blocks of blank cells, or new blank pages for a multipage spreadsheet (see Chapter 6).

With the **R**ow or **C**olumn option, you can point to the row or column ranges you want, in the same way you point to a cell range. This command's only limitation is that sometimes the extra space causes the worksheet to expand beyond the column and row boundaries of the spreadsheet. Such expansion stops the /**I**nsert command from executing.

In the original income statement worksheet (refer to fig. 5.2), row 7 contains the total revenue and is labeled *Designs and Consulting*. In the revised worksheet (refer to fig. 5.13), this row holds figures for the detail line labeled *Designs*. To make room for the other two detail lines and the line for *Total Income*, move the cell pointer to cell A7 and type

/**I**nsert,A7

After you access the Insert menu, you see the options

    Row   Column   Block   Page

Select **R**ow. The prompt line asks for a row range and displays the current row number. Enter multiple rows like the four rows in this example by pressing a colon or period to anchor the beginning of the range, pointing down the next three rows, and pressing Enter. The result is that everything in row 7 and below is moved down and adjusted to reflect the new row addresses. For example, the label *Salaries* in the old format is in row 10; with the new format, the label is in row 14.

To insert the rows necessary in the *Expenses* portion of the statement, repeat the /Insert command at row 15 and then at the new row 19. Two rows are added when you enter /Insert,**R**ow,15; anchor the beginning of the row range by pressing the period key, which defines the single row range 15:15; and press the down arrow twice. You complete the command by pressing Enter.

Now, all the additional rows are inserted. Next, you must perform the following steps:

1. Copy the percent formulas to C7:C9, C15, and C19:C20.

2. Enter all specific text headings and subtotal lines.

3. Change B11 to the formula $+B7+B8+B9$.

4. Enter and change values to reflect the new level of detail.

5. Recopy range B6:C26 to cell D6 to incorporate the changes to the second quarter data area.

The /Delete Command

You use /**D**elete to eliminate the *Other Income* row from the income statement worksheet. Add the *Other Income* amount in row 9 of figure 5.13 to the *Consulting* amount (row 8) so that income is from only designs or consulting. Then use the /**D**elete command to eliminate the *Other Income* row from figure 5.13.

Deleting is much more dangerous than inserting. The /Insert command adjusts all formulas to reflect the new status; however, deleting can cause unexpected problems when you delete rows that are referenced in formulas. Because /**D**elete is a destructive command, it should be used carefully—preferably only after saving a copy of the worksheet to disk.

As an example, after moving the cell pointer to row 9, you can enter

    /**D**elete,**R**ow,9

All formulas that reference a cell in row 9 now display the error message as the solution to the formula, and all formulas referencing a cell with an ERROR also display ERROR (see fig. 5.15).

```
┌─────────────────────────────────────────────────────────────┐
│           A              B        C        D        E         │
│1                   Lateral Designs, Inc.                      │
│2                  Quarterly Financial Statement               │
│3                                                              │
│4              ┌────1st Quarter────┐ ┌────2nd Quarter────┐     │
│5                     $        %         $        %            │
│6          Income                                             │
│7  Designs          25,825   ERROR    36,450   ERROR          │
│8  Consulting       28,680   ERROR    42,000   ERROR          │
│9                                                             │
│10    Total Income  ERROR    ERROR    ERROR    ERROR          │
│11                                                            │
│12         Expenses                                          │
│13 Salaries         35,678   ERROR    51,238   ERROR          │
│14 Copyrights          400   ERROR       400   ERROR          │
│15 Patents             442   ERROR       442   ERROR          │
│16 Rent              3,000   ERROR     3,200   ERROR          │
│17 Supplies          4,200   ERROR     3,550   ERROR          │
│18 Utilities           300   ERROR       350   ERROR          │
│19 Telephone           400   ERROR       350   ERROR          │
│20 Miscellaneous       868   ERROR       868   ERROR          │
│↓ INCBYQ!A9                                                   │
│Width: 25 Memory:    96  Last Col/Row:E25                     │
│   1>                                                         │
│READY F1:Help F3:Names Ctrl-Backspace:Undo Ctrl-Break:Cancel  │
└─────────────────────────────────────────────────────────────┘
```

Fig. 5.15.

ERROR *messages displayed after row 9 is deleted.*

Figure 5.16, a portion of the same spreadsheet displayed with the audit feature //**T**est,/**V**iew,**F**ormula, shows the underlying cell contents (columns are separated by vertical bars). You can see that only the formulas directly referencing a deleted cell actually change to ERROR (cell B10). The remaining formulas are intact and will be correct again when the formula in B10 is fixed. Chapter 13 describes the audit features.

```
┌─────────────────────────────────────────────────────────────┐
│       A             B              C            D             │
│1              Lateral Designs, Inc.                           │
│2             Quarterly Financial Statement                    │
│3                                                             │
│4   "          "────1st Quarter────┐  "┌────2nd Qu            │
│5   "          "$         "%           "$                     │
│6  "Income     "          "                                   │
│7  "Designs    25825      ROUND(+B7/B$10,3)   36450           │
│8  "Consulting 28680      ROUND(+B8/B$10,3)   42000           │
│9                                                            │
│10 "   Total Income  +B7+B8+ERROR  ROUND(+B10/B$10,3) +D7+D8+ERROR │
│11                                                           │
│12 "Expenses                                                 │
│13 "Salaries   35678      ROUND(+B13/B$10,3)  51238          │
│14 "Copyrights 400        ROUND(+B14/B$10,3)  400            │
│15 "Patents    442        ROUND(+B15/B$10,3)  442            │
│16 "Rent       3000       ROUND(+B16/B$10,3)  3200           │
│17 "Supplies   4200       ROUND(+B17/B$10,3)  3550           │
│18 "Utilities  300        ROUND(+B18/B$10,3)  350            │
│19 "Telephone  400        ROUND(+B19/B$10,3)  350            │
│20 "Miscellaneous 868     ROUND(+B20/B$10,3)  868            │
│↓ INCBYQ!A9                                                  │
│Width: 21 Memory:    96  Last Col/Row:E25                    │
│   1>                                                        │
│AUDIT For troubleshooting, search-replace; press / to display the AUDIT menu │
└─────────────────────────────────────────────────────────────┘
```

Fig. 5.16.

The ERROR *messages displayed by* //**T**est/**V**iew,**F**ormula.

To fix this error, you have to reenter the formula in B10. An important point is that this cell would not have generated an error if the formula SUM(B7:B9) had been used rather than +B7+B8+B9. If the SUM function had been used, the formula would have adjusted to

SUM(B7:B8)

Therefore, use SUM wherever possible to avoid the error problem. However, you should always be careful when you use /Delete.

The **C**olumn and **P**age options work like the **R**ow option when you use the /Insert and /Delete commands, with corresponding effects on the worksheet. For deleting files, you are prompted with a **N**o or **Y**es choice after selecting the file. This useful safety net was missing from SuperCalc4.

Block Manipulation: The New Alternative

The /Insert and /Delete commands now have a **B**lock option for inserting and deleting a range within the worksheet. For example, suppose that you have a worksheet with several blocks of data. Without the **B**lock option, adjusting the size of only one area of the worksheet would take quite a bit of copying and moving. With this option, however, the task becomes minimal.

To insert a block, you first must decide which way you want to shift the affected data and cells. You can choose either the **R**ight or **D**own option to push the data to the columns to the right or down to the rows below. With the /Insert,**R**ow and /Insert,**C**olumn options, this choice is already made. When a row is inserted, everything is pushed down; when a column is inserted, everything is pushed to the right. Figure 5.17 demonstrates the two choices for /Insert.

Fig. 5.17.

Effects of the /Insert,Block or /Delete,Block options.

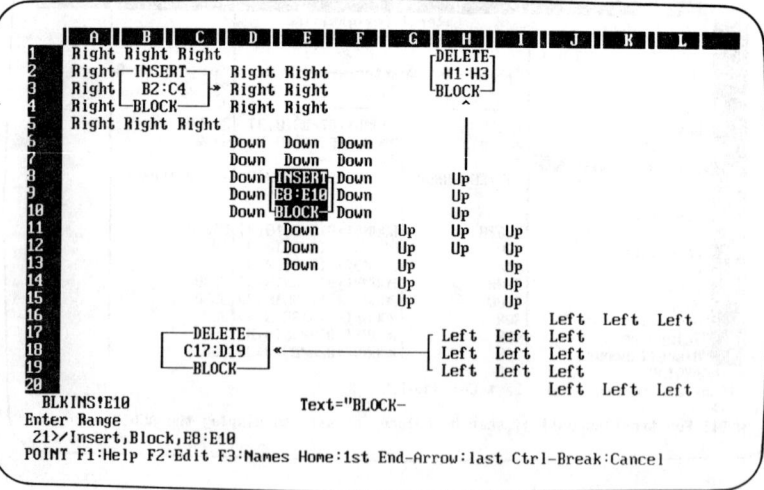

In the block made up of the text Right, a six-cell block is inserted in the middle of the block (B2:C4) and the **R**ight option is selected. The cells affected are pushed to the right two columns. Similarly, with the Down block, a three-cell block is inserted at E8:E10, and the **D**own option is selected. The three displaced cells are squeezed down three rows. The center five cells in the Up block move up three rows because a three-cell block (H1:H3) is deleted, and the **U**p option is selected. (Selecting any three cells in column H above the block would have had the same effect.) The center six cells in the Left block adjust left because a six-cell block (C17:D19) is deleted to the left of the block, and the **L**eft option is selected. This deletion forces everything in the rows to the right of the deleted block to move left.

Row, Column, and Page Moves

Another important command in the worksheet restructuring process is the /**M**ove command. Whereas the /**C**opy command leaves the original range intact and duplicates it in the target range, the /**M**ove command actually takes the source range and places it in the target position, adjusting everything accordingly. Like /**C**opy, /**M**ove also has the **T**ranspose option in SuperCalc5.

As with the /**I**nsert and /**D**elete commands, you can move a row, column, block, or page of a worksheet. In many ways, /**M**ove is similar to /**I**nsert and /**D**elete. Whether you are moving a row, column, or block, and whether you are moving an item up, left, down, or right in the worksheet, the rest of the worksheet adjusts to accept the moved data.

For example, in the income statement example (refer to fig. 5.13), the *Copyrights* row can be moved below the *Patents* row. Move the cell pointer to A15 and enter

   /**M**ove,**R**ow,A15

You move the cell pointer down one row to A16, and press Enter. Old row 15 is now located below the old row 16. In essence, you have swapped the two row locations. Whatever the direction of the move, the remainder of the worksheet located between the two spots adjusts to fill the void.

When your range to be moved involves only text cells, the command works cleanly and simply. But complications arise when formulas are involved. If the formulas include only relative addresses, the /**M**ove command adjusts the formulas to reflect the new position. If, however, the formulas involve any absolute addresses, they are not adjusted.

Block Moves

The **B**lock option of the /**M**ove command is different from the other options (**C**olumn, **R**ow, or **P**age). A column, row, or page move adjusts the cells to fill the void left by the move. The block move leaves a blank range where the source range was and completely replaces the target range.

/**M**ove,**B**lock is a great addition to the SuperCalc tool chest, but this command can be complex. If you are moving text cells, the command is straightforward and harmless. Moving formulas around or moving blocks into areas with formulas can cause problems.

In a block move, absolute references do not always stay absolute and relative references do not always act as if they are relative. Figure 5.18 demonstrates the effect of moving an end cell in a range being referenced by a formula. Column A shows the relationship of three different types of formulas and addresses before the move, and columns C and D show the relationships of the three formulas after the move.

Fig. 5.18.

Moving an end cell of a range referenced in a formula.

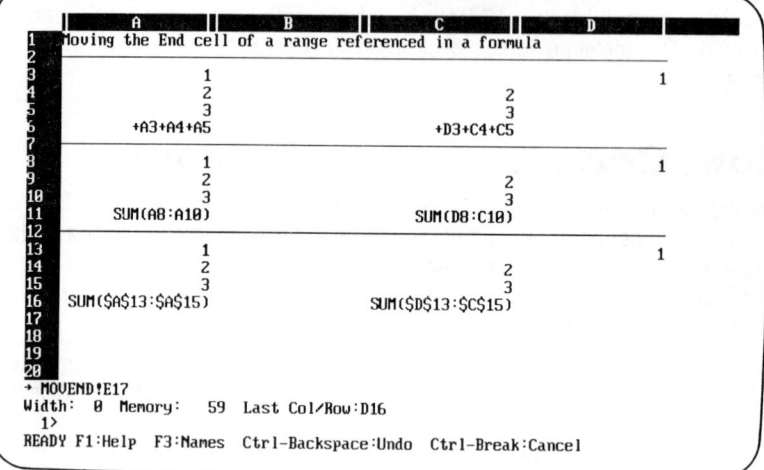

The top formula in column C, +D3+C4+C5 before moving cell C3 to D3, changes to reflect the new location of the value 1. The second formula, SUM(D8:C10) before moving cell C8 to D8, changes to SUM(D8:C10). Although the SUM function (see Chapter 7) returns the same total (6) as the simple arithmetic formula +D3+C4+C5 before the move, the same function may have a completely different value after the move. Any numbers entered in cells D9 and D10 are included in the SUM of the six-block range from D8 to C10. The first formula (+D3+C4+C5), however, returns the same result both before and after the move. Although the bottom formula in column C, (SUM($D$13:$C$15)), has absolute cell references, the formula changes the same way the middle formula in that column changes and now includes a six-block range from D13 to C15.

In figure 5.19, rather than the end cell in each range, the center cell is moved. The formula in cell C6 adjusts to take into account the new location of the value 2. The two SUM formulas remained unchanged and so no longer include 2 in the total. The formulas are not changed because the move occurs in the middle of the range being referenced and does not affect the specific cell references in the formulas.

In figure 5.20, the formulas themselves are moved from column C to the same rows in column D. In each case, the formulas maintain the same cell references as before; they still address the three values in column C, regardless of whether the formula has relative or absolute references. If each formula is copied—instead of moved—to the cell to the right, cell D6 contains the formula +D3+D4+D5, and cell D11 holds SUM(D8:D10), but cell D16 still contains SUM($C$13:$C$15).

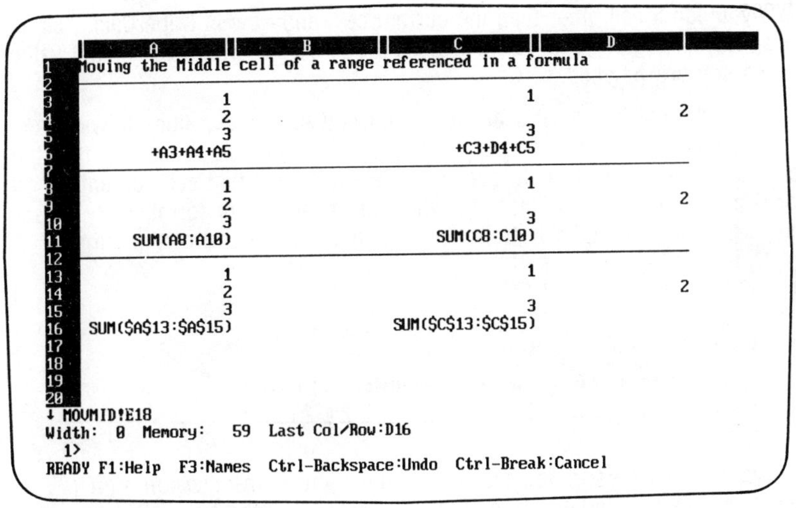

```
  ┌──────┬────────────┬────────────┬────────────┬──────────┐
  │   A  │      A     │      B     │      C     │     D    │
  │1     │Moving the Middle cell of a range referenced in a formula
  │2     │
  │3     │            1                        1
  │4     │            2
  │5     │            3                        3                 2
  │6     │+A3+A4+A5                   +C3+D4+C5
  │7     │
  │8     │            1                        1
  │9     │            2
  │10    │            3                        3                 2
  │11    │SUM(A8:A10)                 SUM(C8:C10)
  │12    │
  │13    │            1                        1
  │14    │            2
  │15    │            3                        3                 2
  │16    │SUM($A$13:$A$15)           SUM($C$13:$C$15)
  │17    │
  │18    │
  │19    │
  │20    │
  └──────┴────────────────────────────────────────────────────┘
  ↓ MOVMID↑E18
  Width:  0 Memory:   59 Last Col/Row:D16
     1>
  READY F1:Help  F3:Names  Ctrl-Backspace:Undo  Ctrl-Break:Cancel
```

Fig. 5.19.

Moving the middle cell of a range referenced in a formula.

```
  ┌──────┬────────────┬────────────┬────────────┬──────────┐
  │   A  │      A     │      B     │      C     │     D    │
  │1     │Moving a formula that references a range of cells
  │2     │
  │3     │            1                        1
  │4     │            2                        2
  │5     │            3                        3
  │6     │+A3+A4+A5                                  +C3+C4+C5
  │7     │
  │8     │            1                        1
  │9     │            2                        2
  │10    │            3                        3
  │11    │SUM(A8:A10)                               SUM(C8:C10)
  │12    │
  │13    │            1                        1
  │14    │            2                        2
  │15    │            3                        3
  │16    │SUM($A$13:$A$15)                     SUM($C$13:$C$15)
  │17    │
  │18    │
  │19    │
  │20    │
  └──────┴────────────────────────────────────────────────────┘
  → MOVFORM↑E18
  Width:  0 Memory:   59 Last Col/Row:D16
     1>
  READY F1:Help  F3:Names  Ctrl-Backspace:Undo  Ctrl-Break:Cancel
```

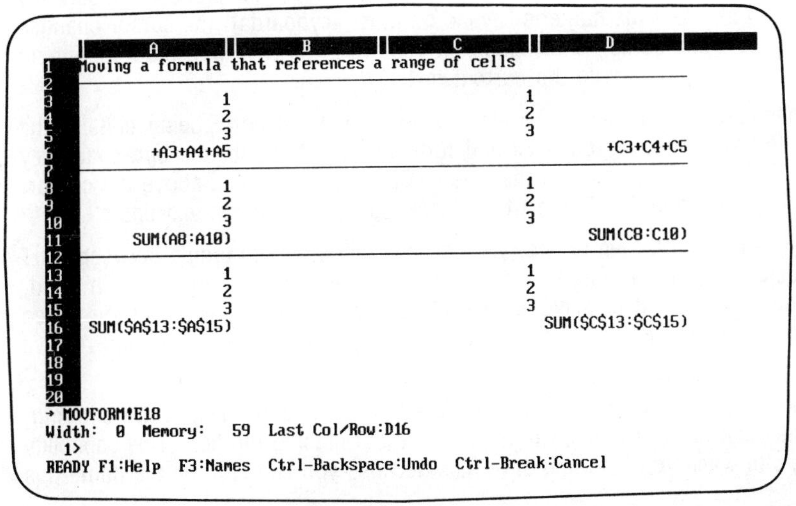

Fig. 5.20.

Moving a formula that refers to a range of cells.

When dealing with formulas, copying the cell to the new location and then blanking the old cell is probably a better method than using the block move. Remember, /**M**ove,**B**lock is a powerful tool to use on text cells but can be dangerous with formula cells.

The /Edit Command

The /**E**dit command is an important modifying tool of SuperCalc. This command was first incorporated into the function keys in SuperCalc4. The F2 function key works the same as the /**E**dit command if you want to edit the cell where the cell pointer is located. The /**E**dit command still lets you edit a cell other than the current cell; and now in SuperCalc5, as an option, you can specify a target cell different from the source cell where the edited value will be placed when you are finished.

When you are editing, the mode indicator at the far left end of the help line shows EDIT. Figure 5.21 shows the dialog panel during an edit of a cell's content. Assuming that the cell pointer is on the cell you want to edit, press the F2 key to pull that cell content up on the entry line for editing. The cursor is placed at the end of the text or formula. By pressing Tab or Home, you can move quickly from the beginning to the end of the entry.

Fig. 5.21.

The dialog panel in EDIT mode.

```
→ INCSTAT!C10              Form=ROUND(+B10/B$10,3)
  Width: 12  Memory:   56  Last Col/Row:E25
   12>ROUND(+B10/█B$10,3)
  EDIT  F1:Help  F3:Names  Ctrl-Backspace:Undo  Ctrl-Break:Cancel
```

Notice in figure 5.21 that the cursor, located just to the right of the division sign (/), is rectangular rather than a thin underline. This cursor indicates that the Insert toggle is on; anything you type now will be inserted on the entry line. When you press the insert key (Ins, located at the bottom of the numeric keypad on most keyboards), the cursor changes from a box cursor to a line cursor, indicating that you are in OVERWRITE mode; anything you type at the cursor will overwrite the current text.

Most of the other cursor-movement keys also move around the entry being edited. The right arrow and left arrow move you back and forth through the line; the backspace key erases text to the left of the cursor; and the delete (Del) key erases text above the cursor. The up and down arrows and Ctrl-E and Ctrl-X insert spaces within the text line.

While you edit a formula on the entry line, you can use the F2 key to toggle between EDIT and ENTRY modes. In ENTRY mode, you can build a formula by pointing. Keep in mind, however, that you cannot point to make changes to addresses in the middle of the edited line; and you cannot use the F4 key in EDIT mode to toggle between absolute and relative addressing.

The F2 key works in COMMAND mode as well. To edit a command line you are entering, press F2. You then can move to the left in the line without erasing the text. This capability is particularly helpful when you load and save files because you can edit the file name this way.

Using the /Title Command

The /Title command is an old friend from early SuperCalc releases. This command is indispensable for spreadsheets that exceed the size of the screen—the "big picture" alluded to at the beginning of this chapter—and most spreadsheets you create probably will exceed the 20-row-by-75-character display area.

This command is useful because, like the income statement example, most spreadsheets are defined with column heading information across the top of the worksheet and row labels down the left side. The /Title command freezes (or locks) these labels on-screen. Only the data range (the unlocked portion of the spreadsheet) changes as you move the cell pointer around the screen.

The four options for working with title locks appear in the menu as

        Horizontal Vertical Both Clear

If you select the **H**orizontal option, only the rows at the top of the worksheet are locked on-screen. With the **V**ertical option, only the columns on the left edge of the screen are locked on-screen. With the **B**oth option, both columns and rows are locked on-screen.

To understand this last and most useful option, look once more at the income statement (see fig. 5.22). Because of the inserted rows, the worksheet has grown larger than the 20-row display. To lock the captions and row and column labels on-screen with the **B**oth option, move the cell pointer to the cell at the intersection of the lowest row and the right-most column that you want to remain frozen on-screen (cell A6 in fig. 5.22). The title lock is set up while the cell pointer is within the title area.

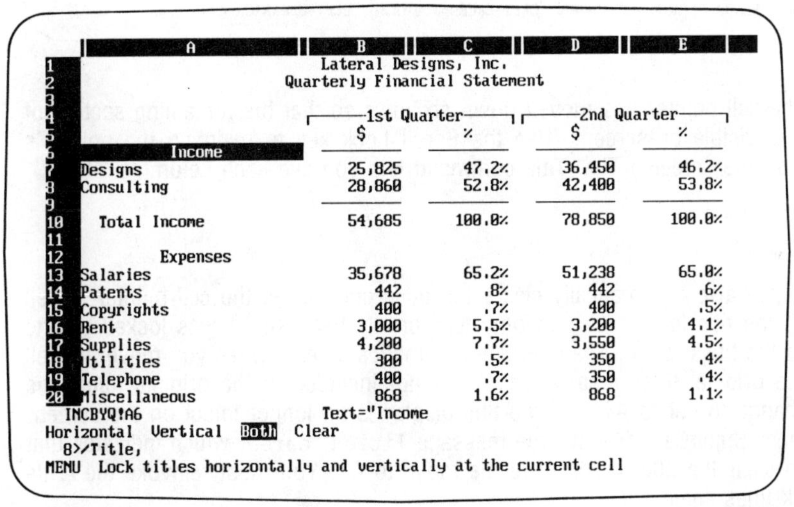

Fig. 5.22.

Setting up a title lock.

To create the locked title area, use the command

  /**T**itle,**B**oth,A6

Nothing appears to change on-screen; but if you move the cell pointer one cell to the right and then try to move the pointer back to the left, you will realize that you are locked out of that part of the screen. If you move the cursor down one cell, you cannot move the cell pointer back to row 6.

Now press the PgDn key or move the cursor across a page. The captions and labels remain on-screen for use with the data in the lower sections of the worksheet. Figure 5.23

shows the income statement with the /Title,**B**oth option set. The first six rows of the spreadsheet and column A are fixed on-screen. The active area of the spreadsheet begins at B7.

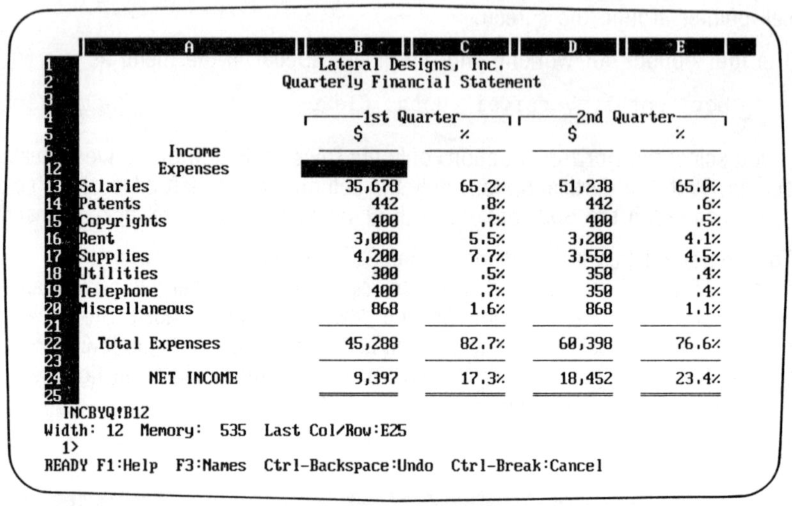

Fig. 5.23.

The income statement with title lock set.

```
               A              B           C             D            E
 1                         Lateral Designs, Inc.
 2                       Quarterly Financial Statement
 3
 4                        ┌──────1st Quarter──────┐ ┌──────2nd Quarter──────┐
 5                               $         %              $          %
 6           Income           ─────     ─────          ─────      ─────
12           Expenses
13  Salaries                  35,678    65.2%          51,238     65.0%
14  Patents                      442      .8%             442       .6%
15  Copyrights                   400      .7%             400       .5%
16  Rent                       3,000     5.5%           3,200      4.1%
17  Supplies                   4,200     7.7%           3,550      4.5%
18  Utilities                    300      .5%             350       .4%
19  Telephone                    400      .7%             350       .4%
20  Miscellaneous                868     1.6%             868      1.1%
21
22       Total Expenses       45,288    82.7%          60,398     76.6%
23
24          NET INCOME         9,397    17.3%          18,452     23.4%
25

     INCBYQ!B12
Width: 12  Memory:   535  Last Col/Row:E25
   1>
READY F1:Help  F3:Names  Ctrl-Backspace:Undo  Ctrl-Break:Cancel
```

In figure 5.23, the cell pointer has moved down six rows so that the remaining section of the spreadsheet is visible on-screen. (Use the Scroll Lock key to maintain the pointer's relative position on the screen.) The /Title command lets you see each column's labels.

To clear the titles, select

/Title,**C**lear

Pressing Home once also automatically clears the titles and places the cell pointer in cell A1. In this case, the title lock is cleared only temporarily because A1 was locked on the display as part of the titles range. The titles are automatically reset when you move the cell pointer out of the original titles area. If cell A1 is not included in the original titles, the display has to change to get to A1; and the title display is no longer intact on the screen. When this happens, SuperCalc displays the message Title Cleared, which indicates that SuperCalc had to clear the title to complete the move to A1. You must reinvoke the /Title command to lock titles again.

In SuperCalc the title locks are used with the /**O**utput command for printing large worksheets. This enhancement is discussed in Chapter 9 along with the other capabilities of the improved /**O**utput command.

Using the /Window Command

The /Window command is a timesaving tool similar to the /Title command. Like the /Title command, /Window segments the screen; but the commands operate in different circumstances. Whereas /Title works only on columns and rows on top and to the left of the display, /Window can be used on rows and columns on the bottom or to the right of the display.

/Window lets you split the screen either horizontally or vertically but has no **B**oth option (unlike the /Title command). When you split the screen, another border row appears and separates the two windows on the worksheet. You can jump between windows, change their formats, and move them in two different directions. By selecting /Window from the main command menu, you can access all the options:

```
Horizontal  Vertical  Clear  Synchronize  Unsynchronize
```

The **H**orizontal and **V**ertical options split the screen at the current column or row location of the cell pointer. The **C**lear option works like the similar option in the /Title command, but /Window,**C**lear always clears away the lower or right window and completes the display from the left or upper screen.

If you choose the **S**ynchronize option, the two windows move in unison when the cell pointer is moved. With a horizontal split, this movement happens when the cell pointer is moved off-screen to the right or left. In a vertical split, both screens adjust when the cell pointer is moved up or down off-screen. If you **U**nsynchronize the two windows, you can position a window in a certain location, move to the other window, and move the cell pointer around that window without affecting the first window.

To move between the displays, press the semicolon (;) or F6. (The semicolon is a holdover from pre-IBM function-key operations.) SuperCalc stores the location of the cell pointer in both windows. The cell pointer is returned to the same cell the pointer was in when you moved to the other window. Because of this feature, you can easily work on two different areas of the spreadsheet at the same time.

The /Global settings can be set to display the same cell range in both windows with one showing underlying formulas and the other displaying values as shown in figure 5.24.

Figure 5.24 demonstrates one of the more exotic combinations of display-altering commands. To create this display, use /Global,**Z**oom overall and /Global,**F**ormulas and /Window,**V**ertical in each spreadsheet display. To fit more lines on-screen, the /Global,**Z**oom command ''squeezes'' each line. Note that where F6 moves between windows in the same spreadsheet, Ctrl-F6 moves between spreadsheets. To make the display even more exotic, you can toggle off the border display in one or both windows of each spreadsheet independently. Multiple spreadsheet displays and multipage spreadsheets are discussed in detail in the next chapter.

Other things can be manipulated within a window. Separate title locks can be set for each window. Any title lock set before the window is split remains in effect for both windows. You cannot print the two windows using the /Output command, however; the top or left window is the only one printed.

Fig. 5.24.

Three spreadsheets
displayed with
windows and zoom.

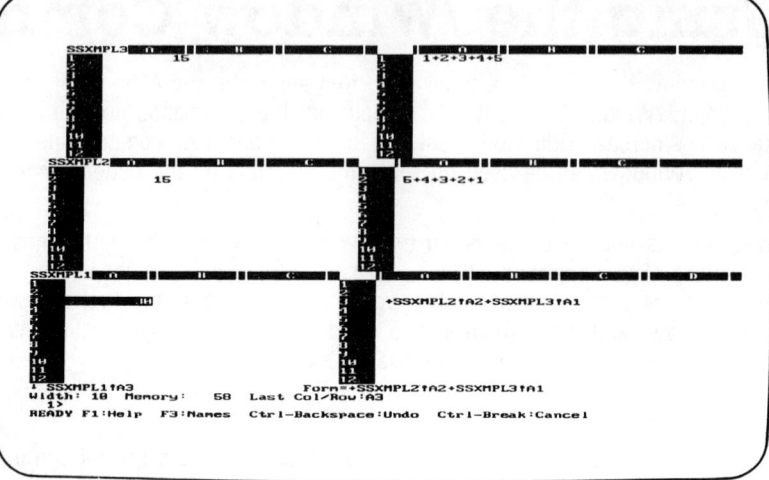

Chapter Summary

This chapter covers several commands and methods to increase your proficiency in Super-Calc. The income statement spreadsheet illustrates a variety of options and features. The more you explore and understand the various SuperCalc methods and tools for spreadsheet development—such as pointing and the special movement keys; absolute and relative referencing; copying, inserting, deleting, and moving; and title locking and window splitting—the more quickly you will develop accurate, professional spreadsheets. As you gain control over the various features of SuperCalc, you will find more and more tasks for this flexible package. In the next chapter, the focus changes to multiple and multipage spreadsheets, exciting new capabilities in SuperCalc5.

Part II

Learning SuperCalc's Intermediate Features

Includes

Adding Another Dimension:
Linked Spreadsheets

Functions: Part I

Functions: Part II

Adding Another Dimension: Linked Spreadsheets

The ability to consolidate important information from disparate spreadsheets and display it in a single summary spreadsheet is vital to obtaining an overview of a company's key financial statements. SuperCalc can enable you to do all this through page and spreadsheet *linking*. Sometimes referred to as three-dimensional spreadsheets, linked spreadsheets and linked pages of single spreadsheets provide powerful means of filtering unneeded details and automatically providing current summary information important for key management decisions.

This chapter focuses on how to link spreadsheets. Examples of linked spreadsheets (called *multiple spreadsheets*) and linked pages of individual spreadsheets (called *multipage spreadsheets*) are given. All commands associated with multiple and multipage spreadsheet manipulation are presented. In particular, emphasis is given to the //**S**preadsheets command and its several options. You learn how to load multiple spreadsheets into memory, remove individual spreadsheets from memory, view several spreadsheets simultaneously, create link references to other spreadsheet cells, create multipage spreadsheets, build supporting spreadsheets, and many other details.

Understanding Linked Spreadsheets

You should understand the terms used in this chapter to refer to multipage and multiple spreadsheets. Previous chapters concentrated on *single* spreadsheets that have no direct relationship with other spreadsheets, so many of the terms you see in this chapter are new.

Important Definitions

A *multipage* spreadsheet contains more than one page. By default, spreadsheets created and displayed in previous chapters were single-page spreadsheets. Each example spreadsheet occupied exactly one page, called page 1, of a potentially large number of pages. (The maximum number of pages in a single spreadsheet is 255.) The practical upper limit of pages a spreadsheet can contain is governed by the size of your computer's memory: the more memory, the more pages that can be created.

Multiple spreadsheets are integrated by cell references. A *consolidating* spreadsheet, providing summary information, may contain one or more formulas with references to cells found in different spreadsheets. These spreadsheet *links* (sometimes called *hot links*) provide the "glue" that binds several spreadsheets together into a cohesive, large model. Once established, the values displayed by these interspreadsheet links are updated whenever the spreadsheet is recalculated and the information they reference changes.

Spreadsheets containing cells or ranges of cells referenced by other spreadsheets are called *supporting* spreadsheets. Any spreadsheet containing a formula referencing another spreadsheet is known as a *dependent* spreadsheet. A spreadsheet can be both a supporting and a dependent spreadsheet simultaneously. Spreadsheets referenced with links may be in memory, on disk, or both.

The *current* spreadsheet is the spreadsheet displayed on-screen or in the case of a multiple-spreadsheet display, the spreadsheet where your cursor is located. The beginning of the status line displays the name of the current spreadsheet.

A spreadsheet is *open* when it is in memory (and is also called *memory resident*). Up to 255 spreadsheets can be open simultaneously, although your computer's memory may not handle that many. Spreadsheets referenced by the current spreadsheet but currently not in memory are called *disk resident*.

Keeping track of what spreadsheets are open (memory resident) can be difficult. The *Open Spreadsheet Directory* (OSD) contains a list of spreadsheet names and corresponding disk file names for each spreadsheet in memory. Similarly, the *Referenced Spreadsheet Directory* (RSD) lists all spreadsheets referenced (linked) by the current spreadsheet for both memory-resident and disk-resident spreadsheets. Both of these directories are described in this chapter.

General Concepts

Multipage and multiple spreadsheet linking provide several advantages previously not available to spreadsheet users. One of the most important advantages provided by linked spreadsheets and multipage spreadsheets is the fostering of hierarchical, structured, and modular spreadsheet model design and implementation. Analogous to hierarchical programming methodology, linked spreadsheets allow you to concentrate on a single spreadsheet at a time without concern for the aggregate, large spreadsheet system being developed. Individuals can be delegated the duties of developing detailed supporting spreadsheets that are part of a larger system, allowing these people to concentrate on

those details. Others can be tasked with developing higher level, dependent spreadsheets that display aggregate information useful for middle and upper management.

Individuals have greater control over parts of the larger spreadsheet system when they can create supporting sheets used by other sheets. Likewise, no one spreadsheet contains all the important details. Rather, the summary spreadsheet comprises several support spreadsheets under the purview of (hopefully) responsible individuals. This "divide and conquer" method provides a high degree of parallelism and saves overall development time. Additionally, a measure of security is provided by the support/dependent spreadsheet structure.

The issue of *where* spreadsheets are stored on disk becomes moot when using SuperCalc on a local area network. Spreadsheet control and storage can be distributed to remote locations best suited to supply supporting, detailed information.

In summary, large spreadsheet models cry out for dissection. No large spreadsheet can be easily understood unless and until it is restructured into linked layers of spreadsheets with successively finer details in supporting sheets and less detail in higher-level summary sheets.

Working with Multipage Spreadsheets

Multipage spreadsheets are handy when you want to work with a group of related spreadsheets always used together. Similar to a file folder containing individual pages, multipage spreadsheets are loaded as a group; you access an individual page to review or change by moving to it (open the folder to a particular page) (see fig. 6.1). You can move forward or backward through the pages. Additionally, you can add or remove one or more pages, just like you can in the file-folder analogy. Each page appears to be an ordinary spreadsheet, but each page following the first displays a page number in the upper left corner of the border. Multipage spreadsheets are also called three-dimensional spreadsheets because you can envision successive pages in a separate plane. The rows and columns are the normal, two dimensions; additional pages (each having their own rows and columns) make up the third dimension.

Multipage spreadsheets are useful in their own right, but interpage cell references (links) show the true power of three-dimensional spreadsheet models. Examples of multipage spreadsheets include summary and support spreadsheet pages in which each support page contains employee labor-hour information—the first page consolidates total hours for each employee and displays total hours for all employees for a particular project. As many individual multipage spreadsheets exist as there are projects in the functional entity. Other examples include summary sales information (page 1) supported by four additional pages containing detailed information about each sales quarter. A 13-page spreadsheet can summarize, in page 1, the total expenses and revenues for each of 12 months in a calendar year, where pages 2 through 13 contain detailed information about January through December.

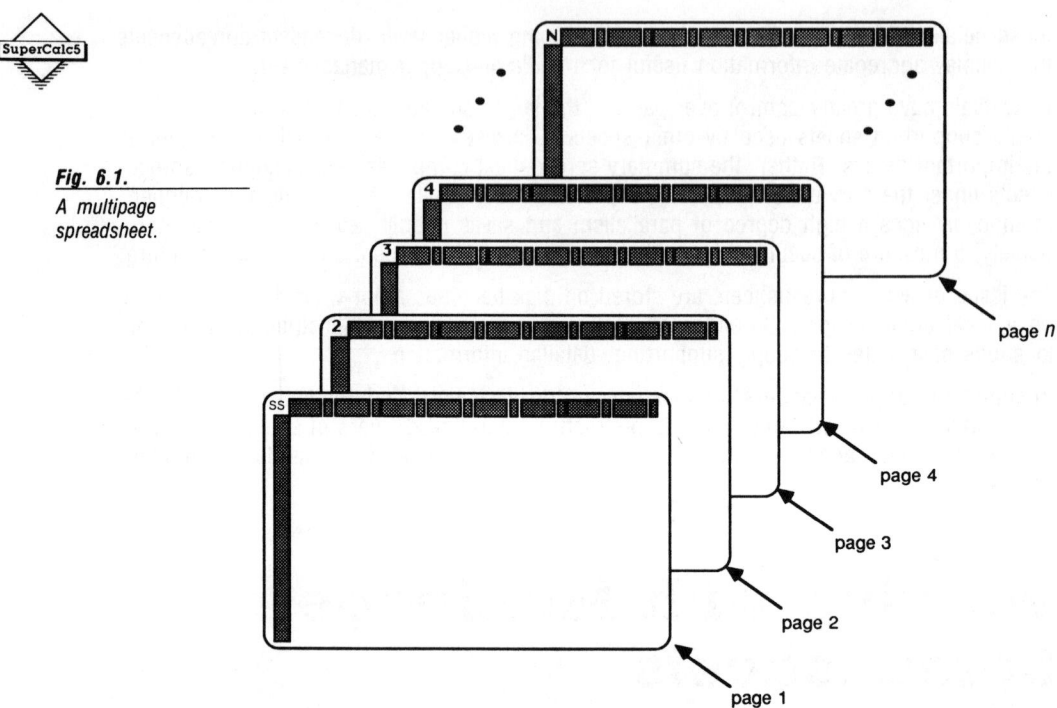

Fig. 6.1.

A multipage spreadsheet.

page *n*

page 4

page 3

page 2

page 1

This section develops a multipage spreadsheet introduced in Chapter 5 (similar to fig. 5.22). Later, this spreadsheet is to be linked to a different spreadsheet that summarizes information from this spreadsheet and others to produce an overview of a company's financial position for several of its divisions.

Creating Pages

Multipage spreadsheets—those with more than one page—are helpful when you want to create a group of related spreadsheets accessed (loaded, saved, and so on) together. A multipage spreadsheet is loaded and saved just like the single-page spreadsheets described in previous chapters. You can build each page of a multipage spreadsheet so that it is independent of the other pages, or you can create links between pages. An example from Chapter 5, the financial statements, is developed here as a spreadsheet containing two pages. Each page of the new spreadsheet contains the data stored previously as two separate spreadsheets. These two financial statements were stored in two independent spreadsheets (see fig. 6.2).

Because these statements are frequently used together, they can be incorporated into a single, two-page spreadsheet, with each quarter in a separate page. Later, when the third- and fourth-quarter financial values are determined, additional pages can be added, resulting in a four-page spreadsheet.

	A	B
5	Income	
6	Designs	$25,825
7	Consulting	28,860
8		
9	Total Income	$54,685
10		
11	Expenses	
12	Salaries	$35,678
13	Copyrights	400
14	Patents	442
15	Rent	3,000
16	Supplies	4,200
17	Utilities	300
18	Telephone	400
19	Miscellaneous	868
20		
21	Total Expenses	$45,288
22		
23	Net Income	$9,397
24		

First quarter

	A	B
5	Income	
6	Designs	$36,450
7	Consulting	42,400
8		
9	Total Income	$78,850
10		
11	Expenses	
12	Salaries	$51,238
13	Copyrights	400
14	Patents	442
15	Rent	3,200
16	Supplies	3,550
17	Utilities	350
18	Telephone	350
19	Miscellaneous	868
20		
21	Total Expenses	$60,398
22		
23	Net Income	$18,452
24		

Second quarter

Fig. 6.2.

First- and second-quarter financial statements from Chapter 5.

The first step to create a multipage spreadsheet is to enter the data for the first page. Whenever you create a new spreadsheet, it is stored in page 1. One way to build the first page of the multipage spreadsheet is to *load* the data from an existing spreadsheet. Load the first-quarter financial data by invoking SuperCalc. Then, load the first-quarter financial statement into the (empty) first page by executing the following command:

/Load,**QUARTER1**,Replace

where *QUARTER1* is the name of the first-quarter financial statement (substitute any appropriate name here). Alternatively, you can invoke SuperCalc and build the first-quarter spreadsheet from scratch.

Creating additional spreadsheet pages is easy. Once data for the first page has been entered, execute the /Insert,**P**age command to create as many additional pages as necessary. Figure 6.3 shows the steps used to create page 2 of the spreadsheet. Following is an explanation of the steps.

Press / and select **I**nsert (see fig. 6.3a). Notice that the last of the four choices displayed on the menu prompt line is **P**age (see fig. 6.3b). Press **P** to insert a new page. Because pages are numbered beginning with 1, you are prompted to enter the number of the page(s) you want to insert. If you enter **2** (indicating that page 2 is to be inserted), all existing pages are incremented by 1 to make room for the *new* page being inserted. If the spreadsheet contains pages 1 through 3, typing **2** moves the current page 2 to page 3, and page 3 to page 4. Press **2** to insert a new page 2 when the following prompt is displayed (see fig. 6.3c):

Enter pages to insert

Notice that after you press Enter to complete the page-insertion operation, the status line includes a page number (1) as part of the cell reference (see fig. 6.3d). This number indicates that the cursor is positioned in page 1, cell A10. When only a single page was in

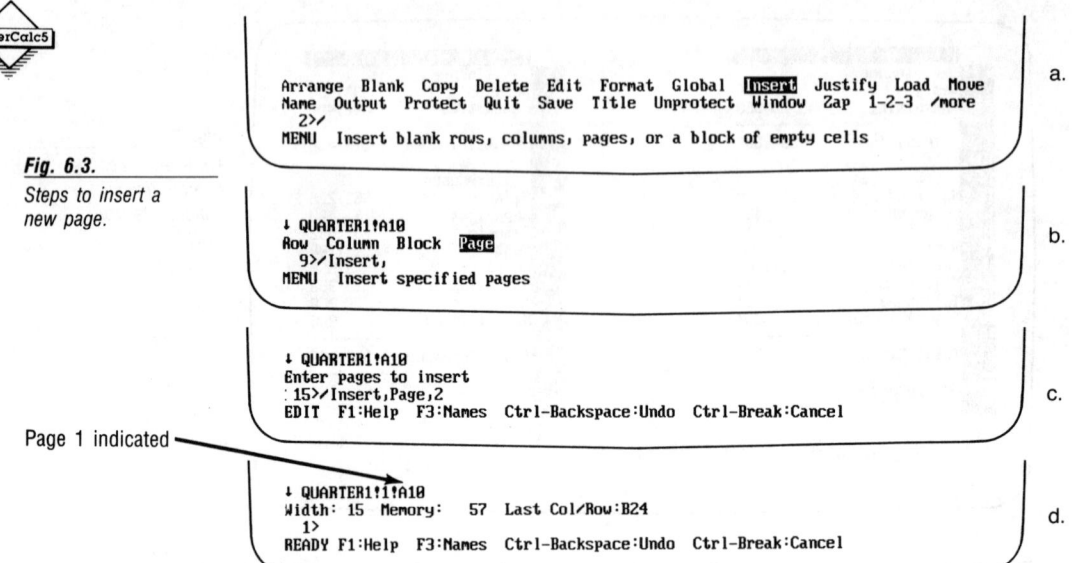

Fig. 6.3.

Steps to insert a new page.

```
                Arrange Blank Copy Delete Edit Format Global  Insert  Justify Load Move
                Name Output Protect Quit Save Title Unprotect Window Zap 1-2-3 /more
                  2>/
                MENU  Insert blank rows, columns, pages, or a block of empty cells
```
a.

```
                ↓ QUARTER1↑A10
                Row Column Block  Page
                  9>/Insert,
                MENU  Insert specified pages
```
b.

```
                ↓ QUARTER1↑A10
                Enter pages to insert
                : 15>/Insert,Page,2
                EDIT  F1:Help  F3:Names  Ctrl-Backspace:Undo  Ctrl-Break:Cancel
```
c.

Page 1 indicated ⟶

```
                ↓ QUARTER1!1↑A10
                Width: 15  Memory:   57  Last Col/Row:B24
                  1>
                READY  F1:Help  F3:Names  Ctrl-Backspace:Undo  Ctrl-Break:Cancel
```
d.

the spreadsheet, the cursor location indicator contained no page reference. This number is your first indication of how to reference cells in multiple pages. The general form of a cell reference is as follows:

spreadsheetname!pagenumber!cellrange

where *spreadsheetname* (QUARTER1 in this example) is separated from *pagenumber* (1 in this example) by an exclamation point. Likewise, *cellrange* is separated from *pagenumber* by an exclamation point.

If you wanted to display, in cell C6 of page 1, the value of cell B9 of page 2 of this spreadsheet, for example, you would move the cursor to cell C6 and enter the following formula:

QUARTER1!2!B9

or

2!B9

Inserting a new page is only half of the process. Creating a new page (using /Insert,Page,2) merely inserts an empty page into memory. Therefore, you must go to page 2 and insert data into it.

Moving to Another Page

To put data into a new page, you must know how to move the spreadsheet cursor to that page—that is, how to go to a particular page. This section explains how to move to page 2 and put the second-quarter financial information into it.

You can use one of several special key sequences to move to different pages in a single spreadsheet. These key sequences begin with either the Ctrl key or the Tab key. To move to the *next* page—the next higher numbered page from the current page—hold the Ctrl key and press the plus (+) key on the numeric keypad. This key is called the *gray plus* key. Press Ctrl-gray minus (hold Ctrl and press the gray minus key simultaneously) to move to the *preceding* page. Other page-movement key sequences are summarized in table 6.1.

Table 6.1
Multipage Spreadsheet Special Keys and Commands
(* means to use the gray keys)

Action	Special Key	Command
Open (insert) new page in memory		/**I**nsert,**P**age,*n*
Load new page into memory		/**L**oad,*spreadsheet*,**S**ingle
Move page(s)		/**M**ove,**P**age
Delete page(s)		/**D**elete,**P**age
Display Open Spreadsheet Directory (OSD)	Ctrl-F4	
Go to next page	Ctrl-plus*	
Go to preceding page	Ctrl-minus*	
Go to particular page	Ctrl-F5 or Ctrl-=	
Go to first page	Tab-Ctrl-Home	
Go to last page	Tab-Ctrl-End	
Go to first page of next spreadsheet	Tab-Ctrl-plus*	
Go to last page of preceding spreadsheet	Tab-Ctrl-minus*	
Move to next display window	Ctrl-F6	
Display multiple pages		//**S**preadsheets,**D**isplay,*n*
Display one page (several windows displayed)	Ctrl-F7	//**S**preadsheets,**D**isplay,**Z**oom,**Y**es
Hide one or more pages		//**S**preadsheets,**H**ide
Unhide one or more pages		//**S**preadsheets,**U**nhide
Toggle between multiple- and one-page display	Ctrl-F7	

Table 6.1—*Continued*

Action	Special Key	Command
Save current spreadsheet (all pages) and quit SuperCalc		/**Q**uit,**S**ave
Quit SuperCalc without saving current spreadsheet		/**Q**uit,**Y**es (repeatedly)
Save all modified spreadsheets		//**S**preadsheets,**S**ave
Save all modified spreadsheets and then clear (blank) current one		//**S**preadsheets,**Z**ap,**S**ave
Save all modified spreadsheets and then quit SuperCalc		//**S**preadsheets,**Q**uit,**S**ave
Abandon all open spreadsheets and quit SuperCalc		//**S**preadsheets,**Q**uit,**Y**es

To move to page 2 of the two-page spreadsheet, press Ctrl-gray plus. You can see which page is currently displayed by looking at the page number in the upper left corner of the screen—at the intersection of the row and column borders. It displays 2, indicating that you have moved to page 2.

The simplest way to fill in the second-quarter financial information (shown in fig. 6.2, on the right) is to /**L**oad it. Assuming that the second-quarter financial information is in a file called QUARTER2, execute the following command and press Enter:

   /**L**oad,**QUARTER2**,**S**ingle,**1**,**R**eplace

Be careful! *Do not* execute the following command:

   /**L**oad,**QUARTER2**,**R**eplace

The second command replaces the entire spreadsheet, not just page 2! Why? Because the /**R**eplace command immediately following the spreadsheet name to be loaded replaces the entire memory-resident spreadsheet, destroying page 1, which contains the first-quarter financial information. To load a single page of a multipage spreadsheet, first create page 2 (/**I**nsert,**P**age,**2**). Then move to page 2 and enter

   /**L**oad,**QUARTER2**,**S**ingle,**1**,**R**eplace

When loading one of several pages, always use /**L**oad,**S**ingle. The **S**ingle option alters only the currently displayed page (be sure that you have moved to page 2), not *all* pages of the memory-resident spreadsheet. Type **1** to change the suggested page to 1. After pressing Enter to complete the last step, the following message displays briefly:

   Loading...

The spreadsheet QUARTER2.CAL is then placed into page 2 (see fig. 6.4) of the memory-resident spreadsheet model being built. Specifying **1** in the command /**L**oad,**QUARTER2**,**S**ingle,**1** loads page 1 of QUARTER2 into page 2 of the open spreadsheet.

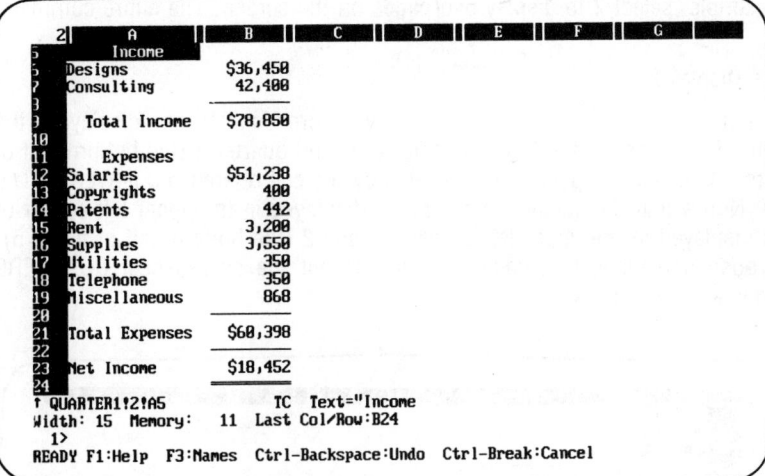

Fig. 6.4.

Page 2 after the QUARTER2 spreadsheet is loaded.

Notice that the upper left corner of the display shows the number 2, indicating that the second page of the spreadsheet is displayed. The cursor location in the status line indicates the spreadsheet name, the page number, and the cell (QUARTER1!2!A5).

Viewing Several Pages Simultaneously

When a spreadsheet contains several pages, it is often convenient to view parts of several pages simultaneously. SuperCalc can display a maximum of three pages at one time. To view parts of the two financial quarters created so far, execute the //Spreadsheets command (be sure to type two slashes). Then select Display. The menu prompt line displays the following choices:

```
    1  2  3  Synchronize  Unsynchronize  Zoom
```

Choices **1**, **2**, and **3** control how many spreadsheet pages (windows) are displayed simultaneously. **S**ynchronize, the default multiple spreadsheet display mode, displays the current spreadsheet with adjacent spreadsheet pages. When you press Ctrl-gray plus or Ctrl-gray minus, the spreadsheets in other windows also move forward or backward. When only one spreadsheet is displayed, **S**ynchronize has no effect.

Unsynchronize has the opposite effect: multiple spreadsheets in separate windows do not move in synchrony when you move to a new page in the spreadsheet window. Each display window is independent of the others.

Zoom toggles between multipage (or spreadsheet) display (**Z**oom,**N**o) and full screen display (**Z**oom,**Y**es) of the current page (or spreadsheet). Pressing Ctrl-F7 has the same effect. Press Ctrl-F7 to display only the current page; press it again to display multiple pages (or spreadsheets).

For the current example, select **2** to display two pages on the screen. The entire command displayed is

//**S**preadsheets,**D**isplay,**2**

After you press Enter to complete the command, two spreadsheets are displayed: the financial statements for quarter 1 (the top half of fig. 6.5) and quarter 2 (the bottom half of fig. 6.5). The cursor is located in page 2 as indicated by the cell reference QUARTER1!2!A5 in the status line. Notice that the spreadsheet name is displayed in the upper left corner of page 1, and 2 is displayed in the upper left corner of page 2 (the bottom half of fig. 6.5). The QUARTER1 open spreadsheet contains two pages, but the spreadsheet QUARTER2 remains in its original form on disk.

Fig. 6.5.

Two-page display example.

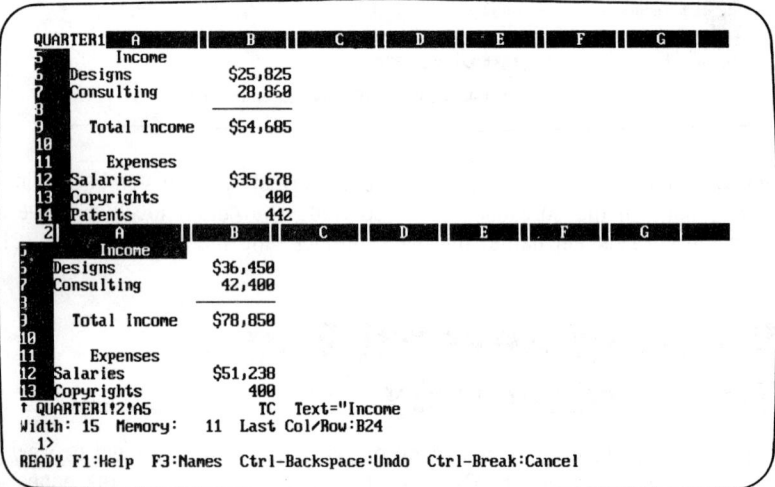

You can move between the spreadsheet "windows" by pressing Ctrl-gray plus or Ctrl-gray minus. Alternatively, you can press Ctrl-F6 to jump between the two pages. When you press Ctrl-F6 repeatedly, the display doesn't change, but the cursor jumps between the two displayed pages. Practice using both Ctrl-gray plus and Ctrl-F6 to see the subtle difference.

To switch back to a single spreadsheet display, press Ctrl-F7 or execute either of the following commands:

//**S**preadsheets,**D**isplay,**1**

//**S**preadsheets,**D**isplay,**Z**oom,**Y**es

To complete the multipage example, create page 3 and page 4 and insert information for the third and fourth quarters into them. Follow these steps for page 3:

1. Execute /**I**nsert,**P**age,**3**.

2. Move to page 3.

3. Fill in page 3 with data shown in column 3 of figure 6.6 (the third quarter).

Repeat these steps for page 4. If you are following the examples in this book and re-creating them in SuperCalc, use figure 6.6 as a guide to fill in the last two pages. The four pages are displayed side-by-side in the figure but are located in pages 1 through 4 as they are displayed (left to right).

	A	B	B	B	B
	Income				
5	Designs	$25,825	$36,450	$62,350	$68,500
6	Consulting	28,860	42,400	14,000	30,450
7					
8					
9	Total Income	$54,685	$78,850	$76,350	$98,950
10					
11	Expenses				
12	Salaries	$35,678	$51,238	$56,000	$61,000
13	Copyrights	400	400	600	400
14	Patents	442	442	555	700
15	Rent	3,000	3,200	3,200	2,900
16	Supplies	4,200	3,550	4,200	3,500
17	Utilities	300	350	400	395
18	Telephone	400	350	700	500
19	Miscellaneous	868	868	567	463
20					
21	Total Expenses	$45,288	$60,398	$66,222	$69,858
22					
23	Net Income	$9,397	$18,452	$10,128	$29,092
24					
		Quarter 1	Quarter 2	Quarter 3	Quarter 4

Fig. 6.6.
The completed four-page display.

Hiding and Unhiding Pages

If some spreadsheet pages contain sensitive information, or if you merely wish temporarily to suppress the display of certain pages, you can hide them. Hidden pages remain in the spreadsheet and in memory but cannot be viewed when you press Ctrl-gray plus, Ctrl-gray minus, or Ctrl-=. When you leaf through spreadsheet pages by repeatedly pressing Ctrl-gray plus, for example, any hidden pages are not displayed—they are skipped. Regardless of the page currently displayed or the window the cursor is in, you can hide selected pages with the following command:

//**S**preadsheets,**H**ide

After you type //**SH**, the following message prompts you to enter the page number to hide:

    Enter sheet, page or page range to hide

You can hide page 3 of the four-page financial statement example by executing the following command:

//**S**preadsheets,**H**ide,**3**

Figure 6.7 shows an overview of what it means to hide a page. You can hide all pages of a spreadsheet by executing

//**S**preadsheets,**H**ide,*spreadsheetname*

If only one spreadsheet is open, however, you cannot hide all its pages.

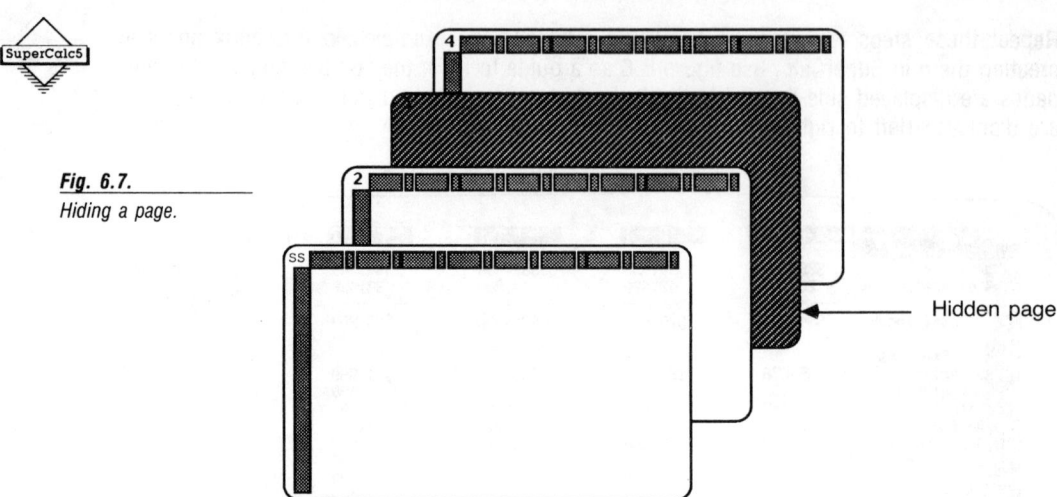

Fig. 6.7.

Hiding a page.

Hidden page

One or more spreadsheets or pages of individual spreadsheets can be unhidden by executing the **U**nhide command. You can unhide pages 3 through 4 by executing the following command:

//**S**preadsheets,**U**nhide,**3:4**

Displaying the Open Spreadsheet Directory

The *Open Spreadsheet Directory* (OSD) displays the name and page number of each spreadsheet loaded into memory. OSD is useful when you want to keep track of the names of spreadsheets loaded and the number of pages in each. The OSD is displayed whenever you press Ctrl-F4. Figure 6.8 shows an example.

Fig. 6.8.

The Open Spreadsheet Directory.

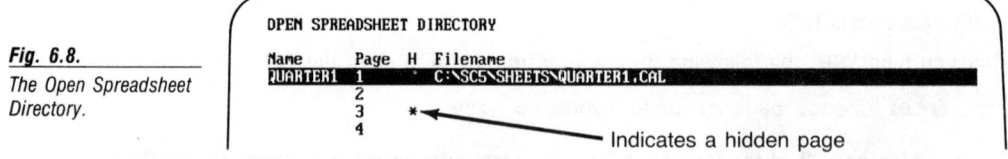

Indicates a hidden page

Four columns are displayed in the OSD. The first column, Name, displays the spreadsheet name. The second column lists the memory-resident pages of the spreadsheet. The third column, H, contains an asterisk (*) if the page is hidden; otherwise, the column is blank. The fourth column lists the fully qualified disk file name of the spreadsheet if it was loaded from other than the default data directory. In figure 6.8, the file name displayed is

C:\SC5\SHEETS\QUARTER1.CAL

Because the default directory is C:\SC5 in this example, the fully qualified file name is displayed. Had QUARTER1 been located in the default directory and loaded from there, QUARTER1 would be displayed in the fourth column (see fig. 6.8). Press Esc to return to the spreadsheet.

Moving and Deleting Pages

To move pages in an open spreadsheet, use the /**M**ove,**P**age command. Then enter the page or page range you want to move. When the following prompt displays, enter the number of the page the selected pages are to *follow*:

    Enter target page position

Executing the following command, for example, moves page 2 to the fourth page (the page following page 3):

    /**M**ove,Page,**2,3**

Page 3 is renumbered to page 2. Any pages preceding the target page are decremented by one. (If more than one page is moved, then pages preceding the target page are decremented by the number of pages moved.) In the preceding command, for example, if pages 4, 5, and 6 existed before page 2 was moved to page 3, then page 3 becomes 2.

One or more pages in the open spreadsheet can be deleted by executing the /**D**elete,**P**age command. Type /**DP** and then enter the page or range of pages to delete. When you press Enter, you are asked to confirm the deletion with the following menu prompt:

    No   Yes

Press **Y** to complete the delete operation. The following command, for example, deletes pages 2 and 3:

    /**D**elete,Page,**2:3**,Yes

Pages following the deleted range of pages are renumbered correspondingly (for example, page 4 becomes page 2, and so on).

Referencing Other Pages with Link Formulas

The multipage spreadsheet created in this chapter consists of four *independent* pages. Creating a four-page spreadsheet is a convenient way of storing pages used together in one spreadsheet. The real power of three-dimensional spreadsheets, however, is not realized until interpage cell references, or *links*, are used. When you link spreadsheets, any cell can contain a reference to a cell or range of cells found in other pages of open spreadsheets or page 1 of any spreadsheet—on disk or open.

Suppose, for example, that you want an easy-to-read summary of the four quarters of information found in the four pages of your financial statement spreadsheet. A fifth (summary) page can be created containing summary information from each of the other four pages. This *dependent* or *consolidation* spreadsheet could contain eight linked cell references to each quarter's *Total Income* and *Total Expenses* cells. The following example builds a simple summary page to show how interpage cell references (links) work.

The first step is to create a new, summary page. Create a new page by executing the following command:

/Insert,Page,1

The summary page is now the first page, displacing existing pages by one page. Now five pages are in memory: the (empty) summary page, and pages 2, 3, 4, and 5, containing information about quarters 1, 2, 3, and 4, respectively. Duplicate the spreadsheet shown in figure 6.9 to begin building the summary page.

Fig. 6.9.

Summary page with labels entered.

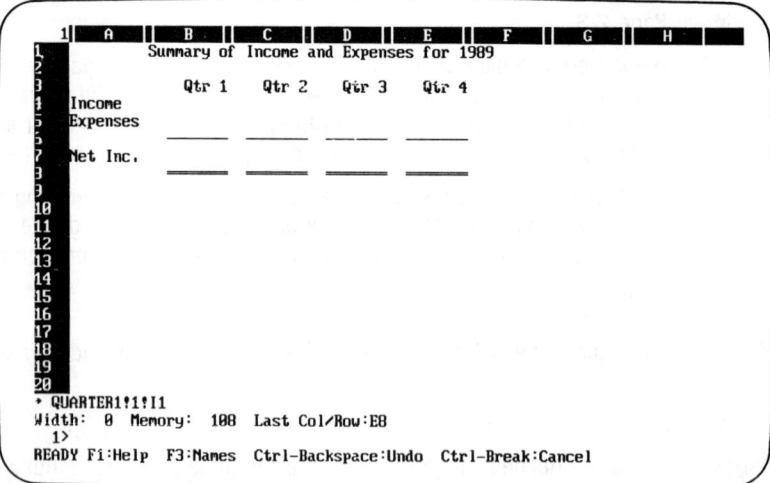

The underlines in row 6 are created by holding down the Alt key and simultaneously pressing the keys 1, 9, and 6 on the numeric keypad (Alt-196). Similarly, the double underlines are created by pressing Alt-205. All text entries in columns B through E are formatted TextRight (see Chapter 4).

Move to cell B4 and enter the formula **2!B9**. This is a link formula that references cell B9 on page 2—the cell containing the *Total Income* for the first quarter. In cells C4 through E4 enter the formulas **3!B9**, **4!B9**, and **5!B9**, respectively. These link formulas reference the *Total Income* (cell B9) found in pages 3, 4, and 5, corresponding to the 2nd, 3rd, and 4th quarters.

Enter into cells B5, C5, D5, and E5 the link formulas referencing *Total Expenses* in each of the four quarters. These formulas are **2!B21**, **3!B21**, **4!B21**, and **5!B21**. The four formulas

in row 7 (B7 through E7) are the difference between *Income* and *Expe* ter: **B4 − B5**, **C4 − C5**, **D4 − D5**, and **E4 − E5**. Figure 6.10 shows the c sheet. It has been split into two windows so that the bottom window (using the /**G**lobal,**F**ormula command) and the top window shows the Examine the lower window carefully, paying particular attention to the li in cells B4 through E5.

```
 1   A   ||   B   ||   C   ||   D   ||   E   ||   F   ||   G   ||   H
 1              Summary of Income and Expenses for 1989
 2
 3            Qtr 1    Qtr 2    Qtr 3    Qtr 4
 4 Income    $54,685  $78,050  $76,350  $98,950
 5 Expenses   45,288   68,398   66,222   69,858
 6
 7 Net Inc.   $9,397  $18,452  $18,128  $29,092
 8
 9

     A   ||   B   ||   C   ||   D   ||   E   ||   F   ||   G   ||   H
 1              Summary of Income and Expenses for 1989
 2
 3            Qtr 1    Qtr 2    Qtr 3    Qtr 4
 4 Income    2!B9     3!B9     4!B9     5!B9
 5 Expenses  2!B21    3!B21    4!B21    5!B21
 6
 7 Net Inc.  B4-B5    C4-C5    D4-D5    E4-E5
 8
 9
10
 + QUARTER1!1!B4        U1      Form=2!B9
 Width:  9  Memory:  107  Last Col/Row:E8
      1>
 READY F1:Help  F3:Names  Ctrl-Backspace:Undo  Ctrl-Break:Cancel
```

Fig. 6.10.

Completed summary page with link formulas to other pages.

Avoiding the Copy Trap

Instead of entering a link formula such as 2!B9 in the summary sheet (as shown in fig. 6.10), why isn't the /**C**opy command used to copy a cell into the summary sheet? Using /**C**opy is a trap, an error, that is demonstrated here. One of the big advantages of establishing "hot links" to cells and cell ranges in other pages is that whenever supporting data changes, the dependent spreadsheet cell containing the link formula changes automatically. Cells in a summary sheet containing data *copied* from other pages do not change when the corresponding data in another page changes. Copied cells are *static* links—not really links at all.

The second, more subtle, problem with copying cells from other pages is that the source cell *contents* are copied to the summary sheet cell—not necessarily the displayed *value* of the cell. The next example illustrates these fallacies. To simplify the example and focus on inherent problems with interpage /**C**opy commands, save the current spreadsheet and clear memory by executing the following command:

/**Z**ap,**S**ave

Next, create a two-page spreadsheet. Insert page 2 with the /Insert,**P**age,**2** command. Display both pages so that you can see both the summary page (page 1), and the support page (page 2). Use the following command to do this:

//**S**preadsheets,**D**isplay,**2**

Move to page 2 (press Ctrl-F6). Enter the value **10000** in cell A1. Enter the value **15000** in cell A2. Enter the formula **SUM(A1:A2)** in cell A3. Now move back to page 1, the summary sheet. In cell A3 enter the link formula **2!A3**. The value 25000 is displayed in cell A3. Next, copy cell 2!A3 (cell A3 in page 2) to cell B3 in page 1 by executing the following /**C**opy command:

/**C**opy,**2!A3,B3**

The problem appears! Cell B3 displays a zero. Figure 6.11 shows the spreadsheet.

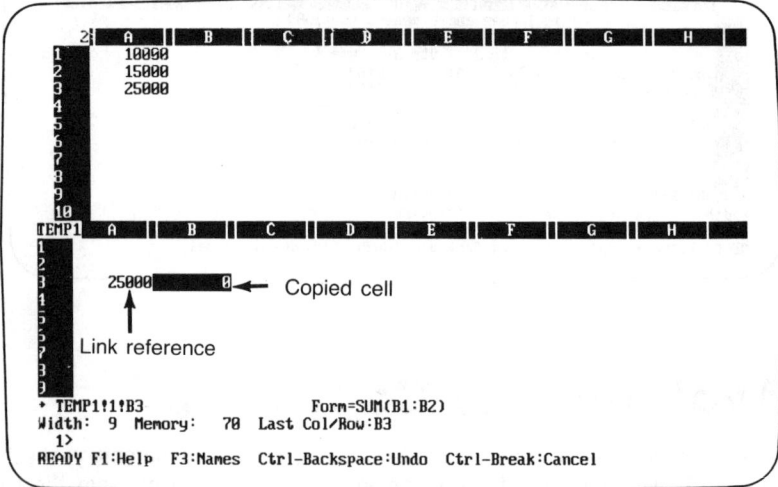

Fig. 6.11.

Link cell reference versus copied cell.

Examine the status line. There's the problem. Cell B3 contains the *formula* SUM(B1:B2). In other words, when you copy a cell from another page, its *contents* are copied (unless you specify the **V**alues option). Cell references in the copied cell are adjusted to reflect the relative movement of the formula from one page to another. If cell A3 in page 2 had contained the following formula, the /**C**opy would have generated the correct results in the target cell (page 1, cell B3):

SUM(2!$A$1:$A$2)

The lesson here is that it's best to use link formulas rather than copy cells from other pages, especially when accuracy is important for dependent cells (those containing the link formulas). Copied values are *static* and don't necessarily reflect the current values of cells from which they were copied.

When is it appropriate to copy cells? Copying cells when you are creating a new page that is a clone of an extant page with minor changes is fine. If you want to create another page (for example, page 6) that contains first-quarter 1990 information in the same form as that of page 2 (containing first-quarter 1989 information), copying the entire page 2 to the new page 6 is correct. Once the cells are copied, you can move to page 6 and fill in the correct financial information for the first quarter of 1990.

Execute /**Z**ap,**Y**es to clear memory (close this example). Load the QUARTER1 spreadsheet that you saved prior to the preceding experiment (see fig. 6.10).

Renaming the Current Spreadsheet

After you have constructed a multipage spreadsheet comprising pages of other spreadsheets and pages you have created manually, you may wish to save it under a different name. The spreadsheet you have been working on is currently called QUARTER1 (refer to fig. 6.10). The //**S**preadsheets,**R**ename command is used to rename one or more *open* spreadsheets (spreadsheets in memory). A renamed spreadsheet can be saved on disk under its new name; in this way, you can avoid altering a disk file spreadsheet listed under the same name.

The steps to rename a spreadsheet are shown in figure 6.12. First, type // and select **S**preadsheets (see fig. 6.12a). Then select the **R**ename option (see fig. 6.12b). When prompted for the new spreadsheet name, type **SUMM1989** and press Enter (see fig. 6.12c). The new spreadsheet name is displayed in the upper left position in the dialog panel (see fig. 6.12d).

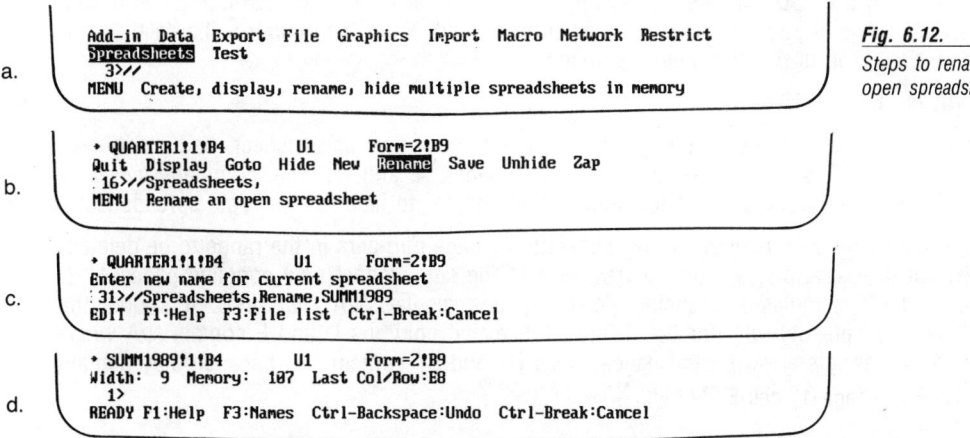

a.
```
Add-in Data Export File Graphics Import Macro Network Restrict
Spreadsheets Test
 3>//
MENU Create, display, rename, hide multiple spreadsheets in memory
```

b.
```
 • QUARTER1↑1↑B4      U1      Form=2↑B9
Quit Display Goto Hide New Rename Save Unhide Zap
 : 16>//Spreadsheets,
MENU  Rename an open spreadsheet
```

c.
```
 • QUARTER1↑1↑B4      U1      Form=2↑B9
Enter new name for current spreadsheet
 : 31>//Spreadsheets,Rename,SUMM1989
EDIT F1:Help F3:File list Ctrl-Break:Cancel
```

d.
```
 • SUMM1989↑1↑B4      U1      Form=2↑B9
Width: 9 Memory: 107 Last Col/Row:E8
 1>
READY F1:Help F3:Names Ctrl-Backspace:Undo Ctrl-Break:Cancel
```

Fig. 6.12.

Steps to rename an open spreadsheet.

You can rename the current spreadsheet no matter where the spreadsheet cursor is positioned (for example, the cursor can be in page 4). The spreadsheet to be renamed, however, must be the *current* spreadsheet. If several spreadsheets are open (if multiple spreadsheets are in memory), move to the spreadsheet you want to rename first. Otherwise, the wrong spreadsheet is renamed.

If you press Ctrl-F4 to display the Open Spreadsheet Directory, observe that both the Name and Filename columns are changed to reflect the new spreadsheet name (see fig. 6.13). (If you were to save the spreadsheet, it would be placed in the default SuperCalc5 directory.)

Fig. 6.13.

The Open Spreadsheet Directory after renaming the spreadsheet.

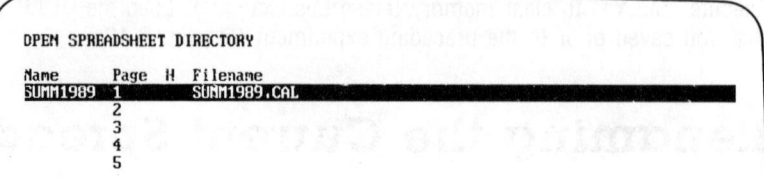

```
OPEN SPREADSHEET DIRECTORY

Name      Page  H  Filename
SUMM1989   1       SUMM1989.CAL
           2
           3
           4
           5
```

Deleting and Clearing Pages

Individual pages of a spreadsheet may be either *deleted* or *cleared*. These two actions are not the same. When you delete one or more pages, all subsequent pages are renumbered. When you clear a page, no pages are renumbered: the cleared page remains part of the spreadsheet, but the page is empty.

Deleting Pages

Pages are deleted with the /**D**elete,**P**age command. Suppose that you want to remove pages 4 and 5 of SUMM1989, for example. Execute the command /**D**elete,**P**age and then enter the range of pages to be deleted when prompted. Enter **Y** to confirm the delete command. Following is the complete command:

/**D**elete,**P**age,**4:5**,**Y**es

If you are following the examples in this book with your own spreadsheet, be sure to save the SUMM1989 spreadsheet before deleting pages 4 and 5. The complete five-page SUMM1989 spreadsheet is needed later in this chapter to illustrate multiple spreadsheets.

Either a period (.) or a colon (:) may separate the page numbers in the range to be deleted. After you press Y, pages 4 and 5 are deleted. The spreadsheet now contains pages 1, 2, and 3. Link formulas referencing deleted pages display N/A. Figure 6.14 shows the SUMM1989 spreadsheet after the delete. Notice that columns D and E contain N/A wherever formulas reference deleted pages. Cells D7 and E7 contain N/A because they contain SUM formulas for cells containing N/A.

Clearing Pages

Individual pages of a multipage spreadsheet can be cleared without closing the entire spreadsheet. Execute /**Z**ap,**P**age to clear the currently displayed page. Be careful! After you press **P**, SuperCalc does not prompt you for confirmation. The current page is cleared immediately. It cannot be recovered unless the undo feature (Ctrl-Backspace) is enabled.

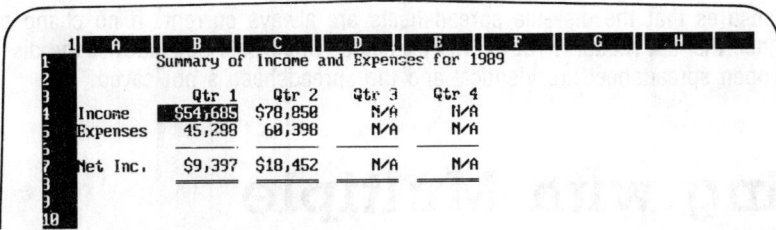

Fig. 6.14.
SUMM1989 after pages 4 and 5 are deleted.

The entire spreadsheet (all of its pages) can be cleared by executing the following command:

/**Z**ap,**Y**es

Again, be careful. After you press **Y**, all pages of the current spreadsheet are cleared. In addition, all pages are removed from memory (*closed*) except page 1, which is empty. Pressing undo (Ctrl-Backspace) restores the spreadsheet pages when undo is enabled. (Undo is enabled by executing /**G**lobal,**O**ptimum,**P**resent,**U**ndo,**Y**es.)

Saving Multipage Spreadsheets

Like the /**L**oad, all the main /**S**ave options work with multipage spreadsheets. You can save multipage spreadsheets in one of three ways. The "usual" way is simply to execute the following command:

/**S**ave,*spreadsheetname*

where *spreadsheetname* is the disk file name under which the spreadsheet is saved. This command saves all the pages of the spreadsheet, even if no modifications have been made since it was loaded.

The second way to save a spreadsheet is to save individual pages. By executing /**S**ave,*spreadsheetname*,**S**ingle, you can save any page in its own disk file. After you press **S**ingle, SuperCalc prompts you for the page number to be saved:

    Enter page number

Enter the page number; the familiar /**S**ave options appear:

    All Values Part Duplicate Level Mode

Select one of the /**S**ave options to save the current page. To save page 3 (second-quarter financial information) in a disk file named SUMMPAG3, for example, execute the following command:

/**S**ave,**SUMMPAG3**,**S**ingle,**3**,**A**ll

A third way to save a spreadsheet is to execute the //**S**preadsheets,**S**ave command. Unlike the /**S**ave command, this command saves all pages of the *current* spreadsheet only if they have been modified. Periodically executing the following command is a good idea:

//**S**preadsheets,**S**ave

This command ensures that the disk-file spreadsheets are always current. If no changes have occurred since the last /Load or /Save was executed, SuperCalc detects that the disk version and the open spreadsheet are identical and the spreadsheet is not saved.

Working with Multiple Spreadsheets

The term *multiple spreadsheets* refers to spreadsheets related to one another by inter-spreadsheet-link formulas. Like a multipage spreadsheet, a group of related spreadsheets contains one or more link formulas that establish a relationship between dependent and supporting spreadsheets. An overview or consolidation spreadsheet can contain summary information retrieved from other support spreadsheets. Support spreadsheets can be in memory (''open'') or they can be on disk. Figure 6.15 illustrates a typical summary/support spreadsheets relationship.

All the commands and features described for *multipage* spreadsheets have analogous commands and features for *multiple* spreadsheets. Cell contents can be copied from one spreadsheet to another, cell ranges found in supporting spreadsheets (either on disk or in memory) can be summed, and several spreadsheets can be memory resident simultaneously. You can move from one open spreadsheet to the next one, move directly to a particular spreadsheet, hide and unhide one or more spreadsheets, and delete or clear open spreadsheets. These and more multiple spreadsheet features are described in this section. A four-spreadsheet model shows the many extraordinary SuperCalc features used to work with multiple related spreadsheets. The example to be used consists of a dependent summary spreadsheet and three supporting spreadsheets.

Creating Multiple Open Spreadsheets

When you create multiple linked spreadsheets, the easiest method is sometimes to build the consolidation or summary spreadsheet-link formulas with all the supporting sheets in memory. This arrangement is not required, but you can use POINT mode to create link formulas as you view both supporting and dependent spreadsheets. A multidivision summary illustrates this procedure.

Leave the SUMM1989 spreadsheet in memory and build two more supporting spreadsheets that summarize income, expenses, and net income for the company's other two divisions. When completed, the summary spreadsheet is to display total income, total expenses, and total net income for the three divisions named Lateral Designs, Rehab Systems, and Consulting Services. Lateral Designs is already completed and open in memory (SUMM1989 shown in fig. 6.10). The following sections explain how to build the Rehab Systems and Consulting Services support spreadsheets.

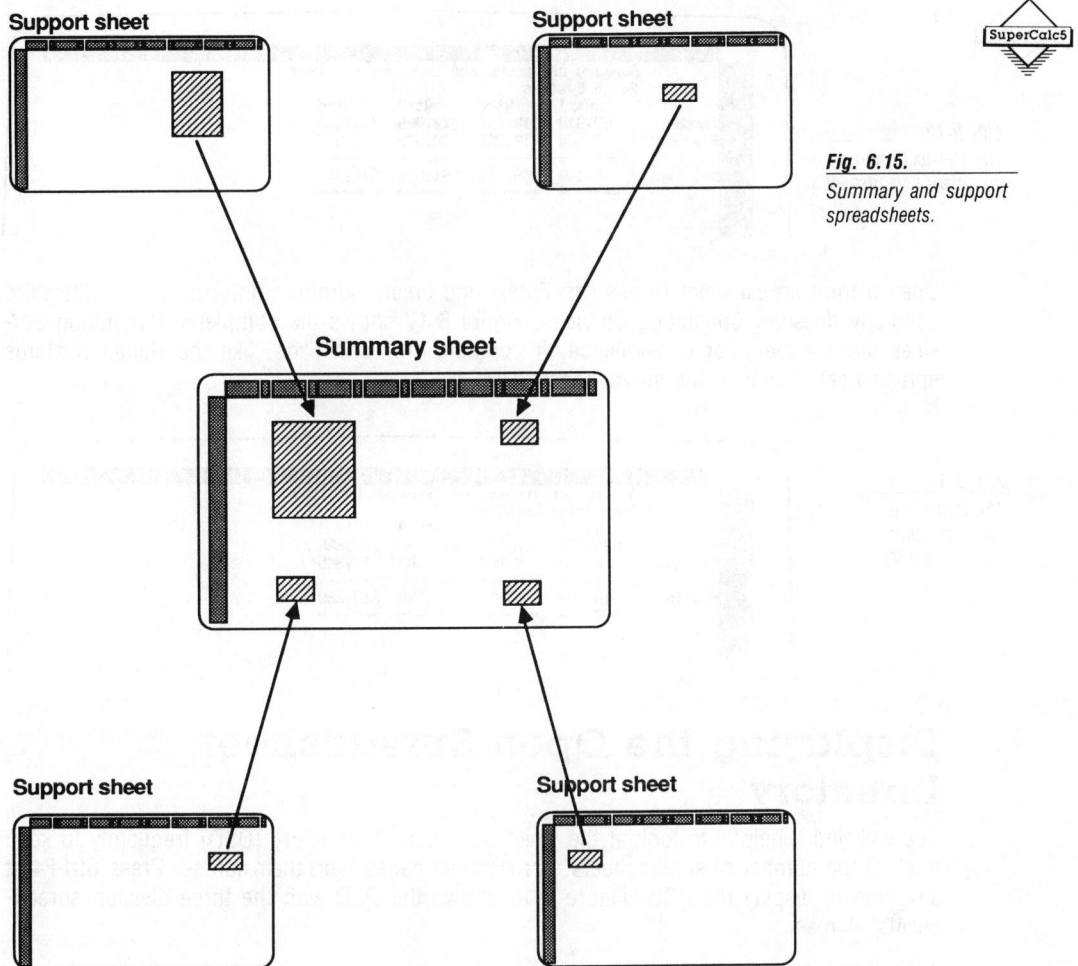

SuperCalc5

Fig. 6.15.
Summary and support
spreadsheets.

Opening a Spreadsheet

Begin by opening a new spreadsheet "frame" in memory. To create a new open spreadsheet, press Ctrl-Enter. For convenience, the Rehab Systems spreadsheet consists of only one page, the summary of all four quarters. The completed Rehab Systems spreadsheet, consisting entirely of numeric constants and text (no references to other pages) is shown in figure 6.16.

Use the command //**S**preadsheets,**R**ename (refer to fig. 6.12) to rename the current spreadsheet to **SUMR1989**.

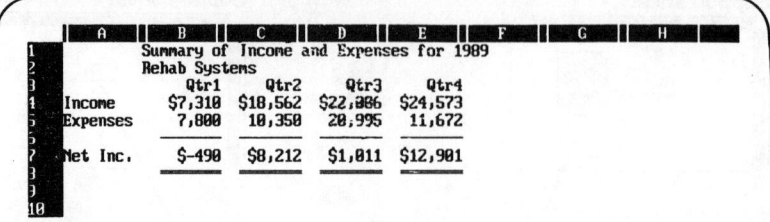

Fig. 6.16.

The Rehab Systems summary spreadsheet.

Open a third spreadsheet (press Ctrl-Enter) and create summary information for the third company division, Consulting Services. Figure 6.17 shows the completed Consulting Services spreadsheet. For convenience, it contains only one page, like the Rehab Systems spreadsheet. Rename this spreadsheet SUMC1989.

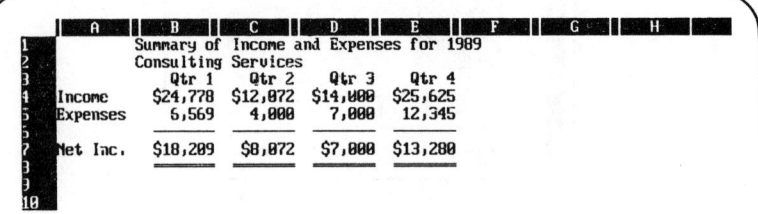

Fig. 6.17.

The Consulting Services summary spreadsheet.

Displaying the Open Spreadsheet Directory

You will find it helpful to look at the Open Spreadsheet Directory (OSD) frequently to keep track of the number of spreadsheets, spreadsheet pages, and their names. Press Ctrl-F4 at any time to display the OSD. Figure 6.18 shows the OSD with the three division spreadsheets' names.

Fig. 6.18.

The Open Spreadsheet Directory with the three division spreadsheets names.

```
OPEN SPREADSHEET DIRECTORY

Name      Page  H  Filename
SUMM1989   1       SUMM1989.CAL
           2
           3
           4
           5
SUMR1989   1       SUMR1989.CAL
SUMC1989   1       SUMC1989.CAL
```

Note that SUMM1989 has five pages; both SUMR1989 and SUMC1989 contain only one page each. The Filename column indicates that the spreadsheets are stored in the default directory when saved. Press Esc to return to the normal spreadsheet display.

Hiding and Unhiding Spreadsheets and Spreadsheet Pages

You can hide or unhide any open spreadsheets or spreadsheet pages. Often, hiding one or more spreadsheets or pages is convenient when you move from one spreadsheet to another by pressing Ctrl-gray plus or Ctrl-gray minus as you create link formulas. When you hide selected spreadsheets or pages, they do not display as you move among the open spreadsheets. Later, you can execute the **U**nhide option to display the hidden items.

In the next section, you create in a summary sheet link formulas that display summary information from each of the supporting division spreadsheets. Because viewing the individual pages of the supporting sheets is unnecessary (only the first page containing the aggregate, four-quarter summary data is referenced), pages 2 through 5 can be hidden. Figure 6.19 illustrates the steps to hide spreadsheet pages. The procedure is identical for hiding one or more complete spreadsheets.

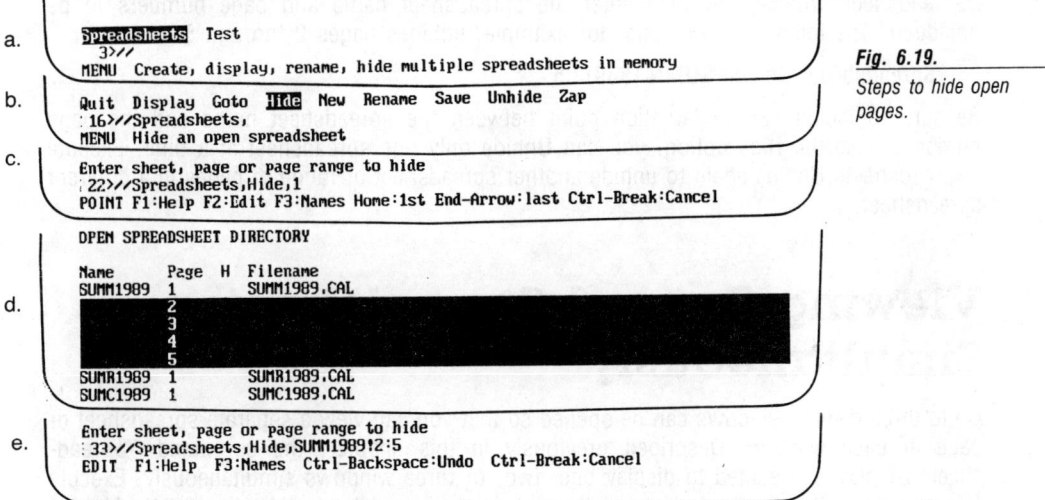

Fig. 6.19.

Steps to hide open pages.

The first step is to execute the //**S**preadsheets command (see fig. 6.19a). Then select **H**ide (see fig. 6.19b). When prompted for the sheet or pages to be hidden (see fig. 6.19c), enter the fully qualified spreadsheet name and page name. The easiest way to do this is to use POINT mode. Press Ctrl-F4 to display the OSD. Then use the arrow keys to move to the first spreadsheet or page in the range to be hidden. Press period (.) to anchor the first reference; then press the down-arrow key to highlight the remaining spreadsheets/pages in the range. Press Enter to complete the range (see fig. 6.19d). The OSD is erased and the current spreadsheet is redisplayed. Press Enter to finalize the range (see fig. 6.19e).

Pages 2 through 5 of the SUMM1989 spreadsheet are now hidden. They are still in memory, but when you use any of the keys to move among spreadsheet displays, the hidden pages are skipped. Press Ctrl-F4 to display the OSD again. Note that each hidden page is indicated by an asterisk (*) in the H column of the OSD (see fig. 6.20).

Fig. 6.20.

The Open Spreadsheet Directory with hidden pages marked.

```
OPEN SPREADSHEET DIRECTORY

Name      Page  H  Filename
SUMM1989   1       SUMM1989.CAL
           2    *
           3    *
           4    *
           5    *
SUMR1989   1       SUMR1989.CAL
SUMC1989   1       SUMC1989.CAL
```

You should know several rules for hiding spreadsheets and pages. Only *one* spreadsheet can be hidden when you execute //**S**preadsheets,**H**ide. To hide other spreadsheets or spreadsheet pages, execute **H**ide repeatedly. You cannot hide all spreadsheets and all spreadsheet pages. At least one spreadsheet or one spreadsheet page must be unhidden. You can hide spreadsheets SUMR1989, SUMC1989, and any four of the five pages of SUMM1989, for example, but one page in SUMM1989 must be unhidden.

You unhide one or more spreadsheets or pages similar to the way they are hidden. Execute //**S**preadsheets,**U**nhide and then enter the spreadsheet name and page numbers to be unhidden. The following command, for example, unhides pages 2 through 5:

   //**S**preadsheets,**U**nhide,**SUMM1989!2:5**

Be sure to include an exclamation point between the spreadsheet name and the page numbers. Like the **H**ide option, you can **U**nhide only one spreadsheet at a time. Execute //**S**preadsheets,**U**nhide again to unhide another spreadsheet or range of pages in a different spreadsheet.

Viewing Several Spreadsheets Simultaneously

Up to three display windows can be opened so that you can view a separate spreadsheet or page in each window. Described previously in this chapter, the command //**S**preadsheets,**D**isplay is executed to display one, two, or three windows simultaneously. Execute //**S**preadsheets,**D**isplay,**3** to show all three division spreadsheets (see fig. 6.21). Making support spreadsheets partially visible facilitates building summary sheets with links to the supporting sheets.

By executing //**S**preadsheets,**D**isplay,**Z**oom, the display toggles between multiple windows and a single window. Ctrl-F7 is equivalent to the //**S**preadsheets,**D**isplay,**Z**oom command. Table 6.2 lists the special keys and commands used with multiple spreadsheets.

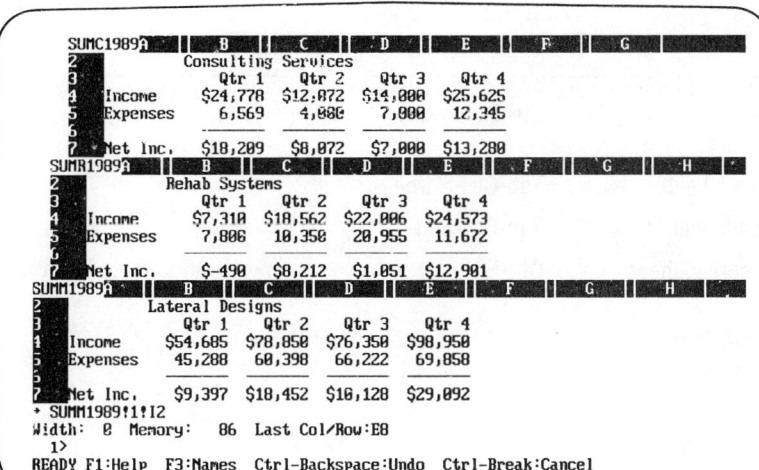

**Fig. 6.21.**
Three spreadsheets
displayed
simultaneously.

Table 6.2
Multiple Spreadsheet Special Keys and Commands
(* means to use the gray keys)

Action	Special Key	Command
Open (insert) new spreadsheet in memory	Ctrl-Enter	//**S**preadsheets,**N**ew
Load new spreadsheet into memory		/**L**oad,*spreadsheet*
Display Open Spreadsheet Directory	Ctrl-F4	
Display Referenced Spreadsheet Directory	Ctrl-F3	
Display Multiple Spreadsheets		//**S**preadsheets,**D**isplay,*n*
Display one/multiple spreadsheets (toggle)	Ctrl-F7	
Hide a spreadsheet		//**S**preadsheets,**H**ide
Unhide a spreadsheet		//**S**preadsheets,**U**nhide
Go to next spreadsheet	Ctrl-plus*	
Go to preceding spreadsheet	Ctrl-minus*	

Table 6.2—*Continued*

Action	Special Key	Command
Go to particular spreadsheet	Ctrl-F5 or Ctrl-=	
Go to first spreadsheet	Tab-Ctrl-Home	
Go to last spreadsheet	Tab-Ctrl-End	
Go to another spreadsheet window	Ctrl-F6	
Save current spreadsheet (all pages) and then close it		/**Q**uit,**S**ave
Close current spreadsheet without saving it		/**Q**uit,**Y**es
Save current spreadsheet and then close it (delete from memory)		/**Z**ap,**S**ave
Clear current spreadsheet		/**Z**ap,**Y**es
Save all modified spreadsheets		//**S**preadsheets,**S**ave
Save all modified spreadsheets and then close all (clear memory)		//**S**preadsheets,**Z**ap,**S**ave
Save all modified spreadsheets and then quit SuperCalc		//**S**preadsheets,**Q**uit,**S**ave
Abandon all open spreadsheets and quit SuperCalc		//**S**preadsheets,**Q**uit,**Y**es

Moving among Open Spreadsheets

Whether multiple spreadsheets are displayed or only one is displayed, you can move from one open spreadsheet to another to edit cells, define range names, copy blocks of cells, and execute any other commands executable when only one spreadsheet is open. Pressing Ctrl-F6 moves you to another open spreadsheet when several are displayed. In a similar way, you can move to the next spreadsheet (or page) by pressing Ctrl-gray plus; move to the preceding page with Ctrl-gray minus—the same as the interpage movement keys described in the first section of this chapter.

Before you create the summary spreadsheet, a few named ranges must be defined in each of the three open spreadsheets. Range names play an important role in linked spreadsheets; they provide a convenient way to write link formulas in the dependent spreadsheet

to refer to one or more cells in a supporting sheet. More important, range names insulate the dependent spreadsheet-link formulas from support-sheet changes that alter the number of cells or their position in the supporting sheet. A brief example explains this last point.

Suppose that you wish to display the total income for Rehab Systems in a separate dependent spreadsheet with a link formula. The link formula (in any cell of the new spreadsheet) could be as follows, to display the sum of the income row in the SUMR1989 (Rehab Systems) spreadsheet:

SUM(SUMR1989!B4:E4)

Similarly, the following formula displays the total expenses for Rehab systems:

SUM(SUMR1989!B5:E5)

Although these link formulas are correct, they are somewhat inflexible. Consider what would happen if the Rehab Systems spreadsheet (shown in fig. 6.21) were reorganized so that *Expenses* were moved to row 7. If the dependent spreadsheet containing the preceding two link formulas were loaded, the cell containing the sum of cells B5 through E5 would display a value that no longer totals *Expenses* in the supporting sheet! Why? Doesn't SuperCalc account for row adjustment and adjust formulas accordingly? Yes, but only within a single spreadsheet. Any movement that occurs outside the spreadsheet containing the formula, however, occurs entirely *independently* from the dependent spreadsheet. What is the solution to this situation, if any? Named ranges solve this problem.

Good spreadsheet technique names any ranges referenced by other spreadsheets (even if it is only one cell). Likewise, dependent spreadsheet-link formulas should refer to named ranges rather than explicit spreadsheet cells. Any changes to cells (that is, any movements) cause the range name to be redefined in the supporting sheet. The dependent spreadsheet refers to the correct range because it uses a range name (adjusted in the supporting sheet).

Because the dependent spreadsheet to be created in the next section uses link formulas to refer to the *Income* and *Expenses* row of each division, create named ranges for *Income* and *Expenses* in each of the three spreadsheets SUMM1989, SUMR1989, and SUMC1989. Because they are open (in memory), move to each spreadsheet in turn and define two range names: INCOME for cells B4 through E4 and EXPENSES for cells B5 through E5.

Saving Changed Spreadsheets

Several spreadsheets have been created in this chapter, but few have been saved—the latest spreadsheets (SUMM1989, SUMR1989, and SUMC1989) remain in memory but have not been stored on disk. SuperCalc provides a convenient command for saving *changed* spreadsheets. Execute the command //**S**preadsheets,**S**ave (see table 6.2). Super-Calc saves only the spreadsheets that have changed since they were loaded. Each spreadsheet is saved in its own disk file. Because all the spreadsheets are new, all are saved. If you execute //**S**preadsheets,**S**ave again without changing any of the spreadsheets, no spreadsheets are saved.

Of course, you can force SuperCalc to save a spreadsheet, even when it is identical to its disk-file version, by executing the familiar **/S**ave command. The current (displayed) spreadsheet is saved on disk. The **/Q**uit,**S**ave command is slightly different: it saves the current spreadsheet and deletes (*closes*) it from memory. Other open spreadsheets are unaffected. Table 6.2 lists other commands for various combinations of saving spreadsheets and leaving SuperCalc. Experiment with each to become familiar with how the methods differ.

Closing Individual Spreadsheets

When you have saved all the division spreadsheets with //**S**preadsheets,**S**ave, remove (close) the SUMR1989 and SUMC1989 spreadsheets, leaving only the SUMM1989 spreadsheet open. To do so, move to SUMR1989 (use Ctrl-gray plus, Ctrl-gray minus, or Ctrl-F6 until SUMR1989 is the current spreadsheet). Then execute the following command:

   /**Q**uit,**Y**es

SUMR1989 is closed and is no longer displayed. Remove SUMC1989 from memory (close it) by moving to it (make it the current spreadsheet) and executing /**Q**uit,**Y**es again. Observe that /**Q**uit,**Y**es removes an *individual* spreadsheet—the one currently displayed.

The only remaining spreadsheet is SUMM1989. Execute //**S**preadsheets,**D**isplay,**1** to restore the full-screen display of SUMM1989, if necessary.

Saving and Closing All Spreadsheets

You can close spreadsheets in a simpler way when you wish to remove all of them from memory. You can remove all spreadsheets from memory by executing the following command:

   //**S**preadsheets,**Z**ap,**Y**es

All spreadsheets are closed (but *not* saved) and a blank spreadsheet is displayed. If you want to save all modified spreadsheets and close them with one command, execute this command:

   //**S**preadsheets,**Z**ap,**S**ave

Modified spreadsheets are saved, and memory is purged of all open spreadsheets. You can abandon all open spreadsheets (not save them) and leave SuperCalc by executing the following command:

   //**S**preadsheets,**Q**uit,**Y**es

To be on the safe side, it is always better to execute the following command whenever you want to leave SuperCalc:

   //**S**preadsheets,**Q**uit,**S**ave

This command first saves any modified spreadsheets before leaving SuperCalc.

Creating Link Formulas

You can now proceed to build the dependent spreadsheet containing summary information about all company divisions. Link formulas are created to reference the three spreadsheets SUMM1989, SUMR1989, and SUMC1989. With these link formulas, key financial information about all company divisions can be displayed. The details remain in the supporting sheets and are not displayed in the "executive summary" spreadsheet.

First, open a new spreadsheet to hold the summary information. Press Ctrl-Enter; then enter text information in preparation for creating spreadsheet links. Figure 6.22 displays the developing summary spreadsheet consisting of text entries only. Labels in rows 4 and 5 are right-justified (use the command /Format,**R**ow,**4:5**,Text**R**ight); the underlines are created by pressing the Alt-196 for single underlines and Alt-205 for double underlines. Format the single and double underlines with the TextRight format. Rename the spreadsheet to COMPANY using the //**S**preadsheets,**R**ename command.

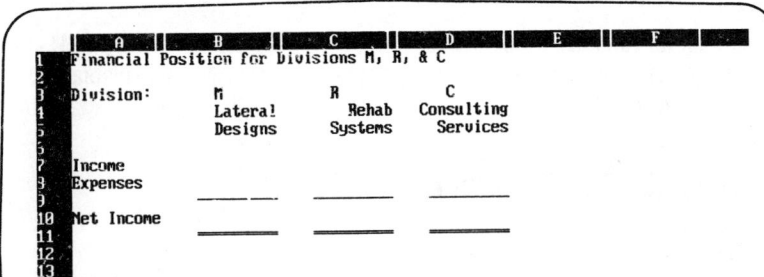

Fig. 6.22.

Summary spreadsheet labels.

Defining Links to Open Spreadsheets

Now you are ready to enter a link formula that gathers and displays information from another spreadsheet. Move to cell B7 in the COMPANY spreadsheet. This cell is to hold the total income for Division M, Lateral Designs. The total is computed by summing the four quarters' income from page 1 of the SUMM1989 spreadsheet, which is still open (in memory). Begin by typing the following partial formula:

    SUM(

The range to be summed is on the resident spreadsheet, SUMM1989. Using the POINT mode, press Ctrl-gray plus to move to that spreadsheet. Because the range to be summed is cells B4 through E4, move the cursor to cell B4 and press period (.) to anchor the first reference. If the cursor is *already* on cell B4, press the exclamation point to anchor the page portion of the cell reference; then press period to anchor the first cell reference. The dialog panel entry line now shows the partial formula SUM(SUMM1989!1!B4 or simply SUM(SUMM1989!B4. (The two formulas are equivalent because page 1 is assumed if the page portion is omitted.)

Press the right-arrow key to highlight (in POINT mode) the remaining cells in the sum range. Figure 6.23 shows the SUMM1989 spreadsheet (for the Lateral Designs division) after the range is highlighted.

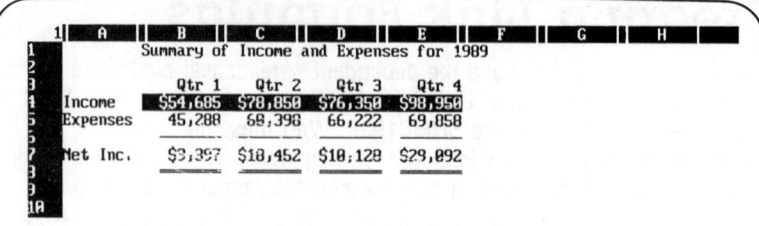

Fig. 6.23.

Creating link formulas in POINT mode.

Type a right parenthesis to complete the sum expression. The screen switches back to the COMPANY spreadsheet when you press the right parenthesis. Press Enter to insert the formula into cell B4 of the COMPANY spreadsheet. To complete the COMPANY spreadsheet, create another link formula in cell B8 that is the sum of expenses (cells B5 through E5) in the SUMM1989 spreadsheet. Follow the preceding steps using POINT mode to create the following link formula stored in B8:

SUM(SUMM1989!1!B5:E5)

Finally, enter the simple formula **B7 − B8** into cell B10. Not linked to the SUMM1989 spreadsheet, this formula references *Income* and *Expenses* in COMPANY and displays the difference between them—*Net Inc.*.

Defining Links to Disk-Resident Spreadsheets

The preceding section explained how to create link formulas to open (memory resident), supporting spreadsheets. Frequently, however, supporting spreadsheets are stored on disk and are not memory resident. Link formulas referencing spreadsheets on disk are created by simply writing the link formulas, including spreadsheet name, page(s), and cell(s). Referenced spreadsheets need not be open for you to reference them. SuperCalc searches various directories on the disk to *resolve* (evaluate) references to nonopen spreadsheets.

Move to cell C7 in the consolidated spreadsheet, COMPANY, and enter the following formula:

SUM(SUMR1989!1!INCOME)

Note that the range name INCOME is used instead of an explicit cell range. Recall that this is the best way to refer to cells in other spreadsheets. Press Enter to complete the expression. Figure 6.24 shows the resultant spreadsheet display.

Oops! Cell C7 contains N/A, and a warning is displayed in the status line indicating that the SUMR1989 spreadsheet could not be located. This warning message means that SuperCalc searched the default disk drive directories looking, unsuccessfully, for the referenced spreadsheet.

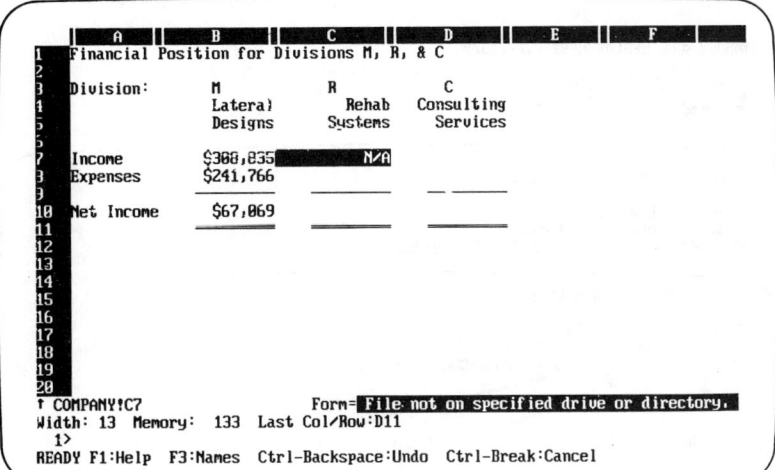

Fig. 6.24.
N/A *is displayed when the referenced spreadsheet cannot be found.*

Using the Referenced Spreadsheet Directory

When a formula in the current spreadsheet references another spreadsheet, you create a *spreadsheet link*. Summary information about all spreadsheet links found in the current spreadsheet page are maintained and displayed in the Referenced Spreadsheet Directory (RSD). The RSD indicates whether a referenced spreadsheet is in memory (Mem), in a disk file (Disk), or not found (N/A). Accessed by pressing Ctrl-F3, the RSD displays three columns of information: the spreadsheet alias name, the spreadsheet location, and the fully qualified spreadsheet file name for each spreadsheet-link reference. Figure 6.25a shows an example of the RSD for the spreadsheet being developed.

When a spreadsheet whose name appears in a link formula cannot be found, N/A is displayed in the Link column of the RSD. Mem is displayed when referenced spreadsheets are in memory. Spreadsheets in link formulas found on disk are noted in the Link column with Disk. The Name column, also called the spreadsheet *alias*, is associated with the file name in the File column. You can edit the File column spreadsheet file name to associate a different file name with the spreadsheet alias name. When you change the file name, all link formulas using the associated alias reference the new file name.

When SuperCalc attempts to calculate the value of a link formula and the referenced spreadsheet cannot be found, the spreadsheet alias is placed in the File column. You can edit this reference and thereby direct SuperCalc to the correct disk directory to find the missing spreadsheet. To change the file name entry for SUMR1989 (the spreadsheet that cannot be located), display the RSD and use the arrow keys to move to the File column.

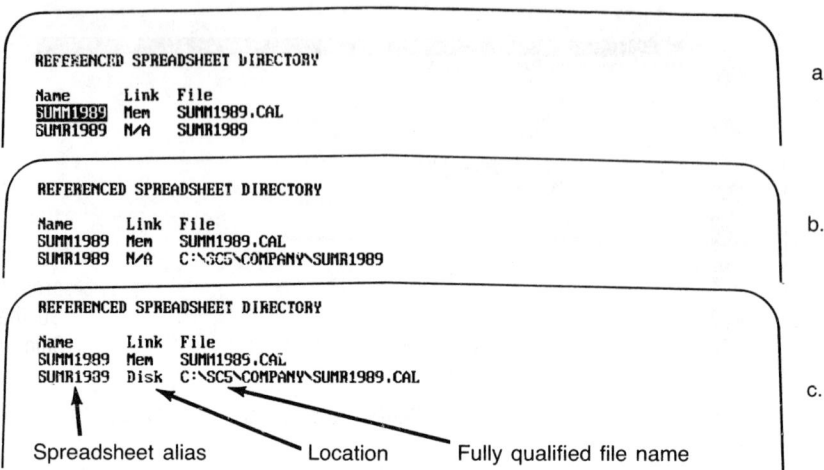

Fig. 6.25.

Steps to edit the Referenced Spreadsheet Directory.

Then change the SuperCalc-suggested file location to the disk directory where SUMR1989 is located. Simply type a full path and file name (substitute *your* disk and path), and press Enter:

C:\SC5\COMPANY\SUMR1989

Figure 6.25b shows the changed drive, path, and file name before pressing Enter. Notice that the Link column shows N/A for SUMR1989. Mem is displayed to the right of SUMM1989, indicating that SUMM1989 is memory resident.

After you press Enter (see fig. 6.25c), SuperCalc immediately searches for SUMR1989 in the updated directory. When it finds the file, SuperCalc changes the Link column to Disk for SUMR1989 to indicate that the referenced spreadsheet was located on disk. Press Esc to display the COMPANY spreadsheet.

Establishing the Spreadsheet Search Path

Changing the file reference in the RSD provides only temporary relief for "lost" spreadsheets. If you write other spreadsheet-link formulas referencing spreadsheets not found in the current directory (the one from which SuperCalc was invoked), the problem persists.

How does SuperCalc search for unopened spreadsheet-link formula references? When you enter a link formula, SuperCalc creates an entry on the RSD. Then the program attempts to find all spreadsheet, range, and cell references and evaluate the formula. SuperCalc searches for spreadsheets in the following order:

1. RAM (open spreadsheets)
2. The current data directory
3. The spreadsheet data path (entered with //**F**ile,**P**ath)
4. The global data path

If the referenced spreadsheet is among the open spreadsheets, the search ends. If not, SuperCalc searches the current directory, the spreadsheet data path, and then the global data path. The search stops when the first occurrence of the referenced spreadsheet is found. The next several paragraphs describe how to establish your own data search paths.

By indicating the names of other disk directories to search for referenced spreadsheets, you can permanently avoid editing the RSD File column manually. So that SuperCalc can locate other referenced spreadsheets (link formulas), inform SuperCalc where to look for other spreadsheets whenever their references appear in formulas.

Figure 6.26 illustrates the steps to define another disk directory where SuperCalc can search for nonresident spreadsheets. The //**F**ile command is used to establish the spreadsheet search path. Execute the //**F**ile command. A menu of three options appears:

        Directory   List   Path

The **D**irectory option allows you to change the default directory; the **L**ist option displays a list of files on the default directory; the **P**ath option allows you to define data paths for SuperCalc to use when it searches for files. Choose the **P**ath option to declare the search path for other spreadsheets on disk.

Two options then appear:

        Global   Spreadsheet

The **G**lobal option lets you define a data path for the whole SuperCalc session (it is a "keepable" value—execute /**G**lobal,**K**eep). Specifying a global data path restricts spreadsheet searches to your personal directories. The **S**preadsheet option lets you define a data path for the *current* spreadsheet (the displayed, open spreadsheet). If you define a spreadsheet data path, it is stored with the spreadsheet.

Choose **G**lobal to restrict searches for the SUMR1989 and SUMC1989 spreadsheets to just one directory. The **E**dit, **C**lear, and **Z**ap options are next displayed. The **Z**ap option resets the global data path to the last one saved with the /**G**lobal,**K**eep command. **C**lear removes the existing global data path for the current SuperCalc *session*. **E**dit lets you enter or change the global data path. Press **E** to select **E**dit.

You are then prompted to enter the global path names (see fig. 6.26a). Press F2 to edit the displayed, current global spreadsheet path name (see fig. 6.26b), or simply type a new one. You can enter several data paths, but be sure to place semicolons between distinct path names. You can establish two search paths with the following command:

   //**F**ile,**P**ath,**G**lobal,**E**dit,**C:\SC5\COMPANY;C:\DIVISION\WESTERN**

Press Enter after completing the search path. Remember to execute the following command if you want to save your new, default data paths:

   /**G**lobal,**K**eep

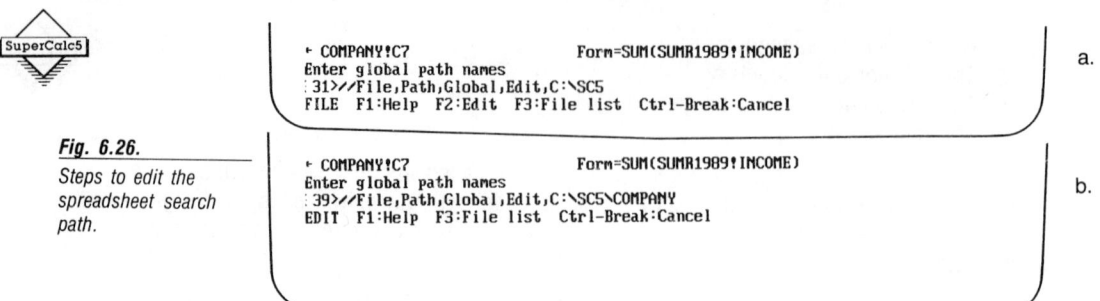

SuperCalc5

Fig. 6.26.

Steps to edit the spreadsheet search path.

```
┌ COMPANY!C7              Form=SUM(SUMR1989!INCOME)
  Enter global path names
  31>//File,Path,Global,Edit,C:\SC5
  FILE  F1:Help  F2:Edit  F3:File list  Ctrl-Break:Cancel
```
a.

```
┌ COMPANY!C7              Form=SUM(SUMR1989!INCOME)
  Enter global path names
  39>//File,Path,Global,Edit,C:\SC5\COMPANY
  EDIT  F1:Help  F3:File list  Ctrl-Break:Cancel
```
b.

Entering More Link Formulas

Complete the COMPANY spreadsheet (as shown in fig. 6.24) by entering the three remaining link formulas to display information about the SUMR1989 and SUMC1989 divisions. Move to cell D7 and enter the following link formula:

SUM(SUMC1989!1!INCOME)

Next, move to cell D8 and enter the formula **SUM(SUMC1989!1!EXPENSES)**. In cell C8, enter the formula **SUM(SUMR1989!EXPENSES)**. The last formula displays the total expenses for the Rehab Systems division. Notice that no page 1 reference is included between the spreadsheet name and cell range. Omitted page references default to page 1. Any other page references (for example, page 2 of SUMR1989) must include the page number: SUMR1989!2!F4:F15. Copy the formula in cell B10 to the cell range C10:D10 to display *Net Income* for all three divisions (use /**C**opy,**B10**,**C10:D10**).

The completed COMPANY spreadsheet with all link formulas in place is shown in figure 6.27. The spreadsheet has been split to show display values in the upper window and the formulas in the lower window.

Auditing Link Formulas: //Test

When you create complicated spreadsheet models containing many link formulas, it is often useful to highlight in a consolidated spreadsheet cells that contain link formulas. The summary spreadsheet with link formulas to division spreadsheets contains several link formulas (see fig. 6.27). Even in this simple spreadsheet, however, it is not obvious which cells contain link formulas to other spreadsheets or spreadsheet pages. Link formulas can be highlighted using SuperCalc's *audit* feature.

```
    |   A    ||   B    ||   C    ||   D    ||   E    ||   F    |
1   Financial Position for Divisions M, R, & C
2
3   Division:        M          R          C
4                 Lateral     Rehab    Consulting
5                 Designs    Systems     Services
6
7   Income        $300,835    $72,451     $76,475
8   Expenses      $241,766    $50,777     $29,914
9
10  Net Income     $67,069    $21,674     $46,561
11
    |   A    ||   B    ||   C    ||   D    ||   E    ||   F    |
4                 Lateral     Rehab    Consulting
5                 Designs    Systems     Services
6
7   Income     SUM(SUMM1989 SUM(SUMR1989 SUM(SUMC1989!INCOME)
8   Expenses   SUM(SUMM1989 SUM(SUMR1989 SUM(SUMC1989!EXPENSES)
9
10  Net Income B7-B8       C7-C8       D7-D8
11
↓ COMPANY!C8                   Form=SUM(SUMR1989!EXPENSES)
Width: 13  Memory:  120  Last Col/Row:D11
  1>
READY F1:Help  F3:Names  Ctrl-Backspace:Undo  Ctrl-Break:Cancel
```

Fig. 6.27.

The completed COMPANY spreadsheet with link formulas.

Highlighting Cells Containing Link Formulas

A complete discussion of the audit feature is presented in Chapter 13. This section presents a subset of audit's powerful command set to highlight link formulas and display the details. The //Test command invokes spreadsheet auditing. Type //T to invoke this command. Once invoked, a complete, independent set of commands and menu prompts is displayed. Control remains exclusively in audit until you press /Quit. After typing //T, you display the main audit commands by pressing /. To highlight link formulas, for example, execute the following command:

/Highlight,Links,Dependent

Figure 6.28 displays the results of this command. Notice that cells B7 through D8 are highlighted to indicate that these cells contain link formulas to other spreadsheets or spreadsheet pages. The following message is displayed on the top right of the dialog panel:

```
The total number of highlighted cells is 6
```

The message indicates the total number of cells on the current page, containing link formulas. You can remove the highlight by executing this command:

/Highlight,Zap

If you leave audit mode by pressing /Quit, any highlighted cells remain highlighted. You can then move around the spreadsheet and inspect the highlighted area, change link formulas, or execute any other SuperCalc command while the formulas are highlighted—a convenient feature.

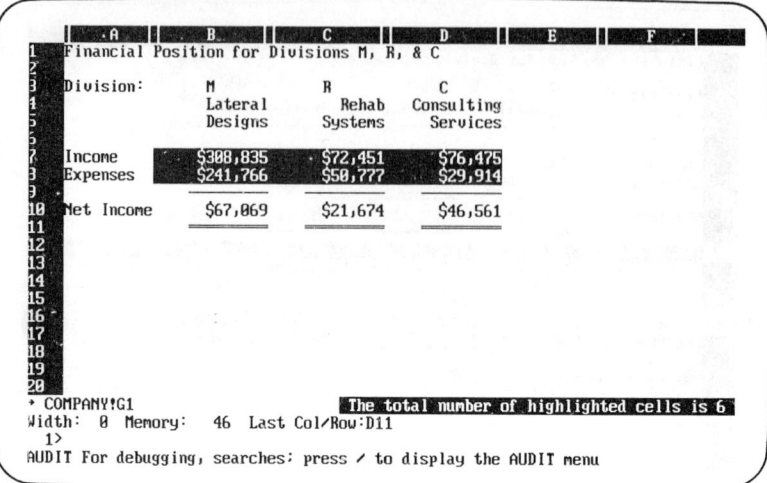

Fig. 6.28.

Highlighted link cells.

Displaying Link Formula Details

You can display more details about highlighted cells by executing the following command:

/**D**etails

The contents of highlighted cells are displayed, one cell at a time, in the bottom portion of the spreadsheet. By pressing the right- and left-arrow keys, you can move to different cell addresses in the details panel and display the contents of each cell. Figure 6.29 shows an example of the details. The contents of highlighted cell D7 are displayed below the double line in the details panel.

Press Esc to remove the details panel. Remember to execute the following command to remove the highlight box(es) from all link formulas before exiting audit:

/**H**ighlight,**Z**ap

Press /**Q**uit to leave audit.

Chapter Summary

SuperCalc provides true three-dimensional spreadsheet capabilities. You can create multipage spreadsheets for related groups of information or summarize information from subsidiary (supporting) spreadsheets with SuperCalc's commands for multiple spreadsheets. Building multipage or multiple spreadsheet models allows different people to build individual models independently of the "master" spreadsheet, which contains summary information.

```
    ┌──A──┐┌──B──┐┌──C──┐┌──D──┐┌───E───┐┌───F───┐
  1 │Financial Position for Divisions M, R, & C
  2 │
  3 │Division:      M          R          C
  4 │            Lateral      Rehab   Consulting
  5 │            Designs      Systems   Services
  6 │
  7 │Income      $308,835    $72,451    $76,475
  8 │Expenses    $241,766    $50,777    $29,914
  9 │
 10 │Net Income   $67,069    $21,674    $46,561
 11 │
 12 │
    │   6 highlighted LINKED cells
    │B7 C7 D7 B8 C8 D8
    │
    │D7:      SUM(SUMC1989!INCOME)
    │
    │
    │+ COMPANY!G1
    │Width:  0  Memory:    46  Last Col/Row:D11
    │   1>
    │AUDIT For debugging, searches; press / to display the AUDIT menu
```

Fig. 6.29.
Link cell details.

Up to 255 spreadsheets can be open at one time, limited only by the amount of memory your computer has. Complicated spreadsheets can reference hundreds of spreadsheets stored on disk or in memory. Because supporting spreadsheets can reside on disk, the number of referenced spreadsheets is unlimited. Spreadsheets or spreadsheet pages can be hidden; you also can display up to three spreadsheets or spreadsheet pages simultaneously on-screen. Movement among open spreadsheets is easy. Several special spreadsheet-movement keys are provided for moving from one spreadsheet to another.

The next two chapters introduce you to SuperCalc's functions, which greatly expand the power of your spreadsheets. SuperCalc offers so many functions that the discussion is divided into two chapters. Chapter 7 introduces the theory and use of functions. If you already understand how to use functions in your formulas, look up (in either chapter) the functions that you want to learn about.

Functions: Part I

SuperCalc's functions are some of its handiest tools. Similar to the modern calculator's hard-wired functions, SuperCalc's functions can sum columns or rows, compute column or row averages, determine the largest or smallest value of a list of values, and search for a value in a table of values. In this chapter, you will see functions providing powerful one-word alternatives to lengthy formulas.

SuperCalc has ten groups of functions: statistical, arithmetic, logical, index, calendar, data management, trigonometric, financial, string, and special purpose. Because SuperCalc provides so many functions, grouping them in one chapter with a single spreadsheet example would be confusing or even intimidating. The first five of these groups are described in this chapter. Because you are moving into more complex spreadsheets with rows or columns that require frequent rearrangement, the /Arrange command also is introduced in this chapter.

The functions explained in this chapter are grouped as follows:

- *Statistical* functions: AVERAGE, COUNT, MAX, MIN, RANDOM, STD, SUM, and VAR

- *Arithmetic* functions: ABS, EXP, INT, LN, LOG10, MOD, ROUND, ROUNDUP, SQRT, and TRUNC

- *Logical* functions: AND, EXACT, IF, OR, NOT, and the special logical functions (ISBLANK, ISDATE, ISERROR, ISNA, ISNUM, ISPROT, ISSTR, ISTIME, ISVAL, ERROR, FALSE, NA, and TRUE)

- *Index* functions: HLOOKUP, LOOKUP, and VLOOKUP (others are discussed in Chapter 8)

- *Calendar* functions are subdivided into two groups:

  - *Date/time entry* calendar functions: DATE, DVAL, DATEVALUE, EDAT, NOW, TIME, TIMEVALUE, TODAY, and TVAL

  - *Date/time reference* calendar functions: DAY, HOUR, JDATE, JTIME, MINUTE, MONTH, SECOND, WDAY, and YEAR

187

The other index functions, the financial functions, the trigonometric functions, the string functions, and the special-purpose functions are described in Chapter 8. The data management functions are discussed in Chapter 12.

The Program Management Spreadsheet

In this chapter, you are introduced to a spreadsheet that records employee hours charged to different projects. This program management spreadsheet illustrates several SuperCalc functions and the /Arrange command.

Looking at the Program Management Spreadsheet

The program management spreadsheet reflects a characteristic of many spreadsheets: you do not know the final boundaries of the spreadsheet when you create it. When you begin designing such a spreadsheet, you may not know the total number of rows or columns you will need. You should recognize that a dynamic model will continue to grow and that you must plan ahead for that growth. Created manually, a dynamic spreadsheet requires a great deal of restructuring before completion. SuperCalc, however, is designed to handle with ease these adjustments and modifications. The program management example in this chapter shows how SuperCalc functions and commands help you design a dynamic spreadsheet model.

A program management spreadsheet is used frequently to help a manager maintain control over the number of labor hours charged to separate projects for which the manager is responsible. This type of spreadsheet shrinks and grows as projects and personnel are removed or added—often on a weekly basis. In addition to providing an overview of expended labor hours, a program management spreadsheet can be included directly in monthly status reports required by contracting officers who fund the projects. Thus, the spreadsheet offers project control and assists report preparation. The program management spreadsheet used to illustrate several SuperCalc functions is shown in figure 7.1.

Building the Program Management Spreadsheet

Beginning with simple labels and labor hours for a few projects, you can construct this spreadsheet in steps that introduce SuperCalc functions. Take an extra moment to study figure 7.1 carefully. Notice that personnel are listed alphabetically down column A, and projects are listed across row 3. The hours charged to a project for each employee appear

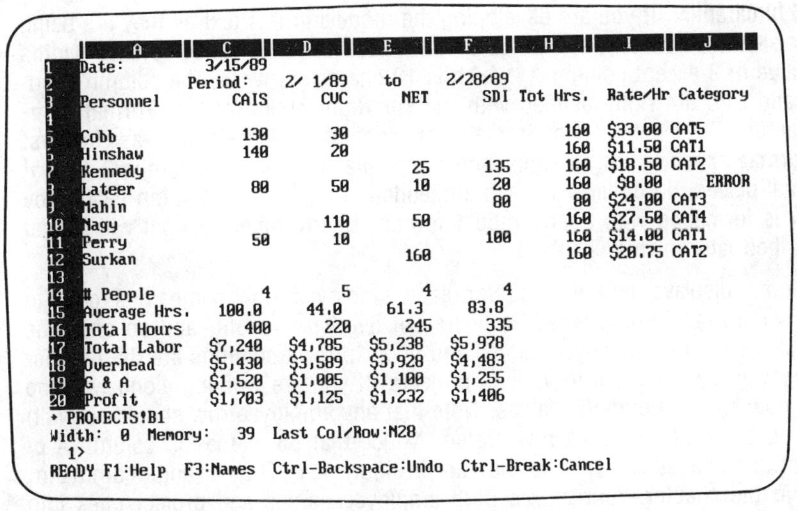

```
    A              C        D        E        F        H        I        J
 1 Date:        3/15/89
 2          Period:    2/ 1/89    to      2/28/89
 3 Personnel      CAIS      CVC      NET      SDI Tot Hrs.  Rate/Hr Category
 4
 5 Cobb            130       30                         160  $33.00 CAT5
 6 Hinshaw         140       20                         160  $11.50 CAT1
 7 Kennedy                            25      135       160  $18.50 CAT2
 8 Lateer           80       50       10       20       160   $8.00      ERROR
 9 Mahin                                       80        80  $24.00 CAT3
10 Nagy                     110       50                160  $27.50 CAT4
11 Perry            50       10               100       160  $14.00 CAT1
12 Surkan                            160                160  $20.75 CAT2
13
14 # People          4        5        4        4
15 Average Hrs.  100.0     44.0     61.3     83.8
16 Total Hours     400      220      245      335
17 Total Labor  $7,240   $4,785   $5,238   $5,970
18 Overhead     $5,430   $3,589   $3,928   $4,483
19 G & A        $1,520   $1,005   $1,100   $1,255
20 Profit       $1,703   $1,125   $1,232   $1,406
* PROJECTS!B1
Width:  0  Memory:   39  Last Col/Row:N20
  1>
READY F1:Help  F3:Names  Ctrl-Backspace:Undo  Ctrl-Break:Cancel
```

Fig. 7.1. *Typical program management spreadsheet.*

at the intersection of a personnel row and a project column. Near the bottom of the sheet are statistical data and figures of interest to a financial officer as well as to the program manager: total labor, overhead, general and administrative (G & A) charges, and profit.

Before discussing functions, let's put some initial nonfunction values into the spreadsheet, establish column widths, and define the display formats. Figure 7.2 is the beginning model for the program management spreadsheet.

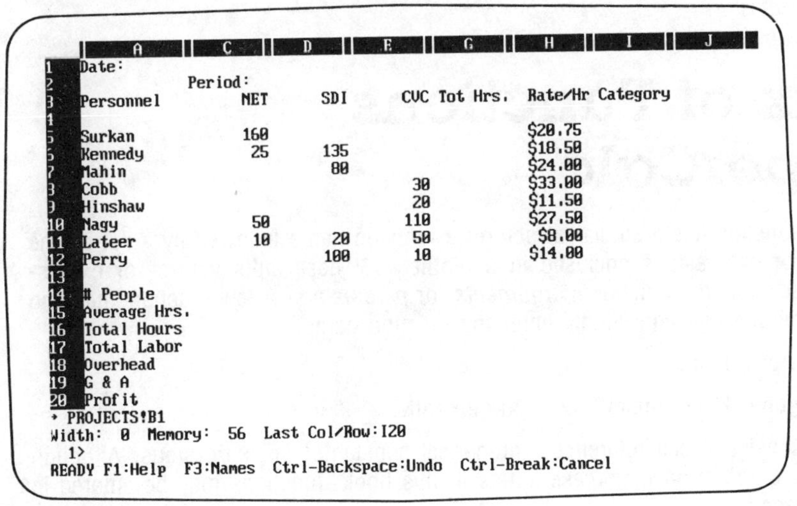

```
    A              C        D        E        G        H        I        J
 1 Date:
 2          Period:
 3 Personnel       NET      SDI      CVC Tot Hrs.  Rate/Hr Category
 4
 5 Surkan          160                              $20.75
 6 Kennedy          25      135                     $18.50
 7 Mahin                     80                     $24.00
 8 Cobb                               30            $33.00
 9 Hinshaw                            20            $11.50
10 Nagy             50               110            $27.50
11 Lateer           10       20       50             $8.00
12 Perry                    100       10            $14.00
13
14 # People
15 Average Hrs.
16 Total Hours
17 Total Labor
18 Overhead
19 G & A
20 Profit
* PROJECTS!B1
Width:  0  Memory:  56  Last Col/Row:I20
  1>
READY F1:Help  F3:Names  Ctrl-Backspace:Undo  Ctrl-Break:Cancel
```

Fig. 7.2. *Beginning program management spreadsheet model.*

Examine figure 7.2 carefully. If you are developing the models in this text as they are being described, enter all the values shown in figure 7.2 before continuing. All column widths have a default value of 9 except column A, which is 12 characters wide. The column headings *NET*, *SDI*, and *CVC* are right-justified with the **T**ext**R**ight option of the /**F**ormat command (see Chapter 4). Finally, two formats are defined (**U**ser-define) as follows: UserNumber1 format specifies dollar signs and 2 decimal places; UserNumber2 format specifies 0 decimal places, no dollar sign, and embedded commas. The column headed by the label *Rate/Hr* is formatted with UserNumber1 format. UserNumber2 format will format other rows described later in this chapter.

The *Rate/Hr* column displays hourly rates for each employee (the company's cost to employ a given person, an "unburdened" rate free of overhead, profit, and so on). The numeric entries to the right of employee names and under project columns are the number of hours, in integer values, charged to various projects. If you are working along with the text, you should now enter all numeric values. Note that any employee row should (or will) add up to 160 hours except employee row *Mahin*. Notice that the names in column A of figure 7.2 are not in alphabetical order as they are in figure 7.1. The /**A**rrange command, introduced later in the chapter, reorganizes both employee names and project titles into alphabetical order.

One remaining note: columns B and F seem to be "lost" in figure 7.2 because they do not appear in the top row of column letters. Columns B and F do exist, but they have been formatted with a width of zero. Having these two "ghost" columns is crucial to being able to add new project columns later in the spreadsheet's development. These extra but unused columns help preserve the integrity of formulas that reference cells in columns located between B and F. This factor is explained more fully when more project columns are added to the spreadsheet.

Syntax of Functions in SuperCalc

Each SuperCalc function has a similar structure: a function name followed by a list of one or more values or expressions enclosed in parentheses. These input values, or expressions, are referred to as the function's *arguments*, or *parameters*. A few functions have no arguments and require that you simply enter the function name.

The general form of a function is

    FUNCTION(argument1,argument2, . . . ,argumentN)

The arguments consist of cell references, numerical constants, or expressions. Although function names are written in uppercase letters in this book, functions may be entered in upper- or lowercase.

Each function computes and displays a single value; and the kind of value computed depends on the function. To learn how to use the rich variety of SuperCalc functions, you must understand the kinds of arguments and their relative order in the argument lists of various functions.

Statistical Functions

Seven of SuperCalc's eight statistical functions have lists or ranges of cells as arguments (RANDOM has no argument). Numbers, cell addresses, range addresses, cell names, and range names (see Chapter 3) can be valid arguments. The statistical functions are listed and described briefly in table 7.1.

Table 7.1
Statistical Functions

Function	Meaning
AVERAGE(list) AVG AV	Returns the average (mean) value of the numeric values in the given range(s). This function is equivalent to SUM(list)/ COUNT(list). A value of zero is returned if no numeric value formulas are found in the list.
COUNT(list)	Returns the number of numeric-valued cells in the list. Blank cells and other nonformula cells are not counted.
MAX(list)	Returns the largest value from a list of cells. Non-numeric cells are ignored.
MIN(list)	Returns the smallest value of the numeric cells in the argument list. Non-numeric cells are ignored.
RANDOM RAND RAN	Returns a pseudo random value in the range from zero to one. The random number is regenerated each time the cell containing the number is recalculated.
STD(list)	Returns the standard deviation for the values in the list and is a measure of how much individual values deviate from the collective list mean. This function is the square root of the variance.
SUM(list)	Returns the sum of all numeric values in the list. Non-numeric values are ignored.
VAR(list)	Returns the variance for the values in the list. VAR is a measure of how much, on the average, the individual values of the list deviate from the mean of the list.

A *list* is composed of one or more arguments. Like all SuperCalc functions, multiple arguments must be separated by commas. Look at the following example:

    MAX(SALESQ1,B12:B20,C25,32765.41)

This MAX function contains four arguments separated by commas: a named range (*SALESQ1*), a cell range (*B12:B20*), a single cell (*C25*), and a literal value (*32765.41*). The MAX function is explained in the section "The MAX and MIN Functions."

Several SuperCalc functions are used in the program management spreadsheet. The first of these functions is AVERAGE.

The AVERAGE Function

The AVERAGE function computes the average value of the values listed as arguments. You can enter a single range of values or a list of several cells or ranges separated by commas. Non-numeric values within any given range are ignored; therefore, the average is computed with actual numeric values. SuperCalc does not use blank cells in the AVERAGE computation, so you do not need to set those cells to zero.

In the spreadsheet, AVERAGE is used in cells C15 through F15 to compute and display the average number of hours per person for a given project (refer to fig. 7.1). To enter the AVERAGE formula into cell C15, move the spreadsheet cursor to that cell and enter the following formula:

AVERAGE(C4:C13)

Both AVG and AV are acceptable abbreviations for AVERAGE. You can type the cell addresses or use the POINT mode to specify the first and last cells in the range to be averaged.

Notice that the first cell in the argument list (C4) is an unoccupied cell just above the first employee row. Likewise, the last cell is one row below the last employee row (see fig. 7.2). Why is a seemingly superfluous row included on each end of the range in the AVERAGE function argument list? Although not important initially, the extra rows become important when the rows are rearranged with the /Arrange command. When this command moves the first and last rows (or columns) to new positions in the spreadsheet, any cell ranges in formulas outside the sorted range are altered to reflect the new row positions. If the formula lists cells that are rearranged, the new formula with the altered cell range becomes incorrect. In particular, suppose that the AVERAGE function is entered as

AVERAGE(C5:C12)

When rows 5 through 12 are sorted by employee name, the formula is adjusted to

AVERAGE(C11:C12)

That function clearly would be incorrect. Therefore, keep the "end point" cell range designations outside any possible future /Arrange block limits (see the discussion of the SUM function).

Another reason for including an unused row above and below a cell range is to ensure that the AVERAGE formula remains accurate when additional rows are added. For example, you could insert a new row 4 (between existing rows 4 and 5) for a new employee record. Similarly, a row could be inserted between rows 12 and 13, creating a new row 13. As long as the cell range argument of any function such as AVERAGE includes these extra rows originally, the new, altered cell range will be adjusted correctly whenever new rows are inserted *within* the cell range. This rule holds for cell ranges consisting of contiguous columns as well.

You now have the single AVERAGE formula in cell C15 of the program management model. Copy the AVERAGE formula to cells D15 and E15 (/Copy,C15,**D15:E15**). The formulas are adjusted automatically after the copy operation. Figure 7.3 shows the program management spreadsheet after this copy operation.

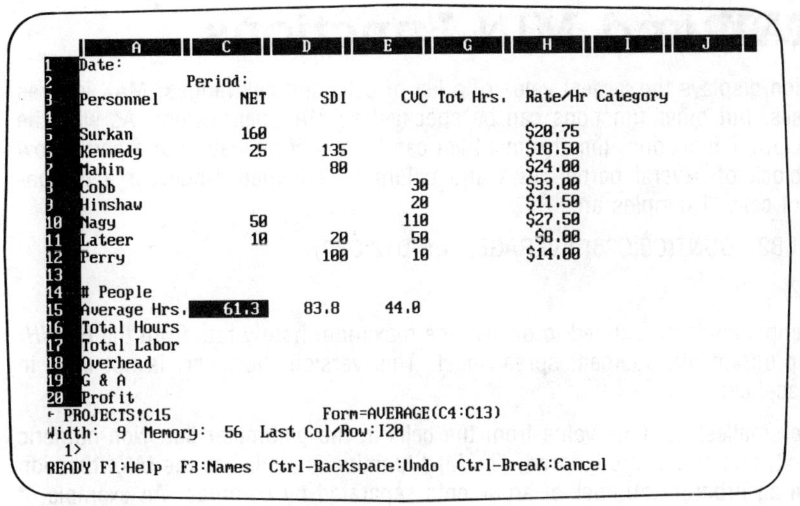

```
          A       C       D       E       G       H       I       J
1  Date:
2              Period:
3  Personnel     NET     SDI       CUC Tot Hrs.  Rate/Hr Category
4
5  Surkan        160                             $20.75
6  Kennedy        25     135                     $18.50
7  Mahin                  80                      $24.00
8  Cobb                            30             $33.00
9  Hinshaw                         20             $11.50
10 Nagy           50              110             $27.50
11 Lateer         10      20       50              $8.00
12 Perry                 100       10             $14.00
13
14 # People
15 Average Hrs.  61.3    83.8     44.0
16 Total Hours
17 Total Labor
18 Overhead
19 G & A
20 Profit
 * PROJECTS!C15              Form=AVERAGE(C4:C13)
Width:  9  Memory:  56  Last Col/Row:I20
  1>
READY F1:Help  F3:Names  Ctrl-Backspace:Undo  Ctrl-Break:Cancel
```

Fig. 7.3.

Spreadsheet with the
AVERAGE functions
added.

The COUNT Function

The COUNT function computes the number of *numeric* values in a list of cells. Blank cells and labels (text entries) within the range are not counted. The list of cells is written after the function name (see table 7.1). As usual, entries are separated by commas, and any number of arguments can be specified. An example is

COUNT(A5:B42,C12,E14:E22)

To determine the number of employees who reported hours for the NET project, place the following COUNT formula in cell C14:

COUNT(C4:C13)

To enter the formula, you type

COUNT(

Then move the cursor to C4, and press the period to anchor the beginning of the range. Next, you press the down arrow until the pointer reaches cell C13, type a right parenthesis, and press Enter. Then copy the formula to cells D14 and D15 so that the employees working on the other two projects are counted.

If you type a formula incorrectly (for example, misspell a function name), SuperCalc interprets the entry as text. Should this happen, you must edit the formula to correct the mistake. Be sure to remove from the formula the SuperCalc-inserted leading quotation marks (inserted automatically when SuperCalc does not recognize a formula) before you press Enter.

The MAX and MIN Functions

The MAX function displays the largest value of a list of cells and cell ranges. MAX ignores non-numeric cells, but other functions can be specified as MAX parameters. As with the AVERAGE and COUNT functions, the argument list can be any combination of a partial row or column, a block of several partial rows and columns, a named range, or a discontinuous group of cells. Examples are

    MAX(A1:A20,B2,COUNT(C5:C25),AVERAGE(14.5,D12:D19))

    MAX(H5:H12)

The second example could be entered to display the maximum hourly rate from the *Rate/Hr* column of the program management spreadsheet. This version, however, is not used in the model spreadsheet.

MIN returns the smallest numeric value from the cells in the parameter list. Non-numeric cells (textual, text, and so on) are ignored. The MIN function is similar to the MAX function and can contain an arbitrary number of arguments separated by commas. An example of MIN is

    MIN(A2,SALESPERSONS,D5:D10)

where SALESPERSONS is a named range. The minimum value found for cell A2, the SALESPERSONS range, and the range D5:D10 is displayed.

The RANDOM Function

Unlike other statistical functions, the RANDOM function has no argument list. When you recalculate a cell containing a RANDOM function, it generates a pseudo random number in the range of zero to one. You can use RANDOM to create data to test spreadsheets. If integer random values are required in a spreadsheet application, use the functions ROUND, INT, or TRUNC with RANDOM. (ROUND, INT, and TRUNC are described in following sections.) You can use the abbreviation RAND or RAN in place of RANDOM.

By using multiplication and addition arithmetic operators, you can create random values in ranges other than zero through one. For example, the hours recorded under each project in the program management spreadsheet can be created initially by entering the formula

    RANDOM*160

In this example, the value 160 is used to expand the range of potential values from the initial range (0 to 1) to a larger range (0 to 160).

Similarly, you can generate random values with lower limits greater than zero by adding a value to the result of RANDOM. To create random values from 40 to 160, you enter the following formula:

    40+RANDOM*120

The value returned by RANDOM is multiplied by 120 to yield a possible range of pseudo random numbers from 0 to 120. Next, the value 40 is added to establish the lower and upper limits of the range as 40 and 160. Multiplying the random number by an integer broadens the range of returned values, and the addition of a positive integer shifts the returned value range.

Because RANDOM values are regenerated whenever the spreadsheet is recalculated, you cannot "freeze" these values. To save a given set of random data as values, save the spreadsheet model with the **P**art,**V**alues option. For example, the command

   /**S**ave,**MYSHEET**,**P**art,**V**alues,**B1:B20**

saves the random function results as *values* for the cell range B1 through B20. Later, you can use /**L**oad to load the saved block of values back into your spreadsheet. This technique "stabilizes" random data so that it doesn't change with each spreadsheet recalculation.

The STD Function

The STD function calculates the standard deviation for the values in the argument list. The *standard deviation* is the square of the variance (see the discussion of VAR) and is the average amount by which each member of the population deviates from the mean. For example, if spreadsheet column A contained heights of people in inches and column B contained the frequency of people in those height categories, the standard deviation of that population would measure the average deviation from the mean height.

For so-called normal distributions, a standard deviation of +1 or −1 on either side of the mean accounts for approximately 68 percent of the sampled population. Correspondingly, a standard deviation of +2 or −2 away from the mean accounts for 95 percent of the sampled population. If you produce a graph in which the heights of many people are on the x-axis and the number of people at each height is on the y-axis, you can create a classic bell curve. An example of the function's use is

   STD(B1:B40)

This function computes the standard deviation of the list of values in cells B1 through B40.

The SUM Function

The SUM function returns the sum of all numeric values in its argument list. Like all argument lists in statistical functions, this list can contain an arbitrary number of arguments separated by commas. Individual arguments can be literal values, cell references, named ranges, or single cells.

You enter the SUM function in several places in the program management spreadsheet. The function is used to

- Total the labor hours for each project
- Total the labor costs for each project
- Total the hours for each employee for all projects

To illustrate SUM, you can total the hours worked by each employee for all projects (see fig. 7.3) and display those totals under the column label *Tot Hrs.* Move to cell G5, enter the formula SUM(B5:F5), and press Enter. If you use the /Name command (discussed in Chapter 3) to label each employee row to match the employee name (/Name,Labels,Right,**A5:F12**), you can create a SUM formula using the named range. For example, entering the formula

SUM(SURKAN)

in cell G5 sums the labor hours for row 5 (SURKAN).

Copy the formula down to cells G6 through G12 with the /**C**opy command. The column *Tot Hrs.* now contains total hours for the period for each employee. Note that the summed range includes the unused columns B and F to accommodate additional project columns and to maintain the integrity of the SUM argument range.

Because cell references are adjusted during the copy operation, the assigned names (KENNEDY, MAHIN, NAGY, and so on) automatically replace the cells in the new SUM functions. Cell G12, for example, will contain the formula SUM(PERRY) after the copy operation. (The project management spreadsheet uses cell ranges rather than range names.)

To compute total hours for the NET project, move to cell C16 and enter the formula **SUM(C4:C13)**, totaling the hours in the partial column representing the NET project. If the cell range C4 through C13 is assigned the name of the project, NET, then you also can enter the formula

SUM(NET)

Remember that the unused rows 4 and 13 are included in the summed range so that rearranging employee rows keeps the SUM function(s) adjusted correctly. The formula for total hours for a project also could be entered as

C4 + C5 + C6 + C7 + C8 + C9 + C10 + C11 + C12 + C13

This formula is clearly more difficult to enter. More important, the formula is static. If one or more employee rows are added, this formula will exclude the new rows from the sum. Using the SUM function instead solves this problem, and SUM is easier to write.

To complete entering the formula, copy the SUM function in cell C16 to cells D16 and E16. Automatic cell adjustment alters each copied formula cell reference to sum the columns for the SDI and CVC projects (see fig. 7.4).

Before entering the total labor SUM functions, you must create three new columns of data. Enter the following formula in row J5:

$H5*C5

The preceding formula is the product of an hourly rate multiplied by the number of hours recorded for a given project. Copy this formula to all cells in the range J5:L12. Column J contains each employee's rate times the hours for the NET project. Column K is the rate times the hours for the SDI project. And column L is the product of rates and hours for the CVC project. These extra columns are needed because they help form the *sum of products* (for example, total labor costs for the NET, SDI, and CVC projects) displayed in cells C17,

D17, and E17 (see figs. 7.4 and 7.5). Move to column I and execute the /Window,Vertical command to produce the split screen shown in figure 7.5.

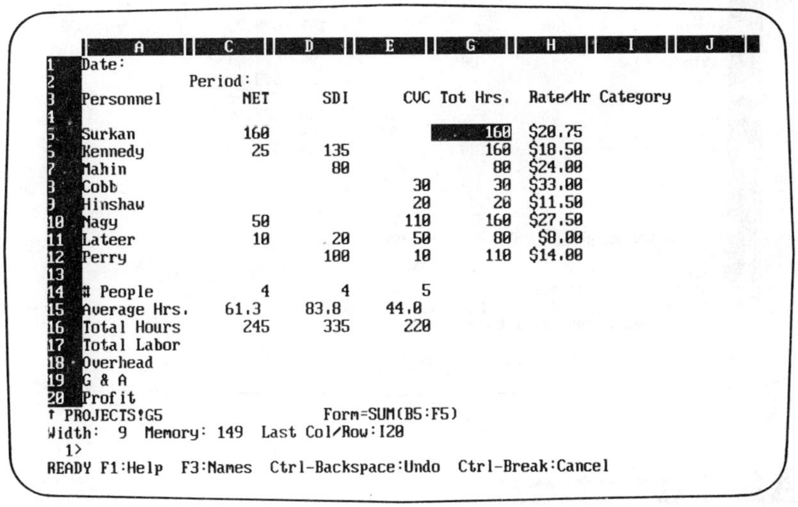

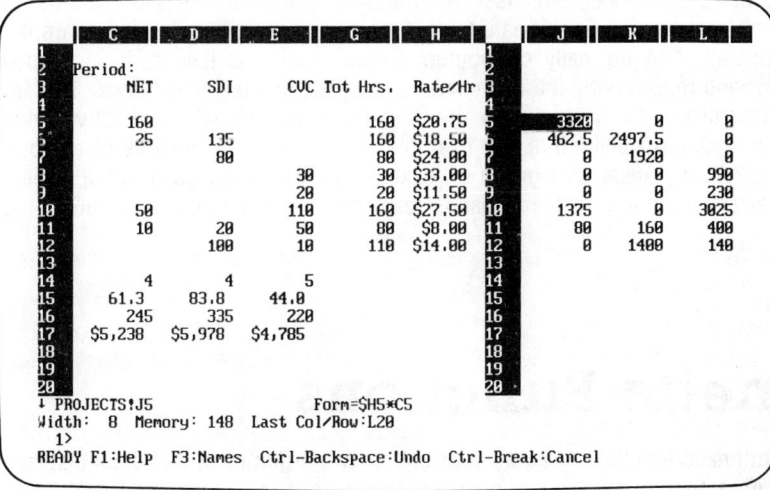

Fig. 7.4.
Program management spreadsheet with SUM functions for total hours.

Fig. 7.5.
Columns containing the products of total hours and hourly rate.

To compute and display the total labor for each project, move to cell C17 and enter the formula

   SUM(J4:J13)

Copy the preceding formula to cells D17 and E17. Figure 7.6 illustrates the program management spreadsheet with sums of total hours per employee (column G), total hours per project (row 16), and total labor costs for each of the three projects (row 17).

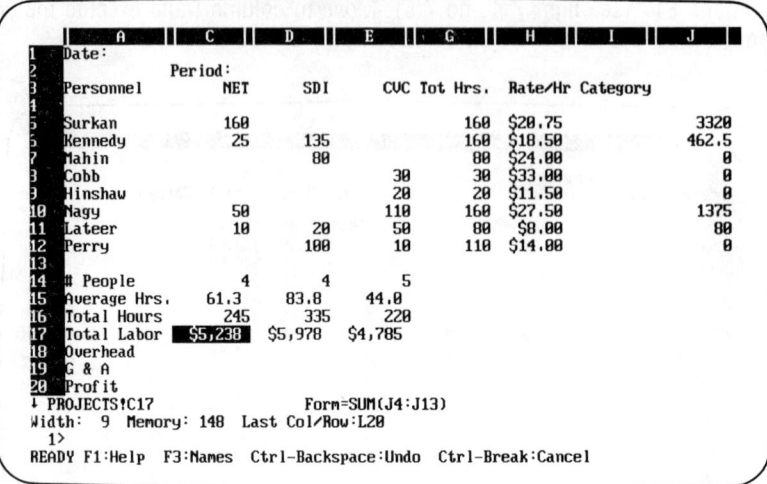

Fig. 7.6.

Spreadsheet with SUM functions.

The VAR Function

VAR is related to the STD function because VAR measures *variance*: the average amount that members of a sample population deviate from the mean or average value (for example, height) of the population. A normally distributed variable, such as height, forms a bell curve. The broader and more gently the bell curve slopes, the greater its variance. That is, a large variance indicates that values vary greatly from the mean, whereas a small variance indicates a narrow, spike-like bell curve (for example, the variance for heights of a group of professional basketball players or a group of jockeys). Although not used in the project management spreadsheet, the variance of labor rates can be computed by entering the formula

VAR(G4:G13)

Arithmetic Functions

Each of the ten arithmetic functions uses a list of one or two arguments, and each displays a numeric value. An argument can be a number, cell address, name, formula, function, or an arbitrarily complex expression. Often, you create formulas by combining the arithmetic functions with other functions. The arithmetic functions are summarized in table 7.2.

Table 7.2
Arithmetic Functions

Function	Meaning
ABS(value)	Returns the absolute value of the argument value entered
EXP(value)	Raises the number *e* (2.71828) exponentially to the power entered
INT(value)	Returns an integer value by dropping the decimal part of the value (truncating)
LN(value)	Returns the natural log base *e* of the value entered. LN is the inverse of the EXP function.
LOG10(value) LOG	Returns the log in base 10 of the value entered
MOD(value1,value2)	Returns the remainder of the first value divided by the second value
ROUND(value,places)	Rounds the value to a specified number of decimal places. If the second argument is negative, the value is rounded to that number of places to the left of the decimal point. Otherwise, the value is rounded to the specified number of places to the right of the decimal point.
ROUNDUP(value,places)	Operates like ROUND except that the value is rounded *up* to the number of indicated decimal places
SQRT(value)	Returns the square root of the value. The value entered must be positive. The ABS function can be used to ensure that the argument is positive: SQRT(ABS(value)).
TRUNC(value,places)	Returns a value truncated to the specified number of decimal places. If the second argument is negative, the value is truncated to that number of places to the left of the decimal point. Otherwise, the value is truncated to the specified number of places to the right of the decimal point.

The ABS Function

The ABS function returns the absolute value of its argument. The function's form is

ABS(value)

The value parameter can be a number, cell address, cell name, formula, or another function. When a formula or function requires a nonnegative value as part of the computation, to avoid the ERROR condition, you can use the ABS function within the formula or function to force the value in the function to be nonnegative. For example, the following formula ensures that the values extracted from the cells named TOTAL HOURS and RATE PER HOUR are made positive in the formula before their product is formed:

>   ABS(TOTAL HOURS)*ABS(RATE PER HOUR)

Note carefully that this formula does not mean that the referenced cells are altered to positive values—only the cells' respective values within the product cell become positive. If the entered labor rates must be positive, you can use an IF conditional function to check new entries of rates and warn the spreadsheet user of data entry errors. The IF function is covered fully in the discussion of conditional logic functions.

The EXP Function

The EXP function raises the number *e* to the power specified in the single argument (see table 7.2). For example, the formula EXP(2) raises *e* (approximately 2.71828) to the second power and displays the result: 7.28906. EXP is the inverse of the LN function; that is, LN(EXP(2)) equals two. (The LN function is discussed following the description of the INT function.)

The INT Function

The INT function forms an integer value from the single cell or formula in the function argument. Values to the right of the decimal point are truncated, not rounded. Therefore, INT(2.378) results in the displayed value of 2. Likewise, INT(−398.765) displays the result as −398.

Note that various forms of the integer can be displayed, such as 2.00 or $2.00 for INT(2.378). The displayed form depends on the format of the cell containing the INT function. If you want a particular integer display in addition to the contents of the integer cell, use the /Format command (for instance, /Format,Entry,Integer).

The LN and LOG10 Functions

The LN function returns the natural log base *e* of the argument value. LN is the inverse of EXP, and the single argument must be positive and numeric. In the following example, the ABS function is included to force the LN argument to a positive value:

>   LN(ABS(A5))

LOG10 returns the log base 10 of the value given. A single argument is specified, and the general form is

>   LOG10(value)

The MOD Function

The general form of the MOD function is

MOD(value1,value2)

This function divides the first argument by the second argument and displays the *remainder* of that division. You can use MOD to constrain values to a certain upper limit. For example, the following formula produces the integer remainder of HOURS divided by 40, and the displayed value is in the range of 0 to 39:

MOD(HOURS,40)

Because 40 is the divisor in the MOD function, any value divided by 40 has a remainder in the range of zero (40 evenly divided HOURS) to 39 (1 less than the divisor). For example, MOD(80,40) returns zero (40 evenly divides 80); however, the formula MOD(79,40) returns 39, because the quotient is 1 and the remainder is 39.

MOD can be used with the RANDOM function to generate random numbers in a given range. For example, if you wish to create a series of random values in the range of 0 to 455, then enter the following formula:

MOD(RANDOM*1000,456)

The ROUND Function

The ROUND function rounds the first parameter value to the number of decimal places indicated in the second parameter. For example,

ROUND(3.141592,3)

rounds 3.141592 to 3 places after the decimal point, resulting in the value 3.142. If you omit the second parameter (the number of decimal places), the value is rounded to a whole number.

Specifying a negative value as the number of decimal places causes rounding to occur to the left of the decimal point. For example,

ROUND(27643.481, −2)

results in the value 27600. Remember that the result shown in this example could be displayed as 27600, 27600.00, or $27,600.00, depending on the format of the cell containing the ROUND function.

To illustrate the ROUND function, let's add to the program management spreadsheet three formulas that calculate those "bottom lines" so dear to a chief financial officer's heart: overhead costs, general and administrative (G & A) costs, and profit. You can compute the overhead formula as a percentage of labor cost with a value of 75 percent. Once you determine overhead, you can calculate general and administrative costs. You can arbitrarily set G & A to 12 percent of total labor plus overhead. Finally, you can calculate profit as a formula of 12 percent of the amount of total labor plus overhead plus G & A. To round the values of overhead, G & A, and profit to whole dollar amounts, you can place the formula for each within the ROUND function like this:

ROUND(formula)

Enter the first formula (for *Overhead*) for project NET (see fig. 7.6) by moving to cell C18 and entering the formula ROUND(75%C17). Move to cell C19, enter the formula for *G & A* as ROUND(12%(C17+C18)). Finally, enter the formula ROUND(12%(C17+C18+C19)) for *Profit* in cell C20. To reproduce these three formulas for the other projects, SDI and CVC, copy the block of three formulas in cells C18, C19, and C20 to corresponding rows in columns D (SDI project) and E (CVC project). Figure 7.7 shows the program management spreadsheet after the three formulas have been entered and copied.

Fig. 7.7.

Rounded values for Overhead, G & A, and Profit.

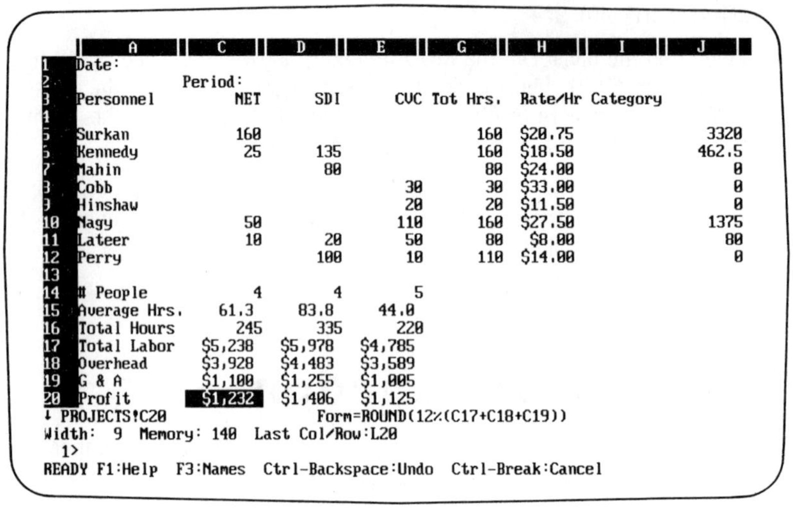

```
    |   A   ||  C   ||   D  ||   E   ||   G   ||   H    ||  I  ||   J   |
1   Date:
2           Period:
3   Personnel      NET    SDI        CVC Tot Hrs.  Rate/Hr Category
4
5   Surkan         160                    160  $20.75          3320
6   Kennedy         25    135             160  $18.50         462.5
7   Mahin                  80              80  $24.00             0
8   Cobb                            30     30  $33.00             0
9   Hinshaw                         20     20  $11.50             0
10  Nagy            50             110    160  $27.50          1375
11  Lateer          10     20       50     80   $8.00            80
12  Perry                 100       10    110  $14.00             0
13
14  # People         4      4        5
15  Average Hrs.  61.3   83.8     44.0
16  Total Hours    245    335      220
17  Total Labor $5,238 $5,978   $4,785
18  Overhead    $3,928 $4,483   $3,589
19  G & A       $1,100 $1,255   $1,005
20  Profit      $1,232 $1,406   $1,125
↓ PROJECTS!C20              Form=ROUND(12%(C17+C18+C19))
Width:  9  Memory: 140  Last Col/Row:L20
    1>
READY F1:Help  F3:Names  Ctrl-Backspace:Undo  Ctrl-Break:Cancel
```

Rounding the contents of a cell and truncating the displayed value of a cell are two different operations. The ROUND function affects the contents of a cell no matter how the contents are displayed in the formatted cell. Figure 7.8 illustrates this distinction. The value 1234.56789 is stored in column A, and four different ROUND functions are placed in columns C through F. Each row is formatted to a different number of decimal places.

Rows 7, 9, 11, 13, and 15 are formatted (**E**ntry level format) to display zero, one, two, three, or four places after the decimal point, respectively (see column B of fig. 7.8). The ROUND function in each formula refers to the same value: 1234.56789 (shown in column A). Cell C9 contains the function

ROUND($A9, −2)

Notice the status line in fig. 7.8. This function and its arguments round the value to two places to the left of the decimal point. One decimal place to the right of the number is displayed because the row is formatted to display one decimal place.

Cell E15 displays the value 1234.5700. Clearly, the number is rounded to two places after the decimal point, but four places after the decimal point are displayed because the entire row is formatted that way. Finally, cell D11 is rounded to the whole number 1235

```
┌─────────────────────────────────────────────────────────────────┐
│      A       B         C          D          E         F          │
│1                 Decimal Places:  /Format Versus ROUND            │
│2                                                                  │
│3            Formatted                                             │
│4   Stored   Decimal                                              │
│5   Value    Places    ROUND(V,-2)  ROUND(V,0)  ROUND(V,2)  ROUND(V,4) │
│6                                                                  │
│7  1234.56789   0          1200       1235       1235       1235  │
│8                                                                  │
│9  1234.56789   1        1200.0      1235.0     1234.6     1234.6 │
│10                                                                 │
│11 1234.56789   2        1200.00     1235.00    1234.57    1234.57│
│12                                                                 │
│13 1234.56789   3       1200.000    1235.000   1234.570   1234.568│
│14                                                                 │
│15 1234.56789   4      1200.0000   1235.0000  1234.5700  1234.5679│
│16                                                                 │
│17                                                                 │
│18                                                                 │
│19                                                                 │
│20                                                                 │
│ ↓ ROUND!C9           V2       Form=ROUND($A9,-2)                  │
│ Width: 13  Memory: 144  Last Col/Row:G16                         │
│    1>                                                             │
│ READY  F1:Help  F3:Names  Ctrl-Backspace:Undo  Ctrl-Break:Cancel │
└─────────────────────────────────────────────────────────────────┘
```

Fig. 7.8.

Rounded values displayed in various formats.

(ROUND($A11,0)) but displays two zeros after the decimal point because of the row format. Therefore, ROUND affects the *value* of a number, but the /Format command affects how the number is *displayed*. Rounding and formatting operations are independent of each other.

The ROUNDUP Function

Unlike the ROUND function, ROUNDUP forces the value in the first parameter to be rounded up to the number of decimal places indicated in the second parameter. For example,

ROUNDUP(3.141592,2)

rounds up 3.141592 to 2 places after the decimal point, to the value 3.15. If you omit the second parameter (the number of decimal places), the value is rounded up to a whole number.

Specifying a negative value as the second parameter causes rounding (up) to occur to the left of the decimal point. For example,

ROUNDUP(27643.481, −2)

results in the value 27700.

The SQRT Function

The SQRT function computes and displays the square root of a value (or cell reference) argument. The argument must be positive. To ensure that the argument is positive, you can include the ABS function to convert the argument to a positive value:

SQRT(ABS(A5))

Always be careful to include as many closing parentheses as you have opening parentheses. Writing too few right parentheses is often the cause of incorrectly interpreted formulas. When the numbers of left and right parentheses do not match, SuperCalc interprets the input expression as text and briefly displays TEXT in the right portion of the screen just after you press Enter.

The TRUNC Function

The TRUNC function forms a truncated value from the single cell or formula in the function argument. TRUNC differs subtly from the INT function, which also produces truncated values: INT always produces integer results, whereas TRUNC can produce values to the right of the decimal point. TRUNC's second argument indicates where truncation is to occur. For example,

TRUNC(76543, −2)

produces the integer 76500. Specifying a positive number as the second argument causes truncation to occur to the right of the decimal point. The expression TRUNC(123.456,1) displays the noninteger value 123.4.

When the second argument in the TRUNC function is zero, then the result is identical to the INT function. For example, the functions TRUNC(754.32,0) and INT(754.32) produce the same result: 754.

Logical Functions

The SuperCalc logical functions are divided into 3 groups:

1. Cell-type test functions

2. Cell-type assignment functions

3. Conditional logic functions

A cell-type test function determines the type of data in the cell or expression supplied as the parameter of the function; the function returns the value of 1 (true) or 0 (false). These functions are usually written as part of a conditional logic function that determines which of two actions the program should take.

The cell-type assignment functions place a value in a cell, rather than test the type of value already in a cell. These functions assign the values ERROR, N/A, TRUE, and FALSE wherever the respective functions are used.

SuperCalc's conditional logic functions are AND, OR, NOT, IF, and EXACT. The IF function is often combined with the other three conditional logic functions to perform one of two possible actions based on the result of a test condition.

Logical Cell-Type Test Functions

Each of the logical test functions returns either 1 (true) or 0 (false) based on the results of a test of the argument. Each function has a single argument, and each function can have either a self-contained expression or a cell reference as an argument.

Table 7.3 provides a list of the logical cell-type test functions and a brief description of what each accomplishes. Two of the functions, ISPROT and ISTIME, are new to SuperCalc5.

Table 7.3
Logical Cell-Type Test Functions

Function	Meaning
ISBLANK(expression) ISB	Determines whether a cell is blank
ISDATE(expression) ISD	Determines whether the cell contains date-type returned value
ISERROR(expression) ISERR ISE	Tests the expression for the ERROR value type
ISNA(expression)	Tests the expression for the Not Available returned value
ISNUM(expression) ISN	Determines whether the expression is a numeric-value type. Text, repeating text, and blank cells are considered numeric types with a value of zero. ISNUM returns 1 (true) for these types of cells.
ISPROT(expression)	Determines whether the expression (or cell address) is protected. True (1) or false (0) is returned.
ISSTR(expression) ISS	Determines whether the expression is text- or string-type data
ISTIME(expression)	Determines whether a cell contains a time value. A cell containing the NOW function does (ISTIME returns 1); a cell containing a text value does not contain a time value (ISTIME returns 0).
ISVAL(expression) ISV	Tests the expression for a numeric-value data type. Unlike the function ISNUM, ISVALUE returns 0 (false) for text, string, and blank cell types.

Following are some examples of how logical test functions and their arguments can be written.

ISBLANK(A5)   (cell reference argument)

ISDATE(DATE(5,12,89))   (expression argument)

Although you can place the logical test functions alone in cells, these functions are often part of a larger conditional logic expression. For example, the following formula contains the ISBLANK function as the test condition, and either `Blank Cell` or `Nonblank Cell` is displayed in the cell containing the IF expression:

IF(ISBLANK(A5),"Blank Cell","Nonblank Cell")

Which of the two text values is displayed depends on whether ISBLANK produces 1 (true) or 0 (false)—whether or not cell A5 is blank. The IF function is discussed later in this chapter.

Figure 7.9 illustrates each logical cell-type test function for each SuperCalc data type. The cell-type test functions are listed in column A. Each function is used in the row with its name. Row 4 shows the type of data tested by functions in the rows below. For example, cell D7 contains the function

ISDATE(D$4)

and cell H12 contains the function

ISSTR(H$4)

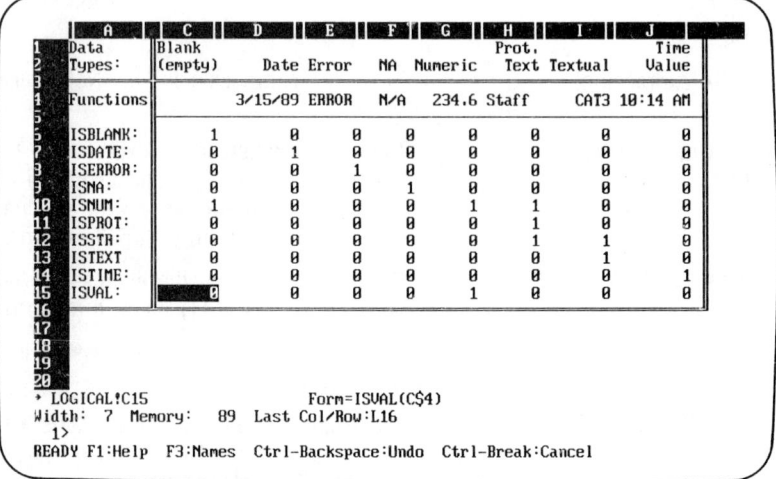

Fig. 7.9.

Logical cell-type test functions.

	A	C	D	E	F	G	H	I	J
1	Data	Blank					Prot.		Time
2	Types:	(empty)	Date	Error	NA	Numeric	Text	Textual	Value
3									
4	Functions		3/15/89	ERROR	N/A	234.6	Staff	CAT3	10:14 AM
5									
6	ISBLANK:	1	0	0	0	0	0	0	0
7	ISDATE:	0	1	0	0	0	0	0	0
8	ISERROR:	0	0	1	0	0	0	0	0
9	ISNA:	0	0	0	1	0	0	0	0
10	ISNUM:	1	0	0	0	1	1	0	0
11	ISPROT:	0	0	0	0	0	1	0	0
12	ISSTR:	0	0	0	0	0	1	1	0
13	ISTEXT	0	0	0	0	0	0	1	0
14	ISTIME:	0	0	0	0	0	0	0	1
15	ISVAL:	0	0	0	0	1	0	0	0

```
* LOGICAL!C15              Form=ISVAL(C$4)
Width: 7  Memory:    89  Last Col/Row:L16
    1>
READY F1:Help  F3:Names  Ctrl-Backspace:Undo  Ctrl-Break:Cancel
```

Columns C through J show the results of each function for eight types of cell contents. All column C functions reference cell C4, which is an empty cell. Functions in column D all refer to cell D4, which contains a date. All cells in the block of cells C6 through J15 display either 0 or 1; a 1 corresponds to true and indicates that the data at the top of the column is the type tested by the function name shown in the left cell in that row. A 0 indicates the result is false. For example, cell J14 displays a 1, indicating that cell J4 displaying the value 10:14 AM is a time type (A14). Cell C15 (where the cell cursor is positioned) indicates that cell C4 is not a value-type cell. Cell C6 displays a 1, indicating cell C4 is empty. The formula

ISBLANK(C$4)

is the *contents* of that cell with a *displayed* value of 1.

Logical Cell-Type Assignment Functions

The logical cell-type assignment functions do not have parameters. Entering ERROR causes ERROR to be displayed. Entering the FALSE or TRUE functions causes 0 or 1 to be displayed, respectively. A cell containing NA displays N/A. (Recall that, in addition to being functions, both ERROR and NA are data types; see Chapter 3.) Table 7.4 lists the logical cell-type assignment functions and describes each briefly.

Table 7.4
Logical Cell-Type Assignment Functions

Function	Meaning
ERROR ERR	Displays ERROR in a cell whose value cannot be calculated
FALSE	Assigns a logical FALSE to a cell and has the numeric value zero
TRUE	Assigns a logical TRUE to a cell and has the numeric value one
NA	Assigns the value Not Available to a cell, displaying N/A

The value ERROR occurs because it is entered directly in a cell or because an expression cannot be calculated by SuperCalc. Look at figure 7.1 and notice that cell J8 displays ERROR because an error exists somewhere in the employee Lateer row. (The rate per hour field is too small and therefore incorrect; thus ERROR is displayed.)

The functions TRUE or FALSE can be placed in cells by themselves, but each function often is used with the conditional logic function IF. An example of use with the IF function is

IF(RATE PER HOUR<12.00,TRUE,FALSE)

In this expression, the function TRUE is invoked (1 is displayed) if the rate per hour is less than $12.00; otherwise, FALSE is invoked (0 is displayed).

Often, the NA function is entered to mark cells in which values are incomplete or yet to be defined. As you develop spreadsheets, place NA in cells you want to define later. The N/A display is a reminder that one or more cells remain undefined.

Conditional Logic Functions

The conditional logic functions include AND, EXACT, IF, NOT, and OR. Table 7.5 lists the conditional logic functions and describes each briefly.

Table 7.5
Conditional Logic Functions

Function	Meaning
AND(value1,value2)	Returns the value 1 (true) if both values are true. Otherwise, returns 0 (false).
EXACT(string1,value2)	Returns the value 1 (true) if both strings (text or labels) match exactly. Otherwise, returns 0 (false).
IF(cond,exp1,exp2)	Tests the condition *cond* and places *exp1* in the cell if the condition is true; otherwise, places *exp2* in the cell
NOT(value)	Places the logical opposite of the value in the cell. If the value is TRUE, places FALSE in the cell, and vice versa.
OR(value1,value2)	Returns the value 1 (true) if either value is true. If both values are false, returns 0 (false).

Expressions involving AND, IF, NOT, or OR are often written with the IF function. The IF function requires three arguments. The first argument is called a *conditional expression* and usually contains a combination of cell references and relational operators ($<$, $>$, $=$, and others). The conditional expression always has a computed value of true or false. The second argument can be an arbitrarily complex expression or a simple expression (for example, C25). The value of the second argument is displayed if the conditional expression is true. If the expression is false, the third argument value is displayed. The general form of the IF function is

IF(conditional expression,true expression,false expression)

If the third argument is omitted and the conditional expression is false, the value zero is returned and displayed.

The AND, OR, and NOT Functions

The AND and OR functions are used to combine elementary logical expressions into more complex logical expressions. Each function has two arguments, and the value returned depends on the logical value of the two arguments. The AND function returns the value true (displays 1) if both argument expressions are true; otherwise, false is returned (0 is displayed). The OR function returns true if either the first or second argument expression is true. If both argument expressions are false, 0 is returned.

The NOT function has a single argument, which is a logical expression. NOT simply reverses the value of the argument. If the argument expression is true, false (0) is returned. Otherwise, true is returned. Examples of AND, OR, and NOT functions related to the program management spreadsheet (but not used in it) are as follows:

AND(TOTAL HOURS<160,HOURLY RATE<12.00)
OR(ISERROR(A1),ISNA(A1))
AND(NOT(ISERROR(A1)),NOT(ISNA(A1)))

The function

> AND(TOTAL HOURS<160,HOURLY RATE<12.00)

returns 1 (true) if the named cell TOTAL HOURS is less than 160 and the named cell HOURLY RATE is less than 12.00. Otherwise, 0 (false) is returned. The function

> OR(ISERROR(A1),ISNA(A1))

returns 1 (true) if A1 displays ERROR *or* contains the "not available" value, NA. If neither of these conditions is true, zero is returned. The third formula, AND(NOT(ISERROR(A1)),NOT(ISNA(A1))), returns results identical to the result of the OR function.

The EXACT Function

The EXACT function, introduced in SuperCalc5, tests whether two labels (text strings) are identical. Its form is

> EXACT(string1,string2)

where *string1* and *string2* are the two labels being tested for equality. EXACT returns 1 (true) if the two strings match, and 0 (false) if they do not. For example, the function

> EXACT("Sales Volume","sales volume")

returns zero, whereas the function

> EXACT("Sales Volume","Sales Volume")

returns one. Note, however, that 0 (false) is returned for the following function, in which one of the strings contains one or more trailing blanks:

> EXACT("Sales Volume","Sales Volume   ")

The IF Function

The IF function is a great tool for validating data entered by spreadsheet users. For example, the program management spreadsheet contains a user-entered date in cell D2 (refer to fig. 7.1). To validate that cell and display a warning message if the date is entered incorrectly, the following expression could be placed in an unused cell near the top of the spreadsheet:

> IF(ISDATE(D2)," ","CELL NOT DATE TYPE")

This IF function contains the conditional expression ISDATE(D2) to determine whether cell D2 is a date entry. If cell D2 is a date entry, a blank value (" ") is returned. The message CELL NOT DATE TYPE is displayed in the cell containing the IF function when cell D2 is not a date-type cell.

Although not currently on the program management spreadsheet, an IF function could be placed in row 14 (refer to fig. 7.7). The function would return the number of people on a project for a certain month or display a warning message if no people reported time for a project. Cells C14, D14, and E14 could contain the following IF function (cell addresses adjusted later for columns D and E):

IF(COUNT(C4:C13) = 0,ERROR,COUNT(C4:C13))

In this function, the ERROR function displays the value ERROR if no one worked on the NET project. If the COUNT function returns a value greater than zero, the third argument value—the count of employees on the project—is displayed.

You could replace nearly every dependent function on the program management spreadsheet with IF functions. If you were to do so, each cell would contain an IF function with a conditional expression similar to the following syntax:

IF(arithmetic result correct?,display arith. result,ERROR)

For example, column G (total hours per person for the month) in figure 7.7 could contain a series of IF functions like the following:

IF(SUM(B5:F5) = 0,"NO SHOW",SUM(B5:F5))

Notice that both the conditional expression tested (SUM = 0) and the value displayed if the data is valid are identical. Almost every spreadsheet formula can be replaced with an IF function testing the formula and returning the formula value or an error indicator. Adding IF functions like these can be useful for identifying data entry errors. For example, the warning NO SHOW is displayed for employee rows containing no hours for the reporting period. This warning probably indicates that hours were omitted inadvertently for one or more employees.

Figure 7.10 shows another popular use of the IF statement: to test a row value against a column value and display a value if a match is found. In figure 7.10, a simple ledger is produced to break out expenses and income into column categories by account number. A transaction, entered in columns A, B, and C of a particular row, appears in one cell in that same row under its associated account number. Transactions are entered as they occur and consist of three parts: transaction date, transaction amount, and assigned account number.

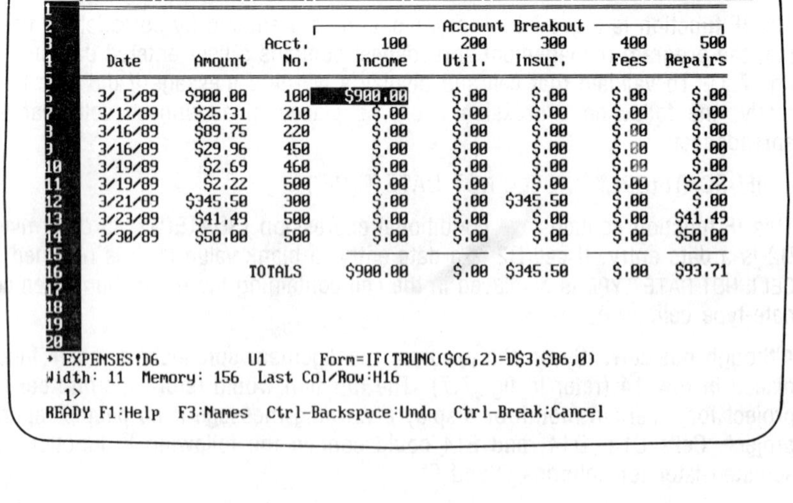

Fig. 7.10.

Using IF to search for row and column matches.

	A	B	C	D	E	F	G	H
						Account Breakout		
			Acct.	100	200	300	400	500
	Date	Amount	No.	Income	Util.	Insur.	Fees	Repairs
6	3/ 5/89	$900.00	100	$900.00	$.00	$.00	$.00	$.00
7	3/12/89	$25.31	210	$.00	$.00	$.00	$.00	$.00
8	3/16/89	$89.75	220	$.00	$.00	$.00	$.00	$.00
9	3/16/89	$29.96	450	$.00	$.00	$.00	$.00	$.00
10	3/19/89	$2.69	460	$.00	$.00	$.00	$.00	$.00
11	3/19/89	$2.22	500	$.00	$.00	$.00	$.00	$2.22
12	3/21/89	$345.50	300	$.00	$.00	$345.50	$.00	$.00
13	3/23/89	$41.49	500	$.00	$.00	$.00	$.00	$41.49
14	3/30/89	$50.00	500	$.00	$.00	$.00	$.00	$50.00
16		TOTALS		$900.00	$.00	$345.50	$.00	$93.71

```
* EXPENSES!D6          U1        Form=IF(TRUNC($C6,2)=D$3,$B6,0)
Width: 11  Memory: 156  Last Col/Row:H16
  1>
READY F1:Help  F3:Names  Ctrl-Backspace:Undo  Ctrl-Break:Cancel
```

An account number appears at the top of its column. Each cell in the range D6 through H14 contains a formula similar to the one displayed in the status line of figure 7.10:

    IF(TRUNC($C6,2) = D$3,$B6,0)

The statement causes a nonzero dollar value from that same row (column B) to be displayed when the row account number matches the column in which the formula is located. Otherwise, zero is displayed. The TRUNC function aids in grouping accounts such as 111, 120, and 145 to be considered a match for the column account 100.

The ledger provides a breakout of expenses and revenues by account and facilitates preparation of other accounting ledgers.

Index Functions

Three table lookup functions (part of the family of *index* functions), LOOKUP, HLOOKUP, and VLOOKUP, are described in this chapter. The remaining index functions are presented in Chapter 8. Before you examine the family of lookup functions, however, add one project to the program management spreadsheet.

A new project, CAIS, has just been acquired by the program manager supervising all major programs. Execute the /Insert,Column command to open a blank column between columns E and F. (Recall from fig. 7.7 that F is an invisible column.) All formulas in cells E14 through E20 are copied to the new column in cells F14 through F20. A new set of hours—130, 140, 80, and 50—are added for employees Cobb, Hinshaw, Lateer, and Perry. You also need to copy the formulas in cells L5 through L12 to cells M5 through M12. This partial column contains the products of total hours and hourly rate for the CAIS project. Figure 7.11 shows the program management spreadsheet after you have inserted the new data and copied the summary information near the bottom of column E to column F.

Notice that as the new hours are added for the previously listed employees, the total hours column (H) is recalculated and displays the new total hours for all employees. Because the SUM formula totaling each employee's hours originally included the unused columns B and F in the range to be summed (refer to fig. 7.4), the cell references are adjusted automatically to the column range of B through G when the new column F is added. Had the original SUM formula for employee row 5 been entered as SUM(C5:E5), the terminal cell reference (E5) would not be adjusted when a new column F is inserted. Therefore, you can see the importance of using empty columns (and rows) to accommodate the addition of columns (and rows). The adjusted SUM formula for cell H5 appears in the dialog panel below the spreadsheet.

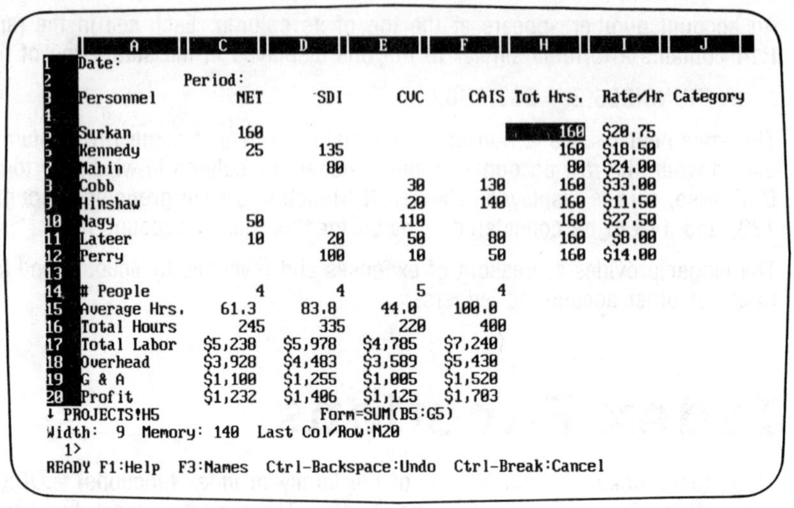

Fig. 7.11.

Spreadsheet with added project column and adjusted SUM formulas.

```
          A    C       D      E       F   H  I       J
 1 Date:
 2         Period:
 3 Personnel   NET     SDI    CVC     CAIS Tot Hrs. Rate/Hr Category
 4
 5 Surkan      160                          160   $20.75
 6 Kennedy      25     135                   160   $18.50
 7 Mahin               80                    80   $24.00
 8 Cobb                        30     130   160   $33.00
 9 Hinshaw                     20     140   160   $11.50
10 Nagy         50            110           160   $27.50
11 Lateer       10     20      50     80    80    $8.00
12 Perry              100      10     50    160   $14.00
13
14 # People      4      4       5      4
15 Average Hrs. 61.3   83.8   44.0   100.0
16 Total Hours  245    335    220    400
17 Total Labor  $5,238 $5,978 $4,705 $7,240
18 Overhead     $3,928 $4,483 $3,509 $5,430
19 G & A        $1,100 $1,255 $1,005 $1,520
20 Profit       $1,232 $1,406 $1,125 $1,703
  ↓ PROJECTS!H5            Form=SUM(B5:G5)
  Width:  9  Memory: 140  Last Col/Row:N20
    1>
  READY  F1:Help  F3:Names  Ctrl-Backspace:Undo  Ctrl-Break:Cancel
```

The LOOKUP Function

The LOOKUP function is the most elementary of the three lookup functions available in SuperCalc. As its name suggests, this function "looks up" a value from a table based on the value of a test variable. This function's general form is

LOOKUP(value,cell range)

(You also can use the abbreviation LU as the function name.) The first parameter, the test variable, can be either a numeric value or a string value. The test variable specifies a value to be looked up in a separate table. This table is specified as the second parameter of the LOOKUP function. Often referred to as the "lookup table," it is usually placed in an out-of-the-way spot in the spreadsheet, although it can be placed in a separate spreadsheet and accessed through SuperCalc's spreadsheet link capability.

You use the LOOKUP function to search a two-row or two-column table for the first occurrence of the largest table value that is less than or equal to LOOKUP's test variable. The lookup table cell range always specifies either the leftmost column (column table) or the topmost row (row table). If the searched table is a pair of columns, the first column contains the values examined by the LOOKUP function. The column to the right contains the list of values returned following a successful search.

Row tables are structured in a slightly different way. The first row contains values to be searched, and the second row contains corresponding values returned as the result of a successful table search. Row tables are searched from left to right (ascending column order), and column tables are searched from top to bottom (ascending row order).

The search method used by the LOOKUP function demonstrates an important point: you must arrange the search row (row tables) or search column (column tables) in *ascending* order. If not, the LOOKUP function will return false results. The LOOKUP function is illustrated in the program management spreadsheet.

The lookup table in the program management spreadsheet is written in two columns to look like the following example. The left column of the labor rate and category table contains labor rates in ascending order; these are boundary values for five labor categories. The second column contains text category names corresponding to the first column's labor rates. Normally considered confidential, the labor rate and category information is located in a table that is not visible when the main portion of the program management spreadsheet is displayed. The labor rate and category lookup table begins in cell I23 and extends to cell J28. The table takes the following form:

Rate	Category
$.00	ERROR
$11.00	CAT1
$16.00	CAT2
$21.00	CAT3
$26.00	CAT4
$31.00	CAT5

The upper left corner of the table contains the value $.00, and the lower right corner contains the text (string) value CAT5. Although unneeded, the labels *Rate* and *Category* above the table help to identify the data in the table and the purpose of each column. To continue building the program management spreadsheet, enter the preceding table in cells I22 (*Rate* label) through cell J28 (CAT5).

Once the lookup table is in place, you are ready to write the LOOKUP function that searches the table. Moving to cell J5 of the program management spreadsheet (see fig. 7.11), enter the formula

LOOKUP(I5,$I$23:$I$28)

The formula contains absolute references to the table so that the copy operation will not adjust the second-argument cell references. Using absolute references in the formula frees you from having to specify **N**o-adjust during any copy operations while you are developing your spreadsheet.

Copy the preceding formula down through the remaining employee rows in column J (cells J6 through J12). This LOOKUP function uses cell I5 as the search value (a labor rate of $20.75 per hour), searches the table specified in the second argument ($I$23:$I$28), and returns the lookup table value found to the right of the highest table value less than or equal to 20.75—CAT2 in the cell J5.

You can use the /**W**indow,**H**orizontal command to display both crucial parts of the spreadsheet simultaneously. Figure 7.12 displays both areas of the program management spreadsheet after you have created the lookup table and placed the LOOKUP function in column J under the label *Category*.

Specifying table range addresses correctly in the LOOKUP function is important. The table range in the preceding function specifies only the first column of the two-column lookup table. Also, the table range references are written in absolute form (the $ precedes both column and row values) so that the range does not adjust when formulas containing the LOOKUP function are copied to other employee rows. The value to look up (I5), however, is a relative cell address. If you were to write the formula

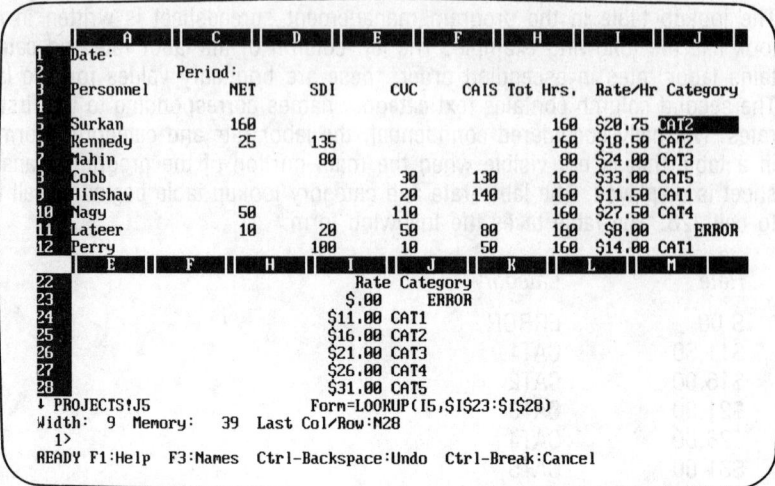

Fig. 7.12.

*Lookup table and
LOOKUP functions.*

LOOKUP(I5,I23:J28)

in cell J5 and then copy that formula to cells J6 through J12, the table-range portion of the LOOKUP formulas in cells J6 through J12 would be adjusted by one for each successive row to which the LOOKUP function is copied. This kind of "moving target" table reference is undesirable.

You could construct a horizontal lookup table, identical to the preceding one, as follows:

$.00	$11.00	$16.00	$21.00	$26.00	$31.00
ERROR	CAT1	CAT2	CAT3	CAT4	CAT5

The shape of the table (vertical or horizontal) determines the way the table range is written in the LOOKUP function. Assuming the preceding table begins in cell I23, you write the LOOKUP function referencing the horizontal table as

LOOKUP(I5,$I$23:$N$23)

Did you notice that the value ERROR appeared in cell J11 of figure 7.12? The LOOKUP function returns this result because the table contains the formula ERROR to the right of the rate $.00. Indicating possible mistakes in labor rates, LOOKUP retrieves the value ERROR from the table whenever the referenced labor rate is less than $11.00 (see the lookup table in fig. 7.12).

The HLOOKUP and VLOOKUP Functions

The HLOOKUP and VLOOKUP functions are similar to the LOOKUP function. Like LOOKUP, both HLOOKUP and VLOOKUP search a table and return a value corresponding to the value supplied as the function's first argument. Both functions have three arguments:

1. A search value to be located in the table

2. A range of cells encompassing the search table

3. A table offset value

The first two parameters are like those in LOOKUP. The table offset value indicates which row or column of the table contains the values to be returned. The general forms of the functions are

HLOOKUP(search value,table address,offset)

and

VLOOKUP(search value,table address,offset)

You can abbreviate HLOOKUP to HLU and VLOOKUP to VLU.

Identical in the way they operate, HLOOKUP and VLOOKUP differ only in the orientation of the lookup table. By definition, HLOOKUP always searches a horizontal table from left to right—across a row of the spreadsheet. VLOOKUP, on the other hand, searches a vertical table from the top to the bottom—down a column. To better understand these concepts, look at some examples of each function and an associated lookup table.

Several examples of the VLOOKUP function are shown in figure 7.13. Two tables containing values to be extracted by VLOOKUP are shown. One table is in cells C4 through F9 and is named EMPID (employee ID) for convenience. The other table is located in cells C15 through D20 and is named PER (performance ratings). The EMPID table is used to look up employees by employee ID number and return the employee's name, sex, or rating evaluation (Rate). The PER table contains a pay rate bonus schedule. If an employee found in the EMPID table has a Rate value of .90, then the PER table reveals that a one-time 10% bonus is due that employee.

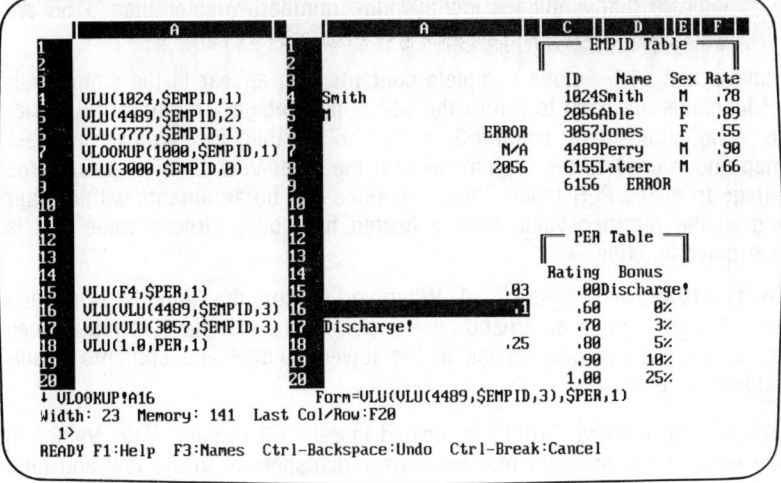

Fig. 7.13.

VLOOKUP functions and vertical lookup tables.

The left window of the figure contains several VLOOKUP formulas, the *contents* of cells A4 through A8 and cells A15 through A18. The values returned by the VLOOKUP function are shown in the right window in column A. For example, the following formula returns the employee's name associated with identification number 1024:

VLU(1024,$EMPID,1)

The first argument is the value to be located in the table during a VLOOKUP search of cells C4 through C9—the search column. $EMPID is the named range of all four table columns. The third-parameter value of 1 indicates that the resulting value should be extracted from the *second* column of the lookup table. This table offset parameter can have values from 0 (''return values from the search column itself'') to the total number of table columns minus 1 (3 for the EMPID table and 1 for the PER table shown in fig. 7.13). Notice that the first column always counts as 0.

Cell A7 contains the formula

VLU(1000,$EMPID,1)

Notice that cell A7 in the right side of figure 7.13 displays N/A. Because the first parameter, the value to be located in the table, is 1000, this value would occur just before the beginning of the lookup table. References to values preceding the beginning of the lookup table always result in N/A being returned by the VLOOKUP, HLOOKUP, and LOOKUP functions.

A formula of special interest is in cell A6 in figure 7.13. Look at the formula:

VLU(7777,$EMPID,1)

The value ERROR is returned because the value being looked up, 7777, is higher than the highest value in EMPID. Because the search value 7777 is above the highest value in the lookup-table search column, VLOOKUP returns the highest table value from the second column of the lookup table. The function ERROR has been placed in the second column of the lookup table to indicate that employee identification numbers greater than 6155 are erroneous.

Look at the formula in cell A16, whose complete contents also appear in the status line. Nested VLOOKUP functions are used to return the bonus percentage. The inner VLU function looks up the rating value (offset column 3 in the EMPID table) for employee number 4489. This returned rate is used as the search value for the outer VLU function and returns the bonus percentage from the PER table. Thus, functions can be arguments within other functions, as long as the returned value from a nested function returns a value that is consistent with the outer function.

The HLOOKUP function is shown in figure 7.14. When you execute the /Window,Horizontal command and the /Global,Formula command, the upper window displays formulas (cell contents). Therefore, you can display values in the lower window and contents simultaneously in the upper window.

The horizontal lookup table (named TABLE) is located in cells C9 through H12. Values in the table could be used in the program management spreadsheet to locate low and high salary values for each category or the number of people in each company category. Organized by ascending text strings from CAT1 to CAT6 in row 9, the table is searched when

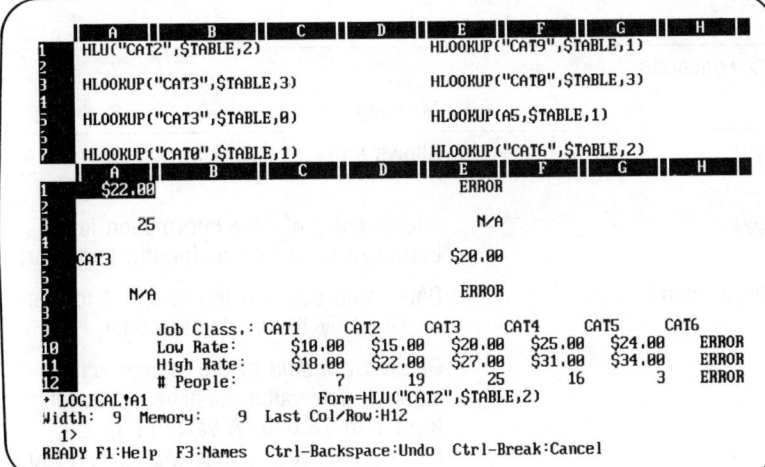

Fig. 7.14.

HLOOKUP functions and a horizontal lookup table.

you supply HLOOKUP with the proper arguments: a category description to locate, table cell addresses, and an offset value. As usual, the offset value specifies the row from which data is to be extracted: 0, 1, or 2.

Notice that the lookup table in figure 7.14 contains a terminal value CAT6 with three ERROR formulas below the CAT6 value. This inclusion permits an error condition to be returned when a category exceeds the allowed maximum value of CAT5. The formulas in cells E1 and E7 (both windows of fig. 7.14) illustrate this condition. The HLOOKUP formula in cell A7 returns N/A (see the lower window of fig. 7.14) because the value "CAT0" is lower than the lowest value in the first row of the lookup table.

Calendar Functions

Calendar functions are divided into two groups: date/time entry functions and date/time reference functions. Calendar functions are often used in applications that require calculations of elapsed number of days, entry of current date, or the number of days invoices are past due. The 18 calendar functions are listed in table 7.6 with a brief description of each function. Nine of these functions are new in SuperCalc5.

SuperCalc stores date values in an unusual way. A modified Julian-calendar numbering scheme represents the 200-year range between March 1, 1900, and February 28, 2100. The internal range of dates consists of days numbered from 1 to 73,049. The calendar functions let you enter a date or time into your spreadsheet and then reference and mathematically manipulate that date or time information. You can use the arithmetic functions of both addition and subtraction with date-type data, but no other arithmetic operators can be used. You also can compare dates and times by using the relational operators (<, >, =, and combinations of these operators).

Table 7.6
Calendar Functions

Date/Time Entry Functions:

Function	Meaning
DATE(mm,dd,yy) DAT	Allows entry of date information
EDAT(dd,mm,yy)	Allows entry of date information in the European format (day, month, and year)
DATEVALUE(string,fmstr)	Date value equal to the string of format specified by the *fmstr* parameter
DVAL(value)	Returns the *date* of the integer value entered. The value must be in the range from 1 to 73,049. A value of 1 corresponds to the date March 1, 1900, and the value of 73,049 corresponds to the date February 28, 2100.
NOW	Returns today's date or time. Obtained from the system date and time kept by the operating system, either the time or date may be accessed and displayed.
TODAY	Reads and displays the system date, which was set by entering the operating system command DATE or by an internal clock that maintains the current date. Unlike the NOW function, the time of day is inaccessible from the TODAY function.
TIME(hh,mm,ss)	The time value of a specified time
TIMEVALUE(string)	Converts a character string expression representing time to a time-formatted value
TVAL(date value)	Returns the time value of the referenced cell containing a date value. It converts the *fractional* portion of the date-valued cell.

Date/Time Reference Functions:

Function	Meaning
DAY(date value)	Returns the number of the day of the month of the referenced cell containing a date value (1 through 28, 29, 30, or 31)

Table 7.6—*Continued*

Date/Time Reference Functions:

Function	Meaning
HOUR(time value)	Returns the hour corresponding to the referenced time value
JDATE(date value)	Returns the Julian date of the date value and ranges from 1 to 73,049. JDATE is the complement of the function DVAL.
JTIME(date value)	Returns a decimal number that is equal to the time found in the referenced date-valued cell
MINUTE(time value)	Returns the minutes portion of a time-valued cell
MONTH(date value) MON	Returns the number of the month of the date value (1 for January, 2 for February, and so on)
SECOND(time value)	Returns the seconds value corresponding to the referenced *time value* cell.
YEAR(date value)	Returns a four-digit year value for the entered date
WDAY(date value)	Returns the number of the day of the week for the entered date (1 for Sunday, 2 for Monday, and so on)

Figure 7.15 shows each of the date/time entry and reference functions. Refer frequently to that figure throughout this section, paying particular attention to the example of each function when it is presented.

Figure 7.15 shows formulas and display-form examples of various date/time entry and date/time reference functions. The right half of figure 7.15 lists the functions you enter, and the left half shows the displayed results. Date/time entry functions are shown in rows 1 through 9; date/time reference functions are in rows 10 through 19.

Date/Time Entry Functions

You can enter a date or a time in a spreadsheet with one of the date/time entry functions: DATE, DVAL, DATEVALUE, EDAT, NOW, TIME, TODAY, TIMEVALUE, or TVAL. If you try to enter a date merely by typing **3/15/89**, SuperCalc computes the value of 3 divided by 15 divided by 89.

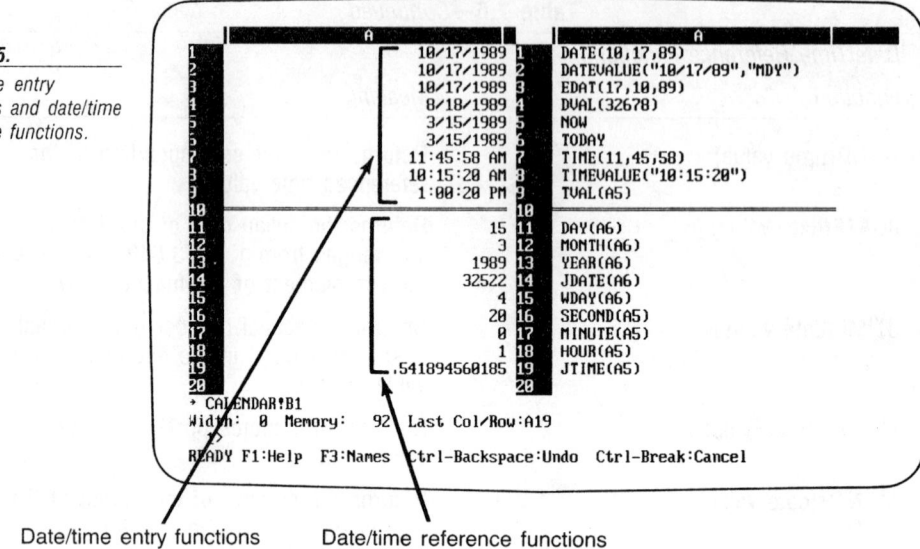

Fig. 7.15.

Date/time entry functions and date/time reference functions.

Date/time entry functions   Date/time reference functions

The DATE Function

You can use the DATE function to enter a date, and type the month, day, and the year as arguments separated by commas:

    DATE(3,15,89)

or

    DAT(3,15,1989)

The default display format is mm/dd/yy (see fig. 7.15, cell A1). Because dates are stored as numbers between 1 and 73,049, dates can be written that span month ranges. For example, the DATE function

    DATE(6,60,89)

displays the date 7/30/89.

The EDAT Function

EDAT permits dates to be entered in the European format by writing the day, month, and year in that order as parameters:

    EDAT(15,3,89)

or

    EDAT(15,3,1989)

The value displayed is identical (month/day/year), regardless of whether you use DATE or EDAT. Keep in mind that if you enter an invalid date such as 6/32/89 or 13/7/89, the date is converted to a valid one and displayed. For example, DATE(6,32,89) converts and displays as 7/2/89, and EDAT(7,13,89) converts to the valid date 1/7/90. In figure 7.15, cell A3 shows an example of EDAT.

The DATEVALUE Function

DATEVALUE has the general form

DATEVALUE(string,format)

where *string* is the character string form of a date and *format* is the format string. The format string is composed of the characters *D*, *M*, and *Y*, corresponding to Day, Month, and Year. The format defines the order of month, day, and year information in the date string. An example is

DATEVALUE("10/17/89","MDY")

which returns the date value 10/17/1989 (see fig. 7.15).

The DVAL Function

The DVAL function displays the date that is equivalent to any number in the range of 1 to 73,049. DVAL(1) corresponds to March 1, 1900, and DVAL(73049) corresponds to February 28, 2100. Like the other date/time entry functions, you can do limited arithmetic operations on date or time values. For example, you can write the formula

DVAL(32678) − 60

to display the date that is 60 days prior to the DVAL-returned date (see fig. 7.15, cell A4).

The NOW Function

The NOW function returns today's date and time as a number. The number represents the number of days since March 1, 1900, and a fraction represents the time elapsed since 12:00 a.m. yesterday. It has no arguments. When used without any other function, NOW displays the date in the same format as the TODAY function.

This function is useful for using your computer's timekeeping capability. NOW gives you access (through the use of the functions associated with time values) to the date and time that are automatically maintained by your internal clock or that you set when you booted up your computer.

Keep in mind that if you do not have an internal clock and you forget to set the clock to the proper date and time, then a bogus time and date will appear in the spreadsheet. If you want to modify the date and time during a SuperCalc session, you can execute the command /**Q**uit,**D**OS to temporarily return to DOS. Then you can execute the DOS DATE and TIME commands and return to your spreadsheet by typing **EXIT** and pressing Enter (see cell A5 in fig. 7.15).

The TODAY Function

Like the NOW function, the TODAY function has no arguments. Wherever TODAY appears, it displays the date obtained from the operating system. TODAY differs from the NOW function in only one way: NOW includes the current time, whereas TODAY does not. Any function returning a time obtained from a cell containing the TODAY function will return 0.

If cells containing the TODAY function display an incorrect date, such as 1/1/80 in 1989, the system date probably was not set when the system was first initialized. To reset the system date, execute /**Q**uit,**D**OS to leave SuperCalc, and fill in the current date. Systems with a built-in clock card automatically maintain the system date.

You also can place dates in cells by referencing other cells containing dates. For example, if cell A1 contains the formula DATE(6,14,89), and the formula

   A1 + 25

is entered in cell B1, the date value 7/9/89 is displayed in cell B1—the date 25 days after the date in A1. Likewise, the formula

   TODAY + 180

displays the date 180 days from the current date.

Another handy feature of date functions is their capability to compute elapsed time between two dates (for example, "How many days behind am I in paying the rent?"), such as,

   TODAY − DATE(6,1,89)

and

   EDAT(1,6,1989) − DATE(1,1,1989)

You can use the TODAY function in the program management spreadsheet featured in this chapter. Place the TODAY function in cell C1 to display the date when the report is created or altered (refer to fig. 7.1). Move to cell C1 and type the function **TODAY**.

You recall that figure 7.1 shows two other cells displaying date information: cells D2 and F2. These cells use date/time reference functions as well as date/time entry functions. Cell A6 in figure 7.15 contains an example of the TODAY function.

The TIME Function

The TIME function provides a way of entering time information into your spreadsheet. The general form of the function is

   TIME(hour number,minute number,second number)

The following are examples of how the TIME built-in function is used:

| TIME(3,30,0) | 3:30 a.m. |
| TIME(23,20,29) | 11:20 p.m. and 29 seconds |

The hour number must be between 0 and 23. The minute number and the second number both must be between 0 and 59. Finally, SuperCalc truncates all but the integer portion of the numeric arguments. SuperCalc formats all time entries as **U**ser-define,**D**ate,**T** by default. Although expressed as numbers, a time entry does not constitute a numeric entry. A time value is a special value that can be referenced only by the time reference functions. However, time values can be used in some arithmetic operations. For example, you can subtract two time values to yield elapsed time. Cell A7 in figure 7.15 shows an example.

The TIMEVALUE Function

The TIMEVALUE function converts   character string into a time-formatted value. The string must match one of the allowed time formats. For example, you can store the time 10:15:20 a.m. in a cell with the formula

TIMEVALUE("10:15:20")

Observe the format difference between TIMEVALUE and the TIME function. TIME requires *integer* values separated by commas as arguments.

The TVAL Function

TVAL converts the *fractional* portion of a value into a time. For example, TVAL(NOW) displays the time (see cell A9 in fig. 7.15). If TVAL references a cell that is empty, 00:00 a.m. is returned. TVAL returns 00:00 a.m. for referenced cells containing integer numbers (only fractional portions of numbers are converted to time values). For example, TVAL(TODAY) displays 00:00 a.m. because TODAY stores only *date* information, not time information.

Date/Time Reference Functions

The nine date/time reference functions are slightly more versatile than the date/time entry functions, especially when the date/time reference functions are used in numeric formulas (see table 7.6). All the date/time reference functions have a single parameter that must be a date/time value, and each function returns a numeric value.

You specify the function followed by a single cell argument that is date or time value. If the referenced cell does not contain a valid date or time, then the function returns ERROR.

Figure 7.15 contains an example of each of the date/time reference functions. Look again at that figure to see examples of how each function is used.

Because the date/time reference functions return numeric results, these functions can be combined with themselves and with date/time entry functions in several meaningful ways. Consider these examples, based on the data in figure 7.15. Suppose that you enter the formula

MONTH(A5) + 1

This function returns the next month. Now, look at a more complicated date/time reference formula:

DATE(MONTH(A5) + 1,1,YEAR(A5))

This formula returns the date of the first day of the next month (4/1/1989). The program management spreadsheet provides another example. The two date entries in cells D2 and F2 (refer to fig. 7.1) indicate a one-month reporting period covered by the spreadsheet. The beginning and ending dates are dependent on (calculated from) the current date stored in cell C1.

Because status reports are usually prepared within 5 to 10 days after the reporting period, the starting date of the reporting period can be derived from the current date. The following formula should be entered into D2 to display the beginning date of the period:

DATE(MONTH(C1) − 1,1,YEAR(C1))

Because cell C1 contains the current date (five days following the end of the monthly reporting period), the value of the expression

MONTH(C1) − 1

is the integer 2. This formula can be plugged into the date function to display the preceding month. You also can type the first part of the date formula as

DATE(MONTH(C1) − 1)

The second argument of the DATE function being entered into cell D2 is 1, the first day of the reporting period. The third argument in the DATE function returns the current year:

YEAR(C1)

This formula displays the first day of the preceding month—the start of the monthly reporting period. Remember that this date is derived from the current date computed and displayed by the TODAY function in cell C1. The current date, in turn, is generated from the system date. If the system date is incorrect, the reporting period starting date also will be incorrect. Always make sure that the system date you enter when you first turn on your computer is correct so that spreadsheets containing dates will be correct.

The ending date for the period is computed from a similar formula. The following formula is entered in cell F2 to display the last date of the reporting period:

DATE(MONTH(D2) + 1,1,YEAR(D2)) − 1

You use the MONTH function to return the current month (numeric) from the reporting-period start date. The value of one is added to the month value returned to produce an intermediate date that is the first day of the next month. (That intermediate date can even fall temporarily into a new year.) The final operation is to subtract one from the entire date value. This method always results in a displayed date that is the last date of the month.

Figure 7.16 shows the current date and the reporting-period dates displayed by the three formulas developed in this section (rows 1 and 2). The content of the ending-period date cell is also displayed in the dialog panel.

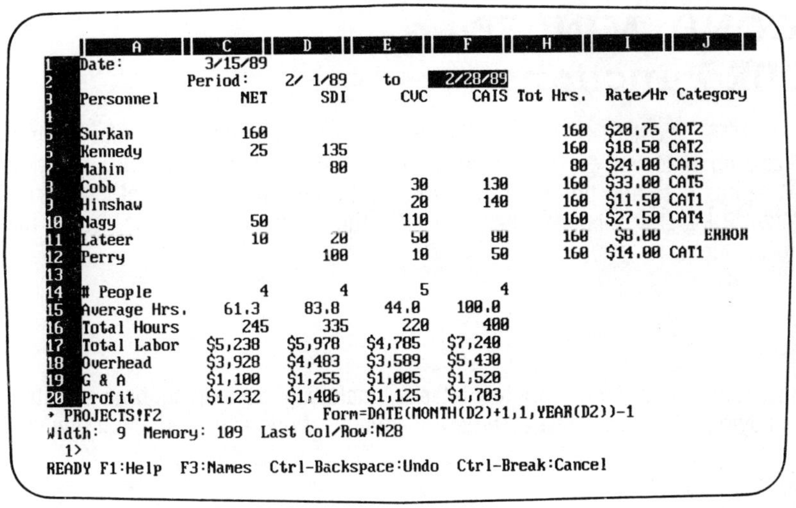

```
    A              C          D          E          F         H       I            J
 1  Date:        3/15/89
 2            Period:    2/ 1/89      to      2/28/89
 3  Personnel       NET        SDI        CVC       CAIS  Tot Hrs.  Rate/Hr  Category
 4
 5  Surkan          160                                      160   $20.75  CAT2
 6  Kennedy          25        135                           160   $18.50  CAT2
 7  Mahin                       80                            80   $24.00  CAT3
 8  Cobb                                   30        130      160   $33.00  CAT5
 9  Hinshaw                                20        140      160   $11.50  CAT1
10  Nagy             50                   110                 160   $27.50  CAT4
11  Lateer           10         20         50         80      160    $8.00       ERROR
12  Perry                      100         10         50      160   $14.00  CAT1
13
14  # People          4          4          5          4
15  Average Hrs.   61.3       83.8       44.0      100.0
16  Total Hours     245        335        220        400
17  Total Labor  $5,230     $5,970     $4,785     $7,240
18  Overhead     $3,920     $4,483     $3,589     $5,430
19  G & A        $1,100     $1,255     $1,005     $1,520
20  Profit       $1,232     $1,406     $1,125     $1,703
* PROJECTS!F2              Form=DATE(MONTH(D2)+1,1,YEAR(D2))-1
Width:  9  Memory: 109  Last Col/Row:N20
  1>
READY F1:Help  F3:Names  Ctrl-Backspace:Undo  Ctrl-Break:Cancel
```

Fig. 7.16.

Date/time entry and date/time reference functions in the program management spreadsheet.

The DAY Function

The DAY function returns the number of the day of the month of the referenced date value (see fig. 7.15). For example, if cell A5 contains the date 5/14/89, then DAY(A5) returns the value 14.

The MONTH Function

Similar to the DAY function, the MONTH function returns the number of the month of the year. If cell A5 contains the date 3/15/1989, then MONTH(A5) returns the value 3 (see fig. 7.15).

The YEAR Function

YEAR returns an integer value corresponding to the year value of a date entry (see fig. 7.15). YEAR(A5) returns 1989 if cell A5 contains 5/12/1989, for example.

The JDATE Function

JDATE returns the Julian date number of a date/time-valued cell. This number has a range of 1 to 73,049 corresponding to the date range of March 1, 1900, through February 28, 2100. Figure 7.15 shows an example of JDATE. The returned value of 32522 corresponds to the date March 15, 1989.

The WDAY Function

WDAY returns the Julian number of the day of the week of a referenced date-valued cell. The values can range from 1 (Sunday) through 7 (Saturday) (see fig. 7.15).

The SECOND, MINUTE, and HOUR Functions

The SECOND, MINUTE, and HOUR functions allow you to extract different units of time from a cell containing time values. For example, if cell A5 contains the NOW function (recall that NOW stores date and time information) and the time portion of that cell corresponds to 1:00:24 P.M. (24 seconds after 1 p.m.), the following functions return the values shown to the right:

HOUR(A5)	1
MINUTE(A5)	0
SECOND(A5)	24

You can use these functions for a variety of tasks, including developing time-sensitive schedules and studying fairly sophisticated time-driven simulations and production queuing problems.

The JTIME Function

JTIME returns the time value of the fractional portion of a date-valued cell (see fig. 7.15). The displayed value is a fraction and is the reciprocal of the TVAL function. Figure 7.15 (cell A19) shows an example in which the referenced time portion of the cell corresponds to 1:00:24 p.m.

The /Arrange Command To Reorganize Rows and Columns

Only one task remains to complete the program management spreadsheet example shown throughout this chapter. That task is to reorganize the employee rows and then to sort the project columns into alphabetical sequence (left to right). The SuperCalc /Arrange command accomplishes both these tasks.

The /Arrange command sorts spreadsheet rows or columns into alphabetical sequence. One of the program's most powerful commands, /Arrange permits three major types of sorts to be performed. You can sort spreadsheet rows by a key column (called a *column sort*), sort spreadsheet columns by a key row (called a *row sort*), or sort a spreadsheet block (called a *block sort*). Whichever method you choose, you can sort only a group of rows or a group of columns.

The *block* option allows you to choose up to three sort keys. The first key chosen is the primary sort key. Second and third sort keys, if chosen, specify additional keys that serve as tie breakers. The second key breaks any first-key ties, and the third key breaks simultaneous first- and second-key ties.

Both *column* and *row* sort operations have a second option that sorts spreadsheet rows or columns by a *secondary* key. The secondary sort is used as a tie breaker for a primary sort. For example, suppose that a spreadsheet similar to the program management spreadsheet contains first and last names of employees in a group of spreadsheet rows. You could execute the /Arrange command to sort rows by last name (the primary-key column) and then by first name (the secondary-key column) to resolve any last-name ties (for example, several employees with last names of Smith).

You can sort rows or columns in either ascending or descending order. If more than two levels of sort are required (for example, sort first by last name, second by first name, and third by middle initial), /Arrange may be executed more than once. Sorting data for more than two key columns or rows is accomplished in steps. To execute multiple key-sort operations, you sort rows or columns by the *least significant* key row or column first. Then sort the partially sorted data again by the *next least significant* key row or column. Finally, sort the data by the most significant key row or column (the primary-sort key row or column) to yield the final form of the reorganized spreadsheet. The ordering of less significant key rows or columns is maintained by each successive execution of /Arrange as long as you specify the same range of rows or columns at each step.

The /Arrange command is illustrated in this section by reorganizing the program management spreadsheet in two important ways. First, the employee rows are rearranged into ascending alphabetic sequence using column A as the key column. Second, the four project columns (labeled *NET*, *SDI*, *CVC*, and *CAIS*) are sorted by the project-name row (row 3) so that the project columns appear in ascending order by project name, left to right. Because data is frequently reorganized only by a *primary key* row or column, /Arrange is illustrated for a single sort key row or column first. Secondary column or row sort options are illustrated in the following section.

Rearranging Rows by a Primary Key

The /Arrange,Column and /Arrange,Row commands have several options. These options specify

1. A column or row sort

2. A key column or row by which the new column or row ordering is determined

3. The block cell range included in the sort

4. Ascending or descending order

5. Adjustment or nonadjustment of formulas

6. A secondary sort if desired

To learn how to use /Arrange, you can reorder the rows of the program management spreadsheet so that the employees' names and their associated rows are placed in ascending sequence by key sort in column A for rows 5 through 12. /Arrange is executed by typing /A or by simply pressing the slash and Enter. Because you specify the range of cells to sort by typing the range of addresses, the cell cursor need not be moved to any particular cell before you execute /Arrange.

Selecting a Column or Row To Sort

After you type **/A**, the first three choices appear: **B**lock, **C**olumn, and **R**ow. Choosing **B**lock lets you further determine whether a key column or key row will be used to determine the sorted sequence. In a similar fashion, **C**olumn and **R**ow allow you to specify whether a key column or key row will be used to determine the sorted sequence. Throughout this section, examine figure 7.17. It contains several parts corresponding to each sort step in the process of sorting the program management rows and columns. The first of these steps is shown in figure 7.17a.

Fig. 7.17.

Executing a key column sort for a range of rows: the /Arrange options.

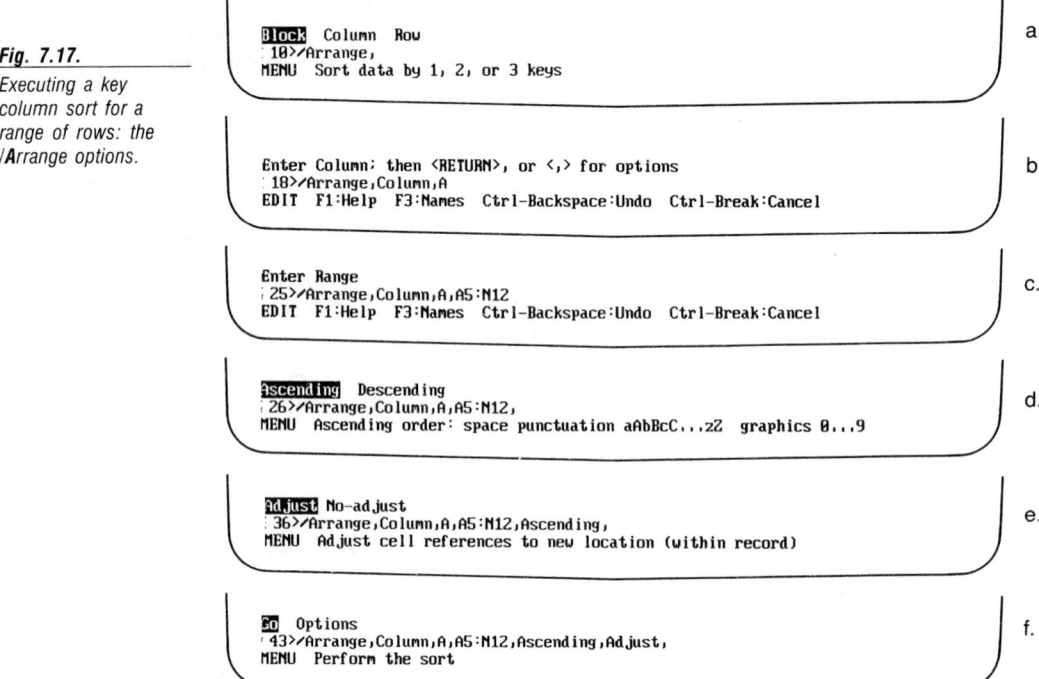

```
Block  Column  Row                                              a.
  10>/Arrange,
MENU   Sort data by 1, 2, or 3 keys
```

```
Enter Column; then <RETURN>, or <,> for options              b.
  18>/Arrange,Column,A
EDIT  F1:Help  F3:Names  Ctrl-Backspace:Undo  Ctrl-Break:Cancel
```

```
Enter Range                                                   c.
  25>/Arrange,Column,A,A5:N12
EDIT  F1:Help  F3:Names  Ctrl-Backspace:Undo  Ctrl-Break:Cancel
```

```
Ascending  Descending                                        d.
  26>/Arrange,Column,A,A5:N12,
MENU  Ascending order: space punctuation aAbBcC...zZ  graphics 0...9
```

```
Adjust  No-adjust                                            e.
  36>/Arrange,Column,A,A5:N12,Ascending,
MENU  Adjust cell references to new location (within record)
```

```
Go  Options                                                  f.
  43>/Arrange,Column,A,A5:N12,Ascending,Adjust,
MENU  Perform the sort
```

The three choices shown in figure 7.17a may be somewhat confusing, and you should be cautious when choosing an option. The choice **B**lock means that you can sort either rows by a key column or columns by a key row. **C**olumn means that *rows* are rearranged according to a key column. Choosing **R**ow means that the order of *columns* is altered according to the values stored in the key row. Remember, then, to choose **C**olumn to sort rows or **R**ow to sort columns. You can choose **B**lock to sort either columns or rows. The difference between the **B**lock option and either the **R**ow or **C**olumn option is that with **B**lock SuperCalc *remembers* the range of cells to be sorted and the key column(s) or row(s). SuperCalc does not remember ranges if you choose either **C**olumn or **R**ow. (Similar to the **B**lock characteristic of remembering ranges is the print range: /**O**utput,**P**rint,**R**ange.) The remainder of this section illustrates the second and third choices: **C**olumn and **R**ow.

Because you want to sort the program management spreadsheet rows by employee last names that are located in column A (refer to fig. 7.16), select the key column option by typing **C**.

Specifying the Key Column

Next, choose the key column. Which column of the program management spreadsheet determines the sort order? Column A does, so type **A** (see fig. 7.17b) and press the comma key. If you type **A** and press Enter, /Arrange immediately sorts the spreadsheet rows using a set of default values. (All rows of the spreadsheet are rearranged in ascending order.) Usually, the default /Arrange options are not desirable, so be careful to specify explicitly all options until you become more familiar with the /Arrange command.

Specifying the Block of Cells
To Be Reorganized

Once the key column has been selected and followed by a comma to request additional /Arrange options, you select range of cells to be sorted.

The range of cells to be sorted is rows 5 through 12—the employee name rows. You have two ways, in this example, to indicate the block or cell range to be sorted. Either specify the entire block of rows by typing **5:12** or specify the block of cells **A5:N12**. The end of the range is N12; the products of labor rates multiplied by hours for each employee and each project are out of view in the block of cells K5 through N12. Type the range **A5:N12** (see fig. 7.17c), and type a comma after the range to indicate that additional options are desired. Notice that if the block of cells were specified as A5:A12, only the key column would be sorted. Furthermore, employees' names would be disassociated from their respective rows after the sort. The prompt, entry, and help lines displayed after the cell range is specified are shown in figure 7.17d.

Choosing Ascending or Descending Sort Order

The key column and its associated block of cells can be reorganized in ascending order (the default) or descending order. Ascending order is selected when **A** is typed, and descending order when **D** is typed. These selections dictate how the key column in this example is reorganized. Because the block of cells participating in the sort operation must always include the key row or column, the block of cells as well as the key cells are reorganized.

To sort employee rows in ascending order, type **A**. The prompt, entry, and help lines displayed are shown in figure 7.17e.

Adjusting Formulas within the Selected Block

The **A**djust and **N**o-adjust options determine whether cell references in the block to be sorted are adjusted. Because formulas often contain references to other cells, you should generally select the **A**djust option. The only time when **N**o-adjust is appropriate is when formulas and the cells the formulas reference are in the same row or the same column. That is, **N**o-adjust is fine when you are sorting rows (by a key column) as long as all formulas in a given row always reference cells within that same row. Likewise, each column to be rearranged by a key row must contain references to cells within the same column only. If either of these conditions is not true, choose the **A**djust option so that formulas are adjusted to reflect the new locations of cells the formulas reference.

Choose the **A**djust option for the program management spreadsheet. Type **A** and the final options appear in the prompt, entry, and help lines (see fig. 7.17f).

You would select the **O**ptions choice to specify secondary sort information. Because the program management key column contains unique names, you select the **G**o option. When you press Enter, /**A**rrange executes.

Following execution of the /**A**rrange command, the employee rows are reorganized, cell references are adjusted, and cell values are recalculated. You can see the results of the sort in figure 7.18. Notice that only rows 5 through 12 have been rearranged. Rows before 5 and after 12 remain unchanged.

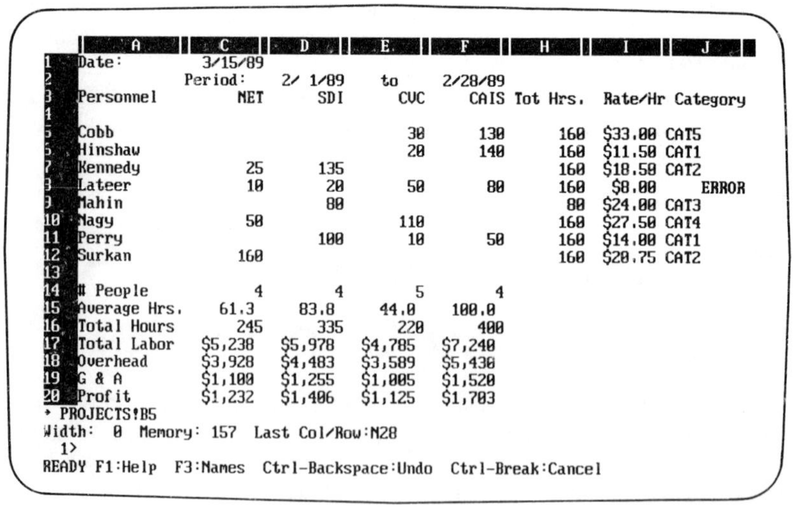

Fig. 7.18.

*Employee rows after /**A**rrange is executed.*

	A	C	D	E	F	H	I	J
1	Date:	3/15/89						
2		Period:	2/ 1/89	to	2/28/89			
3	Personnel	MET	SDI	CVC	CAIS	Tot Hrs.	Rate/Hr	Category
4								
5	Cobb			30	130	160	$33.00	CAT5
6	Hinshaw			20	140	160	$11.50	CAT1
7	Kennedy	25	135			160	$18.50	CAT2
8	Lateer	10	20	50	80	160	$8.00	ERROR
9	Mahin		80			80	$24.00	CAT3
10	Nagy	50		110		160	$27.50	CAT4
11	Perry		100	10	50	160	$14.00	CAT1
12	Surkan	160				160	$28.75	CAT2
13								
14	# People	4	4	5	4			
15	Average Hrs.	61.3	83.8	44.0	100.0			
16	Total Hours	245	335	220	400			
17	Total Labor	$5,238	$5,978	$4,785	$7,240			
18	Overhead	$3,928	$4,483	$3,589	$5,430			
19	G & A	$1,100	$1,255	$1,005	$1,520			
20	Profit	$1,232	$1,406	$1,125	$1,703			

```
* PROJECTS!B5
Width:  8  Memory: 157  Last Col/Row:N28
  1>
READY F1:Help  F3:Names  Ctrl-Backspace:Undo  Ctrl-Break:Cancel
```

Rearranging Columns by a Key Row

The second and final sort operation to be performed on the program management spreadsheet is to rearrange the project columns (C through F) into left-to-right alphabetical sequence by project name. Because the order of columns is determined by the labels at the top of the project columns in row 3, you invoke /**A**rrange,**R**ow (key row). Next, type **3** to indicate that row 3 is the key row.

As in the preceding rearrangement of employee rows, the next option you specify is the range of cells to be rearranged. You choose the range that includes cells C3 through F12. To complete the set of options to rearrange project rows, type a comma after the cell range and select the **A**scending option. Again, the choice of **A**djust or **N**o-adjust is presented. Choose the **A**djust option by typing **A**. The entry line now appears as

    40›/Arrange,Row,3,C3:F12,Ascending,Adjust

Choose **G**o to start sorting the columns.

If you choose **O**ptions rather than **G**o, you can specify a secondary sort key. However, inspection of the column labels (*NET*, *SDI*, *CVC*, and *CAIS*) in the key row reveals no duplicate values. Thus, a secondary sort key is not needed. Type **G** or press Enter to invoke the /**A**rrange command with the full list of options. After you execute /**A**rrange, the four projects are placed into ascending order within columns C through F (see fig. 7.19).

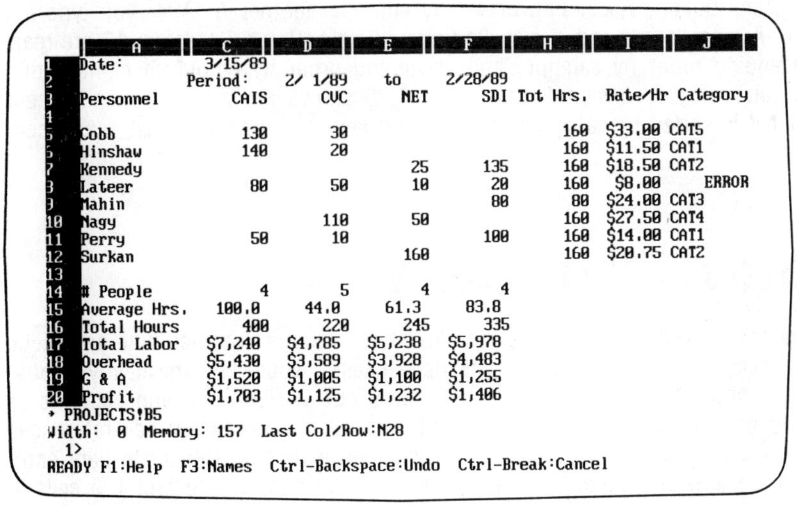

Fig. 7.19.

Project columns after /*Arrange* is executed.

	A	C	D	E	F	H	I	J
1	Date:	3/15/89						
2		Period:	2/ 1/89	to	2/28/89			
3	Personnel	CAIS	CVC	NET	SDI	Tot Hrs.	Rate/Hr	Category
4								
5	Cobb	130	30			160	$33.00	CAT5
6	Hinshaw	140	20			160	$11.50	CAT1
7	Kennedy			25	135	160	$18.50	CAT2
8	Lateer	80	50	10	20	160	$8.00	ERROR
9	Mahin				80	80	$24.00	CAT3
10	Nagy		110	50		160	$27.50	CAT4
11	Perry	50	10		100	160	$14.00	CAT1
12	Surkan			160		160	$20.75	CAT2
13								
14	# People	4	5	4	4			
15	Average Hrs.	100.0	44.0	61.3	83.8			
16	Total Hours	400	220	245	335			
17	Total Labor	$7,240	$4,785	$5,238	$5,978			
18	Overhead	$5,430	$3,589	$3,928	$4,483			
19	G & A	$1,520	$1,005	$1,100	$1,255			
20	Profit	$1,703	$1,125	$1,232	$1,406			

    ◆ PROJECTS!B5
    Width: 0 Memory: 157 Last Col/Row:N28
      1›
    READY F1:Help F3:Names Ctrl-Backspace:Undo Ctrl-Break:Cancel

Using a Secondary Key

You select a secondary sort option whenever the key column or row contains duplicate data. For example, if the program management spreadsheet were sorted by the key column labeled *Category* (column J), employee rows could be placed into ascending order by text category data (see fig. 7.19). Because duplicate values exist in the key column *Category* (two CAT1 values and two CAT2 values), you can use a secondary key to sort duplicate entries into relative order by a secondary key column. Column A (employees' last names) can be used as the secondary key column. To use primary and secondary keys, enter the /**A**rrange command in the same way as before, except type the letter **O** at the prompt so that you can select secondary key sort options.

Go through the steps needed to arrange the employee rows first by category designation and then by employee last name. The prompt line and entry line up to the point in which a secondary sort key is selected appear as follows:

```
Enter Secondary sort column
    49›/Arrange,Column,J,5:12,Ascending,Adjust,Options,
```

Notice that the prompt line requests that a secondary sort column be selected. Because the primary key is a column, the secondary key must be a column as well. Type **A** to select column A—the employee name column. The prompt and entry lines displayed are

```
Ascending Descending
    51›/Arrange,Column,J,5:12,Ascending,Adjust,Options,A,
```

You specify the final option, **A**scending order, by entering another **A**. After you type the final option, the /**A**rrange command is executed immediately. Rows 5 through 12 are rearranged into ascending order by category and ascending order by employee name within groups of duplicate category designations. Figure 7.20 shows the program management spreadsheet after it is sorted by category (primary sort key) and employee last name (secondary sort key).

Chapter Summary

SuperCalc's functions perform calculations that would be arduous if written with arithmetic operators alone. Without functions, some spreadsheet tasks would become nearly impossible. Imagine the difficulties if the SUM function were not available. To add columns or rows, you would have to construct formulas containing all the necessary cell references joined by addition arithmetic operators. A long calculation would be subject to data entry errors and would be time-consuming to enter. (For example, sum up the first 129 cells in column A.)

In this chapter, you have seen SuperCalc's logical functions, statistical functions, arithmetic functions, and calendar functions. You have learned that the /**A**rrange command reorganizes rows and columns of data in ascending or descending order on primary and secondary keys (a key row or a key column). /**A**rrange is used frequently in this chapter so

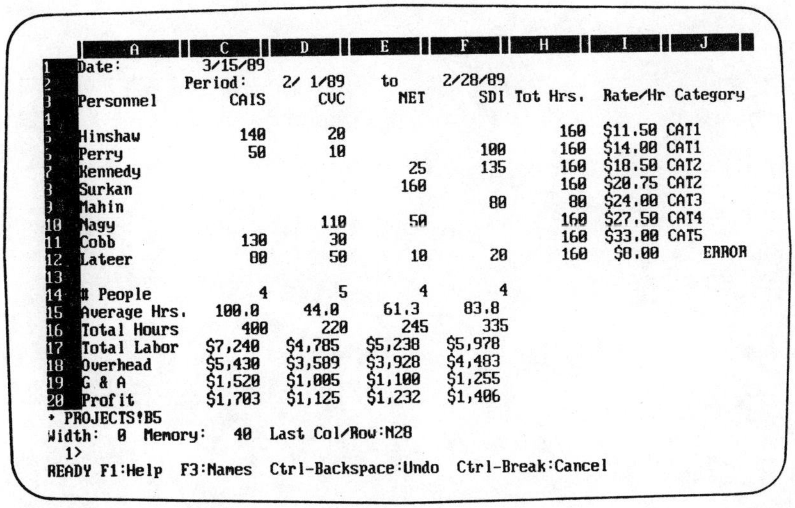

Fig. 7.20.

Project spreadsheet sorted by category and employee name.

	A	C	D	E	F	H	I	J
1	Date:	3/15/89						
2	Period:		2/ 1/89	to	2/28/89			
3	Personnel	CAIS	CVC	MET	SDI	Tot Hrs.	Rate/Hr Category	
4								
5	Hinshaw	140	20			160	$11.50 CAT1	
6	Perry	50	10		100	160	$14.00 CAT1	
7	Kennedy			25	135	160	$18.50 CAT2	
8	Surkan			160		160	$20.75 CAT2	
9	Mahin				80	80	$24.00 CAT3	
10	Nagy		110	50		160	$27.50 CAT4	
11	Cobb	130	30			160	$33.00 CAT5	
12	Lateer	80	50	10	20	160	$0.00	ERROR
13								
14	# People	4	5	4	4			
15	Average Hrs.	100.0	44.0	61.3	83.8			
16	Total Hours	400	220	245	335			
17	Total Labor	$7,240	$4,785	$5,238	$5,978			
18	Overhead	$5,430	$3,589	$3,928	$4,483			
19	G & A	$1,520	$1,005	$1,100	$1,255			
20	Profit	$1,703	$1,125	$1,232	$1,406			

```
* PROJECTS!B5
Width:  8  Memory:    40  Last Col/Row:M28
  1>
READY F1:Help  F3:Names  Ctrl-Backspace:Undo  Ctrl-Break:Cancel
```

that you can become familiar with its use. Chapter 8 introduces index, financial, and trigonometric functions. Data management statistical functions are described in Chapter 12 with the SuperCalc data management commands.

8

Functions: Part II

The power and breadth of SuperCalc built-in functions call for two chapters to describe the complete set of functions. In the last chapter, you learned about the statistical, arithmetic, logical, index, and calendar functions. This chapter focuses on the extensive set of financial functions, the enhanced class of index functions, the full complement of trigonometric functions, and the added set of string functions.

Financial functions, the first group of functions discussed in this chapter, are one of the main reasons spreadsheets were invented. Early in spreadsheet history, @NPV, a function to calculate the net present value of a stream of cash flows, was created for the VisiCalc program. Since then, many more financial functions have been incorporated into spreadsheets. Computer Associates first went beyond the basics when they added 12 new financial functions to SuperCalc4 for a total of 18 functions. The added functions analyzed periodic annuity calculations, lifetime annuity calculations, onetime investments, and periodic investments, and provided three alternative depreciation methods. With the 18 functions provided in SuperCalc, you can analyze different investment decisions from all sides and save a good deal of time creating formulas.

The next group of functions discussed in this chapter is a complete set of trigonometric functions. Included in this discussion is some graphic output that shows the interactions and comparable roles of the functions.

This chapter includes a discussion of an enhanced class of index functions. These functions include the traditional lookup functions for locating a value from a range of cells and another group of functions that converts spreadsheet and range locations and sizes into numeric values for use with macros, cell-reference expressions, and other formulas. The unique ITER function, also grouped with the index functions, identifies the number of times the spreadsheet has been calculated.

Finally, the chapter concludes with a discussion on a completely new set of functions for handling strings and taking care of other special requirements.

To help you learn how to use the financial functions, this chapter gives simple examples that should translate easily to your own situations. Because SuperCalc offers functions for analyzing all sides of financial decisions, each discussion of a financial function includes a question that a specific function may best address. These common investment-decision questions can help you decide which function to use in a particular situation.

235

Financial Functions

SuperCalc has several financial functions that facilitate calculations involving annuities, investments, and depreciation. Look at table 8.1 for definitions of recurring financial-analysis terms that appear in the discussion of these functions.

Table 8.1
Definitions of Terms

Terms	Definition
Period	A unit of time, such as a day, a month, or a year
Rate	The periodic interest rate. For periods shorter than one year, rate adjustment is necessary. The monthly interest rate equal to an annual 12 percent interest rate, for example, is 1 percent (12/12).
Term	The number of periods. If the rate is stated in months, for example, the term also must be expressed in months.
Payment	The periodic payment, such as the monthly mortgage payment
Present value	The value of an investment or loan at the beginning of the term
Future value	The value of an investment or loan at the end of the term

SuperCalc's financial functions are discussed in the following order:

1. Lifetime annuities
2. Periodic annuities
3. Onetime investments
4. Multiple-period investments
5. Depreciation

Lifetime Annuity Functions

Annuities are investments that yield equal periodic payments over a period of time. For a general type of annuity, called an *ordinary annuity*, payments are received at the end of each period. For another type, called an *annuity due*, payments are received at the beginning of each period. All SuperCalc functions default to the ordinary annuity. Table 8.2 shows the SuperCalc functions that relate to lifetime ordinary annuities.

Table 8.2
Lifetime Annuity Functions

Function	Meaning
ANRATE	Periodic interest rate
ANTERM	Number of periods of payments
PMT	Amount of the periodic payment
PV	Current value of a series of payments

These four functions produce results relating to the annuity as a whole. Each function considers a different part of the equation that determines the overall parameters of an annuity. In other words, you look over time at the aggregate values of the annuity instead of looking at a point in time. When using these functions, you must express the rate, payment, and term in the same measurement throughout (days, months, or years, for example).

The most practical example is an ordinary mortgage. The spreadsheet in figure 8.1 is used to show all four lifetime annuity functions.

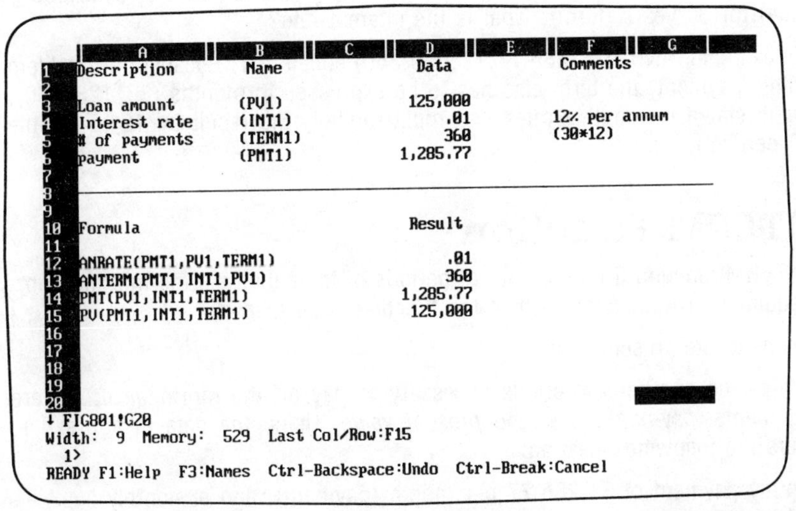

Fig. 8.1.

Using lifetime annuity functions.

In this example, the total principal amount of the mortgage is $125,000. This 30-year mortgage is payable in 360 equal monthly payments at an annual interest rate of 12 percent. The monthly payment, therefore, is $1,285.77. Column D in the top half of the figure lists the factors of the monthly payment. To make the example easier to follow, each cell range name is given in column B. Specifically, the loan amount data range in D3 is named PV1, the interest rate cell is named INT1, the number of payments cell is named TERM1, and the payment amount cell is named PMT1.

The bottom half of the figure demonstrates how each lifetime annuity function, given the other values, provides the solution to one factor. By analyzing this example, you can learn which function to use when you are missing a component of the equation.

A common unknown variable, for example, is the monthly payment amount. You usually know the principal amount, the rate, and the term; but you need to figure a monthly payment. The PMT function can determine the monthly payment you must make. In another case, you may know the monthly payment on a mortgage, the term of the mortgage, and the mortgage rate; and you need to calculate the principal amount. The PV function answers these questions for you. By plugging in any three of the four necessary values, you can determine the fourth value.

The ANRATE Function

You use the ANRATE function when the interest rate of the mortgage is the missing component. The general form of the function is as follows:

ANRATE(payment,present value,term)

This function calculates the periodic interest rate related to an annuity (in this case, a mortgage) based on three arguments: *payment*, *present value*, and *term*. In the example in figure 8.1, ANRATE answers the question:

Given a payment of $1,285.77 per month (payment) on a loan amount of $125,000 (present value) for 30 years (term), what is the interest rate?

In the mortgage example, ANRATE(1285.77,125000,360) equals .01. Because the problem involves a monthly payment, the term also has to be expressed in months (30*12 = 360), and the answer is stated in monthly rate. You must multiply the result by 12 to get the annual rate (12 percent).

The ANTERM Function

You use the ANTERM function if the number of periods of the annuity is the missing component in the equation. The general form of the function is as follows:

ANTERM(payment,rate,present value)

ANTERM calculates the number of periods necessary to pay off the mortgage if you are given three arguments: *payment*, *rate*, and *present value*. Using the data in figure 8.1, ANTERM answers the following question:

Given a monthly payment of $1,285.77 per month (payment), and a monthly mortgage interest rate of 1 percent (rate) on a $125,000 loan (present value), how many months are necessary to repay the loan?

In figure 8.1, ANTERM(1285.77,.01,125000), stored in D13, equals 360. Because both the payment and interest rate are expressed in months, so is the term. To convert the term to years, simply divide by 12, for an answer of 30 years.

The PMT Function

The PMT function is probably the most widely used of the four lifetime annuity functions. PMT solves for the periodic payment amount when you are given the remaining three components of the formula. The general form of the function is as follows:

PMT(present value,rate,term)

This function calculates the periodic payment necessary to reduce the first argument (*present value*) to zero, given the second argument (*rate*) over the number of periods specified in the third argument (*term*). PMT answers the following question:

Given a $125,000 loan with an annual interest rate of 12 percent and a 30-year life, what is the monthly payment?

In the example in figure 8.1, PMT(125000,.01,360), stored in D14, equals $1,285.77. Like the previous examples, both the term and interest rate must be expressed in months in order to get an answer in months.

The PV Function

You use the PV function to calculate the present value of an amount when you are given the remaining three components specified in the formula. The general form of PV is as follows:

PV(payment,rate,term)

The arguments required to solve this formula are *payment*, *rate*, and *term*. In figure 8.1, the PV function answers the following question:

Given monthly payments of $1,285.77 (payment) on a 12-percent loan (rate) over 30 years (term), what is the initial principal balance?

In the example, PV(1285.77,.01,360) equals $125,000. Once again, all the known variables must be stated in similar terms.

The PV function can help you calculate windfall earnings, such as a state or commercial lottery. Suppose that you win $20,000,000; but instead of receiving the complete sum in cash, you are scheduled to get $1,000,000 per year over the next 20 years. The delay in payments means that you may actually receive less than $20,000,000 in current value. You can use the PV function to calculate what the prize is worth to you today. The only thing you must estimate is the interest rate (or investment rate) you want to use in the formula. Assuming that you can invest the sum at 10 percent annually, the formula is as follows:

PV(1000000,.10,20)

This formula is based on the assumption that you get each payment in a single check at the end of every year. Based on these assumptions, the actual current value of your prize is $8,513,563.72. So if someone offers you $9,000,000 cash for it—take it!

The relationships between these four functions (ANRATE, ANTERM, PMT, and PV) are important. Four variables—payment, rate, term, and present value—are needed to explain an annuity. The functions provided by SuperCalc enable the user to solve for any unknown without having to handle the underlying financial formulas. As long as all variables are stated in similar terms, the lifetime annuity functions offered by SuperCalc can prove very useful.

Periodic Annuity Functions

You have just seen how SuperCalc handles lifetime annuities. This section describes the periodic annuity functions, which examine the status of the annuity at one point in time rather than over the full life of the annuity. Once again, SuperCalc defaults to the ordinary annuity, where payments are made at the end of each period. Table 8.3 shows the Super-Calc periodic annuity functions.

Table 8.3
Periodic Annuity Functions

Function	Meaning
BALANCE	Balance remaining after a specified number of payments
KINT	Amount of interest paid for a specified period of an annuity
KPRIN	Amount of principal paid for a specified period of an annuity
PAIDINT	Cumulative interest paid to date through a specified period for an annuity

The periodic annuity functions help you answer specific financial questions concerning both annuities and mortgages. These SuperCalc functions can save you significant time in creating the formulas behind annuities and mortgages.

To help you understand these functions, look at the mortgage example again. Figure 8.2 is the same spreadsheet, but now it displays the four periodic annuity functions.

In the top section of this figure a fifth variable, period, has been added. This variable specifies the point in time to analyze the annuity. In this example, the remaining principal amount, the total interest paid to date, and the breakdown of the current period's payment between principal and interest are calculated for the 12th period of the mortgage.

In cell A16 in the lower section of the figure under *Observations*, several relationships are described to show how these different functions interact.

The BALANCE Function

The BALANCE function calculates the remaining principal balance based on a period you specify, given the initial principal balance, interest rate, and total periods of the annuity. The general form of BALANCE is as follows:

BALANCE(present value,rate,term,period)

In this function, *present value* is the original loan amount (PV1 in fig. 8.2), *rate* is the interest rate of the mortgage (INT1), *term* is the number of payments into which the loan is

```
┌──────────────────────────────────────────────────────────────────┐
│    ║     A        ║║    B    ║║    C    ║║  D  ║║  E    ║║  F  ║   │
│   1║Description     ║    Name   ║  Data    ║     ║Comments     ║    │
│   2║                                                                │
│   3║Loan amount     (PV1)       125,000                             │
│   4║Interest rate   (INT1)          .01          12% per annum      │
│   5║# of payments   (TERM1)         360          (30*12)            │
│   6║Payment         (PMT1)       1,285.77                           │
│   7║Period          (PER1)           12                             │
│   8║─────────────────────────────────────────                      │
│   9║Formula                      Result                             │
│  10║                                                                │
│  11║BALANCE(PV1,INT1,TERM1,PER1)  124,546.40     (BALANCE1)         │
│  12║KINT(PV1,INT1,TERM1,PER1)       1,245.86     (KINT1)            │
│  13║KPRIN(PV1,INT1,TERM1,PER1)         39.90     (KPRIN1)           │
│  14║PAIDINT(PV1,INT1,TERM1,PER1)   14,975.59     (PAIDINT1)         │
│  15║                                                                │
│  16║Observations                                                    │
│  17║                                                                │
│  18║(KINT1+KPRIN1)                  1,285.77                        │
│  19║PV1-BALANCE1                       453.60                       │
│  20║((PMT1 * PER1) - PAIDINT1)         453.60      ████████         │
│  ↓ FIG802!F20                                                       │
│  Width: 9  Memory:  527  Last Col/Row:E20                          │
│    1>                                                               │
│  READY F1:Help  F3:Names  Ctrl-Backspace:Undo  Ctrl-Break:Cancel   │
└──────────────────────────────────────────────────────────────────┘
```

Fig. 8.2.

Using periodic annuity functions.

divided (TERM1), and *period* is the point in time at which you want to evaluate the loan or annuity (PER1). The BALANCE function answers the question:

Given a $125,000 loan with an annual interest rate of 12 percent and monthly payments for 30 years, what is the remaining principal balance after 12 payments?

In the example, BALANCE(125000,.01,360,12) equals $124,546.40 (row 11). This figure clearly shows how little principal is paid in the first year of a mortgage ($453.60)! Once again, all applicable variables (such as rate, term, and period) must be stated in the same terms, this time, months.

The KINT Function

The next two functions, KINT and KPRIN, concern the monthly payment amount. When added together (see row 18 in fig. 8.2), the two functions return the full payment amount. Although each total monthly mortgage or annuity payment is equal, the interest and principal portions of each payment are different. In the early periods of a mortgage, you pay off more interest and less principal, but these proportions reverse in later periods. The KINT function determines what the interest portion of the monthly payment is at a specific period in the term of the loan. The general form of KINT is as follows:

KINT(present value,rate,term,period)

In KINT, *present value* is the original loan amount (PV1), *rate* is the interest rate of the loan or annuity (INT1), *term* is the total number of payments for the loan (TERM1), and *period* is the point where you want to evaluate the loan or annuity. In terms of figure 8.2, KINT answers the following question:

Given a $125,000 loan at an annual interest rate of 12 percent for 30 years, what is the value of the interest portion of the 12th payment?

In the example, KINT(125000,.01,360,12) equals $1,245.86. All variables except present value are stated in the same terms (months). The results of this function and the next function, KPRIN, add up to the monthly payment amount.

The KPRIN Function

The KPRIN function complements the KINT function. KPRIN calculates the principal amount of an annuity at any point in time. The general form of KPRIN is as follows:

KPRIN(present value,rate,term,period)

The arguments required for this function are identical in content and format to the KINT function. Given the initial annuity amount, the interest rate of the annuity, the total term, and the period in question, SuperCalc calculates the principal portion of the payment for that period. KPRIN can be used to answer the question:

Given a $125,000 loan at an annual interest rate of 12 percent for 30 years, what is the value of the principal portion of the 12th payment?

In the example, KPRIN(125000,.01,360,12) equals $39.90. All variables except present value must be stated in similar terms (months). Line 18 of the spreadsheet shows that the interest plus the principal paid in the 12th payment equals the total payment (KINT1 + KPRIN1 = PMT1).

The PAIDINT Function

Although you can think of the KINT and KPRIN functions as period functions, think of PAIDINT as a total-to-date function. PAIDINT calculates the total amount of interest paid on an annuity up to and including the period specified in the function's arguments. The general form of PAIDINT is as follows:

PAIDINT(present value,rate,term,period)

This function requires the same arguments as the other functions in this category: the original annuity amount (*present value*), the interest rate of the annuity (*rate*), the number of payments (*term*), and when to base the calculation (*period*). PAIDINT answers the following question:

Given a $125,000 loan at an annual interest rate of 12 percent over 30 years, what is the total amount of interest paid after 12 payments?

In the example, PAIDINT(125000,.01,360,12) equals $14,975.59. All variables except present value must be stated in the same terms (months).

The PAIDINT function relates to the other functions in the following way. Row 19 of figure 8.2 shows that the present value minus the balance (PV1 − BALANCE1) equals the amount of principal paid during the 12-month period ($453.60). Row 20 shows an alternate method of arriving at this figure; you multiply the number of periods by the payment and subtract the PAIDINT figure ((PMT1*PER1) − PAIDINT1).

The functions presented in this section complete SuperCalc's package of eight annuity-related features. Different combinations of these functions are capable of solving most of your annuity-related problems.

Onetime Investment Functions

This section pertains to investments that basically do not change—investments set up with an initial amount at a fixed interest rate and left to grow. Examples of these onetime investments are certificates of deposit or zero-coupon bonds on the investment side and simple-interest loans on the debt side. Table 8.4 lists the SuperCalc functions that analyze a onetime loan or investment.

Table 8.4
Onetime Investment Functions

Function	Meaning
CTERM	Periods needed to grow a current value into a future value given an interest rate
COMPBAL	Compounded future value after a specified number of periods at a specified rate
RATE	The periodic interest rate needed to grow a current value into a future value over a specified number of periods

The spreadsheet in figure 8.3 shows the three onetime investment functions.

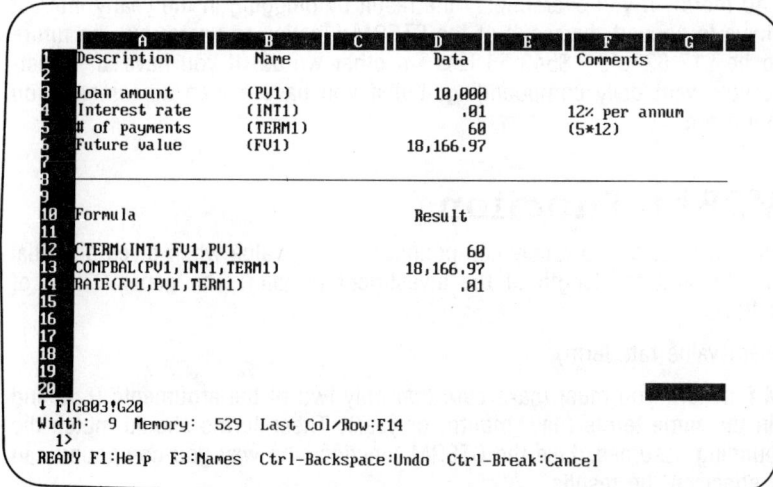

Fig. 8.3.

Using onetime investment functions.

The top section of figure 8.3, similar to figures 8.1 and 8.2, identifies the components of a loan. In this case, the loan amount is $10,000, the interest rate expressed as a monthly rate is .01 (12 percent per year), the number of payments expressed in months is 60 (5 years), and the future value of the loan (the total principal and interest paid for the loan) is $18,166.97. The lower section of the figure shows how the three onetime investment functions in SuperCalc interact in this situation.

The CTERM Function

The CTERM function calculates the number of periods necessary to grow from a present value to a future value at a given interest rate. The general form of CTERM is as follows:

CTERM(rate,future value,present value)

CTERM answers the question:

Given an initial balance of $10,000, with an annual interest rate of 12 percent compounded monthly, how much time is required to reach an ending balance of $18,166.97?

In the example in figure 8.3, CTERM(.01,18166.97,10000) equals 60 months. As with annuity functions, you must state all relevant variables for the onetime investment functions in the same terms (in this case, monthly interest *rate*). You also must state the rate and period in terms of when the compounding takes place. In this example, interest is compounded monthly. (The money is calculated and interest is added by the bank each month.) If you were analyzing a passbook savings account investment in which the bank compounds the investment daily, you should state the rate as a daily equivalent (annual interest rate * 1/360). The result appears as a certain number of days. To convert this result to years, divide the CTERM function by 360 (a simplified figure for the number of days in a year) to arrive at the number of years for the investment. If the example in figure 8.3 had been a daily compound situation rather than monthly, the future value would be $18,219.37 ($52.40 more). If you oversimplify the result by plugging in the yearly interest rate, you do not have to convert the result of the CTERM function to years; but the future value turns out to be $17,623.42—$543.55 less. In other words, if you have an investment opportunity, you want daily compounding; but if you have a loan agreement, you want yearly compounding.

The COMPBAL Function

The COMPBAL function calculates a totally compounded ending value when given an initial value, an interest rate, and the length of the investment or loan. The general form of COMPBAL is as follows:

COMPBAL(present value,rate,term)

Unlike the CTERM function, you must make sure that only two of the arguments (*rate* and *term*) are stated in the same terms (day, month, or year). These terms should match the method of compounding assumed. Like the CTERM function, the way you compound can have a significant effect on the results.

COMPBAL answers the question:

Given an initial balance of $10,000, with an annual interest rate of 12 percent compounded monthly over 5 years, what is the ending balance?

In the example, COMPBAL(10000,.01,60) equals $18,166.97. If interest had been compounded weekly, however, the result would have been $18,208.60 (COMPBAL(10000,.002308,260)).

The RATE Function

The RATE function calculates the interest rate required to produce a given ending balance from a given present value and length of the investment or loan. The general form of RATE is as follows:

RATE(future value,present value,term)

The RATE function answers the question:

What interest rate is necessary to produce a future value of $18,166.97 from an initial value of $10,000 and a term of 5 years compounded monthly?

In figure 8.3, RATE(18166.97,10000.00,60) equals .01. Like CTERM, RATE must be converted to years if an argument (in this case, *term*) is stated in anything other than years. To obtain an annual rate based on the monthly value of this example, simply multiply by 12.

This section has described the onetime investment functions offered by SuperCalc. To apply these functions accurately, you must remember to state the factors in the same terms and to keep the investment static. In other words, once the investment is made, it runs to term with no deposits or withdrawals.

Multiple-Period Investment Functions

This section explains the most complex financial situations, where investments are made and returns are received in several periods. These functions include the "granddaddy" of spreadsheet financial functions: the NPV function. Table 8.5 shows the functions that allow the user to set up calculations for both fixed and variable financial investments.

Table 8.5
Multiple-Period Investment Functions

Function	Meaning
FV	Future value of a stream of even payments invested at a given rate
TERM	Number of periods needed to grow a stream of payments invested at a given rate into a future value
IRR	Internal rate of return: the rate of return needed to offset an initial payment with a stream of predicted cash flows
NPV	Net present value of a steam of cash flows given a rate of investment

As with annuity and onetime investment functions, SuperCalc uses an ordinary annuity situation to calculate the results of these functions—a situation in which payments are made or received at the end of the period. The FC and TERM functions deal with fixed return situations; the IRR and NPV functions deal with variable returns.

Figure 8.4 shows the uses of FV and TERM. In the top section of this example, you see all the components of an investment decision: the interest rate, the number of payments, the payment amount, and the future value. The logic is the same whether the payments are deposited in a savings plan or extended toward paying off a loan. Sitting down at the screen for an afternoon of "what ifs" with this particular example is a good way to analyze what type of retirement plan you require to continue to live in the style to which you have grown accustomed. You can determine the amount you must save per year, your annual return on the investment, and how many years until actual retirement.

Fig. 8.4.

Using the FV and TERM functions.

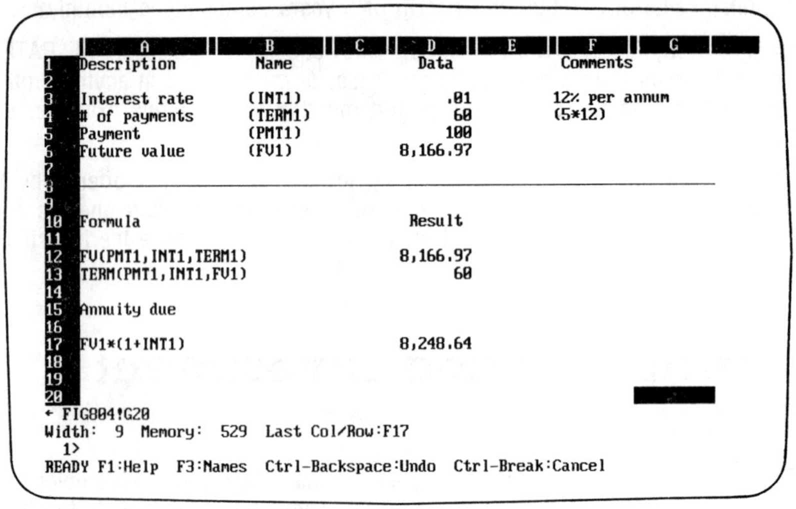

```
           A            B            C      D       E        F       G
 1  Description       Name                  Data            Comments
 2
 3  Interest rate     (INT1)                  .01           12% per annum
 4  # of payments     (TERM1)                  60           (5*12)
 5  Payment           (PMT1)                  100
 6  Future value      (FV1)             8,166.97
 7
 8
 9
10  Formula                            Result
11
12  FV(PMT1,INT1,TERM1)                8,166.97
13  TERM(PMT1,INT1,FV1)                      60
14
15  Annuity due
16
17  FV1*(1+INT1)                       8,248.64
18
19
20
← FIG804↑G20
Width:  9  Memory:  529  Last Col/Row:F17
    1>
READY F1:Help  F3:Names  Ctrl-Backspace:Undo  Ctrl-Break:Cancel
```

The FV Function

The FV function calculates the fundamental unknown amount, the future value of an investment, based on an assumed level of payment, interest rate, and duration. This function is limited in that it applies only to situations where the payments remain constant. The general form of FV is as follows:

FV(payment,rate,term)

The *rate* and *term* arguments must be stated in the same terms. You must match the expected compounding rate (yearly, monthly, weekly, or daily) to get the most accurate result. In terms of the example in figure 8.4, FV answers the question:

What is the value at the end of 5 years of $100 invested at the end of each month at an annual interest rate of 12 percent, compounded monthly?

In the example, FV(100,.01,60) equals $8,166.97. Note that both the interest rate and term had to be restated in terms of months to match the payment time frame. For an annuity due, one where you make investments at the beginning of the month, multiply FV by (1 + INT1). In this case, the result is $8,248.64 ($8,166.97*(1 + .01)).

The TERM Function

The TERM function calculates the number of periods of equal payments required (based on a given interest rate) to attain a specified future value. The general form of TERM is as follows:

TERM(payment,rate,future value)

In figure 8.4, TERM answers the question:

How long do you need to accumulate $8,166.97, assuming monthly payments of $100 payable at the end of the month and a monthly compounded annual interest rate of 12 percent?

In the example, TERM(100,.01,8166.97) equals 60. Because all terms are stated in months, the result is 60 months, or 5 years.

The NPV and IRR Functions

The next two functions, NPV and IRR, evaluate multiperiod situations in which the returns or payments vary. Typically, capital budgeting problems use these two methods to analyze cash flows. Both functions use the time value of money (cash in the future is worth less than cash today) and the assumption that a desired rate of return must be earned. The desired rate is the minimum rate of return that an investment must yield to be acceptable.

In a capital budgeting problem, these functions help you evaluate a series of cash inflows and outflows for a certain amount of return. If the rate of return is higher than the desired rate, the investment is accepted. If the rate of return is lower than the desired rate, the investment is rejected. Figure 8.5 shows the NPV and IRR functions in use.

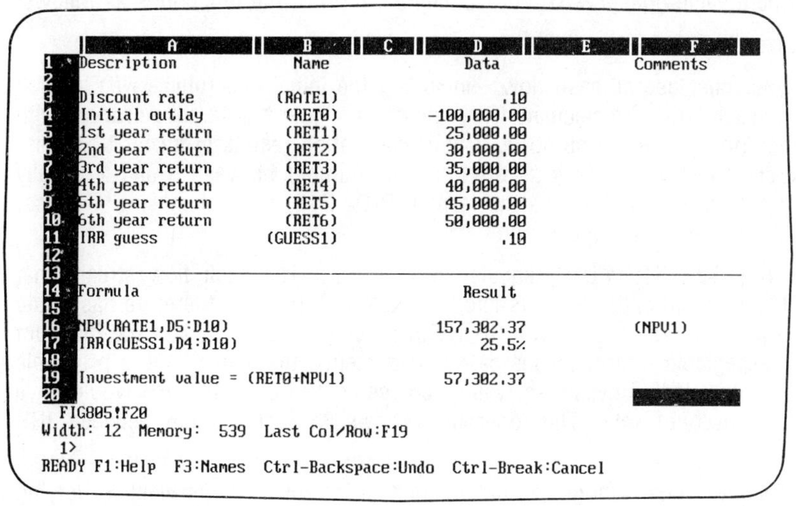

```
           A              B        C        D        E         F
 1   Description          Name              Data              Comments
 2
 3   Discount rate        (RATE1)            .10
 4   Initial outlay       (RET0)     -100,000.00
 5   1st year return      (RET1)       25,000.00
 6   2nd year return      (RET2)       30,000.00
 7   3rd year return      (RET3)       35,000.00
 8   4th year return      (RET4)       40,000.00
 9   5th year return      (RET5)       45,000.00
10   6th year return      (RET6)       50,000.00
11   IRR guess            (GUESS1)           .10
12
13
14   Formula                            Result
15
16   NPV(RATE1,D5:D10)               157,302.37       (NPV1)
17   IRR(GUESS1,D4:D10)                  25.5%
18
19   Investment value = (RET0+NPV1)   57,302.37
20
     FIG805!F20
Width: 12  Memory:  539  Last Col/Row:F19
  1>
READY F1:Help  F3:Names  Ctrl-Backspace:Undo  Ctrl-Break:Cancel
```

Fig. 8.5.

Using the NPV and IRR functions.

In this example, an investment requires an initial cash outlay (RET0) of $100,000. An annual discount rate of 10 percent (RATE1) and 6 years of positive cash flows (RET1 through RET6) are assumed. Based on these assumptions, NPV and IRR are two Super-Calc tools to help you determine whether the investment is financially sound.

The NPV (net present value) function calculates the present value of a stream of cash flows at a given discount rate. The general form of NPV is as follows:

NPV(rate,row/column range)

NPV differs from the PV function because NPV does not require equal cash payments or flows, and the term is implicit in the number of cells included in the *row/column range* argument. You set the discount rate, which is the first argument (*rate*), equal to the minimum acceptable rate of return. The investment value should be positive for the investment to be accepted. The example in figure 8.5 shows a typical cash flow stream, when an initial outflow is followed by successive inflows.

In the example, NPV(RATE1,D5:D10) equals $157,302.37. The RATE1 argument is the discount rate. (Typically, capital budgeting problems use annual data; therefore, the discount rate is an annual rate.) The range of cash flows is D5:D10. Remember that the rate and range must be stated in the same terms (in this case, years). If each cell contained a monthly cash-flow value, the desired discount rate would have to be defined as a monthly rate in order for the function to calculate correctly. Note that the initial cash flow is excluded from the range.

To arrive at the investment value, add the NPV of the cash flow stream to the initial cash flow (RET0 + NPV1). Line 19 of figure 8.5 shows this. The investment value in the example is $57,302.37. Because the number is positive, the investment has a rate of return higher than the desired rate and should be accepted.

The IRR function, known as the Internal Rate of Return, calculates the rate of return for which the investment value equals zero. The conceptual form of the function is as follows:

IRR(stream of cash flows) − initial cash outlay = 0

To set up IRR, you must use all cash flows, including the initial one (unlike NPV, which excludes the initial cash flow). To calculate IRR, you must trigger the iterative process with a "guess" number (to "prime the pump"). If your calculation results in an ERROR message, try a different guess to produce an answer. Any number between 0 and 1 usually produces the correct answer. If you use the form IRR(D4:D10) without making a guess, SuperCalc uses .1 as the default guess number.

In the example, IRR(GUESS1,D4:D10) equals 25.5 percent. The cash flow stream that begins with −$100,000 and ends six years later with a $50,000 inflow therefore has a rate of return of 25.5 percent. As long as the IRR (25.5 percent) is greater than the discount rate (a minimum acceptable return, in this case, 10 percent), the investment is profitable and should be accepted. If the investment value had resulted in zero, the IRR would have been equal to the discount rate. This operation shows the relationship between IRR and NPV.

Both IRR and NPV give you methods to analyze multiperiod investments yielding varying returns. Both functions are valid when only one sign change appears in the cash flow stream. The preceding example had only one sign change: an initial outflow of −$100,000 followed by six positive cash inflows. Both methods resulted in acceptance. The investment value was positive at a discount rate of 10 percent, and the IRR was 25.5 percent compared to the discount rate of 10 percent.

Depreciation Functions

SuperCalc has three depreciation functions. Each function requires information concerning the cost, salvage value, and the life of the asset. Table 8.6 lists the depreciation functions.

Table 8.6
Depreciation Functions

Function	Meaning
DDB	Amount of depreciation for a period using the double-declining balance method
SLN	Amount of depreciation for a period using the straight-line method
SYD	Amount of depreciation for a period using the sum-of-the-years digits method

A depreciation schedule is a means to distribute the expense of a long-term asset across its useful life for tax purposes. Instead of reducing income by the full value of the asset in the year it is purchased, an estimate is made on how long the asset may be useful, and a portion of the cost is absorbed in each year of the asset's lifetime.

The DDB Function

DDB, the double-declining balance function, is an accelerated depreciation method that allows you to capture more of the cost of the asset in the early years. DDB calculates depreciation for a given period based on a double-declining balance.

The general form of DDB is as follows:

DDB(cost,salvage,life,period)

The *cost* argument is the original value of the asset, *salvage* is the estimate of the residual value of the asset (if any), *life* is the number of years the asset may be useful, and *period* is the period of the asset's life for which you want to determine the amount of depreciation. In the underlying formula, you multiply the net book value by 2 and divide by the life of the balance. In figure 8.6, the calculation for the first year for an asset costing $10,000, depreciated over five years, and with a salvage value of $1,000 at the end of the five years (DDB(10000,1000,5,1)), equals $4,000.

The most difficult component of this formula to identify is the salvage value. It should equal the amount you can sell the asset for at the end of the five years. The underlying calculation is ((10000*2)/5). The calculation for the second year is (((10000 − 4000)*2)/5). The function ignores the salvage value in the early years, using it only to adjust the final year's depreciation so that the sum of all years' depreciation equals the cost minus salvage value.

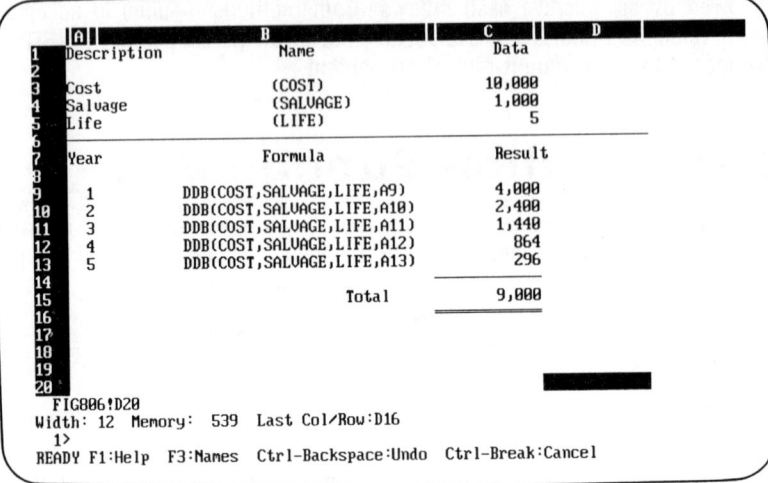

The SLN Function

The SLN, or straight-line, function calculates depreciation based on the straight-line method. Straight-line is the simplest and most commonly used method of depreciation.

The general form of SLN is as follows:

    SLN(cost,salvage,life)

Again, *cost* equals the original value of the asset, *salvage* is the estimated residual value of the asset after its useful life, and *life* is the number of years the asset will be useful. Unlike DDB, no period is necessary because straight-line depreciation takes cost minus salvage and divides by the life of the asset. The amount of depreciation is therefore the same in each period (see fig. 8.7).

The SYD Function

The SYD, or sum-of-the-years digits, function calculates depreciation for a given period using the sum-of-the-years digits method. The general form of SYD is identical to DDB:

    SYD(cost,salvage,life,period)

SYD requires a period because the function is an accelerated depreciation method and the amount of depreciation varies from period to period. In figure 8.8, SYD(10000,1000,5,1) equals $3,000.

The underlying calculation is based on the total of the years. In this case, the total of years is 15:

    1+2+3+4+5

```
 |A|            B               || C  ||    D  |
1  Description            Name              Data
2
3  Cost                  (COST)            10,000
4  Salvage               (SALVAGE)          1,000
5  Life                  (LIFE)                 5
6
7  Year                  Formula           Result
8
9    1          SLN(COST,SALVAGE,LIFE)      1,000
10   2          SLN(COST,SALVAGE,LIFE)      1,000
11   3          SLN(COST,SALVAGE,LIFE)      1,000
12   4          SLN(COST,SALVAGE,LIFE)      1,000
13   5          SLN(COST,SALVAGE,LIFE)      1,000
14
15                       Total             9,000
16
17
18
19
20
  FIG807!D20
 Width: 12  Memory:  539  Last Col/Row:D16
   1>
 READY F1:Help  F3:Names  Ctrl-Backspace:Undo  Ctrl-Break:Cancel
```

Fig. 8.7.
Using the SLN function.

```
 |A|            B               || C  ||    D  |
1  Description            Name              Data
2
3  Cost                  (COST)            10,000
4  Salvage               (SALVAGE)          1,000
5  Life                  (LIFE)                 5
6
7  Year                  Formula           Result
8
9    1          SYD(COST,SALVAGE,LIFE,A9)   3,000
10   2          SYD(COST,SALVAGE,LIFE,A10)  2,400
11   3          SYD(COST,SALVAGE,LIFE,A11)  1,800
12   4          SYD(COST,SALVAGE,LIFE,A12)  1,200
13   5          SYD(COST,SALVAGE,LIFE,A13)    600
14
15                       Total             9,000
16
17
18
19
20
  FIG808!D20
 Width: 12  Memory:  539  Last Col/Row:D16
   1>
 READY F1:Help  F3:Names  Ctrl-Backspace:Undo  Ctrl-Break:Cancel
```

Fig. 8.8.
Using the SYD function.

The first year's depreciation is taken by multiplying the beginning book value ($9,000) by the ratio of the last year to the total (5/15). The second year's depreciation is (9000*(4/15)).

Figure 8.9 compares SuperCalc's three depreciation methods.

Notice that DDB causes you to expense the greatest amount in the first period—almost half the total cost. If you expect most of the asset's productivity to be in the early periods, you should use DDB or SYD to calculate depreciation.

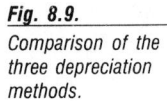

Fig. 8.9.

Comparison of the three depreciation methods.

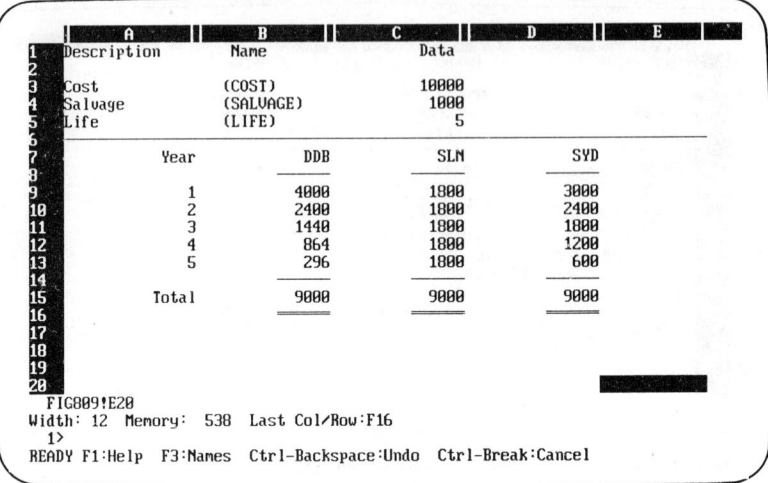

Summary of Financial Functions

With the group of financial functions provided with SuperCalc, you can analyze investment decisions from all sides. Whether you lack the term, rate, future value, or present value of an investment decision; or the investment or loan is a onetime value or a lifetime value; or the investment/loan is a level stream of returns/payments or a variable stream—SuperCalc provides the tools to solve your "what if" questions. In addition, you can use the three major depreciation functions. These powerful functions eliminate much of the time needed to create formulas for these tasks. Instead, in most cases, your investment or loan problems are reduced to entering the correct variable into a cell and letting SuperCalc do all the work.

Trigonometric Functions

SuperCalc has eight trigonometric functions, including PI. Although these functions are of limited use in a financial environment, SuperCalc is well suited for graphically analyzing trigonometric relationships. The trig functions are useful in engineering to analyze wave forms, for example. If you are unfamiliar with trig functions, don't fret. Graphs of their wave forms have been included in this section so that you can recognize the graph's associated waves on a line graph. Figure 8.10 shows the interactions of these functions in numeric form; table 8.7 lists the various trig functions.

```
      A      B       C       D       E      F       G      H       I
1  Degrees° Radians                           ┌─Converted to °─┐ (÷(π/180))─┐
2  (1-360) °* π/180  SIN()   COS()   TAN()  ASIN()  ACOS()  ATAN()  ATAN2()
3
4        0       0        0       1       0       0  .000001      0      90
5       30 .5235988      .5 .866025 .577350      30      30      30      60
6       45 .7853982 .707107 .707107       1      45      45      45      45
7       60 1.047198 .866025      .5 1.73205      60      60      60      30
8       90 1.570796       1       0   ERROR      90      90   ERROR       0
9      120 2.094395 .866025     -.5 -1.7321      60     120     -60     -30
10     135 2.356194 .707107 -.70711      -1      45     135     -45     -45
11     150 2.617994      .5 -.86603 -.57735      30     150     -30     -60
12     180 3.141593       0      -1       0       0 180.000       0     -90
13     210 3.665191     -.5 -.86603 .577350     -30     150      30    -120
14     225 3.926991 -.70711 -.70711       1     -45     135      45    -135
15     240 4.188790 -.86603     -.5 1.73205     -60     120      60    -150
16     270 4.712389      -1       0   ERROR -90.000      90   ERROR     180
17     300 5.235988 -.86603      .5 -1.7321     -60      60     -60     150
18     315 5.497787 -.70711 .707107      -1     -45      45     -45     135
19     330 5.759587     -.5 .866025 -.57735     -30      30     -30     120
20     360 6.283185       0       1       0       0 .000001       0      90
   FIG810!I4                    Form=ATAN2(SINE,COSINE)/(PI/180)
Width:  8  Memory:  526  Last Col/Row:Q20
  1>
READY F1:Help  F3:Names  Ctrl-Backspace:Undo  Ctrl-Break:Cancel
```

Fig. 8.10.

Comparative analysis of the seven trigonometric functions.

Table 8.7
Trigonometric Functions

Function	Meaning
PI	The value 3.14159265359, used for many calculations
SIN	The sine of an angle value defined in radians
COS	The cosine of an angle value defined in radians
TAN	The tangent of an angle value defined in radians
ASIN	The angle value in radians of a specified sine of a value
ACOS	The angle value in radians of a specified cosine of a value
ATAN	The angle value in radians of a specified tangent of a value
ATAN2	The angle value in radians of the specified tangent of a value defined as x and y coordinates

The PI Function

Pi, or the symbol π, is the ratio of the circumference of a circle to its diameter and is equal to 3.14159265359. SuperCalc interprets the function PI as the number 3.14159265359 whenever PI is encountered in a formula. In figure 8.10, PI converts degrees to radians. In B5, the following formula converts 30 degrees to .5235988 radians:

+A4*(PI/180)

In row 12, notice that 180 degrees converts to 3.141593 radians.

The SIN Function

The SIN(value) function calculates the sine of a value specified in radians. The formula in C5 of figure 8.10 is as follows:

SIN(B5)

In row 5, this formula returns .5. At 0, 180, and 360 degrees, the sine of the angle is 0; at 90 and 270 degrees, the sine is 1 and -1, respectively. SIN(value) always returns a value from -1 to 1.

The COS Function

The COS(value) function calculates the cosine of a value specified in the *Radians* column. Like the SIN(value) function, COS(value) always returns a value from -1 to 1. Notice that cosine values are offset by 90 degrees from the sine values. That is, the value in D4 equals the value in C8 (90 degrees away), and the value in D5 equals the value in C9. The two columns of values are offset by four rows (or 90 degrees).

The TAN Function

The TAN(value) function calculates the tangent of a value specified in radians. Notice in figure 8.10 that the tangents of 90 and 270 degrees evaluate as ERROR. The tangent of an angle can also be defined as follows:

SIN(value)/COS(value)

Notice that in rows 8 and 16 the cosine (denominator) of the equation is zero, so the tangent ERROR message is a divide-by-zero error.

The line graph in figure 8.11 graphs the tangent wave, the sine wave, and the cosine wave in order to show their relationships.

Fig. 8.11.

Line graph of SIN, COS, and TAN.

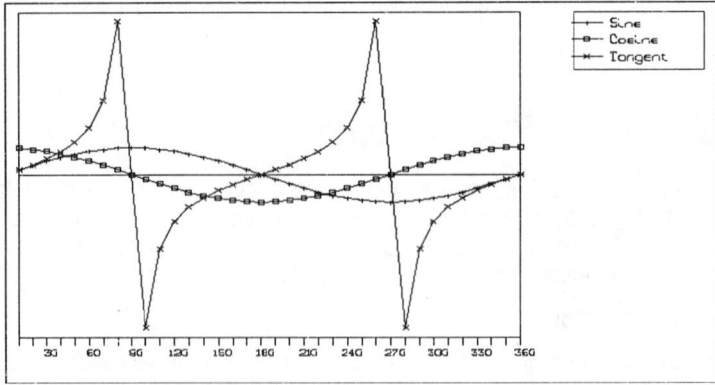

As you can see, this graph demonstrates that the COS and SIN functions have the same curve (and therefore the same values), but the curves are offset by 90 degrees. Tangent spikes up and down because it approaches infinity; that is, the tangent equals SIN divided by COS. As you can see in figure 8.10 in rows 8 and 16, this equality causes the formula to have a denominator of 0 (COS equals 0), and division by 0 is impossible.

The ASIN Function

The ASIN(value)—arcsine—function returns the radian-angle value of the sine value entered in the parentheses. In figure 8.10, cell F5 contains the following formula to convert the sine value back to degrees:

ASIN(C5)/(PI/180)

In row 5, this formula evaluates to 30 degrees—equal to the original degree value in column A.

The ACOS Function

The ACOS(value)—arccosine—function returns the radian-angle value of the cosine value entered in the parentheses. In figure 8.10, cell G5 contains the following formula:

ACOS(D5)/(PI/180)

This formula converts the arccosine value, which solves in radians, into the more recognizable degrees value.

The ATAN Function

The ATAN(value) function converts the arctangent (inverse tangent) of a value into a radian value, which varies in range from −PI/2 to PI/2 or approximately −90 degrees to 90 degrees. The following formula in cell H5 converts the TAN formula in cell E5 back to the original input of 30 degrees:

ATAN(E5)/(PI/180)

In figure 8.10, the ATAN function, like TAN( ), evaluates to ERROR at 90 and 270 degrees.

The ATAN2 Function

The ATAN2(x,y) function calculates a four-quadrant arctangent value of an angle specified in radians. The coordinates of the angle, x and y, can be any value. ATAN returns a value from −PI to PI (−180 to 180) in degrees.

In figure 8.10, the sine and cosine columns hold the x and y coordinates. Figure 8.12 is a graph of the ASIN, ACOS, ATAN, and ATAN2 columns in figure 8.10. As you can see in this graph, the ACOS cycle is a longer cycle than ASIN. ACOS ranges from −180 degrees to 180 degrees, and ASIN ranges only from −90 to 90 degrees. The same relationship occurs between ATAN and ATAN2. ATAN approaches −90 and 90 degrees, but ATAN2 ranges twice the distance between −180 and 180 degrees. Because of this difference, ACOS and ATAN2 intersect the axis only half as many times as do ASIN and ATAN. This graph shows you one way to use SuperCalc's powerful graphics capabilities to analyze these relationships. (See Chapters 9 and 10 for more information.)

Fig. 8.12.

Line graph of ASIN, ACOS, ATAN, and ATAN2.

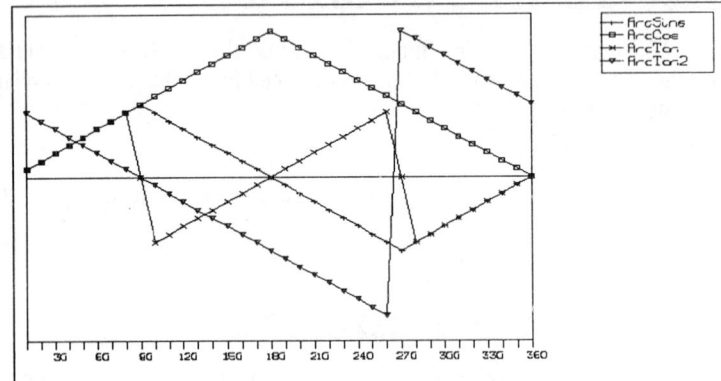

Index Functions

Another category of functions is the continually growing group of indexing functions. Many of these functions provide information useful in creating dynamic macros that execute based on the size, width, or location of a cell range or the location of the cell pointer. Some of these functions can be used to access and reference cells from other cells, commands, and macros; other index functions report the size of the spreadsheet or a specific range within the spreadsheet, the cell pointer location, and the iteration count on which is based the iterative recalculation.

Table 8.8 lists all the index functions provided in SuperCalc. Three of the functions (LOOKUP, HLOOKUP, and VLOOKUP) are described in Chapter 7.

Table 8.8
Index Functions

Function(s)	Meaning
COLCHARS(value)	The column letter(s) equivalent to the specified value (1–255 possible)
CURCOL/CURROW CCOL/CROW	The value of the column or row where the cell pointer is located

Table 8.8—*Continued*

Function(s)	Meaning
CURPAGE/CURSHEET	The value of the page or sheet where the cell pointer is located
CURADDRESS	The cell reference of the cell where the cell pointer is located
LASTCOL/LASTROW LCOL/ROW	The value of the last column or row in the entire spreadsheet
THISCOL/THISROW TCOL/TROW	The value of the column or row containing the formula using this function
ADDRESS(range)	The address of the upper left cell in the range
BEGCOL(range) BCOL BEGROW(range) BROW	The value of the beginning column or row of the range
ENDCOL(range) ECOL ENDROW(range) EROW	The value of the ending column or row of the range
COLS(range) ROWS	The total number of columns or rows in the range
N(range) S(range)	The numeric (N) or string (S) contents of the upper left corner of the range
LOOKUP(value,row/col range) LU	The value in the cell one column to the right or one row below the cell in the specified range containing a value equal to or less than the specified value
HLOOKUP(x,range,row offset) HLU	Like LOOKUP, but only for row lookups and multirow ranges
VLOOKUP(x,range,col offset) VLU	Like HLOOKUP, but for column lookups
INDEX(range,col offset, row offset)	Retrieves a value from the cell in the specified range at the offset coordinates measured from the upper left corner of the range
CHOOSE(offset,value1, value2, . . .)	Retrieves the value from a list of values at the locations specified by the offset values
ITER	Displays the iteration count when recalculating multiple times

The COLCHARS Function

The COLCHARS function takes a value you specify between 1 and 255 (inclusive) and converts it to the column letter(s) equivalent (A through IV). For example, COLCHARS(1) = A and COLCHARS(27) = AA.

This function is helpful in building addresses in a macro based on numeric input. Like other index functions, COLCHARS is most useful when combined with other functions. For example, the function CURCOL returns a value. COLCHARS(CURCOL) converts that value to a column name.

The CURCOL, CURROW, and CURADDRESS Functions

The pair of CURCOL and CURROW functions is one of several pairs of index functions that work in a similar way, except that one function works on columns and the other on rows. CURCOL and CURROW calculate the current coordinates of the cell pointer. CURCOL returns a column number instead of a column letter (that is, columns 1–26 instead of columns A–Z) so that the column values can be used for column offsets and calculations. Each time the spreadsheet is recalculated, these functions update to reflect the new cursor position. Figure 8.13, which includes examples of several of the index functions, shows CURCOL and CURROW in B2 and B3. Either CURCOL and CURROW or CCOL and CROW is acceptable usage.

Fig. 8.13.

Examples of index functions.

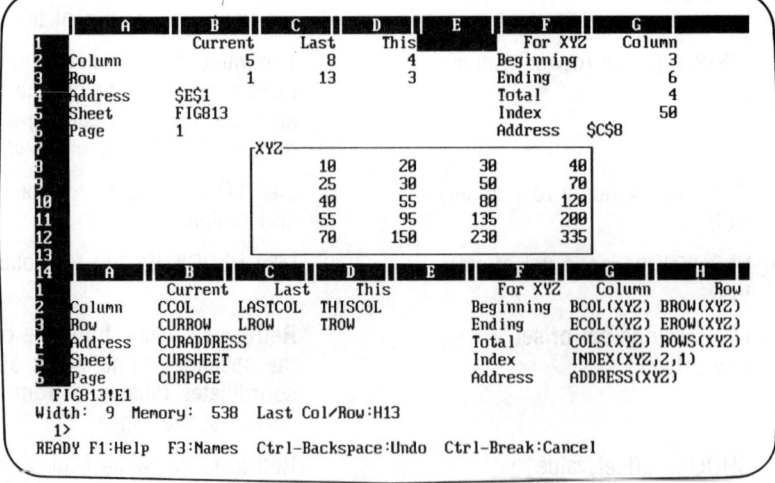

The top window in the figure shows the spreadsheet in READY mode, and the bottom window shows the same cells with /Global,Formulas set to show the formulas behind the answers. The cell pointer is in cell E1 with the following coordinates:

CCOL = 5
CROW = 1

CURADDRESS is a new function in SuperCalc5, that returns the full address of the cell cursor as an absolute reference. In figure 8.13, CURADDRESS is in cell B4 and returns the value $E$1 (the absolute version of the cell reference E1). Unlike CURCOL and CURROW, CURADDRESS has no abbreviation.

All three of the CUR functions remain the same (5, 1, and $E$1) until the spreadsheet is recalculated. If you include these functions in a macro (see Chapter 11), make sure that recalculation takes place when necessary.

The CURPAGE and CURSHEET Functions

Because SuperCalc5 handles multiple spreadsheets at once and up to 255 pages per spreadsheet, the CURPAGE and CURSHEET functions were added. When you enter **CURPAGE** into a cell, the value of the spreadsheet page where the cell pointer is currently located is displayed in a left-justified format. Likewise, if you enter **CURSHEET**, the name of the spreadsheet where the cell pointer is located displays in the cell. If you enter Super-Calc and type **CURSHEET** in cell A1, the CURSHEET function returns the name of the spreadsheet, which the default names TEMP1 because you have not loaded another spreadsheet or renamed the current spreadsheet. Once you name the spreadsheet, CUR-SHEET shows the name of the function.

CURSHEET and CURPAGE are demonstrated in figure 8.13 in cells B5 and B6, respectively. Obviously, CURPAGE is most useful when a spreadsheet has more than one page (fig. 8.13 does not).

The THISCOL and THISROW Functions

Whereas CCOL and CROW relate to the column and row where the cell pointer is located, THISCOL and THISROW relate to the formula address. If THISCOL is in C1, the result is 3 (column C is the third column); if THISROW is in C1, the result is 1. SuperCalc recognizes any of the following entry forms:

```
THISCOL
thisrow
ThisCol
This Row
TCOL
TROW
```

A space can appear between THIS and ROW or COL, and the functions can be written with uppercase or lowercase letters. The program takes out the space and automatically converts the letters to uppercase. TCOL and TROW are acceptable abbreviations. In figure 8.13, THISCOL is entered in D2. As you can see in the upper window of the screen, the row value of column D is 4, so THISCOL = 4; when TROW is entered in cell D3, TROW calculates to 3.

The LASTCOL and LASTROW Functions

LASTCOL (C2 in fig. 8.13) and LROW (C3) refer to the last column and last row of the active spreadsheet. These two functions are the coordinates of the cell that your cursor moves to if you press End-Home. As you can see in figure 8.13, the sample spreadsheet extends only to the lower right corner of the range screen (H13).

The complements to LASTCOL and LASTROW would probably be named FIRSTCOL and FIRSTROW if SuperCalc offered them. Both are unneeded, however; SuperCalc always considers row 1 and column A the first row and column of any spreadsheet, so FIRSTCOL and FIRSTROW would always equal 1.

The BEGCOL, BEGROW, and ADDRESS Functions

Unlike the functions that relate to the entire spreadsheet, these three functions relate to a specific range within the spreadsheet. In figure 8.13, the range to which BEGCOL(XYZ) and BEGROW(XYZ) refer is XYZ bounded by C8:F12. From these two functions, you can see that the range XYZ begins in row 8 of the third column of the spreadsheet. These functions evaluate the actual size of the named range regardless of whether the range is empty. BCOL(XYZ) and BROW(XYZ) are acceptable abbreviations of these functions.

Like CURADDRESS, ADDRESS has been added in SuperCalc5 to combine the functionality of two functions, in this case BEGCOL and BEGROW. ADDRESS(range) returns the beginning address (upper left corner) of the range, described in absolute format. In figure 8.13 the address for range XYZ is $C$8 (G6).

The ENDCOL and ENDROW Functions

ENDCOL and ENDROW fit the pattern of the remaining cell-coordinate index functions. These functions give the number of the last row or column in the specified range. In figure 8.13, ECOL(XYZ) and EROW(XYZ) equal 6 and 12, respectively, as you can see in cells G3 and H3. Unfortunately, there is no ENDADDRESS function in SuperCalc (perhaps in SuperCalc6?).

The COLS and ROWS Functions

COLS(range) and ROWS(range) calculate the total number of columns and rows in the specified range. Figure 8.13 shows four columns and five rows in the range XYZ.

The N and S Functions

To find the first value in a range (upper left value), use the N and S functions. N works only for values and S only for strings. If you enter **N(XYZ)** and **S(XYZ)** in cells in figure 8.13, the value 10 appears in the N cell and nothing appears in the S cell because the contents of the upper left cell in range XYZ is the value 10. Likewise, if you replace the 10 in cell C8 (the first cell in XYZ) with a string such as **TRAIN**, the N cell changes to 0 and the S cell displays the string TRAIN.

INDEX Versus the LOOKUP Functions

INDEX is a function within the class of index functions. This function is a form of the lookup functions (LOOKUP, VLOOKUP, and HLOOKUP, discussed in Chapter 7). Figure 8.13 shows an example of the INDEX function in use. The syntax for INDEX is as follows:

    INDEX(range,column offset,row offset)

INDEX is best used when you know the exact cell location of the value you want in a range. In this spreadsheet, the value in the cell two columns over and one row down from the upper left corner of the range is specified and returns the value 50 (in E10). The first column and row of the range are considered 0 offset.

LOOKUP has the following syntax:

    LOOKUP(value,row/column range)

To use LOOKUP to find a number in range XYZ, you have to know a value and its position relative to the value you want. You also have to know that the value you want to retrieve is in either the row or column adjacent to the specified range. If the defined range is a row,

LOOKUP retrieves the value from the row below the range. If the defined range is a column, LOOKUP retrieves the value in the column to the right of the range. The following formula evaluates to 50 because the value 30 is 2 cells over in row 8 of XYZ, and the value in the cell below is 90 (E9):

LOOKUP(30,C8:F8)

This next formula, however, evaluates to 30:

LOOKUP(30,C8:C12)

In the example in figure 8.13, because the column range C8:C12 has no value of 30, you use the value 25, which is the next lowest number in the ascending values, to reference cell D9, which is in the column next to column C, the defined range.

You could use VLOOKUP to retrieve the value 50 from cell E9. The formula to do that could be similar to the following, where 55 is the value, XYZ is the range, and 2 is the column offset amount:

VLU(55,XYZ,2)

The LOOKUP function also works in the formula where 1 is the row offset:

HLU(30,XYZ,1)

Figure 8.14 shows good use of the INDEX function. The table contained in columns A through H is a detailed table of trig values for each degree in a circle (0 to 360), extending from row 3 to row 363. A similar spreadsheet was used to create the graphs in figures 8.11 and 8.12.

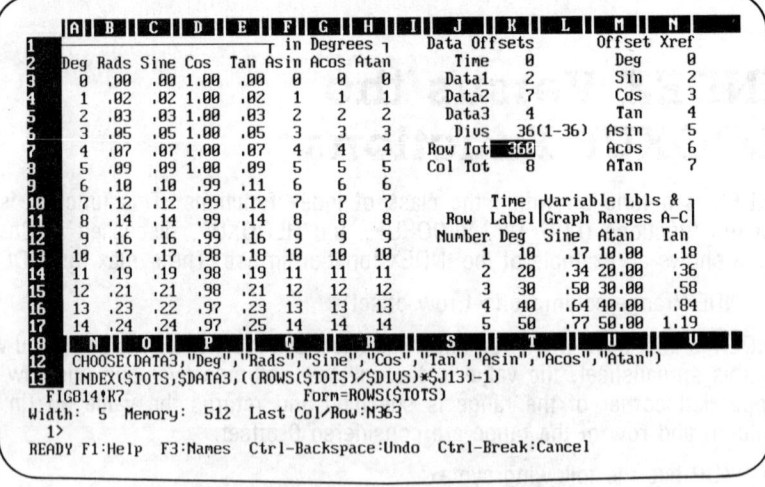

Fig. 8.14.

A practical use for the INDEX function.

The section to the right of the table in columns J through N was created for graphing purposes. Graphing 360 rows of data and still maintaining readable time labels (the x-axis labels) on the graph is cumbersome. This spreadsheet solves the problem by creating a summary, or indexed, table, located to the right with the first data element (*Deg*) starting in cell K13. As you can see, the table to the left increases by one degree per row; the table to the right increases by 10 degrees per row. Using the INDEX function, you can reduce a 360-row table to 36 rows.

The table to the right contains only four time and data columns compared to the eight columns in the detailed table (named TOT). By entering the column number offset for *Time*, *Data1*, *Data2*, and *Data3* (cross-referenced in range N2:N8) in range K2:K5, and the number of divisions into which you want the summary table broken in cell K6, you can combine several elements from the detailed table into varying levels of detail in the summary table. In figure 8.14, for example, *Data2* contains a 7, meaning *ATan* is the second variable to be summarized in the graph table to the right (column M).

The INDEX function is entered in each cell in the summary table. The function uses $TOT (the entire detailed table) as an index range; the values entered in *Time*, *Data1*, *Data2*, and *Data3* are used as column offset values; the following formula is used to calculate the row offset:

((ROWS($TOTS/$DIVS)*$J13) − 1)

In this formula, $DIVS (K6) is the number of equal divisions you want to graph, and $J13 is the current row value from the column entitled *Row Number*. For row 13, this row offset evaluates to ((360/36)*1) − 1 or 9.

Row 14 evaluates to 19 (((360/36)*2) − 1); row 15, to 29; and so on, so that you are pulling out every tenth value. Notice that the values in the first row in the summary table equal the values in the tenth row of the detailed table.

The CHOOSE Function

The general form of the CHOOSE function is as follows:

CHOOSE(x,v0,v1,v2, . . . ,vn)

The parameters *v0* through *vn* reflect a list of values of any type (text, numeric, textual, date, or cell reference), and *x* is the *x*th value from that list, counted from left to right.

In figure 8.14, the CHOOSE function also is used in the bottom window in N12 to select column headers to appear as variable labels in the graph. The function is entered into the column heading of each column in the summary table. These entries cause the program to display the correct column heading based on the column extracted from the detailed table. In cell N12, CHOOSE takes the following form:

CHOOSE(Data3,"Deg","Rads","Sine","Cos","Tan","Asin","Acos"," Atan")

All these strings consist of fewer than nine characters because text strings can be only nine characters long. (Strings can be text, numeric, date values, or cell references.) In the example in figure 8.14, 0 is entered in K2 (*Time*), so *Deg* (the first value in which offset = 0) is the string used in K12. With 2 entered in *Data1*, *Sine* is selected for L12 (the CHOOSE function with *x* = *Data1*). Similarly, *ATan* is selected for M12 and *Tan* for N12.

The ITER Function

ITER is the counter related to one of SuperCalc's most powerful features, a function that can control circular references. A circular reference is a situation that occurs when a cell references itself in a calculation and therefore never resolves.

Problems with Circular References

Entering a circular reference in SuperCalc is certainly possible. If you mistakenly enter **SUM(A1:A5)** in A5, for example, you create a diverging, unsolvable circular reference, which continues to calculate until you press Ctrl-Break to halt the circle. If that formula were entered in A5 and the function ITER in cell B5, however, when you pressed Ctrl-Break, B5 would display the number of times the spreadsheet had calculated before you pressed Ctrl-Break.

In the lower right corner of the screen, the word CIR appears, which indicates you have a circular reference in the worksheet.

Constructive Uses of Circular References and Iteration

Circular references are not necessarily dangerous. Generally, a divergent circular reference, in which the values in the dependent cells continue to grow farther apart, is destructive. Converging circular references, however, can be used to solve simultaneous equations that have no exact answer.

SuperCalc's Global menu provides a way to get control of circular references. Enter /Global,Evaluation,Iteration-control from READY mode. The following selections appear:

```
Quit  Solve  Fixed
```

The **S**olve and **F**ixed options control the iterations. **S**olve is the default. If you select **F**ixed, you can reset the number of times SuperCalc recalculates to solve a circular reference. You are prompted to enter an integer from 1 to 99, which limits the number of times SuperCalc recalculates a circular reference before stopping.

In certain circumstances, you may want to reset this recalculation to 1. In the sample spreadsheet, PAYROLL, provided with SuperCalc, Computer Associates demonstrates a cumulative total example where you can control the way a circular reference calculates the year-to-date gross pay for employees by changing a recalc flag (Recalculate(Y/N)?) and adding a cell to itself. The **F**ixed Iteration-control is set to 1, and the spreadsheet recalculates once to add a cell content (the prior year-to-date gross) to itself plus the current period amount. This operation is an example of controlling a diverging calculation.

A more common use of circular references is to solve a converging dependent relationship. This technique can be used for goal seeking (calculating an optimum value for a situation) or for a situation like calculating a commission based on net income, where the expenses subtracted from gross income include the commissions you need to calculate. When you select **S**olve in the Global Evaluation Iteration-control menu, the following menu appears:

    Quit Delta Range

Delta determines the precision with which you want the converging cells to solve. The default option is set to .01, which means that SuperCalc continues to calculate until the converging cells change less than .01 with each calculation, at which point the reference is considered solved.

By selecting **D**elta, you can point to a cell that contains a delta value for SuperCalc to use in place of .01. If you make **D**elta equal 100, SuperCalc stops when a circular cell value changes less than 100 on succeeding calculations.

With **R**ange, you can specify the range to be tested for convergence. Range is defined as the entire spreadsheet by default but can be redefined as a smaller cell range or a single cell. Any circular references that fall outside the specified range recalculate but are checked for convergence. Figure 8.15 demonstrates converging iteration.

```
          A              ║    B    │    C    │   D   │    E    │
 1 BUDGET                            Dollars  Forecast % of Gross
 2 Gross Income                    1,750,000.00  100.0%
 3
 4 Expenses
 5   Manufacturing                   850,420.00   48.6%
 6   Sales & Marketing               142,500.00    8.1%
 7   General & Administrative        275,000.00   15.7%
 8   Engineering                     220,000.00   12.6%
 9 Total Expenses                  1,487,920.00   85.0%
10
11 Bonus            Enter % of N.I.
12   Manufacturing       16.0%       25,568.78    1.5%
13   Sales & Marketing   16.0%       25,568.78    1.5%
14   General & Administrative 16.0%  25,568.78    1.5%
15   Engineering         16.0%       25,568.78    1.5%
16 Total Bonus           64.0%      102,275.12    5.8%
17
18 Net Income                        159,804.88    9.1%
19 Recalculate(1=yes)                        1
20 Iterations                             1.00
    FIG815!C12           Form=IF($C$19<>1,+C12,+$C$18*B12)
 Width: 13 Memory:  537 Last Col/Row:D20
  1>
 READY F1:Help  F3:Names  Ctrl-Backspace:Undo  Ctrl-Break:Cancel    CIR
```

Fig. 8.15.

Using iteration to determine company bonuses.

In this figure, budgeted bonuses are calculated based on the net income generated from operations. Because these bonuses are included in the calculation of net income, what you might call a "chicken and egg" condition occurs. Column B contains the bonus allocation percentages for each department. The key to solving this problem with iteration is to make these percentages add up to less than 1. If they add up to more than 1, the circular reference diverges instead of converges, and the spreadsheet continues to calculate indefinitely.

Cell C19 in figure 8.15 tells the spreadsheet whether or not to solve the condition. In C12:C15, an IF function is included to set each cell equal to itself if C19 does not equal 1 (see cell C12). Otherwise, each cell equals the bonus percent times the net income. The circular reference can be described as follows:

Gross Income − Total Expenses − Bonus = Net Income
Bonus = Bonus % * Net Income

In cell C20, ITER is used to display the number of iterations necessary to solve the circular reference. During the calculation, SuperCalc displays the number of iterations on the status line but only during the calculation process. ITER is necessary, too, because it displays the iteration count as a reminder until the next time you calculate.

String and Special Purpose Functions

With SuperCalc5 comes the introduction of 22 new functions; 17 are referred to as *string* functions, and the remaining 5 are referred to as *special purpose* functions. Some of these functions can perform all types of extractions, conversions, and combinations on data in a cell or range of cells. Others provide valuable information about the nature of the data in cells or cell ranges, and the rest of these functions orient more toward the structure of the cell itself. This discussion focuses on a functional breakdown of these functions to provide more insight into how they can be combined to perform complex data management.

Fact-Finding Functions

Fact-finding functions are referred to as *special purpose* functions. With these functions, you can find out how wide a cell is (WIDTH), the type of contents it contains (TYPE), or how the cell is formatted (FORMAT). Table 8.9 lists these functions.

Table 8.9
Fact-Finding Functions

Function	Meaning
WIDTH	The column width or column range width in character spaces
TYPE	Character code of the cell type
FORMAT	Format string representing the cell format

The WIDTH Function

From the beginning days of spreadsheet use, one of the first questions asked was the following:

Will this print range fit on my printer?

With the WIDTH(range) you can find that out quickly. If you have named your print range (for example, PRINT1), all you have to do is enter the following in a cell in your spreadsheet:

WIDTH(PRINT1)

A number equal to the cumulative width of the columns in the range then appears in the cell.

The TYPE Function

The TYPE function returns one of the following six possible values describing the cell contents:

Value	Description
B	Blank cell
C	Control text (printer control string)
E	Formatted but empty cell
F	Formula
R	Repeating text (preceded with a single quotation mark)
T	Text

Figure 8.16 shows examples of each of these types of cells. Cell C6 is a control cell because of the vertical bar (I) preceding the \015 (see the status line). Although nothing shows up in either C4 or C8, C8 is empty, not blank, because it has been formatted, as you can see in D8. A blank cell (C4) is an unused cell; when you format a cell (C8), it is used because the format characteristics are stored with it. The cell still appears blank, however, because no value appears on the spreadsheet in that cell.

```
       A       B        C     D      E      B        C     D    E
 1            TYPE     Input FORMAT  1  TYPE      Input FORMAT
 2            Column   Column Column 2  Column    Column Column
 3                                   3
 4    Blank->B                       4  TYPE(C4)         FORMAT(C4)
 5                                   5
 6    Control->C      \015      I    6  TYPE(C6)  \015   FORMAT(C6)
 7                                   7
 8    Empty->E              RU3D1TLP 8  TYPE(C8)         FORMAT(C8)
 9                                   9
10    Formula->F       30.00R $     10  TYPE(C10) 15+15  FORMAT(C10)
11                                  11
12    Repeat->R     RepeatedRepeatedR 12 TYPE(C12) RepeatedRepeatedRepeat
13                                  13
14    Text->T         TRAIN      TL 14  TYPE(C14) TRAIN  FORMAT(C14)
15                                  15
16    DISPLAY->     156  156.00     16  156        DISPLAY(B16,D8,8)
17    STRING->      156156.00       17  156        STRING(B17,2)
18     CHAR->       156   £         18  156        CHAR(B18)
19    CONTENTS->       STRING(B17,2) 19             CONTENTS(C17)
20                                  20

 FIG816!C6            I     Ctrl=!\015
Width:  7  Memory:    539  Last Col/Row:D19
 1>
READY F1:Help  F3:Names  Ctrl-Backspace:Undo  Ctrl-Break:Cancel
```

Fig. 8.16.

Demonstration of special purpose and string functions.

The FORMAT Function

The FORMAT function returns a left-justified eight-character string describing the format characteristics of the cell (refer to D8 of figure 8.16). The displayed string takes the format

JnnDdTjP

where none to all of the positions can contain a value. The following list describes positions 1 through 8:

Position	Description
1	Number justification (L, C, R, or blank)
2–3	Number format (blank, I, *, $, E, G, H, or U1–8)
4–5	Date format (D1–8)
6–7	Text format (TL, TC, TR, or blank)
8	Protected flag (only changes after recalculation)

If by some rare chance (such as the example in figure 8.16) the format string RU3D1TLP appears, it means the referenced cell is formatted with *r*ight-justification for *u*ser-defined format *3*, *d*ate format *1*, *l*eft *t*ext-justification, and the cell is *p*rotected. Rarely are all eight positions filled; a more typical result is the string

"   TL "

like the cell combination C14/D14 or the string

"R $ "

exemplified in C10 and D10. FORMAT works only on a cell formatted with the /Format,Entry version of /Format. If a cell is formatted with the **G**lobal, **C**olumn, or **R**ow option, nothing appears for format. For details on formatting, see Chapter 4.

Value-to-String Functions

Four functions deal with converting a value or formula into a text string, as in table 8.10.

Table 8.10
Value-to-String Functions

Function	Meaning
DISPLAY	String formatted according to a specified format string description and width
STRING	String equivalent of a value displayed with a specified number of decimal places
CHAR	The ASCII character representation of a value between 0 and 255, inclusive
CONTENTS	Contents of a specified cell displayed as a string

The DISPLAY Function

Because the first function, DISPLAY, is closely tied to the FORMAT function described in the preceding section, the same figure (fig. 8.16) can be used. Its syntax looks like this:

    DISPLAY(x,format,width)

In this syntax, *x* is a value or cell reference, *format* is either the result of the FORMAT function as shown in cell C16 or a literal string containing some subset of the characters possible in the FORMAT function, and *width* is the entire width to be used to display the string. As you can see in C16 (the left window), although the column width of column C is 7 (see the status line), the value 156 is in an eight-character-long string that overlaps the cell to the right. The value 8 is used for the width, and that overrides the normal column width (7).

The value of *x* can either be a numeric value or a string value. When you enter

    DISPLAY(A1,"R$TL",20)

in cell A2, the result is a right-justified currency format if A1 contains a number; the result is left-justified if A1 contains a string. Both appear in a 20-space-wide string regardless of the column width. If the format exceeds the width of column B, it displays in continuous format like a normal text string. If nothing is entered in A1, ERROR appears in A2.

The STRING Function

The second function, STRING, is used for converting numeric values into a text string. STRING has a simple syntax:

    STRING(x,n)

In this syntax, *x* is a cell reference or numeric value, and *n* is the number of decimal places used to display the *x* value. If a cell reference containing text or a string entered in quotation marks is used for *x*, a zero value is returned with the appropriate decimal places. Cell C17 in figure 8.16 shows the value from B17 as a string (notice it is left-justified by default).

The CHAR Function

CHAR is the third value-to-string function. It is a specialty function for defining an ASCII character using its ASCII code. All ASCII characters have a value from 1 to 255. As examples, the ASCII value 71 equals the uppercase *G*, value 103 is a lowercase *g*, and value 156 is the British pound sign (£). With the CHAR function, you can enter these values as **CHAR(71)**, **CHAR(103)**, and **CHAR(156)**, respectively. The alternative is to hold down the Alt key and press the ASCII values of the desired characters (71, 103, or 156). C19 shows the value from B18 as ASCII character 156—the British pound sign.

The CONTENTS Function

CONTENTS is the last value-to-string function. Its purpose is to display the underlying formula in a cell. CONTENTS is used in cell C19 to show the formula from C17. CONTENTS is also used several times in figure 8.17 to show cell contents. The function is especially good for debugging formulas.

String-to-Value Functions

Another group of functions have the opposite effects of the value-to-string functions described in the last section. This group of functions convert strings into values. They are listed in table 8.11.

Table 8.11
String-to-Value Functions

Function	Meaning
VALUE	The value equivalent of a valid character string
CODE	The ASCII equivalent of the first character in a specified string
@	Contents of a cell pointed to through a cell address stored in a specified cell
FIND	The starting point of one string within another string
LENGTH	The length of a string

The VALUE Function

The most obvious function in the string-to-value group of functions is the VALUE function. This function has the following syntax:

VALUE(string)

The *string* variable must contain only numbers; the VALUE function converts the string to a number. This function is especially useful if you want to convert imported strings into values quickly. (An imported string is always considered a string, even though it may resemble a number on-screen.) Remember that numbers sort differently than character strings; use this function if you want to sort a column of string values based on a numeric sort.

The CODE Function

Another string-to-value function, CODE, complements the CHAR function in the value-to-string group of functions. Where CHAR converts a number (71) into a character (G), CODE does the opposite. If **CODE(G)** is entered, the value 71 appears.

The @ Function

Another specialty function is @(cell). This function serves as a pointer variable. If @**(A1)** is entered in B1, for example, and you enter the string **HELLO** in C1, the string *C1* is stored in A1, and HELLO appears in B1, too. B1 uses the @ pointing function to address indirectly the contents of C1. The use of the pointer function @ is shown in the following example, which shows the results on the left and contents on the right:

```
    A    B      C                A      B       C

 1 C1   HELLO  HELLO        1   "C1   @(A1)   "HELLO
```

The @ function, like many of the string and indexing functions, may be more useful in macro creation than in any other area.

The FIND and LENGTH Functions

To demonstrate FIND and LENGTH, as well as many of the remaining substring functions in the sections that follow, refer to figure 8.17.

```
 ┌─A─┬───B─────┬═══════════════════C═══════════════════════════┐
 │1  │  GORMAN, ANTHONY < Stored string with last name, first name format
 │2  │
 │3  │ Step    RESULT
 │4  │  1        6      < Find the comma using FIND
 │5  │  2       15      < Calculate the length using LENGTH
 │6  │  3    GORMAN     < Separate out the last name using LEFT and FIND
 │7  │  4    ANTHONY    < Isolate the first name using MID, FIND, and LENGTH
 │8  │  5    ANTHONY GORMAN  < Recombine the name in first last format with &
 │9  │  6    Anthony Gorman  < Convert it to Initial Caps with PROPER
 │10 │  7    Dear Mr. Gorman < Create a salutation with REPLACE
 │11 │
 │12 │
 │13 │ Step    CONTENTS
 │14 │  1   FIND(",",NAM,0)
 │15 │  2   LENGTH(NAM)
 │16 │  3   LEFT(NAM,FIND(",",NAM,0))
 │17 │  4   MID(NAM,FIND(",",NAM)+2,LENGTH(NAM))
 │18 │  5   B7&" "&B6
 │19 │  6   PROPER(B8)
 │20 │  7   REPLACE(B9,0,LENGTH(B7),"Dear Mr.")
 └───┴─────────────────────────────────────────────────────────┘
   FIG817!B14                    Form=CONTENTS(B4)
Width: 16  Memory:  538  Last Col/Row:C25
   1>
READY F1:Help  F3:Names  Ctrl-Backspace:Undo  Ctrl-Break:Cancel
```

Fig. 8.17.

Demonstrating a string transformation using several string functions.

Figure 8.17 demonstrates how the FIND, LENGTH, and substring functions can be combined to perform complex data manipulation. In the figure, the string GORMAN, ANTHONY, shown in cell B1 (which is named NAM), is converted to the string Anthony Gorman (A9) using the steps outlined in the following paragraphs.

In this figure the bottom cells B14:B20 show the formulas from cells C4:C10 using the CONTENTS function. So B14 shows you what formula is used to isolate the comma (B4), B15 shows you what formula is used to calculate the length of the string (B5), and so on. (The cells B14 through B20 are for reference, not for string conversion.)

The first step uses FIND to locate a character within the string. Cell A4 contains the formula that calculates the location of the comma (,) in the string. The comma is the key on which the conversion is based. (Cell B14 displays the formula using the CONTENTS(B4) function.) The result is 6, meaning that the comma is offset 6 places from the left of the string. The first character, G, is in position 0. The third value in the formula is optional and indicates the starting position for the search. If you enter 5 instead of 0, the result is 1 instead of 6 because the comma is offset only 1 position to the right of the starting position.

The second step is to determine the total length of the string. The LENGTH function allows you to do that easily. Using the formula entered in B5 and displayed in B15, you find that the length of the string GORMAN, ANTHONY is 15 characters.

Substring Functions

To go to the next step in figure 8.17, you must understand some substring functions. These functions are presented in table 8.12 and used in the explanation of the conversion procedure that follows.

Table 8.12
Substring Functions

Function	Meaning
LEFT	Display a string of specified length derived from the leftmost characters of a specified string
MID	Display a string of specified length derived from a specified string beginning at a specified position in the string
RIGHT	Display a string of specified length derived from the rightmost characters of a specified string
&	The operator for concatenating multiple strings
PROPER	A string converted to ''proper name'' format (lowercase with initial letters uppercase)
UPPER	A string converted to uppercase
LOWER	A string converted to lowercase
TRIM	Trims unneeded blanks from the left end and between words in a string
REPLACE	Replaces a subset of one string with another string
REPEAT	Repeats a specified character or string a specified number of times

The LEFT and RIGHT Functions

In step 3 of the conversion procedure shown in figure 8.17, the LEFT function (B6/B16) is used to extract the first six characters of the string GORMAN, ANTHONY. LEFT has the following syntax:

LEFT(value,length)

In this syntax, *value* is a string or cell address, and *length* is the number of characters to include, starting from the left end of the string. In figure 8.17, the FIND function was substituted for the length variable so that no matter what length name was entered, just the last name (or all of the characters to the left of the first comma) are used. The RIGHT function is identical to the LEFT function except that RIGHT counts from the right end of the string instead of the left end.

The MID Function

To extract the first name from the middle of the string, use the MID function. MID has the following syntax:

MID(string,startnumber,length)

You have to know the starting position of the substring you want and the length of the substring. The comma's FIND function was substituted in A17 to determine the starting number, offset it two spaces to the right to eliminate the comma and following space, and request the remaining characters of the string up to the full LENGTH.

The & (Concatenation) Function

The & (concatenation) function is singularly important in the string-function world. With &, you can combine into one cell several strings or cell contents (strings and values converted into strings). The & function's general syntax is

string1&string2&string3

In the case of the conversion procedure being described, the & function is used to recombine GORMAN, ANTHONY into ANTHONY GORMAN, using

B7&" "&B6

You can use this function in many ways.

The PROPER, UPPER, and LOWER Conversion Functions

The last step in the conversion procedure being described is to convert ANTHONY GORMAN into Anthony Gorman. You can do this using the PROPER function (initial-letter-uppercase format). Cell B9 demonstrates this transition. B19 shows the content of the formula PROPER(A8).

Two other conversion functions can be used. UPPER converts a string to all caps; LOWER converts a string to all lowercase. Similar to PROPER and UPPER, the syntax for LOWER is

>   LOWER(cell address)

which references the cell containing the string to be converted. With these functions, you can consistently store data in all caps and then convert it to other formats as required.

The TRIM Function

In other software packages offering a TRIM function, especially fixed-field database and file-management packages, the TRIM function can be used to eliminate trailing blanks from the contents of a field. In SuperCalc, trailing blanks are automatically eliminated when you enter the value into a cell. The TRIM function in SuperCalc is designed to eliminate extra blanks within a string and at the beginning (left end) of the string. When this function trims blanks within a string, it replaces a group of blanks with a single blank space. If you apply the functions in figure 8.17 to convert an entire database of names from last-first to first-last format, you can use the TRIM function to eliminate any unexpected blanks lurking out there.

The REPLACE Function

You can alter cell contents by using the REPLACE function. The syntax of REPLACE is as follows:

>   REPLACE(input string,startnumber,length,replace string)

In this syntax, *input string* is a cell reference or literal string, *startnumber* is the position in the input string where you want the replacement to begin (the leftmost character is 0), *length* is the number of positions you want to replace, and *replace string* is the new value. As you can see in cell B20 of figure 8.17, the following formula causes the salutation Dear Mr. Gorman to appear in B10:

>   REPLACE(B9,0,LENGTH(B7),"Dear Mr.")

The REPEAT Function

The last string function is the REPEAT function. Its syntax looks like this:

>   REPEAT(string,n)

In this function, *n* is the number of times you want to repeat *string*. To demonstrate the use of this function, consider the subtotal line that often appears at the end of a column of numbers. Instead of entering a line of dashes to create that line, enter the formula shown in the lower window of figure 8.18 where you would have placed the dashed lines.

This formula is applicable wherever you want to use a subtotal line. You can also enter **CHAR(196)** instead of entering the Alt-196 character in quotation marks as was done in A1 of figure 8.18 to produce the same character. Once you enter the character, the string is

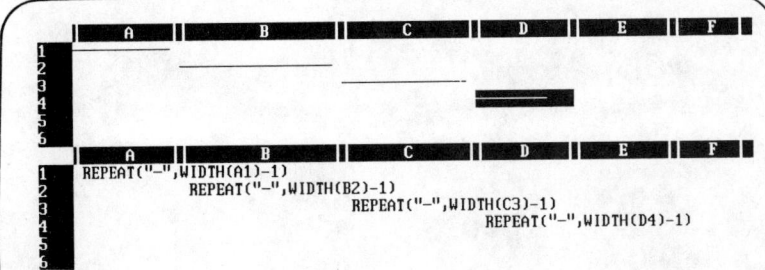

Fig. 8.18.

Using the REPEAT function for subtotal lines.

automatically adjusted to the current column width, as you can see when it was copied to cells B2, C3, and D4. You do not have to alter the line when you change the width of the column; the subtotal line is always one space less than the width of the column. In column D, the column width was changed from 9 to 11, but the string is still 8 characters wide. As you can see in cell D4, the string does not quite automatically adjust—you must press the F4 (calculate) key to adjust the number of characters shown to 10 after you change the width.

The string functions in SuperCalc provide you with the ultimate in flexibility. Of course, in the main example, GORMAN, ANTHONY could have been more simply converted to Dear Mr. Gorman. To create generalized functions that adapt to the length of each name used or to the width of each column (as was done with the REPEAT function), you will find yourself employing all 22 special purpose and string functions provided in SuperCalc.

Chapter Summary

In this chapter, financial functions, trigonometric functions, and index functions were described in a structured format for easy reference and comparison.

The SuperCalc financial functions allow you to analyze and solve for all components of most major financial formulas (such as rate, principal, periods, payment amount, and term of annuity). By understanding which function to use to answer which question, you help improve your use of these functions in decision making.

The trigonometric functions, although not a part of mainstream business use, work well with the graphics capabilities in SuperCalc to help clarify the functions' relationships and for use with wave frequency and form analysis.

Many of the index functions, such as CCOL and LROW, along with the new class of string functions and special purpose functions, become more useful when you begin to work with macros. The index functions are especially useful in cell-address expressions (described in Chapter 11) in macros to help automate command strings. String functions provide a capability to manipulate text in support of SuperCalc's role as a flat-file manager.

Part III of the book, "Creating Reports and Graphs," explains creating output in Super-Calc. In Chapter 9 you learn about the improved report capabilities of SuperCalc.

Part III

Creating Reports and Graphs

Includes

Creating Reports with /Output

Graphing and Plotting

9

Creating Reports
with /Output

Until you can transform a spreadsheet into well-formatted printed output, your work remains unfinished. An otherwise superbly designed spreadsheet is useful only when presented in an understandable style. If other people cannot understand your methods and the results of your analysis, your work is useless. You should determine the best layout, breakdown, and level of detail for your printed output, using SuperCalc's output tools to transform your data into useful information.

The present format of the /Output command was first implemented in SuperCalc4 as a major overhaul of that command. Most of the added features in SuperCalc5 are for handling the enhanced printing capabilities of laser printers. Computer Associates has based most of SuperCalc5's laser-oriented features on two major laser-printing standards: the Hewlett-Packard LaserJet and the PostScript standard. With the added command capabilities in /Output and /Global and the addition of spreadsheet-embedded print strings, SuperCalc's flexibility and power take a back seat to no other spreadsheet package.

In this chapter, you see all the improved features of the /Output command. You learn how to use the /Output command to communicate with your printer and how to use alternative formats and output devices (such as disk files or the screen) for special situations. The chapter begins with the essential tools for generating output and ends with the optional settings and methods that polish your work. SuperCalc's laser printing capability is also explained.

Peripheral Considerations

Before learning the features of the /Output command, you should be aware of some general considerations about printing and your printer.

279

Using /Global To Define Your Printer

Because SuperCalc works with most printers, normal spreadsheets should require no special setup. Printing and plotting, however, are functions of both SuperCalc and the printer or plotter connected to your computer. Before you delve too deeply into SuperCalc, you should know about several features of your printer. Most printer manuals cover all the necessary information. Browse through your printer manual to see what your printer can do and how to use its features.

First, you should know how your printer and computer are hooked together (the *interface*). A *serial* interface sends data in a single stream over a single data line. A *parallel* interface sends data over several lines and so transmits entire computer words (bytes) at one time. Although the parallel port on a computer is used strictly to hook up to a printer, the serial port can be used for other peripherals, such as a modem or a mouse, as well as a printer. To use SuperCalc, you need to know whether your printer interface is serial or parallel and which port your printer is plugged into on your computer.

Once you have identified the type of interface your printer uses, you can set SuperCalc to recognize it using the /Global,Spreadsheet command. You can identify a spreadsheet printing device that is different from your graphics plotting device.

To define your printer as either parallel or serial, from the READY prompt type

    /Global,Spreadsheet

At this point, the following menu options appear:

    Quit Cartridges Device Fonts Options Translation-tables

Cartridges and **F**onts are two new commands (for laser printers) that are discussed in the sections about laser printers in this chapter. **T**ranslation-tables is a new name for a feature previously listed under the **D**evice option name. **D**evice has been redefined for selecting the printer to be used to print spreadsheets.

To specify your printer, select **D**evice. The following two options then appear:

    B&W-printers Color-printers

Determine which category describes your printer. Most printers fall under the first category (close to 120 black-and-white printers are available compared with only 41 color printers). In this case, select **B**&W-printers, which brings up the screen shown in figure 9.1.

This screen lists both specific printers (such as Xerox 4045) and printer brands (IBM, for example). The printer brand choices have additional submenus beneath them, which include specific printers. The default printer, the generic Draft Printer at the top of the list, may be adequate for your situation.

To demonstrate selecting the IBM Graphics Printer, move the menu pointer to IBM and press Enter. The screen changes to a list of IBM printers. IBM Graphics is the first option; press Enter to select it. You then return to the Global Spreadsheet menu. If you do not find

```
DEVICE SELECTION MENU -- Black & White Printers
Current Selection: Draft Printer

Draft Printer      NEC
IBM                OKIDATA
AMADEX DP Series   Postscript Device
CANON              QUADRAM QUADJET
Citizen            RICOH
C.ITOH             SIEMENS
DIABLO             TEKTRONIX 4696
EPSON              TEXAS INSTRUMENTS
FACIT              TOSHIBA
FUJITSU DPL24      XEROX 4045
GENICOM 3000 SERIES
HONEYWELL 4-66/CQ34
HEWLETT-PACKARD
IDS
KYOCERA Laser
MANNESMAN TALLY
MPI Solution

→ TEMP1!A1
Use arrow keys to move cursor. Press ←┘ to select device.
 41>/Global,Spreadsheet,Device,B&W-printers,
MENU  Select Black and White printer for spreadsheet output
```

Fig. 9.1.

The Device Selection menu for choosing a printer.

your specific printer, your printer may emulate one listed, which you can select. Otherwise, selecting a generic category such as the default `Draft Printer` or `IBM Graphics` will probably satisfy most of your requirements.

Once you select your printer you can save your selection for future work sessions with /**G**lobal,**K**eep,**Y**es. If you have more than one printer, you may want to save each to its own configuration file with

/**G**lobal,**K**eep,**T**o,*filename*

Next, you should check to see that SuperCalc has the correct printer interface definition. To do so, select /**G**lobal,**S**preadsheet,**O**ptions, calling up the Spreadsheet Options menu, which shows the information SuperCalc uses to define your printer (see fig. 9.2).

At the bottom of the figure you see eight options:

Quit Auto Parallel Serial DOS Check FormFeed Zap

Your printer is connected to your computer in one of two ways: by a parallel interface or a serial interface. First, you should take advantage of an option new for SuperCalc5, **A**uto. If you select **A**uto, SuperCalc guesses at your configuration based on the printer you select. However, you still must inform SuperCalc whether you have a parallel or serial printer. If your printer is a parallel printer, select the **P**arallel option now. You then must choose one of the three possible parallel ports because you may have more than one parallel port installed in your computer:

1 = LPT1:   2 = LPT2:   3 = LPT3:

Usually, you choose port 1 (**1** = LPT1:).

If you select **S**erial rather than **P**arallel, you must consider a few additional settings. As previously mentioned, because a serial interface can be used for communicating with various devices, you need to define not only to which serial port the printer is attached

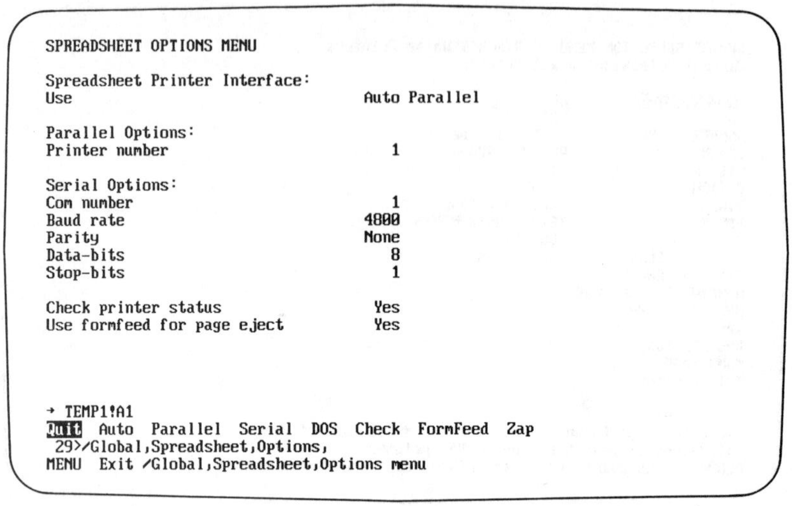

Fig. 9.2.

*The Spreadsheet
Options menu.*

```
SPREADSHEET OPTIONS MENU

Spreadsheet Printer Interface:
Use                                    Auto Parallel

Parallel Options:
Printer number                         1

Serial Options:
Com number                             1
Baud rate                              4800
Parity                                 None
Data-bits                              8
Stop-bits                              1

Check printer status                   Yes
Use formfeed for page eject            Yes



→ TEMP1↑A1
 Quit Auto Parallel Serial DOS Check FormFeed Zap
  29>/Global,Spreadsheet,Options,
 MENU  Exit /Global,Spreadsheet,Options menu
```

(**1** = COM1: or **2** = COM2:) but at what rate the data will be transferred and how many parity bits (0, 1, or 2), data bits (7 or 8), and stop bits (1 or 2) define a packet of data to be transferred. The program defaults for these settings appear in figure 9.2 and are the most common. (Hint: The first thing to check if you have a printing problem is the speed of transfer—9600 baud is a common transfer rate). Serial printers generally require more user knowledge of these communication parameters than do parallel printers.

If you define your printer through DOS using the DOS MODE command, you can select **D**OS on the Options menu rather than **P**arallel or **S**erial.

The remaining three options—**C**heck, **F**ormFeed, and **Z**ap—have nothing to do with the type of interface. **C**heck was on the Global Optimum menu in SuperCalc4, but is now more appropriately placed on this menu. When **C**heck is set to **Y**es, SuperCalc checks whether your printer is on-line and active before printing your output. If set to **N**o, SuperCalc releases the output to the printer without checking. You typically want to have the program check, so the default setting is **Y**es. If **F**ormFeed is left as **Y**es (the default), a formfeed character will be issued to your printer between pages of long documents. If the setting is changed to **N**o, linefeeds will be used instead. If you set **F**ormFeed to **Y**es and then select **P**age-advance (discussed later in this chapter) after printing your report, the page will eject one page length and not to the top of the next page. Because of this page advance characteristic, you may want to keep the **F**ormFeed set to **N**o. Finally, **Z**ap will reset all the **S**preadsheet options to their default settings if you need to start over.

Once you have completed your options specification, select **Q**uit to return to the main Global Spreadsheet menu. Like the **D**evice options, you can save all **S**preadsheet options with the /**G**lobal,**K**eep command.

For normal use of the SuperCalc printing commands, you also need to know the printer setup strings, especially if your printer is a dot-matrix printer. SuperCalc has its own way of specifying a command to be sent to your printer so that characters will print in boldface, in near-letter quality, with underlines, with different character spacing (the distance between characters), or with different line spacing (the number of lines per inch).

Because SuperCalc accepts extended ASCII graphics characters, your worksheet can contain them. A dot-matrix printer may be capable of displaying these characters. To test your printer for this capability, press F1 to call up a SuperCalc AnswerScreen, which almost always contains graphics characters. After you verify that your printer is on and has paper, press Shift-PrtSc. On IBM and compatible computers, this key combination sends a copy of the screen to the printer. If the printer is compatible, the box surrounding the AnswerScreen is printed as it appears on-screen; otherwise, the box appears with a different character substituted for the line.

If your printer does not handle the extended ASCII character set, you can turn off those characters by selecting Translation-table, which is on the Global Spreadsheet menu. The Device Selection menu, shown in figure 9.3, then appears.

```
DEVICE SELECTION MENU -- Character Translation Tables
Current Selection: PC Extended ASCII

PC Extended ASCII
96 Character ASCII
```

Fig. 9.3.
The Device Selection menu for choosing character sets.

On this screen you have two options. The default choice, PC Extended ASCII, will print all the extended graphics characters definable using the Alt-decimal value key combination (discussed in Chapter 11). The optional selection, 96 Character ASCII, will eliminate any of the specialty characters from the extended mode.

Selecting Single-Sheet or Continuous-Form Printing

Some of the options described in this chapter pertain to special printing situations or special printers. The option for single-sheet or a form-feed type printer, which you select with /Output,Printer,Options,Paper, is an example. As you go through this chapter, look for the options that are most useful for your printing requirements.

Considering Page Size

When you work with large spreadsheets, figuring how to structure and fit a seemingly infinite amount of data into a finite amount of printed page can become a time-consuming task. You first need to consider your printer's width. You also have to consider the characters per inch your printer prints, such as 10 characters per inch (pica style), 12 characters per inch (elite style), or even 17 characters per inch (condensed style). You must consider these choices every time you print a spreadsheet.

The /Output Command Structure

To access the printing commands and setups in SuperCalc, you select /Output, which brings up the following menu:

```
Printer  File  Attributes  Grid  Lines  New-page
```

The first choice you must make is where to direct the output. You choose one of the first two choices (**P**rinter or **F**ile) as your destination. **P**rinter is the normal choice in this situation, indicating that you want to direct the output to your printer. **F**ile stores the output in an ASCII text file for later use instead of sending the output to the printer for printing. In an ASCII text file, the file can be edited by a text editor or printed with Sideways®, the utility provided for using a dot-matrix printer to print spreadsheets laterally on the page.

The next three choices (**A**ttributes, **G**rid, and **L**ines) are used with laser printers to define overlay shading, borders, grids, lines, and fonts. Because these are unnecessary unless you have a laser printer, they are discussed in the ''Laser Power'' section in this chapter.

If you select the **N**ew-page option, a new row is inserted in the spreadsheet above the row that you point to with the cell pointer, and the text

```
|::
```

is entered in the cell where the cell pointer is located. If you look at the contents of the cell shown on the status line, you see

```
Ctrl=|::
```

This is an embedded printer control character, which instructs SuperCalc to issue a form-feed command when it encounters that cell, printing the rest of the spreadsheet on a new page. Other embedded printer control strings can be entered directly into cells. (See ''Defining the Printer Setup'' in this chapter.)

The Output Printer Menu

Selecting either **F**ile (by way of selecting a file name) or **P**rinter moves you to the Output Printer menu, which has the following choices:

```
Range  Go  Console  Line-advance  Page-advance  Options  Zap  Align  Width  Quit
```

This is a powerful set of choices. If you define the output range with **R**ange, you can store your output range for future printing. The **G**o choice executes the printing. **C**onsole, a holdover from SuperCalc3, lets you preview your output on the computer screen rather than on the printer. **L**ine-advance and **P**age-advance are options for sending a line-feed or form-feed command to your printer. The **O**ptions selection shows you the many options provided in SuperCalc's /Output command. By selecting **Z**ap, you can reset all the changed settings to the default settings. The **A**lign choice directs SuperCalc and your printer to begin your output at the top of a page. The **Q**uit option leaves the /**O**utput command.

The **W**idth option, which is one of the new features of SuperCalc5, calculates the width of a range that you point to or define.

The Output Options Menu

When you select **O**ptions, the screen displays the Output Options menu, shown in figure 9.4.

```
OUTPUT OPTIONS MENU: (*Indicates options saved with /Global,Keep)
*Report Format          *Layout                     *Paper
  Formatted    Draft      Page-length   66            Wait        Yes
  Contents     No         Width         80            Auto-page   No
  Spool        No         Left          4             Double      No
                          Top           2             Line-feed   Yes
  Titles       None       Bottom        2
  Horiz.       None       Orientation   Portrait     *Borders     No
  Vert.        None      *Copies        1             Character    !
  Headers
  1:
  2:
  3:
  4:
  Footers
  1:
  2:
  3:
  4:
 *Setup String (default)            (Output range is currently empty)

 → TEMP1!A1
 Quit  Report  Layout  Paper  Titles  Copies  Borders  Headers  Footers  Setup
  25>/Output,Printer,Options,
 MENU  Done with output options; return to /Output,Printer or File menu
```

Fig. 9.4.

The Output Options menu.

The Output Options menu is a comprehensive and user-friendly screen; it's like a spreadsheet within the spreadsheet. From this screen you can see the settings of all the options in the output structure. When you debug a report, this screen is indispensable.

This menu has been changed only slightly in SuperCalc5 and mostly to handle laser printers. All laser printer-related options are discussed in the section "Laser Power."

The top third of the Output Options menu screen displays the options for report format, titles, page layout, border printing, and printer page-control settings. You use the middle section to enter multiline headers and footers. The lower part of the screen is for entering the important printer setup string. All sections of the screen are accessible through the options at the bottom of the screen. The first selection, **Q**uit, returns you to the regular spreadsheet display and the Output Printer menu.

Default Settings

The settings shown in figure 9.4 are the default settings for each option. Most of the options are switched off, and those that cannot be switched off are defined for the most general use. For example, because letter-size paper is 66 lines long at 6 lines per inch and is 80 characters wide at 10 characters per inch, **L**ayout,**P**age-length is set at 66 and **W**idth at 80. Any change you make to a default setting is recorded on-screen. After the change, the new setting and its label appear in half-intensity (white rather than yellow on a color monitor) to remind you that you made a change.

Redefinable Default Settings

As the top of the screen in figure 9.4 indicates, you can redefine the default setting for any option preceded by an asterisk (*). To redefine the default setting, make the changes, press Ctrl-Break to return to READY mode, and enter

   /Global,**K**eep,**Y**es

Once you have customized the options for your printer and your situation, save them so that the options will be defined the same way every time you use SuperCalc. For example, if you usually use continuous-form paper and want the printer to continue automatically to the next page, you can change the **W**ait setting to **N**o and retain that setting with the **/G**lobal,**K**eep command. The settings not marked with an asterisk remain set for the spreadsheet in which they are stored but cannot be changed permanently into default settings.

The Basics of Producing Output

Some steps in producing output are mandatory; others are more useful for special circumstances, a special effect, or a special type of printer. Therefore, this discussion is divided into two main parts: the basics (the mandatory steps) and the **/O**utput frills (the specialty steps).

Defining the Range

The most important selection within the **/O**utput command structure is the **R**ange definition. With SuperCalc, once you define an output range, it is stored with the worksheet.

Defining a print range is a good time to point to the range in order to confirm the range selection. This confirmation can be demonstrated with a client contact list. Figure 9.5 shows a portion of the worksheet with the print range defined. With a large print range, you see at one time only a portion of the range highlighted and displayed. In the figure, only A11:C30 is displayed, even though the full range is R3:A30, as indicated on the entry line.

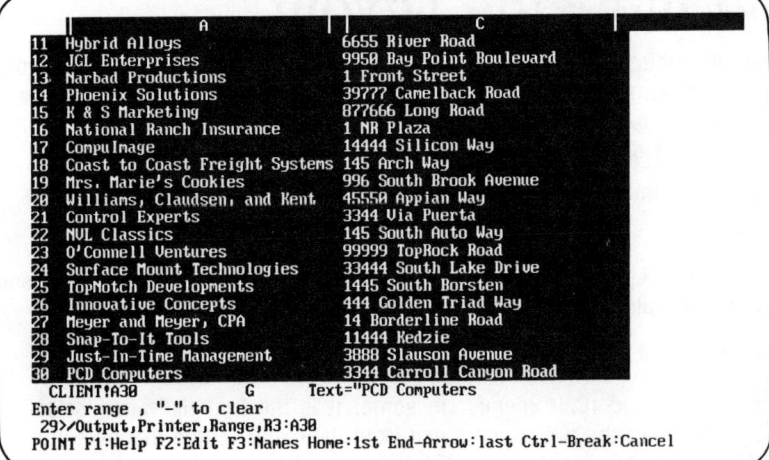

Fig. 9.5.

Defining the output range for a client contact list.

Pointing to the Range

To enter the range, press Home and on the entry line choose

/Output,Printer,Range,**A1**

The current location of the cell pointer appears as the default range because no range was previously entered. To print the entire worksheet, press a colon (:) to anchor the beginning address of the range. Then press End-Home.

The screen changes to display the lower right corner of the worksheet. To move around the four corners of the range, you can press the period key. The cell pointer moves clockwise around the rectangular range that is highlighted in reverse video (blue on a color monitor). Figure 9.5 shows the cell pointer in the lower left corner of the range (A30) after the period was pressed once.

Using a Named Range

Another useful strategy for defining print ranges is to use the /Name command before you print to assign a name to the print range. This operation is useful when you have to print several ranges in the worksheet.

Pointing to the range through the Named Range Directory can speed the selection process even more. When you are ready to define the range, you can either type the name of the output range or press F3 to display the Named Range Directory. Move the selector to the name you want and press Enter. The name appears in the /Output command line, which looks like this:

/Output,Printer,Range,**MAILIST**,

When you incorporate macro commands into a worksheet that has several print ranges, named ranges clarify which macro is associated with which print range (see Chapter 11).

Defining the Page Layout

Another basic step in producing a printed report is to define the page layout. The Layout section of the Output Options menu helps you designate the area you want to consider a page of output. By adjusting and combining specified parameters, you can create a large variety of page styles to fit different situations.

To get to these options from READY mode, at the prompt enter

/Output,Printer,Options,Layout

The Output Options menu appears on-screen, and across the bottom the Layout menu appears and displays the following choices:

```
Quit  Page-length  Width  Left  Top  Bottom  Orientation
```

Quit is an option in many SuperCalc menus. In some, it is the first (leftmost) selection and, along with Esc, is one of the two ways to exit from the menu. Some menus automatically change to the next higher menu or to READY mode after the command process is over; but others, like the Layout menu, require you to exit from the menu. All the options on this menu appear on the Output Options menu in figure 9.4 and can be altered permanently using /Global,Keep,Yes.

Page-length

Page-length, the next Layout menu choice, defines the maximum number of lines that can be printed on a page. The default page length of 66 lines is the number of lines on an 11-inch page printed at the standard 6 lines per inch. You can change the page length from 0 up to 255 lines per page. SuperCalc considers 0 to be a continuous page (with no bottom or top margins) and prints the output continuously, without any page feeds.

Like all print options, you must know how other output options affect the page length. In this case, you have to consider the size of the top and bottom margins and the number of header and footer lines used. To calculate how many data lines will print per page, you must subtract the top and bottom margins from the designated page length. For example, with 2 lines of margin at both the top and bottom, a 66-line page holds only 62 lines of data.

To change the page length, move the menu selector to Page-length for the following prompt:

```
Enter number (0-255), then return.
    44>/Output,Printer,Options,Layout,Page-length,
```

You can enter any length between 0 and 255. In the client list example, 66 lines per page is acceptable. This length means that SuperCalc sends the first 66 lines of the print range to the printer, then a page-feed flag, and then the second page.

Table 9.1 lists common page sizes with the number of lines on each page at six lines per inch and the less common, but useful, eight lines per inch. Most printers have the capability to print at both these standard rates. With some printers, you can even vary the lines-per-inch increment by as little as 1/216 inch. Look for your printer's capabilities in your printer manual.

Table 9.1
Lines per Page for Common Paper Sizes

| Paper Size in Inches | | Printed Lines | Number of Lines |
Width	Length	per Inch	per Page
8 1/2 or 14	11	6	66
8 1/2 or 14	11	8	88
8 1/2	14	6	84
8 1/2	14	8	112
11	8 1/2	6	51
11	8 1/2	8	68
11	17	6	102
11	17	8	138

Width

Select **W**idth to change the number of characters printed on each line on the page. The default is 80 characters per line, which prints on an 8 1/2-by-11-inch page at 10 characters per inch and, on most printers, leaves room for the default left margin. The width, however, can range from 1 to 255 characters. Unlike the page length, the left margin is not combined into this total. Instead, the line width and the left margin added together equal the total width of the page. Therefore, on most printers the 80-character **W**idth setting leaves room for left and right margins of 2 characters each.

When the defined line width exceeds the total characters possible on your printer, the remainder of the line wraps around and prints on the next line. Figure 9.6 shows a worksheet with data wrapped around. As you can see, "wraparound" can be confusing and should be avoided.

If the defined print range is wider than the defined line width, the remaining columns in the range are printed on the next page instead of wrapping around to the next line. You then can lay the pages next to each other and get a clear view of the information. To avoid wrapping the lines of data, try to match the defined width to the printer's maximum width rather than to the width of the print range. Remember, you can now easily identify the width of your print range by using

/**O**utput,**P**rinter,**W**idth

If your printer handles different print pitches, you can stretch the width limits. Most printers offer some alternatives; the most common pitches are 10 (pica), 12 (elite), and 15 or 17 (compressed) characters per inch. Check your printer manual for specific capabilities. Table 9.2 lists some common page sizes, characters per inch (cpi) settings, and

Fig. 9.6.

Output with wrapped lines.

```
                                            Client Call Sheet
          CLIENT.CAL                        For: Jim Palma
                 6/ 06/89
                 Company Name      Address          City         ST   Zip    Phone
                 Contact
          -------------------------  -------------------  ----------------------  --  ------  ------------------  -------

          Zambini's Sports Shops    14 South Vermont     Urbana          IL   65505  ( 217) 434- 2313 Mike Mc
          Mahon
          P and P Communications    14328 Mountain View  Denver          CO   78506  ( 303) 987- 4285 Dick Pi
          ttman
          Miller and Miller Investments  1 Ocean Boulevard  Marina Del Rey  CA   90005  ( 213) 431-RENT  Don Mil
          ler
          North County Air Conditioning  1125 South Northface Drive  Rancho Panasquitos  CA   90001  ( 619) 987- 5454 Ed Holu
          b
          CMD Electronics           1456 Front Street    Woodland Hills  CA   39789  ( 308) 423- 1995 Bob Sau
          cedo
          Lateral Designs, Inc.     124 Fountain Hills Road  Loda        WY   73687  ( 514) 862- 9364 Jane Ru
          th
          Cox Chemicals             6657 South Vernon    City of Industry  CA   90830  ( 213) 744- 7304 Kim Cox
```

line widths. Line width is not always cpi multiplied by the number of inches. Some printer manufacturers use an artificial number less than the total maximum; therefore, your printer's maximum widths may vary from those in the table.

Table 9.2
CPI and Width Settings for Common Paper Sizes

Paper Width (in Inches)	Characters per Inch	Line Width
8 1/2	10	80
8 1/2	12	102
5	15	127
8 1/2	17	144
14	10	132
14	12	168
14	15	210
14	17	238
11	10	110
11	12	132
11	15	165
11	17	187

SuperCalc prints only whole columns, and when text spills over into the columns to the right, these spill-over columns must be included in the range as well. By adjusting the column widths, you may be able to fit more data on a page.

Width is influenced by paper width, printer cpi options, column widths, and left margin width. By manipulating these parameters, you can have a variety of output options. Table 9.3 shows a breakdown of the widths of the 18 columns from the client list example in figure 9.5.

Table 9.3
Summary of Client List Column Widths

Field Name	Column	Width
Company Name	A	30
Address	C	30
City	E	20
State	G	2
ZIP	I	5
Left Parenthesis	K	1
Area Code	L	4
Right Parenthesis	M	1
Phone Prefix	N	4
Dash Separator	O	1
Phone Suffix	P	5
Contact	R	23
Spacer Columns	B,D,F,H,J,Q	6 (1 column apiece)
	Total	132

Total width in the client list example should be set to 132 so that your report will fit across one page. In some cases, you must change an individual column width to match the printer width. In this example, column R, *Contact*, is the most flexible, so it is reduced to 23 from 30 to fit into the total of 132.

Margins

You can adjust the left, top, and bottom margins. Increasing the top and bottom margins reduces the number of lines per page, and increasing the left margin reduces the line width available for printing. The default left margin is four, and the default top margin and bottom margin are two.

A right-margin parameter is not necessary because it is defined as the remainder of the page after the width is offset by the left margin, according to the formula

Right Margin = (Width of Paper) − (Left Margin) − (Line Width)

You can set the margins to any number from 0 to 255. SuperCalc accepts any combination of margins on input; but when you execute the print operation, the following error message may appear in the lower right corner of the display:

```
No room for report; check Output Options menu.
```

This error message means that the margin settings left no room for the report to be printed. This error can be the result of setting the left margin to 255 or the top or bottom margins to 66 (with a 66-line page length).

In the client list example, both the left and right margins should be zero because the data uses 132 character spaces. The top and bottom margins can be left at 2, but more data will fit if both margins are set to zero.

Defining the Printer Setup

The command that actually sets up the printer is closely tied in to all the discussion up to now. SuperCalc's print features, although powerful, are only as powerful as your printer. When turned on, most printers default to 10 cpi and 6 lines per inch. In addition, any dot-matrix printer is likely to be in draft-mode (single-pass) print quality. The printer has either a narrow carriage, which uses only letter-size paper, or a wide carriage, which uses 132-column paper. If your printer does not have hardware switches on the front panel to change from draft to near-letter quality (NLQ) or to 10, 12, or 17 cpi, you must use the Setup String section of the Output Options menu to change these settings.

Several setup-string standards have evolved in the computer industry. Many printers accept the IBM-standard graphics and control codes; the EPSON® character set, also currently popular; and the Diablo character set, an early standard for letter-quality printers. For example, your printer may recognize the IBM lower-order characters, which match closely the characters on your computer keyboard; but your printer may not recognize the extended graphics character set, which includes special engineering, mathematics, and graphics symbols. To learn which setup strings your printer recognizes, look in the control code section of your printer manual.

Using printer codes, however, is standard within the industry. Each code can be represented in an ASCII format, a hexadecimal equivalent, or a decimal equivalent. The IBM-compatible code for compressed printing, for example, is Ctrl-O in ASCII format, 1F in hexadecimal format, and 15 in decimal format.

Table 9.4 lists some common control codes. The first column of the table lists eight popular settings; the second column lists the printer manufacturers; the third column specifies the ASCII code that activates that setting for those printers; and the fourth column specifies the decimal equivalent for that setting. (Notice that Esc + E, for example, means to press and release Esc and then press E.) Your printer's manual contains a similar table, which covers all your printer's capabilities.

Table 9.4
Common Control Code Descriptions and Decimal Equivalents

Description	Manufacturer	ASCII Code	Decimal Code
Compressed print	IBM, EPSON	Ctrl-O	015
Emphasized	IBM, EPSON	Esc + E	027 069
Double strike	IBM, EPSON	Esc + G	027 071
Eight lines per inch	IBM, EPSON	Esc + 0	027 048
Underlining	Okidata	Esc + C	027 067
12 cpi print	Okidata	FS	028
Compressed print	Okidata	GS	029
Correspondence quality	Okidata	Esc + 1	027 049

Although at first glance a printer manual's control-code table appears intimidating, only a few of the control codes are necessary to print most spreadsheets. The codes relating to character spacing, line spacing, character quality, and underlining are the most useful.

SuperCalc5 makes these codes easy to use because you can enter the decimal equivalent for the code as a three-digit decimal number preceded by a backslash (\). The codes range from 000 to 255. Some codes require an additional two numbers. For example, the code for the Esc key precedes many of the setup codes. In table 9.4, the Okidata Correspondence Quality control string illustrates the use of the second code. The decimal equivalent for the Esc key is 27 and a 1 is 49. Some codes require a third code as well. The EPSON code for near-letter quality (NLQ) is

Esc + x + 1

to enter NLQ mode and

Esc + x + 0

to exit (where x is the three-digit code). The EPSON NLQ code operates like most codes: one code switches on the mode and another code switches off the mode.

To enter a code, select **S**etup from the Output Options menu. The cursor moves to the Setup String section of the Output Options menu. To enter a compressed-mode setup string and an emphasized-print setup string for an IBM-compatible printer, type

\015\027\069

Notice that codes can be entered consecutively to combine effects. After typing a backslash, you can enter up to 60 characters with each code. If you want to edit the setup string, press F2 while you are in the string. You can now move the edit cursor back and forth in the code line and add, change, and delete characters from the setup string. When you have completed your changes to the string, press Enter to return to the menu. You cannot use the Esc key to return to the menu because Esc can be part of setup codes (see table 9.4).

Embedding Setup Strings

A new alternative is available with SuperCalc5: now you can embed setup strings in your spreadsheet. To embed the string in the preceding section into your spreadsheet, insert at the beginning of your print range a blank row that will be dedicated to the setup string. In a cell in that row of the range (preferably the leftmost cell within the range), enter

II\015\027\069

SuperCalc recognizes these characters as a control string and executes the string. You also can embed comments in the spreadsheet by typing a single vertical bar before the comment. The comment will not print, even when included in the print range. Once a setup string is included in a row, nothing in the row will print. That is, you must dedicate an entire row to the setup string. Embedding a setup string in a header is discussed in the section ''Creating Headers and Footers'' in this chapter.

Whether you use the **S**etup method or the embedded spreadsheet string method, help yourself take advantage of SuperCalc's full power; take time to learn these setup codes, and keep your printer manual close by. Just remember: experimenting with these codes is fun, and you can easily return to your printer's defaults by switching the printer off and back on.

Executing the Print

After you have defined a range and redefined some of the basic options, you are ready to print. The Output Printer menu contains two selections designed for your direct interaction with the printer: **P**age-advance (page feeding) and **L**ine-advance (line feeding).

Setting Page and Line Options

When you select **P**age-advance from the Output Printer menu, the paper in your printer advances to the end of the page and on to the top of the next page. If the paper is not at the top of the next page, adjust the paper so that the print head is situated in the top left corner of the page. You can select **P**age-advance both before and after you print. Before you print, **P**age-advance helps you align the top of the form. You can also select **P**age-advance after you print, to advance the paper to the end of the current page if you have FormFeed set to **N**o on the Global Spreadsheet Options menu. Otherwise, the **P**age-advance option will eject one full page-length. That way, you can retrieve the report from the form feeds on your printer without rolling the printer platen ahead. This command honors any headers and footers defined by the Output Printer menu and prints these headers and footers during subsequent page feeds.

Instead of advancing to the end of the current form, **L**ine-advance advances the printer one line and adds one line to the line counter. This feature is useful for separating two ranges that you want to print on the same page. The **L**ine-advance command also honors any defined headers and footers. Multiline headers or footers print one line at a time as the **L**ine-advance command is executed.

The **A**lign selection on the Output Printer menu resets the line and page counters. This feature ensures that your counters are set to one. As a rule, you should select **A**lign before each printing and make sure that the paper in the printer is aligned at the top of a page.

Selecting Go

When you select **G**o, SuperCalc begins to print. The setup string and then the report are sent to the printer. You cannot use SuperCalc while the program is printing the report, but keystrokes entered during printing are stored for execution after printing has stopped. Until the end of the report enters the printer or printer memory buffer, the computer waits for the printer to stop.

Interrupting the /Output Command

After selecting **G**o, you can interrupt printing in three ways. You can reboot the computer, losing any unsaved data. One of the other methods is "nonfatal," which means that printing can continue after the interruption. The "nonfatal" way to stop printing is to turn off the printer by pressing the power button on the printer. When you do, the following message appears on-screen:

    Ready printer and press space to continue.

At this point, SuperCalc waits to resume printing where it left off. If you press any key while the printer is off-line, you are returned to READY mode.

You also can stop the printing process permanently by pressing Ctrl-Break—the "fatal" method. This key combination generates the following message in the status line:

    Command terminated

SuperCalc returns you to READY mode after you press another key.

Sending Output to the Screen

To send the report to the screen rather than to the printer, select **C**onsole from the Output Printer menu. The formatted report then is displayed on-screen. **C**onsole displays the first 80 columns of the report. You can see only a small portion of large reports, but the page breaks show you where the data will break and how many pages are in the report. You can save yourself a great deal of wasted paper by learning to use this option. If you have a long report and your computer and monitor have the capability, set /**G**lobal,**Z**oom,**O**n before displaying your output. You will see a much larger part of the report at one time.

The Frills of the /Output Command

Up to this point, the discussion has centered on what can be considered the basics of /Output; after you become familiar with the commands and options discussed in this section, however, you will have your own lists of basics and frills. The following frills are what make the SuperCalc /Output command a state-of-the-art design. They are all accessed through the Output Options menu (shown in fig. 9.4) by typing

/Output,Printer,Options

Printing Titles

The Titles option from the Output Options menu is just as important in printing worksheets as in viewing large worksheets. When a worksheet exceeds the width or length of a page, the remaining columns have to be printed on the following page. Without titles defined, the remaining data is printed without any column or row headings.

When you choose Titles, the following choices appear:

```
Auto  Manual  None
```

With a large worksheet, you may have a title lock already defined. When you select the Auto option, titles that are defined in the spreadsheet by the /Title command carry over for use with the /Output command. For easy reference, the title range is displayed on the Output Options menu. If you are defining a horizontal title, the column labels relating to the data being printed on that page are printed across the top of the page below the header. If you are defining a vertical title, the portion of the title relating to the data being printed on the page is printed down the left edge of the page with the corresponding data printed adjacent to the title.

Manual Titles

If you did not define titles before entering the /Output command or if you want a different set of titles relating to the output data, select the Manual option under Titles. The following menu of choices appears:

```
Quit  Horizontal-range  Vertical-range
```

If you want column labels printed across the top of the page, select Horizontal-range to define the row range containing the column labels. If you want row labels to appear down the side of the page, select Vertical-range to define the column range containing the labels.

After you make your Titles selection, the screen switches to the spreadsheet so that you can point to the row or column range. Figure 9.7 shows the screen during a Horizontal-range title-selection process.

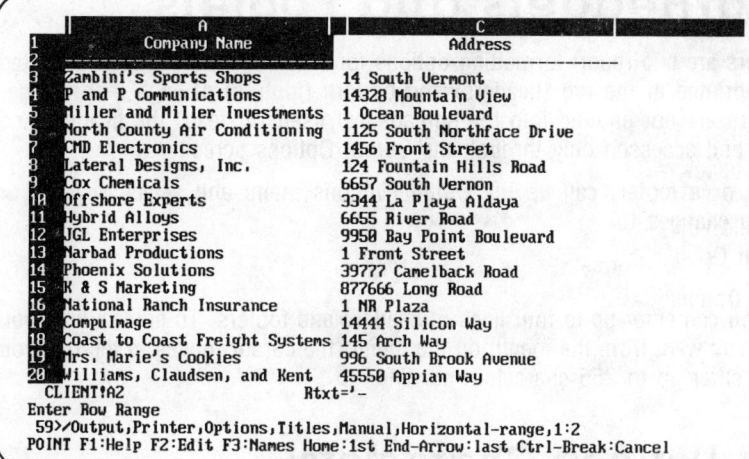

Fig. 9.7.

Defining a Horizontal-range title for printing.

The defined-row range is highlighted in reverse video (blue on a color monitor). After pointing to the range, press Enter. The Output Options menu returns to the screen with the new title range displayed in the Titles section.

Effects on the Defined Range

In figure 9.7, a two-row range is defined. This range subtracts two data lines per page; similarly, vertical titles reduce the number of columns available for data. Any title range you use should not be included in the output range. In the client list example, the range was originally defined to include rows 1 and 2. If the range is not adjusted, rows 1 and 2 will be printed twice on the page: once as a part of the title section and once as a part of the print range. Figure 9.8 shows how the report appears if the print range is not adjusted. When you use **T**itles, define the print range as only the data portion of the worksheet. The range needs to be adjusted to A3:R30 rather than A1:R30.

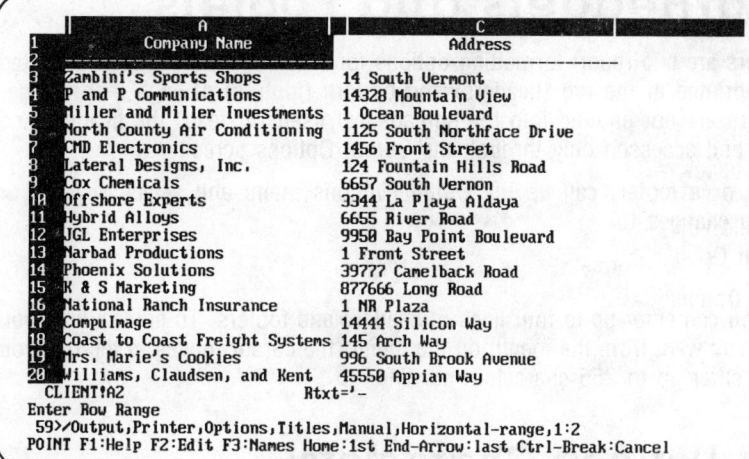

Fig. 9.8.

Labels included in both titles and range.

Creating Headers and Footers

Headers and **F**ooters are two report formatting options for entering report titles and related information to be printed at the top (headers) and bottom (footers) of each report page. Headers and footers are not entered into the spreadsheet itself. Instead, the headers and footers are stored and accessed only through the Output Options screen.

To enter a header or a footer, call up the Output Options menu and select **H**eaders or **F**ooters. The menu changes to

    Quit 1 2 3 4 Fonts

As you can see, you can enter up to four lines of headers and footers. To enter a line, you select the number you want from the menu; on the menu, the cursor moves to the row you selected. You can enter up to 255 characters per line.

Specially Defined Characters:
The |, @1–@8, @P, and @F

You can position your header data on the page with spaces, or you can use special characters to make the task easier. The line-feed character (|, the vertical bar) takes on a special meaning when used in headers. The text after the first vertical bar is centered on the page, and the text after the second vertical bar is right-justified. For the client list example, enter the header text as follows:

    1: |Client List
    2: @F|For: |::\027\071::|Jim Palma|::\027\072::||@2

The report title will be centered in line 1 because there is one vertical bar preceding the title. Of the three pieces of information in line 2, @F will substitute the spreadsheet's file name on the left edge of the spreadsheet and the account representative's name will be centered and printed in an enhanced print style called near-letter quality (NLQ). The NLQ is activated by the

    |::\027\071::|

printer setup string before the representative's name, and it is deactivated by the string

    |::\027\072::|

after the representative's name. All the vertical bars can get confusing, so make sure that you have enough bars to format your printout successfully. The centering bars can save you time in figuring out spacing requirements. Remember, however, that the placement is based on the page **W**idth setting. If the **W**idth is overestimated, the headers and footers will be wrapped and off-center.

In the example, @F is the new SuperCalc5 function for embedding the file name. You could also use @L rather than @F to include the full path where the file is located along with the file name. At the end of the example is another @ sign followed by a 2. This @2 will cause the DOS system date to be substituted using **U**ser-define,**D**ate,**2**. The current DOS date is defined at the system level.

A third special function appears in the client list's footers. @P is a variable that prints the current page count in the header or footer. Enter a footer in line 2 of the client list by selecting **F**ooters from the Output Options menu and selecting **2** from the **F**ooters menu. Enter the footer as

```
1:
2:  |Page: @P
3:
4:
```

Page: will precede the page number (@P), and the vertical bar will center the footer at the bottom of the page.

Uses for Multiple Lines

In this footer, line 1 is left empty, but both 1 and 2 appear in white on-screen (half-intensity with a monochrome screen). Although nothing is entered in the first line, Super-Calc dedicates a line to the first footer line on the printed page, causing a blank line to be left before the page number. SuperCalc does not allot space for any footer lines beneath the data line. The blank line for spacing reduces the lines per page available for data, but the format looks less cluttered.

Altogether, four lines are used for the header and footer in the client list, and 62 out of 66 lines are left for spreadsheet data. However, because this report has two title rows already defined, the data area is reduced further to 60 lines per page.

A demonstration of this breakdown of the lines on a printed page can be seen by looking ahead to figure 9.12, the finished client list report. Because the report is printed with the double-spacing option, the four lines for headers and footers, two lines for the title rows, and 60 lines for the rest of the data become eight lines for headers and footers, four lines for the title rows, and 54 lines for the rest of the data. The lines available for the data are defined as

66 Total − 8 Header/Footer − 4 Titles = 54 Data Lines

Of the 54 lines for data, only half are data lines; the other half are double-spacing lines. Therefore, of 66 total lines, only 27 lines of data are printed before the page is ejected.

If you use **F**ooters, remember to select **P**age after **G**o so that the footer on the last page will be printed. SuperCalc, by default, stops after the last line of the print range. The program does not automatically send a page feed unless you change the **P**aper,**A**uto-page option (see the section ''Auto-page Switch'').

Working with the Borders and Report Options

The **B**orders and **R**eport options, which were available with the first SuperCalc release, are useful only in special circumstances.

Using the Borders Option

Turning on the **B**orders option causes the SuperCalc spreadsheet border (the row numbers and column letters on the screen) to be printed as part of the report. If you select **B**orders from the Output Options menu, the following menu appears:

        Quit Auto Yes No Character

If **B**orders is set to **A**uto, the borders on the printed report will match the borders on the spreadsheet. You can turn off the borders control on the spreadsheet display with the /**G**lobal,**B**order,**N**o command. With the borders off (the default setting), a border does not appear along the edge of the printed range.

The **B**orders,**Y**es option, however, forces the border to be printed regardless of the status of the border on the display. Similarly, the **B**orders,**N**o option, the default value, prevents the border from being printed regardless of the status of the display on-screen.

When you select the **C**haracter option, the following menu prompt line is displayed:

        Enter new border character
         43>/Output,Printer,Options,Borders,Character,

When the border is printed, any character you enter on the command line, rather than the default character (.), will be printed between the column letters. This feature, however, does not change the character display on the screen. After you enter the new character, press Enter twice to return to the main Output Options menu.

Figure 9.9 shows a portion of the client list with the border character changed to the line-feed character (I) in single-space and with the borders set to print. The row numbers are displayed down the left edge; and the column letters, separated by single line-feed characters, are displayed above the spreadsheet data. The headers are placed above the column letters because headers are stored separately in the /**O**utput command structure.

Fig. 9.9.

A portion of the client list report output with borders.

```
                                                      Client Call Sheet
     CLIENT                                             For: Jim Palma
          !              A          ! !          C           ! !        E
     1               Company Name                   Address               City
     2
     3     Zambini's Sports Shops      14 South Vermont        Urbana
     4     P and P Communications      14328 Mountain View     Denver
     5     Miller and Miller Investments 1 Ocean Boulevard     Marina Del Re
     6     North County Air Conditioning 1125 South Northface Drive Rancho Panasq
     7     CMD Electronics             1456 Front Street       Woodland Hill
     8     Lateral Designs, Inc.       124 Fountain Hills Road Loda
     9     Cox Chemicals               6657 South Vernon       City of Indus
     10    Offshore Experts            3344 La Playa Aldaya    San Diego
     11    Hybrid Alloys               6655 River Road         Phoenix
     12    JGL Enterprises             9950 Bay Point Boulevard Petoskey
     13    Narbad Productions          1 Front Street          Providence
     14    Phoenix Solutions           39777 Camelback Road    Phoenix
     15    K & S Marketing             877666 Long Road        Huntington Be
     16    National Ranch Insurance    1 NR Plaza              Newport Beach
     17    CompuImage                  14444 Silicon Way       San Jose
     18    Coast to Coast Freight Systems 145 Arch Way         St. Louis
     ↓ MAILIST!A1                P Text="Company Name
     More... (<RETURN> to continue)
      24>/Output,Printer,Console
     MENU  Display the report on the console
```

Columns A, C, and E in figure 9.9 appear to have two line-feed characters between them; in reality, however, these columns are B and D with a width setting that is too narrow for the letters to be displayed. Figure 9.9 displays the report created by using /Output,**P**rinter,**C**onsole to send the report to the screen rather than the printer. (This option is discussed in "Sending Output to the Screen" in this chapter.)

Using the Report Option

Report Format, located in the upper left corner of the Output Options menu, is a flag for SuperCalc to print the report formatted with headers, footers, titles, and margins or without the optional formatting as one long page of output.

Select **R**eport from the Output Options menu. Your four choices appear as

```
Quit  Formatted  Contents  Spool
```

The **S**pool option, if turned on, causes printer control characters to be embedded in a print file when the /**O**utput,**F**ile command is used. If turned off, **S**pool causes SuperCalc to ignore the printer control characters when writing the report to file. Because you are printing to the printer, the **S**pool option is not applicable.

Select **F**ormatted. The menu changes to

```
Final  Draft  No
```

The first option, **F**inal, is pertinent only to laser printers. SuperCalc ignores any special enhanced characteristics if your printer does not support them, even if you enter them and set the option to **F**inal. If you try to print in **F**inal format and the printer you have defined does not support it, the following message appears:

```
Enhanced output not supported, printing in draft mode
```

To change **F**ormatted to **N**o (not formatted) from the default of **D**raft, enter **N**o or move the cursor to **N**o and press Enter. The output is printed without margins, title, headers, or footers.

The remaining choice for the **R**eport option is **C**ontents. When you select **C**ontents the following menu appears:

```
Yes  No  Highlighted  View
```

Toggle this option to **Y**es; the cell contents are printed by cell address in a single long column with each cell's relevant information. In addition, if the /**G**lobal,**L**abels option is set to **Y**es, the range names appear on the report; otherwise, the actual range coordinates are printed. Figure 9.10 is a portion of the client list printed with **C**ontents and /**G**lobal,**L**abels both set to **Y**es.

If **C**ontents is set to **N**o, the cell contents are printed as they appear on-screen. Whether you print the formulas or the values depends on which way you set the /**G**lobal,**F**ormula option.

Fig. 9.10.

Client list printed with the Contents, Yes option.

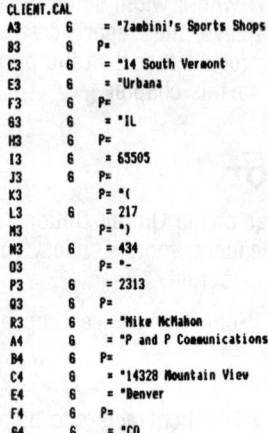

```
                                      Client Call Sheet
                                       For: Jim Palma
     CLIENT.CAL
     A3      6    = "Zambini's Sports Shops
     B3      6    P=
     C3      6    = "14 South Vermont
     E3      6    = "Urbana
     F3      6    P=
     63      6    = "IL
     H3      6    P=
     I3      6    = 65505
     J3      6    P=
     K3      6    P= "(
     L3      6    = 217
     M3      6    P= ")
     N3      6    = 434
     03      6    P= "-
     P3      6    = 2313
     Q3      6    P=
     R3      6    = "Mike McMahon
     A4      6    = "P and P Communications
     B4      6    P=
     C4      6    = "14328 Mountain View
     E4      6    = "Denver
     F4      6    P=
     64      6    = "CO
```

The last two **C**ontents options, **H**ighlighted and **V**iew, were added in SuperCalc5 to take advantage of the //Test command (see Chapter 13). In //Test, you can highlight several cells and analyze them. If you select **H**ighlighted from this menu, the last active set of highlighted cells will be the only ones to print. If you select **V**iew, the report will print formatted according to the last active /View command setting (see Chapter 13). Besides **N**ormal, the default, this setting can be either **F**ormula, which resembles the /**G**lobal,**F**ormula mode, or **M**ap. **M**ap style reduces the spreadsheet to a series of one-character representations of the types of data the spreadsheet consists of, using either a **P**attern map or a **S**tandard map. Figure 9.11 shows the same spreadsheet printed in a standard map format (**C**ontents,**V**iew).

Fig. 9.11.

Client list printed with Contents, View option.

```
                                      Client Call Sheet
                                       For: Jim Palma
     CLIENT.CAL
      .  .  .   .   . .  .            .
     .  .,,, , , ,, , .     . .
     .. . . . . . . .|. ..|..
     ... ....... .|...|..
     .. ......... .|.|..
     .. ....... ..|..|..
     .. ....... ..|..|..
     .. ....... ..|..|..
     .. ....... ..|..|..
     .. ....... ..|..|..
     .. ....... ..|..|..
     .. ....... ..|..|..
     .. ....... ..|..|..
     .. ....... ..|..|..
     .. ....... ..|..|..
     .. ....... .|..|..
     .. ....... .|..|.
     .. .. .... ..|..|..
```

The pound sign (#) indicates a blank cell and a quotation mark (") represents a text cell. If the spreadsheet had any formulas, those cells would appear as an F for "Formula."

Fine-Tuning the Printer Options

Selecting **P**aper from the Output Options menu brings up the following choices:

Quit Wait Auto-page Double-spacing Line-feed

You can use these options to fine-tune the way SuperCalc interacts with your printer.

```
                               Client Call Sheet
CLIENT.CAL                     For: Jim Palma                            6/ 06/89

      Company Name              Address              City      ST  Zip    Phone            Contact

----------------------------   --------------------------   --------------------   -- ------ ---------------  ----------------------
Zambini's Sports Shops         14 South Vermont             Urbana                 IL  65505 ( 217) 434- 2313 Mike McMahon

P and P Communications         14320 Mountain View          Denver                 CO  78506 ( 303) 987- 4285 Dick Pittman

Miller and Miller Investments  1 Ocean Boulevard            Marina Del Rey         CA  90005 ( 213) 431-RENT  Don Miller

North County Air Conditioning  1125 South Northface Drive   Rancho Panasquitos     CA  90001 ( 619) 987- 5454 Ed Holub

CMB Electronics                1456 Front Street            Woodland Hills         CA  39789 ( 308) 423- 1995 Bob Saucedo
```

Fig. 9.12.

The finished client list report.

The Double-spacing Option

The **D**ouble-spacing option is used for the final client list report (see fig. 9.12). This option allows room for further notes to be added by the account representative handling the report.

By changing the **D**ouble-spacing option to **Y**es, you can print only 33 lines per page rather than 66 lines. The headers, footers, and titles rows also are doubled-spaced.

Do not double-space in the spreadsheet. For a double-spaced report, you should single-space the spreadsheet and then use the **D**ouble-spacing option for the printed report. If you single-space in the spreadsheet and wait to add the **D**ouble-spacing option for output only, you can use the /**A**rrange command to sort the data more easily. Use the tab keys to move around the spreadsheet more quickly; more of your spreadsheet is visible on-screen at once. You usually should not leave blank rows between all records in a spreadsheet.

The Wait Option

The **W**ait setting is useful if your printer accepts only single sheets of paper. When you set this option to **Y**es, SuperCalc pauses during printing and displays the message

    Insert paper and press any key

At this point, you can insert another piece of paper and press any key. SuperCalc continues printing where it left off. When the next page is completed, the cycle repeats.

The Auto-page Switch

If the **A**uto-page switch is set to **Y**es, a TOF (top-of-form) or page-feed control character is sent to the printer after each range is printed, and the paper is ejected. As a result, you can print only one range per page.

The **A**uto-page switch is helpful, however, when you are printing a footer on each page. With this capability activated, you no longer need to remember to press **P**age-advance at the end of your report to print the footer on the last page. If, instead of pressing **P**age-advance, you use your printer's form-feed switch or you simply roll the paper forward by hand, the footer is not printed, and the last page of your report is not numbered or identified. By selecting **A**uto-page each time you enter a footer, you no longer need to worry about printing the footer.

The Line-feed Switch

Some printers require a line feed at the end of each line received, and others do not. SuperCalc handles both types of printers with the adjustment of this setting.

By default, SuperCalc issues a line-feed at the end of each printed line. By using the /**G**lobal,**K**eep command, however, you can change the setting to **N**o and then save the current setting for **L**ine-feed and the other **P**aper settings as the program's default values.

Sending Output to a File

As you recall, when you first enter the /**O**utput command, your choices are **P**rinter and **F**ile. You use the **F**ile option to send the data to a disk file rather than to a printer.

You might send output to a disk file for several reasons. If the output is a PRN file on a disk, you can use the DOS PRINT command to print the file in a batch. Or you may want to access the file with your word processor to add information or to combine the file with some other word processed text. This operation is possible because the file is saved in a universally accepted ASCII format. Or if your spreadsheet is too big to fit conventionally on your printer paper, you can send the report to a file and use Sideways (a utility provided as part of the SuperCalc package) to print the file sideways on the page. In addition, you can use the DOS PRINT command to exchange data with another package, such as a database program, by printing the data to an ASCII file, which may be more easily retrieved by the database manager.

When you send output to a file, you must follow the same procedure as you do for the /**S**ave command. First, you give your file a name, such as CLIENTS. Then type the command

　/**O**utput,File,**CLIENTS**,

If you have not specified a file extension (for example, CLIENTS.JTP), SuperCalc attaches the print file extension PRN. If another file has that name already, you can select the file by pressing F3 to access the file directory. SuperCalc asks you whether you want to perform the following activities on the file you selected:

```
Backup   Change   Overwrite
```

Selecting **C**hange indicates that you want to change your file selection, so you are returned to the command line to edit the file name. **O**verwrite replaces the file on disk with the new report you are going to send. The **B**ackup selection copies the file already on disk to another file with the same eight-character name but with a BAK file extension. With this method, you will have the two latest versions of the file on disk. Remember that if you want to store your printer control codes in the print file, you must set the **R**eport,**S**pooled option to **Y**es; otherwise, set the **S**pooled option to **N**o.

Zapping the Output

The final option on the main /**O**utput menu is **Z**ap. You can use **Z**ap to reset all the Output Options settings to the program defaults, much as you use the /**Z**ap command from the main menu. When you select **Z**ap, the Output Options menu appears with the main menu choices. Unlike the regular version of this menu, however, these menu choices have no submenus. You reset all the options of any selection. For example, you have to reset all the **L**ayout options or all the **P**aper options.

Laser Power

Many of the new features in SuperCalc5 provide compatibility with laser printers and take advantage of many of their enhanced printing capabilities, including multiple fonts, area shadings, line graphics, and output orientation. This section describes the various commands blended into the SuperCalc menus for use specifically with laser printers.

Defining Your Printer

As mentioned in the beginning of this chapter, you first must define your printer. The printer definition settings are in the Global Spreadsheet menu. If you select **D**evice, the screen shown in figure 9.1 appears. Many laser printers or classes of printers are shown on the screen. Although your specific one might be listed on this screen, check to see which laser printer standards your printer is compatible with before making your selection.

Two major standards have developed in the industry: the LaserJet standard (under HEWLETT-PACKARD in fig. 9.1) and the PostScript standard. Your printer probably can emulate the LaserJet or is PostScript-compatible. The enhanced output capabilities of SuperCalc are focused on these two standards, so to take full advantage of these enhanced capabilities your printer must be LaserJet- or PostScript-compatible. Of the LaserJets, SuperCalc supports three variations: the LaserJet, the LaserJet Plus, and the LaserJet II. For purposes of this demonstration, select the LaserJet.

Two choices on the Global Spreadsheet menu relate to laser printers: **C**artridges and **F**onts. You must select **C**artridges if you are using a LaserJet or compatible printer in order to define the "pool" of fonts you have plugged into your printer. When you select /**G**lobal,**S**preadsheet,**C**artridges, the screen shown in figure 9.13 appears. You can define up to three cartridges from a list of 25 supported cartridges and three soft fonts from a list of 15.

Fig. 9.13.

Specifying a laser printer cartridge.

```
CARTRIDGE/SOFTFONT DEFINITION MENU

                 Currently Selected Cartridge/Softfont
    Cartridge 1      Internal
    Cartridge 2      Internal
    Cartridge 3      Internal

    Softfont 1       Internal
    Softfont 2       Internal
    Softfont 3       Internal
```

Each cartridge contains the definitions necessary to print the text of your output, using that typeface. Internal, the default, means that you will have only the internally defined fonts as a source for your font selection. For the LaserJet, only a Courier font would be available, and for the LaserJet Plus and LaserJet II, only Courier and Line PR fonts would be available. The selections you make can be saved with the /**G**lobal,**K**eep command.

After you have defined the cartridges and soft fonts, select **F**onts from the Global Spreadsheet menu to define the eight selected fonts. After you select **F**onts, the Font Definition menu appears with all eight fonts defined as the Courier default (see fig. 9.14).

Fig. 9.14.

The Font Definition menu.

```
FONT DEFINITION MENU

    Font                                  Point-
    Number   Currently Defined Typeface   Size    Attributes

    Def.     Courier                       12
      1.     Courier                       12
      2.     Courier                       12
      3.     Courier                       12
      4.     Courier                       12
      5.     Courier                       12
      6.     Courier                       12
      7.     Courier                       12
```

The font definition process is much like the User-defined format process. You can define a default font, which will be used globally for Final output without any further action on your part. You also can define seven additional fonts from which you can select to override the default for print ranges, headers, and footers. To define the default font, choose Default. The following menu of choices appears:

    Quit Face Point-size Bold Italic

These are the four characteristics that you can define for each font. Face is the typeface design, Point-size is a number representing the relative height and width of the character, and Bold and Italic are two soft toggles for boldfacing and italicizing the type.

When you select Face, all the available fonts specified through the Cartridges option will appear for you to select with the arrow keys. (This list can be more than six for a LaserJet type printer, even though you can specify only three cartridges and three soft fonts, because some of the selections represent groups of fonts). If you are using a PostScript-compatible printer, you do not have to specify Cartridges or Softfonts, as you do for a LaserJet-compatible printer, so all 24 SuperCalc-supported PostScript fonts will appear for your selection.

Once you make your selection, you return to the Font Definition menu, shown in figure 9.14—with the screen updated to reflect your choice.

For a LaserJet-type printer, the point size will automatically adjust initially for the font type. You can manually adjust the point size then by selecting Point-size and entering a value between 1 and 99. Point size is a factor representing the relative height and width for each character on the page, and depends on the font (typeface) you choose. Thus, a point size of 12 for Courier will be different from a point size of 12 for Helvetica. Using extreme values here might cause some odd-looking output, so be judicious in your selection.

Finally, turning on the Bold or Italic switches by typing Bold,Yes or Italic,Yes from the menu automatically updates the Font Definition menu to reflect the new feature. Once you complete your selection, you can save these fonts by using /Global,Keep.

Applying Enhanced Features to Your Spreadsheet

Once you make your global font selections, you must go to the Output menus to assign the selections to ranges and to take advantage of the other enhanced output capabilities in SuperCalc. The first menu under /Output contains most of the enhanced output features. As you recall, the menu looks like this:

    Printer File Attributes Grid Lines New-page

If you select Attributes, a menu of laser-specific options for enhancing your output appears. The menu has the following selections:

    Quit Fonts Border Shade

When you choose **F**onts, you can override the default font you specified in /**G**lobal,**S**preadsheet,**F**onts. You can assign one of the other seven fonts to a single cell, range of cells, or the entire spreadsheet. When you select from the menu of eight font choices, the name of the font assigned to that value appears in the help line for your convenience.

You can outline one or all sides of a range of cells with lines by using **B**order. You can select from the menu that appears containing these choices:

```
Quit  Top  Bottom  Left  Right  Outline  Clear
```

Outline will place a border around the entire range, or you can select from **T**op, **B**ottom, **L**eft, or **R**ight to create a range border on selected sides of the range. To eliminate all the borders, select **C**lear from this menu. To eliminate only a specific border, select **C**lear from the menu below each choice.

With **S**hade you can highlight a range of cells to print within a shaded background to offset them from the rest of the output. You can either define the range with **S**et or eliminate it with **C**lear.

One of the problems with this system is that you have no obvious way of knowing whether a cell or range has had enhanced attributes assigned to it. The cells appear on-screen the same as before. The only way to identify enhanced cells is to use **H**ighlight under //**T**est to highlight the cells containing one or more of the output attributes. (See Chapter 13 for details on this command.)

In the main Output menu is the **G**rid selection. With **G**rid you can frame all cells in your output with a grid. This is an "all or nothing" approach, so it isn't effective in all situations.

The **L**ines option allows you to enter line-definition control text into cells and cell ranges. Make sure that you do not try to place the control text in a cell containing data; the line control string will replace the data in the cell. Use this feature only to define blank cells with lines. This feature is useful because you can define either horizontal or vertical and either single or double lines varying in relative thickness from 1 to 5. You can specify more than one line in a single row or column, also. Figure 9.15 shows all possible default lines and the underlying printer control string to define each of them in the column to the right.

The string specifies the direction, row-height (horizontal line), or column width (vertical line) in decimal points, line-shading percent, base-line offset as a percentage of row-height/column width, and line-thickness as a percentage of the row-height/column width. The structure and syntax of **L**ines provide you with much flexibility, so if you have a special requirement for a line, try experimenting with this enhanced output feature.

Although the lines all appear on-screen as single lines of the same thickness, they will appear significantly different on paper, as you can see in figure 9.16, which uses **S**hading, **B**orders, and various fonts.

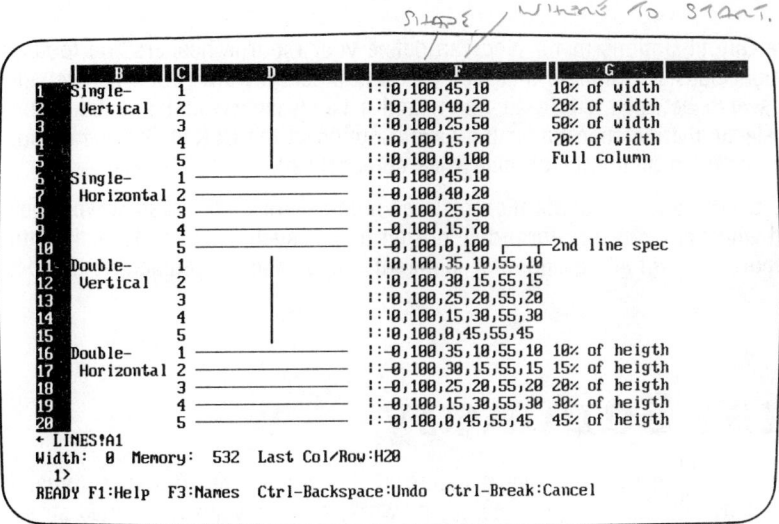

Fig. 9.15.
/Output,Lines
definitions.

Fig. 9.16.
/Output,Lines
definitions printed in
Final format.

Understanding the Enhanced /Output Options

Probably the most important point to remember about enhanced output is that it will not print unless you go to the Output Options menu and switch the **R**eport **F**ormatted option from the default **D**raft to **F**inal. **F**inal prints attributes, grids, and lines in addition to the regular headers, footers, margins, and setup strings printed using **D**raft. This way you can use **D**raft to fix the numbers and placement, and then apply the enhanced features in the final pass.

Also, while in the Output Options menu, you can define your report's headers and footers with one of the eight possible fonts so that they can look different from your data section. Finally, you can switch between a **P**ortrait (long) and a **L**andscape (wide) orientation for your output by selecting **O**rientation under the **L**ayout option in the Output Options menu. **L**andscape mode comes in handy for printing wide spreadsheets.

The affordability, power, and standardization of laser printers are three reasons why they make sense. And when you can transform dull-looking output such as the CLIENT list into an enhanced report with gray scaling and different fonts, the temptation is almost irresistible.

Chapter Summary

The /**O**utput command is an ever-improving feature in SuperCalc. The /**O**utput command gives you the flexibility necessary to produce quality work, and the visually oriented structure of the Output Options menu helps you finish the job quickly. With the introduction of laser printer support, SuperCalc helps you finish the job professionally, also.

In this chapter, you learned how to use the /**O**utput command to print spreadsheet information in a useful format for basic spreadsheets, for more complete spreadsheets, and on a laser printer. In Chapter 10 you learn how to use the powerful graphics capabilities of SuperCalc to present the information in a more easily analyzed format. You also learn how to display graphs on-screen and how to plot them on a printer or plotter.

Graphing and Plotting

An amazing transformation has taken place. Computer Associates made SuperCalc4's powerful and easy-to-use graphics subsystem look like "a little prop job" in the age of jet propulsion when compared to the new SuperCalc5 edition. This graphics package within a package is so powerful, so easy, and so much fun to use that it may become the main reason many people buy the package.

The gurus at Computer Associates are making it tough on themselves, though. With the track record they are developing, people are going to expect this kind of improvement every time around. In this transformation they have added three more graph types (dual, radar, and word), an average of seven variations within each graph type, over 50 new colors, another axis (y2), and titles and labels galore. This time it's 3-D; what's next—holograms?

This chapter acquaints you with this package within a package. For those of you unfamiliar with spreadsheet graphing, this chapter explains the main components and tools of the trade. Then, taking a simple project management spreadsheet, you go through the menu choices and screens used in building a graph. You learn some of the type-specific options that can be employed to make your graph tell the right story in your own unique way. You discover the various considerations in plotting a graph and learn about the added tools provided for managing your charts.

Graph Components: The Anatomy of a Graph

In this chapter, part of the program management spreadsheet introduced in Chapter 6 is used to illustrate SuperCalc's powerful graphing commands. The portions of the program management spreadsheet used are the four rows labeled *Labor*, *Overhead*, *G & A*, and *Profit* for the projects labeled *CAIS*, *CVC*, *NET*, and *SDI*. The graphics produced from this subset of the spreadsheet paint clear financial pictures. The graphs show projects producing the largest profits, the relationship between labor costs and profit, and the relative percentages of the four components in the billable cost (labor, overhead, general and administrative, and profit). The program management data from Chapter 6 is shown in figure 10.1.

Fig. 10.1.

A project revenue spreadsheet example.

	A	B	C	D	E	F	G	H
1			Summary of Project Revenues					
2								
3								
4		SDI	NET	CAIS	CVC	Total		
5								
6	Labor	5978	5238	7240	4785	23241		
7	Overhead	4483	3928	5430	3589	17430		
8	G & A	1255	1100	1520	1005	4880		
9	Profit	1406	1232	1703	1125	5466		
10								
11	Total	13122	11498	15893	10504	51017		
12								

To graph the data in figure 10.1, you use two main command trees. //Graphics takes you to the main Graphics menu. Using this command, you specify the graph type, data ranges, title and labels, the graph name, and plot the graph. (SuperCalc uses the terms *chart* and *graph* interchangeably.) With the second command tree, /Global,Graphics, you specify plotting characteristics. (A third command tree, /View, is the SuperCalc4 graphing command tree, which has been taken off the SuperCalc5 command menu but is "hidden" for downward compatibility. /View's options are completely replaced by //Graphics; even the most nostalgic user will likely abandon /View for the new and improved version).

Before analyzing the command trees in detail, examine a graph of the data in figure 10.1 to demonstrate the various components to be discussed. Figure 10.2 is a three-dimensional bar graph with each of the profit components shown by project plotted against the left axis (y1) along with total revenue in the back plotted against the right axis (y2).

Fig. 10.2.

A bar graph showing graph components.

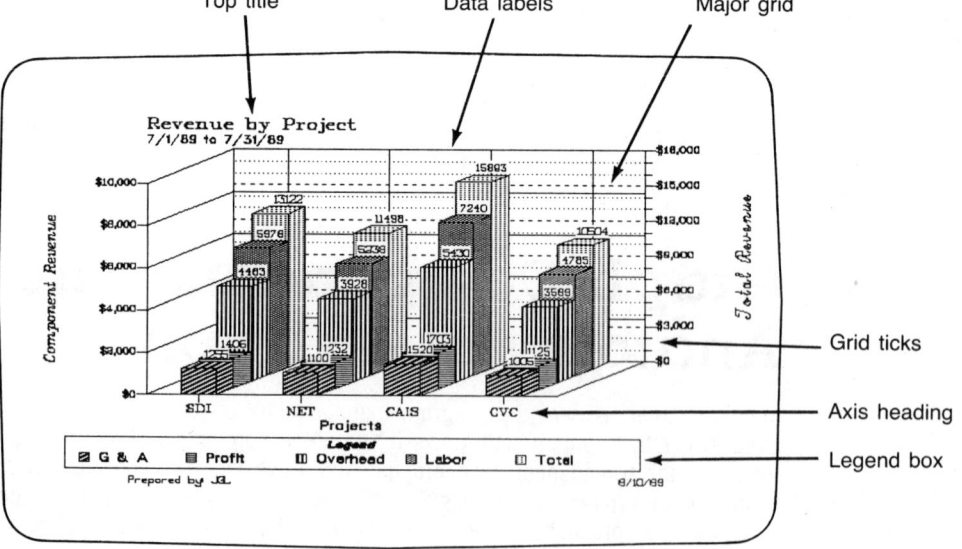

Granted, this example may squeeze in a little more than is normal for one graph, but it demonstrates many graphics features of SuperCalc5:

- Fill type lines (instead of color), which distinguish one series from another
- Grid lines for easier horizontal (relative to both the y1- and y2-axes) and vertical references
- Titles, including the top title, subtitle, and axis-titles
- Axis labels, legend labels, and data labels
- The legend box, axis box, and axis box, each of which can be set in any of 71 different colors
- Three-dimensional graphs
- Different scalings for the y1-axis (0 to 10,000) and the y2-axis (10,000 to 18,000)

Each of these features is described in greater detail in the following sections.

Fill Type

Fill type distinguishes one series of data from another. With color monitors you can define brilliant and contrasting colors to set apart the different series of data. Up to 71 different colors can be selected depending on your monitor. For monochrome output on your dot-matrix or laser printer, however, color may not be possible. SuperCalc therefore provides three variations (narrow, medium, and wide) of five different fill patterns (horizontal, vertical, hatch, cross, and slant). In figure 10.2, *G & A* is slant, *Profit* is horizontal, *Overhead* is vertical, *Labor* is hatch, and *Total* is the cross pattern.

Grid Lines

Grid lines are used to align the vertical and horizontal axis points with values in the graph. In figure 10.2, four vertical grid lines represent each of the projects; five solid horizontal lines represent $2,000 increments of the y1-axis (left side); and three dashed horizontal lines represent $2,000 increments for the y2-axis (*Total Revenue* on the right side). You can have the following types of grid lines:

Solid
Dash
Dot
Dash dot
Medium dash
Dash dot dot
Short dash

At the label end of the grids are tick marks that extend out from the axis box. You can select whether to place these tick marks inside or outside of the axis box. In figure 10.2

the grid marks are outside the box. Minor grid lines also can be defined, which further divide the chart within each axis label. Minor grid lines are defined for the y2-axis in figure 10.2.

Titles

In SuperCalc4, text around the graph was called *headings* and consisted optionally of a main heading, a subheading, an x-axis heading, and a y-axis heading. In SuperCalc5, headings are renamed *titles*.

Five title types are possible in SuperCalc5, of which four are demonstrated in figure 10.2. *Projects*, *Component Revenue*, and *Total Revenue* are the x-, y1-, and y2-axes titles, respectively. *Revenue by Project*, in a larger font size at the top, is called a *top title*. You can define up to three lines of top titles. Below the top title is a subtitle defining the relevant date range of the project revenues. You can define up to two subtitles. At the bottom is a footnote, which is a new feature of SuperCalc5 and can contain up to three lines of text. You also can have a legend title within the legend box. Figure 10.2 shows the legend box between the graph and the footnote. You can make the Legend Title and text string up to 80 characters.

For greater flexibility, in SuperCalc5 you can store title text either in cells in the spreadsheet or directly in title locations within the graph definition. In previous editions you had to store titles or headings in cells.

Labels

Where an axis *title* defines the overall content of the axis (for example, *Projects*), axis *labels* define the individual data points along the axis. The same relationship is true with the legend title and legend labels—the legend title defines the overall legend content but the legend labels define what each fill type, fill color, line, or marker represents in the graph.

Data labels are another set of labels with no title counterpart and are shown just above each bar in figure 10.2. Using the **D**ata-labels menu choice (covered later in this chapter), you can cause the values on which the graph is based to appear in the body of the graph. For the SDI project, for example, the G & A expense was $1,255. This value is shown right above the bar representing the G & A expense for the SDI project. In SuperCalc4, data labels were referred to as *point labels*.

Series

Figure 10.2 consists of five series of data. A *series* is a row or column of spreadsheet values, related graphically. Cells B8 through E8 in figure 10.1 make up the four values in the series represented by the slant-filled bars in figure 10.2. Each cell is one value in the series. As you see later in this chapter, that series of values can appear as bars along an axis, marks on a line, wedges in a pie graph, or bends in a line, once they are identified as a data series.

Scaling

Once you define a series, SuperCalc applies an automatic scaling to the values so that the graph plots within relevant boundaries. Because all the *Component Revenue* values fall below $10,000 in figure 10.2, SuperCalc automatically sizes or scales the graph between 0 and 10,000. Because *Total Revenue* is shown along the y2-axis and all those values fall between $10,000 and $18,000, the y2-axis would have been scaled accordingly. In Super-Calc you can override the automatic scaling and define any minimum and maximum value. (In figure 10.2 the y2-axis scaling was set to 0–18,000 rather than the automatic scaling of 10,000–18,000.) You also can alter the number of major and minor divisions into which the scale is broken.

Design Features

Graphing is where you really can bring your artistic side to the fore. Although you can leave your footprint on a spreadsheet design, in graphing the creative half of your brain takes over in considering the many options available to create your masterpiece. You can manipulate 71 colors and 15 alternate fill types. For most graphs, you can choose between 2-D and 3-D displays. You also can switch from the standard orientation to a horizontal display (where the x-axis is vertical).

You don't need to make decisions about all the features at once in order to get a graph out. The only thing you must do is select a series of cells to use for the data elements and view or plot the graph. For most other features, SuperCalc has system defaults in critical settings or automatic settings derived from choices made in other sections of SuperCalc. You have only to address these features if you want to override the system values or add some optional features.

Of course, the best way to understand graphics is to create a graph. The next sections explain how to do this.

Using the Graphics Menu To Define Your Graph

Using the spreadsheet data in figure 10.1, you begin to build graphs. (Make sure that you have the data on-hand to enter.) The first step is to enter the Graphics menu by typing //**G**raphics. This command brings up the following choices on the Graphics menu:

```
View  Type  Data  Labels  Axis  Options  Global  Name  Plot  Zap  Quit
```

If the message Graphics not enabled appears, your graphics capabilities have been disabled (most likely for more efficient memory use). To re-enable graphics, take the following steps:

1. Type /**G**lobal,**O**ptimum,**N**ext,**G**raphics,**Y**es, and press Enter.

2. Type /**G**lobal,**K**eep, and press Enter twice.

3. Type /**Q**uit,**T**o,**SC5**.

4. Type //**G**raphics.

On the Graphics menu you use the first choice, **V**iew, to show your graph on screen after you have defined it. Alternatively, you can press F10 from the Graphics menu or from Ready mode to view your graph. You choose which of the nine basic graphs you want to create using the **T**ype option. You build your graph using **L**abels, **A**xis, and **O**ptions. You can set a few overall graphics settings (mostly relating to plotting) through **G**lobal; you can name, save, and retrieve an unlimited number of graphs through **N**ame; you can plot the graph to your graphics plotting device using **P**lot. If you want to start all over, select **Z**ap to empty or reset to a default value the fields in all of the graphing screens.

Using the Keyboard

Learning the function of several keys and key combinations for use with the Graphics menu and screens can make your life a little easier. Table 10.1 contains a list of relevant keys and key combinations.

Table 10.1
Graphics Key Functions

Key	Definition
F1	Graphics Help
F2	Edit field contents
F3	Chart List menu
F4	Point to a cell range
F5	Switch data range orientation between column and row
F6	Copy entries to the right
F10	View the current graph
Alt-F10	Plot the current graph
Esc	Exit a graphing input screen
PgDn/PgUp	Move between pages of two-page input screens
Ctrl-Right	Move right between wide-format input screens
Ctrl-Left	Move left between wide-format input screens
Enter	Select from a list
Del	Erase a field input

Field Types

Unlike SuperCalc4, where most of the values were stored in the spreadsheet itself, Super-Calc5 provides input screens (called *menus*) for you to define the graph and uses the spreadsheet itself only as a reference. As you see in this chapter, some input fields must be strictly a cell or range reference (that is, a data range); other fields can be either a cell reference that points to text in the spreadsheet or direct text input (see the Titles Entry menu). Another class of fields, called Selection fields, can be entered directly but must contain valid entries. Instead of typing a response, you can select the correct response from a menu of choices by pressing Enter. Alternatively, you can cycle through the choices by pressing the space bar.

Each type of field is demonstrated in this chapter as you step through the menus for building a graph.

Selecting the Appropriate Graph Type for the Data

To choose a graph type, select //**G**raphics,**T**ype. The following menu of available graph types appears:

```
Bar  Pie  Dual  Line  Area  Hi-Lo  X-Y  Radar  Word
```

These choices are fairly descriptive and some should sound familiar to you. Figure 10.2 is an example of a bar graph (the default graph type). You can change the default graph type by entering /**G**lobal,**K**eep,**Y**es after selecting a different graph type. Two other well-known types are the pie graph and line graph. A dual graph, which is new to SuperCalc5, actually consists of two graphs. The two graphs can be either related or unrelated pie or bar graphs. The bar graph, however, must be a single-column, stacked-bar type, functioning as a square pie graph. Figure 10.3 demonstrates a dual graph of the data in figure 10.1.

On the left side of the figure is a pie graph of the total revenue from each project with the biggest segment, CAIS, exploded (cut out from the pie for emphasis). The lines between the graphs emphasize that on the right side is a breakdown of the individual revenue components of the CAIS project. Dual-graphing is a powerful graphing tool for relating two levels of detail about a data element: how it fits within a larger set of data and how the data elements that comprise it break down. Although figure 10.3 shows two related graphs, you can have two unrelated graphs as well. Dual graphs can be shown in the following combinations: pie-bar, pie-pie, bar-pie, or bar-bar.

Figures 10.4, 10.5, 10.6, and 10.7 show, respectively, an area graph, a Hi-Lo graph, an X-Y graph, and (new with SuperCalc5) a radar graph.

The area graph demonstrates a volume relationship between two series. The Hi-Lo graph demonstrates the extreme high and low values for each point in two or more series of values. The X-Y graph takes two series of data and plots them against each other. The radar graph plots one series as angle values defined in radians against one or more series defined in terms of a radius.

Fig. 10.3.

Project revenues displayed using a dual graph.

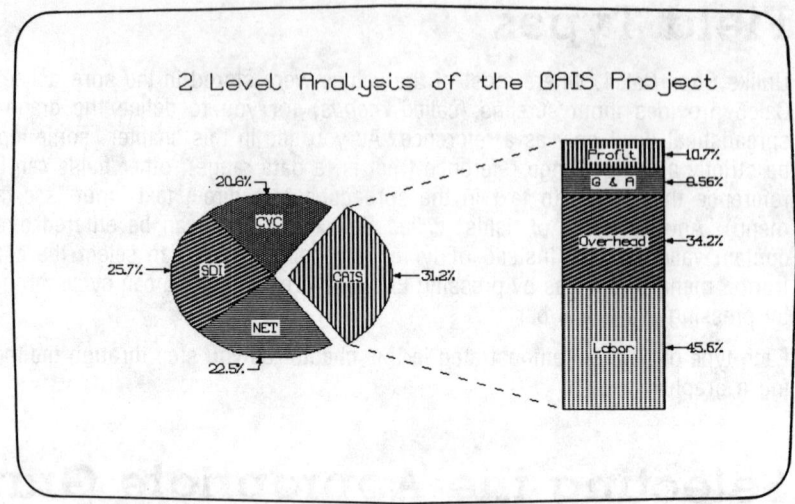

Fig. 10.4.

An area graph.

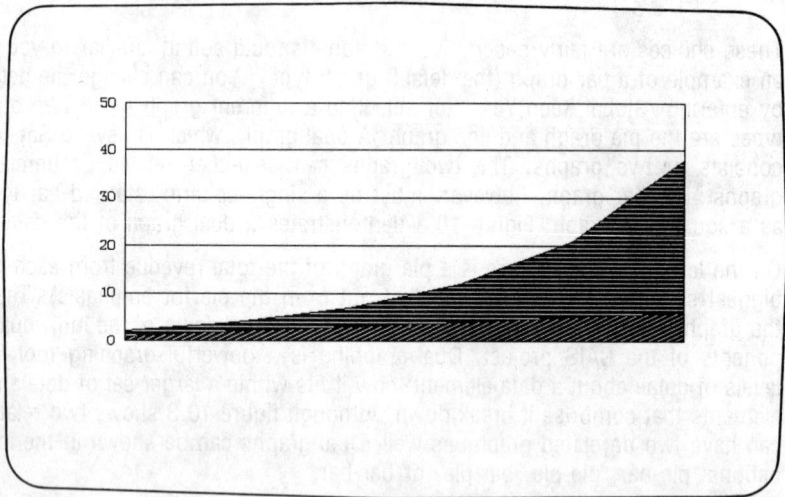

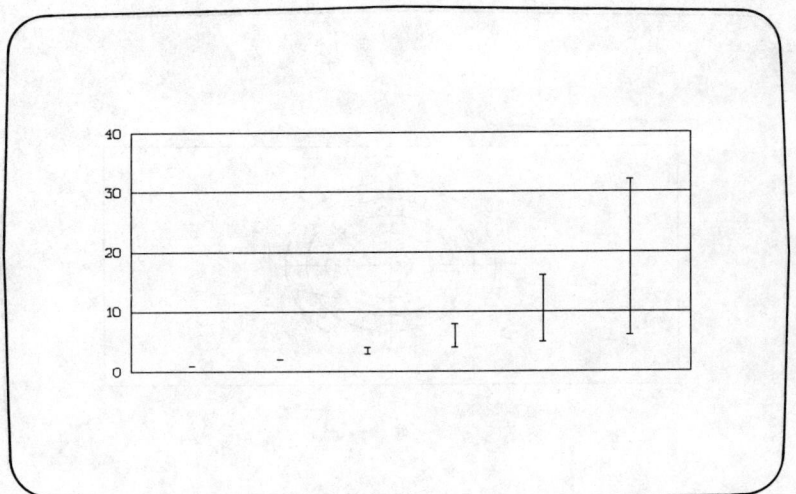

Fig. 10.5.
A Hi-Lo graph.

As you move to the right across the subtotals at the bottom of the screen, the differences become more noticeable. There are two highlighted areas, one showing which month has the greatest sum of all the categories, and one showing the month with the least amount. Press Escape to return your cursor to the View X-Y graph selection of this menu.

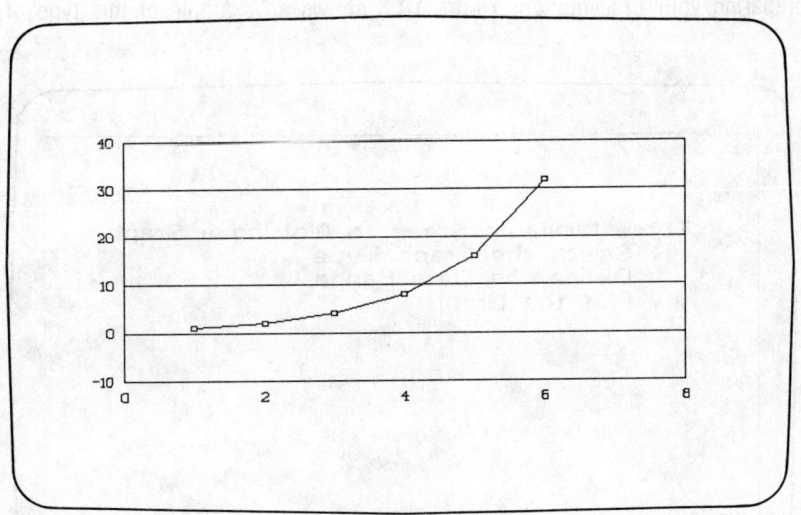

Fig. 10.6.
An X-Y graph.

Fig. 10.7.

A radar graph.

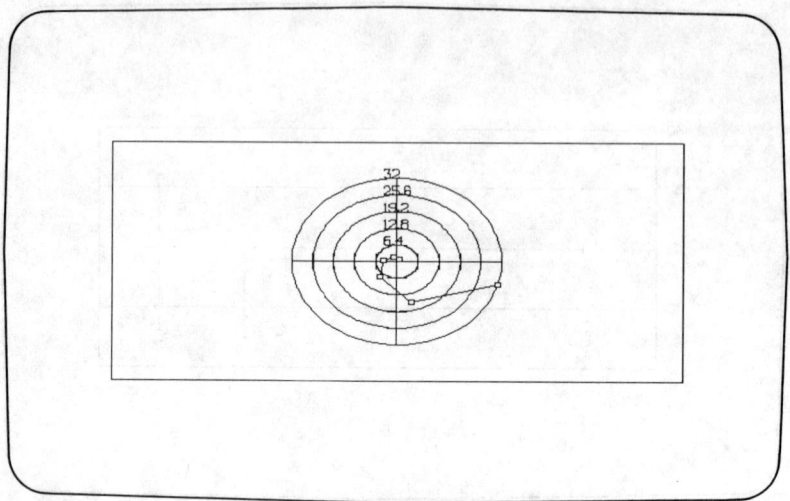

As you move from left to right along the options on the Graphics Type menu, the general trend is toward more scientific graphs until you reach the last graph option, **W**ord, which you could call the word processor of the graph environment. If you ever have had to make an overhead slide for a presentation, you will love the word chart, which takes the ''grunt'' work out of preparing your presentation. Figure 10.8 shows an example of this type of graph.

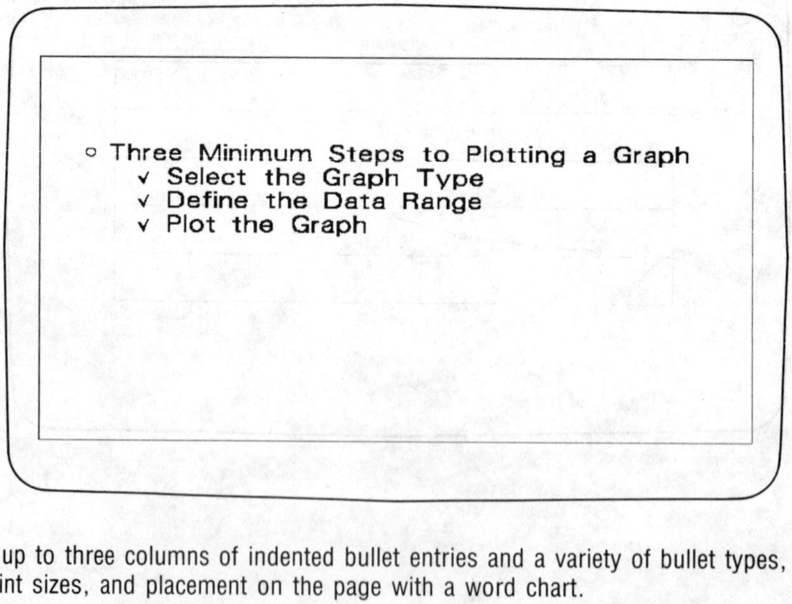

Fig. 10.8.

A word chart.

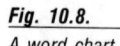

○ Three Minimum Steps to Plotting a Graph
   √ Select the Graph Type
   √ Define the Data Range
   √ Plot the Graph

You can have up to three columns of indented bullet entries and a variety of bullet types, font types, point sizes, and placement on the page with a word chart.

Note: To help even further in preparing for your next presentation, as of the time of this printing, Computer Associates provides an overnight service for transforming your graphs into a variety of media, including slides. Although you pay a premium price for this premium service, setting yourself up with this service costs nothing initially and could save you in a pinch.

Although only nine graph types are available on the Graphics Type menu, many more types are available through the Graphics Options menu options within each type. Table 10.2 lists the optional variations available within each type.

Table 10.2
Variations for Graph Types

Bar	Pie	Dual	Line	Area	Hi-Lo	X-Y	Radar	Word
Simple	Regular	Pie-Bar	Simple	Simple	(Just 1)	XYXY	XYXY	1 column
Stacked	Exploded	Pie-Pie	Stacked	Stacked		XYY	XYY	2 column
Grouped	(All,	Bar-Pie						3 column
100%	List,	Bar-Bar						
Delta	Below,							
	Above,							
	Within,							
	Outside,							
	Smallest,							
	Largest)							

In addition to the basic variations, you can select 3-D and horizontal *orientation* for many of these graphs. After making your graph selection you can select grids, fill types, legend locations, scaling, fonts—and the list goes on. Computer Associates has provided an overflowing tool box.

Defining the Data

If the default graph type is acceptable, the only required choice on the Graphics menu is **D**ata. After selecting **D**ata, the Chart Data Appearance and Options menu shown in figure 10.9 appears for all graphs except for word. Because of its nature, the word graph uses a different menu.

```
┌─────────────────────────────────────────────────────────────────┐
│        CHART DATA APPEARANCE AND OPTIONS MENU      TYPE: BAR    → │
│                                                                   │
│                      1          2          3          4        5  │
│   SERIES RANGE   ████████                                         │
│                                                                   │
│   SERIES OPTIONS                                                  │
│   Color          9LtBlue    10LtGreen  11LtCyan   12LtRed    13LtMagent │
│   Hide           No         No         No         No         No   │
│   Fill Pattern   MediumSlan MediumHori MediumVert MediumHatc MediumCros │
│   Outline Color  Black      Black      Black      Black      Black │
│   Outline Style  Solid      Solid      Solid      Solid      Solid │
│   Outline Width  Auto       Auto       Auto       Auto       Auto │
│   Y-axis         Left       Left       Left       Left       Left │
│   Pie Explosion  No         No         No         No         No   │
└─────────────────────────────────────────────────────────────────┘
```

Fig. 10.9.
The Chart Data Appearance and Options menu.

Although only five columns appear on the screen, five more are available by pressing Ctrl-right arrow once or the right arrow five times. Each data range, called a Series Range, is defined in the first row. The optional characteristics for each series can be altered under Series Options. For each series, you can choose from 71 colors (or none). You can choose whether or not to Hide the range specified and select from 16 fill patterns, including solid, for all object-oriented graph types (bar, pie, dual, or area types). You can also specify 71 outline colors for those objects (pie-slices, bars, areas) and 6 combinations of dashes and dots, solid, or none for the outline style. You can hook each series to either the left y-axis (y1) or right y-axis (y2). You can define specific series to be exploded on a pie graph by setting the Pie Explosion field to Yes for the series (you also must set the Explosion Type field to List on the Pie Chart Options menu, which is described later in this chapter).

Depending on the graph type, you have two choices for defining the series to be graphed. Although 10 numbered series fields (10 columns) exist in the two pages of this menu, you can define many more through just one series. If you have fewer than 10 series of data (spreadsheet columns or rows) to graph, you might consider defining each column or row independently in separate series fields; it takes less time, however, to define the entire range once in one series using a multiple-column or multiple-row range.

To demonstrate, suppose that you want to define an entire graph's data range for the spreadsheet in figure 10.1 through series 1. Move the cursor to the upper left field (Series Range 1) and press F4 to point into the spreadsheet. Move the cell pointer to B6, press the period key to anchor the range, move the cell pointer to E9, and press Enter. The Chart Data Appearance and Options menu reappears. The range entered into the field looks like this:

    B6:E9(R)

The *(R)* indicates that the range is a row-wise multiseries range, meaning that each row is a series and each cell in the row is a point within the series. Because the range you defined is a square four-row-by-four-column range, SuperCalc automatically interprets it as a row-wise range. If there are fewer columns than rows in the range, SuperCalc interprets it as a column-wise (C) range, meaning that each column is a series and each cell in the column is a point in the series. If you actually want the opposite effect, you can toggle between (R) and (C) by pressing F5. Using this method, you can define as many series as you have rows or columns in your spreadsheet instead of the 10 individual series available in the menu.

You use the same method to define 10 individual series. After pointing the first row or column of values and returning to the Chart Data Appearance and Options menu, however, you move the menu pointer right to the next series and point to the next row or column. You continue this process until you have all your rows or columns defined in each series field, respectively.

How you use the series depends on the type of graph you want. A pie graph, for example, uses only the first series. For dual graphs, you only need two of the series: one for each graph. A Hi-Lo graph expects the highest value in the series to be in Series 1 and the lowest value to be in Series 2 (you can use the MAX and MIN functions to extract these values); all other series values plot along the line between the maximum and minimum. If you have a 3-D graph, as shown in figure 10.2, you may want to order the series differently from the way the values are stored in the spreadsheet (lowest average row of values to the highest average row of values) in order to improve the appearance or readability of your graph. To do so, you must specify the series individually, from left to right, entering the lowest average-valued row in Series 1 and the highest average-valued row in Series 5. Likewise, you must order a series for a 2-D graph from left to right within a data point on a 2-D, multiseries bar graph; from the bottom up for a stacked graph; and counter-clockwise for a pie graph.

After completing your data selection, press Esc to exit the Chart Data Appearance and Options menu and return to the main Graphics menu.

Specifying Labels

The next option of concern on the Graphics menu is **L**abels. Selecting **L**abels brings up the following menu options:

> Quit Axis-labels Legend-labels Data-labels Titles

The **L**abels option allows you to specify the text and values that define the graph you have created. Each of the types of labels listed in the Graphics Labels menu is described in the following sections.

Selecting Axis Labels

The **A**xis-labels option allows you to define what each data point along the axis represents. In figure 10.2, the x-axis labels are the project names. Other typical x-axis labels are dates and time values. Because time values are so typical, SuperCalc4 called the x-axis label definition choice **T**ime-labels. To label your axes, select **A**xis-labels, and the menu in figure 10.10 appears.

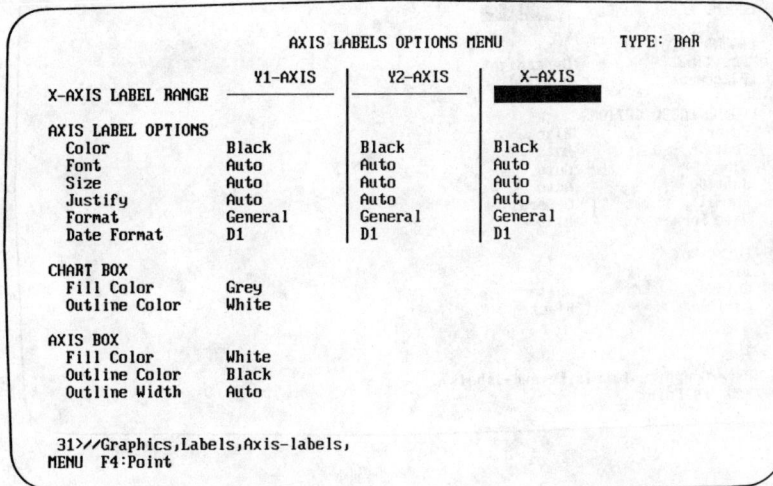

Fig. 10.10.

The Axis Labels Options menu.

Notice in this menu that you can define only the x-axis range. The other two axes are always scaled values measuring the components of the graph and so don't need definition. For the y1- and y2-axes, all you can do is alter the Axis Label Options values, such as the color of the numbers, the font, size, justification, and formats for both numbers and dates (including user-defined formats). At the bottom of the menu are Chart Box and Axis Box fields. Changing the Chart Box Fill Color and Outline Color fields affects the background color of the graph and the outline color of the box.

Note: The chart box outline is the line at the edge of your display that surrounds the chart box. The axis box serves as a background for the bars in bar graphs and the lines in line graphs. The axis box outline is the line that appears around the edge of the axis box. The x- and y-axes cover up the left and lower sections of this outline.

All fields with an Auto setting are system defaults based on other settings and considerations. The Size (font point size) setting, for example, is automatically calculated based on the relative size available on the screen or output page. The Size field can vary from 1 to 12 points and is adjusted depending on the number of titles displayed, the legend size and location, and the number of divisions on the axis. The y1-axis is normally right-justified, and the y2-axis is normally left-justified. When in doubt, leave Auto in place and let SuperCalc do the work.

The x-axis labels for the example in figure 10.1 are the project names stored in cells B4:E4. Once the range is entered or pointed to, you can press Esc to exit the screen.

Selecting Legend Labels

The second labels choice of concern on the Graphics Labels menu is **L**egend-labels. Selecting this option brings up the menu shown in figure 10.11.

Fig. 10.11.

The Legend Label Definition and Options menu.

```
                    LEGEND LABEL DEFINITION AND OPTIONS MENU      TYPE: BAR

    LEGEND LABEL RANGE    ▮▮▮▮▮▮▮▮

    LEGEND LOCATION
      Position            UpperRight
      Placement           Outside

    LEGEND LABEL OPTIONS
      Color               Black
      Font                Auto
      Size                Auto
      Justify             Auto
      Format              General
      Date Format         D1

    LEGEND BOX
      Display             Yes
      Color               White
      Outline             Black



      33>//Graphics,Labels,Legend-labels,
    MENU  F4:Point
```

Legend labels were called *variable labels* in SuperCalc4. Using the Legend Label Definition and Options menu, you can link a description of each series to the graph using a sample of the fill type, marker type, or color of the bar, pie-segment, area, or line. Next to the sample you enter the description. Both the sample and description are in what is called the *legend box*. This legend box is no different from the legend on any street map you read.

Because only one legend-label range can be defined, all the labels you select (by pointing in the spreadsheet) must be stored in adjacent cells and must appear in the same relative position within that cell range as the series that each label represents. In the example in figure 10.2, a separate area in the spreadsheet was created with the labels because the *Total* cell (A11) was separated from the rest of the label cells (A6:A9) and because the data ranges were defined in a different order from that of the spreadsheet in order to appear smallest to largest. Typically, the range adjacent to the data range (in this case, A6:A9) works. In addition to the range, you can define several characteristics of the legend box and contents. In figure 10.2 the legend box is located outside of the axis box (using the Placement field) and at the bottom of the chart (using the Position field). You can place the legend box just about anywhere—to the right, to the left, at the top, at the bottom, or in any corner of the axis box—by overriding the default value (UpperRight) shown in figure 10.11.

Like the axis labels, you can alter the color, point size, font, justification, format, or date format of the legend labels. In figure 10.2, the default values for the legend box were used. If you change the Outline color to None, the outline around the legend box does not appear. If you set the Display field to No, none of the legend box appears on the graph.

Once you have made your selections from the Legend Label Definition and Options menu, press Esc to return to the Graphics Labels menu.

Selecting Data Labels

Although you can set only one x-axis label for each x-axis tick, you can set a data label for each value graphically portrayed. The values placed just above the bars in figure 10.2 are data labels displaying the underlying values represented by the bars. To define the data labels, select **D**ata-labels from the Graphics Labels menu. The Data Labels Options menu appears. Data-label ranges are typically identical to the data ranges. The top row for defining the range has 10 label-range fields just like the Chart Data Appearance and Options menu, and you can point to the same range (B6:E9) from it in the same way.

Because the data label-range is typically the same as the data range, you can switch the third option in the section entitled Data Label Options Source from Range to Data. The data range then is used in place of a range defined in the first row of this menu. To do this, press the down arrow three times from the top of the screen to the Source field. Now use one of the following three methods to change the value in the Source field:

1. Type the word **Data**.

2. Press Enter, point to Data in the selection window that appears (called Source), and press Enter.

3. Press the space bar once.

Figure 10.12 shows the Data Labels Options menu with a selection window.

SuperCalc5

Fig. 10.12.

Selecting from a selection window in the Data Labels Options menu.

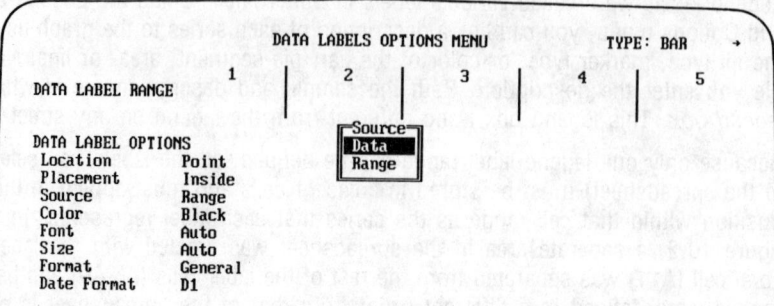

As with other labels, you can change the color, font, size, format, and date format for the data labels. In addition, you can specify the placement of the data labels for bar, pie, or dual graphs as either inside the bar or segment or outside of it. In figure 10.2, the data labels are placed outside the bar. For this example, leave the labels inside and press Esc to return to the Graphics Labels menu.

Establishing Titles

The next option on the Graphics Labels menu, **T**itles, is greatly improved from SuperCalc4. Formerly called **H**eadings, the option allowed you to define only one line each for a main heading, subheading, x-axis heading, and y-axis heading. In addition, the headings had to be stored in a spreadsheet cell. Figure 10.13 shows the Titles Entry menu, the first of two Titles menus. The titles that appear are from the graph in figure 10.2.

Fig. 10.13.

The Titles Entry menu.

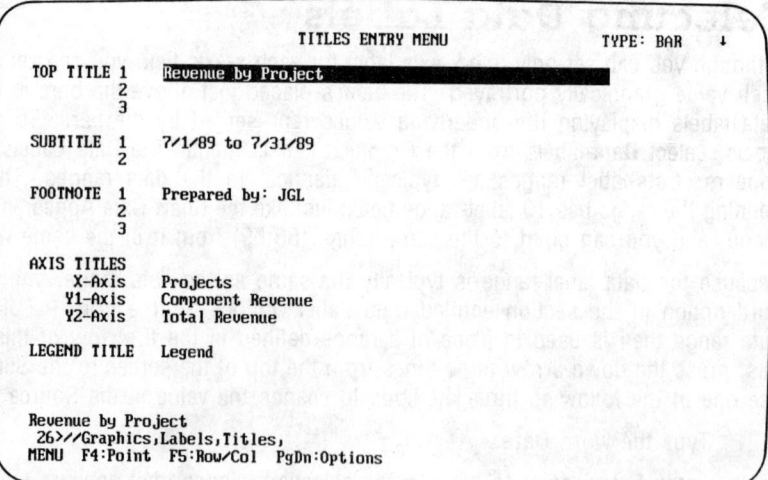

The first screen of the Titles Entry menu is used to enter title text. What is unique about this screen is that you can point to a cell reference containing the title text (as with Super-

Calc4) or you can enter text directly. The dual nature of this screen is helpful because some people like the direct entry mode and others prefer the cell reference style. Sometimes the text you need is already stored in a cell in the spreadsheet; if not, you can enter the text directly without cluttering the spreadsheet. In the top title range, a cell reference was used; in the rest of the titles, direct entry was used.

The top title appears at the top of the graph, the subtitles appear below the top title, the axis titles appear adjacent to each axis, the footnote lines appear below the graph, and the legend title appears within the legend box wherever that box is positioned. SuperCalc automatically adjusts the graph size and spacing on the screen or plot for any title you enter. Space is used only if you enter something into a title field.

Press PgDn to access the second Titles menu, the Titles Options menu (see fig. 10.14).

```
                    TITLES OPTIONS MENU              TYPE: BAR    ↑

                COLOR      FONT       SIZE    JUSTIFY   POSITION

TOP TITLE       Black      RomanBold  8       Left

SUBTITLE        Black      BlockBold  5       Left

FOOTNOTE        Black      Stick      Auto    Center

AXIS TITLES
  X-Axis        Black      HeluLight  Auto    Auto      Auto
  Y1-Axis       Black      Italic     Auto    Auto      Vertical
  Y2-Axis       Black      Script     9       Auto      Vertical

LEGEND TITLE    Black      HeluBoldIt 3               Auto



Black
  26>//Graphics,Labels,Titles,
MENU F4:Point F6:Copy  PgUp:Title Menu
```

Fig. 10.14.
The Titles Options menu.

On the Titles Options menu you can alter the default color, font, size, justification, and position (y-axis only) for each of the titles. Title justification choices are Left, Center, or Right. Although there is a field for the x-axis, the Position column relates only to y-axis titles. The two Position choices for the y-axis are Vertical and Horizontal. If you select Vertical, the y-axis titles appear along the side of the graph, as shown in figure 10.2. Selecting Horizontal makes the y-axis titles appear across the screen above each axis.

Font selection is an important component of defining titles. SuperCalc supports 16 different fonts, based on the following 7 base fonts:

- Stick
- Block
- Roman
- Italic
- Script
- Gothic
- Helvetica

The remaining fonts are boldface or italic versions of these seven fonts. Table 10.3 contains a cross-reference of the fonts used in figure 10.2.

Table 10.3
Font Selection for Figure 10.2

Component	Font
Top title	Roman bold
Subtitle	Block bold
Y1-axis title	Italic
Y2-axis title	Script
X-axis title	Helvetica light
Footnote	Stick
Legend title	Helvetica italic bold
Legend labels	Helvetica light
X-axis labels	Roman

In the example that you are creating, make the top title and subtitle Helvetica Bold and the axis titles Italic. Leave everything else set to Auto, which, by default, is Stick. Exit the menu by pressing Esc. Because you are finished with the Graphics Labels menu, exit it by selecting **Q**uit.

Tailoring an Axis

The next option on the Graphics menu after **L**abels is **A**xis. Using this menu choice, you can tailor the axis scalings. Figure 10.15 shows the first of two Axis Options menus, the Axis Scaling Options menu.

Fig. 10.15.
*The Axis Scaling
Options menu.*

```
                      AXIS SCALING OPTIONS MENU          TYPE: BAR    ↓
                      Y1-AXIS         Y2-AXIS         X-AXIS
     TYPE             Normal                          Normal
     MODE             Auto            Auto            Auto
     LOW VALUE        0               0               0
     HIGH VALUE       0               0               0
     MANUAL LABEL RANGE
     TICKS:
       NORMAL MAJOR
         Divisions    5               5               5
         Increment
       NORMAL MINOR
         Divisions    0               0               0
         Increment
       LOG MAJOR
         Divisions/Decade  1          1               1
         Decades/Division
       LOG MINOR
         Divisions/Decade  9          9               9
         Decades/Division

     Normal
     17>//Graphics,Axis,
     MENU  F4:Point  PgDn:Options
```

Not all of the options on the Axis Scaling Options menu are applicable to every axis or to every graph. The only time you should worry about scaling the x-axis, for example, is for X-Y graphs. Another example has to do with the first field on the screen, Type. With SuperCalc5, you can create a normally scaled graph—one with equal divisions. Alternatively, you can create a logarithmically scaled graph—where each major division represents a power of 10. Because both y1 and y2 must have the same scaling, you cannot select an option for the Type field in the Y2-Axis column. Figures 10.16 and 10.17 demonstrate the difference between these two scaling methods.

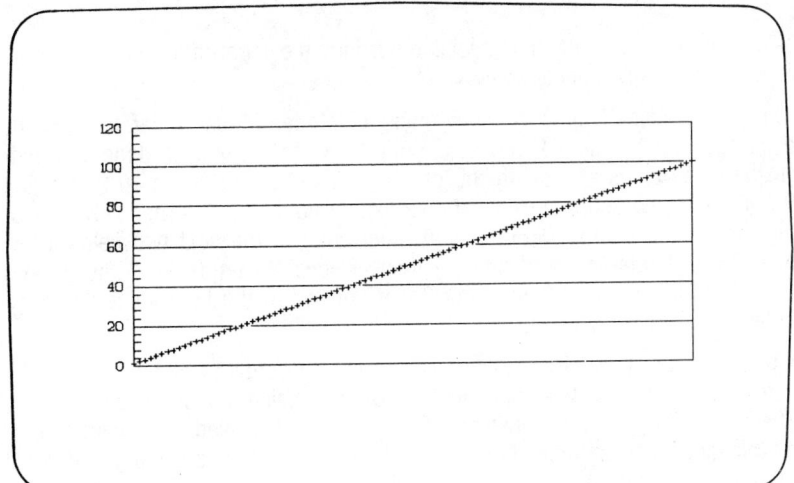

Fig. 10.16.

Normal graph scaling.

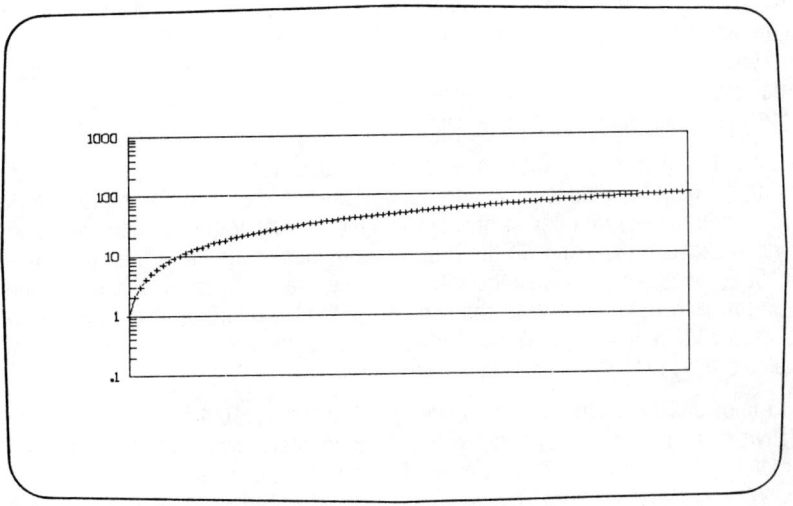

Fig. 10.17.

Logarithmic graph scaling.

The plot is of 100 cells containing integers increasing from 1 to 100. The graph in figure 10.16 breaks the plot into 6 even divisions of 20 integers (labeled) with 5 minor divisions within each major division, increasing by 4 integers each (unlabeled). The major divisions are marked by solid grid lines extending the width of the axis box, and the minor divisions are marked by tick marks projecting into the axis box. The plot is a straight line.

The graph in figure 10.17 has the same data range (1 to 100) but uses a logarithmic scale. Instead of going from 0 to 120, the scale increases exponentially from 0.1 to 1,000, with each major division representing an increase by one power of 10 (one decade) over the last division.

The normal scale is more prevalent in financial reporting; the logarithmic scale is more practical in scientific and mathematical analysis.

The second field on the Axis Scaling Options menu is Mode. Mode is set to Auto by default but can be changed to Manual or Zero. With Auto, the scaling is done automatically so that all the data values appear on the graph. The y1-axis in figure 10.2, ranging from $0 to $10,000, is scaled automatically. The y2-axis in figure 10.2 is manually scaled. When you change the Mode field to Manual, you must enter in the next two fields a low and high value or the cell references containing these values. In figure 10.2 the y2-axis ranges from $0 to $18,000 because *0* and *18000* were placed in the Low Value and High Value fields, respectively, in the y2 column.

Using the next field, Manual Label Range, you can force the contents of the cells in the specified range to appear at each tick mark instead of the scaled values. Scaling is still done as if this field were left blank; but instead of the calculated, scaled values appearing, the values from the range you entered appear. Although you cannot enter a y-axis label range in the Axis Labels Options menu, you can enter such a range into the Manual Label Range fields.

The next section of the Axis Scaling Options menu has to do with the number of divisions (ticks) in the graph. The Ticks section is divided into four parts: Normal Major, Normal Minor, Log Major, and Log Minor. You need evaluate only the two fields that relate to the response in the Type field at the top of the menu. If you selected a normal type of scaling, fill in the Normal Major and Normal Minor fields; if you selected a logarithmic type of scaling, fill in the Log Major and Log Minor fields.

Major divisions are the tick marks labeled with the scaled values. The graph in figure 10.16 contains six major divisions. You can change the number of divisions in one of two ways: You can enter a new number of divisions under Normal Major, or you can enter an incremental value between divisions. In the first method, SuperCalc takes the Low Value and High Value field responses, divides the difference by the number of divisions, and calculates a value for each tick mark. With the second method, SuperCalc takes the difference between the Low Value and High Value field responses, divides it by the incremental value, and calculates the number of major divisions required.

By default, zero minor divisions are defined. In the graph in figure 10.16, the value in the Normal Minor Divisions field was changed from 0 to 5 to make five tick marks appear between each major tick. Minor divisions are not labeled and have no grid showing. In figure 10.2, the Y2-Axis Normal Minor Divisions field was changed to 3. In this field you also can point to a cell in the spreadsheet instead of entering a value directly.

If you choose Logarithmic for the Type field, use the Log Major and Log Minor fields instead of the Normal Major and Normal Minor fields. Detailed discussion of logarithmic scales is beyond the scope of this book.

To see the Axis Appearance Options menu (the second part of the Axis Scaling Options menu), press PgDn. Figure 10.18 shows this screen.

```
                        AXIS APPEARANCE OPTIONS MENU          TYPE: BAR    ↑

                        COLOR       WIDTH      STYLE     POSITION
    X-AXIS
      Axis              Black       Auto       Solid
      Tick              None        Auto                 Outside
      Major grid        None        Auto       Solid
      Minor grid        None        Auto       Solid

    Y1-AXIS
      Axis              Black       Auto       Solid
      Tick              Black       Auto                 Inside
      Major grid        Grey        Auto       Solid
      Minor grid        None        Auto       Solid

    Y2-AXIS
      Axis              Black       Auto       Solid
      Tick              Black       Auto                 Inside
      Major grid        Grey        Auto       Solid
      Minor grid        None        Auto       Solid


    Black
    17>//Graphics,Axis,
    MENU  F4:Point  F6:Copy  PgUp:Axis Menu
```

Fig. 10.18.

The Axis Appearance Options menu.

On this menu you can alter several characteristics for the four major components of each axis: the Axis itself, the Tick marks, the Major grid, and the Minor grid. You can change the color, width, and style (from solid to a combination of dots and dashes) for each component. For the ticks, you can specify the Position (making them stick into the axis box or out from the axis box). In figure 10.2 the Y2-Axis Major grid was changed to a dashed-line style to differentiate it from the y1-axis grid. The two Minor grid fields in each major grid for the y2-axis were changed to a dotted-line style.

Defining Options

The next option on the Graphics menu is **O**ptions. Using this selection, the 9 generic graph types blossom into the 70 or more different variations of graphs possible. The Graphics Options menu choice may seem confusing because the screen that you see when you select this option depends on the type of graph selected with the Graphics Type menu. In fact, if you chose a word chart, which is a text-based chart without any options, nothing happens when you select **O**ptions from the Graphics menu: you remain at the command line. With the other types of graphs, the screens that appear, although similar in format, contain graph-specific information.

Table 10.4 contains cross-references of all the possible fields in the various Options menus that can appear when you select **O**ptions from the Graphics menu and the graph types with which they relate. The *s* marks mean that you can alter that field with a series; *x* marks mean that the field relates to the overall graph appearance or format.

Table 10.4
Chart Options Menu Fields for Each Graph Type

	Bar	Line	Hi-Lo	X-Y	Radar	Area	Pie	Dual
OPTIONS								
Group/Stack #	s							
Bar/Line	s							
Fit Type	s	s	s	s				
Line Style	s	s	s	s	s			
Line Width	s	s	s	s	s			
Marker Type	s	s	s	s	s			
Marker Size	s	s	s	s	s			
TYPE	X	X		X	X	X		X
HORIZONTAL	X	X	X			X		
3D	X	X				X	X	
FILL	X	X				X	X	
DRAW		X		X	X			
%OVERLAP	X							
MARKERS			X					
TREND LINES			X					
SORT SEGMENTS							X	X
PERCENT LABELS								
Display							X	X
Parentheses							X	X
Placement							X	X
EXPLOSION								
Type							X	X
Low Value							X	X
High Value							X	X
LINK CHARTS								X
PROPORTIONAL								X
START ANGLE							X	
DATA SOURCE								
Pie Mode							X	
Series/Point #							X	X

Some of the fields in table 10.4 relate to only one type of graph. You can alter the characteristics of the Markers and Trend Lines fields, for example, only in Hi-Lo graphs. Likewise, the Bar Chart Options menu has Group/Stack #, Bar/Line, and %Overlap fields, which no other graph has. As you can see from the table, the different graph types fall into two general classes. The first class can be called axis-based graphs and includes bar, line, Hi-Lo, X-Y, radar, and area graphs. The other class is nonaxis-based graphs and includes only two types: pie and dual. Because dual is really a limited-option pie-bar graph with an emphasis on pie, the pie graph is really the only nonaxis graph type. Regardless of whether the pie graph constitutes a class of its own or just an exception to the axis-based graph rule, the two classes just named are discussed separately in the following sections.

Axis-Based Graph Options

All the axis-based graphs except the area graph have two categories of options: series-specific options and graph-specific options (you usually use more than one series of data with an axis-based graph). Nonaxis-based based graphs (pie graphs) use only one series per graph.

One of the more comprehensive examples of the Graphics Options menu and series-specific options is the bar graph. The menu shown in figure 10.19 appears when you select **O**ptions if you have selected **B**ar from the Graphics Type menu.

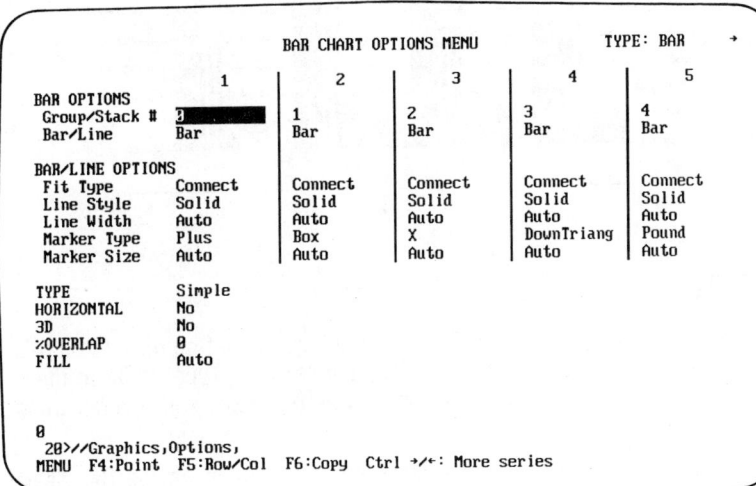

Fig. 10.19.

The Bar Chart Options menu.

Although the Options menu varies by graph type, the variation is more in content than in format. First on the menu come series-specific options and then come the graph-specific options. Like the Chart Data Appearance and Options menu (refer to fig. 10.9), this menu has a column for each of the 10 series (press Ctrl-right arrow to see series 6 through 10) for all types but the area graph.

The Bar Chart Options menu is unique in that it breaks the series-specific options into two sections: Bar Options and Bar/Line Options. The first option under Bar Options, Group/Stack #, is used for a grouped bar graph (see the section "Type" in this chapter). In a grouped bar graph, you can group several series together into one or more stacks. As an example, suppose that a graph has five series. By entering a *1* in columns 1 through 3 and a *2* in columns 4 and 5, you can create a graph with two stacked bars at each x-axis tick: one stack of three bars and one of two bars.

With the second option under Bar Options, Bar/Line, you can change your bar graph into a line graph or a mixture of bars and lines. The default of course, is Bar, but to change one series to a line, move to the correct column and press the space bar once. To demonstrate, suppose that the columns in figure 10.1 represented quarterly results rather than projects. Line graphs are sometimes better for judging a trend, so series 5 (*Total Revenue*), measured on the y2-axis, is changed to Line on the Bar/Line option. Figure 10.20 shows how such a graph might look.

Fig. 10.20.

A bar-line combination graph.

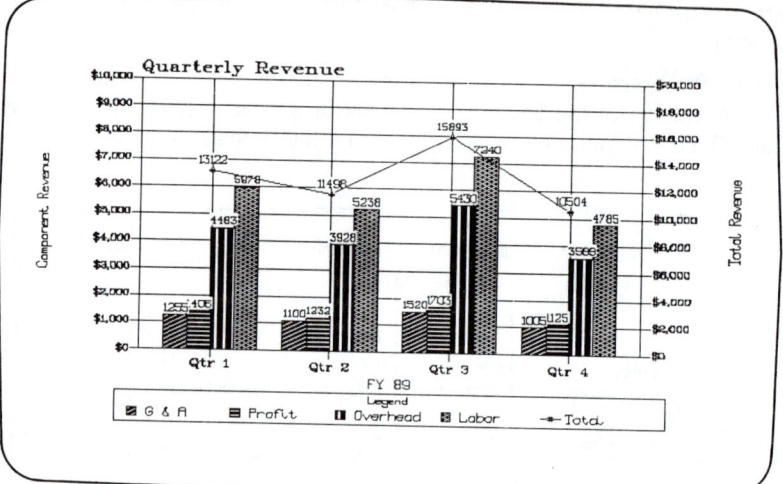

Notice that the graph is now 2-D rather than 3-D. Lines and bars cannot be mixed in a 3-D graph. Nor can they be mixed in a 100% bar graph (see the section "Type"). Given these restrictions, combination graphs are useful for mixing levels of details with overall trend analysis.

If you change any of the series from a bar to a line, the next section on the Bar Chart Options menu becomes relevant. The elements in this section are also in the Line, Hi-Lo, X-Y, and Radar versions of the Options menu (except that the Radar version does not have a Fit Type option).

The first option, Fit Type, is a powerful feature. Using it, you can select one of seven different ways to fit a line to a set of data. The seven alternatives are shown in the following chart.

Fit Type	Description
Connect	Connect points (default)
Stepped	Bar-like horizontal/vertical line connection
Average	Horizontal line equal to the data set average
Linear	Best-fit straight line through the data points
Quadratic	Smooth segment of a parabola

| Cubic | Smooth segment of a third-order polynomial |
| Polynomial | Best-fit curved line through the data points |

To demonstrate these differences, the series 1, 3, 5, 3, and 4 was plotted in the seven different fit types. Figure 10.21 shows the result.

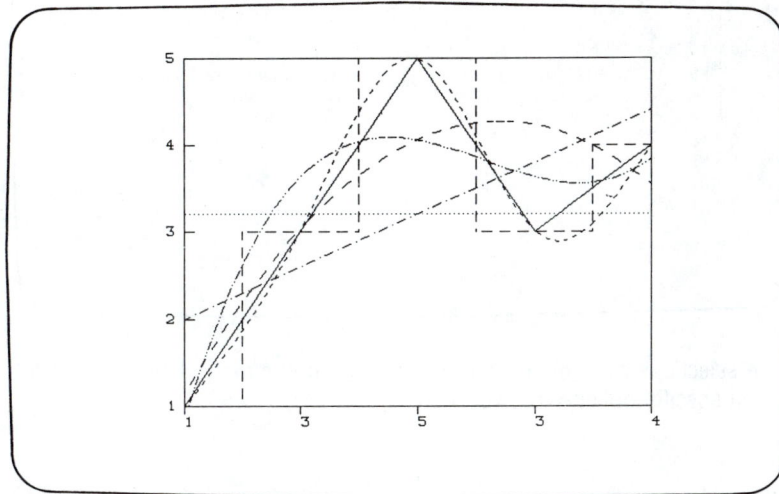

Fig. 10.21.

Seven fit type variations.

In figure 10.21 only the Connect, Stepped, and Polynomial fit types actually intercept the data points; the remaining four (Average, Linear, Quadratic, and Cubic) do not.

Figure 10.21 also demonstrates the eight different line styles (including none) from which you can choose, using the Line Style option. You can select different line widths, as well.

The next two options are Marker Type and Marker Size. These options control the markers placed at each data point on line style graphs. In figure 10.21 markers are turned off so that no markers appear at the data point. Figure 10.20, however, uses a pound-sign marker at each tick in the series. Figure 10.22 shows the 10 marker types from which you can select.

Normally set to Auto to handle graph size changes automatically, the Marker Size option can be set manually from 1 (smallest) to 5 (largest). Figure 10.22 displays the markers with Marker Size set to 5. Marker Size is the last option that can be set independently by series. For all the series-specific options just described, you can copy a setting across the remaining series settings by pressing F6. Once you define series 1 with a Marker Size of 5, for example, press F6 to change the remaining nine fields to 5.

The settings for series-specific options, once set, remain intact regardless of the graph type selected. If you switch the type of graph from bar to X-Y, for example, all the series-specific option responses remain unchanged.

The remaining options on the Bar Chart Options menu apply to the graph as a whole; they are the graph-specific options. The list of overall options varies for each type of graph and,

Fig. 10.22.

The 10 marker types.

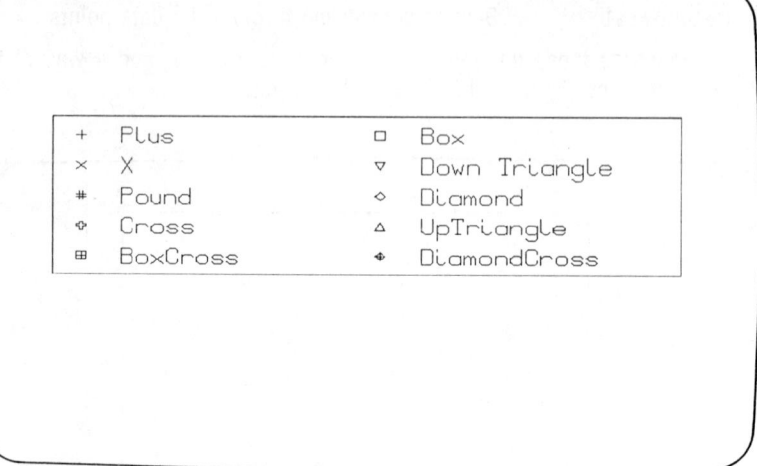

in some cases, the selections available for an option vary. In summary, however, the following are the graph-specific options that you may see:

- Type
- Horizontal
- 3D
- %Overlap
- Fill
- Draw
- Markers
- Trend Lines

The following sections detail the various graph-specific options.

Type

The first option you see in capital letters below Marker Size in figure 10.19 is Type. More bar graph types exist than for any other axis-based graph. As listed in table 10.2, a bar graph can be simple, stacked, grouped, 100%, or delta.

Simple is the standard bar graph type; stacked is a common optional graph type. (In SuperCalc4, as a matter of fact, stacked bar was one of the main graph types.) In Super-Calc5 stacked has been relegated to a bar graph option type and has adopted three powerful cousins (grouped, 100%, and delta). In a simple bar, line, or area graph, each series is calculated and displayed independently. In bar graphs, the bars can share a tick mark, but the heights of the bars are calculated independently. In comparison, a stacked graph stacks the bars, lines, or areas, adding each to the preceding to get a cumulative total.

Figures 10.23, 10.24, 10.25, and 10.26 show a stacked-bar graph and the three new types of bar graphs, respectively.

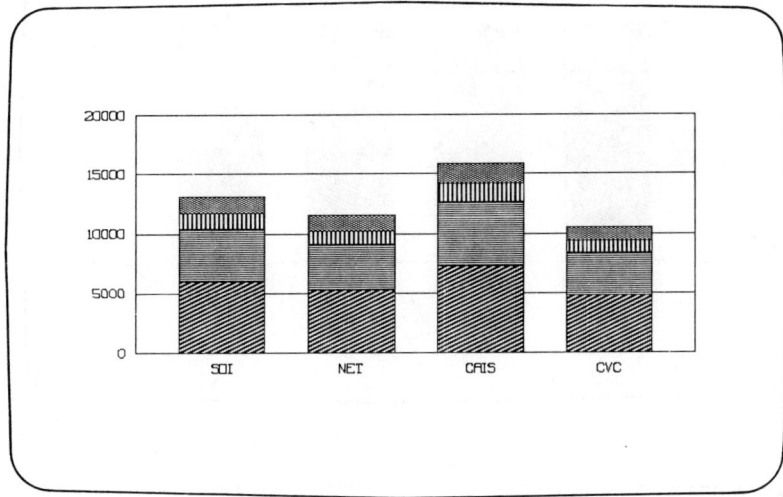

Fig. 10.23.
A stacked-bar graph.

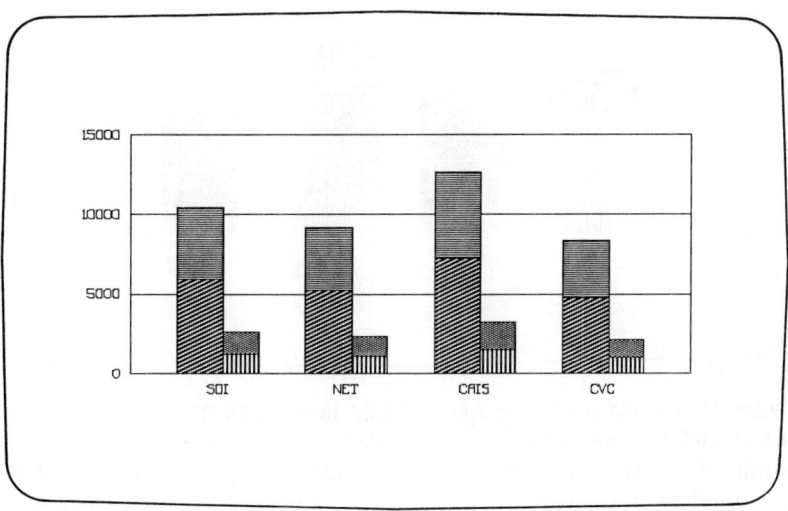

Fig. 10.24.
A grouped-bar graph.

Fig. 10.25.

A 100% bar graph.

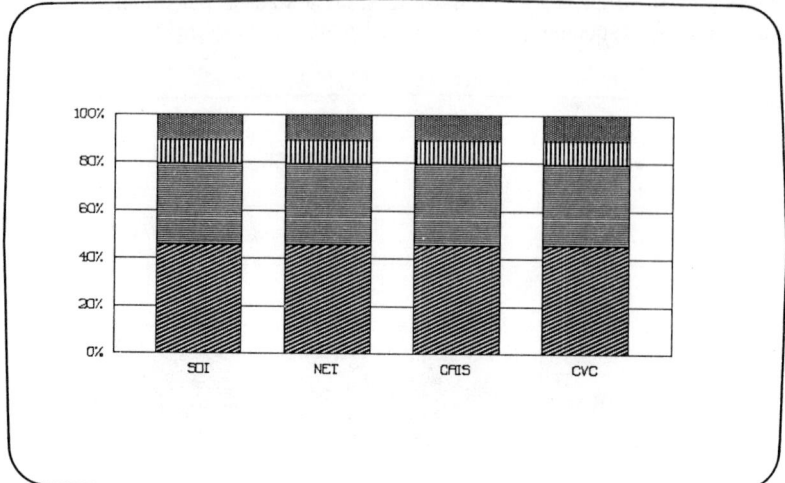

Fig. 10.26.

A delta bar graph.

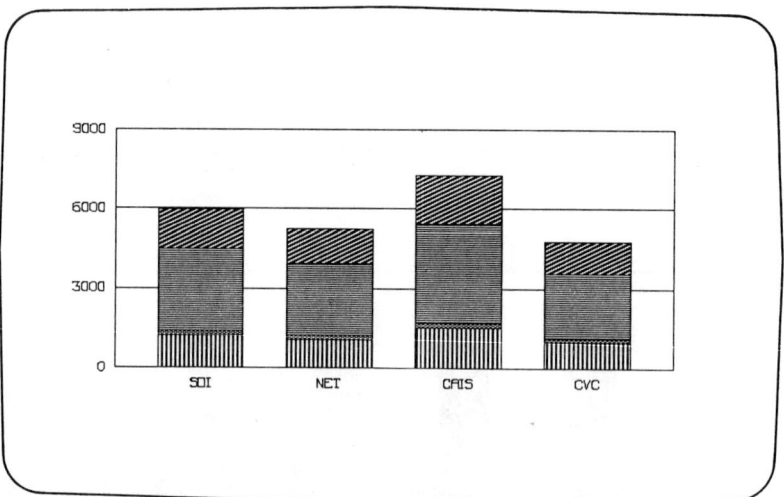

Notice the differences among the graphs in figures 10.23 through 10.26. With a stacked graph, all the bars at each tick are stacked on top of each other rather than next to each other, as is done with simple bar graphs. With a grouped graph, you get a powerful hybrid of simple and stacked graphs that lets you decide whether to stack each series, using the Group/Stack # option discussed earlier in this section.

The 100% type (see fig. 10.25) is a variation of the stacked type. Instead of the y-axis being a measured volume scale, it is a percentage scale that always measures from 0 to 100%. Instead of each stack varying in height relative to the y-axis, each stack always measures to 100% (the full height of the y-axis), and the component bars are sized propor-

tionately. The 100% graph allows you to determine what percent of the total each series bar constitutes and compare it to the other bars in the graph.

With the delta type of graph (see fig. 10.26), you see only the portion of the bar exceeding the height of all the other bars. To generate a delta graph, SuperCalc reorganizes the series order for each tick mark in ascending order, showing the smallest bar in front, with each incremental bar value remaining in the series. In other types of bar graphs, the first series you define (Series 1) is the first value shown across all the tick marks; in the case of a delta bar graph, the first value showing (the bottom bar) depends on the size of each value at that tick rather than the order in which you defined them. In case of equal values, only the first of the two values appears.

As listed in table 10.2, line and area graphs can be either simple or stacked. The Hi-Lo graph has no alternative types, and the X-Y and radar graphs have two unique graph-specific options: XYXY and XYY. The XYXY type causes all odd-numbered series to be plotted against the even-numbered series. In comparison, the XYY type plots series 1 against all the remaining series. Figures 10.27 and 10.28 show two X-Y charts charting the same data: six series (1 through 6, 2 through 7, . . .6 through 11).

Horizontal

You can change the axis orientation for all axis-based graphs (except the X-Y and radar graphs) so that the y-axis is horizontal instead of vertical. To do so, change the Horizontal option to Yes. The y1-axis is then across the bottom, the x-axis is down the left side, and the y2-axis is across the top. In essence, a Horizontal presentation is the mirror image of the graph shown vertically. If you rotated a plot of the Horizontal presentation back so that the x-axis was again across the bottom, y1 would be on the right and y2 on the left.

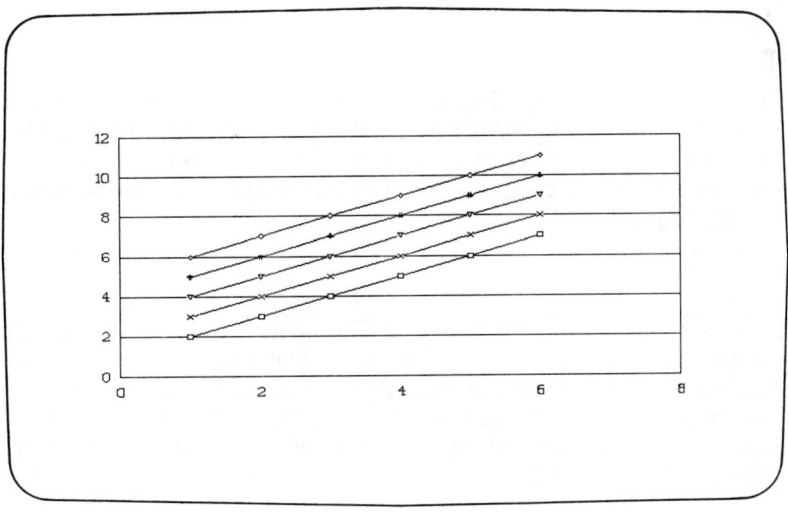

Fig. 10.27.
XYY X-Y graph.

Fig. 10.28.

XYXY X-Y graph.

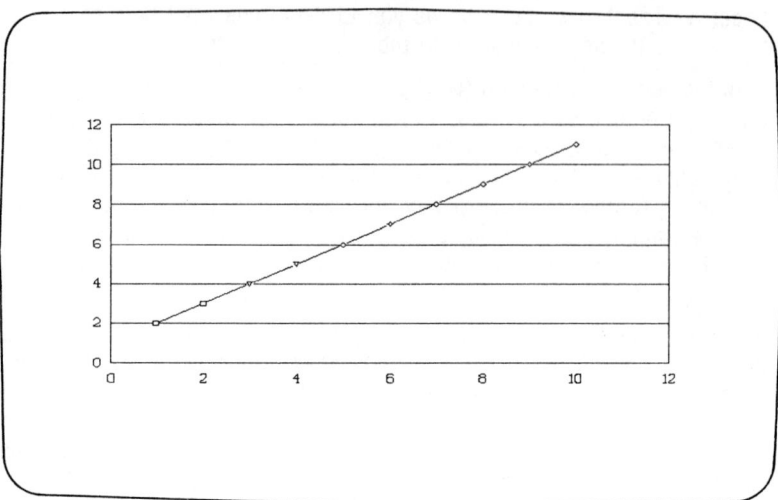

3D

Bar, line, and area graphs can be viewed in three dimensions. Although SuperCalc has three axes, two of them, y1 and y2, are in the same dimension. Because there is no true z-axis, the third dimension cannot be scaled. SuperCalc scales the third dimension automatically based on the number of series defined and the relative scaling of the other two axes. If there was a true third axis, the X-Y graph could be seen in 3-D and would have to be renamed the X-Y-Z type. 3D is the first option, listed in table 10.4, that is shared by axis-based graphs and pie graphs.

%Overlap

Another bar graph option is %Overlap. This option is new to SuperCalc5 and is for use with two-dimensional bar graphs with multiple series. If you enter a value from 1 to 100 in the %Overlap field, the bars at each tick of a simple bar graph overlap by that percent. If you leave %Overlap at 0, every bar appears in full. This option can give a two-dimensional graph the look of a 3-D graph.

Fill

You can select Solid or Patterns for the Fill option. This option also can be controlled by leaving it as Auto and defining your monitor with /Global,Optimum,Next or with //Graphics,Global,Options. If you define a monochrome monitor, patterns are used; otherwise, solid colors are used. Solid colors appear well on-screen, but because many plotters and printers produce only one-color graphics, consider what type of final output you require before selecting one of the fill options.

Draw

You have four selections under the Draw option: None, Lines, Markers, or Both. The Draw option is used for the three line-based graphs (line, X-Y, and radar) but is not available for the bar-line graph. Only the lines connecting the data points appear if Lines is selected; only the markers appear at each data point if Markers is selected; both lines and markers appear if you select Both. Although it may seem odd to select None, where neither lines nor markers appear, you may have a situation requiring the display of only the data labels.

Markers and Trend Lines

Markers and Trend Lines are two options relating only to Hi-Lo graphs. Although these two options refer to the Hi-Lo version of the same markers and lines mentioned in the preceding Draw option, the options are separated into two Yes or No fields.

Nonaxis-Based Graph Options

The pie graph is the principal nonaxis-based graph. The other type included in this section is the dual graph variation of the pie graph. To access the Pie Chart Options menu, select **P**ie under **T**ype on the main Graphics menu and then select **O**ptions from the same Graphics menu. Figure 10.29 shows the Pie Chart Options menu.

```
                    PIE CHART OPTIONS MENU              TYPE: PIE
  DATA SOURCE
    Pie mode             Series
    Series/Point #       1

  3D                     No
  FILL                   Auto
  SORT SEGMENTS          No
  START ANGLE            0

  EXPLOSION
    Type                 List
    Low Value            0
    High Value           0

  PERCENT LABELS
    Display              Both
    Parentheses          Yes
    Placement            Outside


  Series
   20>//Graphics,Options,
  MENU  F4:Point
```

Fig. 10.29.
The Pie Chart Options menu.

Some of the options for the pie graph are the same as for its axis-based counterparts. Pie graphs can be displayed in 3-D or 2-D. The pie segments can be either solid or pattern-filled. The following sections detail the other pie graph options available on the Pie Chart Options menu.

Data Source

The first section of figure 10.29 is called Data Source and has two options. The first option is Pie mode, for which you can select one of two alternatives: Series (default) or Point-Slice. The assumption here is that you may have set up several series as in figures 10.1 and 10.2, where four components of revenue exist for each of four projects. Each component is a series of data. Because a pie graph cannot plot more than one series of data, these two options let you select how to break down the data. If you select Series, all values for one component (one row of data) are used. If you select PointSlice, all the component values for one of the projects (one column of data) are used. You then enter the Series (row) or PointSlice (column) number you want to use.

Sort Segments

The next option unique to nonaxis-based graphs is Sort Segments. If you respond Yes to this option, pie segments are sorted in ascending order counter-clockwise from the starting point defined in the Start Angle option.

Start Angle

If you view a pie graph as the face of a clock, 3 o'clock is the default starting angle (0 degrees), 12 o'clock is 90 degrees, and so on. You can pick a point on the "clock" at which to place the first segment by entering a value from 0 to 360.

Explosion

The next section shown in figure 10.29 allows you to specify explosion options. As you recall, *pie explosion* means that one or all of the slices of the pie are separated for emphasis. The Explosion Type field is used to define what is to be exploded.

If you press Enter to display the selection window for the Type field, the following list of options appears:

Explode Type	What Is Exploded or Set Apart
None	No segments
All	All of the segments
Below	All segments falling below the Low Value
Above	All segments falling above the High Value
Within	All segments falling within the values
Outside	All segments above or below the values
Smallest	The smallest of the segments
Largest	The largest of the segments
List	Manually selected series defined in Data field

The Within option means within or equal to the High Value and Low Value fields. The Outside, Below, and Above options are all exclusive of the values entered in the Low Value and High Value fields. Only one set of explosion parameters can be set for a dual graph.

Percent Labels

Percent labels are also known as segment labels. You can alter three characteristics relating to them.

If you select None for the Display option, no label appears for a segment. If you select Data labels, the data labels you selected in the Data Labels Options menu appear adjacent to each pie segment. Selecting Percent causes the percentage of that segment of the total of the pie to appear. The Both option allows you to show both the data labels and the percent labels at once.

After choosing the format for the label value, you can optionally choose to enclose them in parentheses by selecting Yes in the Parentheses field. The two choices for the Placement field are Inside and Outside, which cause the labels to appear within the body of the pie slice or on the outside of the slice, respectively.

Link Charts

The Link Charts option is valid only for dual graphs. It refers to a pair of lines linking the left graph to the right graph. If you respond No to this option, no lines appear linking the graphs.

Proportional

If you selected a pie graph for both the left and right graphs in a dual graph, you can make the right pie graph appear in relative size to the left graph. The right graph is typically a more detailed breakdown of a slice in the left pie. When the Proportional option is set to Yes, the two graphs appear on the same scale. That is, the right one is only a fraction of the size of the left one. Otherwise, the two graphs appear equal in size.

Plotting Fundamentals and Options

Eventually, you will want to plot your graph. Before doing so, you should check a couple of settings to make sure that the plot comes out right the first time. The settings appear in two principal places: the /Global,Graphics command and the //Graphics,Global command.

The /Global,Graphics Command

In SuperCalc4, the /Global,Graphics command had much greater significance than it does in SuperCalc5. In SuperCalc4 this command was used to define fonts and colors as well as device and other optional settings. Most of these functions have been moved over to the Graphics menu system, but several functions relating to plotting still remain with the /Global,Graphics command.

If you type /**G**lobal,**G**raphics, the following menu appears:

    Quit Device Layout Options

Two of the menu choices, **D**evice and **O**ptions, are similar to the same choices in the Global Spreadsheet menu. Because you can specify a plotting device different from your printing device, two menus are needed. On the Global Graphics Device menu the following three choices appear (instead of just the first two in /**G**lobal,**S**preadsheet):

    B&W-printers Color-printers Plotters

If you select a printer in /**G**lobal,**S**preadsheets,**D**evice,**B**&W-printers (see Chapter 9), the printer selection is carried over to the graphics side until you change those settings. Because the options for the /**G**lobal,**G**raphics,**D**evice command are so similar to their /**G**lobal,**S**preadsheet cousins, the discussion in Chapter 9 should make the selection process for these options clear.

Defining the Size and Orientation of Printed Graphs

The one choice that remains intact from SuperCalc4 is /**G**lobal,**G**raphics,**L**ayout. The options in this menu give you a great deal of control and flexibility over the size and orientation of printed or plotted graphs. The Layout menu in figure 10.30 shows the options available.

Fig. 10.30.

Selecting Page and Chart Size in the Layout menu.

```
LAYOUT MENU: SELECTIONS FOR PLOTTING

Page Size:                 * "Page Size" describes the physical paper you are using
Paper         1              with your graphics printer or plotter. Page Width is the
Width       8.50             direction along which the paper is normally read.
Length     11.00           * "Chart Size" describes where, how large and in which
                             direction the chart is drawn.
Chart Size:                * Size, Rotation and Offset adjust automatically EXCEPT in
Mode          F              Manual Mode. In Manual Mode you can change chart settings.
Rotation      V            * In Horizontal Rotation the chart is viewed in the normal
                             reading direction of the paper. Vertical Rotation is the
Width       9.75             opposite of Horizontal.
Length      7.25           * Chart Width is approximately 1.3 times Chart Length for
                             most graphics devices. If this "aspect ratio" is changed
Chart/Page Offset:           (allowed only in Manual Mode) your Pie charts will look
Top         0.50             like watermelons. If you set Chart Width OR Length to 0.00
Left        0.50             SuperCalc substitutes an appropriate value using the
                             aspect ratio for your device.
                           * "Chart/Page Offset" tells SuperCalc where on the page
                             (measured from the Top and Left) to start the chart.


1 = 8.5" x 11":
 24>/Global,Graphics,Layout
MENU  Specify graph layout - Keepable defaults
```

The Page Size option controls the printer or plotter page size. Two choices are possible: 8.5-by-11-inch (choice 1) or 14-by-11-inch (choice 2). The second choice may be unavail-

able if your plotter or printer device does not use larger size paper. If you cannot select choice 2, make sure that you have configured the program for the printer you are using.

The Chart Size options control the size of the printed graph, its position on the page, and whether it is produced horizontally (portrait mode) or rotated and produced vertically (landscape mode). The Mode option enables you to choose **F**ull, **M**anual, **T**op, **B**ottom, or **Q**uarter. When the default **F**ull mode is set, the Rotation option is automatically set to **V**ertical. The Mode options of **T**op and **B**ottom produce graphs and plots on the top or bottom of the page, respectively. The **Q**uarter option specifies in which of the four quadrants the graph is to be placed. Press 1 to place the graph in the upper left quadrant, 2 to put the graph in the upper right quadrant, 3 to place the graph in the lower left quadrant, or 4 to put the graph in the lower right quadrant. Because of size constraints, setting any of the four **Q**uarter options causes the graph to be rotated and reduced in size. Selecting **M**anual in the Mode option enables the remaining options in the Layout menu: Rotation, Width, Length, Top, and Left.

The //Graphics,Global Command

The remaining plotting settings are in the Graphics Global menu. To access them, select //**G**raphics,**G**lobal. The following choices appear:

```
Quit  Drivers  Options
```

The **D**rivers and **O**ptions selections are described in the following sections.

Drivers

If you select **D**rivers from the Graphics Global menu, three menu choices appear:

```
Normal  PIC  CGI
```

Normal causes the plot to be sent to the graphics plotting device specified in /**G**lobal,**G**raphics,**D**evice. If you did not choose a graphics device, SuperCalc5 tries to send the plot to the printer selected under /**G**lobal,**S**preadsheet,**D**evice.

You have two optional driver settings: **P**IC and **C**GI. The PIC format is the Lotus graphics format used for storing graphs. Once you have saved your plot to a PIC file, you can load it to other graphics and word processing packages supporting the PIC format. The other selection, **C**GI, stands for Computer Graphics Interface. If you make this selection, the following six options appear:

```
Quit  Display  Printer  pLotter  Camera  Metafile  Slide
```

To use these options, you must install the Drivers diskette from your SuperCalc5 package and name the appropriate device driver program in your computer's CONFIG.SYS file. (The CONFIG.SYS file specifies special devices to your computer.) You can add the following two lines to your CONFIG.SYS file:

```
DEVICE = META.SYS /GROUP:OUTPUT
DEVICE = GSSCGI.SYS
```

Computer Associates is trying to provide more general compatibility and standardization with these optional CGI formats. Computer Associates realizes that the plotter or printer is not always going to be adequate for the sophisticated graphics you can create in Super-Calc5. For the power user, Computer Associates supplies some fancy alternatives. You can write the graph to a file to create slides or for camera equipment. Also available are special display, printer, and plotter device drivers.

Options

The other selection on the Graphics Global menu is **O**ptions. Figure 10.31 shows the Global Options menu. The first two options concern monitor settings and are not discussed here.

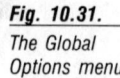

Fig. 10.31.

*The Global
Options menu.*

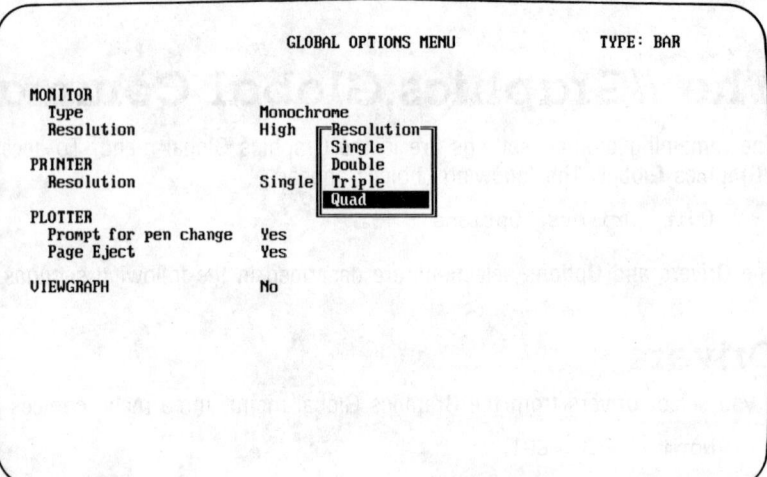

```
                          GLOBAL OPTIONS MENU              TYPE: BAR


     MONITOR
        Type                    Monochrome
        Resolution              High    ┌Resolution┐
                                        │ Single   │
     PRINTER                            │ Double   │
        Resolution              Single  │ Triple   │
                                        │▓Quad▓▓▓▓▓│
     PLOTTER                            └──────────┘
        Prompt for pen change   Yes
        Page Eject              Yes

     VIEWGRAPH                  No
```

The third option on the Global Options menu, Printer Resolution, can be set to one of four levels. Figure 10.31 shows the selection window for the Printer Resolution option. As you work on your plot, you may want to use the single-density format, which plots more quickly but in a less accurate manner. Once the plot is finalized, you may want to change the resolution to Double, Triple, or Quad for the highest quality possible.

Graphics plotters typically have between two and eight pen holders for storing different colored plotting pens. If you have this type of plotter, set the Prompt for Pen Change option On. SuperCalc pauses when the time comes to change colors on the plotter and prompts you to change the pen. If you have adequate holders to handle the colors in your plot, you may want to set this option to No.

The Page Eject option determines how SuperCalc acts after finishing the plot. Because you can plot several graphs on a page by changing the layout options using /**G**lobal,**G**raphics,**L**ayout, you may want the paper to remain in the plotter. If so, set this option to No; otherwise, the paper is ejected after the plot finishes.

If you are going to plot your graph on an overhead transparency, the Viewgraph field should be set to Yes.

Plotting the Graph

One of the big differences between SuperCalc and some of the competitive programs is the ease with which you can plot a graph. If you are in the main Graphics menu, you can select **P**lot. Otherwise, you can press Alt-F10 to begin plotting. Depending on your hardware and optional settings, you may be prompted for pen changes before plotting begins. To interrupt the plot, press Ctrl-Break.

Graph Manipulation

Several support utilities exist in SuperCalc for managing your graphs. These utilities are described in the following sections.

Naming a Graph

You can have as many graph definitions as you like for a spreadsheet. In order to save a graph definition, however, you must give the graph its own identity. To save a graph, select //**G**raphics,**N**ame. The following set of menu choices appears:

    Retrieve Store Delete Zap

Select **S**tore to save the graph description. SuperCalc prompts you for the name of the graph. Enter a name or number up to 31 characters in length. Once you enter the name of the graph, press Enter to return to the main Graphics menu. Unlike other storing operations in SuperCalc, you are not prompted to replace an established graph name if one is already stored; SuperCalc automatically replaces it. If you changed a graph, make sure that you save your spreadsheet as well; graphs are stored as part of the spreadsheet and until the spreadsheet is saved, the graph definitions are not. If you load a SuperCalc4 spreadsheet that has graphs defined, you can retrieve them by using the number assigned to them in SuperCalc4.

In order to load a graph definition stored in the current spreadsheet, select //**G**raphics, **N**ame,**R**etrieve. If you do not remember the graph name, press F3 to display the Chart List menu. Be careful using **Z**ap: all //**G**raphics settings return to their default settings and all ranges, titles, and legends are blanked out.

The /Blank, /Copy, and /Load Commands

In addition to the //Graphics menu utilities, you can use /Blank to blank a graph definition, /Copy to copy a graph definition, and /Load to load just the graph definitions. To blank a graph definition, invoke /Blank. The dialog panel at the bottom of the screen resembles the following:

```
Enter range; then ‹RETURN› or ‹,› for Options
   10›/Blank,A1
```

Normally, you enter a named range or cell range in this location. If you press the asterisk (*) instead, the display changes to the following:

```
From? Enter chart name or ALL
   9›/Blank,*
```

At this point, you can enter the graph definition name or press F3 to select it from the menu. You must use the asterisk to invoke the graph-related option in /Copy as well. You enter the source graph name and the target graph name; then press Enter.

To load a graph description from a spreadsheet on your disk, invoke /Load,Graphs. Then do one of the following: enter a graph name from the spreadsheet, press F3 and select a graph description from the Chart List menu, or enter All to load all the graph settings.

Chapter Summary

Graphics is an extensive subject in SuperCalc5. The improvements over SuperCalc4 are so extensive that an entire book could be written on the subject. This chapter tried to make you familiar with the structure of the //Graphics command and any menu commands required to plot graphs effectively. You learned about the 70 or more different types of graphs available to plot and how to put your signature on a graph by mixing and matching the numerous options and tools available to you.

Chapter 11 begins Part IV of *Using SuperCalc5*: a look at SuperCalc's advanced features, including macros, data management, auditing, and add-in packages. In the next chapter you will learn how to automate your spreadsheet activities, using the macro language.

Part IV

Using Advanced Features

Includes

Automating with Macros

Data Management

Using the Spreadsheet Auditing Tools

Interfacing with Other Packages and Using
Add-In Programs

11

Automating with Macros

Before SuperCalc4, Computer Associates used eXecute (XQT) files to store predefined spreadsheet commands. In SuperCalc4, the developers began using a macro format like 1-2-3's, but built in the option to leave the macros on disk in eXecute files and an automatic macro generator called LEARN. SuperCalc5 adds indispensable debugging tools to enhance your macro reliability and cut your development time. You also have the capability of converting 1-2-3 macros in and out of SuperCalc.

In this chapter, not only do you learn to use macros, but you also use the //**M**acro,**L**earn command, the special SuperCalc development tool, and the rest of the menu-based macro support programs. The chapter begins with an overview of the macro method. After gaining an understanding of the macro system structure, you learn how to create, name, execute, and debug a macro. Using simple macros as examples, the chapter explores specific macro commands and syntaxes. The chapter ends with some practical macros that save keystrokes, use programming commands, and build applications.

Introducing Macros

Macros are neither ominous nor unbelievably complicated. You can use them simply to speed the execution of a frequently used command string, to reduce the number of keystrokes required for a procedure, or even to create complete applications.

The *SuperCalc User's Guide* defines *macro* as a set of instructions that causes SuperCalc to perform certain functions automatically. Macros do such things as move the cursor, enter text and values, perform calculations, adjust the screen, and format the spreadsheet.

If you are familiar with programming, think of macros as programs. If you are unfamiliar with programming or have wondered what programming is like, mastering macros may be your first step toward understanding other programming methods.

351

A major use of macros is to reduce keystrokes by automating routine, tedious, repetitive tasks. For example, the development of a spreadsheet sometimes requires rearranging the contents, reformatting the display, and modifying cell contents. With a little foresight and the tools for developing macros, you can reduce repetitive development commands to single keystrokes. For example, macros can insert rows or columns between lines of data, print reports, format worksheets, and modify and manipulate the data entered.

Another popular use of macros is to create automated spreadsheet templates that address specific functions, such as investment analysis or income tax preparation. These templates are created so that someone who knows little about the structure or mechanics of the spreadsheet can use SuperCalc. A macro can guide novice users through data entry and print the results in a predefined format. Templates are often created by experts who have worked through and tested the spreadsheet to eliminate calculation errors. By using a template, you avoid errors that occur when a new spreadsheet is developed hastily to solve an immediate problem.

With the {MENU} command, an ambitious developer can integrate several spreadsheets into menu-driven applications, such as accounting and file management. The more logically structured an application is, the more likely it can be automated into a set of menu choices using macros.

Understanding the Structure and Capabilities of Macros

Before developing a "micro" perspective on macros, let's begin by looking at the different tools provided in the macro system.

Fundamentals of the SuperCalc Macro System

Unlike most SuperCalc features, the macro system does not depend on menus. You can create a macro by entering a command string directly into a cell, and you can execute the macro without using a menu command. By understanding the menu structure and using it effectively, however, you can use the macro feature to greater advantage.

The //Macro Command

With SuperCalc in READY mode, invoke //**M**acro. The main Macro menu appears:

    Learn Read Write eXecute Analyze Breakpoint Convert Trace

The first selection, **L**earn, is similar to the /**N**ame,**C**reate command. Instead of associating a name with a range, however, you are selecting a range "bucket" to store the keystrokes you will generate while SuperCalc is in LEARN mode. This command only defines the target range; it does not invoke LEARN mode. To toggle on LEARN mode, you press Alt-F4.

Because in LEARN mode your keystrokes are entered into consecutive cells down a column, you need to define a range as only one column wide; the length of the column is the key factor.

The next two selections in the menu are **R**ead and **W**rite. You use **R**ead to load an XQT file macro into the spreadsheet range you select. You then choose to read one of the following options:

```
All  Macros-only  Labels-macros  Comments-macros
```

These choices are a combination of the components of the XQT file. The three columnar components of a macro (discussed in more detail later) are the macro itself, the labels for each macro, and the comments describing the macro's action. With these options, you can read or write the entire eXecute file, the **L**abels-macros columns, or the **C**omments-macros columns. You can write a range of the spreadsheet out to a macro XQT file in the same ways. If the file name you specify already exists, SuperCalc asks whether to overwrite or back up the file on disk.

The next option is eXecute, which is the last of the SuperCalc4-level options. You use the eXecute option to invoke a macro XQT file.

The following options have been added in SuperCalc5 to make life with macros easier. You use **A**nalyze, **B**reakpoint, and **T**race to debug and document macros. These options are discussed in the debugging section, which you will read after you have learned enough about macros to need the debugging tools.

Although you could import Lotus files into SuperCalc4, the macros were not usable in SuperCalc because of differences in the command structure. In SuperCalc5 you can use //**M**acro,**C**onvert to convert 1-2-3 macros into and out of SuperCalc. This command will not, however, convert Supercalc-structured macros into Lotus. Because SuperCalc has added a command to convert to the Lotus menu structure (/**1**-2-3), all that the conversion does for command strings is add a 1 at the beginning so that

  /**FRE**xample~

for /**F**ile,**R**etrieve,**E**xample, becomes

  /1**FRE**xample~

when you use //**M**acro,**C**onvert,**1**-2-3, and the command string changes back again when you use //**M**acro,**C**onvert,**S**uperCalc.

Keyboard and programming macros are converted when necessary so that {BIGRIGHT}, the 1-2-3 key macro for paging right, is converted to {PGRT}. This feature greatly enhances the interface between these two packages.

Text Interpretations of Keystrokes

Textual representations play the most important role in the macro system. Anything you can enter on the keyboard has a text equivalent, which the macro processor can interpret and execute. In some cases, the text equivalent is the literal character; in other cases, the text equivalent is a word that represents the keystroke and is enclosed in braces ({}). For example, the macro representation of Esc is {ESC}; of F6, {WINDOW}; and of Ctrl-Break, {READY}. Studying this chapter will help reinforce your understanding of all the keyboard controls because they all are addressed and represented within the context of the macro processor.

Macro Programming Commands

In addition to the keyboard representations, another class of macro commands is available to perform powerful functions during macro execution. These commands use the same brace ({}) format but do not represent a single keystroke. You can use these commands to structure data input; to control screen activity and movement; and to initiate alternative orders of execution, such as branching to different locations and macro ranges, processing macro subroutines, displaying alternatives in menu format, and conditionally executing subsequent commands. Examples of these commands are {IF cc}, {BRANCH label}, {WINDOWSOFF}, and {MENU label}.

Macro XQT Files

Macro XQT files are used to store macros on disk for general access from all spreadsheets or for the creation of multiple spreadsheet applications. You can create these files in the SuperCalc spreadsheet or with a word processor. The only structural requirement is the statement {MACRO} in the first row of the file. An XQT file consists of labels, macros, and comments.

Named Ranges

For convenience and visibility, macros in spreadsheets should have names, even though the macros can be executed by selecting the cell address of the first command in the macro. The name can be up to 32 characters long. If you use a single letter preceded by a backslash (for example, \A, \B, or \C), you can invoke the macro by pressing Alt plus the range-name letter. Otherwise, you must press Alt-= and then type the range name or select the range name from the Macro Name Directory screen before pressing Enter. You also can use a cell address instead of a range name.

Screen Messages as Road Markers

The screen plays an important role in communicating macro status and error messages and generally helps to clarify the development and execution of macros.

Mode Indicators

When you work with macros, SuperCalc can be in one of five modes: MACRO, STEP, ASTEP, LEARN, or DIRECT. The mode is indicated in the lower right corner of the dialog panel.

The word MACRO normally appears during macro execution. The only time the word does not appear is when the macro is waiting for input or when you choose to execute the macro one command at a time using the STEP or ASTEP modes.

STEP is helpful for "debugging" your macro. When you execute a macro in this mode, the first step in the macro executes, then it pauses, and you have to press F8 to continue to the next step. Using STEP, you can thoroughly analyze your macro at your own pace, which is not possible in the normal MACRO mode.

A variation of STEP, ASTEP, is new in SuperCalc5 and can be invoked only from the STEP mode. It performs the same function as STEP, but it automatically executes all the steps in the macro, only more slowly than in normal MACRO mode. The macro pauses briefly at each step so that you have a chance to witness the action, somewhat like a slow-motion replay.

The other two modes, LEARN and DIRECT, relate to the development phase. When you press Alt-F4, SuperCalc enters LEARN mode, an automatic development tool that echoes your keystrokes directly into the LEARN range, where you can execute them as a macro.

DIRECT is an alternative setting that can be executed only from LEARN mode. Before you can invoke DIRECT mode, the mode indicator must display LEARN. By pressing Alt-F6, you invoke DIRECT mode. The keystrokes you type on the entry line are then entered directly (and only) into the macro LEARN range. In other words, when SuperCalc is in this mode, your keystrokes are not echoed to the LEARN range but are placed directly in it without being executed. To switch back to LEARN mode, you press Alt-F6 again. If you press Alt-F4 instead, you will exit LEARN/DIRECT mode completely.

Prompts

The macro prompts go hand-in-hand with the macro modes. The first two prompts are

    F8 to RESUME

and

    ↵ to RESUME

These prompts appear when a macro command requires user input before the macro can resume execution. For example, {GET} and {?} are two simple input commands that cause the Enter symbol to appear.

Using {SUSPEND} is one way to make SuperCalc display the prompt F8 to RESUME. With {SUSPEND}, you can press Enter without causing the macro to continue execution.

The third and fourth prompts are the two prompts possible during STEP mode. The third prompt is similar to, for example,

    (F8)STEP L:1 \A   A1   /FG$TCW12~

The fourth prompt is, for example,

    F8:STEP@A1/ 10

They have close relatives under ASTEP, except that the (F8) in the third prompt becomes AUTO and F8, in the fourth example, is eliminated. This occurs because pressing F8 is not required to move between steps. When in STEP or ASTEP, you can switch between these two modes by pressing Alt-space bar.

The third prompt, which comes up by default, is a new, more detailed, and more helpful auditing tool. From left to right across the line, the prompt first tells you whether you are in STEP or AUTOSTEP mode. The L:1 indicates that you are at the first level of a macro. (This information is most useful in nested macros, where one is executed within another.) Next comes the name of the macro (\A in this example). To the right is the current macro cell address and finally the actual cell contents of the current macro line with the current command highlighted within the working area. The only shortcoming of this debug screen is that it covers up the first two prompts.

The only way to determine whether either of the first two prompts is showing is to press Alt-space bar to toggle to the other STEP mode. You can still see the cell address and location within the cell through the more abbreviated debug message (the fourth prompt). The x/y positions in this prompt represent the current cell address (A1) and the current character position within the row (10). Each time you press F8, the x and y values change to reflect the command that the macro is executing. This tool is indispensable for debugging macros. With it, you can locate the exact position where the macro error occurs.

Error Messages

A variety of error messages appear while you work with macros. Some are displayed during the development phase; others, during macro execution. The first of these messages is

```
ERROR in Macro at x/y
```

The x/y indicates the cell address and character position of the error that interrupted the macro execution. This error is "fatal" in that the macro terminates and you must reexecute it. The message is constructive, however, because it provides the exact location of the error.

Another message may appear during macro execution:

```
Current macro suspended; cannot invoke another
```

This message appears if you try to invoke a macro while SuperCalc is executing another macro. Only one macro can be executed at a time.

The last message appears if you terminate or interrupt the macro during execution. If you interrupt the macro (by pressing Ctrl-Break), the message

```
User abort at xn/ n
```

appears. The xn/ n represents the cell address and position within the cell of the interrupted macro.

When you are using the //**M**acro,**L**earn command, you may see one or all of three messages. The first is

```
Define Learn range before starting LEARN mode
```

This message appears when you try to toggle on LEARN mode with Alt-F4 before you have defined a target range for the echoed commands.

The second message appears when SuperCalc is not in LEARN mode and you try to toggle on DIRECT mode with Alt-F6:

```
Must be in Learn mode to reach Direct mode
```

You can enter DIRECT only from LEARN mode because creating a macro in DIRECT involves using LEARN mode.

The third message is

```
Learn range full; increase size and start learn again
```

This warning appears all too frequently because of the way SuperCalc stores commands in the LEARN mode. Nearly all keystrokes require a new line of the range except within a command string. If the target range you define through //**M**acro,**L**earn is not big enough to hold the echoed commands, this message appears, and SuperCalc is thrown out of LEARN mode. Before you can enter any more commands, you must enlarge the LEARN range.

Because range naming is so prevalent during macro creation, messages regarding the redefinition of rows, columns, cell addresses, or functions seem to appear frequently. For example, suppose that you want to name a range DATE because you will use it to automate entering a date. DATE is also a SuperCalc function. The program tells you that you are redefining a function but does not stop you from doing so. To prevent much of this redefining from occurring, be careful about range names. Prefixing all macro range names with a backslash (\) to identify them as macro names is also good practice, even though the backslash is required only for single-letter macro names.

Recommended Macro Structure

The two mandatory parts of a macro are the macro itself and its name, which you use to execute the macro. Because macros are usually too cryptic to understand at a glance, including a third part, a comments section, is a good idea. This comments section describes the action and purpose of the macro. Brief comments help you remember what is going on and are essential if anyone else is to understand your macro.

Figure 11.1 is an example of how Computer Associates recommends you structure your macros.

The first column (B) contains the macro label or name, the second column (C) contains the macro itself, and the third column (D) contains the comments and documentation necessary for someone else to understand the macro's function. Because the name is to the left of the first cell of each section, you can name the macro sections by typing

/**N**ame,**L**abels,**R**ight

The column of labels will be linked to the column of macros. Although columns B, C, and D are used in this example, any three columns outside the main spreadsheet area will work.

Fig. 11.1.

Recommended macro structure.

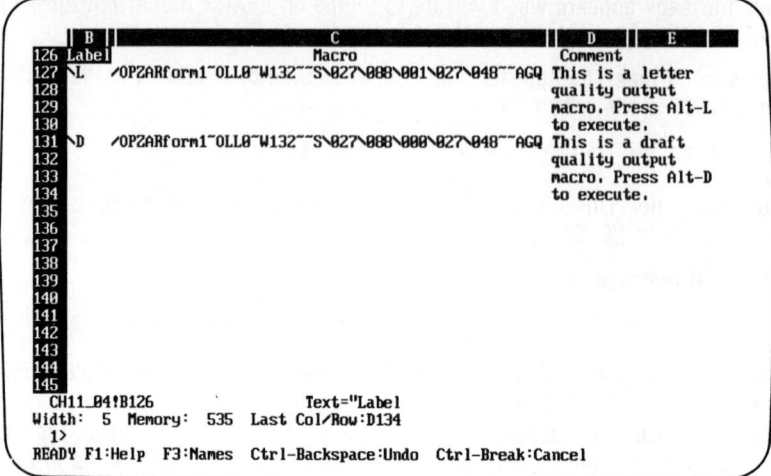

```
      B                       C                    D      E
126 Label                   Macro                Comment
127 \L  /OPZARform1~0LL0~W132~~S\027\000\001\027\048~~AGQ This is a letter
128                                                       quality output
129                                                       macro. Press Alt-L
130                                                       to execute.
131 \D  /OPZARform1~0LL0~W132~~S\027\000\000\027\048~~AGQ This is a draft
132                                                       quality output
133                                                       macro. Press Alt-D
134                                                       to execute.
135
136
137
138
139
140
141
142
143
144
145
    CH11_04!B126              Text="Label
Width: 5  Memory: 535  Last Col/Row:D134
    1>
READY F1:Help  F3:Names  Ctrl-Backspace:Undo  Ctrl-Break:Cancel
```

SuperCalc5 has an added feature that uses comments. If you press Alt-F3 when you are going to invoke a macro, the Macro Name Directory appears on-screen, as in figure 11.2.

As you can see, all the ranges in current memory prefaced with a backslash appear on the screen, along with their spreadsheet name, the page of the spreadsheet where the range is located, the name of the macro, and the comment appearing in the cell to the right of the named macro. This directory is most useful when comments are included. Without comments, its use is limited.

Fig. 11.2.

The Macro Name Directory.

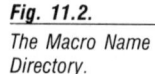

```
MACRO NAME DIRECTORY
Sheet    Page  Name            Comments
CH11_04   1    \D              This is a draft
CH11_04   1    \L              This is a letter
```

Macro Cell Addressing

When you include cell addresses in a macro, you must play by a slightly different set of rules for cell addressing. The main rule to remember is that what is normally a relative address in SuperCalc is an absolute address when used in a macro. Because a macro command string is a text string, the address is not adjusted when you insert or delete rows or copy the macro from one location to another. In a macro, SuperCalc always interprets the address A1 literally as A1.

Relative and Name Addressing

To make a macro cell address relative to the current cell position, you use pointing when you are in LEARN mode or when you are creating a macro command string. For example, to unprotect the range A1:B20, you do not type "**/UA1:B20**~. Instead, you type

"/U.{DN 19}{RT}~

Because the slash command (/) brings up the menus, in a macro you must precede the slash with a quotation mark ("). This mark indicates that you are entering a character string, so SuperCalc allows you to store the command instead of taking you into the menus.

The letter *U* executes the /**U**nprotect command. The remaining part of the macro defines a range by using the pointing method. The period (.) anchors the address at the current cell address so that the address is displayed as a single cell range (for example, A1:A1). The next command is {DN 19}, an abbreviation for {DOWN 19}. During execution, this command moves the cell pointer down 19 rows, defining a 20-cell column range (for example, A1:A20). The next command in the macro string, {RT}, an abbreviated version of the macro keyword {RIGHT}, moves the cell pointer to the right one column so that the range is 20 rows long and 2 columns wide (for example, A1:B20). The last character, the tilde (~), instructs the program to execute Enter, which means the range definition is complete. In this case, the /**U**nprotect command can begin executing.

By using pointing instead of explicitly stating the range A1:B20, the macro is more universally useful. It can work on any 20-by-2 cell range starting wherever the cell pointer is located—not just on the range A1:B20.

An easy way to overcome the problem of defining a relative address is to use named ranges instead of cell addresses as often as possible. For example, if you create an output macro that references range A1:H20, no matter how the spreadsheet changes, cells A1:H20 are printed. If, instead, you name the range, any spreadsheet changes affecting that range are less likely to throw off your output macro range. The output range can expand and contract, move up or down, or move left or right, and the macro range remains intact and valid.

Cell Reference Expressions

SuperCalc provides another longer but more sophisticated cell referencing form, which is especially appropriate for macros. This method is to cell referencing what formulas are to numbers; with this method you derive an address, called a *cell reference expression*. These expressions are not allowed in formulas but can be used in commands (including macro programming commands). You can use these expressions to perform a variety of tasks, including converting numeric range sizing (for example, six columns by six rows) into valid range definitions and creating input screens with SuperCalc's programming logic commands.

A cell reference expression takes the form

[column number;row number]

The brackets ([ ]) tell SuperCalc to expect a cell reference expression. The semicolon separates the column-number identification from the row-number identification. You can combine and compound the expression in a variety of ways.

The main difference between this type of address and a traditional cell address is that columns are defined numerically instead of alphabetically. For example, column A is 1 and column Z is 26. This arrangement makes it easy to create a column address from a value in the spreadsheet. The column reference can be a number such as

[4;]

The column reference can also be a number entered in another cell and referenced by an expression such as

[+ C35;]

If the number 4 is stored in cell C35, the column address of the expression [+ C35;] is 4—the fourth column of the spreadsheet, column D.

The column reference also can be an index function:

[CURCOL;]

You may recall from the discussion of index functions in Chapter 7 that this function represents the value of the column where the cell pointer is located.

You can also use the cell reference expression with a row address to create a full address such as

[+ C35;CURROW]

If 4 is stored in cell C35 and the cell pointer is located at G10, this address is equal to the relative cell reference D10.

The cell reference expression can also be as simple as

[10;15]

In relative form, the preceding address would be J15. You can combine this address to create a range or block, such as

[10;15]:[12;20]

This address is the same as J15:L20.

You can use simple arithmetic in a cell reference expression to derive a cell address. For example, the following command string is valid for copying a single cell to multiple cells if the string is entered on the command line and GEORGE is a named range in the spreadsheet:

/C,A1,[CURCOL + 1;george/4]:[CURCOL + 23;george]~

If this command string in macro form is used in a worksheet, the result looks like figure 11.3.

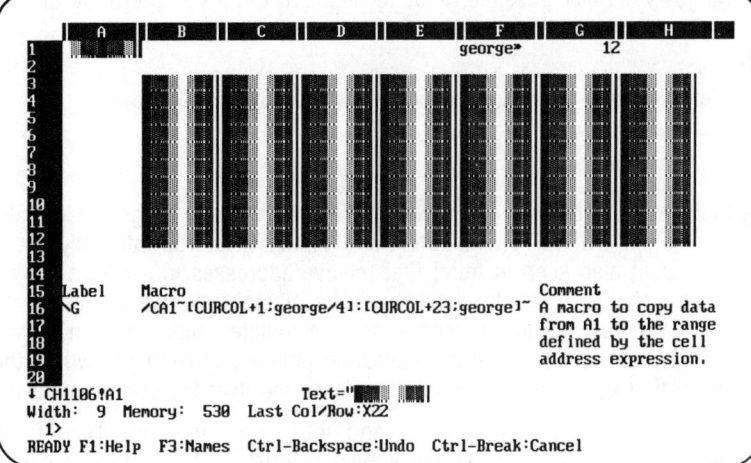

Fig. 11.3.
Macro using cell reference expressions.

This macro, named \G, takes whatever value or string is entered in cell A1 (in this case, a string of ASCII extended characters) and copies that value or string to each cell in the range defined by the cell reference expression. The expression [CURCOL + 1;george/4], which defines the beginning of the range, is equal to the relative address B3. Column B results because CURCOL + 1 equals column 2 (B), and row 3 results because 12 (the value stored in the named range GEORGE) divided by 4 equals 3. The expression [CUR-COL + 23;george], which defines the end or lower right corner of the range, is equal to the relative address X12, where X (the 24th column in the spreadsheet) equals CURCOL (1) plus 23, and 12 is the value stored in the named range GEORGE.

Together the two expressions define a range equal to the relative range B3:X12, given the situation defined in figure 11.3. Changing the value in GEORGE or moving the cell pointer to a different column, however, changes the outcome.

As you see from this example, cell reference expressions provide a way of converting stored values into range definitions. These expressions let you create macros that prompt users for range sizes. You also can define macro ranges by combining cell reference expressions with the index functions described in Chapter 7. You then have ranges sized conditionally, relative to the current cell pointer location, the last row of the spreadsheet or a named range, the size of a range, or a number of other derived parameters.

Helpful Hints

An entire book could be written on helpful hints for using macros, but the following three are fundamental:

1. Save your spreadsheet before executing a macro that will modify spreadsheet structure or content.

2. Use named ranges wherever possible; and, to highlight ranges in the body of the macro, use lowercase letters (this book discusses named ranges in uppercase).

3. Always begin macros with the following command, which turns off the /**G**lobal,**N**ext feature:

   "/G-N

The first hint is self-explanatory, but the other two may not be. Named ranges, especially functionally related names like BUDGET1, AMOUNT, and 4THQTR, let you internally document the macro. You should also keep in mind that relative addresses in a macro are no longer relative. If the size of the spreadsheet changes, the macro's relative addresses do not adjust with the spreadsheet. Using named ranges eliminates this problem. If an address should be relative, define the range by replicating pointing movements within the macro or use the cell reference expression techniques described in the preceding section.

The last hint is applicable only to SuperCalc macros (and not to 1-2-3 macros). This hint is necessary because SuperCalc has what is termed a **N**ext feature. If this feature is set to "on" when you press Enter, the cell pointer moves in the same direction as its last move. **N**ext helps you enter a row or column of figures because you have to enter only the number and press Enter to start the cell pointer advancing automatically down the column or across the row. In this way, you do not have to use a cursor key between entries (which is painful if you have a PC-compatible keyboard that combines the numeric pad and cursor-control keys in one set of keys).

The **N**ext feature in a macro, however, can turn on you. **N**ext can have unpredictable results if the direction is wrong or when the program issues a **N**ext when you really want to remain at a cell location. To have total control over your macro, use the preceding command above the macro or as part of the macro; or use the command manually to neutralize **N**ext before the macro executes.

Gaining Mastery of Macros

You have some flexibility in the way you create, name, execute, and store macros. This section covers the different alternatives available for performing these tasks.

Creating Macros

You can create a macro by entering the text string directly into a cell from the entry line, by using the //**M**acro,**L**earn system of LEARN mode and toggling between LEARN and DIRECT modes within that system, or by editing an eXecute file with an external word processor for disk-based macros. Both of the first two options (entry line or LEARN/ DIRECT) can, of course, be converted to an eXecute file by the //**M**acro,**W**rite command.

Entering Text

The simplest way to create a macro is to type the macro into your worksheet as a text entry. To create a macro command sequence, you must precede the slash (/) with a double quotation mark and then type the first letter of each command. For example, suppose that you want to enter the following command string into a text cell as a macro:

/Format,Global,Left

You type

"/FGL~

In macros, the tilde (~) represents the Enter key. If you did not include the tilde in this macro string, the macro would finish in the middle of the command string, leaving you "hanging" in the Format Global menu with the program expecting more input.

Suppose that you are automating a command string such as

/Format,Row,5,TextCenter

You type

"/FR5~TC~

or

"/FR~TC~

The difference between these two sequences is the range definition. In the first sequence, each time you execute this macro string, row 5 is formatted. In the second sequence, the row in which the cell pointer is located is formatted, so the second command is more generally useful. The second method is a form of relative addressing in which you define the address at the time of macro execution. The tildes are required every time SuperCalc expects the Enter key before continuing with the next command.

To represent range pointing, you need to use a macro keystroke representation. For example, to blank the range C5:C8, you can type at least four different sequences:

"/BC5:C8~

"/B.{DOWN}{DOWN}{DOWN}~

"/B.{DOWN 3}~

"/B[CURCOL;CURROW]:[CURCOL;CURROW+3]~

For the last three sequences to blank the range C5:C8, the cell pointer must be located in C5. The last sequence uses a cell reference expression that works the same as the other three methods. In the second and third sequences, {DOWN}{DOWN}{DOWN} and {DOWN 3} are both acceptable representations of the down-arrow key. You can abbreviate DOWN, CURCOL, and CURROW to DN or D, CCOL, and CROW, respectively.

As you can see in this simple example, you have available a variety of methods for creating macros in SuperCalc. Entering macros directly is difficult because you must envision the command sequence, decide which addressing method works best, and make sure that you place the Enter symbol (~) wherever it is required in the string. As you become fluent with

SuperCalc and start typing command strings instead of using the menu selector, the process of creating a macro string directly will become easier. You just type a double quotation mark on the entry line, close your eyes, and begin typing as if you were actually typing the command string.

Using LEARN Mode

LEARN mode requires more initial setup than entering data directly into a cell, but LEARN mode eliminates much of the thought required to plan and remember the commands. To see how LEARN mode works, you are going to create a macro that formats the spreadsheet globally.

Defining a LEARN Range

The first step in creating a macro with Learn is to define a LEARN range. To avoid having SuperCalc display an error message, define an entire column as a LEARN range. Only when you reach the lower edge of the spreadsheet will you see this error message:

    Learn range full; increase size and start learn again

If you are at the bottom of the sheet, you obviously cannot increase the current range size, so you will have to define another column instead. However, if you have used up a full column for a macro, your macro is very large, and you should try to reorganize the macro in another way. For many reasons, this situation is not likely to occur.

For learning purposes, define column A as the LEARN range by typing

   //Macro,Learn,A

Don't forget to press Enter.

Invoking LEARN Mode

Once you define the LEARN range (column A), you can invoke the processor. Be prepared, however, because after you invoke LEARN, all your input is echoed to the range (including backspaces and typing errors). To continue the learning process, press the Home key to move to cell A1. Press Alt-F4 to invoke LEARN mode. The word LEARN appears in the lower right half of the dialog panel.

With SuperCalc in READY mode and the cursor still in A1, type the following command and press Enter:

   /Format,Global,$,TextCenter,Width,12

Watch the LEARN range (column A) filling in with the commands you are entering.

Move the cell pointer four cells to the right to E1 in order to see how cell-pointer movement is represented by LEARN. Now type

   /Global,-Next

and

   /Global,Evaluation,When,Manual

The first of these two commonly used commands (/**G**lobal,-**N**ext) turns off the automatic cell pointer advance feature. The second command (/**G**lobal,**E**valuation,**W**hen,**M**anual) changes the program to calculate manually. Notice that both commands are stored by LEARN mode in a single cell (A3) as one long character string. LEARN continues to use the same cell for storing keystrokes until you press a key that requires a macro keyword representation to be stored (for example, {RT}). The processor then moves to the next cell down, storing each macro-keyword representation in its own cell.

To demonstrate how to use LEARN mode to store macro-keyword representations, press the down-, left-, up-, and right-arrow keys twice each. Then press Home. The results of these commands and cell pointer movements are shown in figure 11.4.

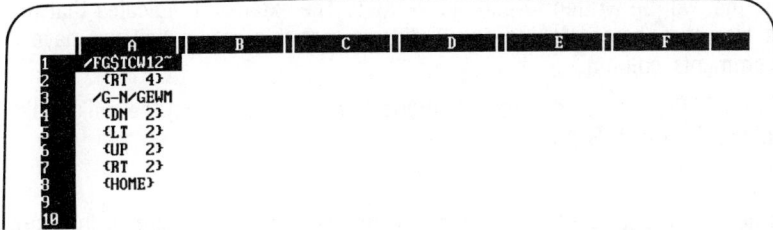

Fig. 11.4.

Creating a macro in LEARN mode.

As you can see, each direction keyword is stored in a separate cell. To avoid using up the LEARN range too quickly, however, the program automatically increments a number inside the keyword (for example, {DN 2}) to indicate that the keyword is repeated more than once. Comparing 19 cells containing the keyword {DN} with one cell containing the keyword {DN 19} demonstrates the significance of this number-incrementing feature.

Using DIRECT Mode

If you want to enter text or commands directly into the LEARN range instead of echoing your spreadsheet input, you can switch to DIRECT mode by pressing Alt-F6.

The macro mode indicator changes from LEARN to DIRECT. To see DIRECT mode work, type the following on the entry line:

    {DN}{RT}/TB~

This expression moves the cell pointer down one row ({DN}) and right one column ({RT}) and executes the command /**T**itle,**B**oth. In DIRECT mode, each keystroke is entered directly into the LEARN range without affecting the rest of the spreadsheet. The spreadsheet changes only when you execute the macro. In DIRECT mode, unlike LEARN, more than one keyword macro command ({DN}{RT}) can be stored in one cell. This flexibility is one advantage of using DIRECT.

To return to LEARN mode, press Alt-F6 again. Anything you type at this point will affect the spreadsheet and be echoed to the macro LEARN range. To get SuperCalc out of LEARN mode, press Alt-F4. The system returns to READY mode. If you reenter LEARN after this, the new commands will be added to the bottom of what is currently in the LEARN range.

Creating and Saving an eXecute File

The commands entered into the LEARN range can be useful each time you begin a new spreadsheet. If you store the commands in a macro (XQT) file, you can execute the macro from any spreadsheet. Macros affecting general formatting, graph and global settings, and printing, as well as macros affecting more than one spreadsheet, are good examples of macros that should be stored in eXecute files. You can consider the eXecute file a program and the spreadsheet a data file. By storing the commands separately, you separate the action steps from the data.

The partially created macro displayed in figure 11.4 can be saved as a file. You type

//**M**acro,**W**rite,**GF,A1:A9,M**acros-only

GF is the file name that will be written to disk as GF.XQT. The extension indicates that the file is an eXecute file. The choice **M**acros-only indicates that this macro will not have a label column or comments column.

The eXecute files are ASCII files stored in alphanumeric format. To see what the a file looks like, type the following at the DOS prompt:

TYPE GF.XQT

The result of this action, a display of the contents of the eXecute file, is shown in figure 11.5.

Fig. 11.5.

Contents of GF.XQT.

```
C>TYPE GF.XQT
{MACRO}
/FG$TCW12~
{RT 4}
/G-N/GEWM
{DN 2}
{LT 2}
{UP 2}
{RT 2}
{HOME}

C>
```

The file version of this macro reads the same as the spreadsheet version. The macro is stored in a simple ASCII format with the contents of each cell stored in a separate row. The /e**X**ecute command goes down the columns and executes the commands consecutively.

Creating a Macro in a Word Processor

Because eXecute files are ASCII (or text) format, you can create or edit them with a word processor. If you create a macro with this method, on the first line of the file, always type

{MACRO}

This word is entered automatically when you use the //**M**acro,**W**rite method.

Naming Macros

Several ways to name macros are available in SuperCalc. Among these are the following commands:

1. /**Na**me,**C**reate creates a single-letter name to be executed with the Alt-key combination.

2. /**Na**me,**C**reate creates a full-name macro that is executable by Alt-F5 plus the macro name.

3. /**Na**me,**L**abels names a range of macros.

4. The \AUTOEXEC file executes automatically when the spreadsheet is loaded.

One-Letter Names

The standard way to name a macro is to assign it a single letter (from A to Z) preceded by a backslash (\). For example, to give the name \G to the macro shown in column A of figure 11.3, you type the following from A1:

/**Na**me,**C**reate,\ **G,A1**

You have to name only the top cell of the macro because the macro processor will continue executing down a column until it encounters a blank cell, regardless of the dimensions of the named range.

Full-Name Macros

If you use more than one letter to name a macro, you have to execute it by a slightly different method. The name can be up to 32 characters long, and you do not have to precede it with a backslash (\). Using the backslash, however, makes macro names easier to identify. To try the naming procedure, move the cell pointer down to the cell in the example that starts with

/G-N

Name this cell \globsets by typing the following:

/**Na**me,**C**reate,\ **globsets,A3**

You can execute the column beginning with A3 by invoking the macro named \globsets using Alt-F5 and then entering the name or pointing to it in the Macro Name Directory, accessed by pressing Alt-F3.

The /Name,Labels,Right Command

If you divide a macro into a label column, macro column, and a comment column (the recommended design), you can name the macro by using the /**Na**me,**L**abels,**R**ight command. Suppose that you insert a column to the left of column A in the example by typing

/**I**nsert,**C**olumn,**A**

Then you can enter labels into the cells in column A and associate them with column B by typing

/**N**ame,**L**abels,**R**ight,**A1:A3**

Figure 11.6 shows this command during execution. The names have been entered in column A to be used as labels.

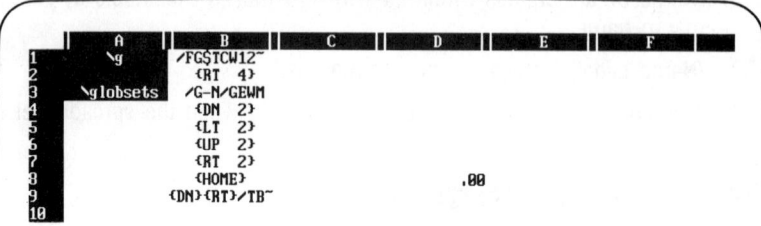

Fig. 11.6.

*Using /**N**ame,**L**abels,**R**ight to name a macro.*

\AUTOEXEC

If you are familiar with batch (BAT) files used by PC DOS and MS-DOS to execute system-level ''macros,'' you may recognize the word AUTOEXEC. If an AUTOEXEC.BAT file is on the disk from which you boot your computer, the commands in that batch file are executed automatically before the machine displays the DOS prompt. The same is true of a macro you name \AUTOEXEC. When you call up a worksheet containing an \AUTOEXEC macro, it is executed before you can access the worksheet.

The \AUTOEXEC feature enables you to create a structured, menu-driven application that begins when the user turns on the system and does not require that the user understand SuperCalc. Assuming that the macro begins in A1, you create this name as you would any other macro name, by typing

/**N**ame,**C**reate,**AUTOEXEC,A1**

In addition to the \AUTOEXEC named range, which executes automatically when the file in which it is stored is loaded, you also have the AUTOEXEC.XQT and AUTOEXEC.CAL file names. When you execute SuperCalc, it looks automatically for an AUTOEXEC.XQT file to load. If the program doesn't find one, it looks for an AUTOEXEC.CAL file to load. You can use these two files to execute a macro by simply typing **SC5**.

Executing Macros

Depending on the way you named or stored your macro, you can execute it in one of several ways.

Invoking Single-Key Macros

If you named the macro using the single-letter method (for example, \G in fig. 11.6), all you have to do to invoke the macro is press Alt-G. The macro processor then takes over. While SuperCalc is executing the macro, MACRO appears in the macro prompt area of the dialog panel.

Invoking Full-Name Macros

If you use more than one letter to name the macro (for example, \globsets in fig. 11.6), you can press Alt-F5 or Alt-=. The entry line changes to

5›=›A1

Now in upper- or lowercase you type **GLOBSETS**. When you press Enter, the macro begins processing. Instead of typing the macro name, you can press Alt-F3 to call up the Macro Name Directory. You can then point to \globsets and press Enter. The Alt-F5 or Alt-= procedure also works if you type or point to the macro's beginning cell address.

Invoking eXecute Files

To invoke the eXecute file GF, you type

//**M**acro,e**X**ecute,**GF**

The macro begins executing. If you do not remember the name of the eXecute file, you can press F3 to get to the File List screen and select the file from the list of XQT files shown.

Although the following sequence does not appear on the main menu, you can also use

/e**X**ecute,**GF**

Computer Associates provides this option to maintain compatibility with previous Super-Calc releases in which /eXecute is a main menu command. This command sequence is still the quickest way to execute a macro file.

Debugging Macros

Macros, like any procedural (programming) language, often do not execute correctly the first time. A macro that does not execute correctly can quickly destroy your data by deleting, copying, inserting, or otherwise altering the data in your spreadsheet.

The first step you can take to prevent damage is to save your worksheet before executing a major macro for the first time. Regardless of the havoc a macro wreaks during execution, you can always retrieve the "premacro" worksheet.

The second step you should take is to put SuperCalc in STEP mode. This mode helps limit the damage to a single command.

A STEP Example

Before executing your macro, press Alt-F2. The word STEP appears in the lower right side of the dialog panel, indicating that when you invoke the macro, SuperCalc will execute one command or keystroke at a time. Try using STEP with the \G macro in the example by pressing Alt-G.

After you press F8 once to execute the first command in the macro, the message at the bottom gives you information about the current step of the macro. In this case, the first step is the slash (/), which leaves the main menu on the screen. The message

```
(F8)STEP L:1  \G                B1        /FG$TCW12~
```

indicates that SuperCalc has halted execution at cell B1. This is only a single-level macro, so L:1 and the macro name (\G) are of limited use. In complex macros, this information is helpful because you find out which level you are at and the name of the current macro (rather than the one you executed). The current keystroke (F) is highlighted in the cell contents displayed on the right end of the help line. You must press the F8 key to proceed.

You can press Alt-space bar and the old STEP mode help line will appear instead of this improved line. It will tell you the current cell and space of the halted macro. If your macro has halted and is waiting for one of the prompts to continue (press Return or press F8) this STEP mode line will cover up the message and you will not be able to see it. The messages will not appear in the new format. You must press F8 to continue with the next step. To return to the new format, press Alt-space bar again.

If you do not want to press F8 each time but you want to observe the macro execute at an observable speed, you can press Alt-F8 to invoke ASTEP mode. Pressing Alt-F8 again toggles back to the manual STEP method. You can move back and forth between these two modes as often as you want.

Processing continues until you complete the macro or abort by pressing Ctrl-Break. By stepping through the macro, you can debug it by seeing at which step the macro begins to go astray. In effect, you are in control of the execution. In normal macro mode, the macro itself is in control of the execution. After locating the error, you can use the F2 key to edit the cell where the error is located, just as you would edit any text string (see Chapter 5).

SuperCalc remains in STEP mode until you press Alt-F2 again.

Macro Menu Support

Two of the options on the Macro menu are closely related to the STEP debugging mode: **T**race and **B**reakpoint. Using **T**race, you can echo the STEP mode help data to a printer or a file. Although organized in a different manner, the printer or file trace data contains the same basic data about the steps: level number, macro name, cell, and contents.

The **B**reakpoint system is a tremendous enhancement to your debugging. In a long macro, you can set up to eight breakpoints so that it will automatically execute until each breakpoint is reached. Then STEP mode will be invoked automatically. This way you do not have to step through each command if you have already narrowed it down to one area of the macro. To set a breakpoint, you select from the //**M**acro,**B**reakpoint. The following menu appears:

```
1  2  3  4  5  6  7  8  Zap
```

If you select **Z**ap at this level, all eight breakpoints will be cleared. To select your first breakpoint, enter **1**, which brings up the following choices:

```
Location  Condition  Zap
```

If you select **Z**ap at this level, only this breakpoint will be cleared. **L**ocation and **C**ondition are the two types of breakpoints you can enter. A **L**ocation breakpoint works as has been described. You specify a step in the macro as the break location, and every time the macro executes, it converts to STEP mode at that location and the message

```
Breakpoint n
```

appears in the error message area, where n is the breakpoint number. The other option, **C**ondition, is used to set a conditional breakpoint. Whereas in **L**ocation you enter a cell(or line number in a file-based XQT macro) within the macro to halt processing, with **C**ondition you specify a cell outside of the macro, containing a conditional value.

To demonstrate, say that you had a macro that contained the {FOR} command, which is used to make your macro repeat a specified number of times. Suppose that you wanted to go into STEP mode only during the fourth time through the macro. The iteration count for the {FOR} command is stored in a separate cell, which increments each time through. We will use B1 for this cell. You can enter the formula **B1 = 4** into cell C1 and define that as the condition cell. Because B1 is initially blank, C1 evaluates to 0 (false).

As the macro executes, B1 increments until it reaches 4, when the solution to B1 = 4 changes to 1 (true). The STEP mode is invoked so that you can step through the macro. The only problem with this method is that you must include a {CALC} command right after the {FOR} command so that the sheet recalculates and C1 (B1 = 4) changes to 1. Otherwise, even though you have automatic recalculation enabled, your spreadsheet does not recalculate during the macro execution. Hopefully this situation will be addressed in future releases.

You can resume normal execution again by pressing Alt-F2 to exit STEP mode.

Documenting Macros

The **T**race option on the Macro menu is a great help in debugging. **T**race is also a method of documenting your macro steps. The last option on the Macro menu to be discussed, **A**nalyze, is another great documenting tool. With //**M**acro,**A**nalyze, you can print all sorts of added information about one or all of your macros. To do this, first select **A**nalyze, which brings up the following selections:

```
Go  Range  Type  Output  Quit
```

This menu resembles the Output menu because **A**nalyze is an output command, but it is used only for macros. You define your range to analyze under **R**ange just like you would an output range. There is a slight difference, however. If you specify the range **A** to print using /**O**utput and it is the address of the beginning cell of a macro, only that initial cell will appear when you print it. If you specify **A** in the analyze range, information relating to the entire macro will be output. You execute the command with **G**o, just like the output command, and under the **O**utput option, you can choose to direct your output to a **P**rinter, **F**ile, or **C**onsole.

The remaining choice, **T**ype, is used to turn on and off several options for output. When you select **T**ype, the following options appear:

    Contents Transfers Modifies

If you did not define at least one of these types of outputs and selected **G**o from the menu above, an error message appears:

    No report type has been selected

With each option, you are choosing whether you want to see the contents of the macro or not, any and what type of transfers to make between macros, and what cells are affected by or changed by the specified macro.

The **C**ontents option is similar to a program listing. The contents for each macro included in the range are printed, one by one. The contents of macro \g in figure 11.6 is shown in figure 11.7.

Fig. 11.7.

Output from the
Contents option of
//Macro,Analyze.

```
Macro Analyzer Output Screen

CONTENTS OF MACRO RANGE \G [B1] :

\G
   [B1]    /FG$TCW12~
   [B2]    {RT  4}
\GLOBSETS
   [B3]    /G-N/GEWM
   [B4]    {DN  2}
   [B5]    {LT  2}
   [B6]    {UP  2}
   [B7]    {RT  2}
   [B8]    {HOME}
   [B9]    {DN}{RT}/TB~




   Press any key to continue, Control-Break to abort...
   20>//Macro,Analyze,Go,
MENU  Start Macro Analysis                               CAPS
```

With **T**ransfers you can select from these options:

To   From   Both   None

The **T**o option lists all macros that are called by other macros and includes the macro name, cell addresses, and cell contents relating to that transfer. **F**rom, on the other hand, lists all macros that call other macros. **B**oth will display both the **T**o and **F**rom responses. If you selected **B**oth, a call would appear twice: once under the **T**o and once under the **F**rom. If you select **N**one, then neither type appears on the output.

Modifies takes the same two-directional approach as **T**ransfers for analyzing the links between macro components: you can see which step modifies a cell and which cell is modified by a step. The choices are

Affects   Changed by   Both   None

Affects selects all macro commands that affect other cells in the spreadsheet in and out of the macro range. This option provides the cell location of the command in the macro and the cell locations of the affected cells. Likewise, **C**hanged by shows, in ascending order, the cells affected by the macro and the command, location within the macro, and the macro name of the affecting cell. If you select **B**oth, both relationships appear on the output.

Although they might not be needed for simple keystroke macros, the documentation tools provided in SuperCalc5 bring macro generation closer to full-fledged programming. Breakpoint analysis and cross-reference lists are both essential tools to creating complex program-style macros.

Understanding Macro Commands and Syntax

As with other more traditional programming languages, such as BASIC, COBOL, PASCAL, and C, to use macros to their fullest extent, you must understand the commands and—more important—their syntax. Fortunately, macros are less syntactically demanding than their programming counterparts. To use several of the commands effectively, however, you must understand their structure and syntax.

In this section, the discussion is divided according to the two main types of macros: keyboard representations and programming macros. The discussion includes both syntax and comparative analysis of the macros' uses.

Keyboard Control Representations

Every key on the keyboard can be represented in a macro. This section provides an overview of the keyboard representations. In most cases, the syntax required is not complicated; but to use the keys in a macro, you must understand the exact effect of each key in different situations and modes.

Cursor-Movement Keys

Cursor-movement commands react differently or not at all, depending on whether Super-Calc is in READY, POINT, MENU, or EDIT mode when you invoke the macro.

READY, POINT, or MENU Mode

All the cursor-control keys work in READY and POINT. Table 11.1 lists the cursor-control keys and the optional syntaxes allowed with macros. The x in the macro versions indicates the number of times SuperCalc is to execute the macro command. When the macro is created with **L**earn, as shown in figure 11.3, the program uses the x method to specify command repetition (for example, {DN 1}). This arrangement makes macro creation and interpretation easier and also saves space.

Table 11.1
The READY or POINT Mode Cursor Controls

Key	Macro Keyword
Down arrow, Ctrl-X	{DOWN},{DN},{DOWN x},{DN x}
Up arrow, Ctrl-E	{UP},{UP x}
Right arrow, Ctrl-D	{RIGHT},{RT},{RIGHT x},{RT x}
Left arrow, Ctrl-S	{LEFT},{LT},{LEFT x},{LT x}
End prefix	{END x} (Works with arrow keys and Home)
Tab prefix	{TAB x} (Works with arrow keys)
Backtab prefix	{BTAB x} (Works with arrow keys)
Home	{HOME x}
Enter	~ (tilde) Input as {~} in LEARN
PgUp	{PGUP},{PGUP x}
PgDn	{PGDN},{PGDN x}
Ctrl-left arrow	{PGLT},{PGLT x}
Ctrl-right arrow	{PGRT},{PGRT x}
Ctrl-Home	{HOMESCR},{HOMESCR x}
Ctrl-End	{ENDSCR},{ENDSCR x}

The cursor controls work in MENU mode; but in a macro, the better method is to move through the menus by typing the first letters of the commands. Table 11.2 lists the cursor controls that work in MENU mode.

Table 11.2
MENU Mode Cursor Controls

Key	Macro Keyword	Description
Cursor arrow	{RT},{LT}	Moves right and left through menu
Cursor arrow	{UP},{DN}	Moves between rows in a two-line menu only
Home	{HOME}	Moves to first selection on menu
End	{END}	Moves to last selection on menu
Space bar	{" "}	Moves right through menu
Tab	{TAB}	Moves between menu pages
Backspace	{BS}	Moves to next higher menu
Esc	{ESC}	Moves to next higher menu

EDIT Mode

Using macros to edit cell contents is a simple way to alter large amounts of data. With macros, you can perform editing tasks that otherwise might not be worth attempting. Knowing how the cursor-control keys work in EDIT mode will help you take advantage of this technique. Table 11.3 lists the cursor-control keys and associated macro commands available in EDIT mode.

Table 11.3
EDIT Mode Cursor Controls

Key	Macro Keyword	Description
Right arrow	{RT},{RT x}	Moves right across entry
Left arrow	{LT},{LT x}	Moves left across entry
Home	{HOME}	Moves to start of entry
End	{END}	Moves to end of entry
Tab	{TAB}	Moves from start to end of entry
INS	{INS}	Toggles on/off INSERT mode

The cursor-control keys enable you to move to specific locations, but you use other keys to delete and add text. Table 11.4 describes those keys.

The last two items in table 11.4 are macro commands that work in relation to the EDIT function. In a macro, {INS} switches the toggle to the opposite of what it was. For example, if SuperCalc is in INSERT mode when you invoke the macro, {INS} invokes OVER-WRITE mode. {INSERTON} and {INSERTOFF} are not toggles. {INSERTON}, regardless of the mode the spreadsheet is in when you invoke a macro, activates INSERT mode. You maintain much more control of the execution by using {INSERTON} and {INSERTOFF} than by using {INS}.

Table 11.4
EDIT Mode Text-Modification Keys

Key	Macro Keyword	Description
INS	{INS}	Toggles on/off INSERT mode
Up arrow	{UP},{UP x}	Inserts spaces in entry
Down arrow	{DN},{DN x}	Deletes character to the right
Del	{DEL x}	Deletes character to the right
Backspace	{BS x}	Deletes character to the left and moves cursor left
Esc	{ESC x} {INSERTON} {INSERTOFF}	Clears/restores entry toggle Initiates INSERT mode Initiates OVERWRITE mode

Program-Control Keys

Program-control keys affect your location in the program, the mode SuperCalc is in, and program interruption. Two of these keys, backspace ({BS}) and Esc ({ESC}), reverse direction within the command string.

The remaining cursor-control keys—Ctrl-C, Ctrl-Z, and Ctrl-Break—interrupt execution of a command string and return SuperCalc to READY mode. In a macro, you use {READY} to represent all three of these keys.

Function Keys

Function keys play an important role in macros. See table 11.5 for a list of the regular function keys, their macro equivalents, and descriptions.

Table 11.5
Function-Key Macro Equivalents

Key	Macro Keyword	Description
F1	{HELP}	Accesses AnswerScreen
F2	{EDIT}	Toggles on/off EDIT mode from ENTRY or POINT; from READY, calls up cell contents to the entry line.
F3	{NAME}	Displays the file directory on Save and Load menus. In /View, F3 displays graph names and, in other modes, displays the Named Range Directory.
F4	{ABS}	Toggles between the four variations in absolute references in ENTRY mode. In the file directory, F4 makes the current directory setting the default.

Table 11.5—*Continued*

Key	Macro Keyword	Description
F5	{GOTO}	Moves to a specific cell location
F6	{WINDOW}	Toggles between windows on the spreadsheet
F7	{TLABELS}	Toggles between name and reference display in formulas
F8		Resumes macro execution
F9	{CALC}	Causes the spreadsheet to calculate or, in ENTRY mode, the entry formula to be solved
F10	{VIEW}	Views the currently selected graph

Another set of actions occur when you press Alt and then the function key. In SuperCalc4, these functions were used strictly in support of the macro function. In SuperCalc5, the original Alt-function keys serve their same purpose, but five new functions are added. Table 11.6 summarizes all of them.

Table 11.6
Alt-Function-Key Macro Equivalents

Key	Macro Keyword	Description
Alt-F1	{AUDIT}	Enters AUDIT mode
Alt-F2	{STEP}	Switches between single-step and normal MACRO execution
Alt-F3	{MACRONAME}	Displays the Macro Name Directory
Alt-F4	{LEARN}	Switches LEARN mode on and off
Alt-F5	{INVOKE}	Executes a specified macro
Alt-F6	{DIRECT}	Switches from LEARN mode to DIRECT mode
Alt-F8	{RESTORE}	Turns on ASTEP mode from STEP mode and restores a string removed with ESC
Alt-F9	{PLOT}	Plots a chart

Alt-F8 takes on a double function. In SuperCalc4 Alt-F8 was used to restore to the entry line a string that was previously erased using the Escape key. The macro name representation is {RESTORE}. Now, the more prevalent use of Alt-F8 is to convert to ASTEP mode when in STEP mode. When not in STEP mode, however, F8 still acts as the restore function.

Multiple Sheet and Multipage Movement Keys

With the advent of multiple active spreadsheets and multipage spreadsheets, a whole new set of keyboard controls have been added to move between sheets and pages and to support that capability. Table 11.7 lists all of their macro equivalents.

Table 11.7
Alt-Function-Key Macro Equivalents

Key	Macro Keyword	Description
Ctrl-F3	{RSD}	Accesses the referenced spreadsheet directory
Ctrl-F4	{OSD}	Accesses the open spreadsheet directory
Ctrl-F5	{GOTOSHEET}	Moves to the specified sheet
Ctrl-F6	{SHEETWINDOW}	Toggles between spreadsheet windows
Ctrl-F7	{ZOOMSHEET}	Zooms in on the active sheet
Ctrl-Enter	{NEWSHEET}	Opens a new sheet
Ctrl-plus	{NEXTSHEET}	Moves to the next sheet in the cycle
Ctrl-minus	{PREVSHEET}	Moves to the previous sheet in the cycle

Most of these keys are a combination of the Ctrl key and another key, whether a function key or other. Two of them ({GOCURRENT} and {GOMACRO}) are really programming keys but support the third-dimensional features and so are included in this section.

Programming Macros

Unlike macro keyboard representations, macro programming commands cannot be created from echoed keystrokes. They must be entered in DIRECT mode. You may find these full-word commands similar to programming language commands. One set of these commands handles errors and controls the user interface (screen-control commands); another set controls the order of execution (logic commands); a third set enters and formats data (data-input commands); and a fourth set controls access to external ASCII storage files.

Screen-Control Commands

With the exception of {BEEP}, screen-control commands can be divided into two types. The first kind includes {ENTRYOFF} and {ENTRYON}, {PANELOFF} and {PANELON}, and {WINDOWSOFF} and {WINDOWSON}. These commands consist of pairs of commands for toggling off or on a specific SuperCalc function.

The second kind includes

{ERRMSG ''xxx''}	{ERRMSG}
{INDICATOR ''xxx''}	{INDICATOR}
{MACROPROMPT ''xxx''}	{MACROPROMPT}
{MESSAGE ''xxx''}	{MESSAGE}
{PROMPT ''xxx''}	{PROMPT}
{STATUS ''xxx''}	{STATUS}

This set consists of pairs of commands for changing a display message and then returning it to the default message. Table 11.8 provides a summary of all the screen-control commands.

Table 11.8
Macro Screen-Control Commands

Command	Result
{BEEP exp}	Sounds computer's bell
{ENTRYOFF}	Clears entry line
{ENTRYON}	Restores normal operation of entry line
{ERRMSG string}	Controls the error message area of status line
{INDICATOR string}	Controls program mode indicator
{MACROPROMPT string}	Controls macro prompt area of help line
{MESSAGE string}	Controls help message area of help line
{PANELOFF}	Clears entry line and holds dialog panels
{PANELON}	Restores normal dialog panel operation
{PROMPT string}	Controls prompt line
{STATUS string}	Controls status line
{WINDOWSOFF}	Holds current window while macro processes
{WINDOWSON}	Restores normal window operation

The best way to see these commands in action is to create a macro. Beginning with cell A1, type the screen-control commands in the order shown in figure 11.8.

Name the macro \A by moving the cursor to A1 (Home) and typing

/Name,Create,\A,A1

To see how each command affects the display, turn on the STEP feature by pressing Alt-F2. To invoke the macro, you press Alt-A. To turn off the enhanced STEP debugging information, press Alt-space bar.

As the macro executes one command at a time, you can see which command changes which on-screen message or feature. Figure 11.9 shows the results of the first command, {PROMPT "prompt"}. In READY mode, the prompt line displays some general spreadsheet

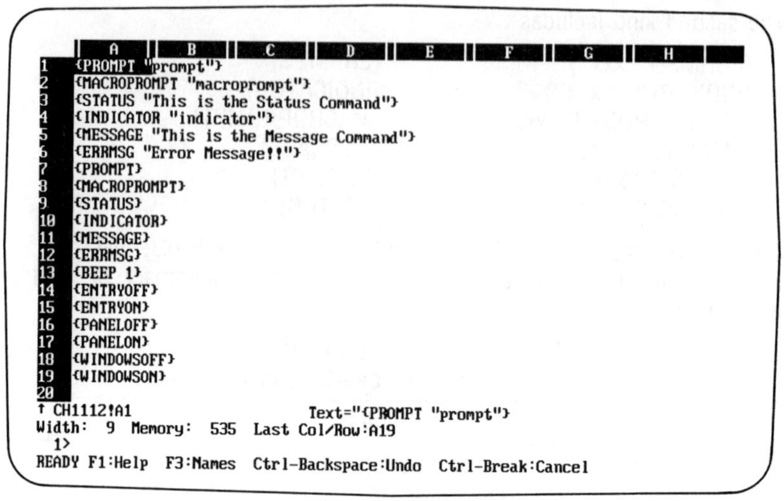

Fig. 11.8.

Screen-control macro.

```
          A       B         C        D       E       F       G       H
 1  {PROMPT "prompt"}
 2  {MACROPROMPT "macroprompt"}
 3  {STATUS "This is the Status Command"}
 4  {INDICATOR "indicator"}
 5  {MESSAGE "This is the Message Command"}
 6  {ERRMSG "Error Message!!"}
 7  {PROMPT}
 8  {MACROPROMPT}
 9  {STATUS}
10  {INDICATOR}
11  {MESSAGE}
12  {ERRMSG}
13  {BEEP 1}
14  {ENTRYOFF}
15  {ENTRYON}
16  {PANELOFF}
17  {PANELON}
18  {WINDOWSOFF}
19  {WINDOWSON}
20
 ↑ CH1112↑A1                     Text="{PROMPT "prompt"}
 Width:  9  Memory:  535  Last Col/Row:A19
     1>
 READY F1:Help  F3:Names  Ctrl-Backspace:Undo  Ctrl-Break:Cancel
```

statistics on current column width, memory available, and the last active cell address. In MENU mode, the prompt line contains the menu selections. You can redefine the prompt line to display any message you want, including a blank (" ") if you want nothing to appear. (The message can be as long as the width of the display.) The {PROMPT} in row 6 resets the prompt line back to the current setting.

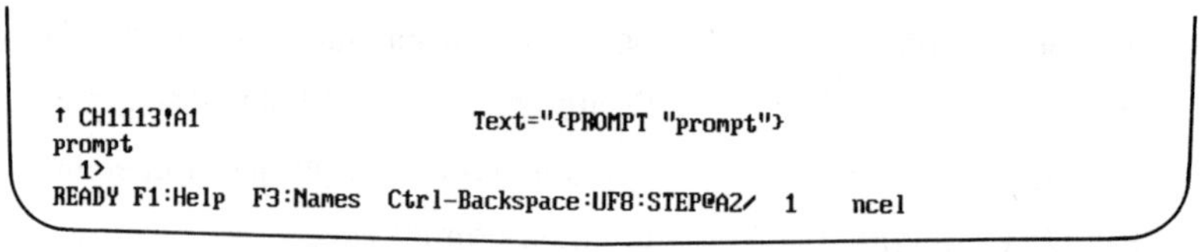

Fig. 11.9.

Dialog panel after {PROMPT "prompt"} is executed.

```
 ↑ CH1113↑A1                     Text="{PROMPT "prompt"}
 prompt
     1>
 READY F1:Help  F3:Names  Ctrl-Backspace:UF8:STEP@A2/  1    ncel
```

Press F8 five times to execute the next five commands: {MACROPROMPT "macroprompt"}, {STATUS "This is the Status Command"}, {INDICATOR "indicator"}, {MESSAGE "This is the Message Command"}, and {ERRMSG "Error Message!"}. Figure 11.10 shows the dialog panel after SuperCalc executes these five commands.

The first command redefines the macro prompt status, which usually displays MACRO, STEP, ASTEP, LEARN, or DIRECT.

The second command redefines the status line, which usually has an arrow indicating which way an Enter would move the cell pointer, the current cell pointer address, and the contents of that cell.

The third command redefines the indicator message, which usually indicates the spreadsheet mode (READY, MENU, EDIT, ENTRY, POINT, FILE, or NAME). Your redefined indicator message can be only five characters long. If it exceeds five characters, SuperCalc truncates the message, as you can see in the lower left corner of figure 11.10 where the word indicator is truncated to indic.

```
This is the Status Command                              Error Message!!
prompt
    1>
indic This is the Message Command        macroprompt
```

Fig. 11.10.
Dialog panel after four
more macro
commands are
executed.

The fourth command in this group redefines the message area on the help line. This command usually displays a help message to assist you in interpreting your choices in the system. The message can be up to 49 characters long.

The last command shown redefines the error message area at the right end of the status line. Up to 76 characters of the string in {ERRMSG "xxx"} will appear in the error message box, in which case it would take up the entire length of the status line.

Execute the next six commands (press F8 six times) and watch these message areas return to their defaults.

{BEEP 1} is the next command (row 13). Press F8 to execute this command. Although the screen's appearance does not change, the computer emits a distinctive (possibly unpleasant) tone. You can experiment by changing the number 1 to another number; but after a few of iterations, beware of the wrath of your coworkers, office mates, neighbors, family, cellmates, or other people within earshot. If you need to interrupt this command, you press Ctrl-Break.

To demonstrate {ENTRYOFF} and {ENTRYON}, located in A14 and A15 in figure 11.8, move the cell pointer to cell F1. Type some text—for example, the much-used

asdf; lkj

Now move the cell pointer to F2 and execute {ENTRYOFF} by pressing F8 once. Notice that the entry line in the dialog panel has been eliminated (no more 1›). Enter some text in F2. As you type, the characters do not appear on the entry line at the bottom of the screen as they normally do. When you press Enter, you see that the text is stored in F2, although the text did not appear as you typed. Figure 11.11 shows the screen as it looks at this stage.

The STEP function shows you that the macro is at F8:A15 /1, positioned before the {ENTRYON} command. Press F8 once again, and the 1› reappears, indicating that the entry line is back in operation. You can enter more text to verify that your text will be echoed on the entry line once more.

{PANELOFF} and {PANELON}, the next two commands in the macro shown in figure 11.8, affect the entire dialog panel. Not only does {PANELOFF}, like {ENTRYOFF}, clear the entry line, but the command freezes the entire dialog panel to look as it appears at the time of execution. Press F8 once to demonstrate. The dialog panel should indicate that the cell pointer is in F3. Then move the cell pointer down to F4, enter some text, and press Enter. As you can see, this command reacts the same way as {ENTRYOFF}. But if you look closely at the screen, which should look like figure 11.12, you will notice that the dialog panel still indicates that the cell pointer is located at F3, although it really is located at cell F5.

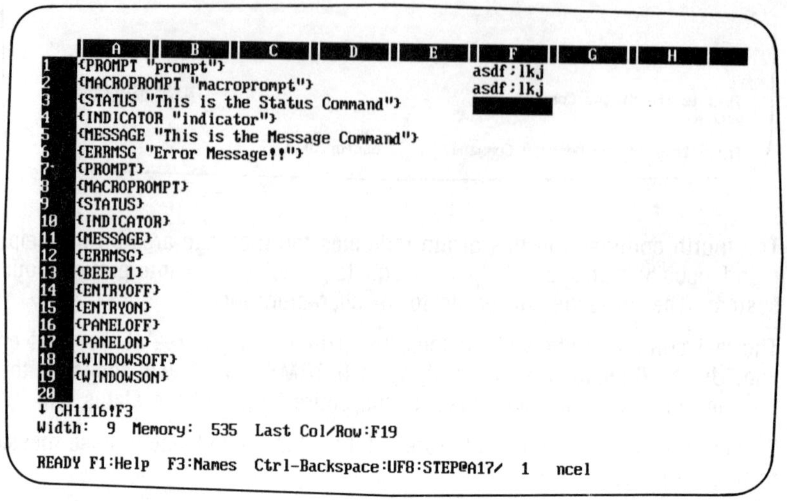

Fig. 11.11.

*Macro with
{ENTRYOFF} executed.*

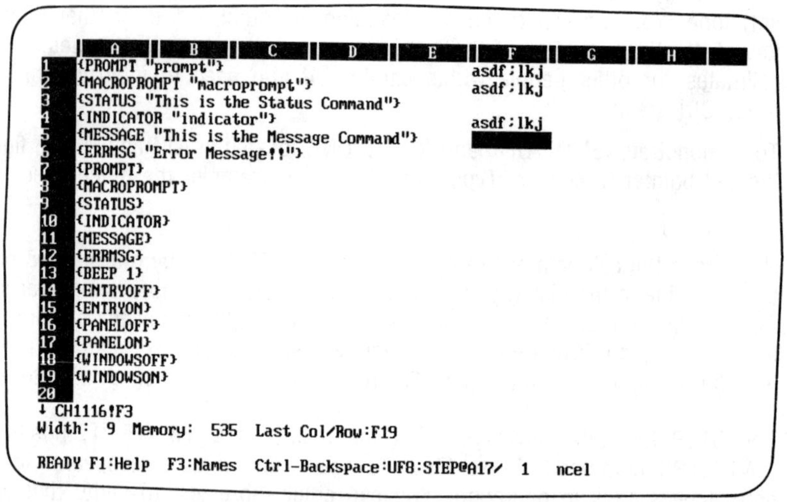

```
     A          B          C          D          E          F          G          H
 1  {PROMPT "prompt"}                                              asdf;lkj
 2  {MACROPROMPT "macroprompt"}                                    asdf;lkj
 3  {STATUS "This is the Status Command"}
 4  {INDICATOR "indicator"}
 5  {MESSAGE "This is the Message Command"}
 6  {ERRMSG "Error Message!!"}
 7  {PROMPT}
 8  {MACROPROMPT}
 9  {STATUS}
10  {INDICATOR}
11  {MESSAGE}
12  {ERRMSG}
13  {BEEP 1}
14  {ENTRYOFF}
15  {ENTRYON}
16  {PANELOFF}
17  {PANELON}
18  {WINDOWSOFF}
19  {WINDOWSON}
20
 ↓ CH1116↑F3
Width:  9  Memory:  535  Last Col/Row:F19

READY F1:Help  F3:Names  Ctrl-Backspace:UF8:STEP@A17/  1   ncel
```

Fig. 11.12.

*Macro with
{PANELOFF} executed.*

```
     A          B          C          D          E          F          G          H
 1  {PROMPT "prompt"}                                              asdf;lkj
 2  {MACROPROMPT "macroprompt"}                                    asdf;lkj
 3  {STATUS "This is the Status Command"}
 4  {INDICATOR "indicator"}                                        asdf;lkj
 5  {MESSAGE "This is the Message Command"}
 6  {ERRMSG "Error Message!!"}
 7  {PROMPT}
 8  {MACROPROMPT}
 9  {STATUS}
10  {INDICATOR}
11  {MESSAGE}
12  {ERRMSG}
13  {BEEP 1}
14  {ENTRYOFF}
15  {ENTRYON}
16  {PANELOFF}
17  {PANELON}
18  {WINDOWSOFF}
19  {WINDOWSON}
20
 ↓ CH1116↑F3
Width:  9  Memory:  535  Last Col/Row:F19

READY F1:Help  F3:Names  Ctrl-Backspace:UF8:STEP@A17/  1    ncel
```

You can move the cursor all over, but the cell pointer location continues to appear as F3 in the dialog panel. All the other status indicators in the panel (for instance, Memory, Last Col/Row, and Width) also remain the same. When you press F8 again, {PANELON} activates the dialog panel again. The panel then updates to reflect the current status. If a {PANELON} is not executed in a macro to reactivate the dialog panel, the command automatically executes at the conclusion of the macro to reactivate the dialog panel for normal operation.

{WINDOWSOFF} is not the macro equivalent of /Window,Clear. This macro command freezes all displayed lines above the dialog panel. You should use {WINDOWSOFF} only when the spreadsheet is on-screen because the command terminates the macro if you use it while an Options Screen is displayed. Press F8 to execute {WINDOWSOFF}. While it is in effect, the cell pointer will not move to match your cursor movements, and SuperCalc will not update the screen when you enter text into the cells. Only if you press Help (F1) will the screen change. When you are done with help, the help screen remains until you press help again, a {WINDOWSON} command executes, or you interrupt the macro.

After you execute the next command, {WINDOWSON}, the system updates the screen to reflect all the changes you have made since the {WINDOWSOFF} was executed. Like {PANELOFF}, {WINDOWSOFF} is canceled by the completion or termination of the macro.

Logic Commands

Logic commands are the source of much of the power of SuperCalc's macro system. Without them, you could not alter the sequential flow of macro execution.

Most program logic can be divided into three groups: sequential, repeating, and conditional. SuperCalc provides methods for handling all three kinds of logic—and some specialty commands as well. See table 11.9 for a summary of the logic commands.

Table 11.9
Macro Logic and Programming Commands

Command	Result
{BRANCH label}	Continues executing macro at another location without returning to original location
{BREAKOFF}	Turns off Ctrl-Break during macro
{BREAKON}	Turns on Ctrl-Break during macro
{CALL label exp,exp}	Continues executing macro at another location, then returns to original location
{COMMENT text}	Stores comments within macros
{DEFINE cell,cell}	Enters {CALL} arguments into specified cells
{DELAY nn}	Delays execution of macro
{DISPATCH}	Causes macro to branch to specified cell location
{FOR count,start,stop, step,start-location}	Repeats the specified macro at start-location ($stop - start$) * $step$ times
{FORBREAK}	Ends a {FOR} repeating macro command
{GOCURRENT}	Returns to the premacro active spreadsheet
{GOMACRO}	The macro spreadsheet becomes the current spreadsheet.

Table 11.9—*Continued*

Command	Result
{IF cc}	Executes a new macro depending on a conditional statement
{LABEL}	Names a location in macro files
{LET location,string}	Places a value in the specified cell
{MACRO}	Indicator of SuperCalc macro file
{MENU label}	Indicator of menu
{ONBREAK location}	Redefines the location after a Ctrl-Break
{ONERROR macro,message loc}	Error handling routine
{QUIT}	Exit the executing macro
{RESTART}	Called macro becomes the master macro
{RETURN}	Returns called macro to master macro

For additional examples of these commands, load the sample macro spreadsheet included with SuperCalc, press Ctrl-Break to exit from macro execution, and print the spreadsheet. This spreadsheet uses in a working macro many of the commands discussed in this section.

Controlling Time with {DELAY exp}

{DELAY exp} is a specialty command that delays the execution of a macro for 1 second to up to 24 hours. The *exp* (expression) can be a number, cell reference, or formula and should be entered in terms of seconds. To delay more than 24 hours, you must use another {DELAY exp} command.

Creating Subroutines with {CALL label exp,exp}

In terms of SuperCalc, a *subroutine* is a set of macro commands located in a different section of the spreadsheet and "called" from the main macro. After performing its task(s), the subroutine passes control to the next command in the main macro. Sometimes you need to execute a set of commands several times in various parts of a macro. You can repeat the commands each time you need them. Using a subroutine call, however, you can put the commands in a different area and call them from specific places in the main macro. The call method reduces the overall length of the macros.

{CALL} is the main command for executing a subroutine, and the syntax is

    {CALL label exp,exp}

In this command, *label* is a named range defined somewhere in the spreadsheet, and each *exp* is any type of expression (for instance, text, values, or cell references) that you want to pass along to use at the new location.

You can nest {CALL} 32 levels deep before SuperCalc loses track. Other related commands are {RETURN}, {DEFINE}, and {RESTART}. A {CALL} executes until the first blank cell is encountered or a {RETURN} is issued. In either case, macro control returns to the statement following the {CALL}. On the other hand, {RESTART} causes the macro to forget the location of the call, and control does not return to the main macro. Instead, the control remains within the called subroutine, which, in essence, becomes the main macro.

You can use {DEFINE} with {CALL} to pass variables to cells for use with the call subroutine. The general syntax for passing variables using {CALL} and {DEFINE} is

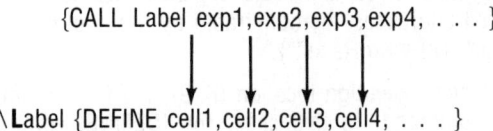

{CALL Label exp1,exp2,exp3,exp4, . . . }

\Label {DEFINE cell1,cell2,cell3,cell4, . . . }

Expressions 1 through 4 in the {CALL} statement are stored in cells 1 through 4 designated in the {DEFINE} command in the subroutine. If *exp1* is the value 100, the {DEFINE} statement defines *cell1* as the location in which the value 100 should be stored. If *cell1* is A1, when the macro encounters the {DEFINE A1} command, 100 is stored in cell A1.

Figure 11.13 is a simplified example of various subroutine calls. The macro in figure 11.13 starts executing when you press Alt-A. The operation begins with cell B2, the location of the range \a. The first step in the macro is to use the /Blank command on the range G2:G20, where the results of this macro appear. The macro then uses the {LET} command (which you learn about in a later section) to store the textual string THE in cell G2. The next step, in cell B3, changes the message area in the dialog panel to read

    This is a Call Example

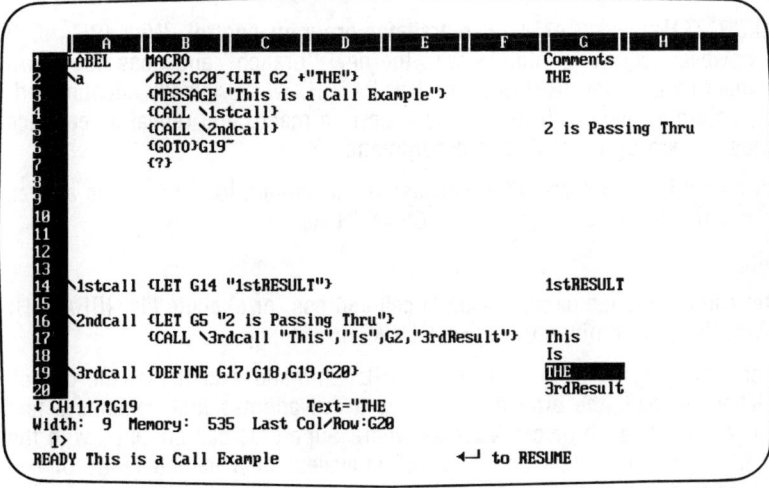

Fig. 11.13.
Subroutine calls.

Then the first {CALL} is executed in B4, causing macro control to transfer from cell B4 to cell B14—the range \1stcall. (The subroutine \1stcall just stores the textual string 1stRESULT in G14.) The macro then transfers control back to the command following the {CALL \1stcall} command in B4, the next {CALL} command in cell B5. This call, {CALL \2ndcall}, transfers control to cell B16, the range named \2ndcall. The first command in this subroutine is a {LET} command that stores the textual string 2 is Passing Thru in cell G5. The next command is another {CALL}, demonstrating that a {CALL} can be executed from within a subroutine macro. This {CALL} command transfers control to the range \3rdcall in cell B19; and, in addition, the command specifies four expressions to be transferred to the subroutine (\3rdcall). The transferred expressions can be textual strings, This, Is, and 3rdResult, as well as cell addresses, demonstrated by the address G2 in the command: {CALL \3rdcall "This", "Is", G2, "3rdResult"}.

To use the expressions transferred to the new execution location (B19), the first command in the subroutine must be a {DEFINE} command. In this case, the {DEFINE} command instructs SuperCalc to store the four expressions that were sent along with the transfer of control—in cells G17, G18, G19, and G20, respectively. As the figure shows, the four expressions are stored in the range G17:G20, as directed. Finally, control is passed back through \2ndcall to the main macro, and the command {GOTO}G19~ is executed, moving the cell pointer to cell G19. The command {?}, located in B7, is then executed, causing the macro to pause; and as the message in the macro prompt area at the bottom of the screen indicates, the macro waits for the user to press Enter to resume macro execution.

Figure 11.13 demonstrates the use of nested {CALL} commands, the {DEFINE} command, and the {LET} command, as well as the types of expressions that are allowed with each command.

Repeating Logic with {BRANCH label} and {DISPATCH cell}

{BRANCH} and {DISPATCH}, like {CALL}, also transfer program control. With {BRANCH} and {DISPATCH}, however, control continues with the new ''branch'' and does not return to the step in the macro where the {BRANCH} or {DISPATCH} was originally encountered. These commands, therefore, allow you to loop back up in a macro and repeat a sequence of macro commands or skip a group of macro commands.

The {BRANCH} command is used more often because it can branch to a macro file as well as a spreadsheet macro. The general syntax for {BRANCH} is

{BRANCH label}

The *label* parameter can be a range name, absolute cell address, or eXecute file. {BRANCH} is demonstrated with the {IF} command in the next section.

The {DISPATCH} command is similar to the {BRANCH} command except that the branch location is not a label. Instead, the branch location is a cell address that contains a text string consisting of a named range or cell address where SuperCalc can continue with the macro. The cell address must contain a text string equivalent of a named range or cell address, not just a named range. For example, if you type the named range **newloc** on the entry line without the preceding double quotation mark, the expression is entered into the cell as a formula, like this:

    form = \newloc

In addition, a zero appears in the cell display. If you enter the expression as

    "\newloc

the expression acts as a text string and appears as \newloc in the cell display, not as 0. A good use of {DISPATCH} is to specify a spreadsheet cell address to execute files that return control of the macro to the spreadsheet.

Using {IF}

{IF} is the primary conditional logic used in SuperCalc. The general syntax for this command is

    {IF cc}

The *cc* parameter is a conditional statement that can be evaluated as either true or false. If the condition is true, the next statement on the same line is executed; otherwise, the statement in the next row is executed.

Using this simple logic, you can set up complex arguments. Figure 11.14 uses the same macro as figure 11.13, but with an {IF} command inserted in cell B7 to cause the macro to execute five times before finishing.

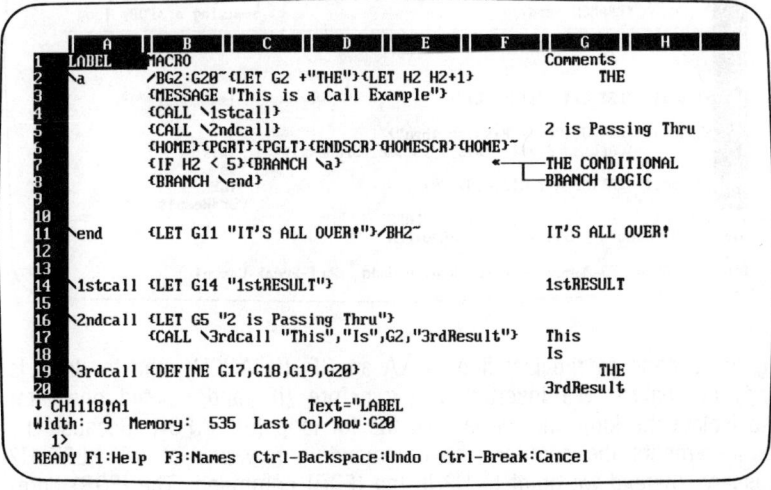

Fig. 11.14.

Demonstration of the {IF} command.

As long as the value in H2 is less than 5, the conditional {IF H2 < 5} command evaluates as true, and control branches back to the beginning of the macro (\a). Coupled with the {IF} command is an added {LET} command in B2. This {LET H2 H2 + 1} command increments the counter cell (H2) value by 1 each time through the macro. When the value in H2 equals 5, the {IF H2 < 5} command evaluates as false, and the macro control is transferred down instead of to the right, causing the command {BRANCH \end} in cell B8 to execute.

Figure 11.14 demonstrates the {IF} command used with a counter cell for conditional execution of a macro. The figure also shows how a {BRANCH} command, used with the {IF} command in B7, causes the program to transfer to another location without returning control to the {BRANCH} point.

Including Logic with {FOR}

Now included in SuperCalc5 is the command {FOR} with the following syntax:

{FOR count,starting value,ending value,increment,start location}

{FOR} replaces many situations where, in SuperCalc4, you would have had to use the commands in the preceding section, {BRANCH} and {DISPATCH}, along with {IF} for repeating logic. Now a loop (repeated logic) can be accomplished by this more advanced command. Figure 11.15 shows how {FOR} would replace {BRANCH} in figure 11.14.

Fig. 11.15.

Demonstrating the {FOR} loop.

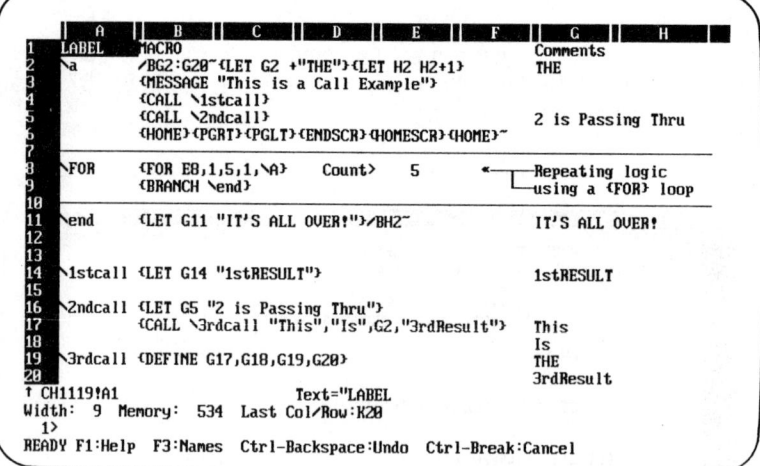

Instead of making the second to the last line of \A an {IF}-{BRANCH}, the for loop is executed as a separate macro. We inserted a row before {IF} and deleted one after {BRANCH \end} to isolate the loop and we labeled the for loop (B8) \FOR. Because the loop automatically increments the counter, the command in row one of \A ({LET H2 H2+1}) is unnecessary. Instead we point to H2 in the {FOR} command. The {FOR} command then means

For H2 incrementing from 1 to 5 by 1 then execute macro \A

To initiate processing, press Alt-F5, Alt-F3, select \FOR from the Macro Name Directory, and press Enter. After the loop is done the logic continues on to the cell below the loop ({BRANCH \end}).

The {FOR} loop, then, combines and replaces three other commands: {IF}, {BRANCH}, and {LET}.

Using {MENU}

{MENU} is a powerful SuperCalc command. With {MENU} you can create custom menus like the SuperCalc menu system. These custom menus use the system's menu cursor controls. The general syntax of the command is

{MENU label}

The *label* parameter is the cell address or file name to which control is transferred when Esc is pressed. If no label is indicated, a {RETURN} is executed, which transfers control to the next line following the menu-related lines. Menus can be stored in the spreadsheet or in eXecute files.

Spreadsheet-Based Menus

Figure 11.16 is an example of {MENU} used in a spreadsheet-based macro. The first line following the {MENU} command contains the menu choices that appear on the prompt line when the macro is executed. Each choice is stored in a separate cell on the line.

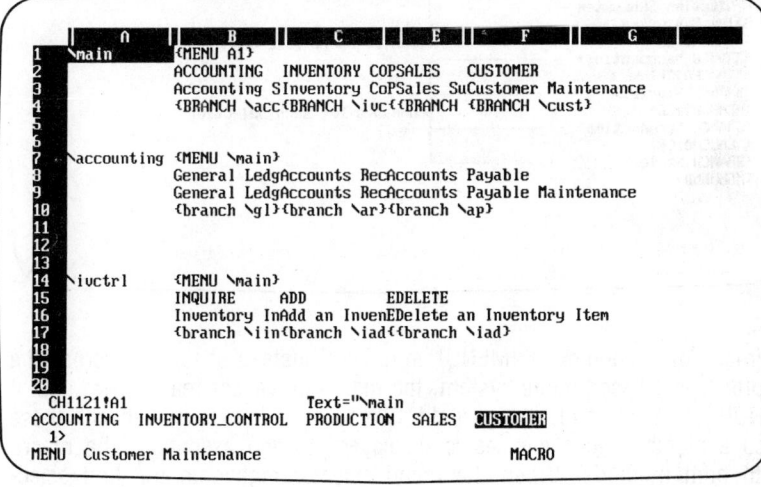

Fig. 11.16.

Execution of the {MENU} command.

The second line below the {MENU} command contains the help messages that appear in the message area of the help line when the macro is executed. Each message is stored in a separate cell on the line below the appropriate menu selection. Each message appears only when the menu selector is located on the selection above the message.

The next line contains the commands that are executed when the related menu choice is selected. Figure 11.16 shows the selections appearing as menu choices when the macro is executed.

eXecute File Menus

The structure of a file-based menu is different from that of a spreadsheet-based menu because only one column is available in an eXecute file. When the {MENU} command is encountered in a spreadsheet-based macro, the macro flow moves across the cells in the following rows, including each cell as a menu choice, and then continues downward through the column in which the selected menu choice is located. To convert this entire process to a single column for eXecute-file macros, three additional macro commands have been added: {MENUHELP}, {MENUCHOICE}, and {MENUEND}. Figure 11.17 shows an eXecute file structure.

Fig. 11.17.

An eXecute file structure.

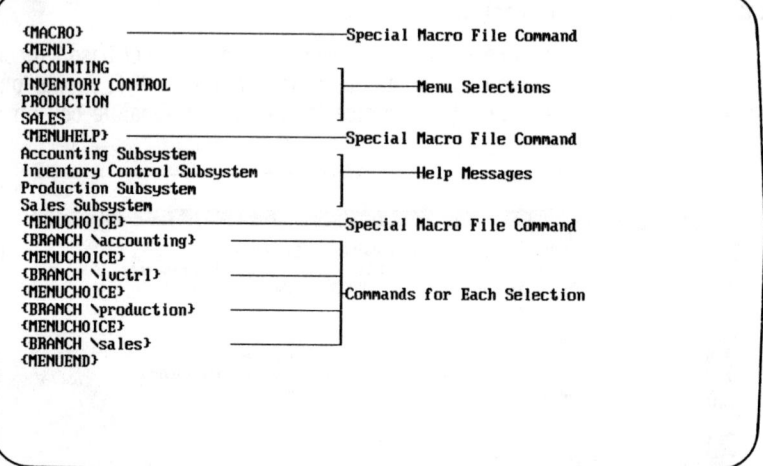

When the macro processor encounters a {MENU} command, instead of reading across the next row as in a spreadsheet-based menu system, the macro processor reads down until it encounters a {MENUHELP} command. In figure 11.17 you have four rows between these two commands, so a menu of four choices is displayed. During execution, the macro looks identical with both methods. When the menu selector highlights the first selection (ACCOUNTING), the associated help message is displayed on the help line. With the macro-file menu, however, instead of reading down the row to get the associated menu help message (Accounting Subsystem) and next command to execute ({BRANCH

\accounting}), the processor looks for the help message in the first row of the {MENUHE-LP} section and locates the first {MENUCHOICE} command. The processor then executes all commands up to the next {MENUCHOICE} command.

Similarly, if SALES, the fourth menu selection, is highlighted and selected, the processor displays the text in the fourth row following the {MENUHELP} command and executes the commands following the fourth {MENUCHOICE} command. The {MENUEND} command is placed at the end of the menu section to serve the same function as an END statement in BASIC language or ENDCASE or ENDDO function in dBASE III.

The //**M**acro,**R**ead and //**M**acro,**W**rite commands automatically convert to this format if you have only one menu in the macro. With more than one menu, SuperCalc translates only the first menu correctly. The system does not recognize the second menu and does not translate it correctly. If you create the eXecute file in a word processor, you will have to organize the file like the example in figure 11.17.

With a multimenu macro, you can create menus in SuperCalc, read them out to an eXecute file one at a time, and combine them again in a word processor. If the macro is complex, however, creating it directly in the word processor may be easier.

Defining Variables with {LET}

{LET} enables you to define variables (cell contents) from a macro. The general syntax is

    {LET cell,exp}

The *exp* expression can be a string, number, function, or cell address.

{LET} is used extensively in figures 11.13 and 11.14 when demonstrating the {CALL} and {BRANCH} commands. Each time the macro executes from the top, the {LET} command is used to increment the counter cell by 1 ({LET H2 H2 + 1}). When the value in H2 equals 5, the {IF} evaluates as false and the macro ends.

Handling Interruptions

{BREAKOFF} disables the use of Ctrl-Break during macro execution. This feature is important when you create applications for other users and do not want them to access the worksheet or interrupt the execution.

{BREAKON} enables the Ctrl-Break key. {ONBREAK label} enables you to redefine what occurs when a Ctrl-Break occurs. SuperCalc resumes execution at the label indicated in the command instead of halting the macro. {ONBREAK} restores normal action.

{FORBREAK} automatically terminates a {FOR} loop whenever it is encountered, no matter what count it is at. The macro control resumes with the cell following the loop.

{ONERROR newloc,messageloc} is used to handle errors that occur during execution. Figure 11.18 demonstrates the {ONERROR} command.

In the example, \E contains an {ONERROR} command and an /e**X**ecute command that is attempting to execute a range which is not on the disk. A cell reference expression is used to store the error messages at the bottom so that more than one message can be seen. With an ordinary cell reference (B16), the old message would be overwritten by the new

Fig. 11.18.

{ONERROR} in action.

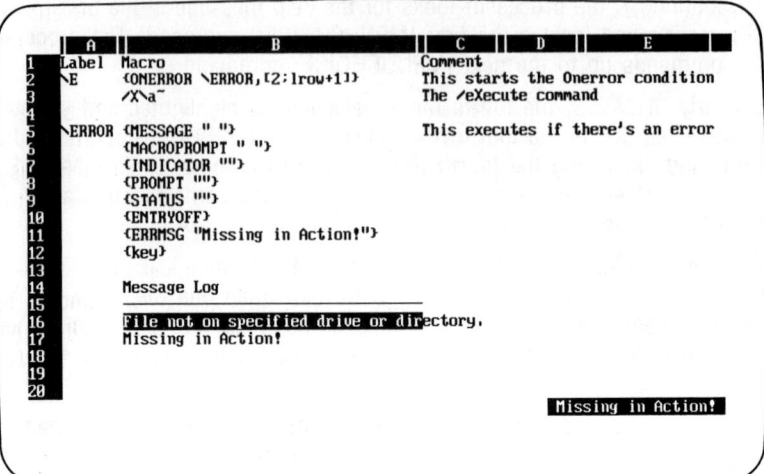

Fig. 11.18.

{ONERROR} in action.

message. When an error is encountered, macro control is transferred to \ERROR, which turns off much of the dialog panel, redefines the {ERRMSG}, and pauses for input using the {KEY} command. The first time Alt-E is pressed the first message is stored and the message Missing in Action! appears in the error message box. When Alt-E is executed again at the {KEY} command, the message Missing in Action! is stored instead of the first message because the error message was redefined as such the first time through the macro.

SuperCalc provides many error and interruption handling commands so that you can take full control of the user's actions if you create comprehensive, user-friendly macros.

Documenting with {COMMENT}

The {COMMENT} command enables you to document a macro. SuperCalc does not execute any line containing the {COMMENT} command. This command has two different versions of syntax:

{COMMENT text}

and

{COMMENT} text

The two are handled differently when the macro is read into the spreadsheet from a macro file. If *text* is within the braces, as in the first syntax, the text is placed in the macro column. If *text* is to the right of the command, as in the second syntax, the text is placed in the *Comments* section in the next column.

Using {MACRO}, {LABEL}, and {QUIT}

{MACRO} and {LABEL} are used in an eXecute file and are created automatically where necessary when you use the //Macro,Write command to create the eXecute file. {MACRO} should be in the top row of the file to identify it as an eXecute file, and {LABEL name} is used with {BRANCH label}. {LABEL} is placed above the beginning of the range of rows the command identifies.

{QUIT} terminates a macro from within the macro. When SuperCalc encounters a {QUIT}, the system stops the macro, then executes the {PANELON}, {BREAKON}, and {WINDOWSON} commands to return full control of the program to the user.

Data Input Commands

The //**D**ata,**I**nput commands are used to interface with the user and to format and limit what the user enters. See table 11.10 for a review of SuperCalc's macro data input commands.

Table 11.10
Macro Data Input Commands

Command	Result
{BACKUP}	Conditional response for creating a file backup when saving a file that is already present on disk
{BLANK location}	Blanks a range of cells
{BLANKC location}	Blanks a range of cell contents only
{GET cell}	Causes a macro to wait for an entry to store in a specified cell
{GETCELLS prompt,cell}	Causes a macro to wait for a cell range to store in a specified cell
{GETCOLS prompt,cell}	Causes a macro to wait for a column range to store in a specified cell
{GETKEY prompt,cell}	Causes a macro to wait for a key to store in a specified cell
{GETNUMBER prompt,cell}	Causes a macro to wait for a value to store in a specified cell
{GETROWS prompt,cell}	Causes a macro to wait for a row range to store in a specified cell
{GETTEXT prompt,cell}	Causes a macro to wait for a label to store in a specified cell
{INSERTOFF}	Deactivates INSERT mode
{INSERTON}	Activates INSERT mode
{KEY}	Causes a macro to wait for the input of a key

Table 11.10—*Continued*

Command	Result
{LETCONTENTS location,exp}	Places expression in *location*
{LOOK location}	Puts character from type-ahead buffer into *location*
{OVERWRITE}	Conditionally saves and overwrites existing file
{READY}	Returns to READY mode
{REPLACE}	Conditional replacement for /**L**oad and /**I**mport
{RECALC range,cond,iter}	Recalculates a range *iter* times
{RECALCCOL range,cond,iter}	Recalculates a range by row *iter* times
{SUSPEND}	Causes a macro to halt until F8 is pressed
{?}	Causes a macro to halt until Enter is pressed
{{}	Inserts an open brace into a macro line
{}}	Inserts a closed brace into a macro line
{~}	Inserts a tilde into a macro, which represents a carriage return

{INSERTON} and {INSERTOFF}

You can use {INSERTON} and {INSERTOFF} only in EDIT mode. Regardless of the current setting in the spreadsheet, {INSERTON} invokes INSERT mode for purposes of entering data.

{INSERTOFF} invokes OVERWRITE mode. These two commands are a more controlled method for selecting INSERT and OVERWRITE modes than is the {INS} macro keyboard representation.

{BACKUP}, {OVERWRITE}, and {REPLACE}

SuperCalc warns you if a file already exists on disk when you use the /**S**ave or //**M**acro,**W**rite commands to save a file. This feature saves you from mistakenly replacing a file on disk, that you do not intend to replace. If SuperCalc finds on the disk a file matching the file name you entered after either of these two commands, the following menu appears:

```
Change  Backup  Overwrite
```

The first option, **C**hange, returns you to the file name part of the command to change the file name you have entered. The second selection, **B**ackup, replaces the CAL extension of the file on disk with a BAK extension and writes the file you want as the CAL version (similar to the method used with word processors to preserve the old version of a file). The third option, **O**verwrite, simply replaces the version of the file on disk with the spreadsheet on-screen (in memory).

This feature is valuable during normal use of SuperCalc, but causes a conditional logic situation within the framework of a macro. If a file already exists on disk with the name you have entered, the program asks whether you want to back up or overwrite that file. If, however, the file is not on disk, the **B**ackup or **O**verwrite option is not necessary and does not appear. For example, for the file EXAMPLE.CAL, suppose that you try using the macro command

"/Sexample.cal~A

meaning

/**S**ave,**example.cal,A**ll

If no file already exists on disk, the macro works. But if you execute the macro again (with the file EXAMPLE.CAL already written to disk once), the program halts at the

    Change Backup Overwrite

menu and beeps. Because this menu occurs conditionally, the commands {BACKUP} and {OVERWRITE} were added to SuperCalc. If, on the menu

    Change Backup Overwrite

you usually select **B**ackup, you use the {BACKUP} command to do the same in a macro. On the other hand, if you usually overwrite the file on disk, you use the {OVERWRITE} command in a macro.

These two commands execute conditionally only if the Backup/Overwrite menu appears, so you have one file-saving macro to cover both situations (write a new file out and replace or back up the existing file). To save EXAMPLE.CAL to disk, you use the macro command

"/Sexample.cal~{OVERWRITE}ALL~

No matter what the situation, this macro executes correctly. In other words, these commands execute only if needed.

The same is true of the {REPLACE} command. When you want to load a spreadsheet using the **R**eplace option, SuperCalc double checks with you before doing it but only if your current spreadsheet has been modified since the last save. To handle this conditional prompt, you can use the string

/Lfile~R{REPLACE}

Commands for Blanking

Two commands have been added in SuperCalc5 to handle blanking. They are {BLANK range} and {BLANKC range}. In SuperCalc4 you had to use the command string /B~ and /B,C to do the respective functions. {BLANK range} will erase the contents and the format of a cell or cell range. {BLANKC range} will blank the contents only of a cell or cell range.

Recalculation Commands

{RECALC} and {RECALCCOL} are two new commands for recalculating a range. {RECALC} calculates by row and {RECALCCOL} calculates by column. The syntax for {RECALC} is

{RECALC range,(condition),iteration}

where *range* is the range to be recalculated, *condition* (optional) will cause the range to recalculate until the condition evaluates as true (1), and *iteration* forces a specific number of recalculations.

{LOOK}

You can find out whether anything is in the type-ahead buffer by using the {LOOK} command. The syntax is

{LOOK location}

where *location* is a cell address to store the type-ahead character if found.

{LETCONTENTS}

New with SuperCalc5, {LETCONTENTS} also places the result of the command into a cell location. Its syntax is

{LETCONTENTS location,"formula"}

where *formula* can be enclosed in quotation marks or not. Unlike its cousin {LET}, this command places the actual formula into a cell instead of the value of the formula, so that

{LETCONTENTS C1,A1 + B1}

places the formula A1 + B1 into cell C1 instead of the value of the solution. If you use a cell address instead of a formula, the cell address will be placed in the location cell. So, to place into the location cell a formula that is stored in another cell, you must use the CONTENTS(loc) function like this:

{LETCONTENTS C1,CONTENTS(C2)}

This function places the formula from C2 into C1 instead of the cell reference itself.

Unformatted Input

Three commands can be used to interrupt execution, ask for user input, and then store the input in the cell in which the cell pointer is located. The commands are {KEY}, {?}, and {SUSPEND}. {KEY} halts macro execution; the next key pressed is entered on the entry line and used in the context of the macro. The {?} command halts execution of the macro until the Enter key is pressed. Until Enter is pressed, the message

↵ to RESUME

is displayed in the macro prompt area in the dialog panel.

{SUSPEND} interrupts execution until the F8 function key is pressed. This command is used instead of {?} in situations where the Enter key is required during the suspended part of the macro. The message displayed is

F8 to RESUME

Figure 11.19 shows a macro that demonstrates the effects of these commands. This figure also shows the use of the {GET . . .} commands, which are described in the following section. Using the commands together emphasizes the difference between the unformatted input commands ({KEY}, {?}, and {SUSPEND}) and the {GET} commands.

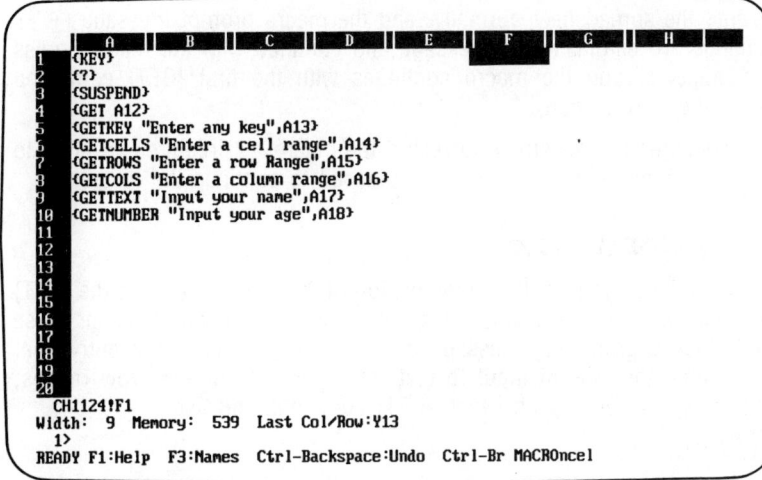

Fig. 11.19.

Alternative methods of input.

To understand these different commands, enter the macro in this figure into your Super-Calc spreadsheet and name cell A1 \A. For this macro, make sure that the /**G**lobal,**N**ext feature is switched on by typing

/**G**lobal, + **N**ext

Then move the cell pointer to cell F1 and press Alt-A to invoke the macro. The word MACRO should be displayed in the macro prompt message area, as in figure 11.19. Now enter **1**. Notice that the message changes to

↵ to RESUME

This message means that the first command, {KEY}, has completed and that you are stopped at the second command, {?}. The 1 was all the input needed to answer the {KEY} prompt. The 1, you notice, remains on the entry line.

Now press the down-arrow key, which stores 1 in F1, and move the cell pointer down to F2. The macro prompt message should not change yet. Type **2** and press Enter. Normally, this action would cause 2 to be stored in F2, and the cell pointer would move to F3. Instead, the 2 remains on the entry line and the macro prompt message changes to

```
F8 to RESUME
```

The {?} interruption has been satisfied, and the {SUSPEND} command in A3 has been encountered. Press Enter once again. This time, the 2 is stored in cell F2, and the cell pointer is moved down one cell to F3. Now type the following (pressing Enter after each)

```
Suspend1
Suspend2
Suspend3
```

This text is entered into the spreadsheet normally, and the macro prompt message F8 to Resume does not change. To eliminate this message and continue with the macro, press F8. The message disappears, and the macro continues with the first {GET} command (which is discussed in the next section).

Remember that {KEY} requires any keystroke to restart the macro, {?} requires an Enter to continue, and {SUSPEND} requires the F8 key to be pressed to continue the macro.

The {GET . . . } Commands

The preceding commands linked your input to the position of the cell pointer, but the {GET} commands redirect your input to the location specified in the command. Most of these commands let you include a prompting message that is displayed above the entry line. These commands also limit the type of input to text, numbers, cell ranges, row ranges, column ranges, or any key, depending on which {GET} command you use.

{GET} and {GETKEY}

The {GET} command is the most general form of the seven {GET . . . } commands. Like the {KEY} command in the preceding section, {GET} interrupts the macro execution, but because the general syntax of {GET} is

```
{GET cell}
```

the key entered is redirected to the cell specified in the command. In figure 11.19, the cell specified in this command (see A4) is cell A12. Continue with the macro started in the preceding section. Even though the cell pointer is located at cell F6, the next printable key you press is entered in A12 (the cell specified in the command), not in F6 (the cell pointer position). Press any key and watch it be stored in cell A12.

The macro stores the keystroke as a textual string in cell A12 in the form

```
Form=("$")
```

instead of simply a text string of the form

```
Text="$
```

This storage form is used by both the {GET} command and the {GETKEY} command, discussed next. SuperCalc does this because, as an expression within a macro, a textual string can be used more universally with formulas and other macro commands.

The {GETKEY} command, which is the next command in the macro, is similar to the {GET} command. The syntax is

{GETKEY prompt,cell}

This command not only redirects your input to the *cell* you specify, but also displays your *prompt* above the entry line, like this:

```
Enter any key
     1›
```

This prompt is entered in the {GETKEY} command in A5 (see fig. 11.19). Any key you press is stored in A13 (the cell specified) as a textual string—not where the cell pointer is still located (F6).

{GETCELLS}, {GETCOLS}, and {GETROWS}

The {GETCELLS}, {GETCOLS}, and {GETROWS} commands work similarly to the {GETKEY} command in that you can specify a prompt and a cell to store the result. In each case, though, you must enter a spreadsheet address range. {GETCELLS} accepts only a valid cell range; {GETCOLS} accepts only a valid column range; and {GETROWS} accepts only a valid row range.

Each command defaults to the address of the cell pointer and invokes POINT mode. That is, when the command is encountered, the address of the cell pointer is automatically entered on the entry line. In the case of {GETCELLS "Enter a cell range", A14} in figure 11.19, the prompt line and entry line look like this:

```
Enter a cell range
     3›F6
```

When you press Enter, the text "F6:F6 is entered in cell A14 as a single cell range.

With the {GETROWS "Enter a row range", A15} command in A7, the prompt line and entry line look like this:

```
Enter a row range
     2›6
```

When you press Enter, the text "A6:IU6 is stored in cell A15, and the macro moves on to the next command.

The {GETCOLS "Enter a column range", A16} command in A8 acts similarly except it expects a column range and defaults to the cell pointer's current column like this:

```
Enter a column range
     2ˆF
```

The text "F1:F2000 (depending on your spreadsheet boundary setting) is stored in A16 if you press Enter to accept the default range.

{GETTEXT} and {GETNUMBER}

The next two commands in the macro, {GETTEXT} and {GETNUMBER}, operate the same as the preceding {GET . . .} commands except that you can enter anything with {GETTEXT} and it is stored as text; but with {GETNUMBER}, you can enter only numbers that are stored as numbers. Figure 11.20 shows the macro from figure 11.19 after the macro ends.

Fig. 11.20.

Input macro after execution.

```
      A         B         C         D         E         F         G         H
1   <KEY>                                                         1
2   <?>                                                           2
3   <SUSPEND>                                         suspend1
4   <GET A12>                                         suspend2
5   <GETKEY "Enter any key",A13>                      suspend3
6   <GETCELLS "Enter a cell range",A14>
7   <GETROWS "Enter a row Range",A15>
8   <GETCOLS "Enter a column range",A16>
9   <GETTEXT "Input your name",A17>
10  <GETNUMBER "Input your age",A18>
11
12  !
13  $
14  F6:F6
15  A6:DW6
16  F1:F2000
17  John Doe
18        65
19
20

↓ CH1125!F6
Width:  9  Memory:  535  Last Col/Row:Y18
    1>
READY F1:Help  F3:Names  Ctrl-Backspace:Undo  Ctrl-Break:Cancel
```

File Control Commands

An entire class of macro commands have been added in SuperCalc5 called *file control commands*. With the commands listed in table 11.11, you can access an external ASCII text file on disk. You can read selective data into SuperCalc from the file and write it out to the file.

The ASCII sequential file format is a traditional format for many programming languages. With the inclusion of this set of file control commands, the SuperCalc macro language moves one step closer to a programming environment. Because of this improvement, one person can access a file on disk using the BASIC language and another can access it using the SuperCalc interface.

How you use these commands will vary greatly, depending on your specific application. Because this concept is new to many spreadsheet users, we will demonstrate with a simple example, which will allow you to complete the cycle (write out to a file and read in from a file) successfully. Figure 11.21 shows the example we will use. Notice that cells D1 through D5 are labeled *Filesize* through *Position*, respectively.

Through the macro you store the list of names in the range labeled *Group* (B16:B20) into an ASCII file called GROUP.DAT; convert them to proper format (initial capitals) as the storage happens; and read and redisplay the converted string stored in the file into the cell to the right. Column D contains several related values that are input to or from the macro.

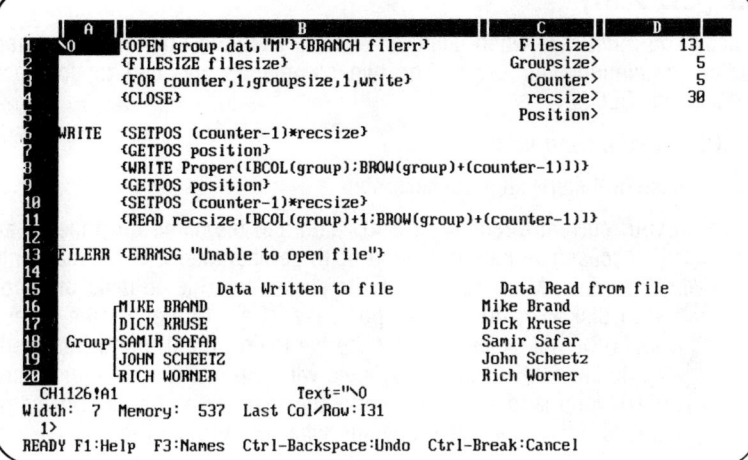

Fig. 11.21.

A file control macro using {WRITE} and {READ}.

Table 11.11
Macro File Control Commands

Command	Result
{CLOSE}	Closes an opened ASCII storage file
{FILESIZE cell}	Size of file in bytes
{GETPOS cell}	Stores file pointer position in a cell
{OPEN filename,access mode}	Opens an external ASCII file for storage
{READ character count,cell}	Reads in a string of characters from a file
{READLN cell}	Reads in a line of characters from a file
{SETPOS pointer value}	Sets a new file pointer position
{WRITE string}	Writes out a string of characters to a file
{WRITELN string}	Writes out a line of characters to a file

{FOR} is used to repeat the macro for each line of the group. With these file commands you will use repetitive logic for each line of data, and you will need to come up with effective ways to calculate rows and positions within the file. The iteration count (*Counter*) that the {FOR} command uses is a helpful tool for positioning the cell pointer. Employing cell reference expressions is also helpful.

{OPEN} and {CLOSE}

The first and last steps you must take when using an external file is to open it for use and close it back up after completing your tasks. The two commands provided to do these operations are {OPEN} and {CLOSE}.

The syntax for the {OPEN} command is as follows:

{OPEN filename, accesstype}failure step success step

Filename can be a file on your current directory or a full path and file name for a file on an alternate drive or directory. *Accesstype* has to be one of three characters: R for read-only access to an established file on disk, M for read and write access to a file on disk, or W for write access for a new file on disk. You must use uppercase letters to identify the access type. *Failure step*, which, like {IF}, will execute only if the file is not found, is not required. However, having an error route like FILERR in the example will help clarify why your macro is not working. If the {OPEN} command does not work, the rest of the file control commands do not execute and it is not immediately obvious what the problem is.

After you complete your work with the file, use the {CLOSE} command to close it.

To create a new file called GROUP.DAT, the following two-line macro will suffice:

{OPEN GROUP.DAT, "W"}
{CLOSE}

As a result, an empty file (0 bytes) named GROUP.DAT will be listed in the directory to which SuperCalc is currently logged.

The access code "M" is used in figure 11.21 because GROUP.DAT is already created. For established files, "M" is used to let the user read from the file and write to the file like the macro in this figure. You might want some users only to read from the file, in which case you would use "R" instead.

{FILESIZE}

The second line of the macro in figure 11.21 is the {FILESIZE location} command. This command calculates the size of the opened file and stores the size in the cell indicated in the *location* argument. In this example, the location is D1. Initially that value is 0 because the file is empty.

{SETPOS} and {GETPOS}

As mentioned, it is important to know the position of the cursor within the file. Two commands, {SETPOS} and {GETPOS}, are included to set the position and identify the position of the cursor in the file, respectively. {SETPOS} has the following format:

{SETPOS value}

where *value* can be a literal value, formula, function, cell reference, or any combination thereof used to identify the character position where you want the cursor placed. When the file is first opened, the cursor is located before the first character in the file, which is position 0.

If you do not know what the position is during macro execution, you can use the {GETPOS location} command to identify the current position and enter it into the cell you specify. In figure 11.21, the value from the {GETPOS} command is entered in the range position (D5). It is very useful for recording the position of the cursor before an action takes place so that you can quickly return to that position.

If you execute the macro in STEP mode, you can see the different positions of the cursor at different steps of the macro. The first command in the WRITE range is {SETPOS (counter − 1)*recsize}. This form of the command is relative to the count of the {FOR} loop. The first time through, (counter − 1)*recsize equals 0 because the record size is being multiplied by counter − 1, which equals 0. The {GETPOS position} command identifies that. After the {WRITE} command, the {GETPOS} command changes cell D5 to 10, which is the number of characters in the first name. To reread the string just written, we repeat the {SETPOS} command, which backs up the cursor 10 spaces to the beginning of the file. In the example, we put the {GETPOS} command after the {WRITE} command to highlight the effects of the {WRITE} command on the cursor. If we had not updated the stored position with the {GETPOS} after the {WRITE}, the second {SETPOS} could have been simplified to

{SETPOS position}

instead of recalculating the original position. This demonstrates how the two commands are closely linked and can be used together effectively.

In this example, we want to create a fixed-length file with all the data stored in one long character string. We use the {SETPOS} command to set the position in increments of 30 characters each time through the macro. So if you were to enter

TYPE GROUP.DAT

at the DOS prompt, the screen would look like figure 11.22.

```
C>TYPE GROUP.DAT
Mike Brand              Dick Kruse              Samir Safar
        John Scheetz            Rich Worner
C>
```

Fig. 11.22.

Example file written using {WRITE}.

Notice the names list in one long string of 30 characters each.

{WRITE} and {READ}

In the figure we use the {WRITE} command to write out the string to the file. The syntax of {WRITE} is as follows:

{WRITE string}

The defined string is written out, and the cursor is positioned on the last character of the string.

The {READ} command, then, has the syntax

{READ stringlength, sheetlocation}

where a string of length *stringlength* is read from where the cursor is positioned and placed in the specified sheet location. The cursor is left positioned at the end of the string in the file.

Although the strings vary in length, each name uses the same space (30 characters) because the cursor is repositioned to an increment of 30 right before the {WRITE} is done.

{WRITELN} and {READLN}

In comparison, {WRITELN} and {READLN} write and read entire lines of data from a file. If we read the GROUP.DAT file using the {READLN} command, all the names appear on one line. This is because these commands use the ASCII carriage-return (CR) character, which is the decimal value 13 in ASCII, and the linefeed (LF) character, which is the decimal value 10 in ASCII characters, together to mark the end of each record and position the cursor (they also add two characters to the size of each record).

When a {WRITELN string} command is used, the CR and LF characters are tacked onto the end of the string so that a new line is created for each string. If you were to enter

TYPE GROUP.DAT

for a file created with the {WRITELN} command, the result would look like figure 11.23.

Fig. 11.23.

Example file written using {WRITELN}.

```
C>TYPE GROUP.DAT
mike brand
dick kruse
samir safar
john scheetz
rich worner

C>
```

Because the computer understands the meaning of the CR and LF combination, it executes a CR to move the cursor back to the left edge of the screen and a LF to move down a line, organizing the data in a much more legible and structured format.

You can mix {WRITE} and {WRITELN} together so that when you create a record such as a mailing list of name, address, city, state, and ZIP, you can write out each field using the {WRITE} command. Then issue a {WRITELN ""} command at the end to write out the CR and LF, or only use the {WRITELN} for the last field in the record (ZIP).

Unlike {READ length,location}, with {READLN location} you do not have to identify the length of string you want because an entire line, up to the next CR and LF, is read. Figure 11.24 is similar to the macro in figure 11.21 except that this macro shows the use of the {WRITELN} and {READLN} commands.

As long as you couple the correct read command with the write command that you used, you will be fine. If your computer recognizes the full ANSI character set (IBM's extended ASCII character set) and you get two characters resembling the ace of spades and a musical eighth note, you will know you are trying to {READ} a {WRITELN}-created file because those two symbols represent the CR and LF characters.

```
     ┌─A─┬──────────────B──────────────┬──────C──────┬──D──┬─
  1 │\0 │{OPEN group.dat,"M"}{BRANCH filerr}  Filesize>     131
  2 │   │{FILESIZE filesize}              Groupsize>       5
  3 │   │{FOR counter,1,groupsize,1,write}  Counter>       5
  4 │   │{CLOSE}                            recsize>      30
  5 │   │                                  Position>      51
  6 │WRITE {GETPOS position}
  7 │   │{WRITELN lower([BCOL(group):BROW(group)+(counter-1)])}
  8 │   │{SETPOS position}
  9 │   │{GETPOS position}
 10 │   │{READLN [BCOL(group)+1:BROW(group)+(counter-1)]}
 11 │
 12 │FILERR {ERRMSG "Unable to open file"}
 13 │
 14 │          Data Written to file        Data Read from file
 15 │       ┌MIKE BRAND                    mike brand
 16 │       │DICK KRUSE                    dick kruse
 17 │  Group┤SAMIR SAFAR                   samir safar
 18 │       │JOHN SCHEETZ                  john scheetz
 19 │       └RICH WORNER                   rich worner
 20 │
    CH1129!A1              Text="\0
    Width:  7  Memory:  537  Last Col/Row:I38
       1>
    READY F1:Help  F3:Names  Ctrl-Backspace:Undo  Ctrl-Break:Cancel
```

Fig. 11.24.

File control macro using {WRITELN} and {READLN}.

The file control commands added with SuperCalc5 are typically used by more experienced users. Analyzing the preceding two simple examples will help you to understand the mechanics, but to use the commands effectively will take much more study on your part. But if the normal //Import and //Export commands do not work to your satisfaction, you might consider trying these file control commands.

Chapter Summary

Macros are an important tool for automating spreadsheet functions and speeding the development and use of SuperCalc. They eliminate the drudgery of repetitive commands and can be fun, too. Everyone who uses SuperCalc will have a use for the macro system. If you are not using macros, you are not using SuperCalc to its fullest potential.

In Chapter 12, you will learn about another specialized area of SuperCalc, data management. As with macros, without understanding and using the //Data tools, you are not using SuperCalc to its fullest potential.

12

Data Management

This chapter describes SuperCalc's data management capabilities. These operations include defining a database, adding and deleting records, reorganizing a database (sorting), locating data records that satisfy specific criteria, and producing a report composed of records selected by query operations.

As in other popular database management systems, *databases* in SuperCalc are tables in which rows are records and columns are fields within records. You will read about three main data management areas of a spreadsheet: the Input area (the database), the Criterion area (for selection and search criteria), and the Output area (for search results). The types of queries discussed include exact-match, formula, and wild-card searches.

Also described in this chapter are the data management statistical functions introduced in SuperCalc4: DAVG, DCOUNT, DMAX, DMIN, DSTD, DSUM, and DVAR. As close relatives of the similarly named statistical functions, each data management statistical function evaluates a set of values from a selected set of data management records and returns a single numeric result.

Finally, the //Data,**A**nalysis, //Data,**B**lock, //Data,**M**atrix, //Data,**P**arse, and //Data,**T**able commands are described. Although not directly related to other data management commands, these five commands are powerful tools that allow you to analyze data relationships, solve linear equations, and parse data—among other operations.

Overview of SuperCalc's Data Management System

SuperCalc's comprehensive data management capability enables you to organize data, search for specific data fields, and extract the results of searches. You can keep track of important information such as mailing lists, parts inventory lists, employee payroll information, and real estate comparable files.

407

This data management capability has features not found in ordinary spreadsheet-only software. Basic data management operations that can be performed on records include add, delete, alter, reorganize (sort), locate (highlight), and extract (report). Adding, deleting, altering, and reorganizing are ordinary spreadsheet operations that have already been discussed. (Adding a record, for example, involves invoking the command to insert a new row, then manually placing data into cells of the new row.) The locate and extract operations are unique to SuperCalc's data management capability and cannot be used during regular spreadsheet operations.

To access SuperCalc's data management facilities, type //Data on the entry line. Notice that you type two slashes, not one, before the D. The first slash indicates that you are invoking a command, and the second slash accesses the following commands: Add-in, Data, Export, File, Graphics, Import, Macro, Network, Restrict, Spreadsheets, and Test.

When you press D, fifteen command menu choices appear on two lines. The upper line of these command options contains Quit, Input, Criterion, Output, Find, Extract, Unique, Select, Remain, and Delete. (See table 12.1 for short definitions of these options).

Table 12.1
Data Management Commands

Command	Meaning
Quit	Leaves the data management portion of SuperCalc
Input	Defines the block constituting the database
Criterion	Defines the area in which search criteria are found
Output	Defines the block in which records are placed that satisfy the search criteria
Find	Searches the database for records satisfying the search criteria, highlighting each one found
Extract	Operates like the Find command but places search results in the Output block instead of highlighting each record
Unique	Works like Extract but copies only one of the identical records to the Output block
Select	Enables the user to select data to be copied to the Output block (variant of Extract command)
Remain	Leaves the spreadsheet cursor in its present position, halts the //Data command, and returns to the idle prompt
Delete	Deletes selected records from the database

The default choice is Quit; note that the command pointer rests on that option (see fig. 12.1). Each of the data management commands, as well as the Analysis, Block, Matrix, Parse, and Table commands, is described in this chapter.

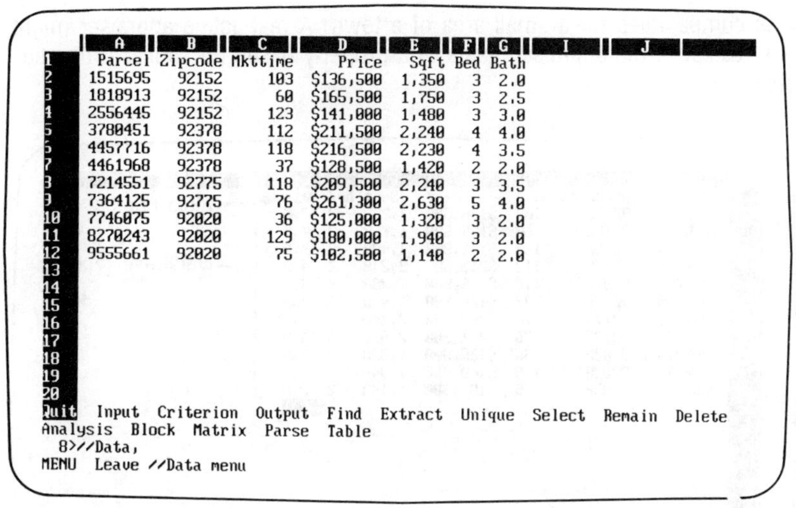

	A	B	C	D	E	F	G	I	J
1	Parcel	Zipcode	Mkttime	Price	Sqft	Bed	Bath		
2	1515695	92152	103	$136,500	1,350	3	2.0		
3	1818913	92152	60	$165,500	1,750	3	2.5		
4	2556445	92152	123	$141,000	1,480	3	3.0		
5	3780451	92378	112	$211,500	2,240	4	4.0		
6	4457716	92378	118	$216,500	2,230	4	3.5		
7	4461968	92378	37	$128,500	1,420	2	2.0		
8	7214551	92775	118	$209,500	2,240	3	3.5		
9	7364125	92775	76	$261,300	2,630	5	4.0		
10	7746075	92020	36	$125,000	1,320	3	2.0		
11	8270243	92020	129	$180,000	1,940	3	2.0		
12	9555661	92020	75	$102,500	1,140	2	2.0		
13									
14									
15									
16									
17									
18									
19									
20									

Quit Input Criterion Output Find Extract Unique Select Remain Delete
Analysis Block Matrix Parse Table
8>//Data,
MENU Leave //Data menu

Fig. 12.1.
SuperCalc's Data menu.

Unlike other commands, the data management command, //**D**ata, retains control after SuperCalc executes an option (for example, **F**ind, **E**xtract, or **I**nput). Additional data management options can be executed in sequence. To return to the SuperCalc idle prompt (1›) after finishing data management tasks, press Enter to execute the **Q**uit command, press R to execute the **R**emain command, or press Ctrl-Break (the data management cancel key).

Data Management Fundamentals

Usually, any spreadsheet created using SuperCalc can be thought of as a database when the spreadsheet conforms to a certain set of rules. Therefore, many of the spreadsheets shown in this book could be considered databases. Like most popular relational database management systems, SuperCalc databases consist of tables made up of rows (or *records*) and columns (or *fields*).

Field Names

The first row of a SuperCalc database is different from the others. Unlike other spreadsheets, SuperCalc requires that the first row of a database contain one or more names of the fields (columns) located in the columns below those names. Therefore, the smallest conceivable database must consist of at least two rows (one field name row and a single record located in the next row) and at least one column. Figure 12.2 shows a small database containing eleven records, each record with seven fields. The records represent a simple list of sales comparables for a small area of a town. A real estate appraiser might use these values to calculate the appraised value of a property based on similar properties that have been sold.

Fig. 12.2.

Small database containing eleven records with seven fields each.

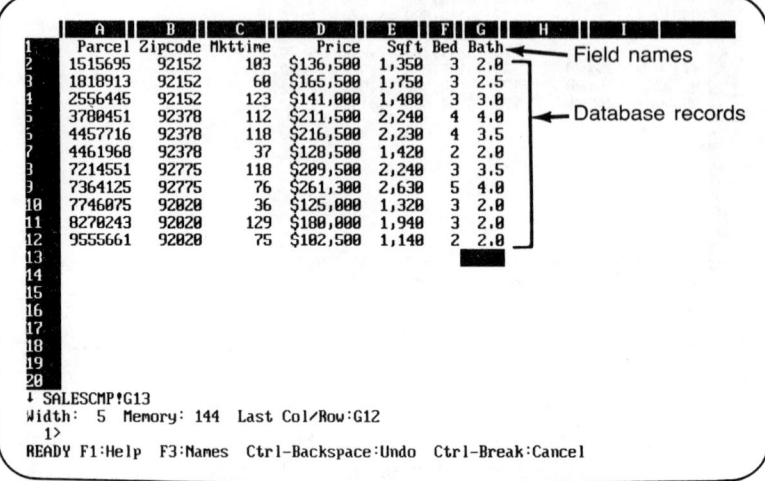

Notice that the top row of figure 12.2 contains the labels *Parcel*, *Zipcode*, *Mkttime*, *Price*, *Sqft*, *Bed*, and *Bath* in columns A through G, respectively. These seven column labels are required to identify the fields of the eleven records (rows) that follow. Of course, labels generally are not needed for spreadsheet columns, but labels are usually required for database search operations. SuperCalc's data management system is often used to search for particular field values by identifying fields by name and giving acceptable value ranges for the fields. Table 12.2 shows the records and fields in the sales comparables database.

The following example illustrates the importance of specifying names at the heads of fields (columns). Suppose that you want to identify in the sales comparables database the properties that are most similar to a 1,925-square-feet house you are appraising. In "noncomputer" form, a query to find such properties might be phrased in this way:

Find all properties with square feet fields within 100 square feet of 1,925.

Without using field names such as *Sqft*, you would have a difficult time creating such a question. A query like this is called a *selective formula* and is written in a more terse way, which SuperCalc can understand:

Sqft > 1824 AND Sqft < 2026

Several queries and query types are discussed in detail later in this chapter.

Table 12.2
Records and Fields in the Sales Comparables Database

Field 1	Field 2	Field 3	Field 4	Field 5	Field 6	Field 7	
↓	↓	↓	↓	↓	↓	↓	
Parcel	*Zipcode*	*Mkttime*	*Price*	*Sqft*	*Bed*	*Bath*◄————	Field Names
1515695	92152	103	$136,500	1,350	3	2.0◄————	Record 1
1818913	92152	60	$165,500	1,750	3	2.5◄————	Record 2
2556445	92152	123	$141,000	1,480	3	3.0◄————	Record 3
3780451	92378	112	$211,500	2,240	4	4.0◄————	Record 4
4457716	92378	118	$216,500	2,230	4	3.5◄————	Record 5
4461968	92378	37	$128,500	1,420	2	2.0◄————	Record 6
7214551	92775	118	$209,500	2,240	3	3.5◄————	Record 7
7364125	92775	76	$261,300	2,630	5	4.0◄————	Record 8
7746075	92020	36	$125,000	1,320	3	2.0◄————	Record 9
8270243	92020	129	$180,000	1,940	3	2.0◄————	Record 10
9555661	92020	75	$102,500	1,140	2	2.0◄————	Record 11

Data Consistency within Fields

Another rule mentioned earlier that distinguishes SuperCalc spreadsheets from SuperCalc databases is the consistent data requirement. Simply stated, the rule is that the data stored in a column must be of the same type and meaning for each database record. For example, storing an alphabetic string in the field labeled *Sqft* violates the consistency rule. Likewise, the *Price* column should contain only numeric values representing the sales prices. A common mistake is to include a column sum or average—AVG(D2:D12), for example—as the last entry in a column (see fig. 12.3). Notice that row 13 contains averages of fields in each column, which are dissimilar from the actual records. Unless carefully excluded, that last row will appear to be just another database record. It is not, however.

To use SuperCalc's data management capabilities, you do not need to organize records in any particular order. For example, you do not have to sort the records in ascending order by square feet or sales price. Doing so might be more pleasing visually, but the data management routines that find or extract records work whether the data is randomly organized or carefully sorted. This is another property common among relational database management systems.

Input, Criterion, and Output Blocks

Any spreadsheet can be either a spreadsheet or a database. By looking at the rows of a spreadsheet on the screen, you cannot tell which of the two (or both) roles the data is playing. What distinguishes a SuperCalc spreadsheet from a database is the explicit identification of rows of data as a database file. To define the boundaries of a database, you specify the range of cells to be included as the Input block.

Fig. 12.3.

*Example of
inconsistent data
in fields.*

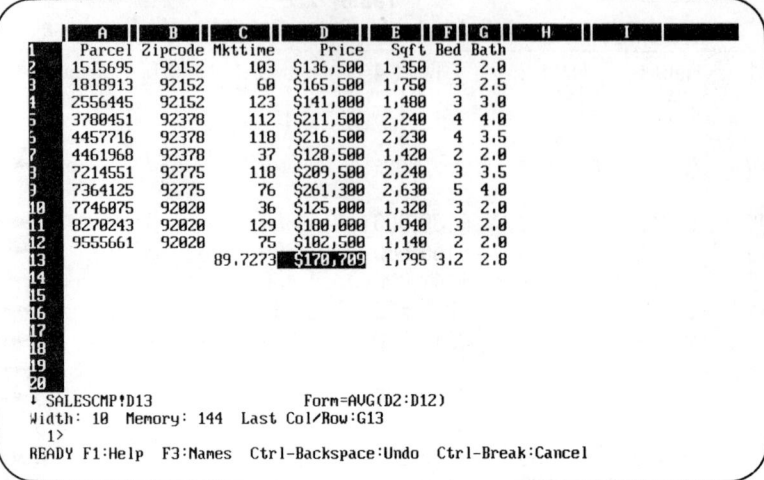

The Input block is the most important of the three database areas to define. After telling SuperCalc what spreadsheet rows are in the database file (the Input block), you can deal with the rows and columns in the usual way. All commands (for example, /Insert, /Delete, and /Arrange) work on the rows in the same way. In addition, however, you can perform database operations.

The other two database spreadsheet areas you must specify are the Criterion block and Output block. The Criterion block is a separate area of the spreadsheet in which you place database search queries. To define search operations, you create database search criteria, place them in cells, and identify those cells as the Criterion block.

The Output block is where the results of database search operations are placed. Although defining the Output block is optional, setting aside an area of the spreadsheet for search results is useful so that you can print the Output block later (using /Output).

An important point to remember is that the three blocks—Input, Criterion, and Output—should never overlap. You also should avoid placing the Criterion block or the Output block to the right or left of any rows of the Input block. If you decide to add a record to the Input block by inserting a new row (/Insert,Row), the Criterion or Output block also will gain a blank row.

Figure 12.4 uses the sales comparables data to illustrate the three blocks. They are labeled for visual identification, but they do not have to be. The **I**nput, **O**utput, and **C**riterion commands establish the cell addresses associated with the Input, Output, and Criterion blocks of a spreadsheet.

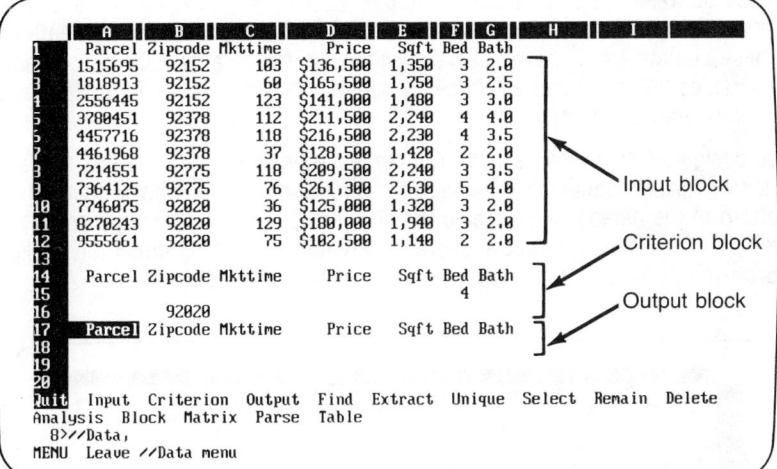

Fig. 12.4.

Three database blocks: Input, Criterion, and Output.

Database Creation: Specifying the Input Block

The process of creating a database containing one or more records is straightforward. However, a few database layout tips can help you establish visual boundaries for the database and also help you avoid inadvertent data loss later. Throughout the rest of this chapter, a sample real estate sales comparables (or simply sales comparables) database is used to illustrate various aspects of SuperCalc data management. Figures 12.1 through 12.4 show the sales comparables spreadsheet that is transformed into a database which can be queried and updated.

Column A contains a unique property parcel number. Column B contains the properties' ZIP codes. Column C indicates how long each property was on the market before being sold. The sales price of each property is found in column D. Property characteristics of square feet of living space (*Sqft*), number of bedrooms (*Bed*), and number of bathrooms (*Bath*) are in columns E, F, and G, respectively. The latter has been formatted to display only one decimal place. The *Price* column displays amounts in whole dollars with inserted commas and a leading dollar sign. All labels in row 1 have been formatted as right-justified in their respective cells (/Format,**R**ow,**1**,**T**ext,**R**ight).

Widths of columns vary from 4 to 10 characters. Column widths have been selected to maximize the amount of information visible on each spreadsheet. You may want to leave all columns (except the *Price* column) at their default width of nine characters for convenience.

Create the database by typing the 11 rows of data the same way you create any other spreadsheet. However, be sure that each column contains only one type of data. The one significant difference between the data shown in figures 12.1 through 12.4 and the data in other spreadsheets is the presence of labels at the top of each column. Although entered the usual way, these column labels have special significance for data management operations. Sales comparables fields are named *Parcel*, *Zipcode*, *Mkttime*, *Price*, *Sqft*, *Bed*, and *Bath* in the sales comparables example.

A useful database design aid that also assists in documentation is to mark the last spreadsheet record in the database. Figure 12.5 shows the same spreadsheet with a double line indicating the bottom of the database. To create the line, enter repeating text into cell A13. Type an apostrophe (') followed by a special character created by holding down the Alt key while typing **205** on the numeric keypad (see the status line in fig. 12.5).

Fig. 12.5.

Spreadsheet with double line to mark bottom of database.

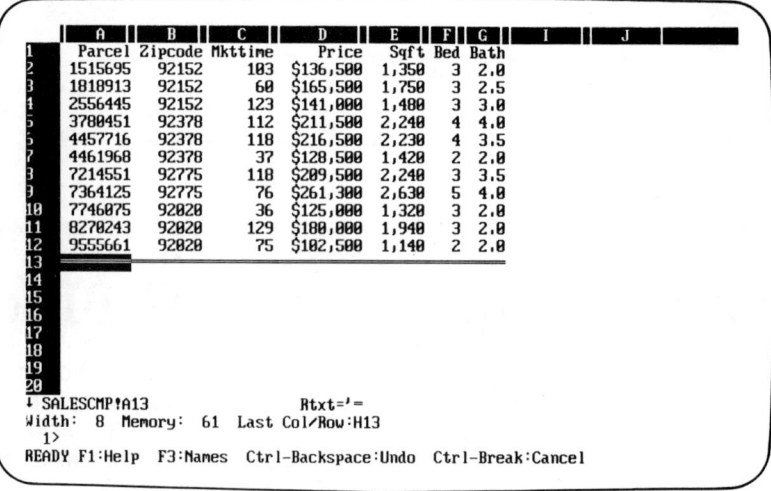

To see a list of the graphics characters you can create, press function key F1. The Help Index appears. Next, highlight the entry `Entering ASCII Chars` in the Help Index and press Enter to display the data entry help screen shown in figure 12.6.

Marking the bottom of the database with a line is an important visual aid when you are adding records to the database. When a record is added to a database, the record is inserted between the current last record and the line marking the bottom. A boundary marker at the top of the database is not needed because the labels in the first row indicate the top.

Defining the Input Block

After you create the spreadsheet records, your next task is to define the limits of the Input block. Enter

    //**D**ata,**I**nput,

```
ASCII Characters                                        SuperCalc AnswerScreen

  ASCII extended character    128 Ç 144 É 160 á 176 ▒ 192 └ 208 ╨ 224 α 240 ≡
  set:                        129 ü 145 æ 161 í 177 ▓ 193 ┴ 209 ╤ 225 ß 241 ±
                              130 é 146 Æ 162 ó 178 ▓ 194 ┬ 210 ╥ 226 Γ 242 ≤
  Hold down ALT key while     131 â 147 ô 163 ú 179 │ 195 ├ 211 ╙ 227 π 243 ≤
  entering the corresponding  132 ä 148 ö 164 ñ 180 ┤ 196 ─ 212 ╘ 228 Σ 244 ⌠
  decimal value for the       133 à 149 ò 165 Ñ 181 ╡ 197 ┼ 213 ╒ 229 σ 245 ⌡
  character. Use the numeric  134 å 150 û 166 ª 182 ╢ 198 ╞ 214 ╓ 230 µ 246 ÷
  keypad. Control characters, 135 ç 151 ù 167 º 183 ╖ 199 ╟ 215 ╫ 231 τ 247 ≈
  decimal 0 to 31, cannot be  136 ê 152 ÿ 168 ¿ 184 ╕ 200 ╚ 216 ╪ 232 Φ 248 °
  used.                       137 ë 153 Ö 169 ⌐ 185 ╣ 201 ╔ 217 ┘ 233 Θ 249 ·
  Examples:                   138 è 154 Ü 170 ¬ 186 ║ 202 ╩ 218 ┌ 234 Ω 250 ·
  · ALT 156 enters £.         139 ï 155 ¢ 171 ½ 187 ╗ 203 ╦ 219 █ 235 δ 251 √
  · ALT 205 entered as        140 î 156 £ 172 ¼ 188 ╝ 204 ╠ 220 ▄ 236 ∞ 252 ⁿ
  Repeating Text produces:    141 ì 157 ¥ 173 ¡ 189 ╜ 205 ═ 221 ▌ 237 ø 253 ²
  ─────                       142 Ä 158 ₧ 174 « 190 ╛ 206 ╬ 222 ▐ 238 ∈ 254 ■
                              143 Å 159 ƒ 175 » 191 ┐ 207 ╧ 223 ▀ 239 ∩ 255

RELATED TOPICS:
ESC=Return to SuperCalc    F2 = How to use Help    F3 = Help Index
```

Fig. 12.6.

Help screen showing special graphics characters.

You may type the cell address limits directly (for example, **A1:G13**) or use the point method. To do the latter, move the cursor to the upper left corner of the database and press the period key. Then use the cursor-movement keys (or press End-Home) to move to the lower right corner cell of the database. Finally, press Enter to establish the Input block cell range. Notice that SuperCalc highlights the Input block as you move the cursor to the lower right corner. Figure 12.7 shows the screen when the point method is used, just before Enter is pressed.

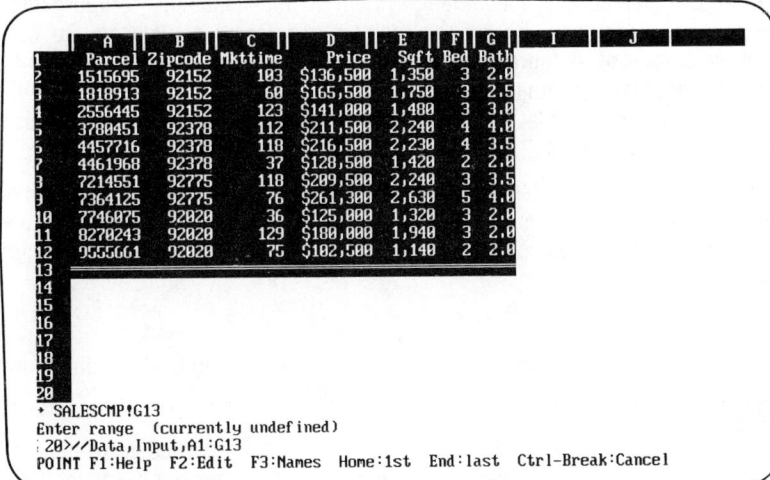

Fig. 12.7.

Using the point method to define the Input block.

You can establish the database's input range by using any combination of opposite corner cell addresses: lower right and upper left, lower left and upper right, and so forth. Super-Calc always sees the cell address limits as a cell range pair: upper left followed by lower right.

Adding Records to the Input Block

The double line just below the last record in the Input block serves to remind you of the location of the bottom of the database. When records are added between the last record and the double line, the Input block is adjusted automatically to include the added record. Why? Because SuperCalc considers the delimiting line the last record in our example. If the database Input block did not include an extra row (that is, a double line) below the last database row and you added a record after the last record in the current Input block, the Input block limits would not be adjusted to include the new record. The record would appear to be in the database but wouldn't be in the defined Input block.

Adding records to the database does not involve redefining the Input block. To add records, you merely use the /Insert,**R**ow command and type the number of the row that is above the last record—in the case of the sales comparables database, above the double line. Then you fill in the fields of the record with the new data to complete the add-record operation.

Reorganizing the Database

A crucial function of any database management system is the capability to reorganize records, either physically or logically, by sorting them into different sequences. To sort records—either database records or spreadsheet rows—you use the /**A**rrange command, not one of the data management commands. In your data management activities, you will find /**A**rrange useful for sorting records into ascending or descending sequence. Because this command is described in Chapter 7, it is described only briefly here.

You can rearrange the sales comparables database in several useful ways. One possibility is to sort the records in ascending order by the *Zipcode* field (refer to fig. 12.5). Execute the following command to place database records in order from lowest ZIP code to highest:

/**A**rrange,**C**olumn,B,2:12,**A**scending,**A**djust,**G**o

You also can organize records by the *Sqft* (square feet) field with the following command:

/**A**rrange,**C**olumn,E,2:12,**A**scending,**A**djust,**G**o

Sorting the sales comparables records by the *Sqft* field helps locate a particular sales comparables item by square footage more quickly, either while using the data management portion of SuperCalc or while manipulating data in normal spreadsheet mode.

Because the database search routines invoked by //**D**ata,**F**ind, //**D**ata,**E**xtract, //**D**ata,**U**nique, and //**D**ata,**S**elect search the database from the first record to the last in response to given search criteria, sorting the database can improve the search speed slightly. In a sorted database, once SuperCalc locates the first of a contiguous group of records satisfying the search criteria, the system finds and highlights subsequent records more quickly. For example, if you sort the sales comparables database in ascending order on the *Zipcode* field, a search request to locate all recent property sales in a particular ZIP code area (for example, ZIP code 92020) finds all these records grouped together. Thus, you minimize the record-to-record search time for the second and subsequent records satisfying the criteria. Because the sales comparables database used in this chapter is so small and all records can be seen on one screen, it is not necessary to sort the database in any particular order.

Database Searches: Designating the Criterion Block

Now that you have created the database and specified the Input block, the next step is to create a spreadsheet area where database search criteria can be placed: the Criterion block.

To prepare for a database search request, you define a Criterion block in your spreadsheet. Once you define the range of cells marking the boundaries of the Criterion block, you place in it search criteria (search questions). The four data management search commands— **F**ind, **E**xtract, **U**nique, and **S**elect—search the data and locate records that match the criteria specified. You can specify the location of the Criterion block before or after entering the search criteria.

Using the sales comparables database as the database to be searched (refer to fig. 12.5), you can experiment with the several database search commands by defining a simple two-row Criterion block and placing search criteria into it.

Defining the Criterion Block

Like the Input block, the Criterion block is a rectangular range of cells defined by its top left and lower right corner cells. The Criterion block must contain at least two rows. The first row is reserved for field names; the second and any subsequent rows contain the search criteria.

To create a two-row Criterion block for the sales comparables database, type //**DC** at the idle prompt and enter the Criterion block cell-range addresses: **A15:G16**. You also can use the pointing method: move the cursor to the top left corner of the criteria area, press the period key, and use the arrow keys to move the cursor to the lower right cell of the block. Then press Enter. Figure 12.8 shows the screen when the pointing method is used to specify the Criterion block (Enter has not yet been pressed).

Fig. 12.8.

Using the point method to define the Criterion block.

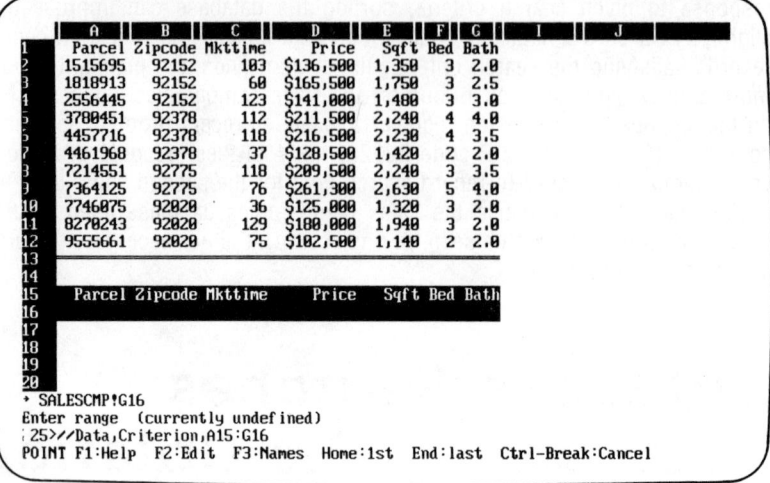

	A	B	C	D	E	F	G	I	J
1	Parcel	Zipcode	Mkttime	Price	Sqft	Bed	Bath		
2	1515695	92152	103	$136,500	1,350	3	2.0		
3	1010913	92152	60	$165,500	1,750	3	2.5		
4	2556445	92152	123	$141,000	1,400	3	3.0		
5	3700451	92378	112	$211,500	2,240	4	4.0		
6	4457716	92378	118	$216,500	2,230	4	3.5		
7	4461968	92378	37	$128,500	1,420	2	2.0		
8	7214551	92775	118	$209,500	2,240	3	3.5		
9	7364125	92775	76	$261,300	2,630	5	4.0		
10	7746075	92020	36	$125,000	1,320	3	2.0		
11	8270243	92020	129	$100,000	1,940	3	2.0		
12	9555661	92020	75	$102,500	1,140	2	2.0		
13									
14									
15	Parcel	Zipcode	Mkttime	Price	Sqft	Bed	Bath		
16									
17									
18									
19									
20									

```
* SALESCMP!G16
Enter range   (currently undefined)
: 25>//Data,Criterion,A15:G16
POINT F1:Help  F2:Edit  F3:Names  Home:1st  End:last  Ctrl-Break:Cancel
```

You must always be careful to specify the exact number of rows needed in the Criterion block. For example, a Criterion block should not be three rows long if only two rows are needed to hold the search criteria. Never include a blank row in the Criterion block. A blank criterion row causes all database records to be located and highlighted during search operations. In other words, a blank row says "Any value for the fields will satisfy the search request."

Entering a Search Request

A simple request is used to introduce database searching. To enter data into the Criterion block, you must leave SuperCalc's data management system and get back to the idle prompt (1>). To do this, either press Enter to execute the **Q**uit command, or press Ctrl-Break or R to execute the **R**emain command. Remember the Criterion block limits (A15 through G16 in this example) so that you can put search data into the block.

The first search request you want to create is to locate all four-bedroom homes (all records whose *Bed* field contains 4).

The first row of the Criterion block is reserved for the names of the database fields that will be searched. The first search request involves only the *Bed* field, so only that field label has to be placed in row 1 of the Criterion block. However, in all likelihood, other records also will need to be located, based on other field values. Therefore, for the sake of possible future search needs, type all field names in row 15, the first row of the Criterion block. The easiest way to do that is to copy row 1 to row 15:

/Copy,1,15

The field names can be in the same order as they are in the database, or they can be specified in a different order. The first row of the Criterion block created for your search request has these labels:

```
Parcel  Zipcode  Mkttime  Price  Sqft  Bed  Bath
```

Each field name in the Criterion block must be spelled exactly as it is spelled in the database field, including spaces and capitalization. For example, the label *Parcel* is not the same as *PARCEL*.

The second Criterion block row (16) contains the data to be used to locate records. Move to the cell below the label *Bed* and type the value **4**. The Criterion block is now complete. It contains a row of field labels matching those of the database and a row with the search criteria:

```
Parcel  Zipcode  Mkttime  Price  Sqft  Bed  Bath
                                        4
```

The criteria placed under each field name (or a blank field name) can be one of three types: exact, nonselective, or selective. The preceding criterion is an example of an *exact* match for the field *Bed*. A *nonselective* field criterion is any blank field under a criterion field name. For example, the nonselective field criteria in the preceding example are the fields *Parcel*, *Zipcode*, *Mkttime*, *Price*, *Sqft*, and *Bath* because the fields below them are blank. Blank fields accept any value for the corresponding field during a search. A *selective* field match can be either a partial text value or a formula. Examples of each of the three types are provided in table 12.3.

Table 12.3
Criterion Match Types

Criterion Match Types		*Sample Criterion Blocks*	
Nonselective:	(a)	Zipcode	Price
	(b)	Parcel Zipcode Mkttime Sqft	
Exact:	(a)	Zipcode 92020	Price 125000
	(b)	Zipcode	Sqft 2100
	(c)	Bath 3.0	
Selective:	(a)	Mkttime C2<50	Price D2<150000
	(b)	Bed F2>2.5	Bath G2>3

Each criterion match type is described in detail later in this section. For now, execute the search for the criteria created. Figure 12.9 shows the Input and Criterion blocks in their current forms, with the database in rows 1–13 and the criteria in rows 15 and 16.

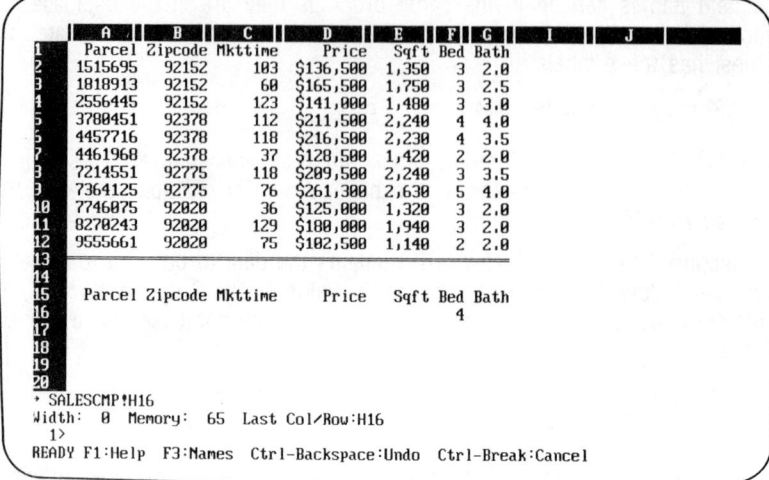

Fig. 12.9.

Input and Criterion blocks.

Executing an Exact Search

With the //**D**ata,**F**ind command, you can search the database for records corresponding to the request in the Criterion block. **F**ind is one of the options in the Data menu.

The **F**ind command uses the Criterion block entries to locate all records that satisfy the request. In figure 12.9, the search request is an exact match. When the //**D**ata,**F**ind command is executed, the database is searched from top (record 1, in row 2) to bottom (record 11, in row 12) to locate records with a *Bed* field equal to 4. The other Criterion block fields are blank; any value in those positions in the database records satisfies the request.

If one or more database records matches the Criterion block request, SuperCalc highlights the first matching record (see fig. 12.10).

Take a close look at the prompt line in figure 12.10. The prompt indicates that you can use the up- or down-arrow key to move the highlight from one record to the next. Pressing the down-arrow key executes the **F**ind command again to locate in the database the next record (if any) that satisfies the search criteria. You can move right or left across fields of a specific record using the right- and left-arrow keys.

The first of two records for homes with four bedrooms is highlighted in figure 12.10. One more record in the database matches the criteria, so pressing the down-arrow key once more locates and highlights this last record. To halt the **F**ind command at any point, press Enter. The prompt line in figure 12.10 reminds you that Enter (Return) is the cancel key for database **F**ind operations.

Pressing the down-arrow key once more causes the following message to appear on the right of the status line:

```
No more matching records
```

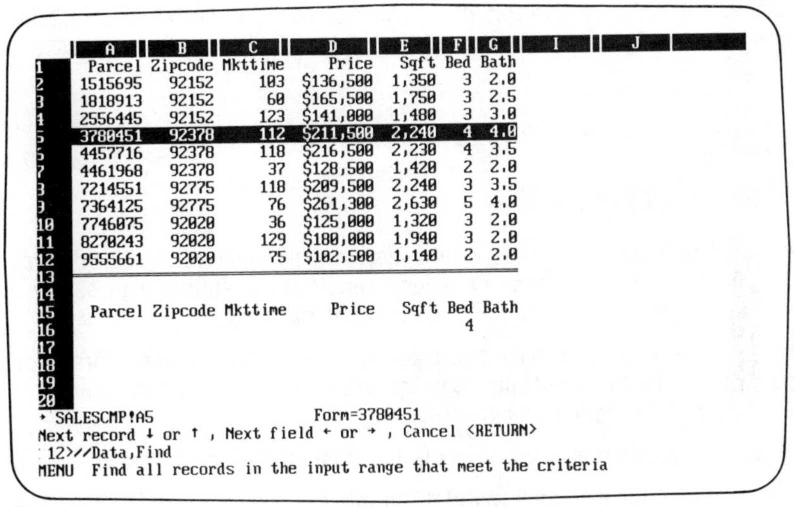

Fig. 12.10.

First located record matching the search criteria.

At any time during the **F**ind operation, you can use the up-arrow key to review other records satisfying the search request. Records above the currently highlighted record are highlighted individually if they match the criteria. Thus, pressing the up-arrow key causes the **F**ind command to search the database in reverse order, from the last record to the first.

Satisfying Multiple Criteria Simultaneously

You can devise a Criterion block search request with several conditions that must be met either simultaneously or separately when the **F**ind command is executed. Suppose that a real estate appraiser wants to locate all recent sales of three-bedroom homes in a particular ZIP code area in order to examine those homes and compare them with a property being appraised. That request might be

Locate all records with the *Zipcode* field equal to 92020 and the *Bed* field equal to 3.

The new Criterion block corresponding to this query, placed in rows 15 and 16, is

```
Zipcode      Bed
  92020       3
```

Two conditions must be met before the record is highlighted: *Bed* must equal 3, and *Zipcode* must equal 92020. Notice that all other field names can be omitted from the Criterion block because they are irrelevant conditions for this search.

To place new criteria data in the Criterion block, you have to exit from the data management part of SuperCalc. Press **R**emain, and then press Ctrl-Break or Enter. Place the new value(s) into the Criterion block and press //**D**ata,**F**ind to use the new search criteria.

The preceding search request is an example of an *and* operation in which two conditions must be true simultaneously for a record to satisfy a search request.

Satisfying Any One of Multiple Criteria

Suppose that you want to locate all records with a *Zipcode* field equal to 92152 or a *Bed* field equal to 4. Criteria in which any one of several conditions is sufficient to satisfy a search are created by placing each condition in its own criteria row.

For the preceding example, you must make two changes to the Criterion block. First, you must enlarge the Criterion block to accommodate an additional row. Second, you must place new search data in the Criterion block.

To change the limits of the Criterion block, execute the //**D**ata,**C**riterion command.

Then type the new cell limits for the block (**A15:G17** in this example) and press Enter. The new Criterion block looks like this:

```
15   Parcel   Zipcode   Mkttime   Price   Sqft   Bed   Bath
16   92152
17                                               4
```

If you execute the **F**ind command with the new criteria, SuperCalc locates the five records that satisfy the search request.

Remember the following important points about Criterion block contents and layout. You use a single row of the Criterion block to specify search criteria containing conditions that are to be met simultaneously. To specify conditions that can be met separately, however, you use separate rows—one row for each condition.

When more than one value or formula is placed in one row of the Criterion block, they are called *and* conditions. In this case, all conditions must be met for a database record to be highlighted. Individual values placed on separate Criterion block lines are called *or* conditions, and the screen displays a database record matching any one of the Criterion block rows.

Conversely, a Criterion block such as the following represents a request for records with a *Zipcode* field equal to 92020, a *Bed* field equal to 4, and a *Bath* field equal to 3.0.

```
15   Parcel   Bed   Bath
16   92020     4    3.0
```

Again, notice that several of the Criterion block field names have been eliminated in this example; they are not necessary to perform the search. These search criteria are obviously more restrictive than others shown in this chapter so far.

Avoiding Blank Rows in the Criterion Block

You must not expand the Criterion block (by redefining its cell limits) to include any blank rows. Because the Find command considers each row of the Criterion block separately, a blank line means "or locate any record in the database," and SuperCalc will highlight all database records. Therefore, never include blank rows in the Criterion block.

Remember that the first row of the Criterion block is reserved for labels, whether or not you choose to place labels there. Criterion blocks without field labels in the first row are used to pose selective formula searches. These types of searches are described along with the Select and Extract commands later in this chapter.

Database Reports: Specifying the Output Block

In many database applications, the desired result of a database search is a report containing records that meet the search criteria. The //Data,Find command locates records satisfying the search criteria, but the records can be viewed only on the screen.

If you want to print or use records in a report, you must use three other database search commands: Extract, Unique, and Select. These commands use the Criterion block as a filter, just as Find does, but they also copy records into the Output block. Then you can print the records or use them in reports.

Defining the Output Block

As you did with the Input and Criterion blocks, you specify the Output block in a separate area of the spreadsheet and define it by specifying two cells at opposite corners of a rectangle. To define the Output block, type //Data,Output and the two cell addresses that define the block.

For example, you can define a small Output block for the sales comparables records in figure 12.10, in rows 18–20 and columns A–G, by typing the following and pressing Enter:

//Data,Output,**A18:G20**

You can also use the pointing method to define the Output block.

The Extract and Unique commands automatically place records matching the search criteria in the Output block, whereas the Select command requires confirmation before placing each record in the block. Therefore, consider the size of the Output block carefully. For example, the number of Output block rows for a 500-record database will never exceed 501 rows and may be much smaller, depending on the search criteria constraints. If a search results in more records than the Output block can hold, the remaining selected records are discarded, and the following warning message appears on the right end of the status line:

    Output area full

You can change the size and location of the Output block at any time. If the block proves to be too small, you can enlarge it. Make sure, however, that the block does not overlap either the Input or Criterion block; otherwise, unpredictable things can occur. In addition, it is a good idea not to place either the Output or Criterion blocks adjacent to the Input block, occupying some of the same rows as the Input block. If you later add or delete records from the Input block, rows in either the Criterion or Output block may be altered inadvertently.

You have now defined the sales comparables database's Input, Criterion, and Output blocks. Your next task is to search the database with **E**xtract, **U**nique, and **S**elect.

Creating and Using Names To Expedite Searching

Before using the **E**xtract and **S**elect database search commands, use the /**N**ame command to create names for the database fields. This practice makes criteria entries easier to construct. Names created with the /**N**ame command are different from field names placed in the top row of the Input, Criterion, and Output blocks. The difference is that names specified with the /**N**ame command can be used in formulas placed in the Criterion block, but the field names in the first row of the Input block cannot. Names will be created with the /**N**ame command and used in several Criterion block entries.

Creating names that are identical to the field names in the Input block makes sense. You can do so easily by invoking the /**N**ame command repeatedly to establish the range names used in place of cell addresses. Because the database field names are located above their respective fields, we can take advantage of that and use the /**N**ame,**L**abels,**D**own command to equate field names in the first Input block row with their respective cells in the second Input block row. That is, the range name PARCEL is equated to cell A2, ZIPCODE to cell B2, and so on. Execute the command

   /**N**ame,**L**abels,**D**own,**A1:G1**

to create the seven range names corresponding to the database field names (see fig. 12.10).

Note that the name is associated with only the first cell address of the field, not the entire column. This fact is important to remember. After establishing range names, to enter text labels (such as *Parcel* or *Price*), you must type a leading double quotation mark before the text label (that is, "**Parcel**). Otherwise, if you enter **Parcel**, a value (cell B2) is displayed because SuperCalc interprets *Parcel* as a range name, not a text entry. Be careful entering text entries after you have established range names.

After executing the /**N**ame command, SuperCalc registers the field names in row 1 as synonyms for the cell addresses A2 through G2. These cell names are used in formula searches, described in the following paragraphs.

Using Selective Formula Searches

Selective formula searches differ from exact searches (see table 12.3) in that formulas can specify nonexact conditions or search criteria. Exact match search techniques are quite different. For example, you can create an exact-match search for *Price* equal to $136,000 by placing the value **136000** under the Criterion block label *Price*. SuperCalc then will locate and highlight only records with a *Price* field exactly equal to 136000.

It is often difficult, inconvenient, or imprecise to state some search criteria in exact-match form. In these instances you must use the formula search criterion. For example, suppose that you want to locate all homes that sold for less than $128,000. To create the formula, you type into the second row of the Criterion block either of the following formulas:

D2<128000

or

PRICE<128000

Like exact-match criteria, the first row of the Criterion block is reserved for labels. The first formula refers to the first nonlabel cell in the database column (labeled *Price*), and the **F**ind, **E**xtract, **U**nique, or **S**elect command automatically searches the entire column by incrementing the row value (D2, D3, D4, and so on).

The second formula uses the previously assigned name PRICE. The search commands operate with either names or explicit cell addresses. Using names is easier than specifying non-mnemonic cell addresses because names are easier to remember.

When formula search criteria are used, Criterion block field names, located in the first row, are not needed. You do not have to remove them; however, they no longer serve any useful purpose. You can write exact-match criteria as formulas by using the equal relational operator. For example, the formula PRICE=142000 can be used instead of typing the value 142000 below the Criterion block label *Price*. You will find that formula searches are more versatile and easier to use than exact-match searches, and any exact-match search can be written as a formula search criterion.

Copying Records to the Output Block with Extract

The //**D**ata,**E**xtract command searches the database and copies into the Output block all records meeting the search criteria. The Output block was previously defined, so all that remains to execute an **E**xtract search is to form a few Criterion block queries and watch what happens.

Start by asking for records with a *Price* field less than 128,000. With the command line in idle mode (1›), move to the Criterion block cell A16, type **PRICE<128000**, and press Enter. Because PRICE is a defined range name, you can type it as any combination of upper- or lowercase letters (see fig. 12.11).

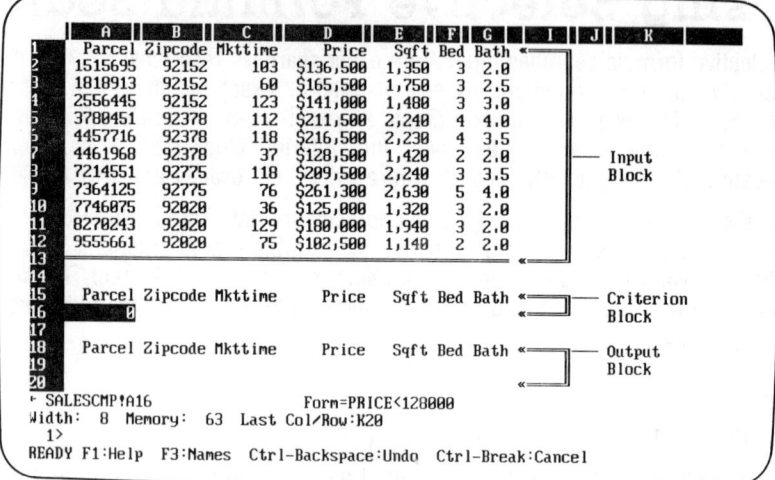

Fig. 12.11.

Criterion search using a formula and //Data,Extract.

Notice that cell A16 displays the value 0, indicating that the first record does not match the criterion. Blank out any other entries in the Criterion block and make sure that the Criterion block area includes only two rows (cells A15 through G16). You can use the //Data,Criterion command to check the current bounds of the Criterion block and adjust them if necessary. Make sure that the Criterion block does not include any blank rows—especially below row 16. Blank rows play havoc when a search request is executed because all records satisfy a blank Criterion block row.

To execute the Extract search, type //Data,Extract and press Enter.

Figure 12.12 shows the screen after the search has been executed. Notice that the Output block now contains two records: the two that satisfy the specified search criteria.

The database command //Data,Unique is similar to the //Data,Extract command in all ways except one: if an identical record is encountered during the Unique database search operation, the duplicate (and any subsequent duplicate records) is not copied into the Output block. As with the Extract command, the database is searched from the first record to the last record. Likewise, any records that satisfy the search criteria are copied into the Output block. Database records that are identical to a previously extracted record are ignored—not placed in the Output block. If two records satisfy the search criteria and all fields of both are identical except for one, both records are placed in the Output block.

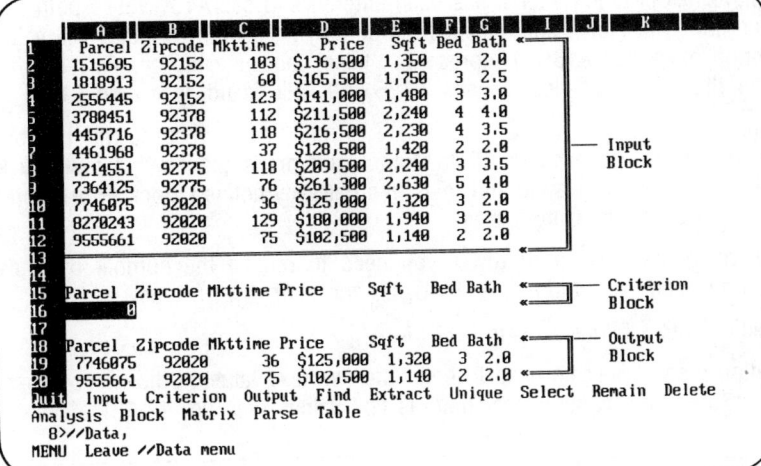

Fig. 12.12.

Screen following execution of the //*Data,Extract* command.

Copying Records to the Output Block with Select

Select works almost exactly like **E**xtract, except that SuperCalc asks you whether you want to copy into the next empty Output block row each highlighted record matching the search criteria. You create Criterion block search criteria in the same manner, and you specify the **S**elect command after invoking the //**D**ata command.

To demonstrate the **S**elect command, search criteria quite different from those shown so far will be used. It is often useful in evaluating properties to look at the cost per square foot. This value can aid in deciding whether a database property is truly comparable to another one. Using the same sales comparables database, formulate search criteria to locate all properties in the database in which the cost per square foot is less than $95. After the search criteria have been entered, you can invoke the **S**elect command to copy selected records to the Output block.

You may notice two important points about the proposed search criteria. First, no database field contains the value of cost per square foot. Second, the search criteria must be a selective formula because values less than $95 for the computed result of *Price* divided by *Sqft* are being requested.

The more interesting of these two observations leads to the obvious question of how to type a query about a nonexistent field—cost per square foot. SuperCalc supports database formulas containing relational operators and arithmetic combinations of existing Input block fields. For instance, the cost per square foot for any sales comparables record is its *Price* field divided by its *Sqft* field. To locate sales comparables properties whose price per square foot values are less than $95, type into the second row of the Criterion block the formula

PRICE/SQFT<95

Figure 12.13 displays this criterion after it has been entered into cell A16. Notice both cell A16 and the status line. The status line displays the underlying search formula. The value displayed in Criterion block cell A16 (0) represents "false" because the simple relational formula is false for the first Input block record ($136,500/1350 is not less than $95).

You should enlarge the Output block to accommodate as many as 11 records (the number of records in the database), so execute //**D**ata,**O**utput and press the down-arrow key 9 times. This process is the easiest way to add rows to an already defined block. Press Enter to complete the expansion of the Output block.

In addition to enlarging the number of rows, you need to reduce the number of fields captured in the Output block. In columns A, B, C, D, and E of row 18 type

"Zipcode "Bed "Bath "Price "Sqft

The double quotation marks must be used to enter the five text values; otherwise, Super-Calc interprets them as range names rather than as text values (see fig. 12.13).

Fig. 12.13.

Search criterion combining record fields.

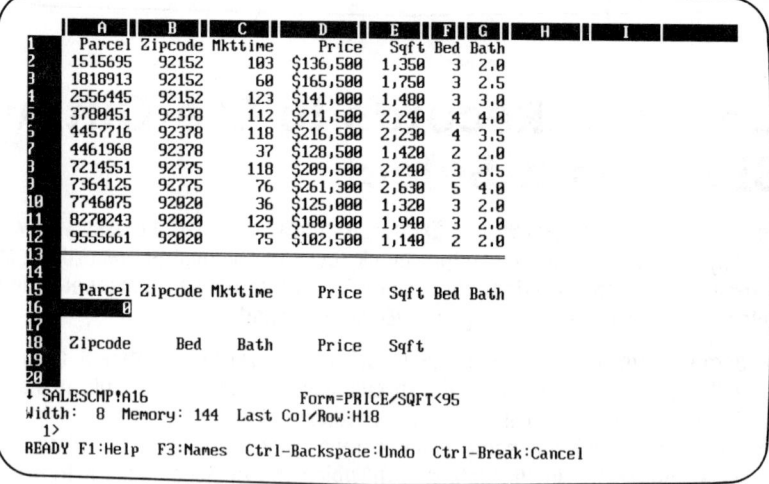

By omitting the labels *Parcel* and *Mkttime* from the first row, you cause SuperCalc to display only the listed five fields in the Output block.

You have typed the criteria and modified the Output block, so you can now execute the **S**elect search command. Enter

//**D**ata,**S**elect

SuperCalc highlights the first record (see fig. 12.14). The system prompts you to press Y to accept the record or N to reject it.

To place the highlighted record in the Output block, press Y; otherwise, press N. In either case, SuperCalc locates and highlights the next record with a computed cost per square foot less than $95. This process continues until the system finds no more records matching the criteria. Figure 12.15 shows the Output block after the last record is located. The dialog panel returns to //**D**ata.

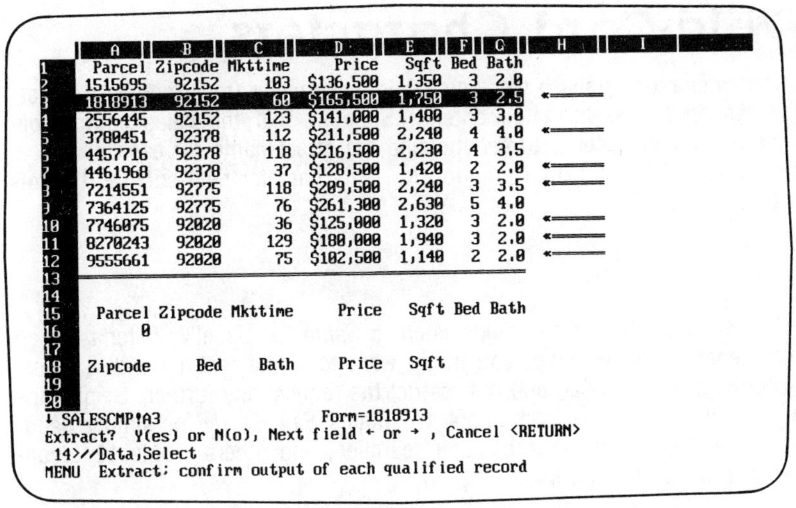

Fig. 12.14.
Executing the //Data,Select command.

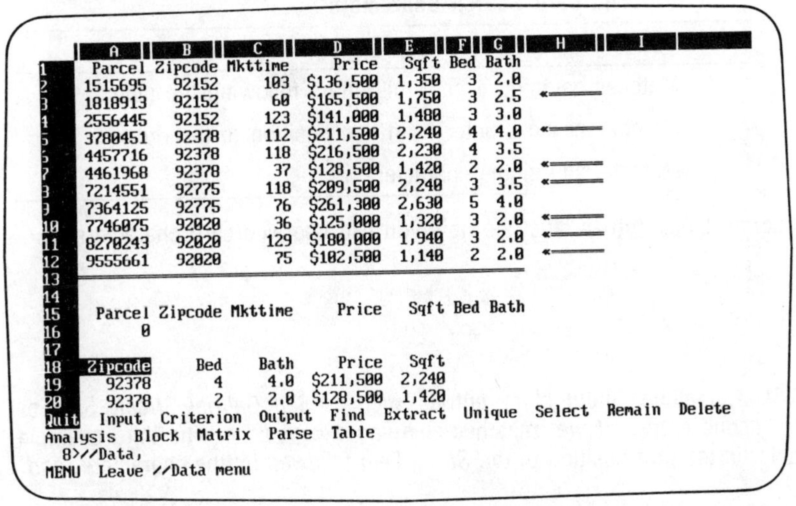

Fig. 12.15.
Output block after execution of //Data,Select.

The arrows in figures 12.14 and 12.15 have been added to the spreadsheet merely to point to the seven records satisfying the formula PRICE/SQFT<95. Notice, however, that the Output block in figure 12.15 contains only two records. No records are in the rows beyond row 20. During the search process, Y was pressed in response to only two of the seven candidate records; therefore, only those two were copied into the Output block.

Using Wild-Card Characters

When typing search criteria for database fields containing characters (for example, a street-name field), you can specify exact-match criteria. Suppose that the sales comparable database contained an additional field, *Street*, holding the street name for each property. You could specify an exact-match search criterion for that character field such as the following Criterion block entry:

```
Street      Parcel    Zipcode
Santa Fe
```

This entry specifies records with a *Street* field matching *Santa Fe*. Usually, criteria search requests are more general. For example, you might want to locate records with a *Street* field beginning with the characters *San* and not restrict the request any further. Or perhaps you want to know whether the sales comparables contains *San Gabriel* or simply *Sand*. Wild-card characters enable you to perform such searches, and others. Table 12.4 contains a list of the wild cards you can use.

Table 12.4
Wild-Card Search Characters

Wild Card	Meaning
~ (tilde)	Matches anything except the letters following the tilde
* (asterisk)	Matches any character from this position to the right
?	Matches any single character

The following Criterion block entries illustrate how you can use wild-card characters:

```
Street      Parcel    Zipcode
San*
~Lane
?and
```

The first entry, *San**, matches Input block entries such as *San Gabriel Street*, *San*, or *Sandy Land*. The second entry, *~Lane*, matches anything except *Lane*. The third example allows any character in the first position of the *Street* field followed by the characters, *and*, to match.

Database Maintenance: Deleting Records

You can easily remove records from the Input block. There are two methods. You can use the SuperCalc /Delete,Row command, or you can use the data management command //Data,Delete. The former is often easier to specify for small databases, but the data management Delete command can be safer for databases containing a large number of records.

With large databases, you can easily remove all records whose ZIP codes match 92020. Or you can remove all records whose *Mkttime* field is greater than 110 days.

To delete records, you establish a Criterion block containing the conditions for selecting records to be deleted. The Criterion block follows the same rules as described for the **S**elect and **E**xtract statements. That is, you select an unused part of the spreadsheet, use the //**D**ata,**C**riterion command to define the Criterion block cell range, place at least one database field name in row 1, and place the selection criteria in the second and subsequent rows. Either exact-match or formula-match selection criteria can be specified to delete records. Remember, however, to exclude blank rows from the Criterion block.

Deleting records from the Input block is simple. After establishing the Input and Criterion blocks, execute the //**D**ata,**D**elete command. Database records satisfying the criteria are highlighted, one after the other.

Experiment with //**D**ata,**D**elete by removing all records in which the *Mkttime* field is greater than 110. Doing so removes properties that sold more than 110 days after they were first listed as available for sale.

Blank the Criterion block. Next, move to cell A16 and enter the deletion criteria formula

    MKTTIME>110

and press Enter. MKTTIME is a range name, so you can type it in either upper- or lower-case. Next, set the Criterion block range to cells A15 through A16. Note that the first row of the Criterion block (cell A15) is empty. Press //**DC** to check the current Criterion block limits, and adjust them if necessary.

From the idle prompt, execute //**D**ata,**D**elete to delete records. Figure 12.16 shows the Input block in the upper window and the Criterion block in the lower window. The lower window is formatted to show formulas (press //**GF**).

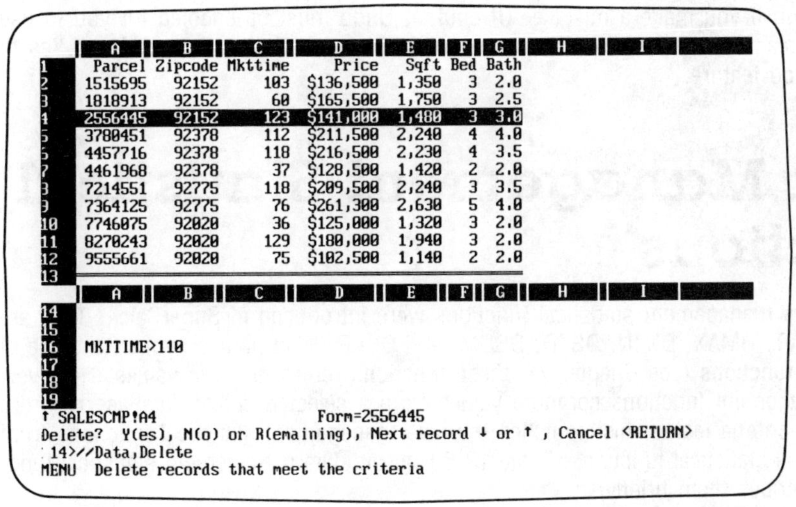

Fig. 12.16.

Deleting records from a database.

Records satisfying the Criterion block formula are highlighted individually. Notice that the record in row 4 is the first of several records highlighted. The prompt line indicates that you can take several actions. You can delete the current record (press Y), not delete the current record (press N), delete all remaining records satisfying the criteria (press R), or examine each candidate record to be deleted by pressing the up- or down-arrow keys.

Press R to delete the highlighted record and all subsequent records satisfying the criteria. After you press R, all records with *Mkttime* greater than 110 are removed (see fig. 12.17).

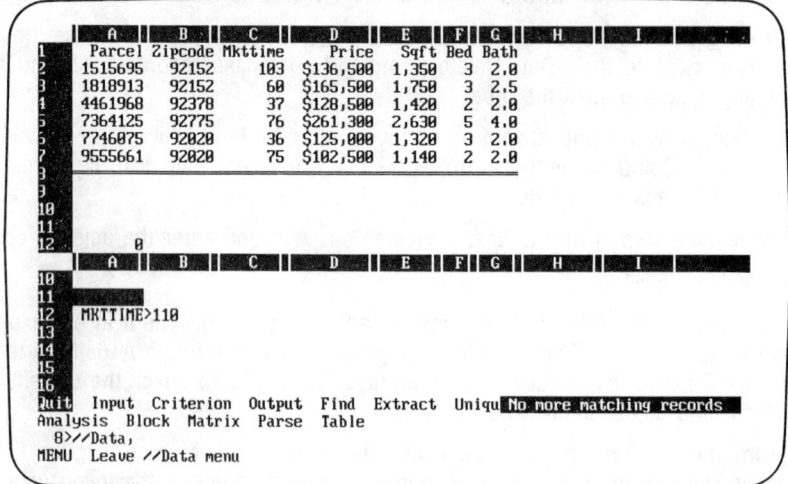

Fig. 12.17.

Database after executing //Data,Delete command.

Remember that you can press the Undo key (Ctrl-Backspace) to restore the Input block to its original form if you make a mistake. Of course, Undo must be enabled for you to use this handy spreadsheet restoration feature. Execute /**G**lobal,**O**ptimum,**P**resent,**U**ndo,**Y**es to enable the Undo feature.

Data Management Statistical Functions

The seven data management statistical functions were introduced in SuperCalc4. They are DAVG, DCOUNT, DMAX, DMIN, DSTD, DSUM, and DVAR. With names similar to those of the statistical functions (see Chapter 7), these functions return numeric values. However, the data management functions compute values from a selected set of database records. This selection-criteria feature distinguishes the data management statistical functions from general purpose statistical functions. Table 12.5 lists the data management statistical functions and describes them briefly.

Table 12.5
Data Management Statistical Functions

Function	Meaning
DAVG	Returns the average (mean) value of the numeric values in the selected records
DCOUNT	Returns the number of numeric-valued cells in the selected records for the specified offset field. Blank and zero-valued cells are not counted.
DMAX	Returns the largest value in the specified offset column of the input range meeting the specified criterion
DMIN	Returns the smallest value in the specified offset column of the input range meeting the specified criterion
DSTD	Returns the standard deviation for the values in the offset column of the input range, that meet the specified criterion. DSTD is a measure of how much individual values deviate from the collective list mean and is the square root of the variance.
DSUM	Returns the sum for the values in the offset column of the input range, that meet the specific criterion
DVAR	Returns the variance for the values in the offset column of the input range, that meet the specific criterion

The general form of all the functions is

function name(database,offset,criterion)

Function name is one of the seven function names. The first parameter, *database*, defines the range of cells in the database. The database range consists of a top row of unique labels serving as the database field names and rows that contain database records.

The *offset* parameter identifies the database column number for which the function computes a value. The offset is a zero-based value. That is, the first database field is at offset zero, and the third database field is selected by an offset value of two.

The third parameter is *criterion*. Similar to the Criterion block for nonfunction database operations, this parameter is a range of cells that includes

1. A top row with one or more labels matching at least one of the labels in the database range

2. A second row containing the database record selection criteria

The input and criterion parameters need not match existing Input block or Criterion block ranges. The first rows of both the Input and Criterion ranges must contain field names, and the Criterion field name must match exactly one of the database names.

The following examples use the same database presented throughout this chapter. Figure 12.16 shows the 11 database records used to illustrate the data management statistical functions. To simplify references to the database, you can execute the //**N**ame,**C**reate command and enter the range name **DBASE**. Then, assign the cell range A1 through G12. The name DBASE is used in all functions shown in this section because the database range name is easier to use and recall than a cell range.

DAVG

DAVG computes the average of the database field specified by the offset value for all records satisfying the criteria. To illustrate, enter a DAVG function that computes the average price for three-bedroom homes. The condition ". . . for three-bedroom homes" is the criterion; the database field to be averaged is at offset value 3 (the fourth database field); and the database range is cells A1 through G12. Place these criteria in cells H2 and H3:

    Bed
      3

Remember to type a double quotation mark preceding *Bed* so that text, not the range name BED, is entered into cell H2. After entering the criterion, type the following DAVG function into cell A14:

    DAVG($DBASE,3,H2:H3)

The value displayed is 159583.33 (rounded to two places after the decimal point).

So that the difference between the DAVG and AVG functions is clear, enter the formula **AVG(D2:D12)** in any unoccupied cell and compare the results of the two functions. AVG displays the average price for all database records, whereas DAVG computes the average price for selected database records.

Figure 12.18 illustrates the DAVG function, as well as the Criterion block in cells H2 and H3. The seven data management statistical functions are shown in the lower window. That window has been formatted to display formulas. Displayed values corresponding to each function are shown in column E of the lower window.

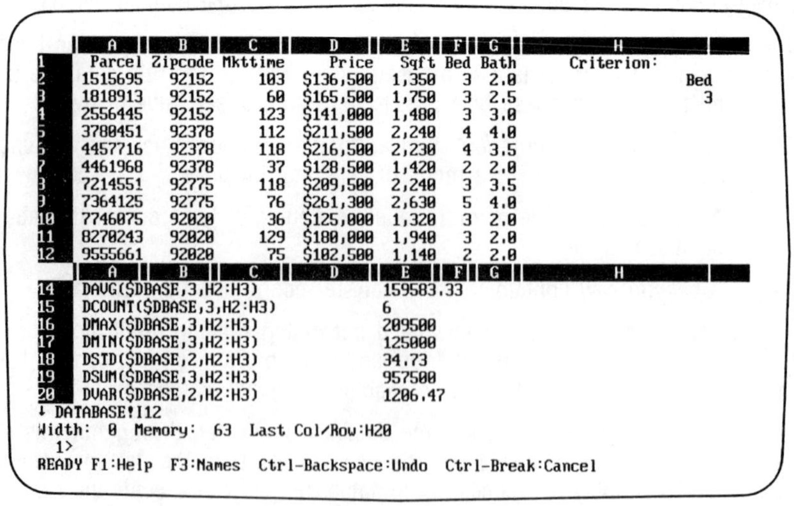

Fig. 12.18.

Examples of data management statistical functions.

	A	B	C	D	E	F	G	H
	Parcel	Zipcode	Mkttime	Price	Sqft	Bed	Bath	Criterion:
1								
2	1515695	92152	103	$136,500	1,350	3	2.0	Bed
3	1818913	92152	60	$165,500	1,750	3	2.5	3
4	2556445	92152	123	$141,000	1,400	3	3.0	
5	3700451	92378	112	$211,500	2,240	4	4.0	
6	4457716	92378	118	$216,500	2,230	4	3.5	
7	4461968	92378	37	$128,500	1,420	2	2.0	
8	7214551	92775	118	$209,500	2,240	3	3.5	
9	7364125	92775	76	$261,300	2,630	5	4.0	
10	7746075	92020	36	$125,000	1,320	3	2.0	
11	8270243	92020	129	$180,000	1,940	3	2.0	
12	9555661	92020	75	$102,500	1,140	2	2.0	

	A	B	C	D	E	F	G	H
14	DAVG($DBASE,3,H2:H3)				159583.33			
15	DCOUNT($DBASE,3,H2:H3)				6			
16	DMAX($DBASE,3,H2:H3)				209500			
17	DMIN($DBASE,3,H2:H3)				125000			
18	DSTD($DBASE,2,H2:H3)				34.73			
19	DSUM($DBASE,3,H2:H3)				957500			
20	DVAR($DBASE,2,H2:H3)				1206.47			

```
↓ DATABASE!I12
Width:  8  Memory:  63  Last Col/Row:H20
 1>
READY  F1:Help  F3:Names  Ctrl-Backspace:Undo  Ctrl-Break:Cancel
```

DCOUNT

DCOUNT returns the number in the offset range of nonblank, nonzero cells that meet the search criteria. The value is computed from the column specified by the offset parameter, whereas the criteria select which records are included in the counting operation.

For example, suppose that you want to know how many three-bedroom homes are in the database. The criterion needed to select only those records has been placed in cells H2 and H3 (see fig. 12.18). Recall that *Bed* is the required first-row label matching the field in the database; and 3 is the number of bedrooms to be matched.

The DCOUNT function that counts the number of three-bedroom homes in the database is

DCOUNT($DBASE,3,H2:H3)

Type the function in cell A15. The value returned by the DCOUNT function is 6 (see fig. 12.18).

DMAX

DMAX searches the database range given as the first argument, uses the Criterion range to select records, and computes the maximum value from the database column specified by the offset parameter. Like all data management statistical functions, DMAX chooses the values evaluated in three increasingly restrictive ways: first, by database range; second, by records selected from the database (the criterion); and third, by a specific column of the subset of records.

DMAX can display the maximum *Price* value (offset parameter value 3) for three-bedroom homes. The selection criterion has already been specified and used by the DAVG and DCOUNT functions. The following function is entered into cell A16:

DMAX($DBASE,3,H2:H3)

The returned value (cell E16 shows the display form) is 209500 and is the highest price for three-bedroom homes in the database (see fig. 12.18).

DMIN

DMIN computes the minimum value from a specified database column (field) of a selected group of records. To find the minimum sale price (column D or offset 3) for records with *Bed* fields equal to 3, enter the following function in cell A17:

DMIN($DBASE,3,H2:H3)

The returned value, 125000, is the lowest price of a three-bedroom home in the database (see fig. 12.18). Note that it is not, however, the least expensive home in the entire database.

DSTD

The DSTD function calculates the standard deviation of the selected database field values. By measuring how much individual values vary from the group average, the standard deviation indicates how representative the average value is for the sampled group. The smaller the standard deviation, the more representative the value is.

Let's look at the standard deviation of the *Mkttime* field. Because our database is small, the DSTD value for selected *Mkttime* values is apt to be large. The sampled values are restricted to those of three-bedroom homes. The function to compute the standard deviation of *Mkttime* values for three-bedroom homes is

DSTD($DBASE,2,H2:H3)

Cell E18 of figure 12.18 shows the result of the DSTD function, and the text representation of the function is in cell A18.

DSUM

DSUM is used to add selected field values of the database. An example is

DSUM($DBASE,3,H2:H3)

The *Price* field (offset 3) is summed for records selected by the Criterion range (cells H2 and H3). The criterion selects only records with *Bed* values of 3. Row 19 of figure 12.18 displays the sum of *Price* values for three-bedroom homes in the sales comparables database: $957,500.

DVAR

The DVAR function returns the variance of selected values. Similar to the standard deviation, variance is a measure of how much the average of a selected population varies from individual members in the sample.

Cell A20 in figure 12.18 contains a DVAR function. Cell E20 shows the value of that function. It displays the variance of the *Mkttime* field for three-bedroom homes. The variance is quite large (1206.47) due to the small sample size; only six records are in the selected group.

You can use the data management statistical functions to check for data errors or omissions. For example, a high variance or standard deviation for a field of a large database may indicate that the field contains errors. The power and versatility of these functions will become even clearer after you have used them for a while.

Special Purpose Data Analysis and Manipulation Commands

Five special purpose data analysis and data manipulation commands are described in this section. They have been called *special purpose* commands because they are used less frequently in business applications than the other //**D**ata commands described in this chapter. The special purpose commands include **B**lock, **A**nalysis, **P**arse, **T**able, and **M**atrix.

The //Data,Block Command

The **B**lock command is used to fill ranges of cells with series of numbers that increase or decrease by a specified increment. For example, you can easily create a spreadsheet row containing a series of dates, a series of arithmetically increasing numbers, or a series of geometrically increasing numbers. Values can be placed into adjacent cells in one or more columns (the default) or in one or more rows.

To illustrate this command, create a column of numbers representing a series of home sale prices so that you can later study the distribution of sales prices. Invoke the command to create a series of numbers by typing //**D**ata and selecting the **B**lock option (see fig. 12.19a). Then, either by pointing or by typing, enter the cell range to contain the series of sales prices—H4:H9 (see fig. 12.19b).

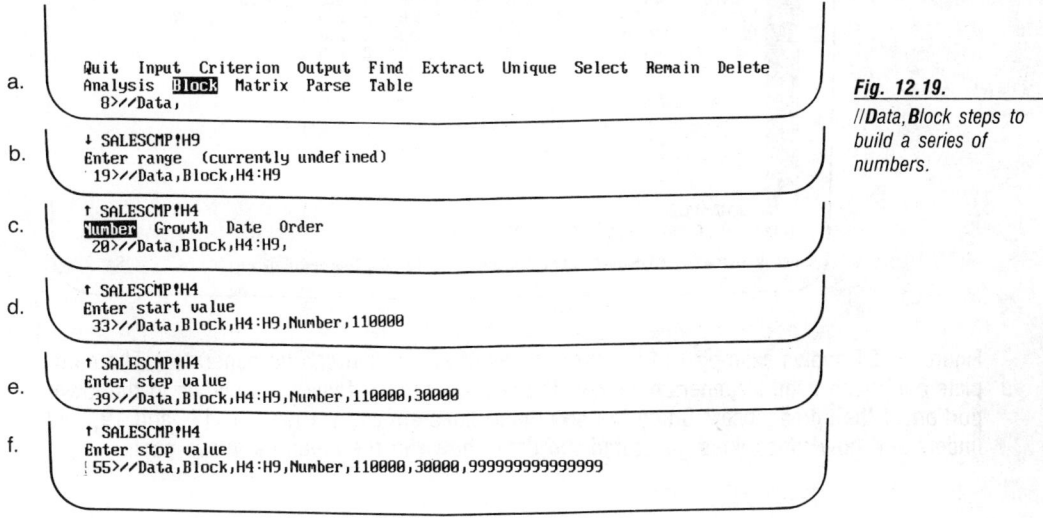

a.
```
Quit  Input  Criterion  Output  Find  Extract  Unique  Select  Remain  Delete
Analysis  Block  Matrix  Parse  Table
    8>//Data,
```

b.
```
↓ SALESCMP!H9
Enter range  (currently undefined)
  19>//Data,Block,H4:H9
```

c.
```
↑ SALESCMP!H4
Number  Growth  Date  Order
  28>//Data,Block,H4:H9,
```

d.
```
↑ SALESCMP!H4
Enter start value
  33>//Data,Block,H4:H9,Number,110000
```

e.
```
↑ SALESCMP!H4
Enter step value
  39>//Data,Block,H4:H9,Number,110000,30000
```

f.
```
↑ SALESCMP!H4
Enter stop value
  55>//Data,Block,H4:H9,Number,110000,30000,999999999999999
```

Fig. 12.19.

//*Data,Block* steps to build a series of numbers.

After you select the range, press Enter to display the next set of options (see fig. 12.19c). The first three choices determine what type of values are to be generated: **N**umber, **G**rowth, or **D**ate. The **N**umber choice causes evenly spaced numbers to be generated; the **G**rowth choice creates a series of numbers in a geometric relationship (each new number equals the preceding number times the quantity 1 plus the step value). If you choose **D**ate, a series of date values is generated. Dates are incremented to create successive values by a number of days, weeks, or months. The fourth choice, **O**rder, specifies whether the range will be filled downward (by column) or across (by row) from the upper left corner of the range to be filled.

Continuing with this example, select **N**umber and then enter the starting value, **110000**, and press Enter (see fig. 12.19d). Next, enter the step (increment) value. It can be a positive or negative number. Type **30000** and press Enter (see fig. 12.19e). The Super-Calc-suggested limit of 999999999999999 shown in figure 12.19f is more than adequate, so press Enter.

A series of numbers, beginning with 110000, is generated in cells H4 through H9. Each successive number is derived by adding the step value 30000 to the preceding number. Figure 12.20 shows the spreadsheet containing the generated series of numbers in the range H4:H9.

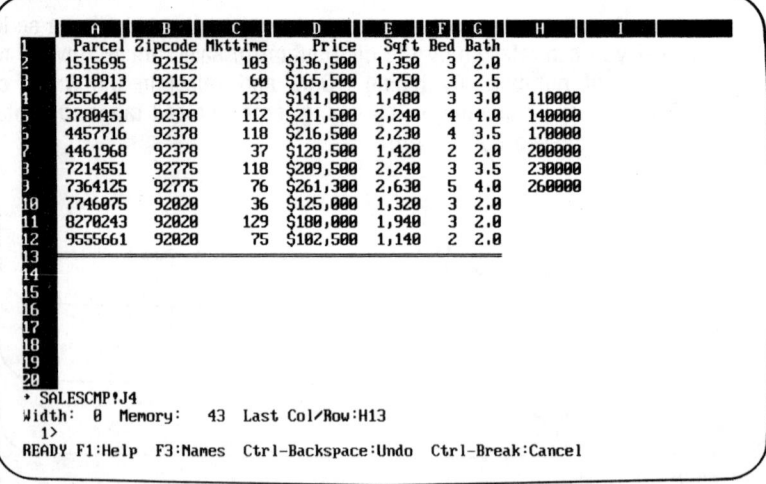

Fig. 12.20.

Spreadsheet after //Data,Block operation.

Figure 12.21 shows examples of the three types of series that can be generated. The complete command used to generate each of the column series of values is shown in the lower portion of the spreadsheet. Study the command lines shown in rows 15, 17, and 19, and understand how those lines generated the data shown in the columns above each.

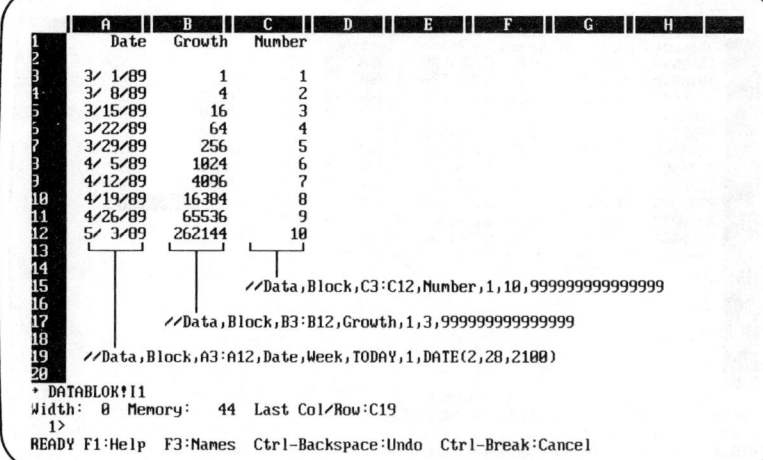

Fig. 12.21.

Examples of
//Data,Block.

The //Data,Analysis Command

The **A**nalysis command is invoked by typing //**D**ata,**A**nalysis from the Ready prompt. Two types of data analysis can be performed: distribution and regression.

Analyzing Data Distribution

The //**D**ata,**A**nalysis,**D**istribution command performs a frequency distribution analysis of a set of data. A *frequency distribution* describes the relationship between a set of classes and the frequency of occurrence of members of each class. The frequency distribution provides a mapping between a large number of data points and a smaller number of classes of data points. For example, a list of home sale prices (refer to fig. 12.20) illustrates why frequency analyses can be helpful.

To use the **D**istribution command, select //**D**ata,**A**nalysis,**D**istribution. Then specify the cell range of the input data to be analyzed—the sale prices of homes found in cells D2 through D12. Once the input data range is defined, the final step is to indicate the location of the set of data bins for which the frequency analysis is performed: cells H4 through H9. The entry line looks like this:

```
42>//Data,Analysis,Distribution,D2:D12,H4:H9
```

The bin range must be in ascending order. The input range of cells is compared to the bin range of cells, and frequency counts are placed into the column to the right of the bin range indicating the frequency of input cells that correspond to each bin range class.

When you press Enter after defining the bin range, SuperCalc performs the frequency analysis and places the generated frequency values into the column to the right of the bin range—in this case, column I (see fig. 12.22).

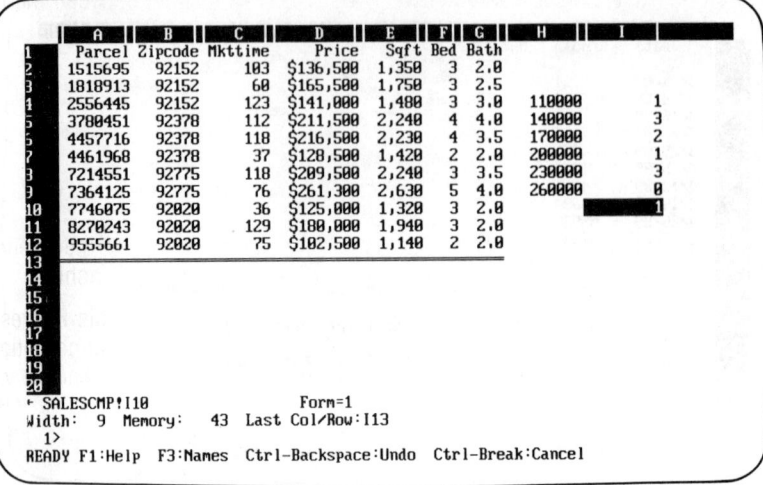

Fig. 12.22.

Spreadsheet after //Data, Analysis, Distribution is executed.

The values in the frequency column represent the frequency of distribution of the numbers in the input values range for each interval. The first interval in the bin range is for values greater than zero and less than or equal to 110,000 (the first bin range value). The second is for values greater than 110,000 and less than or equal to 140,000, and so on. The last value in the results column, in cell I10 (just below the last row in the bin range), shows the frequency of numbers greater than the greatest value in the bin range.

If you examine column I in figure 12.22, you can see that the smallest frequency is for home sales in the price range $231,001 to $260,000.

Using Data Regression Analysis

The data regression command provides the tools necessary to determine the relationship between one set of values, called the *independent variables*, and another set of values, called the *dependent variables*. The results of the regression analysis are summarized in an output range. There are several uses of regression analysis in the business world, including forecasting profit, sales, research and development funds amounts, minimal inventory levels, and advertising budgets. Accurate forecasting using regression analysis is possible only if a strong relationship—a *reliable correlation*—exists between the dependent and independent variables. Regression analysis measures the strength of the relationship between variables.

Relying on past observation and measurement of variables, linear regression analysis is a way of determining the best fit of a linear equation through a series of data points. For example, a marketing director might want to determine what next year's marketing budget should be to maximize sales. Using data gathered from several past months' marketing costs and sales volumes, regression analysis can be used to determine whether increasing the marketing budget has a direct effect on sales volume, resulting in increased sales.

Further, if regression analysis indicates a strong relationship between marketing expenses and sales volumes, what marketing expenses are necessary to attain a particular sales goal? That is, does regression analysis reveal that any trend found is likely to continue into the future?

Using the sales comparables data as an example, regression analysis is used to determine if there is a relationship between the number of square feet in a home and its sale price. If there is a strong enough relationship, then the value of square feet can be reliably used to forecast the sale price of a home based on its square footage. Although you suspect there is a relationship, one question answered by regression analysis is the strength of that relationship (for example, no relationship through very strong relationship).

You invoke the regression command by typing //**D**ata,**A**nalysis,**R**egression (see fig. 12.23a). The choices shown in figure 12.23b appear. Use the **X**-range option to select one or more independent variables for the regression. Up to 87 independent variables can be specified. Independent variables are columns of data, so any rows of data you want to include must be converted to columns (use /**C**opy,**T**ranspose to copy rows to columns). In our example, the X-range is the partial column containing square feet, E2:E12 (see fig. 12.23c). Press Enter to complete the X-range specification.

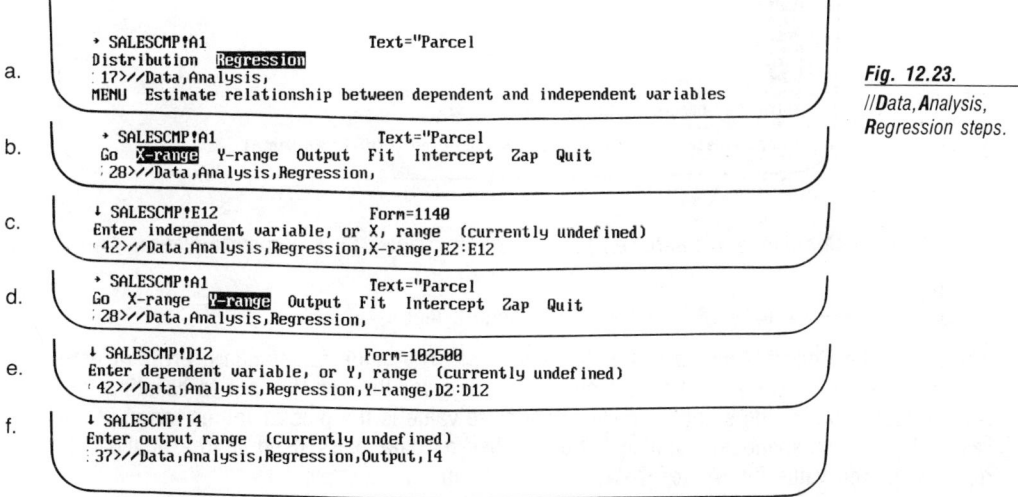

a.
```
 • SALESCMP!A1                 Text="Parcel
 Distribution Regression
 : 17>//Data,Analysis,
 MENU  Estimate relationship between dependent and independent variables
```

b.
```
 • SALESCMP!A1                 Text="Parcel
 Go X-range  Y-range  Output  Fit  Intercept  Zap  Quit
 : 28>//Data,Analysis,Regression,
```

c.
```
 ↓ SALESCMP!E12                Form=1140
 Enter independent variable, or X, range  (currently undefined)
 : 42>//Data,Analysis,Regression,X-range,E2:E12
```

d.
```
 • SALESCMP!A1                 Text="Parcel
 Go  X-range  Y-range  Output  Fit  Intercept  Zap  Quit
 : 28>//Data,Analysis,Regression,
```

e.
```
 ↓ SALESCMP!D12                Form=102500
 Enter dependent variable, or Y, range  (currently undefined)
 : 42>//Data,Analysis,Regression,Y-range,D2:D12
```

f.
```
 ↓ SALESCMP!I4
 Enter output range  (currently undefined)
 : 37>//Data,Analysis,Regression,Output,I4
```

Fig. 12.23.
*//Data,Analysis,
Regression steps.*

The **Y**-range option specifies the dependent variable—the sales price in the sales comparables example. Press **Y** to specify the dependent variable (see fig. 12.23d). Enter the partial column cell range for the variable: **D2:D12** (see fig. 12.23e). Like the X-range, the Y-range must be a column. Press Enter to complete the Y-range specification.

The **O**utput option specifies the upper left corner of the results of the regression analysis. This area should be an unused portion of the spreadsheet because the output of the analysis overwrites existing data in the output range. Minimally, the output occupies nine rows and four columns. Although you can specify a cell range, typing a single cell is sufficient. Enter **I4** (see fig. 12.23f) for the sales comparables example and press Enter.

Figure 12.24 shows the outcome of the //**D**ata,**A**nalysis,**R**egression command in the square feet versus sales price example. The results include the value of the constant and the coefficient of the single independent variable specified for the X-range. The results (cells I4 through L12) include several statistics that describe the strength of the linear relationship between square feet and sales price. In particular, the value for *R Squared* (.989, rounded) indicates a very strong relationship. *R squared* values close to zero would indicate no apparent direct relationship.

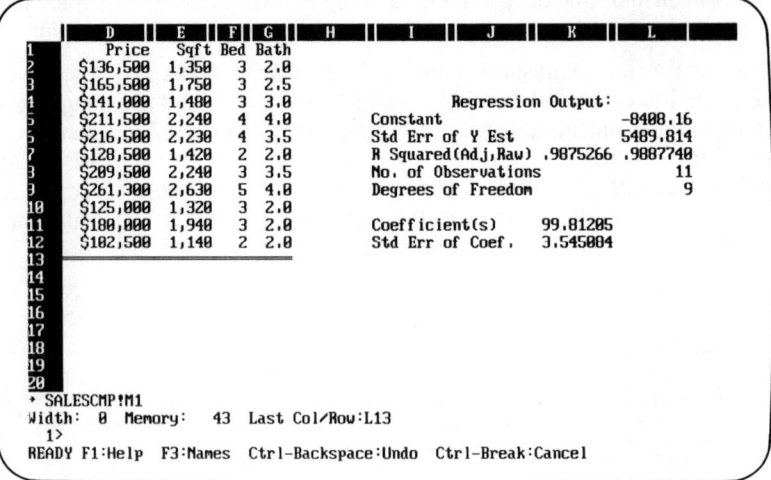

Fig. 12.24.

*Spreadsheet after //**D**ata,**A**nalysis, **R**egression is executed.*

The values for *Constant* and *Coefficient(s)* indicate the values for the linear equation Y = a + bX:

Sales price = −8408.16 + 99.81205 * square feet

where *a* is the *Constant* and *b* is the *Coefficient(s)*. The value for standard error of estimate—*Std Err of Y Est*—is a hedge factor accounting for the fact that our forecasting tool is imperfect. That is, the standard error of estimate value is the plus or minus range of the values for the independent variable. The number of data pairs used in the analysis is reported as the value for *No. of Observations*—11 in our example.

If the *R squared* value is not close to one (for example, 0.55), this value may suggest that the changes in the independent variable (square feet) do not wholly account for corresponding changes in the dependent variable (sales price). Further analysis is required to determine whether changes in the dependent variable are a result of more than one independent variable (perhaps square feet and number of bedrooms together more accurately forecast sales price).

The //Data,Parse Command

The //Data,Parse command is used to convert a column of cell labels into a series of individual columns of cell labels and values. You may encounter a situation in which you want to load your spreadsheet with data obtained from another software product (ASCII data from a word processor document, for example) or a remote computing resource. Frequently, data obtained from a nonspreadsheet is in the form of characters (both alphabetic characters and numeric values). Data not in spreadsheet form can be imported into your SuperCalc spreadsheet by using the //Import,Text command (described in Chapter 14). Data is read into a spreadsheet as a column of cell labels, and each record is placed in one column as a long label (spilling over into adjacent cells if necessary). Numeric data imported into the spreadsheet as part of a long label cannot be used in calculations because they are part of a label. In order to manipulate numeric information, you must be able to separate out, or parse, a label into its component parts.

The //Data,Parse command is a handy means of extracting numeric or string information from a column of long labels (information contained wholly in one column but perhaps displaying across several columns). Parse converts a column of information into one or more separate columns using a format line that indicates how each long label line is to be dissected into its constituent parts. This special line is called the *parse format line*. For example, suppose that you have just imported the data in figure 12.25 and you want to convert it into a series of columns for mathematical manipulation.

```
    │    A    │    B    │    C   │    D    │    E   ││    F    ││    G    ││    H    │
 1  │1515695    92152      103   136500    1350    3  2
 2  │1818913    92152       60   165500    1750    3  2.5
 3  │2556445    92152      123   141000    1400    3  3
 4  │3780451    92378      112   211500    2240    4  4
 5  │4457716    92378      118   216500    2230    4  3.5
 6  │4461968    92378       37   128500    1420    2  2
 7  │7214551    92775      118   209500    2240    3  3.5
 8  │7364125    92775       76   261300    2630    5  4
 9  │7746075    92020       36   125000    1320    3  2
10  │8270243    92020      129   180000    1940    3  2
11  │9555661    92020       75   102500    1140    2  2
12  │
13  │
14  │
15  │
16  │
17  │
18  │
19  │
20  │

* SALESCMP:A1                   Text="1515695    92152      103  136500  1350  3
Width:  9  Memory:    44  Last Col/Row:A11
  1>
READY F1:Help  F3:Names  Ctrl-Backspace:Undo  Ctrl-Break:Cancel
```

Fig. 12.25.

Real estate data after importing (///Import,Text).

Notice the status line in figure 12.25. It indicates that the imported data (Text=''1515695. . .) is contained in column A, although the individual data fields seem to be in separate cells.

To invoke //**D**ata,**P**arse, move the cursor to the first cell in the column to be parsed and type //**DP**. Seven options are displayed:

        Go Create Edit Input Output Zap Quit

The **C**reate option creates a parse format line, **E**dit alters an existing parse format line, **I**nput selects the range that you want parsed, and **O**utput specifies the upper left corner of a block of cells that will hold the parsed data. Additionally, **Z**ap resets any previously selected parse Input and Output ranges. **Q**uit exits the **P**arse command and returns to the Ready prompt. **G**o performs the parse using the Input range and Output range information to parse the data.

Perform the following operations to parse the data displayed in figure 12.25. First, type //**DP** and select **C**reate. Then, enter the cell to contain the parse format line in response to the prompt

        Enter cell

Usually, this is the cell that contains the first row of the data to be parsed. For the example shown in figure 12.25, enter **A1**. A parse format line is inserted just above the first row of the imported data. SuperCalc does a good job of guessing what the format line should contain by examining the first line of data (see fig. 12.26).

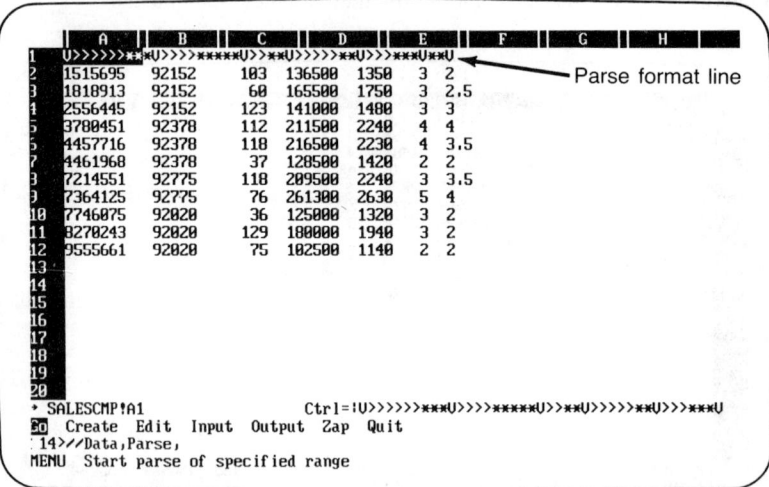

Fig. 12.26.

Parse format line generated with //Data,Parse,Create.

If an incorrect parse format line is created, you can use the **E**dit command to alter the parse line. Special codes are inserted into the parse line to indicate how to treat each line of data. These codes are summarized in Table 12.6.

Table 12.6
Parse Format Line Symbols

Format Code	Meaning
"	The first character of a text field
V	The first character of a value field
D	The first character of a date field
T	The first character of a time field
S	Skip the character below during parsing (this code must be entered manually by editing the parse line)
>	Continuation character for the current field type
* (asterisk)	The "don't care" character. If the character below this position is blank, ignore it. Otherwise, treat the character as part of the current field.

Next, specify the range of cells containing the data to be parsed by typing

　//**D**ata,**P**arse,**I**nput,**A1:A12**

and press Enter. Be sure that the Input range includes the parse format line as well as the entire data column. Finally, select an unused area of the spreadsheet in which to place the parsed results by typing

　//**D**ata,**P**arse,**O**utput,**A14**

and press Enter. Notice that only the upper left corner of the output range need be specified.

Once the parse format line and the Input and Output ranges have been established, the final step is to perform the parse operation. Figure 12.26 illustrates the spreadsheet with parse format line in place just prior to pressing **G**o.

Figure 12.27 illustrates the result. Parsed data begins in row 14. Notice that individual data fields have been placed into separate columns. For example, compare row 2 with row 14.

After the data has been parsed, you can delete the original imported rows.

The //Data,Table Command

Like all other commands described in this chapter, the table-building command is a data management command accessed by typing //**D**. The **T**able command lets you place different values into a formula and view the results for each of several input values (variables). With this command you can perform "what if" analyses—for example, "What if this inventory reorder point is varied in the inventory valuation formula?"—without the added work of creating multiple copies of a formula. Only one model formula is needed to generate a result for each of the input variables. The "what if" process is automated through iteration: sets of values are substituted one at a time into the target formula, and a table of

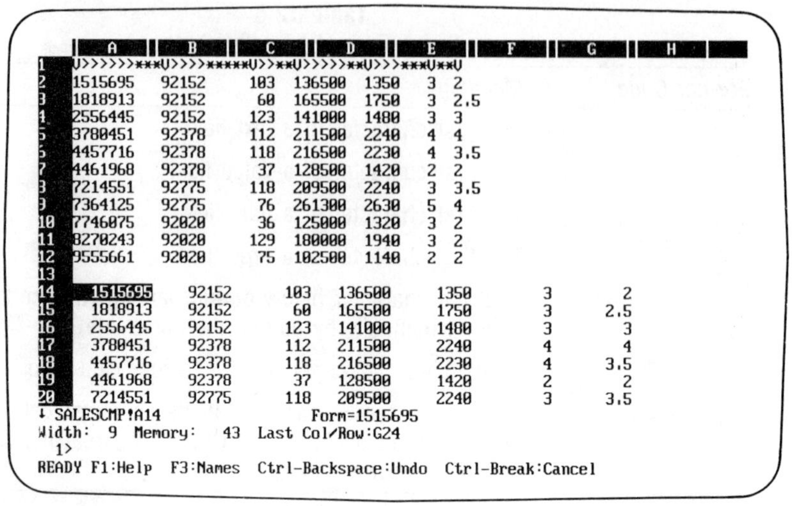

Fig. 12.27.

Spreadsheet after //Data, Parse, Go is executed.

	A	B	C	D	E	F	G	H
1	U>>>>>***U>>>*****U>>**U>>>>***U>>>***U**U							
2	1515695	92152	103	136500	1350	3	2	
3	1818913	92152	60	165500	1750	3	2.5	
4	2556445	92152	123	141000	1400	3	3	
5	3780451	92378	112	211500	2240	4	4	
6	4457716	92378	118	216500	2230	4	3.5	
7	4461968	92378	37	128500	1420	2	2	
8	7214551	92775	118	209500	2240	3	3.5	
9	7364125	92775	76	261300	2630	5	4	
10	7746075	92020	36	125000	1320	3	2	
11	8270243	92020	129	180000	1940	3	2	
12	9555661	92020	75	182500	1140	2	2	
13								
14	1515695	92152	103	136500	1350		3	2
15	1818913	92152	60	165500	1750		3	2.5
16	2556445	92152	123	141000	1400		3	3
17	3780451	92378	112	211500	2240		4	4
18	4457716	92378	118	216500	2230		4	3.5
19	4461968	92378	37	128500	1420		2	2
20	7214551	92775	118	209500	2240		3	3.5

```
↑ SALESCMP!A14                    Form=1515695
Width:  9  Memory:   43  Last Col/Row:G24
   1>
READY F1:Help  F3:Names  Ctrl-Backspace:Undo  Ctrl-Break:Cancel
```

resultant values is formed. You provide the values to be substituted into the formula, and SuperCalc automatically records the results in the spreadsheet. Either one or two sets of input values can be evaluated.

To see just how this table-building process works, let's suppose that you want to build a simple table of production costs for a product. The model formula for product cost is a simple one:

Product cost = $1,500 + $20 * number of units produced

in which there is a fixed setup cost, $1,500, plus an incremental (variable) cost of $20 per unit that is produced. By substituting various production quantities for the single variable, you can generate a table of production costs.

Begin by creating in one column the input values representing the number of product units. Enter values 10 through 80 in cells A6 through A13 (as in fig. 12.28). Next, enter the formula for calculating product costs in cell B5:

1500 + 20*B1

where B1 is the input cell (currently, it is empty) in which each of the eight input values is placed by SuperCalc to calculate the resulting product costs. Type //Data,Table and then specify the table range. The table range must include the input column, the formula result column, and the model formula. Enter the cell range A5:B19. The formula result column is always placed to the right of the input column, and the model formula(s) is placed in the cell just above the result column. The final step is to identify the input cell. The input cell must be the cell referenced in the model formula (B1 in the example). Press Enter and the resulting values are calculated and placed in cells B6 through B13. Figure 12.28 shows the completed table.

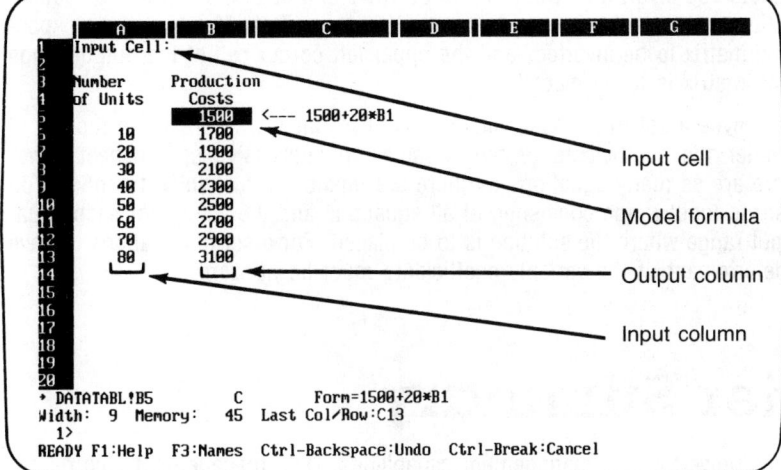

Fig. 12.28.
//Data,Table,1 example.

Cell C5 contains the text equivalent of the model formula stored previously in cell B5.

You generate a table to study the effects of two variables in a single formula by executing //**D**ata,**T**able,**2**. As in the case of the one-variable table, you identify the input values column, the model formula, which is in the upper left corner of the table range (just above the first variable value), and the two input cells. Values for the second variable are entered to the right of the formula and across the row. Tables are not recalculated when the spreadsheet is recalculated. The table result columns are, after all, simply values requiring no recalculation. To recalculate table result values after you have altered input values, press Alt-F9, the table key.

The //Data,Matrix Command

The //**D**ata,**M**atrix command is a special purpose mathematical command that performs a variety of useful matrix operations. You can multiply matrices, invert matrices, and find the solution to a set of linear equations. Of the three matrix operations, the latter is most frequently used in business settings. When you select //**D**ata,**M**atrix, three options are displayed:

    Multiply Invert Solve

Multiply performs matrix multiplication on two rectangular matrices using the rules of matrix algebra. The number of columns of the first matrix must equal the number of rows of the second. The resulting matrix has the same number of rows as the first matrix and the same number of columns as the second matrix. You must specify three ranges to perform multiplication: matrix 1, matrix 2, and the output range where the product is placed. The maximum size of any matrix to be multiplied is 90 rows by 90 columns.

The Invert option lets you invert a matrix of up to 90 rows and columns. It must be square and nonsingular (its determinant must not be zero). You type //**D**ata,**M**atrix and then specify two ranges: the matrix to be inverted, and the upper left corner cell of the output range where the inverted matrix is to be placed.

The **S**olve option solves a set of n linear equations with n unknowns. To solve the set of equations, you enter the coefficients of the variables in successive spreadsheet rows, ensuring that there are as many equations as there are unknowns for which to solve. You enter two ranges: the Input range consisting of all equations and the values for each equation and the Output range where the solution is to be placed. For a set of equations to have a solution, the determinant of the variable coefficients must be nonzero.

Chapter Summary

SuperCalc provides powerful data management capabilities. Data management records are rows and columns of data. The column headings are field names. Although the data of one column may be different from another column, if the data within the individual columns is the same type, you can treat that spreadsheet as a database.

Convenient data management commands permit you to find records that satisfy certain conditions. These conditions are called the search criteria. With the **E**xtract and **U**nique commands, you can locate records and place them in the Output block—a designated separate area of the spreadsheet. The **S**elect command acts like the **E**xtract command except that you are asked whether a highlighted record should be placed in the Output block. You can choose to include some records and exclude others from the Output block.

The data management statistical functions are DAVG, DCOUNT, DMAX, DMIN, DSTD, DSUM, and DVAR. Like similarly named statistical functions, the data management statistical functions calculate averages, sums, counts, and so on. These functions differ from their statistical function cousins in that you can restrict the scope of statistical operations with selection criteria.

SuperCalc's special purpose data analysis and manipulation commands provide regression analysis, block filling, data distribution, text parsing, and a rich variety of matrix manipulation commands. These special purpose commands are powerful components of the data management command set.

SuperCalc's data management system, associated data management statistical functions, and special purpose data analysis commands provide sophisticated and fast data management capabilities. Coupled with SuperCalc's powerful spreadsheet capabilities, the data management system makes SuperCalc a powerful integrated system.

13

Using the Spreadsheet Auditing Tools

SuperCalc's spreadsheet auditing and debugging tools are available through the //Test command. The mode indicator switches to AUDIT when you execute //Test or press Alt-F1. AUDIT mode helps you ensure the accuracy and integrity of your spreadsheet models by providing numerous commands and functions that highlight potential inconsistencies and faults. Use AUDIT mode to

- Locate information
- Locate problems and confusing patterns arising from spreadsheet design or layout
- Identify formulas that reference text or blank (empty) cells
- Trace intercellular relationships
- Locate and list named ranges that reference cells outside spreadsheet boundaries
- Search for and (optionally) replace cell contents and partial contents

Understanding and Invoking AUDIT Mode

To execute any of the auditing commands, simply press the slash key (/) while in AUDIT mode to display the Audit main menu. AUDIT is a "sticky" mode: that is, any command you execute while in AUDIT mode clears the command line and returns control to AUDIT mode. To exit AUDIT mode and return to READY mode, execute /Quit.

449

The first example, illustrating several auditing features, is a summary spreadsheet showing real estate sales by ZIP code in a selected area. Seven independent support spreadsheets supply summary information (see fig. 13.1). The summary spreadsheet includes several important features: extensive use of link formulas referencing supporting spreadsheets, correct and incorrect range name definitions, unused range names, range names that exceed the spreadsheet boundaries, formulas that contain ranges referencing empty or text cells, and column- and entry-level cell formatting. The several subtle errors in the real estate sales spreadsheet demonstrate SuperCalc's many powerful auditing features.

Fig. 13.1.

Real estate sales example with link formulas.

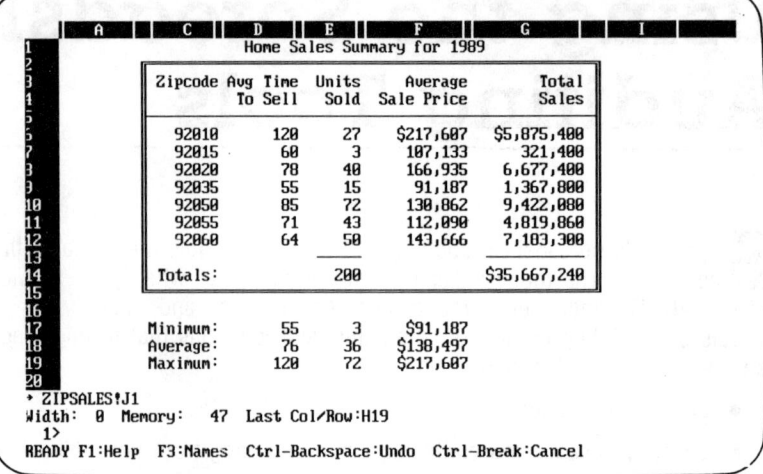

```
                A      C    D    E       F           G        I
1                            Home Sales Summary for 1989
2
3              Zipcode Avg Time Units   Average      Total
4                      To Sell  Sold  Sale Price     Sales
5
6               92010    120     27   $217,607    $5,875,400
7               92015     60      3    187,133       321,400
8               92020     70     40    166,935     6,677,400
9               92035     55     15     91,187     1,367,000
10              92050     85     72    130,862     9,422,000
11              92055     71     43    112,090     4,819,860
12              92060     64     50    143,666     7,103,300
13                                   _____
14              Totals:          200             $35,667,240
15
16
17              Minimum:   55      3    $91,187
18              Average:   76     36   $138,497
19              Maximum:  120     72   $217,607
20
  ⟩ ZIPSALES!J1
  Width:  0  Memory:   47  Last Col/Row:H19
     1⟩
  READY F1:Help  F3:Names  Ctrl-Backspace:Undo  Ctrl-Break:Cancel
```

You invoke AUDIT mode by issuing //Test or pressing Alt-F1. The mode indicator in the lower left corner of the screen changes to AUDIT, and the entry line is cleared. Press / again to display the main Audit menu. The following commands are displayed:

    Details Highlight Names Replace Squeeze View Quit

Each command performs an auditing task. /Details shows further information on the results of the most recent /Highlight test. /Highlight locates specific cells, based on your criteria, and highlights the cells on-screen. /Names identifies named ranges that may require further inspection: overlapping named ranges, ranges that exceed spreadsheet boundaries, and so on. /Replace searches for and replaces text, formulas, control text, or numbers. (/Replace examines cell contents). /Squeeze stores formulas either in their original form or in compressed form when they are copies of other similar formulas. This command can reduce disk space required for saved spreadsheets. /View displays information in one of two formats: in a map format that identifies groups of formulas, text, macros, and numbers using special symbols; or in a formula format showing the cell formulas (contents). The /Quit command returns you to SuperCalc READY mode. These commands, except for /Quit and /Squeeze, are further explained in this chapter.

Displaying Formulas and Cell Patterns: /View

Formulas, numbers, and text entries often appear in recognizable patterns within your spreadsheet. A related group of formulas, for example, may appear in one particular column. Numeric data may appear in a rectangular range of cells, or text may precede every formula cell in a repeating pattern of rows. The /View command highlights these repeating and often standard patterns by replacing the normal spreadsheet display with symbols. These symbols simplify the display and help you to spot disruptions in text, number, and formula patterns. Unlike some AUDIT commands, you also can use /View to return to normal spreadsheet display. The following sections discuss using the /View options.

Displaying Cell Patterns

Invoke /View by pressing /V from AUDIT mode. Three options are displayed: **N**ormal, **F**ormula, and **M**ap. Select **M**ap by pressing **M**. The two **M**ap options, **S**tandard and **P**attern, both display a pattern of common elements by replacing the normal display with the pattern display (**P**attern also displays families of formulas). The unique characters are shown in table 13.1.

Table 13.1
AUDIT Symbols and Their Meanings

Symbol	Stands for
"	Text
'	Repeating text
#	Number
f	Formula
i	Invariant formula
m	Macro

If you discover cells that do not match an evident pattern, you can use the /View,**M**ap,**P**attern command to show relationships among formulas. This command often reveals which formulas are unique and which are related. Figure 13.2 shows this pattern view of the spreadsheet shown in figure 13.1.

The symbols displayed, representing cell contents, are identical to the standard map symbols in table 13.1. In addition, uppercase letters (for example, A, B, C, D, and E in figure 13.2) indicate families of related formulas. Notice that cells E13 and G13 contain B, indicating that these two formulas are similar and thus related. Similarly, the letter A in cells F6 through F12 indicates that these formulas are all similar (link formulas of the same type). If the letter *G* appeared in cell F9, for example, this apparent break in the normal pattern would merit further investigation. The f in some cells indicates a reference to a linked spreadsheet.

Fig. 13.2.

Map pattern view of the real estate sales spreadsheet.

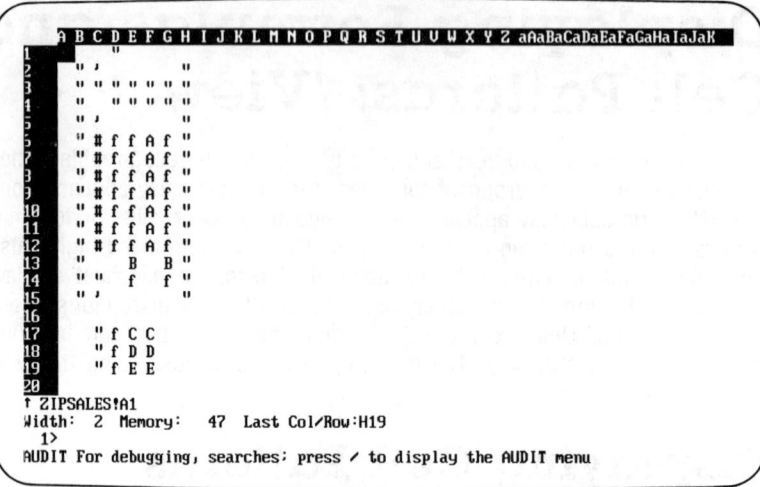

Once you are satisfied that the displayed pattern is correct—that all cells form a regular, consistent pattern—you can return to the normal spreadsheet display by issuing /**V**iew,**N**ormal. You remain in AUDIT mode, however, and you can execute other AUDIT mode commands. Press /**Q**uit to return to READY mode.

Displaying Formulas

You can display and check formulas in your spreadsheet by entering the command /**V**iew,**F**ormula from AUDIT mode. Because this command works only in AUDIT mode, be sure first to press Alt-F1 or //**T**est to switch to AUDIT mode from READY mode.

Formulas displayed by /**V**iew,**F**ormula are much easier to read than those displayed by executing the usual SuperCalc command /**G**lobal,**F**ormula. /**V**iew,**F**ormula presents an organized, partitioned-cell display, whereas /**G**lobal,**F**ormula does not always display entire formulas when column widths are small. Figure 13.3 shows the real estate sales summary spreadsheet (refer to fig. 13.1) after the /**V**iew,**F**ormula command has been issued.

To return to normal display, type /**V**iew,**N**ormal. The familiar spreadsheet display replaces the formula display.

```
   ||   C    ||     D        ||      E           |    F         ||
 7 |92015     |AVG(ZIP92015!MKTTIME|COUNT(ZIP92015!PRICE|G7/E7        |
   |          |)             |)             |              |
 8 |92020     |AVG(ZIP92020!MKTTIME|COUNT(ZIP92020!PRICE|G8/E8        |
   |          |)             |)             |              |
 9 |92035     |AVG(ZIP92035!MKTTIME|COUNT(ZIP92035!PRICE|G9/E9        |
   |          |)             |)             |              |
10 |92050     |AVG(ZIP92050!MKTTIME|COUNT(ZIP92050!PRICE|G10/E10      |
   |          |)             |)             |              |
11 |92055     |AVG(ZIP92055!MKTTIME|COUNT(ZIP92055!PRICE|G11/E11      |
   |          |)             |)             |              |
12 |92060     |AVG(ZIP92060!MKTTIME|COUNT(ZIP92060!PRICE|G12/E12      |
   |          |)             |)             |              |
13 |          |              |REPEAT("-",WIDTH(E13|             |
   |          |              |)-2)          |              |
14 |"Totals:  |              |SUM(E6:E11)   |              |
15 |'=        |              |              |              |
16 |          |              |              |              |
17 |"Minimum: |MIN(SALETIME) |MIN(UNITS)    |MIN(AVGPRICE) |
18 |"Average: |AVG(SALETIME) |AVG(UNITS)    |AVG(AVGPRICE) |
19 |"Maximum: |MAX(SALETIME) |MAX(UNITS)    |MAX(AVGPRICE) |
 • ZIPSALES!D7          Form=AVG(ZIP92015!MKTTIME)
Width: 21 Memory:    47 Last Col/Row:H19
   1>
AUDIT For debugging, searches; press / to display the AUDIT menu
```

Fig. 13.3.

Displaying formulas in AUDIT mode.

Replacing Cell Contents: /Replace

The **/R**eplace command searches for text, control text, formulas, or numbers, and replaces them with other data. **/R**eplace is often used when you find that you have consistently misspelled a label throughout a spreadsheet and want to correct the label, or when you want to make the same change in many formulas within a range of cells. For example, you could use **/R**eplace to change all occurrences of the AVG function to the MAX function. Because **/R**eplace searches cell contents rather than displayed values, it can save a great deal of work when you want to change selected parts of formulas that are in many cells in your spreadsheet.

Performing the /Replace Operation

Select **/R**eplace from AUDIT mode (see fig. 13.4a). The **/R**eplace options are displayed. Only three basic steps are required to replace one string with another:

1. Specify the **O**ld-string.

2. Specify the **N**ew-string.

3. Select **G**o to execute the replacement(s).

Select **O**ld-string to tell SuperCalc what cell contents to locate and ultimately replace (see fig. 13.4b). After selecting **O**ld-string, type the contents (referred to as a *string*) to be

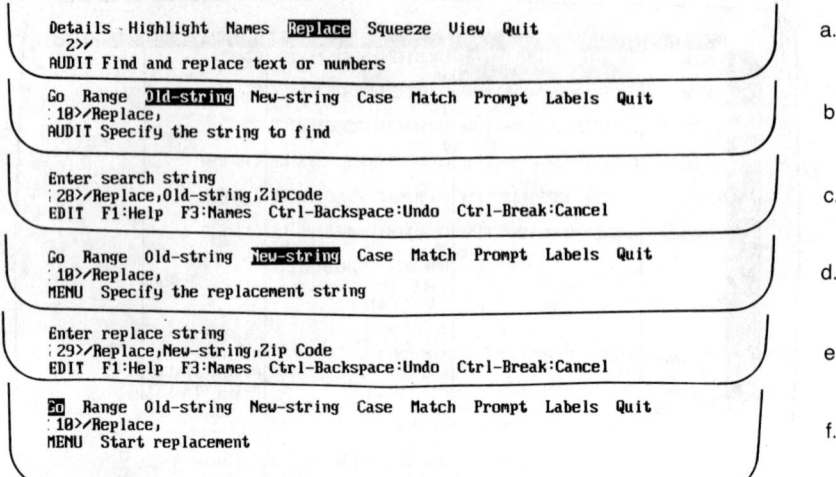

Fig. 13.4.

Example of steps to replace one string with another.

located (see fig. 13.4c). If the case of the string (upper- or lowercase) is important, be sure to type the search string carefully. Press Enter to end **O**ld-string selection.

Next, select **N**ew-string to enter the replacement string (see fig. 13.4d). Enter the replacement string in the same way you entered **O**ld-string (see fig. 13.4e). Again, be sure to specify the replacement string precisely. Press Enter to finish your replacement string choice.

The main Replace menu reappears after you specify the replacement string. Select **G**o to begin the search-and-replace operation (see fig. 13.4f). By default, SuperCalc prompts you with the following choices when the old string is located:

        Yes No Remaining

Choose **Y**es to replace the old string with its replacement, **N**o not to replace it, or **R**emaining to replace this occurrence and all others found throughout the spreadsheet. Notice that the choice **R**emaining replaces all the old strings without prompting you. You probably don't want to select **R**emaining until you feel comfortable with the /**R**eplace command.

When the /**R**eplace command is finished, a message on the right side of the status line indicates the total number of strings that were replaced:

        The total number of replacements was 1

If the old string cannot be located in the spreadsheet, then the message

        Old-string not found

is displayed instead.

Using the Other /Replace Options

The options described in these paragraphs permit you to refine or restrict the **R**eplace operation. **R**ange, for example, restricts the search/replace range. If the options are not specified, they take on "safe" defaults. (Each option's default is noted when it is discussed.) An option can be specified any time before selecting **G**o (see fig. 13.4f).

The Range Option

If you want to restrict the range of cells searched, then you use the **R**ange option (see fig. 13.4b). Select **R**ange from the main Replace menu. The entire spreadsheet is highlighted (in POINT mode), suggesting that the default search area for small spreadsheets (set using the command /**G**lobal,**O**ptimum,**N**ext,**B**oundary) is the range A1 through BK254. Change this unlimited range by pressing the Esc key and typing the appropriate range. For example, type the range **B1:H19** to limit the /**R**eplace search scope to the active portion of the real estate sales spreadsheet shown in figure 13.1. Be sure to press Enter to register this range.

SuperCalc remembers all your /**R**eplace options. On future search-and-replace operations, /**R**eplace will search only the area specified by the **R**ange option you last entered. Remember to change the **R**ange option if needed before executing subsequent /**R**eplace commands.

The Case Option

The **C**ase option (see fig. 13.4b) determines whether or not exact capitalization in **O**ld-string is important. Two options appear when you select **C**ase:

    Exact Any

Exact causes only exact (case sensitive) matches to be found and replaced, whereas **A**ny causes any matching string (regardless of capitalization) to be replaced. The default option is **A**ny.

The Match Option

The **M**atch option (shown in fig. 13.4b) allows you to specify whether the location of **O**ld-string within a candidate cell is important. Five options are available when you select **M**atch:

    Begins Contains Exact Terminates Word

Choose **B**egins if the search string must *begin* a possibly longer string. Choose **C**ontains if the search string can match *any part* of a string. **E**xact restricts matches to cells whose contents *completely* match **O**ld-string. **T**erminates restricts matches to cells that *end* with **O**ld-string. **W**ord restricts matches to strings *surrounded by spaces* and matching **O**ld-string.

The Prompt Option

You may choose to accept or reject each replacement individually by selecting the **P**rompt option (see fig. 13.4b). The **P**rompt options are **Y**es and **N**o. Select **Y**es to control each replacement. During the search-and-replace operation, SuperCalc prompts you each time a candidate string is located with the choices

        Yes No Remaining

Choose **Y**es, the default, to replace this string with the new string. Select **N**o to skip this string and continue to the next occurrence. Select **R**emaining to replace all remaining occurrences automatically without waiting for your confirmation.

The Labels Option

The **L**abels option (see fig. 13.4b) specifies whether **N**ew-string will contain cell references or named ranges. The menu choices are **Y**es and **N**o. The default is **Y**es. If you specify **L**abels,**Y**es, then formula references in **N**ew-string are recognized as named ranges. If you specify **L**abels,**N**o, then formula references in **N**ew-string are recognized as cell references.

Reviewing Range Names: /Names

You should almost always use range names rather than explicit cell references in formulas. You gain many advantages by using range names. Range names document formulas, and spreadsheet debuggers and maintainers can more easily understand the intent of formulas when they contain names rather than cell ranges and cell references. Range names assist you in spreadsheet development as well, because remembering a range name is easier than trying to recall the equivalent range of cells when writing formulas. Naming ranges is explained in Chapter 3.

However, range names can lead to inaccuracies, errors, and redundancies. Many incorrect results are generated from ill-defined range names. Potential errors when creating and using range names include

- Range names exceeding a spreadsheet's boundaries
- Duplicate range names
- Overlapping range names
- Unreferenced range names

AUDIT's /**N**ames command provides a handy mechanism to review range name assignments and point out potential range name errors. The real estate sales spreadsheet shown in figure 13.1 contains several range names—some defined correctly and others incorrectly—that are used to illustrate the powerful /**N**ames command. A list of the named ranges in that spreadsheet is shown in table 13.2. Refer to this table frequently as you read this section.

Table 13.2
Range Names and Their Cell Ranges for the ZIPSALES Spreadsheet

Range Name	Assigned Cell Range
AVGPRICE	F6:F12
FIRSTZIP	C6:I6
GRANDTOTAL	G14
PRICEAVR	F6:F12
SALETIME	D5:D14
UNITS	E6:E12

Invoke the /Names command by typing /Names while in AUDIT mode. The /Names options are displayed:

    Bounds Duplicate Overlap Reversed Unreferenced

Each of these options is described in the following sections.

Locating Range Names That Exceed Spreadsheet Boundaries

Select **B**ounds to display range names that exceed spreadsheet boundaries (see fig. 13.5). Any range names listed are potential errors because they are defined on a cell range that contains more columns or more rows (or both) than the spreadsheet. Any such range name exceeds the range defined by the cells A1 through the cell reached by pressing End-Home (the lower right corner of the spreadsheet).

```
        NAMED RANGE DIRECTORY -- BOUNDS
        FIRSTZIP       C6:I6
```

Fig. 13.5.
Range name that exceeds spreadsheet boundaries.

Press Esc to redisplay the spreadsheet.

Locating Duplicate Range Names

Duplicate named ranges are probably a mistake. Difficult to spot in a spreadsheet, duplicate range names are distracting and confusing, and can lead to more serious mistakes when you write formulas. Select /**N**ames,**D**uplicate to see the applicable range names. An example from the real estate sales summary is shown in figure 13.6.

The first of several duplicate range names is listed in the first column. The second column contains a list of all range names defined over the same range as the highlighted range name. AVGPRICE and the name to its right, PRICEAVR, are duplicates. (Likewise, if you

```
NAMED RANGE DIRECTORY -- DUPLICATE
AVGPRICE      F6:F12                    PRICEAVR       F6:F12
PRICEAVR      F6:F12
```

Fig. 13.6.

Duplicate range names displayed.

moved to PRICEAVR, AVGPRICE would appear to the right.) After reviewing the duplicate named range display, press Esc to return to the spreadsheet.

Locating Overlapping Range Names

Overlapping range names are names that have at least one cell in common. Overlapping range names can cause functions that reference cells in the overlapping ranges to "double count" or "double sum" values that are thought to be distinct and in mutually exclusive ranges. Select **O**verlap from the Names menu to display any overlapping ranges. Figure 13.7 shows an example.

Fig. 13.7.

Overlapping range names displayed.

```
NAMED RANGE DIRECTORY -- OVERLAP
AVGPRICE      F6:F12                    FIRSTZIP       C6:I6
FIRSTZIP      C6:I6                     PRICEAVR       F6:F12
PRICEAVR      F6:F12
SALETIME      D5:D14
UNITS         E6:E12
```

The first column contains a list of all unique range names that overlap others. AVGPRICE is highlighted in figure 13.7. The right-hand column indicates all range names that overlap the highlighted name. The range names FIRSTZIP and PRICEAVR each contain at least one cell in common with the highlighted range name AVGPRICE. Press the down arrow to review other range names and their duplicates. As you move down the first column, the second column displays overlapping range names.

Locating Reversed Range Names

The **R**eversed option locates range names that are defined as a "lower right:upper left" cell range. For example, a range name defined by the range H12:A1 (rather than the customary form of A1:H12) would be highlighted. Reversed range names pose no threat to your spreadsheets.

Locating Unreferenced Range Names

Range names that are defined but unused in a spreadsheet may be mistakes. Type /Names,**U**nreferenced to display a list of unreferenced range names. Figure 13.8 shows two such names: FIRSTZIP and GRANDTOTAL.

```
NAMED RANGE DIRECTORY -- UNREFERENCED
FIRSTZIP          C6:I6
GRANDTOTAL        G14
```

Fig. 13.8.

Unreferenced range names displayed.

Study the unreferenced range names and eliminate unneeded ones. Press Esc to redisplay the spreadsheet.

Keep in mind that not all unreferenced range names are mistakes. For example, suppose that you define a range name WHOLESHEET by typing

/**N**ame,**C**reate,**WHOLESHEET**,

If you then press Home, type a colon, and press End-Home, this range name includes the entire active spreadsheet. Later, when you print your spreadsheet by executing /**O**utput,**P**rinter, you can type **WHOLESHEET** for the **R**ange to print instead of typing an easily forgotten explicit cell range. If you use this technique, the range name will appear among the unreferenced range names because no cell formulas reference that name.

Highlighting Cells with Specific Characteristics: /Highlight

/**H**ighlight is the most comprehensive and powerful of the AUDIT mode commands. /**H**ighlight options locate and highlight specific cells based on your criteria. You can locate and highlight cells containing formulas, particular output attributes, circular references, supporting cells, dependent cells, and more. The /**H**ighlight options are displayed when you type /**H** from AUDIT mode:

```
Area  Block  Cells  Find  Links  Modified  Output-attr  Pre-zap
Relationships  Zap
```

The **P**re-zap option serves a special purpose: it lets you combine /**H**ighlight test results so that multiple test results are displayed simultaneously. Two options, **Y**es and **N**o, are displayed when you select **P**re-zap. **Y**es, the default, means that each /**H**ighlight operation clears any previous highlights before testing and highlighting other cells. Selecting **No** combines highlighting from several tests.

The other /**H**ighlight options are described in the sections that follow. For all examples, **P**re-zap is left at its default **Y**es value so that each highlight result is independent of previous tests.

Highlighting Formulas

You can highlight formulas containing various kinds of information. Among these formulas are link formulas, formulas containing text references, formulas referencing blank cells, formulas referencing null cells, and so on.

Link Formulas: Links

Formulas containing links to other spreadsheets and other spreadsheet pages, called *link formulas*, can be highlighted by selecting the **L**inks option and then selecting the **D**ependent option. The full command is

/**H**ighlight,**L**inks,**D**ependent

All link formulas are highlighted, and a message on the right side of the status line indicates how many cells contain link formulas. Figure 13.9 shows the highlighted link formulas found in the real estate spreadsheet.

Fig. 13.9.

Link formulas highlighted.

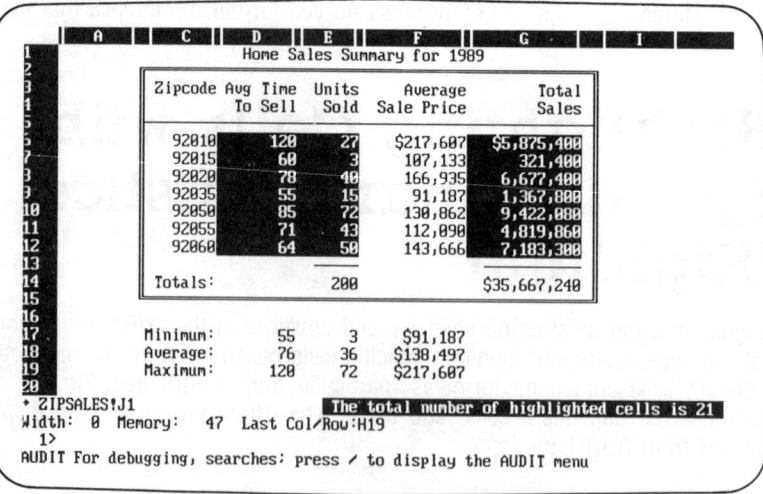

Link formulas remain highlighted even when you execute /**Q**uit to leave AUDIT mode. This useful feature permits you to move around a spreadsheet—inspecting link formulas and making any needed changes—and still view the highlighted cells.

Viewing Details: /Details

You can view additional details about any highlighted cells (link formulas in this particular example) by executing the AUDIT mode command /**D**etails. A separate area of the screen displays detailed information about highlighted cells. Figure 13.10 shows the command used for cell E9. You can use the right- and left-arrow keys to view formulas (cell contents) for any of the cells listed in the details box. Formulas are displayed below the double line. Press Esc to erase the details box from the screen.

```
      A        C      D      E        F          G            I
1                     Home Sales Summary for 1989
2
3          Zipcode Avg Time  Units    Average      Total
4                   To Sell   Sold  Sale Price     Sales
5
6            92010    120     27    $217,607   $5,875,400
7            92015     60      3     107,133      321,400
8            92020     70     40     166,935    6,677,400
9            92035     55     15      91,187    1,367,800
10           92050     85     72     130,862    9,422,000
11           92055     71     43     112,090    4,819,860
12           92060     64     50     143,666    7,183,300
     21 highlighted LINKED cells
D6 E6 G6 D7 E7 G7 D8 E8 G8 D9 [E9] G9 D10 E10 G10 D11 E11 G11 D12 E12 G12

E9:     COUNT(ZIP92035!PRICE)



* ZIPSALES!J1
Width:  0  Memory:     47  Last Col/Row:H19
   1>
AUDIT For debugging, searches; press / to display the AUDIT menu
```

Fig. 13.10.

Displaying link formula details.

Formulas Referencing Empty or Text Cells: Cells

Occasionally, formulas reference a range of cells that includes empty cells or text cells. For example, the formula SUM(G5:G13) stored in cell G14 displays the total sales for all ZIP codes (refer to fig. 13.1). The summed range includes one cell above total sales for the first ZIP code and one cell below the total sales for the last ZIP code. This technique aids in adding other ZIP codes above and below the listed ZIP codes. You can highlight this formula and others like it—formulas referencing blank or text cells—by executing

  /**H**ighlight,**C**ells,**B**lank-ref

Cells with formulas that reference empty or text cells are highlighted. Blank cells referenced by other cells are not necessarily dangerous. Often, cell ranges that are part of a SUM function summing up a column will include an extra blank cell both above and below the actual cell values. Using /**H**ighlight,**C**ells,**B**lank-ref can help verify that this is indeed the case.

Limiting the Area Highlighted: Area

The **A**rea option (type /**H**ighlight,**A**rea) limits the area of the spreadsheet on which tests are performed. In addition, you can select cells on which to base tests. This option does not actually highlight the cells; it merely limits which cells are considered by other /**H**ighlight options.

You can restrict subsequent highlight operations in two ways: to a limited range of your spreadsheet or by a filter based on a particular cell. After typing /**H**ighlight,**A**rea, two options appear: **R**ange and **F**ilter.

Limiting Highlighted Cells to an Explicit Range

Executing /**H**ighlight,**A**rea,**R**ange limits any subsequent /**H**ighlight operations to a range of cells. The default is the entire spreadsheet. For example, if you execute

/**H**ighlight,**A**rea,**R**ange,

the entire spreadsheet (A1 through BK254 for small spreadsheets) is the suggested default range. Press Esc to alter that range. Type the range **C6:G14** to limit subsequent /**H**ighlight commands to those cells in the real estate sales spreadsheet (refer to fig. 13.1). SuperCalc remembers the range. Execute /**H**ighlight,**A**rea,**R**ange and press the hyphen (-) to set the range back to the entire spreadsheet.

Limiting Highlighted Cells to a Cell Type

If you want to examine one group of cells (for example, the original and each of its clones), enter

/**H**ighlight,**A**rea,**F**ilter,**C**urrent

This command sets a "filter" so that any subsequent /**H**ighlight,**R**elationships, /**H**ighlight,**C**ells, and /**H**ighlight,**F**ind tests are based solely on the current cell. After you type **C**urrent, the entry line clears. Alternatively, you can press Alt-F1 to toggle through four possible filters. The mode indicator indicates the filter: AUD-A (all cells), AUD-C (the current cell), AUD-H (currently highlighted cells), or AUD-N (cells not highlighted). Alt-F1 works only after /**H**ighlight is selected.

You can experiment by highlighting a group of related cells. *Related* cells are cells that have the same general form—cells that were copied from an original formula. Start by placing the spreadsheet cursor in cell F6, which displays the average sale price for ZIP code 92010. Next, execute the command

/**H**ighlight,**A**rea,**F**ilter,**C**urrent

Subsequent /**H**ighlight tests are now based on the current cell, F6. Using the following technique, you can identify a range of cells that are related. If you discover that this range doesn't include all the cells that it should, you can leave AUDIT mode and fix the problem cell(s).

To highlight a group of related cells, execute /**H**ighlight,**R**elationships,**G**roup. Finally, select **A**ll to highlight all formulas in the same family as cell F6.

All cells in that family—cells such as F8—are highlighted. The results are shown in figure 13.11. Cell F6 appears darker because it is the cell for which the family of cells has been located.

```
  A   · C    D     E      F         G        I
1              Home Sales Summary for 1989
2
3       Zipcode Avg Time Units  Average     Total
4               To Sell  Sold Sale Price    Sales
5
6       92010     120    27   $217,607   $5,875,400
7       92015      60     3    107,133      321,400
8       92020      78    40    166,935    6,677,400
9       92035      55    15     91,187    1,367,800
10      92050      85    72    130,862    9,422,080
11      92055      71    43    112,090    4,819,860
12      92060      64    50    143,666    7,183,300
13
14      Totals:          200             $35,667,240
15
16
17      Minimum:   55     3    $91,187
18      Average:   76    36   $138,497
19      Maximum:  120    72   $217,607
20
→ ZIPSALES!F6        U1     Form The total number of highlighted cells is 7
Width: 12 Memory:   47 Last Col/Row:H19
  1>
AUDIT For debugging, searches; press / to display the AUDIT menu
```

Fig. 13.11.

Highlighted family of similar cells.

Once you have observed the group of highlighted cells and confirmed that cells F6 through F12 are, rightfully, part of one family of cells, you can clear the highlight by executing

/**H**ighlight,**Z**ap

Try the experiment again by placing the cursor on cell C6 and finding the family of cells cloned from C6 (first type /**H**ighlight,**A**rea,**F**ilter,**C**urrent). The other /**H**ighlight,**A**rea,**F**ilter options (**A**ll, **H**ighlighted, and **N**ot-highlighted) are advanced features and are beyond the scope of this chapter.

Highlighting Cell Relationships: Relationships

Highlighting intercellular relationships provides one of the most useful and frequently used auditing displays. You can limit the range tested and highlighted by executing /**H**ighlight,**A**rea,**R**ange. Highlighting the relationships between cells provides a graphic view of cell relationships and allows you to spot quickly inconsistent patterns of cell references and relationships. You invoke this auditing tool with /**H**ighlight,**R**elationships. Four cell relationship choices appear:

Supporting Dependent Circular Group

The **S**upporting option highlights cells that support one or more cells. **D**ependent highlights cells that depend on one or more cells. **C**ircular highlights circular references. **G**roup highlights a group of related cells.

Highlighting Supporting Cells

Supporting cells are cells that are referenced by a cell or a group of cells. For example, a cell containing the formula SUM(B4:B9) is supported by cells B4 through B9. That is, cells B4 through B9 serve a supporting role for the SUM formula. Highlighting supporting cell relationships will quickly point out cell range errors to you. For example, display the supporting cells for the formula found in cell E14 (refer to fig. 13.1). That formula represents the total units sold in all ZIP code areas. Isolate highlighting to single cell relationships by first executing

> /**H**ighlight,**A**rea,**F**ilter,**C**urrent

Subsequent /**H**ighlight commands are restricted to the currently highlighted cell. Next, move the cursor to cell E14 and execute

> /**H**ighlight,**R**elationships,**S**upporting,

Two menu choices are displayed: **D**irect and **N**ested. **D**irect highlights only those cells that directly support (are referenced by) the current cell—the one where the spreadsheet cursor is located. **N**ested highlights cells that directly or indirectly (to an arbitrary depth) support the current cell. For this example, select **D**irect. Figure 13.12 shows the highlighted supporting cells. That is, the cell range E6:E11 is referenced by the current cell, E14.

Fig. 13.12.

Highlighted cells directly supporting the current cell.

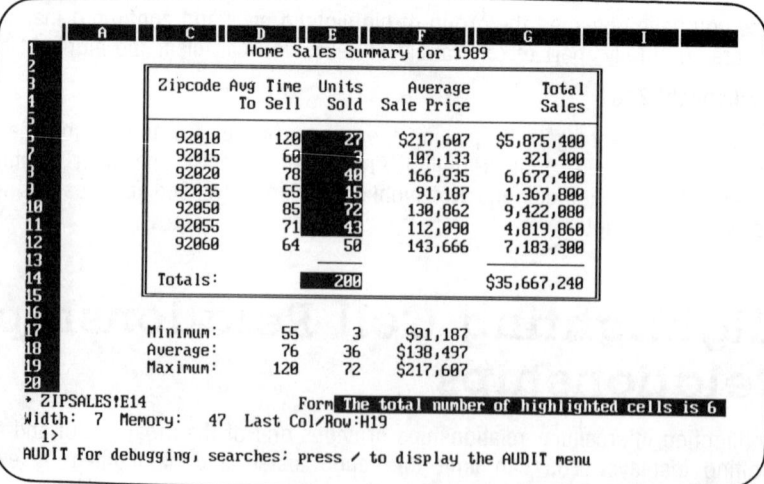

Notice that cell E12 is not among the highlighted supporting cells; it should be. Clearly, highlighting provides a quick way to spot errors. In this case, the formula in cell E14 is corrected to display the total units sold: either SUM(E6:E12) or SUM(UNITS).

When cells indirectly support the current cell or group of cells and you want to highlight these nonprimary support cells, select the **N**ested option. For example, in figure 13.1 cells that support cell F17 (the minimum average sale price) to any degree can be highlighted by moving the cursor to cell F17 and executing

/**H**ighlight,**R**elationships,**S**upporting,**N**ested

Figure 13.13 shows highlighted support cells, both direct and indirect, that are referenced by the formula in cell F17. Cell range F6:F12 directly supports cell F17 (MIN(F6:F12)). Cell ranges E6:E12 and G6:G12 indirectly support the formula in F17.

```
        A      C       D      E        F            G          I
                  Home Sales Summary for 1989
1
2
3           Zipcode Avg Time  Units  Average      Total
4                   To Sell   Sold   Sale Price   Sales
5
6            92010    120      27    $217,607    $5,875,400
7            92015     60       3     107,133       321,400
8            92020     78      40     166,935     6,677,400
9            92035     55      15      91,187     1,367,800
10           92050     85      72     130,862     9,422,080
11           92055     71      43     112,090     4,819,860
12           92060     64      50     143,666     7,183,300
13
14          Totals:          250                $35,667,240
15
16
17          Minimum:    55      3    $91,187
18          Average:    76     36    $130,497
19          Maximum:   120     72    $217,607
20
  ↓ ZIPSALES!F17      U1     For The total number of highlighted cells is 21
  Width: 12 Memory:   47 Last Col/Row:H19
    1>
  AUDIT For debugging, searches; press / to display the AUDIT menu
```

Fig. 13.13.

Highlighted cells directly and indirectly supporting the current cell.

Highlighting Dependent Relationships

When you highlight dependent cells, you can easily locate all cells whose values depend on the current cell. For example, examine one of the spreadsheets that supports the ZIPSALES spreadsheet (refer to fig. 13.1): ZIP92035. That spreadsheet contains sales information for one ZIP code, 92035, and summary information including minimum, average, and maximum market time, as well as minimum, average, and maximum sales price. Suppose that you want to highlight all cells whose values depend on one of the individual sales price cells. Execute the following AUDIT mode command to ensure that only the current cell determines the dependent relationships:

/**H**ighlight,**A**rea,**F**ilter,**C**urrent

To highlight all cells that depend on cell B7, for example, move the spreadsheet cursor to that cell and then execute the command

/**H**ighlight,**R**elationships,**D**ependent,

Two menu choices are displayed: **D**irect and **N**ested. **D**irect highlights only those cells that directly depend on the current cell. **N**ested highlights cells that directly or indirectly depend on the current cell. Select **D**irect for this example.

Cells that depend directly on the current cell are highlighted. If you notice highlighted cells that should not be dependent on the current cell, those highlighted cells are in error and their formulas should be corrected. Figure 13.14 shows the ZIP92035 spreadsheet with dependent cells highlighted. The highlights indicate that cells F8, F9, and F10 each depend, at least in part, on cell B7, the current cell for this operation. Execute /**H**ighlight,**Z**ap to clear the highlights.

Fig. 13.14.

Highlighted cells dependent on the current cell.

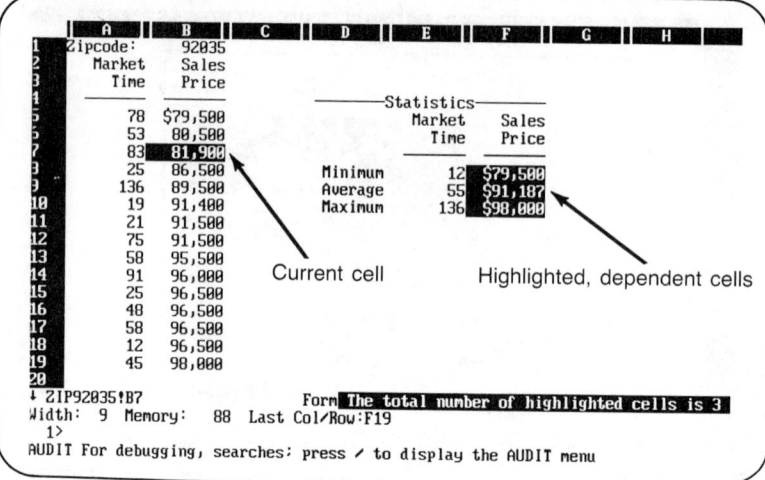

Move the spreadsheet cursor to another cell (for example, any of the cells in column A) and again execute

/**H**ighlight,**R**elationships,**D**ependent,**D**irect

to highlight other dependent cell relationships. You can highlight indirectly dependent cells by executing

/**H**ighlight,**R**elationships,**D**ependent,**N**ested

Cells highlighted are those that depend, either directly or indirectly, on the current cell or group of cells.

Highlighting Circular and Group Relationships

If you have circular relationships in your spreadsheet, the indicator CIR is displayed in the lower right corner of the screen. Locating cells involved in the circular relationship can be difficult. To display them, execute

/**H**ighlight,**R**elationships,**C**ircular

The /**H**ighlight,**R**elationships,**G**roup is used earlier in this chapter. Recall that you can highlight cells whose form and contents are similar to the current cell.

Highlighting Cells with Particular Characteristics: Cells

When you are interested in locating cells that have certain characteristics—such as protected cells, cells with a particular format, or empty cells—the /**H**ighlight,**C**ells option is useful. /**H**ighlight options described previously illustrated how to locate groups of related cells: link formulas, formulas referencing empty or text cells, and supporting and dependent cells. The **C**ells option ignores cell relationships and interaction.

Perform independent-cell highlight operations by executing /**H**ighlight,**C**ells. (You can use /**H**ighlight,**A**rea,**R**ange to limit the range tested.) When you type /**H**ighlight,**C**ells, a menu of options appears:

```
Attribute  Blank-ref  Constant  Date  Error  Formula  Hidden  Invariant  Lone
Macro  NA  fOrmat  Protected  Referenced  String  Time  Unprotected  emptY
```

A brief summary of each /**H**ighlight,**C**ells option is given in table 13.3.

Table 13.3
Cell Auditing Options (/Highlight,Cells)

Option	Locates These Types of Cells
Attribute	Cells containing control text
Blank-ref	Formulas that reference blank text
Constant	Numeric constants (self-defining values)
Date	Date type display
Error	Cells containing ERROR function or that result in ERROR
Formula	Formulas that are variant
Hidden	Cells formatted as hidden at the entry level
Invariant	Expressions (not constants) whose values never change
Lone	Cells not referenced by any other cell (orphans)
Macro	Cells containing \ or { as the first character, indicating macro definitions
NA	Cells containing NA or resulting in N/A
f**O**rmat	Cells formatted individually (entry-level formatting) and either empty or nonempty
Protected	Protected cells
Referenced	Cells referenced by another cell

Table 13.3—*Continued*

Option	Locates These Types of Cells
String	Cells containing text or string values
Time	Cells containing time values
Unprotected	Unprotected cells
empt**Y**	Empty cells that have been formatted at the entry level

The purpose of several of the options is probably obvious to you. Cell tests highlight control text cells (**A**ttribute), cells containing constants (**C**onstant), and cells containing date (**D**ate) values. Additionally, you can locate protected (**P**rotected), unprotected (**U**nprotected), error (**E**rror), hidden (**H**idden), text (**S**tring), macro (**M**acro), and time (**T**ime) cells. Cells that are not referenced by any other cell(s) are highlighted with the **L**one option. Cells referenced by other cells are highlighted by choosing **R**eferenced. **R**eferenced and **L**one are mutually exclusive. Cells that return N/A are highlighted with the **N**A option. Three of the most frequently used options are explained next.

Highlighting Formulas That Reference Blank Cells

Formulas that reference blank cells can cause trouble, often resulting in misleading values. To locate cells containing these types of formulas, execute

/**H**ighlight,**C**ells,**B**lank-ref

Formulas containing range names that include blank cells are also highlighted.

For example, you can determine whether the ZIP92035 supporting spreadsheet (sales for ZIP code 92035) contains any formulas that reference blank cells. After typing /**H**ighlight,**C**ells,**B**lank-ref, the results show that some potentially inaccurate formulas exist (see fig. 13.15).

Although not apparent from the figure, cells E8, E9, and E10 contain formulas that reference the cell range A5:A20—for example, cell E8 contains MIN(A5:A20). Cell A20 is empty.

Highlighting Cells Containing Formulas

You can highlight cells containing formulas whose values can change by executing

/**H**ighlight,**C**ells,**F**ormula

Formulas whose values cannot change—such as MAX(13,52,37)—called *invariant* formulas, are not highlighted. Figure 13.16 shows an example of highlighted formulas.

```
      A        B        C        D        E        F        G        H
1  Zipcode:   92035
2   Market    Sales
3    Time     Price
4
5      78    $79,500                    ─Statistics─
6      53     80,500                      Market    Sales
7      83     81,900                       Time     Price
8      25     86,500
9     136     89,500           Minimum      12     $79,500
10     19     91,400           Average      55     $91,187
11     21     91,500           Maximum     136     $98,000
12     75     91,500
13     58     95,500
14     91     96,000
15     25     96,500
16     48     96,500
17     58     96,500
18     12     96,500
19     45     98,000
20
 * ZIP92035!I1                      The total number of highlighted cells is 3
Width:  0  Memory:   75  Last Col/Row:F19
   1>
AUDIT For debugging, searches; press / to display the AUDIT menu
```

Fig. 13.15.

Cells containing formulas that reference blank cells.

```
      A        B        C        D        E        F        G        H
1  Zipcode:   92035
2   Market    Sales
3    Time     Price
4
5      78    $79,500
6      53     80,500                    ─Statistics─
7      83     81,900                      Market    Sales
8      25     86,500                       Time     Price
9     136     89,500           Minimum      12     $79,500
10     19     91,400           Average      55     $91,187
11     21     91,500           Maximum     136     $98,000
12     75     91,500
13     58     95,500
14     91     96,000
15     25     96,500
16     48     96,500
17     58     96,500
18     12     96,500
19     45     98,000
20
 * ZIP92035!I1                      The total number of highlighted cells is 6
Width:  0  Memory:   75  Last Col/Row:F19
   1>
AUDIT For debugging, searches; press / to display the AUDIT menu
```

Fig. 13.16.

Cells that contain formulas highlighted.

Notice that highlighting cell formulas can give results different from highlighting supporting and dependent cell relationships (described earlier in this chapter). To uncover all formulas, always use the /Highlight,Cells,Formula command. When you are interested in intercellular relationships, use the /Highlight,Relationships command.

Highlighting Cells Formatted at the Entry Level

You also can highlight cells that were formatted at the entry level (individually formatted with the /Format,Entry command). You can choose to highlight either empty cells or all cells. The emptY option displays empty cells formatted at the entry level. The fOrmat option highlights any cell formatted at the entry level. Figure 13.17 shows an example of highlighted cells that are formatted at the entry level (not with /Format,Global,Column, or /Format,Global,Row).

Fig. 13.17.

Cells formatted at the entry level (with /Format,Entry).

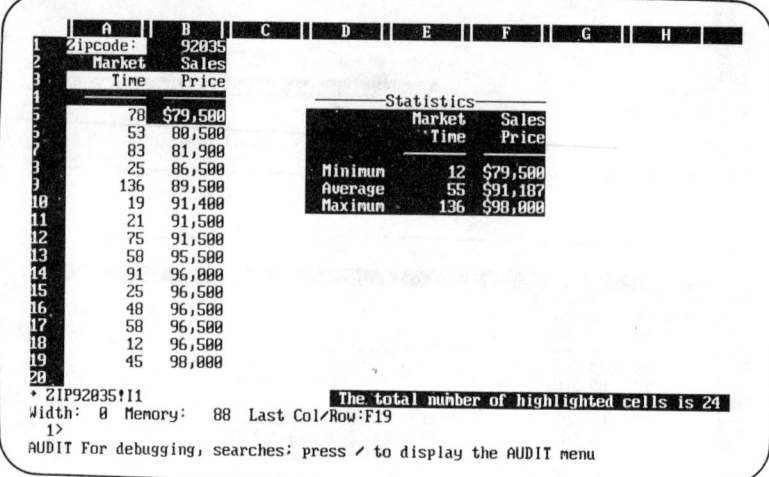

Highlighting Recalculated Cells: Modified

A particularly easy way to debug troublesome spreadsheets is to highlight cells that are changed when the spreadsheet is recalculated. You can uncover subtle intercellular relationships by executing the /Highlight,Modified command. The two options displayed are Yes and No.

Select Yes to highlight cells whenever their display values change. Select No to turn off the Modified option. Once you activate /Highlight,Modified, changed cells are highlighted whenever you change a cell's value, whether or not you are in AUDIT mode.

At first, the /Highlight,Modified and /Highlight,Relationships,Dependent,Nested commands may appear to produce identical results. After all, couldn't you merely highlight cells depending on a particular cell to see affected cell ranges? No—that approach isn't the same. The following example illustrates the subtle differences between the two /Highlight commands.

Load the ZIPSALES summary spreadsheet and then press Alt-F1 to invoke AUDIT mode. Next, turn on modified cell highlighting by typing

/**H**ighlight,**M**odified,**Y**es

Move the spreadsheet cursor to cell E8 while in either AUDIT or READY mode, and enter the value **10** into that cell. Figure 13.18 shows the altered values highlighted.

```
    A      C     D     E       F          G      I
1                      Home Sales Summary for 1989
2
3         Zipcode Aug Time  Units    Average      Total
4                 To Sell   Sold   Sale Price     Sales
5
6          92010   120      27    $217,607    $5,875,400
7          92015    60       3     107,133       321,400
8          92020    78      10     667,740     6,677,400
9          92035    55      15      91,187     1,367,800
10         92050    85      72     130,862     9,422,000
11         92055    71      43     112,090     4,819,860
12         92060    64      58     143,666     7,183,300
13                                 _____
14         Totals:         220               $35,667,240
15
16
17         Minimum:    55    3    $91,187
18         Average:    76   31   $210,041
19         Maximum:   120   72   $667,740
20
  * ZIPSALES!J1
  Width:  8  Memory:   47  Last Col/Row:H19
     1>
  AUDIT For debugging, searches; press / to display the AUDIT menu
```

Fig. 13.18.
Highlighting modified cells.

Look closely at the highlighted cells. Cells E14, E18, F8, F18, and F19 are highlighted because their values changed during recalculation. However, notice that cells E17, E19, and F17 are not highlighted. Clearly, the value 10 entered in cell E8 did not change the value of the minimum number of units sold (cell E17), even though cell E17 depends on cell E8. Similarly, cell F17 is not highlighted because the minimum average sale price didn't change. Cell F17 does depend on cell E8 indirectly for its value, however. Now the difference is clear. Only values that change are highlighted by setting /**H**ighlight,**M**odified to **Y**es.

If you entered the value **2** in cell E8, the value in cell E17 would change because a new minimum number of units sold exists. Previous highlights clear when you enter new values into other cells and before you highlight new changed cells. Remember that you can always view details about highlighted cells by pressing the space bar. Once you have uncovered errors, you can turn off the modified cell highlight feature by entering /**H**ighlight,**M**odified,**N**o from AUDIT mode.

Highlighting Cells with Assigned Output Attributes: Output-attr

The /**H**ighlight,**O**utput-attr command highlights cells that have been assigned output attributes with the /**O**utput command (see Chapter 9). Highlighting these cells helps you check the expected printer output on-screen. The menu options displayed are

        All Border Fonts Shade

Like all /**H**ighlight commands, you can limit the tested cell range by executing /**H**ighlight,**A**rea,**R**ange.

The **A**ll option highlights all cells that have any output attributes (fonts, border, or shade). **B**order highlights selected cells assigned borders. Further **B**order options highlight any cells with borders (**A**ll), cells bordered on the **T**op, cells bordered on the **B**ottom, or cells bordered on the **L**eft or **R**ight.

The **F**onts option highlights either all cells (**A**ll) assigned a font or those assigned selected fonts (**1** through **7**). For example, execute

        /**H**ighlight,**O**utput-attr,**F**onts,**3**

to highlight cells assigned font number 3.

The **S**hade option highlights cells assigned shading with the /**O**utput,**A**ttribute,**S**hade command. Execute the command by typing /**H**ighlight,**O**utput-attr,**S**hade.

Searching for Particular Cell Contents and Values: Find

You can use the AUDIT mode command /**H**ighlight,**F**ind to locate and highlight cells containing particular contents or displayed values. /**H**ighlight,**F**ind,**C**ontents locates cells based on their cell formulas (contents), whereas /**H**ighlight,**F**ind,**V**alue locates cells based on their displayed values. /**H**ighlight,**F**ind is similar to the /**R**eplace command, described previously in this chapter, except that located values are not replaced with new values; they are simply highlighted.

Be mindful of the difference between cell contents and cell values. Cell contents are the underlying strings, formulas, and functions stored in the cell. Cell values are the computed values of those formulas. In addition, the displayed values for cells may not equal the cell values because displayed results may be formatted. For example, the contents of cell E18 in the sales summary spreadsheet (refer to fig. 13.13) is the formula AVG(E6:E12), and the computed value of that cell is 35.714. The displayed value of cell E18, however, is 36. Only the displayed value is currently visible on the sales summary spreadsheet shown in figure 13.13 because that cell has been formatted. As you learn about the /**H**ighlight,**F**ind,**V**alue command in this section, remember these subtle differences.

Searching Cells for Particular Contents

You can locate formulas and text cell contents by executing the command /**H**ighlight,**F**ind. The two menu options, **C**ontents and **V**alue, are displayed. Select **C**ontents to search a spreadsheet for a particular formula or text. Seven **C**ontents options are displayed:

    Go Case Labels Match Relation String Quit

Go executes the search. **C**ase specifies whether the search is case-sensitive (matches exact capitalization). **L**abels specifies whether the search string will contain cell references (**Y**es) or not (**N**o).

The **M**atch option specifies where the specified string must occur in the cell contents. You can choose from the following options:

    Begins Contains Exact Terminates Word

The **R**elation option determines whether cells that match the string (**E**qual) or that do not match the string (**N**ot-equal) are highlighted. The **S**tring option prompts you to enter the text string you want to locate. The **Q**uit option terminates the operation and clears the entry line, remaining in AUDIT mode. The following example illustrates some of these features.

Suppose that you want to locate cell contents that contain the AVG function throughout the spreadsheet. First, enter the command

    /**H**ighlight,**F**ind,**C**ontents

to indicate to SuperCalc that you want to search for cell contents rather than cell values. Next, specify the string you want to locate by selecting the **S**tring option, typing **AVG**, and pressing Enter. The Highlight Find Contents menu is redisplayed:

    Go Case Labels Match Relation String Quit

Select the **M**atch option to tell SuperCalc where in the candidate cell contents to locate the string. Because you want only formulas that begin with the letters *AVG*, select the **B**egins option from the possible choices displayed:

    Begins Contains Exact Terminates Word

After you select **B**egins, the Highlight Find Contents menu reappears. The final step is to begin searching for the string by selecting **G**o. The highlighted cells indicate which cells contain formulas beginning with *AVG* (see fig. 13.19).

If you select either of the **M**atch options **C**ontains or **W**ord rather than **B**egins, additional, superfluous cells would be highlighted (for example, cells D3, F17, and F19 in fig. 13.19). This error occurs because the string *AVG* is found as a named range reference in cells F17 and F19, and as a label in cell D3.

SuperCalc5

Fig. 13.19.

Finding cell contents beginning with AVG.

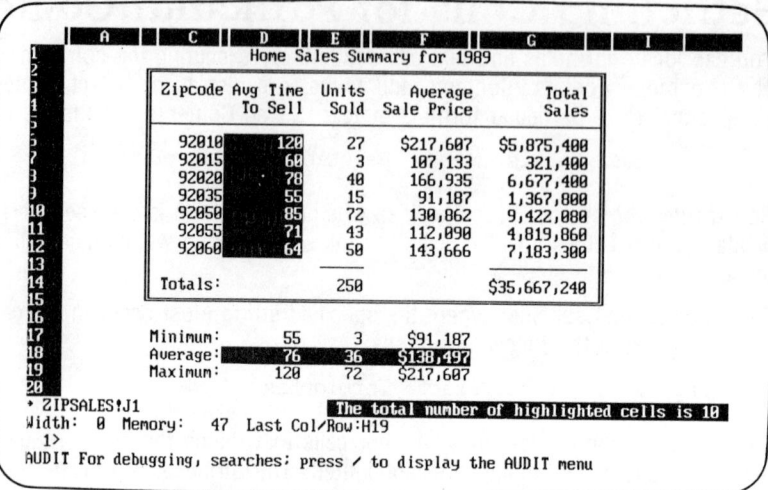

Zipcode	Avg Time To Sell	Units Sold	Average Sale Price	Total Sales
92010	120	27	$217,607	$5,875,400
92015	60	3	107,133	321,400
92020	78	40	166,935	6,677,400
92035	55	15	91,187	1,367,800
92050	85	72	130,862	9,422,000
92055	71	43	112,090	4,819,860
92060	64	50	143,666	7,183,300
Totals:		250		$35,667,240
Minimum:	55	3	$91,187	
Average:	76	36	$138,497	
Maximum:	120	72	$217,607	

Home Sales Summary for 1989

• ZIPSALES!J1   The total number of highlighted cells is 10
Width: 0 Memory: 47 Last Col/Row:H19
  1>
AUDIT For debugging, searches; press / to display the AUDIT menu

Searching Cells for Particular Values

You can locate cell values or self-defining entries (entries whose *displayed* values exactly match what you entered) by executing the command /**H**ighlight,**F**ind,**V**alue. Two **V**alue options are displayed: **N**umbers and **T**ext.

If you select **T**ext to locate cells containing labels (self-defining text entries), the menu line

    Go   Case   Match   Relation   String   Quit

is displayed. These options are identical to those for **C**ontents searches described in the preceding section.

If you select **N**umbers to locate cells with a particular computed numeric value, four options appear:

    Go   Relation   Value   Quit

Go executes the search. The **R**elation option specifies the criteria relationship between the search value and candidate cell values: **E**qual, **N**ot-equal, **A**bove, **B**elow, **G**reater/equal, or **L**ess/equal. For example, selecting **E**qual locates cell values that are equal to the search value; selecting **A**bove locates cell values that are greater than the search value; and so on. The **V**alue option prompts you to enter the search value you want to locate. **Q**uit clears the entry line, remaining in AUDIT mode.

An example illustrates how to search for a numeric display value and also points out a trap you should beware of. Search the sales summary spreadsheet for the total sales values (column G in figure 13.19) that fall below the average total sales values for all ZIP code areas. In this way, you highlight lower-than-average sales performance values.

Two steps are involved: restrict the search range to the *Total Sales* figures in cells G6 through G12, and specify the search value. First, restrict the search range by executing the command

　　/**H**ighlight,**A**rea,**R**ange

Press Esc to erase the suggested default search range (the entire spreadsheet). Type the new search range, **G6:G12**, and press Enter.

The second step, specifying the value to locate, is initiated by executing

　　/**H**ighlight,**F**ind,**V**alue,**N**umbers,**V**alue

When you invoke **V**alue, SuperCalc prompts you to enter the search value:

　　　Enter numeric expression

You can enter a value such as **5095320** (your estimate of the average total sales), or you can enter a formula (an expression). The latter is a better choice because you can define a formula whose computed value is used as the search criterion. Self-defining terms or arbitrarily complex expressions can be entered, as long as any expression you enter is error-free (noncircular, not N/A, etc.). For this example, enter the expression **AVG(G6:G12)** as the search value and press Enter. Press **R**elation, **B**elow, and then **G**o to execute the value search. Figure 13.20 shows the results of this search: *Total Sales* values below the average total sales value are highlighted (cells G7, G9, and G11).

```
┌────────────────────────────────────────────────────────────┐
│  ║ A ║   C ║   D ║ E ║   F   ║   G   ║ I ║                  │
│1                  Home Sales Summary for 1989                │
│2                                                             │
│3              Zipcode Avg Time Units   Average    Total      │
│4                      To Sell  Sold  Sale Price   Sales      │
│5                                                             │
│6               92010   120     27    $217,607  $5,875,400    │
│7               92015    60      3     187,133     321,400    │
│8               92020    78     40     166,935   6,677,400    │
│9               92035    55     15      91,187   1,367,800    │
│10              92050    85     72     130,862   9,422,000    │
│11              92055    71     43     112,090   4,819,060    │
│12              92060    64     50     143,666   7,183,300    │
│13                                     ───────               │
│14              Totals:         250             $35,667,240   │
│15                                                            │
│16                                                           │
│17              Minimum:    55      3    $91,187             │
│18              Average:    76     36   $138,497            │
│19              Maximum:   120     72   $217,607            │
│20                                                          │
│ * ZIPSALES!J1              The total number of highlighted cells is 3 │
│ Width:  0  Memory:   47  Last Col/Row:H19                  │
│     1>                                                     │
│ AUDIT For debugging, searches; press / to display the AUDIT menu │
└────────────────────────────────────────────────────────────┘
```

Fig. 13.20.

Finding below-average total sales values.

Avoiding a Nasty Trap

There is one particularly difficult trap you should beware of when you search for values (using /**H**ighlight,**F**ind,**V**alue). When you want to locate and highlight values that match a particular value, remember that many displayed spreadsheet values may be formatted to omit some digits. This formatting means that values appearing as whole numbers, for example, may have computed values that contain several digits after the decimal point, which can confound exact-value searches.

For example, suppose that you want to locate all values in the sales summary that equal 36. (Cell E18 displays that value). You first ensure that the search area is the entire spreadsheet (/Highlight,Area,Range) and then execute the command

/**H**ighlight,**F**ind,**V**alue,**N**umbers,**V**alue,**36**

Press Enter, and select **G**o to execute the value search. No cells are found, and the message

Search string not found

appears on the status line. Clearly, SuperCalc couldn't find the value 36, but cell E18 displays 36. The trap is that most cells on this spreadsheet (see fig. 13.20) have been formatted to integer values (rounded to the nearest whole value). The true computed value stored in cell E18 is 35.714. In most cases, the cure for this trap is not to execute exact value match searches. Instead, execute

/**H**ighlight,**F**ind,**V**alue,**N**umbers,**R**elation

Select any choice except **E**qual (the default choice) from the menu that appears:

Equal   Not-equal   Above   Below   Greater/equal   Less/equal

To find numbers in a narrow range of values even when their displayed values are slightly different from their stored values, you must execute the /**H**ighlight command twice. Suppose that you want to find all values in the range of 39 to 42. Find numbers that are less than or equal to the highest value in the range and greater than or equal to the lowest value (called an *intersection operation*—the intersection of two criteria). Follow these steps:

1. Execute /**H**ighlight,**F**ind,**V**alue,**N**umbers specifying **39** and a **R**elation of **G**reater/ equal. Select **G**o to highlight those cells.

2. Execute /**H**ighlight and press Alt-F1 until AUD-H appears in the dialog panel, limiting the highlighted range to those cells already highlighted.

3. Execute /**H**ighlight,**F**ind,**V**alue,**N**umbers,**R**elation, and select **L**ess/equal. Then specify **42** as the value to highlight. Select **G**o to locate values that are less than or equal to the upper end of the value range (42). Only already highlighted cells are candidates to be searched.

Chapter Summary

Auditing is a particularly powerful tool for debugging spreadsheets. AUDIT mode provides more than 100 options that help you reveal hidden subtle errors in your spreadsheets. In AUDIT mode you can locate cell formula patterns with /**V**iew, search for and replace cell contents with /**R**eplace, and review named ranges with /**N**ames. You can display details of highlighted cells when you issue /**D**etails or press the space bar.

/**H**ighlight is the most comprehensive AUDIT mode command. You can highlight link formulas, cells having particular attributes, cells with specified contents or computed values, cell and formula relationships, and cells that are modified during recalculation. You also can highlight cells containing output attributes assigned by /**O**utput, as well as groups of related cells (cells cloned from an original). Chapter 14 describes two powerful, general purpose operations: interfacing with foreign files and invoking SuperCalc add-in functions and programs.

14

Interfacing with Other Packages and Using Add-In Programs

The capability of exchanging information with other software products is one of Super-Calc's most important features. Most businesses have stored in computer files information created with other software programs. This data can include accounts receivable and accounts payable files stored as database records, payroll and pay-rate information stored as flat files for input to COBOL programs, and spreadsheet files used by other spreadsheet programs.

SuperCalc provides an easy-to-use facility to transfer files between SuperCalc and other software packages. This feature incorporates data from dBASE files into SuperCalc spreadsheets; converts SuperCalc files to a format that can be accepted by dBASE; and exchanges data files between SuperCalc and BASIC programs, VisiCalc spreadsheets, and several others. Transferring information from these data files to SuperCalc files and vice versa saves time and provides SuperCalc's invaluable analysis capability for these other files.

The add-in facility provides a vehicle for incorporating other software producers' add-in software products seamlessly into SuperCalc.

Introducing the SuperCalc Interfacing Commands

An imaginary boundary between SuperCalc-loadable files and foreign data files provides a method of communication between the programs. This boundary, often called an *interface*, is the meeting point of two dissimilar formats or devices. The two SuperCalc commands

479

that provide this interface, //Import and //Export, eliminate the need to type information a second time.

The //Import and //Export commands allow data to move smoothly between SuperCalc and programming-language files, word processing files (WordStar, for example), database files (such as dBASE III), and other spreadsheet products. The //Import command converts and transports files from external formats to SuperCalc spreadsheets. The //Export command transports files from SuperCalc and converts them to formats that can be used directly by other software products. For example, SuperCalc spreadsheets can be converted to Word-Star format, to VisiCalc spreadsheet format, and to dBASE format. Correspondingly, files from WordStar, dBASE, and VisiCalc can be converted easily to SuperCalc format by using the //Import command. The //Import and //Export commands link SuperCalc to a wide array of other software products and make it an integrated software business tool.

In previous versions of SuperCalc, the //Import command was necessary to work with 1-2-3 spreadsheets. Correspondingly, previous versions of SuperCalc required the //Export command to save SuperCalc spreadsheets in 1-2-3 form. Now, SuperCalc5 loads and saves 1-2-3 files transparently. Therefore, interfacing with 1-2-3 files is not presented in this chapter because the normal /Load and /Save commands can be used to load and save 1-2-3 files directly. Similarly, previous versions of SuperCalc spreadsheet files (SuperCalc3 and SuperCalc4) can be loaded and saved with the Level option of both the /Save and /Load commands.

Like other SuperCalc commands, //Import and //Export are easy to understand and use. The //Import and //Export commands are part of a family of commands that are invoked by typing // (double slash).

Importing Data from Foreign Files

The //Import command converts data files created by other software products to a format that can be loaded directly into SuperCalc spreadsheets. To import a file, first place the spreadsheet cursor in the cell that will be the upper left corner of the imported spreadsheet. Press I (or //I from a blank entry line) to invoke the //Import command. The seven types of files that can be imported to a spreadsheet are displayed on the prompt line (see fig. 14.1).

Fig. 14.1.
//Import command
options.

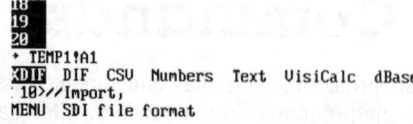

The highlighted default file choice is **X**DIF (eXtended Data Interchange Format). Other choices are **D**IF (Data Interchange Format), **C**SV (Comma Separated Values), **N**umbers, **T**ext, **V**isiCalc, and d**B**ase. Each choice refers to the type of external file you may want to convert to SuperCalc format and load. For example, to load a VisiCalc file, choose **V**. The d**B**ase choice imports database records directly from dBASE database files. The **X**DIF, **D**IF, **C**SV, **N**umbers, and **T**ext choices may be less obvious. Each is discussed in this chapter.

Importing Comma Separated Values (CSV) Files

Comma Separated Values files contain data fields with individual elements separated by commas. CSV files are a useful method of interfacing between SuperCalc and other software products because many products can produce the CSV file format. SuperCalc can import data CSV files produced by a virtually unlimited number of high-level languages and assembler languages. BASIC programs, for example, easily create CSV output files and permit sharing of data between SuperCalc and entire systems written in BASIC. Only values are imported or exported, and no details about formulas or cell formatting are stored in CSV format.

Importing files from other products is a straightforward process. Summary information gathered from U.S. census information is imported to SuperCalc to illustrate this simple procedure. The format of the file being imported is Comma Separated Values. In the raw data file, character fields are enclosed in quotation marks and all fields are separated by commas.

The census data illustrated in this section contains information about selected cities in the United States. Each record contains data about one city. Data fields include city name, state abbreviation, population, per capita income, and per capita retail sales. To keep the example easy to understand, the data to be imported is restricted to only one state: Indiana. Figure 14.2 shows the input data file with its character and numeric-valued fields. Notice the commas that separate the fields. Also notice that the records vary in length. The census data file is named CENSUS.CSV for convenience.

After you invoke the //Import command, the next step to import the file CENSUS.CSV is to choose **C**SV. Then, type the name of the file to be imported. Because SuperCalc automatically adds the extension CSV to files specified without extensions, be sure to type the entire file name if its extension is not CSV. In this case, simply type **CENSUS**.

After you press the comma key to indicate that the import file name is complete, four choices appear:

    Replace All Consolidate Part

Specify whether to replace the current spreadsheet (**R**eplace), import the entire file (**A**ll), import a consolidation (**C**onsolidate), or import a part of the file (**P**art). Press Enter or type **R** to replace the current worksheet and import all records of the CSV file.

The import process takes only a few seconds, and the imported spreadsheet is displayed almost instantly. The imported census data is shown in figure 14.3.

Fig. 14.2.

Census data to be imported as a CSV file.

```
"Anderson","IN",61020,10173,6582
"Bloomington","IN",52500,8513,7298
"East Chicago","IN",36950,7905,2450
"Elkhart","IN",44100,10194,11455
"Evansville","IN",129400,10040,7433
"Fort Wayne","IN",172900,10276,6813
"Gary","IN",136790,7400,2516
"Hammond","IN",86300,9045,4390
"Indianapolis","IN",719020,10036,5040
"Kokomo","IN",45610,10714,8775
"Lafayette","IN",44240,10272,9516
"Marion","IN",35010,9265,7650
"Michigan City","IN",35600,8852,6902
"Mishawaka","IN",41400,10037,9301
"Muncie","IN",72600,8979,6409
"New Albany","IN",37260,9499,4930
"Portage","IN",28420,10139,2907
"Richmond","IN",39030,9126,8133
"South Bend","IN",107190,10154,5647
"Terre Haute","IN",57920,8643,9007
```

Fig. 14.3.

Spreadsheet after importing the Comma Separated Values file.

```
         A            B      C        D        E        F        G
1   Anderson        IN      61020    10173    6582
2   Bloomington     IN      52500    8513     7298
3   East Chicago    IN      36950    7905     2450
4   Elkhart         IN      44100    10194    11455
5   Evansville      IN      129400   10040    7433
6   Fort Wayne      IN      172900   10276    6813
7   Gary            IN      136790   7400     2516
8   Hammond         IN      86300    9045     4390
9   Indianapolis    IN      719020   10036    5040
10  Kokomo          IN      45610    10714    8775
11  Lafayette       IN      44240    10272    9516
12  Marion          IN      35010    9265     7650
13  Michigan City   IN      35600    8852     6902
14  Mishawaka       IN      41400    10037    9301
15  Muncie          IN      72600    8979     6409
16  New Albany      IN      37260    9499     4930
17  Portage         IN      28420    10139    2907
18  Richmond        IN      39030    9126     8133
19  South Bend      IN      107190   10154    5647
20  Terre Haute     IN      57920    8643     9007
+ CENSUS:A1                         Text="Anderson
Width: 15  Memory:   43  Last Col/Row:E20
   1>
READY F1:Help  F3:Names  Ctrl-Backspace:Undo  Ctrl-Break:Cancel
```

Column A in figure 14.3 has been formatted to display 15 characters. Other than that change, the spreadsheet has not been formatted in any special manner—default format conditions apply. The spreadsheet can be formatted to suit your needs at this point. For example, columns D and E, representing per capita income and retail sales, could be formatted with the **$** option.

Formulas and Repeating Text

Besides text and number values, CSV files may contain formulas (arithmetic expressions, functions, and the like) and repeating text. You enclose formulas to be imported from CSV files with backslashes (\). You enter a formula such as SUM(A1:C1) in the CSV file as

> \SUM(A1:C1)\

and separate it from other values in the same record by commas:

> 10,20,30,"Sum Formula",\SUM(A1:C1)\

Place repeating text in a CSV file by enclosing the apostrophe and repeating character(s) in quotation marks. For example, repeating text composed of equal signs is represented as

> "'="

You can use a word processing program to add formulas and repeating text entries to a CSV file produced by another software product. If you use WordStar to alter a CSV file to include repeating text and formulas, be sure to edit the file in nondocument mode. Editing in DOCUMENT mode causes special characters to be inserted in the file, and SuperCalc will misinterpret these special characters when the file is imported.

Details That Cannot Be Imported

CSV files cannot represent certain details about imported data. Most notable among the missing details is formatting information. Individual entries take on the format characteristics established in the SuperCalc spreadsheet to which they are being imported—not the format of the CSV file.

An example of CSV data that does not import directly to SuperCalc is the dBASE logical data type. Elements of that type have the value true or false and are represented by *T* or *F* in dBASE. If a database containing a logical field is sent to a CSV file, the logical fields are written as the letter *T* or the letter *F* without enclosing quotation marks. SuperCalc does not correctly convert text-like values that are not enclosed in quotation marks. Therefore, be careful when attempting to import logical values.

Importing VisiCalc Files

The //Import,**V**isiCalc option converts a file stored in VisiCalc format to SuperCalc format and displays the imported file on the active spreadsheet. SuperCalc can re-create the VisiCalc spreadsheet details precisely.

When you select the **V**isiCalc option and type the file name, the options **R**eplace, **A**ll, and **P**art appear. When you select **R**eplace or **P**art, the entire spreadsheet is imported. The default file name extension VC is assumed if you do not specify an extension.

Formulas and values are converted precisely with only a few exceptions. VisiCalc AND and OR functions are converted to nested AND and OR equivalent expressions up to 240 characters long. ERROR appears if the converted formula exceeds 240 characters. Boolean functions are represented as 1 or 0 in place of VisiCalc's TRUE or FALSE representation.

Because leading plus signs are not needed in SuperCalc expressions, any leading plus signs are removed from formulas. A VisiCalc formula of

+A1*B2/B1

is converted to the SuperCalc form of

A1*B2/B1

Repeating text extends farther in SuperCalc than in VisiCalc. In the converted format, repeating text extends to the first occupied cell encountered—not just to the width of one cell as in VisiCalc.

Finally, SuperCalc maintains the cursor position as last stored in a VisiCalc file. Because VisiCalc displays 21 spreadsheet rows—one more than SuperCalc—however, the top row of the converted spreadsheet displays row 2 so that the cursor is maintained in the bottom row (21) of the display.

Although VisiCalc supports the DIF® format, you do not need to use that format to import a VisiCalc spreadsheet. In fact, importing the VisiCalc spreadsheet directly is the best method. The following sections describe the DIF file. After reading about DIF, you will understand that formulas and other spreadsheet details are lost by using DIF files to form the interface between VisiCalc and SuperCalc. A DIF file must be used, however, to export a SuperCalc spreadsheet to VisiCalc because the //Export command does not support a direct VisiCalc file format creation.

Importing DIF and XDIF Files

When you select //Import,**DIF**, you can choose from the options **R**eplace, **A**ll, **C**onsolidate, and **P**art. **X**DIF permits all //Import options: **R**eplace, **A**ll, **V**alues, **C**onsolidate, and **P**art. These two forms are well suited for communicating with programming languages that can parse the more complicated XDIF or DIF data for use in other software systems. The XDIF format stores information about the format, the display characteristics, and the location of data, in addition to the data itself. Although DIF and XDIF do not store the original formulas used to create the data, they can be used to communicate with several other spreadsheet products.

DIF import operations also have a unique option not available for any other file type: the file can be imported in either column or row order regardless of which method was used to create the file. This capability allows you to rotate the spreadsheet 90 degrees by importing the DIF file rowwise if the file was created in column order or columnwise if the file was created in row order. (Of course, you also can rotate a spreadsheet by using the /**C**opy,**T**ranspose command.) This rotation is especially useful if you have a complex spreadsheet that has, for example, 5 rows and 20 columns. Difficult to view on the monitor, the spreadsheet can be rotated 90 degrees counterclockwise so that it displays 20 rows and 5 columns. Then you can see the entire spreadsheet on the screen.

The file extension DIF is automatically added to the specified file name for DIF import operations unless you type the file name extension (for example, LABOR.AMT). XDIF file names are assumed to have the extension SDI (SuperData Interchange™) unless you specify a different extension.

Both XDIF and DIF files are written in ASCII format, and they can be printed or displayed on the monitor and examined. (Examples of XDIF and DIF files are given in the section "Exporting SuperCalc Spreadsheets to Other File Formats" in this chapter). DIF and XDIF files store only values and not the formulas used to derive the values. This feature is similar to saving a SuperCalc spreadsheet using the **V**alues option rather than the **A**ll option.

More information about cells is retained in the XDIF file than in the DIF file. The biggest difference between the two file forms is that XDIF files contain more information about the format of cells than do DIF files. The DIF form, however, is more widely accepted than the XDIF form. More software products can produce the DIF format because it has been a defined standard for a longer time than the XDIF form. The greatest portability and compatibility with other products are achieved by using DIF files rather than XDIF files. Moreover, some software applications may not be able to read XDIF files properly.

Importing Numbers and Text Files

The //Import,**N**umbers option (refer to fig. 14.1) efficiently imports data that consists of numbers and text. (//Import,**T**ext, on the other hand, puts each row into column A.) Text values must be enclosed in quotation marks. When imported, each number or text value is placed in a separate cell. Text is left-justified in the SuperCalc spreadsheet, and numbers are right-justified. Each data record in a file imported under the **N**umbers option corresponds to a row of a SuperCalc spreadsheet. Although numbers files look identical to CSV files, the numbers and the text in numbers files are separated by one or more spaces, not by commas as in CSV files. Moreover, numbers files cannot contain formulas.

An example of **N**umbers data to be imported is the sales comparables data shown in previous chapters. Originally, the data was obtained from a remote computing source in ASCII form. Figure 14.4 illustrates the sales comparables data to be imported.

1515695	92152	103	136500	1350	3	2
1818913	92152	60	165500	1750	3	2.5
2556445	92152	123	141000	1400	3	3
3700451	92378	112	211500	2240	4	4
4457716	92378	118	216500	2230	4	3.5
4461968	92378	37	128500	1420	2	2
7214551	92775	118	209500	2240	3	3.5
7364125	92775	76	261300	2630	5	4
7746075	92020	36	125000	1320	3	2
8270243	92020	129	180000	1940	3	2
9555661	92020	75	102500	1140	2	2

Fig. 14.4.

Data file containing numbers to be imported.

From the ready prompt, invoke //Import,**N**umbers. Type the name of the file to be imported (**SALESCMP** in this example) and press Enter. The following options are displayed after the full numbers file name is typed:

```
Replace  All  Part
```

You can choose to import the entire file by pressing **R** or **A**, or choose to import only part of the file by pressing **P**. If you choose the latter option, a prompt requests cell range information:

```
From? (Enter Range)
37>//Import,Numbers,SALESCMP,Part,A2:C3
```

At the prompt, indicate what portion of the file is to be imported. Next, SuperCalc requests the destination range:

```
To? (Enter Cell)
40>//Import,Numbers,SALESCMP,Part,A2:C3,C5
```

Press Enter to complete the //Import command for the numbers-file import operation. Figure 14.5 illustrates the sales comparables data after being imported using the **R**eplace option to pull in the entire file. Notice that each field is in a separate column.

Fig. 14.5.

Spreadsheet after importing numbers from a numbers file.

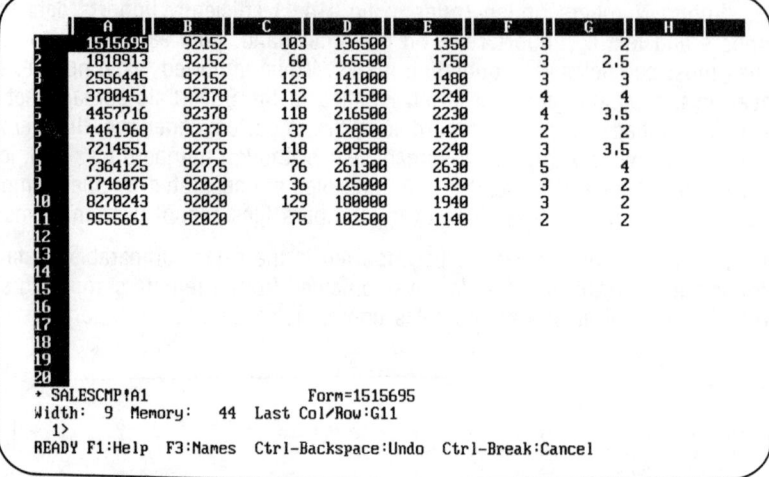

Text files are imported by selecting the //Import,**T**ext option. Similar in nature to numbers files, text files can contain any characters (including quotation marks), but the text does not need to be enclosed in quotation marks. One line of a text file is imported into one SuperCalc spreadsheet cell. If you consider this page as a text file, for instance, each line would be in a new cell. The first line of this page would be placed in cell A1, the second in cell A2, and so on. Each line imported is limited to 240 characters. Like numbers files, text files can be imported entirely (select **R**eplace or **A**ll) or in part (select **P**art). Choosing the **P**art option allows you to select the records to import. The following prompt and entry lines indicate that records (lines) 2 through 5 of the text file are to be imported:

```
Enter Record Range to import
32>//Import,Text,SALESCMP,Part,2:5
```

Following specification of the record range, you can select the upper left spreadsheet cell to be the destination of the first text file record. Text that is too wide for a single cell spills over into adjacent cells in the same spreadsheet row. The maximum length of a text string is, however, 240 characters. If you import a WordStar text file, for example, only the first 240 characters of each paragraph are imported. (A "hard" carriage return marks the end of a line.) Chapter 12 includes an example of importing text data.

An important distinction between importing with the **T**ext and **N**umbers options is that the **T**ext option places each record into the first cell of the range. To separate various imported fields in each record into individual columns, you can use the //**D**ata,**P**arse command to place each record field into a distinct column for all rows (see Chapter 12).

Importing dBASE Files

The power of the dBASE database management system can be used to organize, update, and retrieve information from relational databases. Selected dBASE data records can be imported directly into your SuperCalc spreadsheet, and you can then use SuperCalc functions and commands to further analyze the data. Importing dBASE files is illustrated with a small portion of the census data file shown in a previous section (census data for selected cities in Indiana) and stored in a dBASE database format. Several of the terms you learned in Chapter 12 are used here: Criterion block, Input block, and Output block. The procedure works for dBASE IV as well as for dBASE III and dBASE III Plus.

Importing All Records from a dBASE File

Importing an entire dBASE database is straightforward. To illustrate this simple process, a sample census database stored in dBASE file format is imported into a SuperCalc spreadsheet. Figure 14.6 shows the contents of the dBASE form of the census database. The columns labeled *INCOME* and *SALES* represent per capita income and sales for each listed city.

To import the entire database, execute //**I** to list the main import options. Then press **B** to import a dBASE file. Next, type the database file name (in this case **CENSUS**), specifying only the primary name. If you omit an extension, SuperCalc assumes it is DBF. When you press Enter to enter the dBASE file name, four choices appear:

    Replace All Extract Names

Replace and **A**ll import the database into your spreadsheet; **E**xtract (discussed later) allows you to select particular dBASE records to import; **N**ames imports only the dBASE field names—not database records.

The last step is to select the **R**eplace option. Quickly, SuperCalc reads the dBASE database file and imports it into the spreadsheet. Figure 14.7 shows the result of executing these //**I**mport steps.

Fig. 14.6.

dBASE database to be imported.

```
Record#  CITYNAME      STATENAME POPULATION INCOME SALES
      1  Anderson      IN            61820   10173  6582
      2  Bloomington   IN            52500    8513  7298
      3  East Chicago  IN            36950    7905  2458
      4  Elkhart       IN            44180   10194 11455
      5  Evansville    IN           129480   10048  7433
      6  Fort Wayne    IN           172900   10276  6813
      7  Gary          IN           136790    7488  2516
      8  Hammond       IN            86380    9845  4390
      9  Indianapolis  IN           719820   10836  5048
     10  Kokomo        IN            45610   10714  8775
     11  Lafayette     IN            44240   10272  9516
     12  Marion        IN            35810    9265  7658
     13  Michigan City IN            35600    8852  6982
     14  Mishawaka     IN            41400   10037  9301
     15  Muncie        IN            72600    8979  6489
     16  New Albany    IN            37260    9499  4930
     17  Portage       IN            28420   10139  2907
     18  Richmond      IN            39030    9126  8133
     19  South Bend    IN           107190   10154  5647
     20  Terre Haute   IN            57920    8643  9007
```

Fig. 14.7.

Spreadsheet after importing a dBASE database.

```
       |      A      |    B    |    C    |    D    |    E    |    F    |    G    |
     1 | CITYNAME    |STATENAMEPOPULATIOINCOME    SALES
     2 | Anderson    | IN         61820   10173    6582
     3 | Bloomington | IN         52500    8513    7298
     4 | East Chicago| IN         36950    7905    2458
     5 | Elkhart     | IN         44180   10194   11455
     6 | Evansville  | IN        129480   10048    7433
     7 | Fort Wayne  | IN        172900   10276    6813
     8 | Gary        | IN        136790    7488    2516
     9 | Hammond     | IN         86380    9845    4390
    10 | Indianapolis| IN        719820   10836    5048
    11 | Kokomo      | IN         45610   10714    8775
    12 | Lafayette   | IN         44240   10272    9516
    13 | Marion      | IN         35810    9265    7658
    14 | Michigan City IN        35600    8852    6982
    15 | Mishawaka   | IN         41400   10037    9301
    16 | Muncie      | IN         72600    8979    6489
    17 | New Albany  | IN         37260    9499    4930
    18 | Portage     | IN         28420   10139    2907
    19 | Richmond    | IN         39030    9126    8133
    20 | South Bend  | IN        107190   10154    5647
     • CENSUS!A1                    Text="CITYNAME
    Width: 15  Memory:    43  Last Col/Row:E21
      1>
    READY F1:Help  F3:Names  Ctrl-Backspace:Undo  Ctrl-Break:Cancel
```

Data in figure 14.7 is unformatted. All the SuperCalc default format information is used, except that column A was formatted to display 15 characters. You need not format a spreadsheet in any special way before executing the //Import command. Once the data is imported from dBASE, you may wish to format the columns in a particular way to make the data easier to read and understand.

Importing Selected Records from a dBASE File

When dealing with a large database, you may want to restrict the records imported into your spreadsheet. You can do this by executing dBASE commands that produce another database file containing only the records you want to import, or you can select specific records to import from within SuperCalc. The latter method is faster and easier. To illustrate how to import selected database records, the database shown in figure 14.6 is imported into SuperCalc. However, a few additional SuperCalc commands are used to specify which dBASE records are selected and imported into the SuperCalc spreadsheet. Follow these steps, which are explained in detail in the following paragraphs:

1. Start with an empty spreadsheet (use //**Z**ap,**Y**es) and define a Criterion range consisting of at least two rows.

2. Import the dBASE database field names.

3. Define a two-row Input range to hold each record temporarily so that it can be tested against the selection criteria.

4. Define a block of cells as the Output range. Be sure to include a sufficient number of rows to hold selected database records.

5. Copy the imported dBASE field names (retrieved in step 2) to the first rows of the Input and Output ranges (use /**C**opy).

6. Place the selection criteria into the second row of the Criterion range (use either a formula or one or more values placed under a field name).

7. Execute the **E**xtract command (//**I**mport,d**B**ase,**E**xtract) to search the database and import selected rows.

To prepare to import selected dBASE records, you must define three blocks in your empty spreadsheet: an Input block, a Criterion block, and an Output block. These three blocks are defined in distinct, nonoverlapping areas of your spreadsheet. (Chapter 12 describes defining these three blocks.) The Criterion block determines which dBASE records will be selected. The first row must contain dBASE field names; second and subsequent rows in the Criterion block contain values and formulas that define the selection criteria. Define as many rows as necessary to contain the selection criteria.

To create a two-row, five-column criteria range, execute the //**D**ata,**C**riterion command to define the Criterion block (see fig. 14.8a). In this example, select the cell range A1:E2 (see fig. 14.8b). After defining the Criterion block, execute **Q**uit to return to READY mode.

The simplest way to extract dBASE field names and place them in the first Criterion row is to execute the //**I**mport command. First, type //**I**mport,d**B**ase. Type the name of the database file (**CENSUS** in this example), and press Enter (SuperCalc assumes the file extension DBF if you omit it). Select the **N**ames option (see fig. 14.8c).

After you press **N**, the message

        Importing...

Fig. 14.8.

Fig. 14.8.

Steps to import dBASE field names.

```
Quit Input Criterion Output Find Extract Unique Select Remain Delete
Analysis Block Matrix Parse Table
    8>//Data,
MENU  Range holding criteria to match/qualify records (include field names)
```
a.

```
+ IMPORTDB!E2
Enter range   (currently undefined)
; 23>//Data,Criterion,A1:E2
POINT F1:Help F2:Edit F3:Names Home:1st End-Arrow:last Ctrl-Break:Cancel
```
b.

```
↑ IMPORTDB!A1
Replace All Extract Names
; 23>//Import,dBase,CENSUS,
MENU  Import using data criterion and data output range
```
c.

briefly appears in the second line of the dialog panel. In a few seconds, SuperCalc imports the dBASE field names and places them in the first row of the Criterion block (as in fig. 14.9). If you haven't defined the Criterion block prior to this step, you see the warning message

```
Criterion range not defined
```

when you attempt to import dBASE field names. Press Ctrl-Break to clear the input line, define the Criterion block, and execute //Import,d**B**ase,**CENSUS**,**N**ames again.

The next steps are to define the Input range and the Output range. The Input range is used to hold temporarily each candidate dBASE record and test it against the selection criteria. Consisting of only two rows, the input block must contain text field names. After defining the Input range (cells A4 through E5 in the example), copy the field names from the first row of the Criterion range to the first row of the Input range.

Similarly, define the Output block. The first row must contain text field names (again, copy them from the first row of the Criterion block), and there must be as many additional rows as there are potential records satisfying the selection criteria. The Output block cannot overlap the Input block. Define the Output block range of cells by entering //D**ata**,**O**utput,**A7:A19**.

The selection criteria are placed in the second (and subsequent) rows of the Criterion block. You can, for example, select records for which the *POPULATION* field is greater than 100,000. The selection criterion is placed in the second row of the Criterion range. Formulas placed there always refer to one or more of the cells in the second row of the Input range. To select cities whose population is greater than 100,000, place the formula

C5>100000

in cell C2. C5 refers to the *POPULATION* column in the second Input range row. Figure 14.9 shows the spreadsheet with the three ranges defined and the selection criteria in row 2 (the status line reveals the formula stored in cell C2).

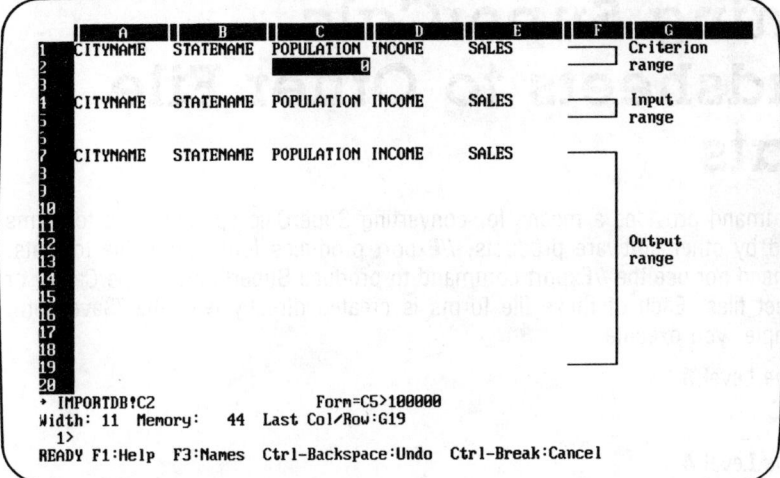

Fig. 14.9.

Criterion, Input, and Output ranges defined.

The last steps execute the //Import command. From the ready prompt, select //Import,dBase, and the dBASE file name **CENSUS**. Then press **E** to execute the **E**xtract option. SuperCalc quickly searches the dBASE database CENSUS and returns selected records, placing the results in the Output range. Figure 14.10 shows the extracted database records—those records for which the *POPULATION* field is greater than 100,000.

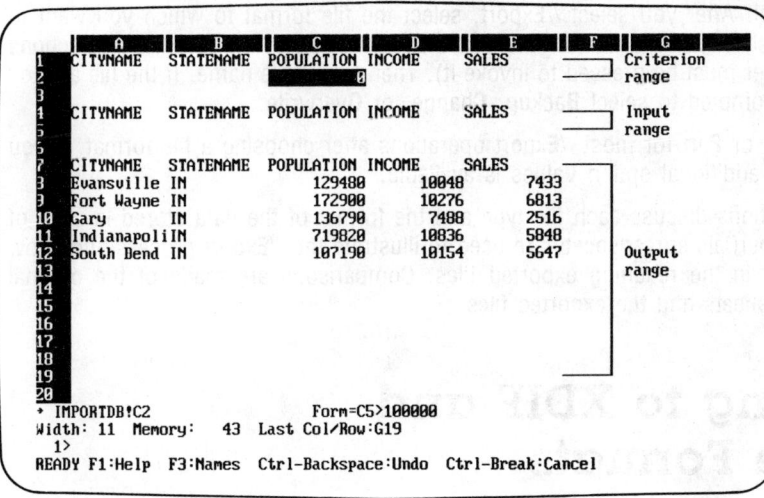

Fig. 14.10.

Extracted dBASE database records.

Exporting SuperCalc Spreadsheets to Other File Formats

The //Export command provides a means for converting SuperCalc spreadsheets to forms that can be used by other software products. //Export produces four output file formats. Recall that you need not use the //Export command to produce SuperCalc3, SuperCalc4, or 1-2-3 spreadsheet files. Each of these file forms is created directly with the /Save command. For example, you execute

/**S**ave,*filename,*Level,**3**

or

/**S**ave,*filename,*Level,**4**

to save a SuperCalc spreadsheet in the SuperCalc3 or SuperCalc4 file formats, respectively. Similarly, to save a SuperCalc spreadsheet in 1-2-3 form, you simply type

/**S**ave,*filename.***WK1**

Invoke the //Export command. Four data formats are supported: XDIF, DIF, Comma Separated Values (CSV), and dBASE. These choices are indicated by the menu choices of

        XDIF   DIF   CSV   dBase

in the dialog panel. After you select //Export, select the file format to which you want to export the spreadsheet data. (Note that the d**B**ase choice is one of the few menu selections whose second letter must be pressed to invoke it). Then type a file name. If the file already exists, you are prompted to select **B**ackup, **C**hange, or **O**verwrite.

You can select **A**ll or **P**art for most //Export operations after choosing a file format. If you choose **X**DIF, the additional option **V**alues is available.

The following sections discuss each file type and the format of the data stored in each of them. Several SuperCalc spreadsheets are used to illustrate the //Export process and show the level of detail in the resulting exported files. Comparisons are made of the original SuperCalc spreadsheets and the exported files.

Exporting to XDIF and DIF File Formats

The **X**DIF and **D**IF options convert spreadsheets to the eXtended Data Interchange Format and to the Data Interchange Format, respectively. The DIF format, as you recall, is a subset of the XDIF format; a great deal more information concerning formulas is carried in the XDIF format than in the DIF format. In addition, //Export doesn't support VisiCalc output; use the DIF form instead.

To export a spreadsheet to XDIF format, press //**EX** from READY mode to select //**E**xport,**X**DIF. Type the name of the file (**STATES**) and press Enter. The default extension supplied by SuperCalc is SDI for XDIF export operations and DIF for DIF export operations.

SuperCalc presents three options. Choose **A**ll to export the entire spreadsheet, including formulas. Choose **V**alues to export only the spreadsheet values (no formulas). Choose **P**art to export a selected block of spreadsheet cells. If you select **P**art, then SuperCalc prompts you for a range of cells to be exported. In this case, type the cell range and then press Enter to complete the export command. If you select **A**ll, SuperCalc briefly displays the message

    Exporting...

and returns to READY mode after completing the export operation.

Exporting to DIF format is almost identical to exporting to XDIF. To begin the operation, enter //**E**xport,**D**IF. Supply the name of the export file—**STATES** in the example—and press Enter. Two options not available with XDIF appear:

    Colwise   Rowwise

These options are used to specify whether the DIF file is written in column order or in row order. Although the distinction normally does not make much difference, these options can be used to transpose spreadsheet rows to spreadsheet columns (or vice versa). For example, a spreadsheet can be exported in column order and later imported in row order, rotating the spreadsheet 90 degrees. Select **C** to export in column order.

After selecting the export order, the choices **A**ll and **P**art appear (see fig. 4.11). Press **A** to export the entire sheet or **P** to export only a subset of the spreadsheet. Press Enter to complete the //**E**xport command. In a few seconds, the entry line clears and the prompt reappears. The exported file is stored in column order (in a file named STATES.DIF in the example).

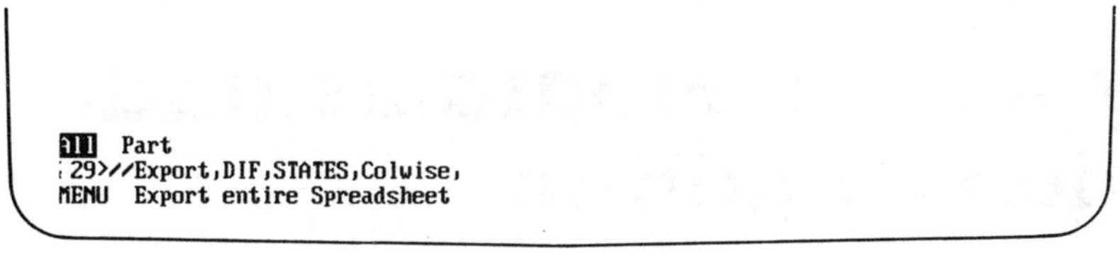

All Part
; 29>//Export,DIF,STATES,Colwise,
MENU Export entire Spreadsheet

Fig. 14.11.
Exporting to a DIF file.

Exporting to CSV Files

When you choose the **C**SV option, the SuperCalc data is converted to Comma Separated Values format. In this format, all text values are enclosed in quotation marks and all non-text values (formulas, numeric expressions, and functions) are converted to numeric values. Arithmetic expressions, for example, are evaluated and the numeric results are placed in the CSV file. Each line of the CSV file corresponds to a spreadsheet row, and entries in each output line are separated by commas.

Enter the export file name after you select **C**SV. If you don't type a file extension, Super-Calc supplies CSV automatically. You can specify either **A**ll or **P**art after entering the CSV file name. The **A**ll option converts the entire spreadsheet, including blank cells. Repeating text is enclosed in quotation marks and contains an apostrophe followed by the repeating text character(s). Textual values are treated like text values. Neither formulas nor any format information is converted. Only formula results are placed in a CSV file.

To export part of a spreadsheet, select **P**art and then specify the spreadsheet cell range to be exported—for example,

//**E**xport,**C**SV,**STATES**,Part,A1:E20

The cell range A1 through E20 is chosen using POINT mode in this example. When you press Enter to complete the //**E**xport command, the spreadsheet range A1:E20 is exported to CSV format.

Exporting to dBASE Files

You can easily export spreadsheets into dBASE form. SuperCalc thus provides a method of moving data back and forth between SuperCalc and dBASE. Invoke //**E**xport,d**B**ase to select dBASE export format.

Because SuperCalc has no way of knowing the target dBASE field names, be sure that the first row of the exported spreadsheet cell range contains text strings—one string for each column in the export cell range. If you forget to include these strings, strange dBASE field names are generated.

Enter the dBASE file name (**STATES**, for example) and press Enter. Select either **A**ll or **P**art to export the entire spreadsheet or a subset. Within seconds of pressing Enter to complete the command, your spreadsheet file is exported to an equivalent dBASE format.

Using Add-In Programs and Functions: //Add-in

Several programs and functions that extend SuperCalc's features and capabilities are available from software vendors. Notable among these programs are Silverado and Oracle, two relational database management programs. You can attach add-in programs to SuperCalc and invoke them from within your spreadsheets. You also can attach add-in functions, usually available from independent software vendors, to extend SuperCalc's set of predefined (built-in) functions.

You attach programs and functions to SuperCalc with the //**A**dd-in command. An add-in program (such as Silverado) can be invoked automatically whenever you start up Super-Calc (only one program can be automatically invoked, however), or a program can be invoked from within SuperCalc with a command or a function key. Add-in functions, unlike add-in programs, are invoked automatically whenever they are used in formulas—just as the SuperCalc built-in functions, like SUM, are involked.

After you have attached one or more programs or functions, you can save the names of attached software and associated control information by executing

   /**G**lobal,**K**eep

SuperCalc stores information about attached software in a file named ADN.CFG. Whenever you attach new programs or detach others, you should save the new add-in settings with /**G**lobal,**K**eep. SuperCalc uses the settings in ADN.CFG if that file exists.

You can deactivate any program or function by detaching it. Once you have detached a program or function from SuperCalc, the add-in is removed from memory and cannot be invoked from within SuperCalc.

Attaching Programs and Functions

You attach application software by selecting //**A**dd-in. A list of attached programs appears in the Add-In List screen displayed after you invoke //**A**dd-in (see fig. 14.12).

```
┌─────────────────────────────────────────────────────────────────┐
│   ADD-IN LIST                                                     │
│   Name                                              Key    Auto   │
│                                                                   │
│                                                                   │
│                                                                   │
│                                                                   │
│                                                                   │
│                                                                   │
│                                                                   │
│                                                                   │
│                                                                   │
│                                            ┌──────────────────┐   │
│                                            │ No Add-ins attached│  │
│   █Attach█ Detach  Invoke  Zap  Quit        └──────────────────┘  │
│   : 1B>//Add-in,                                                  │
│   MENU  Attach an add-in program                                  │
└─────────────────────────────────────────────────────────────────┘
```

Fig. 14.12.
*Add-In List screen displayed when //**Add**-in is executed.*

Because no programs are currently attached, the message No Add-ins attached is displayed in the lower right corner. Choose **A**ttach to attach a program. When the file-name prompt appears, type the name of the program or function you are attaching. You must enter the drive name and directory where the program or function is located. For this example, type the program name **ORACLE**, which is in the default directory (see fig. 14.13a).

You can associate an add-in program with a function key by selecting a number from 1 to 10, indicated as 1 through 0 on the screen (see fig. 14.13b). If you choose one of the function keys (1 in fig. 14.13b), you can invoke the program while in SuperCalc by pressing the Shift key and the assigned function key—for example, Shift-F1. If you select **N**one, no function key is associated with the add-in program. Select **N**one when attaching add-in functions because they are invoked automatically when their names are part of a formula.

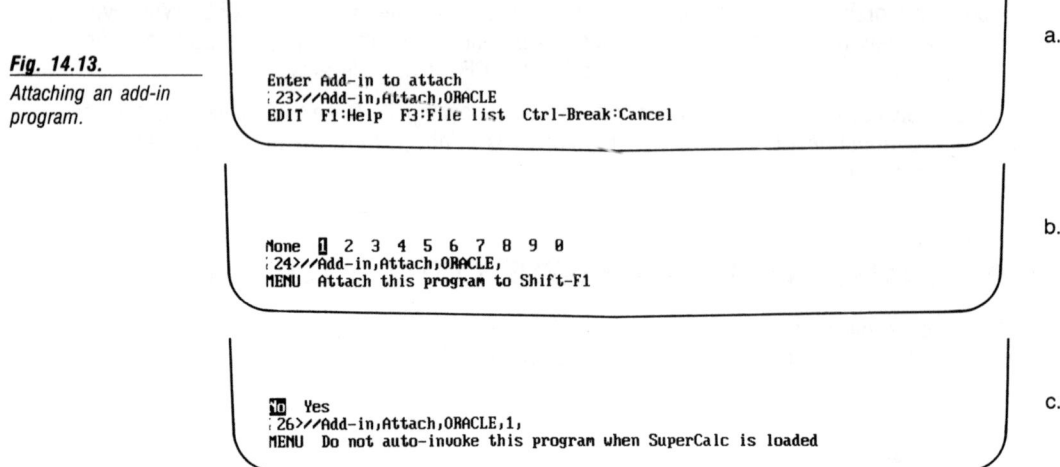

Fig. 14.13.

Attaching an add-in program.

a.
```
Enter Add-in to attach
: 23>//Add-in,Attach,ORACLE
EDIT  F1:Help  F3:File list  Ctrl-Break:Cancel
```

b.
```
None [1] 2  3  4  5  6  7  8  9  0
: 24>//Add-in,Attach,ORACLE,
MENU  Attach this program to Shift-F1
```

c.
```
[No]  Yes
: 26>//Add-in,Attach,ORACLE,1,
MENU  Do not auto-invoke this program when SuperCalc is loaded
```

After specifying the file name and assigning a function key, you can indicate whether you want a particular add-in program to be invoked automatically whenever you start SuperCalc (see fig. 14.13c). Remember, only one program can be automatically invoked. If you select **N**o, you must invoke the program by a function key or by a command. Programs not assigned to function keys are manually invoked with the command

    //**A**dd-in,**I**nvoke

followed by the program name. You can select the file name from the Add-In List screen (refer to fig. 14.12) or type the file name.

Detaching Programs and Functions

You also can detach programs or functions from SuperCalc. When programs or functions are detached, you no longer can invoke them—they are removed from memory and are not available. Executing

    //**A**dd-in,**D**etach

removes a selected program or function from memory. You are prompted for the name of the program or function to detach from memory. You can specify the name by selecting it from the Add-In List screen (refer to fig. 14.12) or by typing its name (including drive and subdirectories, if necessary). Remember to execute /**G**lobal,**K**eep before exiting SuperCalc to store the updated add-in list in the add-in configuration file ADN.CFG.

You can remove all add-in software by executing //**A**dd-in,**Z**ap. SuperCalc prompts you to verify that you really want to detach all add-in programs and functions. You have the opportunity to cancel that command by pressing **N** when the choices

    No   Yes

are displayed. Pressing **Y** confirms your decision to detach all add-in programs, and they become unavailable. You must reattach detached add-in programs and functions before you can invoke them in any way (automatically, with Shift-function keys, within a formula, or with the //**A**dd-in,**I**nvoke command). You leave the //**A**dd-in command by executing **Q**uit when it is displayed on the main Add-in menu (refer to fig. 14.12).

Chapter Summary

Using the //**I**mport and //**E**xport commands can save you time and expense. //**I**mport provides a bridge to SuperCalc from other software products. //**E**xport provides a bridge in the opposite direction, letting SuperCalc provide spreadsheet data in formats usable by other software products. The most elementary form of data for importing and exporting is CSV format. A more sophisticated data file is possible using the DIF form or (better yet) the XDIF form.

The most sophisticated interface file types are the dBASE //**I**mport and //**E**xport formats and the VisiCalc //**I**mport format. (//**E**xport is not allowed with VisiCalc.) All formulas, format characteristics, and other corresponding data between SuperCalc and VisiCalc are available and stored in the DIF file format.

The //**A**dd-in command permits you to invoke other software add-in products directly from SuperCalc. Add-in functions, like SuperCalc's built-in functions, are automatically invoked when their names are used in SuperCalc formulas. One add-in program can be invoked automatically when SuperCalc is started, and you can invoke one or more programs from within SuperCalc. The //**A**dd-in command adds a new level of flexibility and power to SuperCalc. You can use the tremendous capability of SuperCalc now and incorporate powerful add-in programs later on as they become available.

This book was written as a reference work as well as a tutorial. Keep it on your shelf and refer to it often. We hope that you will now put this book to the test—by using it to produce spreadsheets that help you manage your business and create graphics to present information to customers and management.

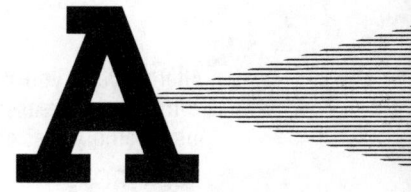

PrivacyPlus

PrivacyPlus is provided with SuperCalc and allows you to encode one or more files so that their contents are scrambled and unreadable. The process of scrambling the contents is called *encryption*. Files can be unscrambled (decrypted) with PrivacyPlus, yielding the original file. You can use PrivacyPlus to protect any files you have, including program files (with EXE or COM file extensions), SuperCalc spreadsheet files (CAL), and documents.

PrivacyPlus uses the approved National Bureau of Standards encryption algorithm called *Data Encryption Standard* (DES). The DES algorithm is publicly known, and its implementation prevents information from being disclosed because files are encrypted with a password that you alone know. This password used by the algorithm consists of up to 32 characters. Once files are encrypted with your key, they are virtually undecipherable. (It is estimated that *years* of high-speed computation would be needed for an adversary to make a systematic attempt to decipher any file.)

Invoking PrivacyPlus

PrivacyPlus is easy to use. It can be used in one of two modes: *nonresident* or *resident*. When you invoke PrivacyPlus directly from DOS, it operates in nonresident mode, and when you load it in memory and invoke it with a *hot key*, it operates in resident mode.

To encrypt (lock) or decrypt (unlock) one or more files, PrivacyPlus needs only this information:

- The option **L**ock or **U**nlock
- The file name(s) to be locked or unlocked
- A password the algorithm uses to lock or unlock files

In nonresident mode, PrivacyPlus is invoked much like other programs. You type **PP** at the DOS prompt and press Enter. You then can lock or unlock files and exit from the program.

Alternatively, you can make PrivacyPlus memory-resident so that you can invoke it when you press a preassigned pair of keys known as PrivacyPlus' *hot key*. To load PrivacyPlus into memory (resident mode), type

    PP /RES

at the DOS prompt. As with other terminate and stay resident (TSR) programs, PrivacyPlus is loaded into memory and then the DOS prompt reappears. PrivacyPlus becomes transparent, occupying approximately 58K of memory. PrivacyPlus is only "asleep" and can be awakened by pressing the hot key Alt-Left Shift (Alt with the Left Shift). You can remove PrivacyPlus from memory by typing

    PP /UNRES

at the DOS prompt.

Locking Files

Whether PrivacyPlus is in resident or nonresident mode, the steps to lock a file are the same. Suppose that you want to lock a SuperCalc spreadsheet after saving it. Invoke PrivacyPlus (in nonresident mode) by typing **PP**. Four options are displayed:

    Lock   Unlock   Dir   Quit

Lock is the highlighted default operation. Select **L**ock by typing **L** or pressing Enter.

Next, PrivacyPlus prompts you for the name of the file(s) you want to lock:

    File to lock

If you forget the file names, you can select the **D**ir option to display a directory and use the arrow keys to point to the file name you want to lock. Otherwise, you simply type the file name. You can either specify an explicit file name, or you can use DOS's asterisk wild-card character (*) to designate a group of files. For example, to lock all SuperCalc spreadsheet files, type ***.CAL** after the PrivacyPlus file name prompt. This specification encrypts all files with the same password, which you supply in the next step.

After entering a file name specification, PrivacyPlus prompts you for a password:

    Enter password

Be especially careful at this prompt. Passwords consist of 3 to 32 printable characters. PrivacyPlus distinguishes uppercase letters from lowercase letters. If you type a password such as **Stirling**, remember the capitalization as well as the spelling. If you later forget the password for a locked file, you have no way to unlock the file!

As you type the password, the screen displays # for each character you type to mask the actual password. If you make a mistake, use the Backspace key to erase the characters and then retype the password. When the password is complete and correct, press Enter. PrivacyPlus then prompts you to enter the password again to ensure that you haven't made

a typing error. After you enter your password a second time, a bar moves across the top of the dialog box indicating how much of the file has been encrypted, as shown in figure A.1.

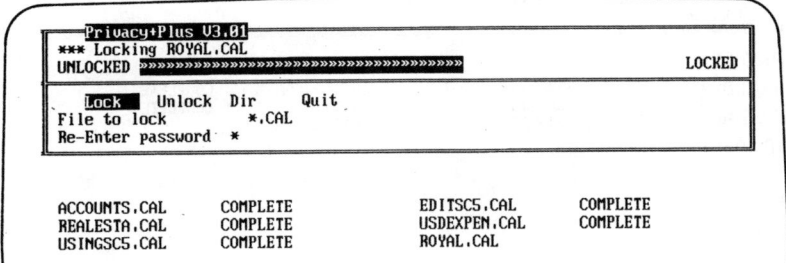

Fig. A.1.
Locking several files with one password.

As each file is locked (when an asterisk is used in the file name specification), the file name is displayed below the dialog box, indicating that the file has been locked. If you press Esc while PrivacyPlus is locking a file, the program stops, and your file is restored as if nothing had happened.

Unlocking Files

Unlocking encrypted files is equally easy. Invoke PrivacyPlus either by typing **PP** or (if PrivacyPlus is memory-resident) by pressing Alt-Left Shift. Select **U**nlock when the PrivacyPlus dialog box is displayed. PrivacyPlus prompts you for the file name(s) to unlock:

        File to unlock

Type the full file name (including extension) and press Enter. PrivacyPlus then prompts you for the password. Enter the correct password (with matching capitalization) and press Enter. As you type the password, the character # is displayed for each character typed to mask your password from peeping eyes. The message WRONG PASSWORD is displayed if you enter a password that does not match the original password used to lock your file. Press the Esc key if you want PrivacyPlus to halt the unlocking operation.

PrivacyPlus begins to unscramble the file(s) you specified. A progress bar appears at the top of the dialog box to indicate how much of the file has been unscrambled. Figure A.2 shows an example of unlocking SuperCalc CAL files. The file specification entered is *.CAL. If PrivacyPlus encounters a file that is not locked, the message

        *** FILE NOT LOCKED

is displayed and the file is ignored. Unscrambling proceeds with the next file.

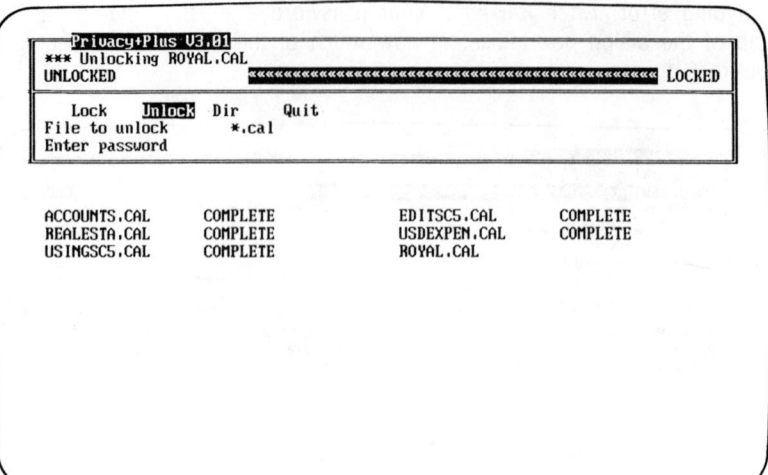

Unlocking several spreadsheet CAL files.

B

Hidden Commands

The commands listed here are available in SuperCalc5 but are "hidden": they do not appear in any command line, but they can be invoked. They are carried over from earlier versions of SuperCalc for convenience and upward compatibility.

Hidden Command	Equivalent SuperCalc5 Command
/e**X**ecute	
/**F**ormat,**D**efine	/**F**ormat,**U**ser-define,**N**umber
/**G**lobal,**A**uto	/**G**lobal,**E**valuation,**W**hen,**A**uto
/**G**lobal,**C**olumn	/**G**lobal,**E**valuation,**O**rder,**C**olumn
/**G**lobal,**D**ependent	/**G**lobal,**E**valuation,**O**rder,**D**ependent
/**G**lobal,**I**teration-control	/**G**lobal,**E**valuation,**I**teration-control
/**G**lobal,**M**anual	/**G**lobal,**E**valuation,**W**hen,**M**anual
/**G**lobal,**O**ptimum,**A**ttribute	/**G**lobal,**O**ptimum,**N**ext,**A**ttribute
/**G**lobal,**O**ptimum,**B**oundary	/**G**lobal,**O**ptimum,**N**ext,**B**oundary
/**G**lobal,**O**ptimum,**C**heck	/**G**lobal,**S**preadsheet,**O**ptions,**C**heck
/**G**lobal,**O**ptimum,**E**xpanded	/**G**lobal,**O**ptimum,**N**ext,**E**xpanded
/**G**lobal,**O**ptimum,**I**nternational	
/**G**lobal,**O**ptimum,**M**emory	/**G**lobal,**O**ptimum,**N**ext,**M**emory
/**G**lobal,**O**ptimum,**V**ideo	/**G**lobal,**O**ptimum,**N**ext,**V**ideo
/**G**lobal,**R**ow	/**G**lobal,**E**valuation,**O**rder,**R**ow
/**O**utput,**C**ontents	
/**O**utput,**P**rinter,**O**ptions,**R**eport,**C**ontents	

503

Hidden Command   *Equivalent SuperCalc5 Command*

/**O**utput,**D**isplay

/**O**utput,**P**rinter,**O**ptions,**R**eport,**C**ontents,**N**o

/**R**eplicate   /**C**opy

/**V**iew   //**G**raphics

//**E**xport,**1**-2-3   /**S**ave,*filename.***WK1**
                                                    /**S**ave,*filename.***WKS**

//**E**xport,**S**C3   /**S**ave,*filename,***L**evel,sc**3**

//**I**mport,**1**-2-3   /**L**oad,*filename.***WK1**
                                                    /**L**oad,*filename.***WKS**

Index

More Computer Knowledge from Que

SELECT QUE BOOKS TO INCREASE
YOUR PERSONAL COMPUTER PRODUCTIVITY

MS-DOS User's Guide, 3rd Edition

by Chris DeVoney

This classic guide to MS-DOS is now better than ever! Updated for MS-DOS, Version 3.3, this new edition features several new extended tutorials and a unique new command reference section. The distinctive approach of this text lets you easily reference basic command syntax, while comprehensive tutorial sections present in-depth DOS data. Appendixes provide information specific to users of DOS on COMPAQ, Epson, Zenith, and Leading Edge personal computers. Master your computer's operating system with *MS-DOS User's Guide*, 3rd Edition—the comprehensive tutorial/reference!

Using WordPerfect 5

by Charles O. Stewart III, et al.

WordPerfect 5 is the latest version of the popular word processor and Que's new *Using WordPerfect 5* is the perfect WordPerfect guide. This comprehensive text introduces you to WordPerfect basics; helps you learn to use macros, Styles, and other advanced features; presents information on outlining, referencing, and text columns; and shows you how to use WordPerfect for desktop publishing. Also included are numerous Quick Start tutorials, a tear-out command reference card, and an introduction to WordPerfect 5 for 4.2 users. Become a WordPerfect expert with *Using WordPerfect 5*!

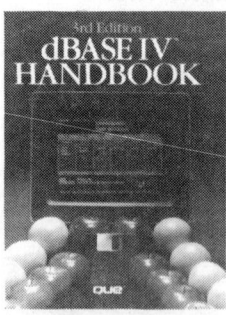

dBASE IV Handbook, 3rd Edition

by George T. Chou, Ph.D.

Learn dBASE IV quickly with Que's new *dBASE IV Handbook*, 3rd Edition! dBASE expert George Chou leads you step-by-step from basic database concepts to advanced dBASE features, using a series of Quick Start tutorials. Experienced dBASE users will appreciate the extensive information on the new features of dBASE IV, including the new user interface, the query-by-example mode, and the SQL module. Complete with comprehensive command and function reference sections, *dBASE IV Handbook*, 3rd Edition, is an exhaustive guide to dBASE IV!

Using Harvard Graphics

by Steve Sagman and Jane Sandlar

Using Harvard Graphics is an ideal book for anyone using this popular presentation graphics program! This well-written text presents both program basics and presentation fundamentals as the reader learns how to create bar, pie, line, and other types of informative charts. Help your customers get the most from Harvard Graphics—and put on the most effective presentations—with Que's *Using Harvard Graphics!*

ORDER FROM QUE TODAY

Item	Title	Price	Quantity	Extension
838	MS-DOS User's Guide, 3rd Edition	$22.95		
852	dBASE IV Handbook, 3rd Edition	23.95		
843	Using WordPerfect 5	24.95		
941	Using Harvard Graphics	24.95		

Book Subtotal _____
Shipping & Handling ($2.50 per item) _____
Indiana Residents Add 5% Sales Tax _____
GRAND TOTAL _____

Method of Payment

☐ Check   ☐ VISA   ☐ MasterCard   ☐ American Express

Card Number _____ Exp. Date _____

Cardholder's Name _____

Ship to _____

Address _____

City _____ State _____ ZIP _____

If you can't wait, call **1-800-428-5331** and order TODAY.
All prices subject to change without notice.

ORDER FROM QUE TODAY

FOLD HERE

_____

_____

_____

_____

Que Corporation
P.O. Box 90
Carmel, IN 46032

REGISTRATION CARD

Register your copy of *Using SuperCalc5*, 2nd Edition, and receive information about Que's newest products. Complete this registration card and return it to Que Corporation, P.O. Box 90, Carmel, IN 46032.

Name _____ Phone _____

Company _____ Title _____

Address _____

City _____ State _____ ZIP _____

Please check the appropriate answers:

Where did you buy *Using SuperCalc5*, 2nd Edition?
- ☐ Bookstore (name: _____)
- ☐ Computer store (name: _____)
- ☐ Catalog (name: _____)
- ☐ Direct from Que _____
- ☐ Other: _____

How many computer books do you buy a year?
- ☐ 1 or less   ☐ 6–10
- ☐ 2–5   ☐ More than 10

How many Que books do you own?
- ☐ 1   ☐ 6–10
- ☐ 2–5   ☐ More than 10

How long have you been using SuperCalc?
- ☐ Less than 6 months
- ☐ 6 months to 1 year
- ☐ 1–3 years
- ☐ More than 3 years

What influenced your purchase of *Using SuperCalc5*, 2nd Edition?
- ☐ Personal recommendation
- ☐ Advertisement   ☐ Que catalog
- ☐ In-store display   ☐ Que mailing
- ☐ Price   ☐ Que's reputation
- ☐ Other: _____

How would you rate the overall content of *Using SuperCalc5*, 2nd Edition?
- ☐ Very good   ☐ Satisfactory
- ☐ Good   ☐ Poor

How would you rate the *tear-out command chart*?
- ☐ Very good   ☐ Satisfactory
- ☐ Good   ☐ Poor

How would you rate *Chapter 11: Automating with Macros*?
- ☐ Very good   ☐ Satisfactory
- ☐ Good   ☐ Poor

How would you rate *Part I: Learning the SuperCalc Spreadsheet*?
- ☐ Very good   ☐ Satisfactory
- ☐ Good   ☐ Poor

What do you like *best* about *Using SuperCalc5*, 2nd Edition?

What do you like *least* about *Using SuperCalc5*, 2nd Edition?

How do you use *Using SuperCalc5*, 2nd Edition?

What other Que products do you own?

For what other programs would a Que book be helpful?

Please feel free to list any other comments you may have about *Using SuperCalc5*, 2nd Edition.

_____

_____

_____

_____

_____

FOLD HERE

_____

_____

_____

_____

Que Corporation
P.O. Box 90
Carmel, IN 46032